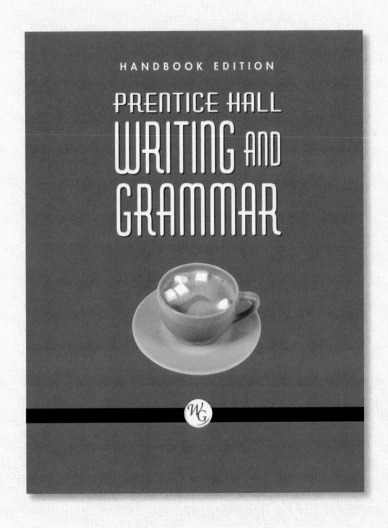

HANDBOOK EDITION

PRENTICE HALL
WRITING AND
GRAMMAR

Grade Ten
Handbook Edition

PEARSON

Prentice
Hall

Upper Saddle River, New Jersey
Boston, Massachusetts

WRITING AND GRAMMAR

Handbook Edition

Grade Ten

ISBN 0-13-201001-1

2 3 4 5 6 7 8 9 10   10 09 08 07

Go Online
PHSchool.com

Use *Writing and Grammar,* your textbook online!

Includes every grammar exercise in this book!

- instant feedback on interactive grammar exercises
- interactive writing tools and writing tutorials
- access to the *Prentice Hall Online Essay Scorer*

Interactive Textbook is also available on CD-ROM.

Go on-line to get instant help on the Writing and Grammar Web site!

- additional grammar practice opportunities
- scoring rubrics with scored student models for different modes of writing

Here's how to use the Writing and Grammar Web site:

Look for these Web Codes in your book:

> eek-1001
> eek-1002

Here's how to use Web Codes:

1. Go on-line. Enter URL: PHSchool.com

2. If you want instant feedback on interactive grammar exercises, enter Web Code: eek-1002

   Choose the appropriate chapter from the menu that appears.

3. If you want to review writing rubrics and scored student models, enter Web Code: eek-1001

   Choose the appropriate chapter from the menu that appears.

Program Authors

The program authors guided the direction and philosophy of *Prentice Hall Writing and Grammar: Communication in Action*. Working with the development team, they contributed to the pedagogical integrity of the program and to its relevance to today's teachers and students.

Joyce Armstrong Carroll

In her forty-year career, Joyce Armstrong Carroll, Ed.D., has taught on every grade level from primary to graduate school. In the past twenty years, she has trained teachers in the teaching of writing. A nationally known consultant, she has served as president of TCTE and on NCTE's Commission on Composition. More than fifty of her articles have appeared in journals such as *Curriculum Review, English Journal, Media & Methods, Southwest Philosophical Studies, Ohio English Journal, English in Texas,* and the *Florida English Journal.* With Edward E. Wilson, Dr. Carroll co-authored *Acts of Teaching: How to Teach Writing* and co-edited *Poetry After Lunch: Poems to Read Aloud.* Beyond her direct involvement with the writing pedagogy presented in this series, Dr. Carroll guided the development of the Hands-on Grammar feature. She co-directs the New Jersey Writing Project in Texas.

Edward E. Wilson

A former editor of *English in Texas*, Edward E. Wilson has served as a high-school English teacher and a writing consultant in school districts nationwide. Wilson has served on the Texas Teacher Professional Practices Commission and on NCTE's Commission on Composition. With Dr. Carroll, he co-wrote *Acts of Teaching: How to Teach Writing* and co-edited the award-winning *Poetry After Lunch: Poems to Read Aloud.* In addition to his direct involvement with the writing pedagogy presented in this series, Wilson provided inspiration for the Spotlight on Humanities feature. Wilson's poetry appears in Paul Janeczko's anthology *The Music of What Happens.* Wilson co-directs the New Jersey Writing Project in Texas.

Gary Forlini

Gary Forlini, a nationally known education consultant, developed the grammar, usage, and mechanics instruction and exercises in this series. After teaching in the Pelham, New York, schools for many years, he established Research in Media, an educational research agency that provides information for product developers, school staff developers, media companies, and arts organizations, as well as private-sector corporations and foundations. Mr. Forlini was co-author of the *S.A.T. Home Study* program and has written numerous industry reports on elementary, secondary, and post-secondary education markets.

National Advisory Panel

The teachers and administrators serving on the National Advisory Panel provided ongoing input into the development of *Prentice Hall Writing and Grammar: Communication in Action.* Their valuable insights ensure that the perspectives of teachers and students throughout the country are represented within the instruction in this series.

Dr. Pauline Bigby-Jenkins
Coordinator for Secondary English
  Language Arts
Ann Arbor Public Schools
Ann Arbor, Michigan

Lee Bromberger
English Department Chairperson
Mukwonago High School
Mukwonago, Wisconsin

Mary Chapman
Teacher of English
Free State High School
Lawrence, Kansas

Jim Deatherage
Language Arts Department
  Chairperson
Richland High School
Richland, Washington

Luis Dovalina
Teacher of English
La Joya High School
La Joya, Texas

JoAnn Giardino
Teacher of English
Centennial High School
Columbus, Ohio

Susan Goldberg
Teacher of English
Westlake Middle School
Thornwood, New York

Jean Hicks
Director, Louisville Writing Project
University of Louisville
Louisville, Kentucky

Karen Hurley
Teacher of Language Arts
Perry Meridian Middle School
Indianapolis, Indiana

Karen Lopez
Teacher of English
Hart High School
Newhall, California

Marianne Minshall
Teacher of Reading and Language Arts
Westmore Middle School
Columbus, Ohio

Nancy Monroe
English Department Chairperson
Bolton High School
Alexandria, Louisiana

Ken Spurlock
Assistant Principal
Boone County High School
Florence, Kentucky

Cynthia Katz Tyroff
Staff Development Specialist
  and Teacher of English
Northside Independent School District
San Antonio, Texas

Holly Ward
Teacher of Language Arts
Campbell Middle School
Daytona Beach, Florida

Grammar Review Team

The following teachers reviewed the grammar instruction in this series to ensure accuracy, clarity, and pedagogy.

Kathy Hamilton
Paul Hertzog
Daren Hoisington
Beverly Ladd

Karen Lopez
Dianna Louise Lund
Sean O'Brien

CONTENTS IN BRIEF

Chapters 1–15

Part I: Writing............1

Chapter 1 The Writer in You 2

2 A Walk Through
the Writing Process. 4

3 Sentences, Paragraphs, and
Compositions: Structure and Style . 16

4 Narration
Autobiographical Writing 32

5 Narration: Short Story. 48

6 Description 62

7 Persuasion: Persuasive Essay 76

8 Persuasion: Advertisement 92

9 Exposition
Comparison-and-Contrast Essay . 106

10 Exposition
Cause-and-Effect Essay 122

11 Exposition
Problem-and-Solution Essay 138

12 Research Writing. 154

13 Response to Literature. 176

14 Writing for Assessment 194

15 Workplace Writing. 204

Chapters 16–28

Part 2: Grammar, Usage, and Mechanics . 213

Chapter 16 Nouns, Pronouns, and Verbs 214
17 Adjectives and Adverbs 240
18 Prepositions, Conjunctions, and Interjections 258
19 Basic Sentence Parts 272
20 Phrases and Clauses 298
21 Effective Sentences 338
22 Verb Usage 366
23 Pronoun Usage 386
24 Agreement 404
25 Using Modifiers 424
26 Miscellaneous Problems in Usage. 438
27 Capitalization 456
28 Punctuation 470

Chapters 29–33

Part 3: Academic and Workplace Skills . . 545

Chapter 29 Speaking, Listening, Viewing, and Representing 546
30 Vocabulary and Spelling 566
31 Reading Skills 588
32 Study, Reference, and Test-Taking Skills 608
33 Workplace Skills and Competencies 628

Test Preparation Handbook 640

Resources

Citing Sources and Preparing Manuscript 672
Penmanship Reference 672
Internet Research Handbook 679
Commonly Overused Words 682
Commonly Misspelled Words 684
Abbreviations Guide 686
Proofreading Symbols Reference 690
Student Publications 691
Sentence Diagraming Workshop 692
Index 704

CONTENTS
PART 1: WRITING

Chapter 1

The Writer in You 2

Writing in Everyday Life 2
What Are the Qualities of Good Writing? 3
Reflecting on Your Writing 3

Chapter 2

A Walk Through the Writing Process 4

2.1 What Is Prewriting? 6
2.2 What Is Drafting? 10
2.3 What Is Revising? 11
2.4 What Are Editing and Proofreading? 14
2.5 What Are Publishing and Presenting? 15

Chapter 3

Sentences, Paragraphs, and Compositions
Structure and Style 16

3.1 **Sentence Combining**
Writing Effective Sentences 17
Inserting Words and Phrases 17
Using Compound Elements 18
Forming Compound Sentences 19
Using Subordination 20

3.2 **Writing Effective Paragraphs**
Main Idea and Topic Sentence 21
Writing Topic Sentences 22
Writing Supporting Sentences 23
Placing Topic Sentences 24
Unity and Coherence 25

3.3 **Paragraphs in Essays and Other Compositions**
The Parts of a Composition 27
Types of Paragraphs 28

3.4 **Writing Style**
Developing Style 30
Formal and Informal English 31

Chapter 4 Narration

Autobiographical Writing 32

4.1 What Is Autobiographical Writing? 33

4.2 Prewriting
  Choosing Your Topic 34
    You Were There!. 34
    Consider the Moment. 34
    Make a Blueprint. 34
    Topic Bank 35
  Narrowing Your Topic. 36
    Use Carbon Paper to Narrow a Topic. 36
  Considering Your Audience and Purpose 36
  Gathering Details 37
    Gather Details About the Characters. 37
    Gather Details About the Setting. 37

4.3 Drafting
  Shaping Your Writing 38
    Create a Plot 38
  Providing Elaboration 39
    Add Dialogue. 39
    Explode the Moment 39

4.4 Revising
  Revising Your Overall Structure 40
    Revision Strategy: Deleting Unrelated Details 40
  Revising Your Paragraphs. 41
    Revision Strategy: Analyzing Paragraphs 41
  Revising Your Sentences 42
    Revision Strategy: Color-Coding to Achieve
    Sentence Variety 42
  Revising Your Word Choice. 43
    Revision Strategy: Color-Coding Personal Pronouns . 43
  Peer Review. 45
    Use a Peer Review Work Sheet 45

4.5 Editing and Proofreading
  Focusing on Punctuating Dialogue 46

4.6 Publishing and Presenting
  Building Your Portfolio 47
  Reflecting on Your Writing 47
    ☑ **Rubric for Self-Assessment**. 47

Student Work
IN PROGRESS

Featured Work:
  "The Ultimate Challenge"
  by Erica Jackson
  Boone County High School
  Florence, Kentucky

Using Blueprinting to
Find a Topic. 34
Elaborating by Exploding
the Moment. 39
Deleting Unrelated Details. 40
Color-Coding Personal
Pronouns 43

INTEGRATED SKILLS

▶ **Grammar in Your Writing**
The Nominative and Objective
Cases of Pronouns 44
Paragraphing and
Punctuating Dialogue 46

Chapter 5 Narration

Short Story 48

5.1 What Is a Short Story? 49

5.2 Prewriting
Choosing Your Topic 50
    Sketch a Character or Setting 50
    Browse Through Quotations 50
    Freewrite 50
    Topic Bank 51
Narrowing Your Topic 52
Considering Your Audience and Purpose 52
    Create a Purpose Planner 52
Gathering Details 53
    Gathering Details About Characters 53
    Gathering Details About Setting 53

5.3 Drafting
Shaping Your Writing 54
    Make a Plot Diagram 54
Providing Elaboration 55
    Use Dialogue to Develop and Reveal Character 55
    Use Dialogue to Further the Plot Events 55

5.4 Revising
Revising Your Overall Structure 56
    Revision Strategy: Identifying the Purpose of
    Plot Events 56
Revising Your Paragraphs 56
    Revision Strategy: Using Contractions in Dialogue . . 56
Revising Your Sentences .57
    Revision Strategy: Color-Coding Passive Sentences . 57
Revising Your Word Choice 59
    Revision Strategy: Evaluating the Use of Tag Words . 59
Peer Review 59
    "Say Back" 59

5.5 Editing and Proofreading
Focusing on Punctuation 60

5.6 Publishing and Presenting
Building Your Portfolio 61
Reflecting on Your Writing 61
☑ Rubric for Self-Assessment 61

Student Work
IN PROGRESS

Featured Work:
"Horror Movie"
by Ian Venokur
Columbia High School
Maplewood, New Jersey

Freewriting to Discover a
Topic 50
Gathering Details About
Setting 53
Color-Coding Passive
Sentences 57

INTEGRATED SKILLS

▶ **Grammar in Your Writing**
Verbs: Active and Passive
Voice 58
Formatting and
Punctuating Dialogue 60

Chapter 6 Description 62

6.1 What Is Description? 63

6.2 Prewriting
  Choosing Your Topic 64
    Draw or Sketch 64
    Browse in a Calendar 64
    Make a Blueprint 64
    Topic Bank 65
  Narrowing Your Topic 66
    Make a Web 66
  Considering Your Audience and Purpose 66
  Gathering Details 67
    Use the Cubing Technique 67

6.3 Drafting
  Shaping Your Writing 68
    Create a Mood 68
  Providing Elaboration 68
    Create Figurative Language 68

6.4 Revising
  Revising Your Overall Structure 69
    Revision Strategy: Outlining Details to Check Your
    Organization 69
  Revising Your Paragraphs 69
    Revision Strategy: Color-Coding to Check Unity 69
  Revising Your Sentences 70
    Revision Strategy: Adding Modifiers 70
  Revising Your Word Choice 72
    Revision Strategy: Circling and Replacing 72
  Peer Review 73
    Create a Plus-and-Minus Chart 73

6.5 Editing and Proofreading
  Focusing on Commas 74

6.6 Publishing and Presenting
  Building Your Portfolio 75
  Reflecting on Your Writing 75
  ☑ **Rubric for Self-Assessment** 75

Student Work
IN PROGRESS

Featured Work:
  "Phantom Finish"
  by Leslie Harris
  Sunnyslope High School
  Phoenix, Arizona

Cubing to Gather Details . . 67
Adding Modifiers 70
Replacing Vague Words . . . 72

INTEGRATED SKILLS

▶ **Grammar in Your Writing**
Dangling and Misplaced
Modifiers 71
Using Commas Correctly . . .74

Chapter 7 Persuasion

Persuasive Essay 76

7.1 What Is a Persuasive Essay? 77

7.2 Prewriting
Choosing Your Topic 78
    Scan Newspapers 78
    Make a Quicklist 78
    Use Sentence Starters 78
    Topic Bank 79
Narrowing Your Topic 80
    Narrow a Topic by Looping 80
Considering Your Audience and Purpose 81
    Create a Purpose Planner 81
Gathering Evidence 82
    Find Unbiased Research 82
    Conduct Interviews 82
    Make a Pro-and-Con Chart 82

7.3 Drafting
Shaping Your Writing 83
    Use TRI/PS/QA to Structure Paragraphs 83
Providing Elaboration 84
    Build Your Argument With Evidence 84

7.4 Revising
Revising Your Overall Structure 85
    Revision Strategy: Color-Coding to Identify Support . . .85
Revising Your Paragraphs 86
    Revision Strategy: Forming Parallel Structures 86
Revising Your Sentences .88
    Revision Strategy: Color-Coding Clues to
    Sentence Types 88
Revising Your Word Choice 89
    Revise Informal Language 89
Peer Review 89
    Use Point/Counterpoint 89

7.5 Editing and Proofreading
Focusing on Spelling 90

7.6 Publishing and Presenting
Building Your Portfolio 91
Reflecting on Your Writing 91
  ☑ **Rubric for Self-Assessment** 91

Student Work
IN PROGRESS

Featured Work:
    "Volunteering Is Vital"
    by Sharon Goldberg
   Miami-Palmetto High School
    Pinecrest, Florida

Using Sentence Starters
to Choose a Topic 78
Looping to Narrow a Topic . .80
Gathering Evidence With
a T-Chart 82
Color-Coding to Identify
Support 85
Making Use of Parallelism . 86
Color-Coding Sentence
Types 88

INTEGRATED SKILLS

▶ **Grammar in Your Writing**
Adding Parallel Clauses . . . 87

Words That End in *-ance*
and *-ence* 90

Chapter 8

Persuasion
Advertisement 92

What Is an Advertisement? 93

8.1 Model From Literature
Costa Rica Advertisement 94

8.2 Prewriting
Choosing Your Topic 95
    Conduct a Survey 95
    Blueprint. 95
    Topic Bank 95
Narrowing Your Topic 96
Considering Your Audience and Purpose 96
    Choose Your Words Carefully 96
Gathering Details 97
    Gather Details for a Product 97
    Gather Details for a Campaign 97
    Gather Details for an Event 97

8.3 Drafting
Shaping Your Writing 98
    Order Details From Most Important to Least
    Important 98
Providing Elaboration 98
    Include Testimonials, Statistics, and Graphics 98

8.4 Revising
Revising Your Overall Structure 99
    Revision Strategy: Experimenting With Placement
    of Your Main Idea. 99
Revising Your Paragraphs 99
    Revision Strategy: Circling the Important Details . . . 99
Revising Your Sentences 100
    Revision Strategy: Color-Coding End Marks 100
    Revision Strategy: Extending an Idea 101
Revising Your Word Choice 102
    Revision Strategy: Replace Dull Words 102
Peer Review 102
    Question a Peer 102

8.4 Editing and Proofreading
Correct Use of *Your* and *You're* 103

8.6 Publishing and Presenting
Building Your Portfolio 104
Reflecting on Your Writing 104
☑ **Rubric for Self-Assessment** 104

Student Work
IN PROGRESS

Featured Work:
  "Bash at the Lake"
  by Ever Chapa
  La Joya High School
  La Joya, Texas

Gathering Details for an
Event 97
Circling Important Details . . 99
Coding to Identify Sentence
Types 100
Final Draft **105**

INTEGRATED SKILLS

▶ **Grammar in Your Writing**
The Four Functions
of Sentences 101

Homophones 103

Exposition: *Comparison-and-Contrast Essay* 106

9.1 What Is a Comparison-and-Contrast Essay? . 107
9.2 Prewriting
  Choosing Your Topic 108
    Freewrite 108
    List 108
    Topic Bank 109
  Evaluating Your Topic 110
    Use a Venn Diagram. 110
  Considering Your Audience and Purpose 110
  Gathering Details 111
    Use Personal Experience. 111
    Use Primary Sources 111
    Use Secondary Sources 111
9.3 Drafting
  Shaping Your Writing 112
    Use Subject-by-Subject Organization 112
    Use Point-by-Point Organization 112
  Providing Elaboration 113
    Give Examples 113
    Provide Facts 113
    Cite Quotations and Figures 113
9.4 Revising
  Revising Your Overall Structure 114
    Revision Strategy: Color-Coding by Subject 114
  Revising Your Paragraphs 115
    Revision Strategy: Using TRI/PS/QA 115
  Revising Your Sentences 116
    Revision Strategy: Using Conjunctions to Combine
    Sentences 116
  Revising Your Word Choice 118
    Revision Strategy: Reading Aloud 118
  Peer Review 118
    Ask Questions 118
9.5 Editing and Proofreading
  Focusing on Punctuation 119
9.6 Publishing and Presenting
  Building Your Portfolio .120
  Reflecting on Your Writing 120
  ☑ **Rubric for Self-Assessment** 120
Connected Assignment: Consumer Report 121

Student Work
I N   P R O G R E S S

Featured Work:
  "Life in Britain Versus
    Life in the U.S."
    by Emily Agy
  Pleasant Valley High School
    Pleasant Valley, Iowa

Using Point-by-Point
Organization 112
Color-Coding to Check
Structure 114
Adding Conjunctions to
Connect 116

I N T E G R A T E D
S K I L L S

▶ **Grammar in Your Writing**
Conjunctions 117
Punctuating Compound
Sentences 119

Chapter 10 Exposition
Cause-and-Effect Essay 122

10.1 What Is a Cause-and-Effect Essay? 123

10.2 Prewriting
  Choosing Your Topic 124
    Sketch a Scene 124
    Make a Listing 124
    Scan a Newspaper 124
    Topic Bank 125
  Narrowing Your Topic 126
    Use the Cubing Technique 126
  Considering Your Audience and Purpose 126
  Gathering Details .127
    Collect Note Cards 127
    Make a Chain of Events 127

10.3 Drafting
  Shaping Your Writing 128
    Choose a Logical Organization 128
  Providing Elaboration 129
    Use the SEE Technique for Elaboration 129

10.4 Revising
  Revising Your Overall Structure 130
    Revision Strategy: Circling to Identify
    Relationships 130
  Revising Your Paragraphs 131
    Revision Strategy: Color-Coding to Identify
    Related Details 131
  Revising Your Sentences 132
    Revision Strategy: Clarifying Relationships 132
  Revising Your Word Choice 134
    Revision Strategy: Underlining Repeated Words
    and Forms of Words 134
  Peer Review 134
    "Say Back" 134

10.5 Editing and Proofreading
  Focusing on Commonly Confused Words 135

10.6 Publishing and Presenting
  Building Your Portfolio 136
  Reflecting on Your Writing 136
  ☑ **Rubric for Self-Assessment** 136

Connected Assignment: Documentary 137

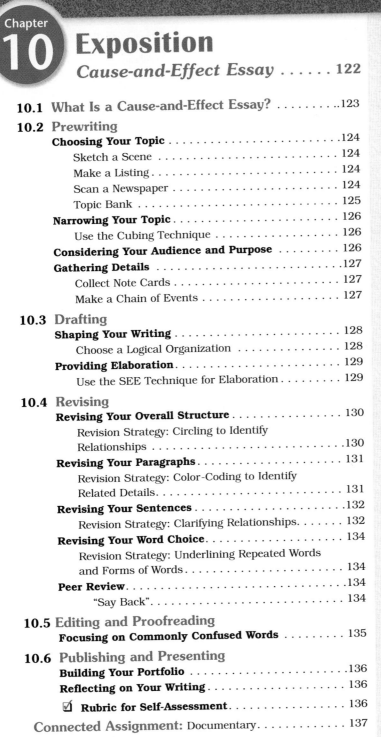

Student Work
IN PROGRESS

Featured Work:
"El Niño"
by Jennifer Hoss
Bel Air High School
El Paso, Texas

Doing a Newspaper Scan
to Find a Topic 124

Showing Causes
and Effects 127

Using SEE to Elaborate . . 129

Color-Coding to Identify
Related Details 131

Clarifying Relationships
With Transitions 132

INTEGRATED SKILLS

▶ **Grammar in Your Writing**
Transitional Phrases 133

Using *Since, Because, Then,*
and *Than* Correctly 135

Chapter 11 Exposition

Problem-and-Solution Essay . . 138

11.1 What Is a Problem-and-Solution Essay? 139

11.2 Prewriting

Choosing Your Topic 140

Talk With a Peer 140

Use Sentence Starters 140

Topic Bank 141

Narrowing Your Topic 142

Use Looping to Narrow Your Topic 142

Considering Your Audience and Purpose 142

Gathering Information 143

Gather Various Types of Details 143

11.3 Drafting

Shaping Your Writing 144

Start With the Problem 144

Providing Elaboration 145

Expand on Your Outline 145

11.4 Revising

Revising Your Overall Structure 146

Revision Strategy: Connecting Ideas 146

Revising Your Paragraphs 147

Revision Strategy: Questioning Your Paragraph
Choices 147

Revising Your Sentences 148

Revision Strategy: Naming Each Tense 148

Revising Your Word Choice 150

Revision Strategy: Highlighting Key Words 150

Peer Review 150

Key Questions 150

11.5 Editing and Proofreading

Focusing on *That* and *Which* 151

11.6 Publishing and Presenting

Building Your Portfolio 152

Reflecting on Your Writing 152

☑ **Rubric for Self-Assessment** 152

Connected Assignment: Advice Column 153

Student Work IN PROGRESS

Featured Work:
"Parking Permits Needed to
Regulate Student Parking"
by Patrick Swan
Muncie Central High School
Muncie, Indiana

Collecting Details 143

Expanding on an Outline . 145

Focusing a Paragraph . . . 147

Fixing Verb Tenses 148

INTEGRATED SKILLS

▶ **Grammar in Your Writing**
The Six Tenses of Verbs . . 149

Restrictive and
Nonrestrictive Clauses . . . 151

Chapter 12 Research Writing... 154

12.1	What Is Research Writing?.................. 155
12.2	**Prewriting**
	Choosing Your Topic 156
	Narrowing Your Topic 158
	Use Research Clues to Narrow Your Topic 158
	Considering Your Audience and Purpose 158
	Use Formal Language....................... 158
	Gathering Information.......................159
	Perform Library Research................... 159
	Take Organized Notes 160
	Doing Investigative Research 161
12.3	**Drafting**
	Shaping Your Writing 162
	Choose an Organizational Strategy 162
	Prepare an Outline 163
	Providing Elaboration....................... 164
	Elaborate on Notes........................ 164
12.4	**Revising**
	Revising Your Overall Structure 165
	Revision Strategy: Using Marginal Notes to Identify the Structure 165
	Revising Your Paragraphs..................... 166
	Revision Strategy: Coding to Identify Structure ... 166
	Revising Your Sentences 167
	Revision Strategy: Color-Coding to Identify Subject-Verb Patterns...................... 167
	Revising Your Word Choice.................... 169
	Revision Strategy: Deleting Empty Words........ 169
	Peer Review.................................169
	Review With a K-W-L Chart 169
12.5	**Editing and Proofreading**
	Preparing a Reference List 170
	Focusing on Proofreading.................... 170
12.6	**Publishing and Presenting**
	Building Your Portfolio 172
	Reflecting on Your Writing.................. 172
	☑ **Rubric for Self-Assessment.**................. 172

Student Work
IN PROGRESS

Featured Work:
"Robert Capa"
by Michael S. Dougherty
Central Bucks West
High School
Doylestown, Pennsylvania

Guiding Research with a
K-W-L Chart 159
Taking Notes 160
Preparing an Outline 163
Elaborating on Notes 164
Color-Coding to Identify
Patterns............. 167
Final Draft.......... **173**

INTEGRATED SKILLS

▶ **Grammar in Your Writing**
Special Problems With
Agreement............ 168
Citing Sources......... 171

Chapter 13 Response to Literature 176

13.1 What Is a Response to Literature?......... 177

13.2 Prewriting
Choosing Your Topic......................... 178
    List 178
    Review Your Journal 178
    Browse a Bookshelf 178
    Discuss With a Peer 178
    Topic Bank 179
Narrowing Your Topic....................... 180
    Make a Web.............................. 180
Considering Your Audience and Purpose 180
Gathering Details 181
    Use Hexagonal Writing to Gather Details 181

13.3 Drafting
Shaping Your Writing 182
    Draft a Thesis Statement 182
Providing Elaboration........................ 183
    Cite Passages From the Work 183

13.4 Revising
Revising Your Overall Structure 184
    Revision Strategy: Underlining Details.......... 184
Revising Your Paragraphs..................... 185
    Revision Strategy: Using a Checklist to Revise
    Paragraphs 185
Revising Your Sentences 186
    Revision Strategy: Color-Coding Elements 186
Revising Your Word Choice................... 188
    Revision Strategy: Reading and Replacing 188
Peer Review 188

13.5 Editing and Proofreading
Focusing on Mechanics 189

13.6 Publishing and Presenting
Building Your Portfolio....................... 190
Reflecting on Your Writing.................... 190
☑ Rubric for Self-Assessment................. 190

Student Work
IN PROGRESS

Featured Work:
  "Telemachus in
  Homer's *Odyssey*"
  by Sheetal Wadera
  Hightower High School
  Missouri City, Texas

Using Hexagonal Writing . 181
Citing Passages from
Literature 183
Underlining Details 184
Color-Coding Characters
to Check For Clarity 185
Final Draft......... 191

INTEGRATED SKILLS

▶ **Grammar in Your Writing**
Pronouns
and Antecedents 187
Styling Titles of Poems,
Stories, and Novels 189

Chapter 14 Writing for Assessment 194

What Is Assessment? 195

14.1 Prewriting
Choosing Your Topic 196
    Skim the Questions 196
    Look for Key Words 196
    Identify the Format 196
    Topic Bank 196
Narrowing Your Response 197
    Identify Key Words 197
    Match Key Words to the Thesis 197
Considering Your Audience and Purpose 197

14.2 Drafting
Shaping Your Writing 198
    Choose an Organizational Model 198
Providing Elaboration 199
    Give Supporting Details 199

14.3 Revising
Revising Your Overall Structure 200
    Revision Strategy: Listing Main Points 200
Revising Your Paragraphs 200
    Revision Strategy: Locating and Ranking Main Ideas . 200
Revising Your Sentences 201
    Revision Strategy: Checking Sentence Beginnings . 201
Revising Your Word Choice 201
    Revision Strategy: Replacing or Deleting "Empty
    and Hedging Words" 201

14.4 Editing and Proofreading
Focusing on Spelling 202

14.5 Publishing and Presenting
Building Your Portfolio 203
Reflecting on Your Writing 203
☑ **Rubric for Self-Assessment** 203

Student Work
IN PROGRESS

Featured Work:
"Why the United States
Entered World War I"
by Tricia Bushnell
Buena High School
Ventura, California

Elaborating With
Supporting Details 199
Deleting Empty and
Hedging Words 201

INTEGRATED SKILLS

▶ **Grammar in Your Writing**
Spelling *ie* and *ei* Words . . 202

Chapter 15 Workplace Writing 204

What Is Workplace Writing? 205
15.1 Business Letter
What Is a Business Letter? 206
    Model Business Letter 206
    Topic Bank 207
15.2 Meeting Minutes
What Are Meeting Minutes? 208
    Model Meeting Minutes. 208
    Topic Bank 209
15.3 Forms and Applications
What Are Business Forms? 210
    Model Fax Cover Sheet 210
    Model Application. 211

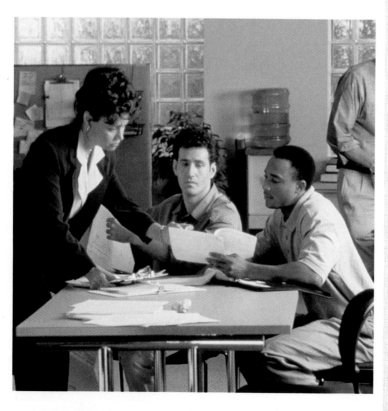

PART 2: GRAMMAR, USAGE, AND MECHANICS

Chapter 16

Nouns, Pronouns, and Verbs 214
▶ **Diagnostic Test**. 215
16.1 Nouns 216
▶ **Section Review** 219
16.2 Pronouns 220
▶ **Section Review** 227
16.3 Action Verbs and Linking Verbs 228
▶ **Hands-on Grammar**. 234
▶ **Section Review** 235
16.4 Verb Phrases 236
▶ **Section Review** 239

Chapter 17

Adjectives and Adverbs 240
▶ **Diagnostic Test**. 241
17.1 Adjectives 242
▶ **Hands-on Grammar**. 250
▶ **Section Review** 251
17.2 Adverbs 252
▶ **Section Review** 257

Chapter 18

Prepositions, Conjunctions, and Interjections 258
▶ **Diagnostic Test**. 259
18.1 Prepositions 260
▶ **Section Review** 264
18.2 Conjunctions and Interjections 265
▶ **Section Review** 270
▶ **Hands-on Grammar** 271

Contents • **xxi**

Chapter 19

Basic Sentence Parts 272
  ▶ **Diagnostic Test**. 273
  19.1 Subjects and Predicates 274
    ▶ **Section Review** 279
  19.2 Hard-to-Find Subjects 280
    ▶ **Hands-on Grammar**. 285
    ▶ **Section Review** 286
  19.3 Direct Objects, Indirect Objects, and
        Objective Complements 287
    The Direct Object 287
    The Objective Complement 292
    ▶ **Section Review** 293
  19.4 Subject Complements 294
    Subject Complements. 294
    The Predicate Adjective. 296
    ▶ **Section Review** 297

Chapter 20

Phrases and Clauses 298
  ▶ **Diagnostic Test**. 299
  20.1 Phrases 300
    Prepositional Phrases 300
    Appositives and Appositive Phrases 303
    Verbal Phrases. 307
    ▶ **Section Review** 320
  20.2 Clauses 322
    Independent and Subordinate Clauses 322
    Adjective Clauses 323
    Adverb Clauses 328
    Noun Clauses 332
    ▶ **Hands-on Grammar**. 335
    ▶ **Section Review** 336

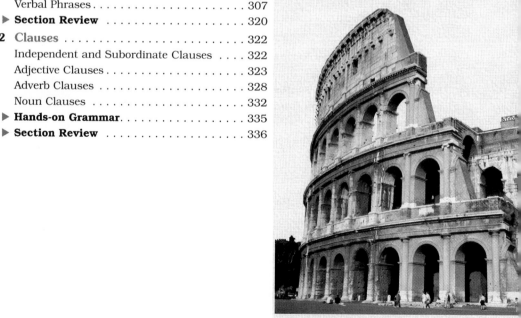

Chapter 21

Effective Sentences 338

▶ **Diagnostic Test** 339

21.1 The Four Functions of a Sentence 340

▶ **Section Review** 342

21.2 Combining Sentences 343

▶ **Hands-on Grammar** 348

▶ **Section Review** 349

21.3 Varying Sentences 350

▶ **Section Review** 353

21.4 Avoiding Sentence Problems 354

Recognizing Fragments 354

Correcting Phrase Fragments 356

Correcting Clause Fragments 358

Correcting Run-on Sentences 359

Recognizing Misplaced Modifiers 361

Revising Sentences With
Misplaced Modifiers 363

▶ **Section Review** 365

Chapter 22

Verb Usage 366

▶ **Diagnostic Test** 367

22.1 Verb Tenses 368

▶ **Hands-on Grammar** 379

▶ **Section Review** 380

22.2 Active and Passive Voice 382

▶ **Section Review** 385

Chapter 23

Pronoun Usage 386

▶ **Diagnostic Test** 387

23.1 Case 388

▶ **Section Review** 395

23.2 Special Problems With Pronouns 396

▶ **Hands-on Grammar** 402

▶ **Section Review** 403

Chapter

24

Agreement 404
▶ **Diagnostic Test**. 405
24.1 Subject and Verb Agreement 406
▶ **Hands-on Grammar**. 414
▶ **Section Review** 415
24.2 Pronoun and Antecedent Agreement . . 417
▶ **Section Review** 423

Chapter

25

Using Modifiers 424
▶ **Diagnostic Test**. 425
25.1 Degrees of Comparison 426
Recognizing Degrees of Comparison 426
Regular Forms 427
Irregular Forms 428
▶ **Section Review** 431
25.2 Making Clear Comparisons 432
Using Comparative
and Superlative Degrees 432
Making Logical Comparisons 433
▶ **Hands-on Grammar** 436
▶ **Section Review** 437

Chapter

26

Miscellaneous Problems
in Usage 438
▶ **Diagnostic Test**. 439
26.1 Negative Sentences 440
Recognizing Double Negatives 440
Forming Negative Sentences Correctly 441
▶ **Section Review** 443
26.2 Common Usage Problems 444
▶ **Hands-on Grammar** 454
▶ **Section Review** 455

Chapter 27

Capitalization 456

▶ **Diagnostic Test**. 457
   Using Capitals for First Words. 458
   Using Capitals for Proper Nouns 461
   Using Capitals for Proper Adjectives 465
   Using Capitals for Titles 466
▶ **Hands-on Grammar**. 469

Chapter 28

Punctuation 470

▶ **Diagnostic Test**. 471
28.1 End Marks 472
▶ **Section Review** 475
28.2 Commas 476
▶ **Section Review** 491
28.3 Semicolons and Colons 493
▶ **Hands-on Grammar** 502
▶ **Section Review** 503
28.4 Quotation Marks and Underlining 504
▶ **Section Review** 519
28.5 Dashes, Parentheses, and Hyphens . . . 520
▶ **Section Review** 533
28.6 Apostrophes 534

Chapter 29

Speaking, Listening, Viewing, and Representing 546

29.1 Speaking and Listening Skills 547
29.2 Viewing Skills 554
    Interpreting Maps and Graphs 554
    Viewing Information Media Critically 557
    Interpreting Fine Art 559
29.3 Representing Skills................ 560
    Creating Visual Aids 560
    Using Formatting 562
    Working With Multimedia 563
    Producing a Video 564
    Performing or Interpreting 565

Chapter 30

Vocabulary and Spelling 566

30.1 Developing Your Vocabulary 567
    Reading, Listening, and Discussing 567
    Recognizing Context Clues 568
    Denotation and Connotation 569
    Recognizing Related Words 570
    Using Related Words in Analogies 571
30.2 Studying Words Systematically 572
    Using Resource Materials 572
    Remembering Vocabulary Words 573
30.3 Studying Word Parts and Origins 574
    Recognizing Word Roots 574
    Using Prefixes 575
    Adding Suffixes 576
30.4 Improving Your Spelling............ 578
    Keeping a Spelling Notebook 578
    Studying Problem Words 579
    Developing Memory Aids 580
    Applying Spelling Rules 581
    Proofreading Carefully 586

Chapter 31

Reading Skills 588

31.1 Reading Methods and Tools.......... 589
31.2 Reading Nonfiction Critically 596
31.3 Reading Literary Writing 602
31.4 Reading From Varied Sources 606

Chapter 32

Study, Reference, and Test-Taking Skills 608

32.1 Basic Study Skills 609
32.2 Reference Skills 611
32.3 Test-Taking Skills 624

Chapter 33

Workplace Skills and Competencies 628

Working With People 629
Learning Teamwork 631
Moving Toward Goals 633
Solving Problems and Thinking
Creatively 634
Managing Time 636
Managing Money 637
Applying Math Skills 638
Applying Computer Skills 639

Test Preparation Handbook 640

Resources

Citing Sources and Preparing Manuscript . . 672
Penmanship Reference 672
Internet Research Handbook 679
Commonly Overused Words 682
Commonly Misspelled Words 684
Abbreviations Guide 686
Proofreading Symbols Reference 690
Student Publications 691
Student Diagraming Workshop 692
Index 704

Writing

Femme Cousant, Henri Lebasque, Christie's Images

The Writer in You

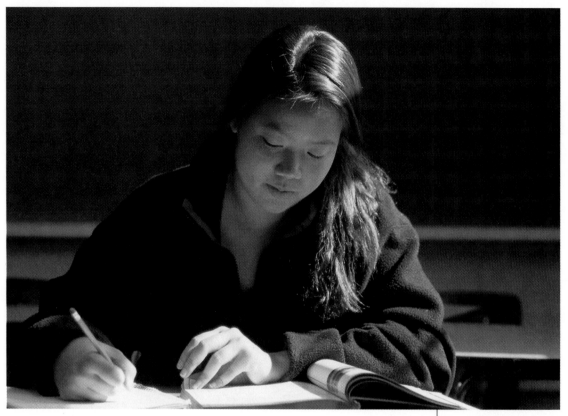

▲ **Critical Viewing**
Suppose you wanted
to interview this stu-
dent about her writ-
ing habits. Name
three questions you
might ask. **[Classify]**

You weren't born knowing how to speak. You learned to
speak by listening to others and, eventually, by using words
yourself. The more you spoke, the better you became at it. The
same is true of writing. The best way to discover the writer in
you is, naturally, to write!

Writing in Everyday Life

Writing is already and will continue to be an important part
of your everyday life. The writing you do can be as simple as
jotting down a phone message or writing yourself a quick
reminder or as complex as developing a research paper on a
historical event or preparing a science lab report. You probably do some form of writing—either simple or complex—just
about every day. In this chapter, you will learn strategies to
help you fully take advantage of each writing opportunity so
that you can continue to develop your skills as a writer.

What Are the Qualities of Good Writing?

Ideas Strong ideas are the starting point for good writing. Try to begin each piece of writing by focusing on a topic that interests you. In addition, consider whether an idea you are writing about will interest your audience. If not, you may want to consider writing about something else.

Organization Present your ideas and details in a consistent, organized manner that will be easy for readers to follow. Often, your topic and the type of writing that you are doing will dictate a particular method of organization. For example, if you are telling a story, you'll probably want to present events in the order in which they occur.

Voice Voice refers to all of the qualities that make your writing different from that of others. It includes the way you use words and sentences, the types of topics you write about, and the perspective that you bring to those topics. Whenever you write, let your personal voice come through in your writing.

Word Choice Words are the building blocks of a piece of writing. The stronger each block is, the stronger the finished piece will be. Carefully choose each word you use. Make sure that it conveys your intended meaning as precisely as possible. In addition to conveying your meaning, your words should also capture your attitude toward your subject.

Sentence Fluency Read your work aloud to see that each sentence flows smoothly from one to the next. Use transitions to connect your sentences, and vary the length and structure of your sentences to help build a rhythm.

Conventions Don't let errors spoil the impact of your work. Take care to ensure that you have followed the conventions of English grammar, usage, mechanics, and spelling.

Reflecting on Your Writing

Self-questioning is useful for honing your writing skills. Here are some questions that can lead you to discover more about the writer in you:

- Which of your recent writing projects was most successful? Why did you connect so well with this project?

- What specific obstacles have you faced when writing? What strategies might you use to overcome these obstacles?

- What writers do you admire? How does reading their work suggest ideas you can apply to your own writing?

A Walk Through the Writing Process

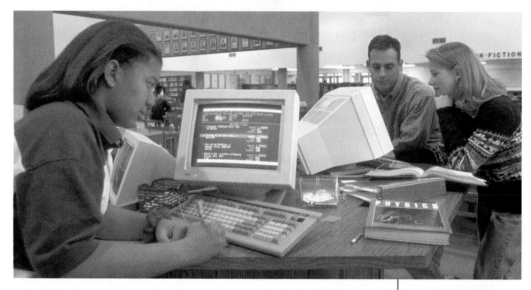

Writing, in one form or another, is an essential component of your daily life. Whatever your final product, the writing process—a systematic approach to writing—can help you achieve it. From prewriting to publishing and presenting, being familiar with and using the stages of the writing process will help you write better.

▲ **Critical Viewing**
Identify one way in which computers in the library can improve your writing process. **[Analyze]**

Types of Writing

There are many types of writing. The various types can be grouped into **modes**, a word that refers to the central purpose of a piece of writing. The chart at right shows the modes you'll encounter in this book.

Writing can also be divided into two broader categories: reflexive and extensive, based on the source of inspiration and audience for a piece of writing. When you write reflexively, you choose what to write, what format to use, and whether to share your writing with others. **Reflexive writing**—such as a journal entry, a personal essay, or a list—is writing you do for yourself. **Extensive writing**, which focuses on topics outside of your imagination and experience, is writing that you do for others. Examples of extensive writing include research papers, persuasive essays, and book and theater reviews.

The Modes of Writing
- Narration
- Description
- Persuasion
- Exposition
- Research
- Response to Literature
- Assessment
- Workplace

The Process of Writing

The process of writing occurs in several stages:

- **Prewriting** includes exploring topics, choosing a topic, and beginning to gather and organize details before you write.
- **Drafting** involves getting your ideas down on paper in roughly the format you intend for the finished work.
- **Revising** is the stage in which you rework your first draft to improve its content and structure.
- **Editing and proofreading** involve correcting errors in grammar, spelling, and mechanics.
- **Publishing and presenting** are the sharing of your work with others.

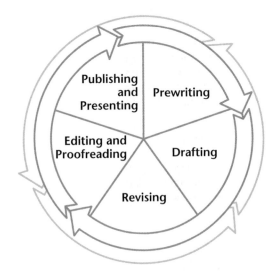

These stages may appear to follow a set sequence, but as writers work, they often skip stages or shift back to earlier stages. For example, as you draft, you may begin making revisions in your work; or as you revise, you may discover that you need to go back and gather more ideas.

A Guided Tour

Use this chapter as a guided tour of the stages of the writing process. Familiarize yourself with the activities of writing. Learn new strategies, look at the way other effective writers employ them, and try them out yourself. In the chapters that follow, you'll see how to apply these and other strategies to specific types of writing.

Most writers feel challenged when faced with a blank sheet of paper. Writers may grapple with what topic to write about, or they may wonder just how much they have to say about a subject. The prewriting stage helps to get a writer's creative juices flowing. Just as musicians prepare for a performance by practicing, you can warm up to write with your own set of prewriting strategies and techniques.

Choosing Your Topic

To begin writing, you must have a topic. Usually, it is best to write about what you know or about what you find interesting. Take time to explore subjects, issues, and experiences that are meaningful to you. You can use a wide variety of strategies to generate topics. Try this sample strategy:

SAMPLE STRATEGY

Blueprinting When you blueprint, you draw a map of a place you know well. To try this strategy, draw a floor plan of a classroom in your school. Fill in the room plan with symbols for desks, chairs, computers, chalkboards, bookshelves, windows, doorways, pictures, and whatever else is appropriate. Think about significant events that this room calls to mind, and list the ideas on your blueprint. From that list, select a topic to develop.

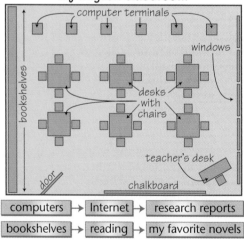

My English Classroom

⊘ Learn More

For additional prewriting strategies suited to specific writing tasks, see Chapters 4–15.

Narrowing Your Topic

Once you have selected a writing topic, make sure it is not so general that you can't cover it thoroughly in a short piece of writing. Consider whether you can narrow your topic by focusing on a single subtopic or aspect of it. One strategy you might use is shown below.

SAMPLE STRATEGY

Looping to Narrow a Topic Looping is a way of discovering and focusing on the features of a topic that are most important or interesting to you. Begin by freewriting on a general topic, such as sports, friends, or favorite books. Write for five minutes. Then, review what you have written. Circle the most important or significant word. Next, freewrite based on that word for five more minutes. Once again, circle the most important or significant word, and freewrite about it. Continue looping until you are satisfied that your topic is narrow enough. Look at this example:

Looping

Broad topic: Reading
   I think I enjoy the time I spend reading because it is private time.

   Reading is something I can really get lost in. When I'm reading a

great book, not much can distract me.

   Reading gives me an alternative to the everyday realities of my own

life and is a great way to disregard anything that annoys me.
Great book:
   Novels especially appeal to me for lots of reasons. Sometimes

characters seem really strange and foreign to me, and other times

I can really relate to them. I like to be pulled into the life of another

character, to feel like I'm experiencing the world being presented in

that novel, and to learn new things.
Narrowed topic:
   The characters in novels make reading appealing to me.

Considering Your Audience and Purpose

After you've narrowed your topic, identify your audience—the person or people who will read your work—and your purpose—what you want your writing to accomplish. Your audience and purpose will affect the type of language you use and the types of information you present.

Considering Your Audience It is best not to develop a piece of writing without thinking about who is going to read it. Consider your audience's age, interests, and knowledge of your subject. If you are writing for young children who know little about your topic, use simple language and include the most basic details. If, on the other hand, you are writing for experts or enthusiasts in the field, use sophisticated language and leave out extended explanations of basic details.

Develop an audience profile by asking and answering questions about your audience, such as those on the notepad below. Refer back to your audience profile as you develop your writing.

Considering Your Purpose Identify what you hope to accomplish with your writing. You may be writing to persuade, to entertain, to inform, or to achieve a variety of other specific purposes. Keep your purpose in mind as you decide which details to include, which to leave out, and what type of language to use.

Audience Profile

1. What does my audience already know?

2. What do they need to know?

3. What details will interest or influence my audience?

Gathering Details

Regardless of your subject, it is essential that you back up the points you make with examples, facts, and details. Generally, it is most effective to take some time to gather details before you begin writing. This may involve research in the library or on the Internet or interviews with experts. Consider these strategies for gathering details:

SAMPLE STRATEGY

Using Hexagonal Writing

Hexagonal writing helps you gather details about a literary work in order to write a well-balanced, complete analysis. Create a chart like the one at right. Then, follow the directions shown here to fill it out.

PLOT

EVALUATION — Decide whether you liked the work.

Summarize or paraphrase the work.

PERSONAL ALLUSION — Note ideas or experiences the selection suggests to you.

LITERARY ALLUSION — Name other literature with a similar theme.

Cite evidence to support the theme.

THEME — State the message the work conveys.

ANALYSIS

SAMPLE STRATEGY

Generating Sensory Word Bins When you are writing description, the words you use create an image for your reader. Identify your topic, and then list words that appeal to each of the senses. Look at this example:

Sensory Word Bin: A Summer Storm				
SIGHTS	**SOUNDS**	**SMELLS**	**TASTES**	**PHYSICAL SENSATIONS**
glistening foggy murky	thunder splashes muffled	freshness springlike		heat breeze

▶ APPLYING THE PREWRITING STRATEGIES

1. Construct a blueprint of a special place. Then, use your blueprint to identify potential writing topics.
2. Use looping to narrow a topic generated by your blueprint.
3. Identify two different audiences, and devise corresponding audience profiles for an account of a memorable vacation.
4. Use hexagonal writing to gather details about a short story or novel you have recently read.

🖥 Internet Tip

Using an Internet browser, you can conduct a keyword search on your topic. Be as specific as possible when entering key words, so that you don't come up with more information than you can manage.

2.2 What Is Drafting?

Shaping Your Writing

Match Purpose and Form Each form of writing is linked to a specific purpose. Make sure that your purpose in writing matches that of your chosen form. For instance, if you are writing an editorial, your purpose should be to influence the way others think or act. If you are writing a report or how-to essay, your purpose should be to inform or explain. The purpose of your chosen form will shape your writing, from the details you include to the organization you use. Keep your form and purpose in mind as you draft.

Pull Readers In With an Enticing Lead Begin with an interest-grabbing first paragraph to attract your audience's attention and to stoke their desire to keep reading. To hook with a powerful "lead," employ a controversial quotation, a little-known fact, a bizarre bit of dialogue, or a striking description.

⊘ Learn More

You can learn about all of the various forms of writing in the writing chapters that follow.

Providing Elaboration

As you draft, elaborate on your main ideas, providing supporting facts, examples, statistics, and other details to help readers understand and accept your points. The SEE method is one strategy that you can use for elaboration.

SAMPLE STRATEGY

Using the SEE Method To use the SEE method (Statement, Extension, and Elaboration), begin each paragraph with a statement that conveys a main idea. Extend that idea by restating or explaining the first sentence. Elaborate on your explanation or restatement by providing supporting details.

STATEMENT:	Family reunions can be fun.
EXTENSION:	When you get together with relatives, you can enjoy the funny stories they tell.
ELABORATION:	No matter how many times you hear about your brother's first report card, you'll still find the exaggerations of the story amusing.

▶ APPLYING THE DRAFTING STRATEGIES

1. Write a humorous or startling lead sentence for a description of a basketball game.
2. Complete the following statements. Then, use the SEE technique to elaborate your ideas.
   My favorite actor is ___?___.
   I'd like to travel to ___?___.

2.3 *What Is Revising?*

Using a Systematic Approach to Revision

Revision is probably the most important stage of the writing process. However, many writers also find it to be the most difficult. In this textbook, you will learn a systematic approach to revision called **ratiocination** (rash´ ē äs ə nā´shen). In everyday use, *ratiocination* refers to the process of reasoning using formal logic. In writing, it refers to the use of a logical step-by-step process to color-code, analyze, evaluate, and rework your writing.

Start by evaluating the overall structure of your work. Then, look at paragraphs, sentences, and words. Throughout the process, use a simple system of highlighting and color-coding to draw your attention to areas that need improvement.

Writers in
ACTION

In The Elements of Style, *William Strunk, Jr., and E. B. White say:*
"Revising is a part of writing. Few writers are so expert that they can produce what they are after on the first try."

Revising Your Overall Structure

There are a variety of things to look for when revising the overall structure of your work, including the following:

- Check to see that your organization makes sense and that it is consistent. You may find it necessary to reorganize parts of your paper.

- Make sure that your introduction will grab your readers' interest and that your conclusion will leave a lasting impression.

- Determine whether you have provided enough support for your main idea. One strategy you can use for this purpose is shown next.

SAMPLE STRATEGY

▶ **REVISION STRATEGY**
Color-Coding Support for Your Main Point

With a red pencil, underline the sentence or sentences that convey the main point of your paper. Then, use a blue pencil to underline the support you've provided for your main point. Once you've finished, you should find that much of your paper is underlined in blue. If not, you probably don't have enough support for your main point. Add more facts, details, or examples to strengthen your writing. In addition, you may want to consider whether all of the passages you have not underlined are necessary.

Revising Your Paragraphs

Once you've reviewed the structure of your draft, check to see that each paragraph focuses on a single aspect of your topic and that all of the sentences within a paragraph relate to one another. Eliminate any sentences that are not clearly related to the others, and look for places where transitions can link the ideas within a paragraph.

Learn More

You will learn more about how to achieve greater sentence variety in Chapter 21.

SAMPLE STRATEGY

▶ **REVISION STRATEGY**
Using Steps, Stacks, Chains, and Balances

- **Steps** When a paragraph presents a series of events or explains a series of steps, check to see that you have used transitions to make the sequence clear to readers. If not, add words such as *first, then,* and *finally.*

- **Stacks** When a paragraph presents a series of related ideas, add transitions such as *in addition* and *as well as.* If certain ideas are more important than others, make sure that you have indicated this with transitions such as *most important.*

- **Chains** When a paragraph explains a cause-and-effect relationship, add transitions such as *consequently* and *as a result* to clarify the relationships among your details.

- **Balances** When the paragraph shows contrast or choice, add words such as *similarly, however, although,* and *rather.*

Revising Your Sentences

Next, study your sentences. Check to see that you have varied their length and structure. Using too many sentences of the same types can make your writing sound choppy.

SAMPLE STRATEGY

▶ **REVISION STRATEGY**
Bracketing Sentence Openers

Use a colored pen to bracket the first three words of each sentence. Review your paper, focusing only on the bracketed words. If you have begun most of your sentences in the same way, rework some of them to produce greater variety.

Revising Your Word Choice

Complete the process of revision by analyzing words you have used. Look for places where you can replace vague or general words with ones that more precisely convey your meaning. Also, check to see whether you have overused certain words. The following strategy will help:

SAMPLE STRATEGY

▶ **REVISION STRATEGY**
Highlighting Repeated Words

Use a highlighter to mark any words you have used more than once. Review the words that you have marked, and consider replacing some to make your writing more lively. Look at this example:

Peer Review

Once you've finished revising on your own, you may want to enlist the help of classmates. Often, others can see problems that are hard for the writer to identify. Use these tips to get the specific feedback you want:

EVALUATING REPEATED WORDS

The ~~snow began falling~~ early in the morning. *first flakes of snow began drifting down from the sky*

By early afternoon, the ground was covered with ~~several inches of snow.~~ *fluffy white crystals* When evening came, it was still snowing heavily ~~the snow was still falling,~~ and by that time, ~~there~~ *the landscape* ~~was at least a foot of snow on the ground.~~ *was layered with at least a foot of soft white powder*

Focusing Peer Review	
Purpose	**Ask**
Evaluate introduction	What part of the introduction was most interesting?
Test argument	Which reason was most convincing?
	Which point was least compelling?

▶ **APPLYING THE REVISION STRATEGIES**

Select a piece of writing you did last year. Use the revision strategies presented here to make improvements in this piece. Identify four changes the strategies helped you make.

What Are Editing and Proofreading?

Once you have finished revising for content, proofread your work carefully to find and eliminate errors in grammar, usage, mechanics, and spelling. These types of errors will distract readers and may cause them to respond negatively to your work—even if the content is excellent.

Focusing on Proofreading

To check your writing for errors, get in the habit of reviewing your draft several times. Each time, focus on a specific proofreading topic. Consider these key areas:

Scrutinize Your Spelling The spell-check function of a word-processing program is never fully dependable. Refer to a dictionary to check the spelling of questionable words.

Follow the Conventions of Grammar, Usage, and Mechanics Apply these conventions to everything you write. Examine each sentence, and correct capitalization and punctuation. Check your grammar and usage, and eliminate problematic language or grammatical structures.

Eliminate Run-on Sentences One specific type of error that you may uncover while proofreading is a run-on sentence—two main clauses that are not adequately separated by punctuation. Look at this example:

CORRECTING RUN-ON SENTENCES

> Some whales weigh as much as twenty elephants, they have blood vessels wide enough for a trout to swim through!

Below are two ways to correct a run-on sentence:
- Break it into two simple sentences.

> Some whales weigh as much as twenty elephants. They have blood vessels wide enough for a trout to swim through!

- Rewrite it as a compound sentence.

> Some whales weigh as much as twenty elephants, and they have blood vessels wide enough for a trout to swim through!

▶ **APPLYING THE EDITING AND PROOFREADING STRATEGIES**

With a partner, identify two grammar, usage, or mechanics errors in a recent piece of your writing. Then, discuss ways to locate and correct such problems during the proofreading stage.

Technology Tip

If your word processor has a spell-check feature, use it, but don't expect it to do the job of a good proofreader. Both *where* and *wear* will pass a spell check, but you may not have used the word you wanted.

2.5 What Are Publishing and Presenting?

Moving Forward

This preview of the writing process provides just a glimpse of the strategies and techniques you can employ in your writing process. Each lesson in this section provides specific strategies that will aid you as you write.

Building Your Portfolio Your finished writing products are valuable, so be sure to organize and save them in a folder, a box, or some other secure place. View your portfolio as a record of your development as a writer. Occasionally, you may return to it to compare your latest writing with something you wrote a while ago.

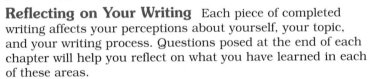

PORTFOLIO

You can also use your portfolio as a repository for future writing ideas, including unfinished writing and thought-provoking photographs or clippings.

Reflecting on Your Writing Each piece of completed writing affects your perceptions about yourself, your topic, and your writing process. Questions posed at the end of each chapter will help you reflect on what you have learned in each of these areas.

Assessing Your Writing A rubric, or set of criteria, on which your work can be evaluated is offered at the end of each chapter. To ensure that you are addressing the main points of the particular mode, refer to the rubric throughout the writing process.

▶ ## APPLYING THE PUBLISHING AND PRESENTING STRATEGIES

1. Reexamine the prewriting activities you used in this introduction to the writing process. Choose one you want to work into a fully developed piece of writing at a later time. Place it in your portfolio. Speak with a writing partner about what made you choose that particular activity.
2. In your writing journal, reflect on your writing process by responding to the following questions:

   • Which techniques helped you the most? Explain.
   • What are your strengths as a writer?

Sentences, Paragraphs, and Compositions
Structure and Style

What Are Sentences, Paragraphs, and Compositions?

A *sentence* is a group of words with a subject and a predicate that expresses a complete thought. Sentences are the building blocks of your writing.

A *paragraph* is a group of related sentences that presents a unit of thought. Paragraphs provide organization and focus to your writing. When you read, a new paragraph is indicated by visual clues, such as the indentation of the first word of the first sentence or an extra line of space between lines of text.

A *composition* is a connected series of paragraphs on a single topic. There are many types of compositions, including essays, research papers, and workplace writing. The specific types of compositions will be covered in later chapters.

▲ **Critical Viewing**
Explain how creating a garden is like constructing an effective paragraph. **[Connect]**

3.1

Sentence Combining

Writing Effective Sentences

Effective sentences are the key to appealing and interesting writing. A sentence that is effective by itself, however, may seem uninteresting if it is one in a series of short sentences. Such a series can produce a choppy, repetitive effect.

To keep your sentences interesting, you need to consider sentence variety. By combining two or more short sentences, you can vary your sentences. At the same time, you can show connections between events, stress important information, and create a smooth flow of ideas.

Inserting Words and Phrases

You may combine two related sentences by taking key information from one and inserting it into the other. The information to be inserted may be a word or it may be a phrase. To combine sentences successfully, you may have to change the form of the words and use additional punctuation.

▼ Critical Viewing
How is constructing a building, such as this building by Antoni Gaudí, like combining sentences in a paragraph? [Connect]

EXAMPLE: The Spanish artist Joan Miró worked in many
                      different media. Miró is a world-famous artist.

INSERTING   The **world-famous** Spanish artist Joan
A WORD: Miró worked in many different media.

EXAMPLE: Miguel de Cervantes was born outside Madrid.
                      He is the author of *Don Quixote*.

INSERTING   Miguel de Cervantes, **the author of**
A PHRASE: ***Don Quixote,*** was born outside Madrid.

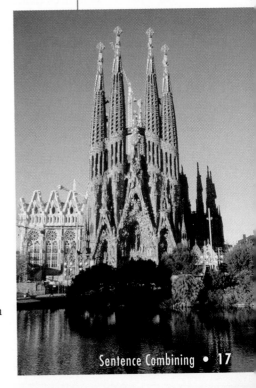

▶ **Exercise 1** Combining With Words and Phrases
Combine each pair of sentences by inserting key information from one sentence into the other. Add commas as necessary.

1. Antoni Gaudí was a famous architect. He was from Spain.
2. Gaudi is probably best known for the Church of the Sagrada Familia in Barcelona. It is unfinished.
3. The Prado contains collections of paintings by artists such as El Greco, Velázquez, and Goya. The Prado is located in Madrid, Spain.
4. The Canary Islands are located in the Atlantic Ocean off the coast of Africa. They are part of Spain.
5. The wild canary bird is generally green, unlike the canaries bred as pets. It takes its name from the islands on which it lives.

Using Compound Elements

Related sentences may be combined by joining elements from each to form compound subjects, verbs, or objects.

EXAMPLE: Spain is on my list of places to go on vacation. Gibraltar is also on my list.

COMPOUND   **Spain and Gibraltar** are on my list of places
SUBJECT: to go on vacation.

EXAMPLE: We visited the Alhambra in Granada, Spain. Then, we toured the gardens and parks.

COMPOUND   We **visited the Alhambra** and **toured the**
VERB: **gardens and parks** in Granada, Spain.

EXAMPLE: In the Straits of Gibraltar, tourists can see dolphins. They can also see whales.

COMPOUND   In the Straits of Gibraltar, tourists can see
OBJECT :   **dolphins and whales.**

EXAMPLE: Gibraltar is famous for its caves. It is also known for the wild Barbary apes.

COMPOUND   Gibraltar is famous **for its caves and the**
PREPOSITIONAL **wild Barbary apes.**
PHRASE:

ⓘ Learn More

For additional information about objects, see Section 19.3; for additional information about prepositional phrases, see Section 20.1.

▶ **Exercise 2** Using Compound Sentence Elements Combine each pair of sentences using compound elements.
1. Seville is a city in southern Spain. Córdoba is another city in southern Spain.
2. Catalan, a Romance language, is spoken in Catalonia. It is also spoken in Roussillon.
3. Spain is known for its sunny climate. It is also known for its beautiful castles and cathedrals.
4. Spanish fishers catch squid and sardines. They also catch tuna and octopuses.
5. The entertainers in the café danced the flamenco. They played the guitar, too.
6. The Prado, Madrid's great museum, is a main attraction for visitors. El Escorial, a palace outside Madrid, is another.
7. The Spanish are the inventors of *paella*, a rice-based dish. They also invented *gazpacho*, a cold tomato soup.
8. The Spanish parliament, known as the Cortes, is divided into two houses. It has more than 500 members.
9. The Spanish people elect members of the Chamber of Deputies, the lower house of the Cortes. They also vote for the Senate, the upper house of the Cortes.
10. You can see traces of Spain's history in the ruins left by the ancient Romans. You can also see them in the alcazars (palaces) built by the Moors of North Africa.

Forming Compound Sentences

A **compound sentence** consists of two or more independent clauses joined by a comma and a **coordinating conjunction** (*and, but, for, nor, or, so,* or *yet*) or by a semicolon.

EXAMPLE: Soccer is the most popular sport in Spain. Many cities have soccer stadiums that seat tens of thousands of spectators.

COMBINED: Soccer is the most popular sport in Spain, **and** many cities have soccer stadiums that seat tens of thousands of spectators. (comma and coordinating conjunction)

You may also use a semicolon or a semicolon and a transition word called a **conjunctive adverb,** such as *however, nevertheless,* and *consequently.* Notice that you are not simply linking two ideas: You are expressing a relationship between them.

EXAMPLE: We were exhausted after six days of touring. We went on to Madrid anyway.

COMBINED: We were exhausted after six days of touring; **nevertheless,** we went on to Madrid. (semicolon and conjunctive adverb)

To Combine Independent Clauses
Use a coordinating conjunction and a comma.
Coordinating Conjunctions: and, but, for, nor, or, so, yet
Use a semicolon and a conjunctive adverb.
Conjunctive Adverbs: consequently, furthermore, however, otherwise, therefore

Learn More

For additional information about compound sentences, see Section 21.2; for additional information about using semicolons, see Section 28.3.

Exercise 3   **Forming Compound Sentences** Using the strategy in parentheses, combine each pair of sentences to form a compound sentence.

1. The Strait of Gibraltar connects the Mediterranean Sea with the Atlantic Ocean. The Suez Canal links the Mediterranean Sea with the Red Sea. (comma and coordinating conjunction)
2. Spain is only eight miles from Morocco across the Strait of Gibraltar. The two countries lie on different continents. (semicolon and conjunctive adverb)
3. Rabat is the capital of Morocco. Casablanca is the largest city in Morocco. (comma and coordinating conjunction)
4. Arabic-speakers make up nearly 65 percent of Morocco's population. Berber-speakers constitute the rest of the population. (semicolon)
5. Morocco exports leatherwork and rugs. It imports oil. (comma and coordinating conjunction)

Using Subordination

When one sentence explains more about an idea in another sentence, you can combine the two sentences by rewriting the first sentence as a subordinate clause. Although a **subordinate clause** has a subject and a verb, it cannot stand by itself as a sentence. An **adjective clause** is a subordinate clause that modifies a noun or pronoun by telling *what kind* or *which one*, using a relative pronoun such as *who, whom, whose, which,* or *that*.

EXAMPLE: The Sahara is the world's largest desert. The Sahara includes portions of eleven countries.

COMBINED: The Sahara, **which includes portions of eleven countries,** is the world's largest desert.

An **adverb clause** is a subordinate clause that answers the question *where, when, in what way,* or *why*. All adverb clauses begin with subordinating conjunctions such as *after, although, as, because, before, if, in order that, unless, until, where,* or *wherever*.

EXAMPLE: Most of Libya is covered by the Sahara. For this reason, most of Libya is uninhabitable.

COMBINED: Most of Libya is uninhabitable **because it is covered by the Sahara.**

(?) Learn More

For additional information about clauses, see Section 20.2; for additional information about pronouns, see Section 16.2.

Subordinating Conjunctions			
after	because	in order that	unless
although	before	since	until
as	even though	so that	when
as if	if	than	while

► **Exercise 4** Using Subordination Combine each pair of sentences using subordinate clauses.

1. The northernmost point in continental Africa is in Tunisia. Tunisia is bordered on the north and east by the Mediterranean Sea. (adjective clause)
2. Most people who live in the Sahara use camels for transportation. Camels can travel far without food or water. (adverb clause)
3. Sometimes, camels use the fatty tissue in the hump for energy. Then, the hump gets smaller and softer. (adverb clause)
4. Scientists believe that camels originated in North America. There are no native camels in North America today. (adverb clause)
5. Our trip to Algeria ended with a visit to the city of Algiers. Algiers is my parents' city of origin. (adjective clause)

3.2 *Writing Effective Paragraphs*

Main Idea and Topic Sentence

In a good paragraph, all of the sentences work together to present and develop one main idea. Often, the main idea is directly stated in a single sentence called the *topic sentence*. All of the other sentences in the paragraph support the topic sentence with examples, details, facts, or reasons.

Sometimes, a paragraph's main idea is *implied*, not directly stated. In such cases, all of the sentences work together to develop the main idea and communicate it to readers.

WRITING MODELS

from **The Cabuliwallah**
by Rabindranath Tagore
Translated From the Bengali Language

Mini, my five-year-old daughter, cannot live without chattering. I really believe that in all her life she has not wasted one minute in silence. Her mother is often vexed at this and would stop her prattle, but I do not. To see Mini quiet is unnatural, and I cannot bear it for long. Because of this, our conversations are always lively.

In this paragraph, the stated topic sentence is shown in blue italics. The other sentences support, develop, and illustrate the topic sentence.

from **Imitating Nature's Mineral Artistry**
Paul O'Neil

The chemical ingredients for a man-made gem are easy to obtain, since most gems consist of relatively common chemical compounds. The art of gem synthesis lies in the technique by which the gem material is liquefied, in a melt or a solution, and then allowed to crystallize slowly and evenly.

Notice that this paragraph does not contain a topic sentence. Instead, all of the sentences work together to communicate an implied main idea: Creating synthetic gems is an art that requires expertise.

> **Exercise 5** Identifying a Stated Topic Sentence Identify the stated topic sentence of the following paragraph:

A medieval feast was designed to appeal to the senses. The dishes were colorful, such as green eel stew, and highly spiced, such as rabbit seasoned with ginger, cinnamon, saffron, sugar, cloves, and nutmeg. Regarding flavor, two words that appeared often in medieval cooking were *aigre*, a popular sour flavor, and *doux*, meaning "not salty."

> **Exercise 6** Identifying an Implied Main Idea Identify the implied main idea of the following paragraph:

We arrived at the gym an hour before the pep rally started. Helen and I hung red and white streamers from the bleachers, while Alex hung posters from the chalkboards. After twenty minutes, the band filed in, pumping marching music with a rhythmic beat. Next, the bell rang, and suddenly the entire class was piling in, stepping clunkily onto the bleachers. Once everyone was seated, the state champion soccer team stormed the floor, and the crowd went wild.

Writing Topic Sentences

In most of the writing you'll do in school—with the exception of stories and other types of creative writing—you will want to focus on writing paragraphs that contain topic sentences. Following are some tips for writing strong topic sentences:

TIPS FOR WRITING TOPIC SENTENCES

1. Review the details you've gathered for a piece of writing.
2. Identify groups of details to focus on specific topics or subtopics.
3. Jot down a few words to capture the main idea that connects each group of details.
4. Develop a sentence that thoroughly and concisely captures the main idea of a group of details.
5. Once you've completed a paragraph, review your topic sentence, and make sure it still sums up the main idea expressed in the other sentences. Revise it if necessary.

> **Exercise 7** Writing Topic Sentences Write a topic sentence for a paragraph on each of the following topics:
1. How computers have changed the quality of life
2. The value of holding a position in student government
3. Building-accessibility for the physically challenged
4. Funding for boys' and girls' sports
5. The high cost of concert tickets

Writing Supporting Sentences

A paragraph's topic sentence should be accompanied by a series of sentences that develop, explain, or illustrate. These other sentences are called *supporting sentences.* Following are some of the types of information that you can include in your supporting sentences:

Use Facts Facts are statements that are provable. They support your key idea by offering backup or proof.

TOPIC SENTENCE:	Our car is almost ready for "retirement."
SUPPORTING FACT:	Our state has just instituted a strict, new automobile inspection policy.

Use Statistics A statistic is a fact stated with numbers.

TOPIC SENTENCE:	Our car is almost ready for "retirement."
SUPPORTING STATISTIC:	It has 235,000 miles on it, and we've owned it for 12 years.

Use Examples, Illustrations, or Instances An example, illustration, or instance is a specific person, thing, or event that demonstrates a point.

TOPIC SENTENCE:	Our car is almost ready for "retirement."
ILLUSTRATION:	Last week, the car broke down, and we had to have it towed.

Use Details Details are the specifics—the parts of the whole. They make your main idea or key point clear by showing how all the pieces fit together.

TOPIC SENTENCE:	Our car is almost ready for "retirement."
DETAIL:	When our car broke down on the highway last week, it sputtered, slowed down, and finally came to a complete standstill. While we waited for the tow truck, we felt isolated on the highway and annoyed with ourselves for not listening to our trusted mechanic's advice.

▲ **Critical Viewing**
What topic sentence and supporting sentences would you use to describe this car? **[Describe]**

Exercise 8 **Writing Supporting Sentences** Write two supporting sentences for each of the following topic sentences. Use a variety of types of support.
1. The library is a place in which people should gather.
2. Many college students choose a vegetarian diet.
3. It's important to drink plenty of water when you exercise.
4. Music can be beneficial for both the mind and the body.
5. Being on a team builds self-esteem.

Placing Topic Sentences

Most often, topic sentences appear at the start of a paragraph. They can also be placed in the middle or at the end of a paragraph to create different effects. Place a topic sentence

- **at the beginning of a paragraph** so that readers will immediately see the focus of the paragraph and know what to expect in the sentences that follow.

- **in the middle of a paragraph** when you need to provide sentences that lead into or introduce your topic sentence.

- **at the end of a paragraph** when you want to drive home your main point, leaving the point fresh in readers' minds.

Paragraph Patterns Paragraphs can follow a variety of different patterns, depending on the placement of the topic sentence. One common pattern is called TRI (Topic, Restatement, Illustration). A TRI paragraph begins with a topic sentence, which is followed by a restatement of the main idea and one or more sentences illustrating the main idea through facts and examples. The elements of a TRI paragraph can be reorganized to follow other patterns, such as ITR and TIR.

T R I	Planting perennial beds, borders, or gardens is an investment in years of floral beauty. Most perennial varieties multiply annually, so the initial costs and efforts of planting reap incremental returns in years to come. Under favorable conditions, daffodils, for instance, can cover almost twice as much space in the garden in their second year.

I T R	Daisies standing guard along the garden border, snapdragons peeking out between holly bushes, and cosmos waving near the side of the house are arranged in colorful groupings. Masses of lavender, lilacs, and forsythia add a brilliant backdrop. The garden is a bright spot in the yard. It presents a splash of color against the expanse of green.

Exercise 9 Placing a Topic Sentence Arrange the sentences below into a TRI pattern. Add transitions as necessary. Then, add two new sentences. Next, reorganize the sentences into a new pattern. Explain the effect created by each pattern.

- Some students do spend hours alone with their computers.
- The fear is that these students will become so used to predictable machines that they will be unable to function with real, fallible human beings.
- Many people think that computers isolate students.

Unity and Coherence

Maintain Unity

A paragraph has unity when all of the sentences support, illustrate, explain, or develop the topic sentence or main idea. To ensure unity as you draft, think about whether each sentence you write connects clearly and logically to the paragraph's topic sentence. When you revise, strengthen the unity of each paragraph by deleting those details or sentences that do not contribute to the support, development, or explanation of the main idea. Look at this example:

> The Russian Revolution resulted in the destruction of the monarchy. During the February Revolution of 1917, Czar Nicholas II was forced to leave the throne of Russia. ~~The term Soviet Union was not used until 1917.~~ With the removal of Nicholas's family, the Romanov dynasty was erased. The Russian Empire had been ruled by czars for hundreds of years; it ended when the reign of Nicholas II ceased. ~~Nikolai Lenin died seven years after the revolution, in 1924.~~

▶ **Exercise 10** **Revising for Unity** On a separate sheet of paper, copy the following paragraph. Mark for deletion the two sentences that interfere with the unity of the paragraph.

The communist government recognized the need for a strong military. Russia signed a treaty with Germany in 1918. There were factions across Russia that did not readily support the new regime. Officials foresaw rebellion and resistance among these groups and needed a well-trained, powerful military force to oppose and put down resisters. To this end, the Red army was established; participation in it became compulsory for city workers and peasants. More than 20 million Russians died during the civil war, which lasted from 1918 to 1921.

▼ Critical Viewing
What can you infer, or conclude, about Russian Czar Nicholas II based on this picture? **[Infer]**

Create Coherence

For a paragraph to have coherence, the supporting ideas must be arranged in a logical order and the sentences must be clearly connected. Following are common organizations:

- **Chronological order** places details in time order.
- **Spatial order** arranges details according to the position in which they appear.
- **Order of importance** presents details from most to least important, or vice versa.
- **Comparison-and-contrast order** discusses all of the details related to one subject, followed by a discussion of all the details related to the other subject; or two or more items are compared point by point.

In addition to using a consistent organization, use transitions to show connections among details.

Learn More

To learn more about creating coherence in various types of writing, see Sections 4.4, 6.4, and 10.4.

COMMON TRANSITIONS

To Show Chronological or Sequential Relationships	To Show Spatial Relationships	To Show Comparison- and-Contrast Relationships	To Show Logical Relationships
first	through	along with	if
second	next to	together with	whether
then	above	as well as	unless
next	below	also	therefore
finally	in front of	by the same token	thus
before	behind	similiarly	hence
after	connected to	although	henceforth
at the same time	north	though	in fact
later	south	however	albeit
immediately	inside	despite	
soon	outside	yet	
daily	centered	but	
frequently	middle	on the other hand	
recently	on	in contrast	
when	at the top of	except for	
	at the bottom of		

Exercise 11 **Revising for Coherence** Revise this paragraph to create coherence. Reorganize sentences and add transitions.

The view was the most beautiful thing Rebecca had ever seen. He was never going to let her talk him into a "little hike" again. She remembered her hiking companion. Hot and tired, he trudged toward her. She looked back down the trail to see Jim.

3.3 *Paragraphs in Essays and Other Compositions*

Writers rarely use paragraphs in isolation. Most writing consists of a series of connected paragraphs that work together to form a composition, such as an essay or a research paper, or another type of writing, such as a short story or an anecdote.

The Parts of a Composition

As you'll learn in the chapters that follow, there are many types of compositions. Compositions include just about any type of writing you do in school, aside from creative writing. While compositions can vary widely in form and purpose, they generally consist of the following elements:

The Introduction

Usually the first paragraph of a composition, the *introduction* introduces the topic, hooks the reader's interest, and presents the thesis statement. The *thesis statement* is a one- or two-sentence summary of the key point of the essay. The thesis statement may be accompanied by a few sentences outlining the subtopics to be covered in the body of the essay.

SAMPLE THESIS STATEMENTS

- Mikhail Gorbachev's policies of openness during the 1980's paved the way for the dismantling of the Soviet Union.
- Hitting a golf ball effectively involves choosing the correct club, assuming the proper position, and swinging smoothly and evenly.

The Body

The *body* of an essay consists of two or more paragraphs that develop and support the thesis. Each body paragraph should focus on a single subtopic and should provide examples, details, facts, reasons, and other types of support. Most often, each body paragraph should include a topic sentence that clearly indicates the subtopic being developed.

The Conclusion

The *conclusion* is the essay's final paragraph. It should reinforce or restate the thesis and offer readers final thoughts on the topic. Ideally, the final sentence should be a forceful, witty, or memorable statement called a *clincher*.

② Learn More

To learn more about writing introductions, body paragraphs, and conclusions for various types of compositions, see Sections 10.4 and 13.4.

▶ **Exercise 12** Analyzing a Composition Find an article in a newsmagazine that follows the preceding format. Explain each element.

Types of Paragraphs

There are a number of types of paragraphs you can use in compositions and pieces of creative writing.

Topical Paragraphs

A topical paragraph consists of a topic sentence and several sentences that support or illustrate it. All of the paragraphs on the preceding pages are examples of topical paragraphs.

Functional Paragraphs

Functional paragraphs are used to achieve a specific purpose in an extended piece of writing. Unlike topical paragraphs, they often do not contain a topic sentence. In addition, they are often shorter than topical paragraphs—in some cases, they are only a single sentence. Functional paragraphs may do the following:

- **Indicate dialogue.** One of the conventions of written dialogue is that a new paragraph begins with each change of speaker.

- **Make a transition.** A short paragraph can help a reader move between the ideas of two topical paragraphs.

- **Create emphasis.** A paragraph of a sentence or two that reinforces a main point in a piece of writing will leave a lasting impression with readers. (See the example below.)

WRITING MODEL

from **The Laugher**
Heinrich Böll

I go through life with an impassive expression, from time to time permitting myself a gentle smile, and I often wonder whether I have ever laughed. I think not. My brothers and sisters have always known me for a serious boy.

So I laugh in many different ways, but my own laughter I have never heard.

Because the second paragraph is so brief and direct, it emphasizes the contradiction at the heart of the excerpt: This man goes through life wearing a serious expression, but he laughs inwardly in many different ways.

Paragraph Blocks

Occasionally, you may have so much information that you will need to develop a single idea over several paragraphs. Such "blocks" of paragraphs all support the same main idea or topic sentence. By separating the development of the contributing ideas into paragraph blocks, your ideas become clearer and more accessible.

Topic Sentence ⟶ | The unexpected weather patterns seemed to result from both natural and artificial, or man-made, factors.

Natural Factor 1 with elaboration

Natural Factor 2 with elaboration

Artificial Factor 1 with elaboration

Artificial Factor 2 with elaboration

Four paragraphs working as a block

Exercise 13 Analyzing Functional Paragraphs and Paragraph Blocks Choose a descriptive essay or factual report. Then, choose a story containing dialogue. In both, locate examples of functional paragraphs that create emphasis, indicate dialogue, and make transitions. Also, locate an example of a paragraph block. Explain to a partner how the functional paragraphs and the paragraph block work within the context of the longer pieces of writing.

▼ Critical Viewing
What topic sentence might you come up with if you were writing a description of this storm? **[Describe]**

Developing Style

You express yourself through your "personal style." It includes your music preferences, the way you dress, how you speak. Style also refers to how you express yourself in writing. These elements work together to determine your writing style:

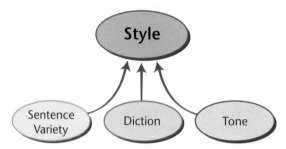

Sentence Variety One of the keys to developing a strong writing style is learning to vary the length and structure of your sentences. Sentences that are all short will sound choppy to readers; sentences that are all very long or all begin in the same way will become boring or hard to follow. Use a mixture of short and long sentences to create a rhythm and emphasize key points. For instance, you can follow a series of long sentences with a short one to drive home an important idea.

Diction Diction refers to a writer's choice of words. When you write, choose your words carefully to have the effect you desire. For example, if you are writing an essay about a serious topic, you will want to use formal language that will command your reader's respect. If, on the other hand, you are writing an amusing story for your friends, you will want to use informal language that matches the way you speak.

Tone The tone of your writing is your attitude toward your subject. Your tone may be formal or informal, friendly or distant, personal or impersonal. A writer offering advice on a serious topic may still choose a lighthearted, amusing tone. When expressing intense personal thoughts about an important topic, however, a writer's tone might reflect awe or respect.

🔵 Learn More

When you revise, you can often achieve better sentence variety by combining your short sentences into longer ones. For instruction on combining sentences, see Section 3.1.

▶ **Exercise 14** Analyzing Sentence Variety Read the Writing Models on pages 21 and 28. Compare and contrast the sentence lengths and structures, the word choice, and the tone of each. Then, write paragraphs of your own, modeled on the style of each piece.

Formal and Informal English

Standard English can be either formal or informal. It is best to use formal English for serious or academic purposes. Informal English is appropriate for stories and casual writing.

Formal English

Formal English should be used for essays, newspaper articles, formal reports, speeches, letters of application, and most school assignments. When using formal English,

- Avoid contractions.
- Do not use slang.
- Use standard English and grammar.
- Use a serious tone and sophisticated vocabulary.

Informal English

The "everyday" English we speak is informal English. You can use informal English when you write dialogue, stories, personal essays, poems, letters to friends, and journal entries. Writing informally allows you to

- Use contractions.
- Use slang and popular expressions, especially to capture the natural sound of speech.

▲ **Critical Viewing** How would you describe this platter of sushi using informal English? How would you describe it using formal English? **[Describe, Compare and Contrast]**

FORMAL ENGLISH:	Sumo wrestling, a special Japanese form of wrestling, may be the most Japanese sport of all. Wrestlers perform ceremonial actions that have traditional significance, like squatting deeply to show respect.
INFORMAL ENGLISH:	I don't think I've ever seen people so crazy about baseball. There's a game every night of the week! It's excellent watching games with a crowd that's totally psyched!

Exercise 15 **Using Formal and Informal English** Rewrite the following sentences. Use formal English for those written in informal English. Use informal English for those written in formal English.

1. In Japan, the contrast of old and new is very striking.
2. This week, I checked out Tokyo.
3. Sushi and sashimi, two types of raw fish dishes, are eaten with soy sauce.
4. Some people are grossed out by the idea of eating raw fish.
5. If you've never tried sushi or sashimi, you may be floored to discover that they don't have a fishy taste.

Chapter 4

Narration

Autobiographical Writing

A Tough Story, John G. Brown, North Carolina Museum of Art

Autobiographical Narration in Everyday Life

Think for a moment about a typical school day. To whom do you talk? What do you say? Chances are, you probably talk with friends about your experiences since you last met. When you tell a friend about what you did during the weekend or describe a funny thing that happened to you, you are engaging in **autobiographical narration**—telling a story from your own life. These stories may be funny or sad, short or long.

Autobiographical narration sometimes takes written form. You may, for example, write a letter to a cousin about a concert you heard, or you may relate a story about yourself on a job or college application.

▲ **Critical Viewing** Judging from the details in this piece of fine art, what sort of life story might these boys have to tell? **[Analyze]**

What Is Autobiographical Writing?

Autobiographical writing tells a story about an event or experience in the writer's own life. An autobiographical narrative can be as simple as a description of a recent car trip or as complex as the entire story of a person's life.

Autobiographical writing usually includes

- the writer as the main character.
- a sequence of events.
- conflict or tension between characters or between a character and an outside force.
- an insight gained by the writer.

To preview the criteria on which your autobiographical narrative may be evaluated, see the Rubric for Self-Assessment on page 47.

Types of Autobiographical Writing

Following are some types of autobiographical writing:

- **Eyewitness accounts** are retellings of events personally witnessed by a writer.

- **Personal narratives** are stories that reveal a writer's opinions, feelings, and insights about an experience.

- **Autobiographical incidents** tell of a memorable or pivotal event in a writer's life.

- **Memoirs** contain a writer's reflections on an important person or event from his or her own life.

- **Anecdotes** are brief, true, and usually humorous stories that contain a definite conclusion.

Writers in
ACTION

American writer and poet Muriel Rukeyser understood the importance of storytelling. In "The Speed of Darkness," she observed the following:

"The universe is made of stories, not of atoms."

PREVIEW
Student Work
IN PROGRESS

Erica Jackson, a student at Boone County High School in Florence, Kentucky, wrote a personal narrative called "The Ultimate Challenge." Follow along as she prewrites, drafts, and revises her work.

4.2 *Prewriting*

Choosing Your Topic

Choose a topic for your autobiographical narrative that you find important or interesting. Following are some ideas for generating topics:

Strategies for Generating Topics

1. **You Were There!** Choose as a topic an exciting event that you witnessed. For example, you could tell about a championship playoff game you attended or about a fantastic concert you heard.

2. **Consider the Moment** Write the following words on a sheet of paper: *Funny, Exciting, Interesting, Puzzling.* Then, try to recall moments in your life that fit each of these categories. Finally, choose one of these moments as the basis of your narrative.

3. **Make a Blueprint** Draw a floor plan of a significant place in your life. Label the rooms or areas, and, if you like, draw in details like furniture or trees. Then, make a list of words, phrases, sentences, names, or activities that come to mind as you "walk through" this special place. Review your ideas, and choose one as the basis of your narrative.

Try it out! Use the interactive Blueprinting activity in **Section 4.2**, on-line or on CD-ROM.

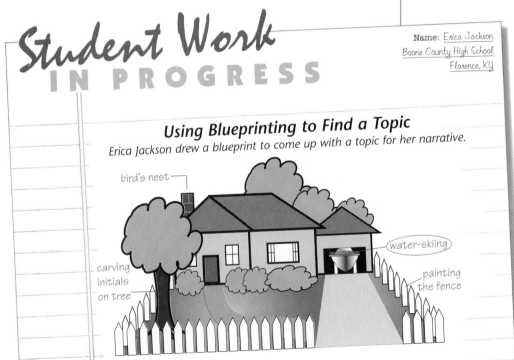

Student Work
IN PROGRESS

Name: *Erica Jackson*
Boone County High School
Florence, KY

Using Blueprinting to Find a Topic
Erica Jackson drew a blueprint to come up with a topic for her narrative.

bird's nest

water-skiing

carving
initials
on tree

painting
the fence

TOPIC BANK

Consider these suggestions if you are having difficulty coming up with your own topic:

1. **Anecdote About a Surprise** Recall a time when you were truly surprised. In a brief anecdote, tell the story of the situation and your actions.

2. **Memoir** Think of a person who has influenced your life in a positive way. In a memoir, recount one incident that shows why that person is a worthy role model.

3. **Personal Narrative About a Time of Change** Write about a period of transition in your own life. Describe fully the people and events that prompted such a change.

Responding to Fine Art

4. Look closely at *Backgammon* by Jane Freilicher. Why might the scene pictured inspire a piece of autobiographical writing? Study the setting and characters in the painting, and write an autobiographical narrative that comes to mind.

Backgammon, 1976, Jane Freilicher, Utah Museum of Fine Arts

Responding to Literature

5. "Occupation: Conductorette" is a real-life story taken from the autobiography of writer Maya Angelou. After reading the story, recall some of the goals you've struggled to achieve. Write an autobiographical essay about one of these goals and how you dealt with the obstacles in your path. You can find "Occupation: Conductorette" in *Prentice Hall Literature, Penguin Edition,* Grade 10.

⏱ Timed Writing Prompt

6. There is an old saying that "Laughter is the best medicine." A good joke or funny incident can pull us out of a bad mood or turn around a difficult situation. Write an autobiographical narrative about a moment when something humorous happened to you. **(30 minutes)**

Narrowing Your Topic

Once you have chosen your topic, narrow it so that the scope of your narrative is manageable. Use the following technique for narrowing the scope of your topic.

Use Carbon Paper to Narrow a Topic

1. Insert carbon paper between two sheets of notepaper.
2. Using an empty pen or a pen that is "unclicked," write on the top sheet anything that comes to mind about your topic. Write for at least five minutes.
3. Remove the top sheet and the carbon paper, and review what you wrote. Choose the aspect of your topic that interests you most.

Considering Your Audience and Purpose

Your audience and purpose for writing will have an impact on the details that you choose to include and the type of language that you use. The following chart highlights strategies for achieving your purpose, depending on your audience.

Type of Narrative	Audience	Purpose	Strategy
Anecdote about a humorous event	Classmates	To entertain	• Use lighthearted, informal language • Emphasize or exaggerate absurd or comical situations
Memoir about an influential friend	General audience	To inform	• Include ample background information since the audience may not be familiar with the subject • Develop details about the subject that explain his or her actions

Technology Tip

If you are working on a computer, use the following strategy to narrow your topic:
1. Open up a word-processing document on your computer.
2. Turn off the monitor so that you can't see the document.
3. Freewrite about your general topic for five minutes. Type anything that comes to mind.
4. Turn the monitor back on, and review what you wrote. Choose the aspect of your topic that interests you most.

Gathering Details

Begin gathering details that are necessary to the narrative and interesting to the reader.

Gather Details About the Characters

Before you write your autobiographical narrative, gather details about your characters that will help bring them to life for your readers. Use a character profile like the one that follows to help you gather details about characters—the people in your narrative.

CHARACTER PROFILE

- What is the character's name, age, profession, and background?

- How would you describe the character's personality, habits, and likes or dislikes?

- What dreams or goals does this character have?

- What has this character achieved in life?

- What do other characters in your narrative think about this character?

- Why is the character important to the narrative you are going to relate?

Gather Details About the Setting

The setting is the time and place in which the events of the narrative unfold. The setting locates your reader in your narrative, explaining when and where the action of the story takes place. Fill out a setting chart like the one that follows to help you get started.

Time/Year	Place	Physical Details
nineteenth century	A school in Springfield, MA	A room inside the schoolhouse, hardwood floors

Try it out! Use the interactive Setting Chart in **Section 4.2,** on-line or on CD-ROM.

Drafting

4.3

Shaping Your Writing

During the drafting stage, give your narrative its shape. Decide where and how to begin and end it, which characters to develop fully, and which events to highlight.

Create a Plot

Just like fictional stories, autobiographical stories should capture and hold the readers' interest. Think about your real-life story as if it were fiction. To do so, identify the timeline of events and decide on where to begin and end your story.

- List the events, and identify the climax, or high point of interest, in the story.
- Then, arrange the rest of the events so that they follow the structure of a plot diagram.

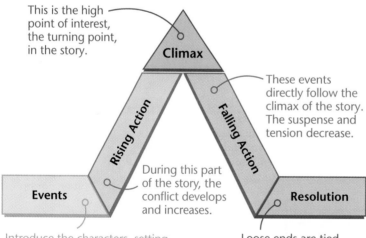

This is the high point of interest, the turning point, in the story.

Climax

Rising Action

Falling Action

These events directly follow the climax of the story. The suspense and tension decrease.

Events

During this part of the story, the conflict develops and increases.

Resolution

Introduce the characters, setting, and conflict. *Conflict* refers to a struggle that takes place in the story. It can occur between characters, between a character and a force of nature (such as a tornado), or within a character's mind.

Loose ends are tied up and questions are answered in this part of the story.

Technology Tip

In your word-processing program, write several ending paragraphs for your narrative, and then cut and paste each one in your narrative. Which one ties up the loose ends most effectively? Choose one that leaves readers with the strongest image.

Providing Elaboration

To *elaborate* means "to develop in detail." Make your narrative compelling to readers by using elaboration.

Add Dialogue

One way to add interest to your narrative is to provide dialogue that re-creates conversations or that reveals the thoughts that went through your head while you were in a particular situation. As you draft, develop your character and the characters of others through dialogue.

Explode the Moment

In everyday life, a moment of time passes quickly; there's little opportunity to observe it in detail. In a narrative, a moment can be "exploded." As a writer, you have the luxury of putting it under a magnifying glass, turning it upside down and inside out, and examining it from a variety of angles. Asking questions about an action or event is one way to get started.

Collaborative Writing Tip

Work with a partner to help you explode a moment in your writing. Describe a moment to your partner. Then, have your partner ask you questions about the moment. Use the details that answer the questions to help you explode the moment.

Student Work
IN PROGRESS

Name: *Erica Jackson*
Boone County High School
Florence, KY

Elaborating by Exploding the Moment

To give depth to her autobiographical narrative, Erica used the technique of exploding the moment.

"Ready!" I called out with clenched fists. The motor raced for the third time, and I felt a gush of wind hit my face. The hair blew off my neck, and I could see the white foam on the peaks of the wake from the boat.

I held on for dear life as the boat pulled me behind it. Wow! What a feeling I had. I was actually skiing!

The highlighted passages "explode the moment," giving readers a vivid sense of Erica's experience.

Revising

Revising Your Overall Structure

A first draft is not a final product. To make it into something wonderful, you need to trim, shape, and polish it. Following are some aspects you should look at as you begin to revise your narrative:

Create Unity

Review the individual elements of your autobiographical narrative to make sure they are unified and that they work together. Each paragraph should help develop the overall impression you want to leave with your readers. Sentences within each paragraph should work to develop the paragraph's main idea.

▶ **REVISION STRATEGY**
Deleting Unrelated Details

Each sentence in the narrative should have a clear relationship to the sentences around it. Delete those sentences or details that do not move events forward or create an image for the readers.

Interactive Textbook

Get instant help! For assistance in creating unity, use the Unity and Coherence Revision Checker, accessible from the menu bar, on-line or on CD-ROM.

Timed Writing Hint

When writing under timed conditions, spend a few minutes revising to delete unrelated details.

Student Work IN PROGRESS

Name: Erica Jackson
Boone County High School
Florence, KY

Deleting Unrelated Details

When Erica reviewed her draft for unity, she discovered that she had included some unrelated details. When she deleted them, her narrative became more focused.

Because these details stray from the main idea of the paragraph, Erica deleted them.

"Are you ready?" my sister shouted from the boat. ~~My sister is an expert water-skier. She's won several local competitions over the years for swimming, diving, and water skiing.~~ I paused for a moment, swallowed hard, and nodded.

Revising Your Paragraphs

Form Functional Paragraphs

As you revise, make sure that your paragraphs perform specific narrative functions. Following are major functions your paragraphs might serve:

▶ **REVISION STRATEGY**
Analyzing Paragraphs

To sustain interest: Reread the longer paragraphs in your work to evaluate their ability to hold the readers' interest. If necessary, revise these paragraphs by breaking them into shorter ones that keep the readers involved in the story.

To achieve desired effects: Intersperse short one- or two-sentence paragraphs with longer ones to achieve desired effects, such as indicating a shift in time, a change in mood, or the occurrence of a major event.

To signify a change in speaker: Indicate which character is speaking by beginning a new paragraph each time a different character begins to speak. Because these paragraphs show that another character is speaking, they allow you, the writer, to avoid repeating "he said" or "she said." In the following example, a long paragraph was made into shorter, functional paragraphs.

Draft: In this version, an exchange of dialogue appears in a single paragraph. It is dense to read and doesn't have much of an impact.

> As Bryan and I rode up the mountain in the chair lift, I peppered him with questions about skiing. "What trail should we take?" I asked. "Can I handle an intermediate trail?" "Well," Bryan replied, "we'll just see what's there when we jump off the lift." "Jump off the lift?" I said. "You mean the lift doesn't stop for us?" "No," Bryan said, "the lift keeps moving and you jump off." "Oh," I said, in a small voice.

Revision: By breaking the large paragraph into smaller paragraphs, it's easier to follow the exchange of dialogue. The final line spoken by the narrator has more impact because it stands alone.

> As Bryan and I rode up the mountain in the chair lift, I peppered him with questions about skiing. "What trail should we take?" I asked. "Can I handle an intermediate trail?"
>
> "Well," Bryan replied, "we'll just see what's there when we jump off the lift."
>
> "Jump off the lift? You mean the lift doesn't stop for us?"
>
> "No," Bryan said, "the lift keeps moving and you jump off."
>
> "Oh," I said, in a small voice.

Grammar and Style Tip

Avoid stringing together too many short sentences with the words *and* or *but*. Varying connecting words is just as important as varying sentence length and structure.

▼ **Critical Viewing**
If this were a movie scene, what lines of dialogue might these skiers be speaking? **[Speculate]**

Revising Your Sentences

Vary Your Sentence Lengths

In narrative writing, variety in sentence length can "spice up" your narrative. Make your writing more expressive by breaking up passages that have consecutive short sentences or consecutive long sentences. Use different sentence types to help make your writing more interesting and mature.

▶REVISION STRATEGY
Color-Coding to Achieve Sentence Variety

Review your draft, and use a blue pencil to highlight sentences of six words or less. Highlight longer sentences in green. Then, examine the balance of sentence lengths and make the following revisions, if necessary.

- Short, simple sentences, which contain only one complete idea, can be combined into compound and complex sentences.

- Long compound and complex sentences can be split into two or three simple sentences.

interactive Textbook

Get instant help! For assistance in revising sentences, use the Sentence Length Revision Checker, accessible from the menu bar, on-line or on CD-ROM.

Simple Sentences: Express only one main idea.		The students wanted to play football. The hailstorm made it impossible to play.
Compound Sentences: Contain two or more complete ideas.	Ideas are joined with the words *and, but, or,* or a semicolon.	The students wanted to play football, **but** the hailstorm made it impossible to play. The students wanted to play football; the hailstorm made it impossible to play.
Complex Sentences: Contain an independent clause with one main idea and one or more subordinate clauses with less important ideas.	Subordinate clauses are introduced by conjunctions, such as *although, because, before, since,* and *while.*	**Although** the students wanted to play football, the hailstorm made it impossible to play.

Revising Your Word Choice

Evaluate Your Use of *Me, Myself,* and *I*

When you are writing a narrative from the first-person point of view—such as a *memoir, personal narrative,* or *eyewitness account*—you will probably use the personal pronouns *me* and *I*. It's particularly important, therefore, to make sure that you use these pronouns correctly. *I* and *we* are **subject pronouns;** they act as the subjects of a sentence. *Me* and *us* are **object pronouns;** these pronouns receive the action of the verb.

▶ **REVISION STRATEGY**
Color-Coding Personal Pronouns

Read through your draft, and circle each use of the personal pronouns *I, myself,* and *me.* Then, examine each usage, and make sure that you've chosen the correct pronoun based on its function in the sentence. A chart explaining the nominative case and objective case of pronouns appears on the following page.

Student Work
IN PROGRESS

Name: Erica Jackson
Boone County High School
Florence, KY

Color-Coding Personal Pronouns

Erica checked her use of personal pronouns and corrected an error she had made. She also deleted an unnecessary use of the word myself.

He had been wanting me to try the whole summer, but (I) hadn't gotten up the nerve to do it. (My) sister and (me) had always been competitive, and she was an expert water-skiier. Also, the thought of making a fool of (myself) in front of everyone didn't sound appealing. At first, (I) was unsure (myself) whether (I) really wanted to undertake skiing, but what did (I) have to lose? . . .

Grammar in Your Writing
Pronoun Case

Case is the form of a noun or pronoun that indicates its use in a sentence. Use the **nominative case** for the subject of a verb and for a predicate nominative. Use the **objective case** for the object of any verb, preposition, or verbal.

Nominative Pronouns	Examples
Subject	*She* is the president of the class. *I* gave my coat to the clerk.
Predicate Nominative	The president is *she*.
(Formal Usage)	It is *I*.
(Informal Usage)	It is *me*.

Objective Pronouns	Examples
Direct Object	Our family praised *her*.
Indirect Object	The organization gave *us* a check.
Object of Preposition	Between *us*, there are no secrets.
Object of Participle	The noise scaring *them* was outside.
Object of Gerund	Helping *them* was my foremost thought.
Object of Infinitive	They want to ask *me* to lead the team.

Find It in Your Reading Read through a recent newspaper editorial. Write down three sentences in which the author uses the personal pronouns *I*, and *me*. Then, explain why each is *nominative case or objective case*.

Put It in Your Writing Review your draft to see whether you've used the objective case of a pronoun following a linking verb. If so, replace the objective case pronoun with a subject pronoun and examine the effect on your writing. Decide which better suits your audience and purpose.

For more on pronoun usage, see Chapter 23.

Peer Review

Use a Peer Review Work Sheet

A peer reviewer can help you assess the clarity and effectiveness of your narrative and spot any errors that you have missed.

- Make a Peer Review work sheet like the one below.
- Photocopy the work sheet and distribute it to peer reviewers, along with a copy of your narrative.
- Have reviewers respond by filling in the work sheet.
- Consider the comments of your peer reviewers as you prepare your final draft.

Try it out! Use the interactive Peer Review Work Sheet in **Section 4.4**, on-line or on CD-ROM.

Title_____

Intended Audience_____   Intended Purpose_____

Question:	Response/Suggestions for Improvement
Does the opening of the story grab your interest? Would you read on if you came across this story in a magazine?	
Are the characters and settings described well? Why or why not?	
Are the language and details in the story appropriate for the intended audience?	
Are there any story passages that get bogged down in unnecessary detail?	
Are there any other areas that need improvement or other suggestions that you would make?	

Editing
and Proofreading

Before sharing your narrative, check it for errors in grammar, spelling, punctuation, and capitalization. Since most narratives contain a lot of details involving characters, make sure that you have used pronouns consistently and correctly. Then, use the following strategy to give your narrative a final polish.

Focusing on Punctuating Dialogue

Review the use of dialogue in your draft to be sure you've punctuated dialogue correctly. Use the tips below for further help:

Timed Writing Hint

If you are given thirty minutes to complete an essay, plan to spend three to five minutes proofreading for punctuation and spelling errors.

Grammar in Your Life
Paragraphing and Punctuating Dialogue

Quotation Marks Dialogue should be set off with quotation marks. Begin a new paragraph with each new speaker. Look at this example:

"These students are very bored," I said. "They need interesting games that they can play inside in the winter."

"Well, then, perhaps you could invent a new game," the doctor replied.

Punctuation Marks Place punctuation marks that indicate the way in which the dialogue is spoken inside the final quotation mark:

"How about that!" exclaimed Judy.

"Who's there?" asked the leader.

Find It in Your Reading Find two examples of dialogue within a story you have read. Think about why the dialogue is punctuated as it is.

Find It in Your Writing Review the use of dialogue in your narrative. Be sure that you've correctly punctuated each instance of dialogue. Also, check to be sure that you've begun a new paragraph with each new speaker.

For more on the use of quotation marks, see Chapter 28.

4.6 Publishing and Presenting

When you've completed your narrative, share it with others and save a copy for yourself. Following are additional ideas for publishing and presenting your writing:

Building Your Portfolio

1. **Publish in a Print Medium** Submit your narrative to a school newspaper or to a national magazine that publishes student writing. Consult your teacher or librarian to find out about publications that might publish your narrative.

2. **Tell Your Story** Rehearse reading your story aloud. Mark up a copy of the story, and underline words that you plan to emphasize. Also, mark passages you'd like to read more slowly or more quickly. Finally, assemble a group of peers or family, and tell your story to them.

Reflecting on Your Writing

Think for a moment about what it was like to create a piece of autobiographical writing. Then, respond to the following questions, and save your responses in your portfolio.

- As you wrote, what insights did you gain about yourself?
- What "tricks of the trade" did you learn about telling a good story?

 Internet Tip

To see model narratives scored with this rubric, go on-line:
PHSchool.com
Enter Web Code:
eek-1001

Rubric for Self-Assessment

Evaluate your autobiographical narrative using the following criteria.

	Score 4	Score 3	Score 2	Score 1
Audience and Purpose	Contains details that engage the audience	Contains details appropriate for an audience	Contains few details that appeal to an audience	Is not written for a specific audience
Organization	Presents events that create an interesting narrative; told from a consistent point of view	Presents a clear sequence of events; told from a specific point of view	Presents a confusing sequence of events; contains a point of view that is inconsistent	Presents no logical order; is told from no consistent point of view
Elaboration	Contains details that create vivid characters; contains dialogue that develops characters and plot	Contains details that develop character and describe setting; contains dialogue	Contains characters and setting; contains some dialogue	Contains few or no details to develop characters or setting; no dialogue provided
Use of Language	Use of language creates a tone; contains no errors in grammar, punctuation, or spelling	Uses vivid words; contains few errors in grammar, punctuation, and spelling	Uses clichés and trite expressions; contains some errors in grammar, punctuation, and spelling	Uses uninspired words; has many errors in grammar, punctuation, and spelling

Narration
Short Story

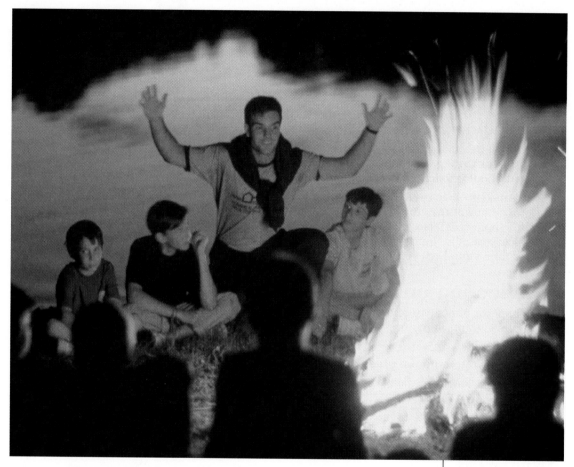

Short Stories in Everyday Life

Storytelling is a part of everyday life. Some stories are true: They relate what happens in the lives of our friends and family. Other stories are fictional: They may teach or caution or amaze the listener. These are the stories you read at bedtime and tell around the campfire. These stories, although fictional, say something about the teller's beliefs, hopes, and ideas of truth and beauty.

▲ **Critical Viewing** What sort of story might this storyteller be relating? Explain. **[Speculate]**

What Is a Short Story?

Narration is writing that tells a story. A **short story** is a particular kind of narration. It is always fictional and always brief. These stories are meant to be read in a single sitting. Using relatively few words, the writer of a short story aims to create a powerful impression on the reader. Most short stories contain

- a main character, who undergoes a change or learns something during the course of the story.
- a setting, the time and location in which the story takes place.
- a single plot, or series of events, which leads to a climax, or high point of interest.
- a theme, or main message, that is revealed by the story's end.

To preview the criteria on which your short story may be evaluated, see the Rubric for Self-Assessment on page 61.

Writers in
ACTION

Writer Maxine Hong Kingston finds that the process is similar for creating both fiction and nonfiction narratives:

"Narration has to do with movements and story and events and the adventures that we all have in our lives. There's an ongoing movement through time. And when I am writing a story, I am very aware of action that happens now—and then what? Then what happens next? And this way we keep moving."

Types of Short Stories

Although a short story is a specific type of literature, the stories themselves, like longer fictional works, vary widely. Following are a few examples:

- **Adventure stories** keep readers in suspense as they follow the plot twists and turns to the final outcome.
- **Fantasies** depart from reality to explore worlds and characters that stem from the writers' imaginations.
- **Fables** often contain animals as characters, and they convey a specific lesson or observation about life.
- **Science-fiction stories** combine elements of fiction and fantasy with scientific fact.

PREVIEW
Student Work
IN PROGRESS

In this chapter, you'll follow the progress of Ian Venokur, a student at Columbia High School in Maplewood, New Jersey, as he drafts his suspenseful short story "Horror Movie."

Prewriting

Choosing Your Topic

Sometimes, ideas for stories come easily and quickly to writers; other times, writers use various strategies to come up with ideas. Below are several strategies you can use to generate ideas for your short story:

Strategies for Generating Topics

1. **Sketch a Character or Setting** Use your imagination to sketch a character or setting. Then, review your sketch, and jot down story ideas that stem from it. Choose one idea to develop into your short story.

2. **Browse Through Quotations** "There is nothing to fear but fear itself!" "One is the loneliest number." Sometimes, looking through a book of quotations can provide you with a theme for a story. Find a quotation or theme that intrigues you, and then build a story around it.

3. **Freewrite** Freewrite for ten minutes about whatever pops into your mind. Review what you have written, looking for an interesting theme or idea. Then, develop your short story around that idea.

Try it out! Use the interactive Freewriting activity in **Section 5.2**, on-line or on CD-ROM.

Student Work
IN PROGRESS

Name: Ian Venokur
Columbia High School
Maplewood, NJ

Freewriting to Discover a Topic

Ian Venokur decided to freewrite about events in his own life to find inspiration for his short story. He began by writing about the events of the previous weekend. When he reviewed his prewriting, he found that a number of details in his freewriting were like elements of a scary movie. Because he was working to catch ideas quickly, Ian's freewriting included sentence fragments. These sentence errors can be corrected in a final draft.

The weekend. After school Friday went skateboarding, dull. Was home alone at night. Mom and dad went out. Gave me the usual business about locking up, etc., etc., etc., Rented a couple horror movies.

A horror story about watching horror movies!

TOPIC BANK

For more specific story ideas, consider the possibilities below:

1. **Story With a Theme** Write a short story around the theme "All's well that ends well." The theme may be implied or directly stated.

2. **Story About a Struggle With Nature** Conflict is the heart of a short story. Develop a conflict between a character and a dangerous foe—nature. Hurricanes, anacondas, a sudden flash flood along a remote hiking trail—you choose the specific force with which the character clashes.

Responding to Fine Art

3. Study the images presented in *Students of Modeling and Painting,* shown at right. Use the characters or setting within the painting to spark story ideas.

Responding to Literature

4. "The Monkey's Paw" by W. W. Jacobs is a chilling short story. First, read the story. Then, write your own short story in response. Your story may update the original version or continue Jacobs's story. "The Monkey's Paw" appears in *Prentice Hall Literature, Penguin Edition,* Grade 10.

Students of Modeling and Painting Anonymous, Private Collection

Timed Writing Prompt

5. Some of the greatest writers have followed the advice, "Write what you know." Now it's your turn. Write a short story set in your hometown. Use the streets and buildings that you see everyday and other details from your hometown to make the story believable. **(30 minutes)**

Narrowing Your Topic

A short story has to be short, containing a single main character, a limited setting, and a focused plot. To ensure that your story will be narrow and focused, answer the following questions as you plan your story. Refer to your answers to help you draft and revise.

- Who is the main character?
- What is the main character's problem?
- Will the main character solve the problem?
- What does he or she learn during the course of the story?

Considering Your Audience and Purpose

Though your general purpose for writing a short story is probably to entertain, you should focus on a more specific purpose as well. This purpose will affect the language and details you choose.

Create a Purpose Planner

Because short stories are meant to convey a single strong impression, think about the impression you want your story to leave on the reader. This will become your purpose for writing. Once you identify your purpose, develop a plan for achieving that purpose.

Create a purpose planner like the one below. Use the purpose planner as you gather details for your short story.

Purpose	Details to Achieve This Purpose
To amuse	Create eccentric characters; use exaggeration
To teach	State your theme; use main character as example
To horrify	Create a mood of horror through word choice; leave things unsaid and mysterious; create suspense by fore-shadowing, or by dropping hints about the story's outcome

Timed Writing Hint

When writing under timed conditions, focus your story on one main character. If you introduce other characters, you may not have time to develop them.

Gathering Details

While the plot is the "engine" of your story, details help to develop the characters, and setting helps to bring your short story to life for your readers. Before you begin drafting your story, gather details about your characters and setting.

Gathering Details About Characters Characters are people, animals, alien life forms, or other creatures that take part in the action of a narrative. Effective characters are memorable, believable, and understandable. Before you begin drafting, jot down details about each character.

Gathering Details About Setting The setting is the time and place in which story events unfold. It includes the historical period, year, season, and time of day; it also includes the planet, country, city, block, or building, as well as specific physical features—such as furniture, plants, and weather conditions. To gather details about the setting, make a setting chart like the one shown below.

Try it out! Use the interactive Setting Chart in **Section 5.2,** on-line or on CD-ROM.

Name: *Ian Venokur*
Columbia High School
Maplewood, NJ

Gathering Details About Setting

Ian used a chart to gather details about the setting of his story.

Time	Place	Weather/ Other
weekend early evening to very late at night	house, 163 Willowbend Lane family room: brown sofa; the basement: dark (burnt-out light bulb), cold concrete floor, spooky banister leading down	howling winds, thunderstorm, lightning

5.3 Drafting

Shaping Your Writing

As you draft your narrative, keep your central conflict in mind and shape the story around it. You may want to use a plot diagram to plan the events leading up to and following the climax of your plot.

Make a Plot Diagram

A plot usually contains the following elements:

- In the **exposition,** the characters and setting are introduced, as is the **conflict**—the struggle between characters or between a character and some other force.
- During the **rising action,** the tension builds as the conflict becomes more evident.
- The **climax** is the high point of interest in the story, during which one of the battling forces wins and the conflict is resolved.
- The **falling action** refers to the events that immediately follow the climax.
- The section of the story in which loose ends are tied up is called the **resolution.**

> ⏰ **Timed Writing Hint**
>
> When writing with a deadline, use a diagram like the one on this page to shape your plot quickly.

Doug's parents arrive home just as Doug panics.

CLIMAX

RISING ACTION

FALLING ACTION

EXPOSITION

Doug's parents go away, leaving Doug alone for the first time.

Doug watches horror movies. He wakes up, alarmed at a noise. He decides to check the basement door. He gets locked in the basement.

Doug explains to his parents why he was in the basement.

RESOLUTION

Doug realizes that he learned an important lesson about himself.

Providing Elaboration

Use Dialogue to Develop and Reveal Character

Often, the most effective way to convey the traits and attributes of your characters is through dialogue. Dialogue is the exact words that your characters say aloud or think to themselves. Through dialogue, you show rather than tell readers about the characters in your story. As you draft, look for opportunities to use dialogue rather than description.

Telling Through Description

Terence caught sight of Pat and enthusiastically greeted him in the hallway. Pat, feeling acutely embarrassed, tried to avoid his friend but had no choice. At first, Terence noticed nothing unusual about his friend's behavior, but puzzled by Pat's reluctance to talk, Terence eventually left.

Showing Through Dialogue

"Hey, pal! Great to see you!" boomed Terence, catching sight of Pat.

"Yeah," Pat said weakly, "great to see you too."

"What luck, running into you here and all."

"Yeah, luck, . . . huh?"

"Anything wrong, Pat? You seem kinda quiet."

"No, no, . . . everything's okay."

"Right," said Terence uneasily, "I guess I'll catch you later."

Use Dialogue to Further the Plot Events

When drafting your story, avoid always having your narrator explain what events happened next. Instead, let the dialogue sometimes reveal what happened to whom.

Description of Plot Events

Jenny was very angry with her friend Bob for forgetting to drive her to the cast party after the show. After all, Jenny was in the play and had worked hard all month during rehearsal. Now, she just wanted to cry.

Plot Events Revealed Through Dialogue

"Bob! How *could* you leave me behind? I've worked so hard all month, rehearsing and rehearsing this play so I'd be good in it. And you leave for the cast party without me! I could just cry."

Revising

Revising Your Overall Structure

Critically examine your short story to ensure that it's fast-moving and interesting. The following strategies will help you evaluate the plot of your story.

▶ **REVISION STRATEGY**
Identifying the Purpose of Plot Events

Short stories that contain too many plot events may be slow-moving and boring. Stories containing plot events that are not clearly connected to the rest of the story may be confusing and hard to follow. Review your draft critically, examining your story's plot events. Then, fill in a chart like the one at right, in which you identify plot events and evaluate their usefulness to the plot. Cut plot events that do not further the plot, and make clear connections between the other plot events to show readers how they relate to each other.

PLOT ANALYZER

How Does It Further Plot?	What Is Its Purpose?
Event A:	

Revising Your Paragraphs

Revise the Dialogue to Make It Realistic

The challenge in writing dialogue is to make it sound as if your characters are real people, speaking as they would in the real world. For example, in the real world, people often use sentence fragments and slang in conversation. Use the following strategy to help make your dialogue more realistic:

▶ **REVISION STRATEGY**
Using Contractions in Dialogue

Only in rare situations would you encounter someone who avoids contractions in everyday speech. When revising your dialogue, combine word pairs, such as *I will* and *have not,* to make contractions.

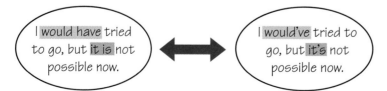

I would have tried to go, but it is not possible now. ⟷ I would've tried to go, but it's not possible now.

Revising Your Sentences
Change the Passive Voice to Active Voice

Your short story should engage and hold the interest of your readers. One way to do this is to write it in the active voice. The active voice, in which the subject performs the action, is livelier and more direct than the passive voice, in which the action is performed on the subject. The use of too many passive sentences may result in clunky and lifeless writing.

▶**REVISION STRATEGY**
Color-Coding Passive Sentences

Use a colored highlighter to mark instances of passive voice in your narrative. Passive verbs always have two parts: a form of *be* plus the past participle of a transitive verb. Once you've color-coded passive voice passages, review them carefully. If your use of the passive voice is unintentional, revise the passage to be in the active voice.

Learn More

For more instruction on passive and active voice, see the Grammar in Your Writing feature on page 58.

Student Work
IN PROGRESS

Name: *Ian Venokur*
Columbia High School
Maplewood, NJ

Color-Coding Passive Sentences
Ian color-coded the passages containing the passive voice. To give his story energy and interest, he changed the passive voice to active voice.

his parents left him alone
It was the first time ~~he had been left alone by his parents~~
for a night. Doug couldn't be happier. He had prepared
for it all week by picking out the movies he wanted to see
and the junk food he wanted to eat. "Now, the doors *keep*
~~should be kept~~ locked,........."

Grammar in Your Writing
Verbs: Active and Passive Voice

Differences Between Active and Passive Voice

There are two voices in English: **active** and **passive.** Only action verbs show voice; linking verbs do not. The voice is determined by the relationship between the subject and the verb. In a sentence in the active voice, the subject performs the action expressed by the verb. In the sentence below, the subject is *balloonists.*

Active Voice: Two balloonists sought the trophy.

In a sentence in the passive voice, the subject receives the action expressed by the verb. In the sentence below, the subject is *trophy.* Note that a passive voice verb contains a form of the helping verb *be* and the past participle of the main verb.

Passive Voice: The trophy was sought by two balloonists.

Use Voice Correctly

Because the active voice is more direct and lively, you should generally use it in your writing. However, if you want to emphasize the receiver of the action rather than the performer of an action, use the passive voice.

Use the passive voice to emphasize the receiver of the action: George Ramirez was awarded Student of the Year by school officials.

The passive voice is also effective when the performer of the action is not important or is not known.

Use the passive voice when the performer of the action is unknown: The mysterious package was left in the cafeteria.

Find It in Your Reading Find two examples of active voice in a story you have read. Explain how the passages would differ if they had been written in the passive voice.

Find It in Your Writing Find an instance of passive voice in your short story. Then, decide whether its meaning would be better served in the passive voice or if the passage would have more impact if written in the active voice.

For more on passive and active voice, see Chapter 22.

Revising Your Word Choice

▶**REVISION STRATEGY**
Evaluating the Use of Tag Words

Tag words describe the way a character in a narrative speaks. For example, "he *said*" and "they *whispered*" are examples of tag words. When the same tag words are used repeatedly, writing may get repetitive and dull. On the other hand, the overuse of tag words or too large a variety of tag words may be annoying to readers. Keep the following tips in mind as you revise your draft:

- Rely mainly on *said* as a tag word, and let the actual dialogue convey the *emotion*—the way the line would be stated:

EXAMPLE: "Are you coming?" Stephen asked. "It's getting late, and I'm rather tired."

"Yes, I'm coming" Miranda said.

- Try to limit the use of tag words in extended passages of dialogue. It has to be clear to readers, however, who is addressing whom.

EXAMPLE: Stephen and Miranda discussed leaving the party.

"Are you coming? It's getting late, and my dad needs the car back."

"Yes, I'm coming."

- Vary the use of tag words to avoid repetition:

EXAMPLE: "Are you coming?" Stephen demanded. "It's getting late, and my dad needs the car back."

"Yes, I'm coming," sulked Miranda.

Try it out! Use the interactive "Say Back" Sheet in **Section 5.4**, on-line or on CD-ROM.

Peer Review

Consult with peer reviewers as you revise your short story. Use the "Say Back" Sheet for getting useful feedback from peer reviewers.

"Say Back"

Assemble a group of four or five peer reviewers. Read your story aloud to them once. Then, distribute a work sheet to them like the one shown at right. Read your story again to the group, and instruct them to fill out the work sheet. Consider the comments of your peer reviewers as you revise your short story a final time.

"SAY BACK" SHEET

What I liked about the story: _____

_____

What I'd like to know more about: _____

_____

Editing
and Proofreading

An error-free, clearly written story will be easier for readers to follow and enjoy. When you have finished revising your narrative, check for errors in grammar, spelling, and punctuation.

Focusing on Punctuation

Check your short story to be sure that you have correctly punctuated passages of dialogue. First, read through your draft and locate all opening quotation marks. Then, make sure that for each opening quotation mark, there is a closing quotation mark. Also, check to see that you have correctly placed end marks in passages of dialogue.

Technology Tip

Use the Find feature of your computer's word-processing program to quickly locate all opening quotation marks. Then, check to see that each has a corresponding closing quotation mark.

Grammar in Your Writing
Formatting and Punctuating Dialogue

Because short stories often make extensive use of dialogue, it's particularly important to understand how to format and punctuate it correctly.

- A character's exact words are enclosed in quotation marks.
- Commas separate quotations from words that identify the speaker. The comma always appears inside the closing quotation mark.
- A new paragraph begins each time the speaker changes.
- When a paragraph ends while a character is still speaking, quotation marks do not appear at the end of that paragraph. However, quotation marks do appear at the beginning of the next paragraph.

Find It in Your Reading Find an example of dialogue in a short story. Explain the conventions used for punctuating and formatting the character's dialogue.

Find It in Your Writing Find the first passage of dialogue in your short story. Look at the end punctuation to be sure that it matches the way in which a character is speaking. For example, if the character is surprised, use an exclamation mark. Then, check to be sure that the dialogue is punctuated and formatted correctly.

For more on punctuating and formatting dialogue, see Chapter 28.

5.6 *Publishing and Presenting*

Following are a few ideas for publishing and presenting your short story:

Building Your Portfolio

1. **Verbal Sharing** With a partner, take turns reading your narratives aloud or organize a reading in which several people read their short stories. Place a copy of the story or a tape of the reading into your portfolio.

2. **Anthology** Present your short story as part of a larger collection of short stories. In your anthology, include works written by your classmates. Organize the stories by theme.

Reflecting on Your Writing

Think back for a moment about your experience writing a short story. Then, answer the following questions, and save your responses in your portfolio.

• Which part of writing a story appealed to you most? Why?

• If you were to write another short story, on which stage of the writing process would you spend more time?

Internet Tip

To see model stories scored with this rubric, go on-line:
PHSchool.com
Enter Web Code:
eek-1001

Rubric for Self-Assessment

Use the following criteria to evaluate your short story.

	Score 4	Score 3	Score 2	Score 1
Audience and Purpose	Contains details that engage and impact the audience	Contains details that appeal to an audience	Contains few details that contribute to its purpose or that appeal to an audience	Contains no purpose; is not written for a specific audience
Organization	Presents events that create an interesting, clear narrative; told from a consistent point of view	Presents sequence of events; told from a specific point of view	Presents a confusing sequence of events; contains inconsistent points of view	Presents no logical order; is told from no consistent point of view
Elaboration	Contains details that provide insight into characters; contains dialogue that reveals characters and furthers the plot	Contains details and dialogue that develop characters	Contains characters and setting; contains some dialogue	Contains few or no details to develop characters or setting; no dialogue provided
Use of Language	Uses word choice and tone to reveal story's theme; contains no errors in grammar, punctuation, or spelling	Uses interesting and fresh word choices; contains few errors in grammar, punctuation, and spelling	Uses clichés and trite expressions; contains some errors in grammar, punctuation, and spelling	Uses uninspired word choices; has many errors in grammar, punctuation, and spelling

Description

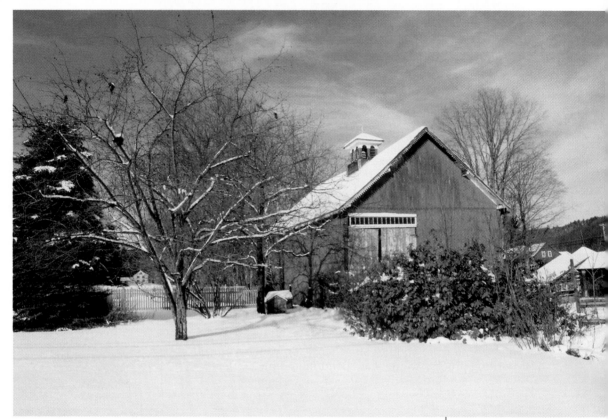

Description in Everyday Life

Before you leave your home each day, you probably use description. For example, you might describe how well you slept or how a new cereal tasted. Through description, patients tell doctors about their illnesses, travel agencies tempt homebodies to new horizons, victims lead detectives to criminals, and screenwriters portray environments for movie producers to build or find.

Description also takes written form. For example, you might write a description about last night's championship game in an e-mail to a friend, or you might describe a chemical reaction in a report for your chemistry class. In the workplace, too, description plays a vital role. Precise descriptions may convey company procedures, explain benefits packages, or provide detailed instructions for accessing a phone-mail system.

▲ **Critical Viewing**
If you were to describe the scene pictured above, what words would you select? Why?
[Interpret]

What Is Description?

You experience your world through your senses: sight, hearing, taste, smell, and touch. **Description** is writing that enables you to re-create your experiences vividly and share them with others. Most descriptive writing contains

- sensory language that shares what the writer sees, hears, tastes, smells, and touches.
- precise language, including vivid verbs and precise nouns.
- figurative language, such as personification, exaggeration, simile, and metaphor.
- a logical organization, such as chronological or spatial order.

To see the criteria on which your final essay may be evaluated, preview the Rubric for Self-Assessment on page 75.

Types of Description

Most writing contains description. Following are a few types of writing that depend heavily on descriptive language:

- **Descriptions of a person, place, or thing** contain sensory details that bring to life actual people, places, and things.
- **Observations** describe an event the writer has witnessed. Often, the event takes place over an extended period of time.
- **Travel brochures** contain factual information as well as persuasive language to encourage tourism.
- **Character sketches** describe fictional characters—their appearances, personalities, hopes, and dreams.

Writers in ACTION

Colleen J. McElroy, poet and author, often uses descriptive details in her writing. Like most writers, she understands the power of description. She has the following to say about finding inspiration for writing a description:

"What makes a description good for me is not so much reporting it, but finding the impression. You're looking for that thing that's in the corner of the eye—or that smell that sort of drifts by—and it reminds you of some place."

PREVIEW
Student Work
IN PROGRESS

Leslie Harris, a student at Sunnyslope High School in Phoenix, Arizona, wrote a description of her impressions during the seconds before the start of a footrace. Follow along as Leslie plans, drafts, and revises her writing.

Prewriting

Choosing Your Topic

Memorable people, remarkable places, unusual events, and intriguing ideas all make great topics for description. Following are more ideas for coming up with a topic for description.

Strategies for Generating Topics

1. **Draw or Sketch** Use a drawing pencil and paper to sketch a person, place, thing, or event you find interesting. Your sketch may be as abstract or realistic as you like. When you are finished sketching, choose an aspect of the drawing to develop into a description.

2. **Browse in a Calendar** Look through this year's or last year's calendar or date book to spark memories of people and events of the past year. For example, a certain date might remind you of someone you met, a game you played, or your grandfather's birthday party. Choose one of those memories to form the heart of your description.

OCTOBER

Sunday	Monday	Tuesday	Wednesday	Thursday	Friday	Saturday
					1 Mom's Surprise Party	2
3	4	5	6	7	8	9
10 Pumpkin Picking	11	12	13	14	15 Choir Concert in Gym	16
17	18	19	20	21	22	23
24	25					

3. **Make a Blueprint** Draw the floor plan of a place you know well. Next, label each room or area with a name that makes it personal for you, such as *My Studio*, *Kai's Hideout*, or *Mom's Den*. Also, jot down memories or ideas you associate with each room. Then, select the most interesting idea, and make it the topic of your description.

TOPIC BANK

To get more specific writing ideas for a description, read the following suggestions:

1. **Describe an Idea: Democracy** Think about the concept of democracy and the images it conjures up for you. For example, you may think of a person voting, a town meeting, or a king losing his crown. Then, develop this idea, and write a description of "democracy."

2. **Recall a Challenging Moment** What was the last big challenge you faced? Write some adjectives or sensory images that arise from your memory of facing that challenge. Then, work your ideas into a description.

Studio Interior, 1982, Jane Freilicher, Tibor De Nagy

Responding to Fine Art

3. *Studio Interior* by Jane Freilicher depicts a picture within a picture. Imagine yourself in the artist's studio, and write a description of what you see, as though speaking to a friend far away. You may describe what is actually in the picture or what you imagine lies beyond the window.

Responding to Literature

4. In "Jazz Fantasia," the poet Carl Sandburg uses vivid descriptive language to bring to life jazz music. Write a description in response to this poem by bringing to life your ideas about jazz or any other type of music you like. "Jazz Fantasia" appears in *Prentice Hall Literature, Penguin Edition*, Grade 10.

Timed Writing Prompt

5. Write a description of your favorite place in the world. It can be anywhere from a corner of your room to an interesting place you once visited. Use sensory details to create a sense of your chosen place for your reader. **(35 minutes)**

Narrowing Your Topic

Use a topic web to explore several aspects of a topic. Then, choose the aspect that most interests you to write about.

Make a Web

Write your broad topic at the top of a piece of paper, and then write subtopics in circles connected to your broad topic by lines. Following is an example:

HER ADULT LIFE: Rhodes scholar, historian, world traveler

COLLEGE YEARS: attended Winston College, degree in history, class president, soccer club, Phi Beta Kappa

AUNT BERTIE

HER CHILDHOOD: born in 1950's, wore braces, was into soccer

Considering Your Audience and Purpose

Choose details for your description that your audience will understand and appreciate. Your choice of details and your tone, or attitude toward your subject, will also help you to achieve your purpose, your overall reason for writing. In the following example, the details and writer's tone vary because the audiences and purposes differ.

Audience: Friends
Purpose: To impress

I lunge through the pressing cluster of runners near the finish line. I push so hard I twist my right ankle. Despite the shooting pain, I manage to limp over the finish line first.

Audience: Doctor
Purpose: To diagnose

The right Achilles tendon is so tight and numb that my foot will flex no more than an inch. Inward and outward motion of the foot is difficult, and I feel a shooting pain with each slow step.

Timed Writing Hint

When you are given a prompt, read it carefully to determine the audience for your writing.

Gathering Details

Gather a wide range of descriptive details using the cubing technique, which is explained below.

Use the Cubing Technique

Just as a cube has six sides or aspects, so may your description topic have different aspects. Following are six ways to look at your topic. Jot down your responses to the directions. Then, use your responses as you draft your description.

1. **Describe It** Provide details about your subject's appearance, importance, or personality.
2. **Associate It** Tell what related thoughts come to mind when you think of your subject.
3. **Apply It** Provide examples of what you can do with or learn from your subject.
4. **Analyze It by Breaking It Into Parts** Describe your subject aspect by aspect, using factual terms.
5. **Compare or Contrast It** Tell what your subject is similar to or different from.
6. **Argue for or Against It** Give details that explain your subject's value or problems.

Student Work **IN PROGRESS**

Name: Leslie Harris
Sunnyslope High School
Phoenix, AZ

Cubing to Gather Details
Leslie used cubing to gather details for her description.

pride; victory; self-worth

like horses preparing to run

Associate It
Describe It
Apply It
Compare or Contrast It
Analyze It
Argue for or Against It

footracing; before starting gun, during race, and after; concentration; effort

psych yourself up; think positively

tension; relaxation; final push

builds self-esteem; promotes health

Drafting

Shaping Your Writing

Create a Mood

Once you have gathered a wide range of details that appeal to the senses, choose the ones that create an overall mood, or atmosphere. The mood your description provides will add to your readers' understanding and to their enjoyment of your writing.

In the following models, the choice of descriptive details gives each description a definite mood:

Joyous Mood The morning sunlight hit the window above my bed and sent dizzying rays of light dancing over the wall. I sprang up and looked outside. The whiteness was almost blinding in its brilliance. It had snowed!

Awed Mood The morning sun was different that morning. It was shining, clear and true, throwing intricate, mysterious patterns onto the wall. With bemused anticipation, I sat up and peered out the window. Snow had fallen overnight, transforming the town into a heartbreakingly beautiful wonderland.

▲ Critical Viewing
What mood does the image in this photograph convey? Explain. **[Analyze]**

Providing Elaboration

Create Figurative Language

As you draft, use figurative language to make your description memorable and unique. Following are some commonly used types of figurative language:

Simile	A simile compares two unlike things using the words *like* or *as.*	The dog was *as fast as* a rocket.
Metaphor	A metaphor compares two unlike things by stating that one thing *is* the other.	The *ball of fire* rises each morning over the horizon.
Hyperbole	Hyperbole is exaggeration that is usually used to create a comic effect.	The guard was *twelve feet tall, with muscles of steel.*
Personification	Personification applies human qualities or behavior to something nonhuman.	The washing machine *danced* across the basement floor!

6.4 *Revising*

Revising Your Overall Structure

Review your description to be sure that you've used a consistent, logical, and effective structural organization.

▶ **REVISION STRATEGY**
Outlining Details to Check Your Organization

Create an outline to show the content and order of each paragraph in your description. Then, review your outline and rearrange paragraphs, if necessary, to make your description more effective. Following are some organizational strategies you might want to use as you reorganize your description:

- **General to Specific** Use this structure when describing a person, thing, or an idea.
- **Chronological Organization** Use chronological, or time, order to bring events to life for readers.
- **Spatial Organization** Use spatial organization to describe where things are located in relation to each other; for example, a place, a building, or an object.

Revising Your Paragraphs
Check Unity

Review the paragraphs in your description to be sure that the main idea of each describes an aspect of your overall topic. Also, make sure that individual sentences within a paragraph support the topic sentence.

▶ **REVISION STRATEGY**
Color-Coding to Check Unity

With a highlighter, color-code the main idea of each paragraph. If any main ideas do not support the topic of your description, rewrite or delete them. Then, use a different-colored highlighter to call out the sentences within each paragraph that support the main idea. Rewrite or delete sentences that stray from the paragraph's main idea.

Jasmine's singing voice had the power to enthrall an audience. Her voice range was impressive, spanning three octaves. An octave is a set of eight notes on a diatonic scale. An easy way to remember what an octave is is the song "Do, a deer." But it was the bell-like quality of her voice that truly set Jasmine apart as a singer.

Interactive Textbook

Get instant help! To create your outline, use the Essay Builder, accessible from the menu bar, on-line or on CD-ROM.

Revising Your Sentences

Add Modifiers to Enhance Your Description

Enliven your description by adding modifiers to dull sentences. Through the use of modifiers, you give more information about the subject or verb of a sentence. Modifiers may be single words (adjectives and adverbs) or they may be in the form of a phrase (adjectival and adverbial phrases and clauses).

▶ **REVISION STRATEGY**
Adding Modifiers

First, read through your draft and circle any passages that seem terse, dull, or incomplete. Then, add descriptive details, answering the questions *Who? What? Where? When? Why?* and *How?* through the use of modifiers. Your modifiers may be single words, phrases, or clauses.

Student Work
IN PROGRESS

Name: Leslie Harris
Sunnyslope High School
Phoenix, AZ

Adding Modifiers

Leslie added some modifiers to her description to add depth and to enhance her readers' understanding of her subject.

Leslie's thoughts are more fully explained with this detail.

The gun explodes₍, sentencing me to a half mile, while at the same time setting me free,₎ and a rush of adrenaline

shoots through my body. I start out hard,

₍sprinting in front of the others, and₎ cutting to the inside lane. Extend, extend, I

This detail was added to help define "start out hard."

remind myself. Relax, stretch it out. More arms.

Faster.₍ As I run by the bleachers,₎ Spectators are screaming

By telling "when," this helps clarify the sentence for readers.

encouragement, but the only sound I hear is that

shot signaling my final lap.

Grammar in Your Writing
Dangling and Misplaced Modifiers

A **modifier** is a word or phrase that helps describe nouns or verbs in a sentence. An essential ingredient of clear writing is effectively placed modifiers. A modifier should be placed as close as possible to the word it modifies.

Misplaced Modifiers

A **misplaced modifier** appears to modify the wrong word in a sentence. In the sentence below that contains the misplaced modifier, the reader may at first think that "we" were covered with cobwebs and mold, not the cabinet.

Sentence with misplaced modifier: Covered with cobwebs and mold, we cleaned the old cabinet.

Corrected sentence: We cleaned the old cabinet that was covered with cobwebs and mold.

Dangling Modifiers

A **dangling modifier** appears to modify either the wrong word or no word at all because the word it should logically modify is missing. In the sentence below that contains the dangling modifier, the reader may wonder what, exactly, is "pistoning like spark plugs"?

Sentence with dangling modifier: Pistoning like spark plugs in a human engine, the track was pounded.

Corrected sentence: Pistoning like spark plugs in a human engine, the runner's feet pounded the track.

Find It in Your Reading Review a story you have written. Locate three sentences that contain modifiers. On a separate sheet of paper, circle each modifier and the word it modifies. Observe where the modifier appears in relation to the word it modifies. Then, answer the following question for each word-modifier combination you identified. Could the modifier be closer to the word it modifies, or does the sentence work fine as is?

Find It in Your Writing Review your draft to identify and correct any dangling or misplaced modifiers. Be sure you have placed your modifiers near their subjects. Be particularly careful about sentences that contain passive voice; they are more likely to contain dangling modifiers.

For more on misplaced and dangling modifiers, see Chapter 21.

Revising Your Word Choice
Replace Vague Words

A vague word—whether it is a noun, a verb, or a modifier—cannot communicate your unique experience. Reread your draft, and replace words that are vague with more precise words.

Vague Words	Precise Words
good	delicious, excellent, well-mannered
looked	stared, glanced, peered, squinted
store	grocery, delicatessan, boutique
cold	freezing, chilly, brisk, frigid

▶ **REVISION STRATEGY**
Circling and Replacing

Read through your description, and circle words that are vague, dull, or inaccurate. Then replace those circled words or phrases with choices that better reflect what it is you are describing.

Student Work
IN PROGRESS

Name: Leslie Harris
Sunnyslope High School
Phoenix, AZ

Replacing Vague Words
*Leslie replaced vague words with more precise words
to make her narrative more engaging.*

I am ~~sure~~ (determined) that I am going to win. All the way through, I ~~think~~ (mentally chant) run all the way through the finish line. And then, as ~~soon~~ (abruptly) as I started, I am ~~done~~ (finished), drained of nervousness and the ability to remain standing. I open my eyes, knowing that I am now ~~ready~~ (prepared) and confident enough to run.

Peer Review

One way to get feedback on your description is to work with a group of peers and have them comment on the effectiveness of your writing. Use the following activity as you edit your description.

Create a Plus-and-Minus Chart

Use the following guidelines as you work with your peers to revise your description:

1. Work in a group of three to five students.
2. Prepare a chart like the one shown, and give copies to peers.
3. Read your description aloud to your peers.
4. Then, read the first entry on the chart, and ask your peers to make a thumbs-up sign if their response is positive and a thumbs-down sign if their response is negative. Enter your peers' responses on your chart.
5. Review the responses, and make revisions to your draft as necessary.

▲ **Critical Viewing**
Why is it useful to compare and contrast reviewers' reactions to your writing? [**Apply**]

Plus-and-Minus Chart

	Reviewer #1	Reviewer #2	Reviewer #3
1. The title is appropriate and interesting.	+	+	-
2. The description contains details like vivid verbs and precise nouns.	-	-	+
3. The description creates a definite mood, or atmosphere.	-	-	-
4. The writing is unified.	+	+	+
5. Each sentence is clear, with no misplaced or dangling modifiers.	+	+	-

Editing
and Proofreading

Before you share your description with others, take time to polish it. Correct errors in grammar and punctuation, and make sure that you have spelled everything correctly.

Focusing on Commas

Review your description carefully, and check to be sure that you have correctly used commas to separate adjectives of equal rank and to separate a series of adjectives.

⏲ Timed Writing Hint

When you write quickly, you may make careless punctuation errors. Allow two or three minutes to check your writing for correct use of commas and other punctuation.

Grammar in Your Writing
Using Commas Correctly

Commas are used to separate items in a series and to separate certain kinds of adjectives.

Serial commas: Use commas to separate three or more words, phrases, or clauses in a series. In the example below, the first two adjectives are followed by a comma. The third adjective does not need a comma.

Example: The restless, tired, and hungry crowd gathered near the mountaintop.

Adjectives of equal rank: Use commas to separate adjectives of equal rank, called coordinate adjectives. In the sentence below, the adjectives *moist* and *delicious* could be switched without changing the meaning.

Example: The moist, delicious pie was a hit after dinner.

Adjectives of unequal rank: If one adjective has a closer relationship to the noun than the other, no comma appears between them. Below, the adjective *talented* has a closer relationship to *acrobats* than does *twenty*.

Example: Twenty talented acrobats appeared in the circus ring.

Find It in Your Reading Read through a short story, and find adjectives that the writer does not separate with commas. Explain why commas are not needed.

Find It in Your Writing Check your description to make sure that you have used commas with adjectives correctly. Find items in a series of adjectives. If there are none, challenge yourself to add a series of adjectives.

To learn more about the correct use of commas, see Chapter 28.

6.6 *Publishing* and *Presenting*

Use the following ideas for sharing your description with others:

Building Your Portfolio

1. **Display** Request a bulletin board at school where you can post your description. Place photos or illustrations around your paper to further enhance its effectiveness.
2. **Audiotape** Capture your description on audiotape. First, rehearse yourself reading your paper. Mark on your copy where you will pause and what words require special emphasis. Then, record your reading. Play the tape back for family and friends.

Reflecting on Your Writing

After you have finished your description, think about the experience of writing it. Use these questions to direct your reflection, and record your responses in your portfolio.

- What did you learn about the subject you chose?
- Which strategy for choosing a topic would you use for a future descriptive essay?

🖥 Internet Tip

To see descriptions scored with this rubric, go on-line:
PHSchool.com
Enter Web Code:
eek-1001

Rubric for Self-Assessment

Use the following criteria to evaluate your description.

	Score 4	Score 3	Score 2	Score 1
Audience and Purpose	Contains details that work together to create a tone	Creates a tone through use of details	Contains extraneous details that detract from the tone	Contains details that are unfocused and create no tone
Organization	Is organized consistently, logically, and effectively	Is organized consistently	Is organized, but not consistently	Is disorganized and confusing
Elaboration	Contains creative use of figurative language, creating interesting comparisons	Contains figurative language that creates comparisons	Contains figurative language, but the comparisons are not fresh	Contains no figurative language
Use of Language	Contains sensory language that appeals to the five senses; contains no errors in grammar, punctuation, or spelling	Contains some sensory language; contains few errors in grammar, punctuation, and spelling	Contains some sensory language, but it appeals to only one or two of the senses; contains some errors in grammar, punctuation, and spelling	Contains no sensory language; contains many errors in grammar, punctuation, and spelling

Persuasion
Persuasive Essay

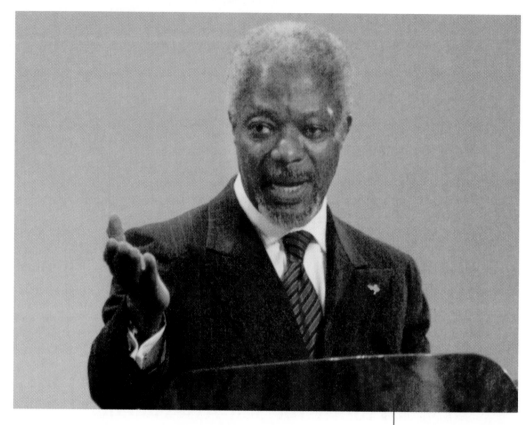

Persuasion in Everyday Life

The art of persuasion—getting others to do something or to think as you do—is a part of daily life. Persuasion may involve convincing a friend to see a movie with you or bargaining over the cost of a comic book at a flea market. Persuasion sometimes is verbal, sometimes visual, sometimes written, and often a combination of all these elements.

Persuasion is often a part of various types of writing, as well as a type of writing itself. For example, a character in a short story may speak persuasively to a group of friends, or a poem may contain a plea to readers about an important issue. Persuasive writing gives you an opportunity to make your voice heard and to express your opinion on an issue about which you feel strongly. In this chapter, you'll learn how to create a persuasive essay that is clear, organized, and forceful.

▲ **Critical Viewing**
Kofi Annan, pictured above, is giving a speech in his role as Secretary General of the United Nations. Why might a member of the United Nations find persuasive skills useful? **[Connect]**

What Is a Persuasive Essay?

A **persuasive essay** is a piece of writing that tries to convince readers to accept a particular viewpoint or to take a certain action. Most effective persuasive essays contain

- a clearly stated opinion or argument on an issue that has more than one side.
- evidence to support the opinion or argument.
- memorable and convincing details and vivid, persuasive language.
- an effective, logical organization.

To preview the criteria on which your persuasive essay may be evaluated, see the Rubric for Self-Assessment on page 91.

Writers in
ACTION

Dean Rusk, former secretary of state, shares the following insight about the art of persuasion:

"One of the best ways to persuade others is with your ears—by listening to them."

Types of Persuasive Essays

In addition to persuasive essays, there are many other forms of persuasion:

- **Editorials and letters to the editor** appear in newspapers. Editorials express the newspaper's stand on a current issue; letters to the editor present readers' viewpoints.
- **Persuasive speeches** are an oral form of a persuasive essay. They often contain allusions and sound devices to make them stirring and memorable.
- **Position papers** address one side of a controversial issue. They are often directed at a person or group with some power to shape policy on a particular issue.
- **Grant proposals** make a request for financing a program or a project of the writer's. They are usually addressed to members of a government agency or private corporation.

PREVIEW
Student Work
IN PROGRESS

In this chapter, you'll follow the work of Sharon Goldberg, a student at Miami-Palmetto High School in Pinecrest, Florida, as she drafts a persuasive essay that expresses her opinion on the importance of volunteerism.

Choosing Your Topic

To write a powerful persuasive essay, start with a topic that is important to you. For help in generating topics, use the strategies below:

Strategies for Generating Topics

1. **Scan Newspapers** Scan a newspaper, looking for stories that matter to you on a personal level. What do you see that makes you angry, strikes you as unfair, or cries out "this needs to be changed"? Use one of the news stories to provide you with a topic for your persuasive essay.

2. **Make a Quicklist** Come up with a topic for your persuasive writing by listing types of issues. For example, write headings like Community Issues, Political Issues, and Social Issues at the top of a sheet of paper, and quickly list ideas inspired by each. Review your lists, and choose the issue that interests you most as the topic of your persuasive essay.

3. **Use Sentence Starters** To come up with a topic, copy the following sentence starters and fill in the blanks. Then, review your completed sentences. Choose one issue as the topic of your persuasive essay.

   - If I became (mayor/president/school principal), the first thing I would do is ___?___ .

   - Something that needs to be changed at this school is ___?___ .

   - Teenagers today should ___?___ .

Get instant help! To make your Quicklist, use the Essay Builder, accessible from the menu bar, on-line or on CD-ROM.

Student Work
IN PROGRESS

Name: Sharon Goldberg
Miami-Palmetto High School
Pinecrest, FL

Using Sentence Starters to Choose a Topic
Using sentence starters helped Sharon Goldberg focus on an issue that was important to her.

- Something that needs to be changed at this school is *cafeteria food*

- Teenagers today should *help others*

TOPIC BANK

If you are having difficulty finding a suitable topic for your persuasive piece, use one of the following:

1. **Persuasive Speech** Choose a global issue—child labor laws or deforestation, for example—about which you would like to take a stand. Write and deliver a persuasive speech in which you support your opinion.

2. **Persuasive Essay** Write an essay in which you support one candidate over another. Candidates may be actual, perhaps someone running for student council president, or imaginary, as in Hero of the Year.

Responding to Fine Art

Arrivals and Departures, 1999, Chester Arnold, The Seven Bridges Foundation, Greenwich, CT

3. Study *Arrivals and Departures* by Chester Arnold. Determine what you think the artist's message is. Then, write a persuasive essay in which you agree or disagree with that message.

Responding to Literature

4. In his Nobel lecture, Alexander Solzhenitsyn argues that writers have the power and responsibility to change the world by telling the truth. Read the speech and write a persuasive essay in which you agree or disagree with Solzhenitsyn's assertion. You can find the speech in *Prentice Hall Literature, Penguin Edition,* Grade 10.

Timed Writing Prompt

5. Some people argue that no one under the age of twenty-one should be allowed to drive. They cite statistics that show teenaged drivers are involved in more accidents than older drivers. Write a persuasive essay explaining why you agree or disagree with this position. Use examples from your personal experience and the experience of people you know to support your argument. **(35 minutes)**

Narrowing Your Topic

Once you've chosen a general topic, narrow it into one you can argue effectively. Looping is one strategy you can use to ensure that your topic isn't too broad.

Narrow a Topic by Looping

1. Write freely on your general topic for about five minutes.
2. Read what you have written. Circle the most important idea.
3. Write freely on that idea for about five minutes.
4. Repeat the process until you have found a topic that is narrow enough to address in your persuasive essay.
5. If you keep writing, you may even be able to identify a thesis statement, or main idea, that you want your persuasive essay to communicate.

Student Work
IN PROGRESS

Name: Sharon Goldberg
Miami-Palmetto High School
Pinecrest, FL

Looping to Narrow a Topic
Sharon used looping to narrow her broad persuasive topic.

Broad Topic: Helping Others
It's important to help others. Those in service industries—like nursing and the fire and police departments—devote their lives to the public. Some people prefer to help in other ways. From retirees who help care for children in need to families who donate food to the hungry to teenagers who work in their communities, everyone can make a difference.

More Narrowed Topic: Everyone Can Make a Difference
Working with others gives volunteers a sense of perspective. Volunteering their extra time keeps teens focused and gives them a sense of responsibility and accomplishment. Schools should offer course credit to teens who take on a volunteering role in the community. Everyone in the community—from elementary-school children to people who have retired—should take time to help others.

Thesis Statement: Volunteerism is vital.

Considering Your Audience and Purpose

As you draft, identify your audience and their opinions. This will help you achieve your purpose—to persuade them.

Write for Various Audiences

A hostile audience is one that will not be immediately receptive to your argument. A friendly audience is one that is likely to be more sympathetic. Depending on whether you expect your audience to be hostile, friendly, or a mix, vary your argument accordingly.

EXAMPLE: Imagine that you are writing an editorial calling for a ban on bicycle traffic from a park pathway.

Hostile Audience: Bicycle Riders

Emphasize alternative paths that would remain available for people who ride bicycles.

Friendly Audience: Families With Small Children

Emphasize the dangers that are posed when bikes and pedestrians mix.

Create a Purpose Planner

Ultimately, you hope your persuasive writing will change the thinking or behavior of your audience. To do so, choose details that will lead your audience to think or behave in a certain way. A purpose planner can help you achieve your particular goals. Use the following purpose planner as a guide for making your own.

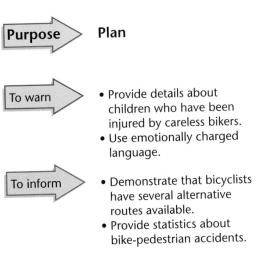

Purpose > **Plan**

To warn >
• Provide details about children who have been injured by careless bikers.
• Use emotionally charged language.

To inform >
• Demonstrate that bicyclists have several alternative routes available.
• Provide statistics about bike-pedestrian accidents.

> ⏱ **Timed Writing Hint**
>
> Read the prompt carefully at least twice to make sure you understand the purpose of your writing and its audience.

Gathering Evidence

You'll need facts and details from a variety of sources to support your position. Follow these strategies as you gather the evidence you need:

1. **Find Unbiased Research** The foundation of an effective persuasive essay should contain reliable evidence in support of its position. Evidence from biased or unreliable sources will weaken your argument. As you perform research for your editorial, find sources of information that are objective and bias-free.

2. **Conduct Interviews** For some issues, the most powerful evidence you can use to support your argument is evidence that you collect yourself. Interview an expert in that field. His or her words will prove more persuasive than a quotation from an unqualified person.

3. **Make a Pro-and-Con Chart** Make a chart to help you see both sides of an issue. In the left column, list your arguments, or "pros"; in the right column, list opposing arguments, or "cons." When it's complete, note the evidence in the "Opposing" column. Brainstorm for ways to counter-argue the evidence listed there.

Student Work
IN PROGRESS

Name: Sharon Goldberg
Miami-Palmetto High School
Pinecrest, FL

Gathering Evidence With a T-Chart
Sharon made a T-chart to examine both sides of the issue about volunteering.

Supporting	Opposing
✓ Volunteering helps the community.	Paying taxes is enough help.
✓ Volunteers learn life skills.	Volunteering takes away from study and homework time.
✓ Volunteering can build self-esteem.	Sports and clubs build self-esteem.

7.3 *Drafting*

Shaping Your Writing

Structure your persuasive writing in the way that best suits your argument and your evidence.

Use TRI/PS/QA to Structure Paragraphs

As you draft paragraphs, think first about what you want to say and then choose a logical organization for each. Following are some ideas for organizing your paragraphs:

TRI stands for **T**opic, **R**estatement, **I**llustration. This type of organization helps readers follow along as you explain your ideas. The elements TRI can occur in any order within a paragraph (TIR). You could also include two illustrations, or even three, within the same paragraph (TRII).

T
R — **Example:** Ursuline Avenue should and must be converted to a one-way street. It cannot support two-way traffic because it is too narrow and it has too much traffic.

I — For example, in a three-month period last year, there were eleven accidents on Ursuline Avenue and at least thirty traffic tie-ups caused by traffic-flow problems.

PS stands for **P**roblem and **S**olution. This type of organization emphasizes the problem-and-solution relationship between the facts you are presenting. To use this type of structure, begin by stating a problem. Follow it with one or more solutions to that problem.

P — **Example:** Our town has been severely damaged by floods over the past ten years. Local officials must look

S — into the solutions of people in areas that have experienced similar problems. Starting from scratch won't gain us anything. We must use the knowledge and experience of others as a starting point so that we can solve our flooding problems soon.

QA stands for **Q**uestion and **A**nswer. Use this method of organization when you anticipate that your audience will have specific questions about your topic. Begin by posing a question or problem. Then, present your answer or answers in response to the question.

Q — **Example:** Why is it necessary to build a new computer laboratory? The future is now. Students must become

A — familiar with current technology in order to better their chances of developing viable work skills. Current software applications will not run on our old computers, so many students miss out on becoming familiar with those all-important workplace tools.

Providing Elaboration

Elaborate on your ideas by providing details that explain, restate, illustrate, or expand on them.

Build Your Argument With Evidence

As you draft, build and support your argument by providing evidence or support. Choose details of various types from various sources. Following are types of evidence you should consider including in your persuasive essay:

- **Historical details** may be provided through excerpts from government records, war records, and almanacs.

EXAMPLE: The Central School Stage Band has been in existence since 1922.

- **Statistical information** may be researched or gathered firsthand. This type of information may come from results of surveys, polls, scientific data, and weather records.

EXAMPLE: Four out of five high-school musicians go on to higher education.

- **Expert testimony** is provided by someone who is considered extremely knowledgeable about or familiar with your topic.

EXAMPLE: Dr, Rita Sohns, head of the American Student Agenda, strongly advocates music programs in schools. She said, "There is no better way to learn discipline, art, and camaraderie, than through participation in music programs."

- **Textual evidence** may come from literature, letters, and personal documents.

EXAMPLE: In an open letter to Principal Ordonez, the band requested "funding for new sheet music and new instruments."

Timed Writing Hint

When writing a persuasive essay under timed conditions, include strong examples to support your argument.

▼ Critical Viewing If you were to persuade someone to take up a musical instrument, what reasons would you give? **[Relate]**

7.4 *Revising*

Revising Your Overall Structure

Once you've completed your first draft, make sure that it contains the details needed to be effective. Also, check to be sure that you develop and support your argument in the body of your paper.

▶ REVISION STRATEGY
Color-Coding to Identify Support

Reread your essay to see whether you have included enough supporting details to make your argument successful. As you read, use a colored pencil to circle each topic sentence. Then, use a different-colored pencil to circle supporting details.

Next, review your markings. If a topic sentence has fewer than two supporting details, add more evidence to support it or reconsider whether the point is worth including.

▲ **Critical Viewing**
In what ways can hospital volunteers improve the quality of patient care? **[Speculate]**

Student Work
IN PROGRESS

Name: Sharon Goldberg
Miami-Palmetto High School
Pinecrest, FL

Color-Coding to Identify Support
Sharon used color-coding to identify the types of support she used in her essay. She revised accordingly and added a different type of support—a quotation—to give this paragraph more depth.

Not only is it necessary to perform community-service hours to graduate from high schools, but it is also essential to provide time and commitment voluntarily to the surrounding community. Young students, for example, should assist at a hospital or a nursing facility as much as possible without interfering with their schoolwork. These services should provide the satisfaction of knowing that the volunteers have made a difference in someone's life.

"Don't give until it hurts, but give until it feels good" is a statement that accurately describes how an individual should volunteer.

Revising Your Paragraphs

Make the main points in your essay memorable by using *parallelism*—the use of patterns or repetitions of grammatical structures. Parallelism adds rhythm and balance to your writing. Use it to emphasize important points and to forge links between related ideas.

▶ REVISION STRATEGY
Forming Parallel Structures

To form parallel structures in your draft, locate an important word, phrase, clause, or question. Then, experiment with building upon that word, phrase, clause, or question to make it into a passage containing parallelism.

PARALLEL QUESTIONS:	Who will step up first? Who will lead the way? Who will win the day?
PARALLEL PHRASES:	If you care, if you can, and if you would, lend a hand now.
PARALLEL CLAUSES:	Although we strive for greatness, although we work hard, although we deserve the best, sometimes, it's just not enough.

Student Work
IN PROGRESS

Name: Sharon Goldberg
Miami-Palmetto High School
Pinecrest, FL

Making Use of Parallelism

As she revised, Sharon made use of parallelism to make her introduction more memorable and stirring.

Reading a book to a blind person. ~~At a nursing home,~~
(cap) feeding a debilitated patient_∧ at a nursing home. Tutoring a younger child.
These are examples of community service projects that
provide the performer of such deeds with feelings of self-
worth and gratification. By serving others in the
community, the individual is helping himself or herself
to grow and to acquire knowledge and wisdom.

Grammar in Your Writing
Adding Parallel Clauses

A **clause** is a group of words with its own subject and verb. One way to make your persuasive essay memorable is by adding **parallel clauses.** These are clauses within a sentence that have matching grammatical forms or patterns.

Following are some tips for revising your sentences to form parallel clauses.

1. Make sure that the verbs in each clause are in the same tense.

NOT PARALLEL: The Garden Group planted, the Garden Group hoed, the Garden Group was persevering, and the Garden Group triumphed.

PARALLEL: The Garden Group planted, the Garden Group hoed, the Garden Group persevered, and the Garden Group triumphed.

2. Don't change the subject in subsequent clauses.

NOT PARALLEL: After his efforts on our behalf, after Matt's sacrifices on our behalf, and after his achievements on our behalf, isn't it time to elect him president of the class?

PARALLEL: After Matt's efforts on our behalf, after his sacrifices on our behalf, and after his achievements on our behalf, isn't it time to elect him president of the class?

3. Always use the same type of subordinate clause:

NOT PARALLEL: The corporation will sponsor only those projects that are worthy and it thinks have a chance at winning awards.

PARALLEL: The corporation will sponsor only those projects that are worthy and that might win awards.

Find It in Your Reading Find an example of parallelism in an essay you have read. Explain the impact that parallelism has on the passage.

Find It in Your Writing As you revise your essay, look for two examples of parallel clauses. If you cannot identify any, revise to insert them.

For more on parallel clauses, see Chapter 20.

Revising Your Sentences

Add Variety to Your Sentences

Writing is much more persuasive if it is interesting. One way to add interest to your writing is to use a variety of sentence types and lengths. Review your draft, and analyze the sentences you have used. If you tend to use too many sentences of one type and of one average length, revise to make your writing more interesting to read and hear.

▶ **REVISION STRATEGY**
Color-Coding Clues to Sentence Types

Use this strategy to analyze the sentence variety in your writing:

1. Read through your essay. Underline declarative sentences in red, interrogative sentences in green, exclamatory sentences in blue, and imperative sentences in black.

2. Review the underlined material. If you have little or no variety in sentence types, revise to make your writing more interesting.

Learn More

To learn more about revising to create effective sentences, see Chapter 21.

Student Work
IN PROGRESS

Name: *Sharon Goldberg*
Miami-Palmetto High School
Pinecrest, FL

Color-Coding Sentence Types

When Sharon discovered that she used only declarative sentences in this paragraph, she revised a sentence to provide sentence variety. Her revised sentence is circled.

"Don't give until it hurts, but give until it feels good" is a statement that accurately describes how an individual should volunteer. These services should provide the satisfaction of knowing that the volunteer has made a difference in someone's life. Similarly, community service activities serve as a learning tool for those involved. ~~Although traditional teaching~~ *Why* ~~techniques require students to~~ sit in a classroom and study from books or that which is written on a traditional chalkboard *when* community service projects give individuals hands-on experiences?

Revising Your Word Choice

Revise Informal Language

The words you choose can influence the power of your essay. Using slang and informal language can mean that your writing may not be taken seriously. Instead, use formal language that reflects the seriousness of your topic.

Informal Language

The town dump has to be cleaned up before it makes everyone really sick.

Formal Language

Conditions at the town's garbage collection center must be made more sanitary before it poses a health risk for residents.

🌸 Grammar and Style Tip

Use a thesaurus to come up with alternative, more formal word choices for your persuasive writing.

Peer Review

Use Point/Counterpoint

Anticipating counterarguments can strengthen your editorial. Share your revised draft with a partner who takes on the role of the opposition. Together, make a list of the main points in your writing. Then, ask your partner to come up with counterpoints, or opposing arguments for these points.

When your partner has finished, find evidence to weaken the opposition's argument. Incorporate that evidence into your draft to strengthen your own argument.

▶ Critical Viewing
Why is it useful to work with a peer while revising?
[Reflect]

Editing
and Proofreading

Before you revise your final draft, proofread your writing, and correct errors in grammar, spelling, and punctuation.

Focusing on Spelling

Your readers will equate careless writing with a careless argument. Make sure that your persuasive essay is free of spelling errors. As you proofread, look for words you frequently misspell, as well as words with tricky endings, such as -*ance* and -*ence*.

Grammar in Your Writing
Words That End in -*ance* and -*ence*

Word endings that sound similar are sometimes difficult to spell. Among the most misspelled word endings are -*ance* and -*ence*.

If a noun ends in -*ance*, the corresponding adjective will end in -*ant*. If the noun ends in -*ence*, the corresponding adjective will end in -*ent*.

abundance/abundant   independence/independent

> **Common Words Ending in -*ance*:** abundance; acquaintance; appearance; brilliance; defiance; importance; radiance; resonance; romance; tolerance
>
> **Common Words Ending in -*ence*:** absence; convenience; correspondence; difference; excellence; independence; patience; presence; reference; violence

Find It in Your Reading Find two words within an essay you have read that end in -*ance* and two that end in -*ence*. Practice writing and spelling those words.

Find It in Your Writing As you proofread your essay, check to be sure that you have spelled words ending in -*ance* and -*ence* correctly.

For more on spelling word endings, see Chapter 30.

7.6 *Publishing and Presenting*

Building Your Portfolio

The purpose of persuasive writing is to influence your audience. To achieve this goal, find a way to share your work with others. Below are a few possibilities for presenting your finished work:

1. **School Paper** If the topic of your persuasive writing is school- or community-related, publish it in your school newspaper.

2. **Local Newspaper** The editorial page of your local newspaper is a place to make your voice heard. Contact the paper for the proper procedures for submitting a letter to the editor, and revise your writing to conform to the newspaper's guidelines.

Reflecting on Your Writing

Once you have completed your persuasive essay, reflect on the experience of writing it. Answer the following questions, and record your responses in your portfolio:

- What did you discover about your topic as you wrote about it?

- What did you learn about the process of writing persuasively? Can you apply what you learned to other types of writing?

Internet Tip

To see persuasive essays scored with this rubric, go on-line:
PHSchool.com
Enter Web Code:
eek-1001

Rubric for Self-Assessment

Use the following criteria to evaluate your persuasive writing:

	Score 4	Score 3	Score 2	Score 1
Audience and Purpose	Demonstrates effective word choice; clearly states focus on persuasive task	Demonstrates good word choice; states focus on persuasive task	Shows some good word choices; minimally states focus on persuasive task	Shows lack of attention to persuasive task
Organization	Uses clear, consistent organizational strategy	Uses clear organizational strategy with occasional inconsistencies	Uses inconsistent organizational strategy; illogically presented	Lacks organizational strategy
Elaboration	Provides specific, well-elaborated reasons that support the writer's position	Provides two or more moderately elaborated reasons to support the writer's position	Provides several reasons, but only one is elaborated	Provides no specific reasons or elaboration
Use of Language	Incorporates many transitions to provide clarity of expression; has very few mechanical errors	Incorporates some transitions to help flow of ideas; has few mechanical errors	Incorporates few transitions; does not connect ideas well; has many mechanical errors	Fails to connect ideas; has many mechanical errors

Persuasion
Advertisement

Advertisements in Everyday Life

Advertisements are all around you. For example, when you watch television, you probably spend at least fifteen minutes every hour watching commercials—advertisements of various companies pitching their products. Advertisements also appear on magazines and billboards and even on T-shirts and hats. In recent years, ads have become common sights on the Internet as well, blinking and winking to grab the attention of those surfing the Web.

▲ Critical Viewing
Judging from this photograph, why might it be important for an advertisement to be eye-catching?
[Connect]

What Is an Advertisement?

An **advertisement** is a persuasive message paid for by an individual or company. Ads attempt to persuade people to buy something, accept an idea, vote for a candidate, or support a cause.

Advertisements take many forms—from media ads on television and radio to print ads in newspapers, magazines, and flyers to creative visual ads, such as skywriting or walking billboards.

Most effective advertisements contain

- a slogan or catchy phrase that grabs the audience's attention.
- reasons the customer should purchase the product or service.
- details that tell who to call or where to purchase the product or service.

To preview the criteria upon which your advertisement may be evaluated, see the Rubric for Self-Assessment on page 104.

Writers in
ACTION

As a person who did fund-raising for and advanced the ideas of the Asia Society in New York City, Sayu Bhojwani has firsthand experience writing persuasively:

"The most important aspect of persuasive writing is to be able to convey to your reader a certain emotion or concept. In the type of work that I do, it's usually a concept. . . . We want to convey a sense of innovation and newness, to get a reader in."

Types of Advertisements

Although most people think of advertising as only commercial ads used to sell consumer products, advertisements can take many forms:

- **Public-service announcements,** sent out by nonprofit organizations, discuss topics such as public safety or health.
- **Merchandise ads** are print, broadcast, or visual messages about products that consumers can purchase.
- **Service ads** are print, broadcast, or visual messages about services—cleaning, entertaining, or self-improvement.

PREVIEW
Student Work
IN PROGRESS

In this chapter, you'll follow the progress of Ever Chapa, a student at La Joya High School in La Joya, Texas, as he drafts an advertisement for a college fair. Follow along as Ever uses prewriting, drafting, and revising strategies to develop his ad. Ever's completed advertisement appears at the end of the chapter.

The following advertisement appeared in a magazine about nature and travel.

This advertisement contains an interesting use of language. The text is like a recipe that creates something wonderful—Costa Rica.

This statistic is presented in an appealing way.

Parallel structure runs through this advertisement: Each sentence is an imperative.

The ad's tag line—no artifical ingredients—continues the recipe metaphor.

Reading Writing Connection

Writing Application: Use Creative Language
You'll notice that the ad above contains creative use of language. As you prepare to write your own ad, think about creative ways you can use language.

8.2 *Prewriting*

Choosing Your Topic

You can write an advertisement for a product, a political candidate, or a service. Use the following strategies to help you come up with a topic for your advertisement:

Strategies for Generating Topics

1. **Conduct a Survey** Ask the following survey question: What gift would you most like to receive for your birthday? Review the responses, and choose one to form the topic of your advertisement.

2. **Blueprint** Draw the floor plan of a room in your everyday environment. Fill the room of your drawing with appropriate gadgets, clothes, or art objects. As you draw the items, decide which object appeals to you most. Make that one the subject of your advertisement.

Try it out! Use the interactive Blueprint activity in **Section 8.2,** on-line or on CD-ROM.

TOPIC BANK

If you need a specific topic for your advertisement, follow these suggestions:

1. **Advertisement for a School Function** Write and design a poster publicizing a school music festival.

Responding to Literature

2. In the ancient Greek tragedy *Antigone,* a woman defies the order of a stern king and gives her dead brother an appropriate burial. Think of images from this or another play that would make an exciting poster for a theatrical production. Then, create such a poster. You can read *Antigone* in *Prentice Hall Literature, Penguin Edition,* Grade 10.

🕐 Timed Writing Prompt

3. Everyone has a favorite class in school. Write a letter to your principal that explains why you enjoy your favorite class. Describe what makes your favorite class educational and enjoyable. **(35 minutes)**

Narrowing Your Topic

An advertisement should almost always have a narrow focus: Most effective ads are short and memorable. To narrow your topic for your advertisement, answer the following questions:

- What product/person/service am I selling or promoting?
- What is the one thing I'd like to communicate to my audience about this product/person/service?

As you draft your ad, refer to your responses to ensure that your focus has remained narrow.

Considering Your Audience and Purpose

As you think about the advertisement you are going to write, consider whom it is you are trying to persuade. Then, decide on the language and details that will impress them most.

Choose Your Words Carefully

One way to achieve your purpose is to choose words that will most appeal to your audience. Select your words carefully, taking into consideration their denotation and connotation. A word's *denotation* is its dictionary meaning. Its *connotation* is the positive or negative association the word conjures up. In your ad, take advantage of a word's connotation as well as its denotation.

Audience: Sporty Women

Audience: Romantic Women

Gathering Details

Put yourself in the place of your audience. Then, answer the questions you, as the audience, have about the product, service, or person you are promoting. Be sure to answer those questions somewhere in the advertisement you write.

Gather Details for a Product

• What is it?

• What makes it special or different?

• How much does it cost?

• Where can I buy it?

Gather Details for a Campaign

• What are his or her qualifications?

• What is his or her stand on ___?___?

• Who else supports this candidate?

Gather Details for an Event

• Who is sponsoring the event?

• Where is the event to be held? At what time?

• How much is the cost of admission?

Student Work
IN PROGRESS

Name: Ever Chapa
La Joya High School
La Joya, TX

Gathering Details for an Event

Because Ever was writing an ad for an event, he made a list of questions his audience would want answered.

Who? Representatives from colleges

What? College fair

When? Saturday, August 9, 2000
12:00 P.M. to 8:00 P.M.

Where? Westside Lake Park

Why? To provide information about colleges, tuition, courses, requirements, etc.

How much? Free

Drafting

Shaping Your Writing

When drafting your ad, be sure to grab the audience's attention right away. To do this, start with the most appealing characteristic of the product.

Order Details From Most Important to Least Important

Know what is most important to your audience, and tell them about that up front. Then, follow with details that your audience will also want to know.

In the advertisement at right, details are arranged in descending order of importance: The most important detail is that the lawn service is half price. The least important detail is that referrals are available.

Providing Elaboration

Include Testimonials, Statistics, and Graphics

Elaborate your advertisement, using pictures, quotations, and facts that will convince your audience of your product's superiority:

Testimonials are quotes from satisfied users:

Mary Kay Louis of Denver, Colorado, says "I'll never leave home without my Timetip wristwatch!"

Statistics are numerical facts that favor the use of the product or service being advertised:

More than 70 percent of the people polled by Dennton University say that they'd like to try a Timetip wristwatch.

Attractive graphics could include photographs of people using your product or service, diagrams that show the benefits of your product, or illustrations of the product or service.

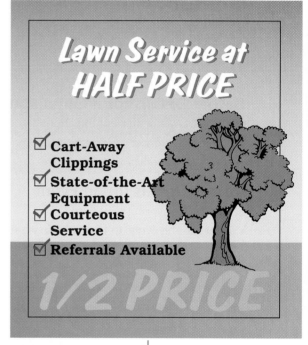

Lawn Service at HALF PRICE

☑ **Cart-Away Clippings**
☑ **State-of-the-Art Equipment**
☑ **Courteous Service**
☑ **Referrals Available**

1/2 PRICE

8.4 *Revising*

Revising Your Overall Structure
Prominently Place the Main Idea

In most advertisements, the most important idea occupies the most prominent place. (If your advertisement is written for radio, you will probably want to lead off with your most important idea.)

▶ **REVISION STRATEGY**
Experimenting With Placement of Your Main Idea

Critically examine the layout of your advertisement, and juggle the placement of your most important idea until it achieves the maximum impact.

Revising Your Paragraphs

▶ **REVISION STRATEGY**
Circling the Important Details

Trim unnecessary information from your paragraphs so that every detail and concept is essential to the message and its delivery. To do this, circle the most important details and delete uncircled material.

Technology Tip

Explore formatting options your word-processing program has to offer. Then, experiment with formats as you revise your advertisement. Choose the format that best suits your purpose.

Student Work IN PROGRESS

Name: *Ever Chapa*
La Joya High School
La Joya, TX

Circling Important Details

Ever Chapa circled the most important details in his advertisement. Then, he deleted or rewrote the uncircled details.

(Attention all SENIORS!) ~~You know who you are.~~ (Come join the fun) at the first annual Bash at the Lake. ~~Who said getting the scoop on what colleges have to offer you has to be boring?~~ (Come out and learn more about local scholarships and grants.)

Revising Your Sentences

Vary Sentence Types

Any writing is more enjoyable and engaging when its rhythms vary. By varying sentence type, you vary the rhythm of your prose. There are four basic sentence types: declarative, interrogative, exclamatory, and imperative.

▶ **REVISION STRATEGY**
Color-Coding End Marks

Read through your draft, and use a colored pen or pencil to call out various end marks. By doing this, you'll be able to see whether, for example, you have mostly declarative or imperative sentences, interrogative sentences, or exclamatory sentences.

First, draw a circle around periods, a square around question marks, and triangles around exclamation marks. Then, review your draft. If you have too many end marks of one shape, you may want to vary your sentence types to make your advertisement more interesting to read.

⏱ Timed Writing Hint

When revising your writing under timed conditions, check that you have varied sentence types and lengths to engage your reader.

Student Work IN PROGRESS

Name: Ever Chapa
La Joya High School
La Joya, TX

Coding to Identify Sentence Types

When Ever reviewed his draft, he found that too many of his sentences were declarative. He made the following changes to enliven his writing and keep the interest of his audience.

BASH AT THE LAKE

Attention all seniors ！

What's happening with your future ?

Come to the first annual Bash at the Lake to find out!
Learn about various colleges and what they have to offer

YOU .

Why not Get the *real scoop* on local

scholarships and grants ?

Create Parallel Structure

Although it can be effective to vary your sentence types in an advertisement, you can make your advertisement memorable if you create parallel structure by repeating sentence types for effect. In the following example, three interrogative sentences are followed by an exclamatory sentence to create an impact.

EXAMPLE: Is your breakfast cereal boring? Is it bland? Is it full of sugar? Then, try Crackle, a new type of cereal that is sure to enliven your mornings!

▶ **REVISION STRATEGY**
Extending an Idea

Read through your draft, and locate an idea that you'd like to emphasize. Then, build on that idea by creating short sentences of the same type to make the idea memorable to readers.

Grammar in Your Writing
The Four Functions of Sentences

Just as sentences can have varied structures, they can have varied functions as well. Try to include declarative, interrogative, exclamatory, and imperative sentences in your writing.

The Four Functions of Sentences Every sentence fulfills one of the following four functions:

Declarative—a sentence that makes a statement
Example: This product whitens and brightens your teeth.

Interrogative—a sentence that asks a question
Example: Do you need a new bicycle?

Exclamatory—a sentence that expresses strong emotion
Example: Try our great-tasting soup!

Imperative—a sentence that gives a command
Example: Be the first to buy this product.

Find It in Your Writing Review your draft to identify sentences that fulfill each of the four functions. Be sure that you have used the appropriate end marks. If you cannot identify all four functions, challenge yourself to add at least one more to your writing.

To learn more about types of sentences, see Chapter 21.

Revising Your Word Choice

In advertising, you want to keep your sentences short and powerful. You don't want to use too many words, so choose carefully. Verbs, especially, can help you stimulate the readers' imagination or motivate them to do something.

Timed Writing Hint

It is fine to cross out unnecessary words neatly when you revise your timed writing.

▶REVISION STRATEGY
Replace Dull Words

When you want to attract attention, use verbs that vividly describe the action you want readers to take.

	DULL VERBS	VIVID VERBS
Example:	*Get* into our car.	*Jump* into our car.
Example:	*See* Williamsburg, Virginia, and *see* the eighteenth century.	*Come* to Williamsburg, Virginia, and *relive* the eighteenth century.

Peer Review

Question a Peer

With a partner, exchange advertisement drafts. Then, have your partner answer the following questions, or create questions of your own that you'd like to have answered.

- What is the main idea conveyed by my advertisement?
- Do any images within the ad seem distasteful? If so, which?
- Which words seem weak or inappropriate? What replacements do you suggest?
- Is any information left out of the ad that you would like to know? If so, what?
- Does my ad need to be enlivened with graphics, charts, or photographs? What type would be effective?
- If you could change one thing about my advertisement, what would it be?

Review the responses of your partner. Then, incorporate changes into your ad, and review it again.

Interactive Textbook

Get instant help! For assistance in replacing dull words, use the Word Bins, accessible from the menu bar, on-line or on CD-ROM.

8.5 Editing and Proofreading

Correct Use of *Your* and *You're*

Homophones—words that sound the same—are sometimes used incorrectly. For example, you might write the contraction *you're* instead of the possessive *your*. Read through your advertisement carefully to make sure that you have chosen the correct homophones.

EXAMPLE:	These walking shoes are made for you're comfort.
CORRECT:	These walking shoes are made for your comfort.
EXAMPLE:	Your going to notice the cushioned insole.
CORRECT:	You're going to notice the cushioned insole.

Grammar in Your Writing
Homophones

Homophones are words that sound the same but have different spellings and meanings. Some homophones that are commonly confused include the following:

It's	Its	
By	Buy	
Who's	Whose	
To	Too	Two

Find It in Your Reading Find a homophone in an advertisement from your favorite magazine. Then, write down the related homophones and their meanings.

Find It in Your Writing As you proofread your advertisement, check that you have written all homophones correctly.

For more on spelling homophones, see Chapter 30.

Publishing and Presenting

Building Your Portfolio

Use the following suggestions for sharing your advertisement:

1. **Post It** If your advertisement is for a real product or service, get permission to post it throughout your school or in your community.
2. **Record It** Rework your advertisement for radio presentation. Add sound effects and tape-record your efforts. Play the ad for your peers.

Reflecting on Your Writing

Consider the experience of writing your advertisement. Then, answer the following questions, and record your responses in your portfolio.

- In the process of writing, what did you learn about how you relate to your audience?
- Which strategies for prewriting, drafting, revising, or editing might you recommend to a friend?

 Internet Tip

To see an advertisement scored with this rubric, go on-line:
PHSchool.com
Enter Web Code:
eek-1001

Rubric for Self-Assessment

Use the following criteria to evaluate your advertisement.

	Score 4	Score 3	Score 2	Score 1
Audience and Purpose	Presents effective slogan; clearly addresses persuasive task	Presents good slogan; addresses persuasive task	Presents slogan; minimally addresses persuasive task	Does not present slogan; shows lack of attention to persuasive task
Organization	Uses clear, consistent organizational strategy	Uses clear organizational strategy with few inconsistencies	Uses inconsistent organizational strategy; creates illogical presentation	Demonstrates lack of organizational strategy; creates confusing presentation
Elaboration	Successfully combines words and images to provide convincing, unified support for a position	Combines words and images to provide unified support for a position	Includes some words or images that detract from a position	Uses words and images that do not support a position
Use of Language	Successfully communicates an idea through clever use of language; includes very few mechanical errors	Conveys an idea through adequate use of language; includes few mechanical errors	Misuses language and lessens impact of ideas; includes many mechanical errors	Demonstrates poor use of language and confuses meaning; includes many mechanical errors

8.7 Student Work
IN PROGRESS

FINAL DRAFT

Ever Chapa
La Joya High School
La Joya, Texas

Come join the fun at the first annual BASH AT THE LAKE.

Learn about various colleges and what they have to offer YOU.

Get the *real scoop* on local scholarships and grants.

BASH AT THE LAKE

Attention all seniors!

Representatives from more than
ninety colleges!
Five hot bands!
Food!

Westside Lake Park
Saturday, August 9, 2000
12:00 P.M. to 8:00 P.M.

Free of charge for everyone

High-school seniors are encouraged to attend.
(10 Senior Points for those who come!!!)
Parents are also encouraged to attend.

Capital letters emphasize the main idea.

Details that make the event more attractive are featured to the side of the main ad.

Colorful text emphasizes the time and place of the event.

Ever used boldface text to highlight the fact that the event is free.

Colloquial terms like "real scoop" appeal to the audience of high-school students.

Exposition
Comparison-and-Contrast Essay

Comparing and Contrasting in Everyday Life

Comparing and contrasting are processes that you perform every day. Whether you're deciding which movie to see or which jacket to buy, you analyze the similarities and differences between the choices and make judgments about the positive qualities or shortcomings of each one.

Developing your ability to compare and contrast is useful any time you have to make a major decision. When the time comes to decide which college to attend or which job offer to accept, being able to clearly assess your options will help you take the best possible course of action.

▲ **Critical Viewing**
What sort of features or qualities might these shoppers be comparing and contrasting? **[Analyze]**

What Is a Comparison-and-Contrast Essay?

To *compare* is to show how two or more things are similar. To *contrast* is to show how two or more things are different. An essay exploring the similarities and differences between two or more subjects is a **comparison-and-contrast essay.**

Most effective comparison-and-contrast essays contain

- two or more subjects that are being compared and contrasted.
- details that reveal the similarities and differences between the subjects.
- transitions that make relationships between the subjects clear.
- an effective structure, such as point-by-point or subject-by-subject organization.

To preview the criteria on which your comparison-and-contrast essay may be evaluated, see the Self-Assessment Rubric on page 120.

Types of Comparison-and-Contrast Essays

Topics for a comparison-and-contrast essay range widely. Following are some examples:

- significant events from history
- works of art, literature, or music
- lives and achievements of historical figures
- effects of different laws or policies

Writers in ACTION

Journalist and author Joseph Epstein considers himself lucky to have discovered at an early age that essay-writing was his preferred form of expression. He reveals the following insight about what makes essay-writing so appealing:

"Writing an essay has for me tended to be an act of self-discovery. By this I mean that I come to the writing of an essay not knowing what I think of the subject, except in an [unformed] way; or if I believe I know what I think, the writing itself leads me into aspects of the subject whose importance or even existence I hadn't earlier recognized."

PREVIEW *Student Work* IN PROGRESS

Follow the progress of Emily Agy, a student at Pleasant Valley High School, in Pleasant Valley, Iowa, as she drafts a newspaper article that explores the similarities and differences between life in the United States and life in England.

Prewriting

Choosing Your Topic

Choose two or more subjects to explore in a comparison-and-contrast essay. For help getting started, consider the strategies below:

Strategies for Generating Topics

1. **Freewrite** Freewrite for five minutes about recent decisions you have made. For example, have you recently purchased one brand of clothing over another brand? If so, why? Review your freewriting, and use an idea from it to form the basis of your comparison-and-contrast essay.

2. **List** First, choose a broad subject area, such as music, art, history, sports, or characters in a novel. Then, list items that come to mind within that subject area—your favorite examples or ones that you find particularly interesting. Finally, examine your list to find connections between the two or more items you recorded. Strong connections between items indicate that they might be effective subjects for a comparison-and-contrast essay. If so, choose those items and build your comparison-and-contrast essay around them. Here's an example:

Get instant help! Freewrite or list your items using the Essay Builder, accessible from the menu bar, on-line or on CD-ROM.

SPACE	Broad Subject Area
Moon	
Sun	
Saturn	
Andromeda	Topic: Comparison and Contrast of Galaxies
Jupiter	
Black holes	
Asteroids	
Milky Way Galaxy	

TOPIC BANK

For more specific suggestions for your comparison-and-contrast essay, consider the following ideas:

1. **Historical and Current Situations** Write an essay in which you compare and contrast an event or situation from history with one that is occurring today. For example, you could compare and contrast the Information Age with the Industrial Revolution.

2. **Two Products** Select two competing products that you would consider buying. In your essay, focus on the merits or shortcomings of each one. Finally, provide the reader with a recommendation about which one is the better product or the better value.

Responding to Fine Art

Minor League, Clyde Singer, Butler Institute of American Art

3. Study *Minor League*, by Clyde Singer. Then, write a comparison-and-contrast essay about two favorite athletes or baseball today compared with baseball of the 1920's.

Responding to Literature

4. Compare and contrast the excerpts from "Touch the Top of the World" by Erik Weihenmayer and "Swimming to Antarctica" by Lynne Cox. You can find both selections in *Prentice Hall Literature, Penguin Edition*, Grade 10. Focus on the similarities and differences in the narrators, the dangers they face, and the character traits they exhibit.

⏱ **Timed Writing Prompt**

5. Write an essay in which you explain to an eighth grader the differences and similarities between middle school and high school. Identify two ways in which middle school and high school are similar and two ways in which they are different. **(40 minutes)**

Evaluating Your Topic

Evaluate your topic to make sure the subjects you have chosen share a valid basis for comparison. Don't compare dissimilar subjects, such as the work of an artist with that of a musician, unless you have a compelling reason for doing so.

Also, make sure that the focus of your comparison isn't too broad. For example, the complete body of work of two writers is too much to handle in a single essay; two of their works or characters is a much more manageable challenge.

Use a Venn Diagram

To evaluate whether or not your subjects have enough points of comparison and contrast, use a Venn diagram.

Try it out! Use the interactive Venn Diagram in **Section 9.2**, on-line or on CD-ROM.

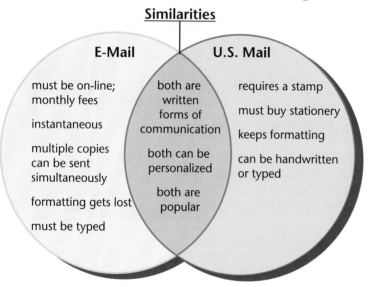

Similarities

E-Mail

must be on-line; monthly fees

instantaneous

multiple copies can be sent simultaneously

formatting gets lost

must be typed

both are written forms of communication

both can be personalized

both are popular

U.S. Mail

requires a stamp

must buy stationery

keeps formatting

can be handwritten or typed

Considering Your Audience and Purpose

The audience and purpose for your essay will affect the type of information you include in it. Use these questions to help you consider your audience:

- Who will read your essay? Peers? A review panel?
- How familiar will they be with the topic? What aspects of the topic will be most interesting to them?

Use these questions to help you consider your purpose:

- What aspects of the topic are most important to emphasize?
- How will your audience use the information you are providing?

Gathering Details

Gather enough details, descriptions, facts, examples, and reasons to provide your audience with a clear understanding of each subject being compared and to support your statements about the similarities and differences between them. Below are three ways to gather details:

Use Personal Experience

Experience counts. Use yours if you are comparing products, places, or things with which you have direct experience or if you are comparing works of art, literature, or music. For example, if you are comparing two products, use your own experience with each of them as evidence.

Use Primary Sources

Primary sources include original documents, such as scientific reports, company brochures, speeches, diary entries, journals, letters, or interview responses. Primary source material provides the words or works of people who were participants in or eyewitnesses to an event.

Use Secondary Sources

Secondary sources come from a published work in which the writer presents ideas about a subject based on evidence from several primary sources. For example, a biography of a president of the United States would be a secondary source. To write one, its author would draw upon primary sources, including letters from the president and interviews with people who worked with the president.

The following chart gives examples of different types of details gathered in various ways:

Subjects	Personal Experience	Primary Source	Secondary Source
two mountain-bike models	your experience riding each model	specification sheets from the manufacturers	newspaper article on this year's mountain-bike models
tornadoes and hurricanes	your experience with those types of weather phenomena	interviews with people who survived a category 5 hurricane	encyclopedia entry on hurricanes

 Internet Tip

If you are comparing and contrasting two or more products in your essay, take advantage of official company Web sites. Many companies maintain Web sites with detailed information (including technical specifications) about their products. Use a search engine to find the company's URL, or Web address.

Drafting

Shaping Your Writing

An effective comparison-and-contrast essay is usually organized in one of two ways:

Use Subject-by-Subject Organization

In a subject-by-subject organization, first discuss all the aspects of one subject and then discuss all the aspects of the second subject. For example, you could discuss figure skating first and then discuss hockey skating.

Use Point-by-Point Organization

In a point-by-point organization, each aspect or point of comparison and contrast is discussed in turn. You might, for instance, discuss the cost of product A and the cost of product B, and then discuss the appearance of product A and that of product B, and so on.

Timed Writing Hint

Make a quick outline based on the subject-by-subject or the point-by-point organization to plan your essay under timed conditions.

Try it out! Use the interactive Point-by-Point activity in **Section 9.3**, on-line or on CD-ROM.

Student Work
IN PROGRESS

Name: Emily Agy
Pleasant Valley High School
Pleasant Valley, IA

Using Point-by-Point Organization

Emily decided to structure her article using point-by-point organization. She wrote each point of comparison on a self-sticking note so she could rearrange the order in which she planned to present each point of comparison.

Point A: Driving
- England
- U.S.

Point B: Curfews
- England
- U.S.

Point C: School Uniforms
- England
- U.S.

Point D: Sports and Activities
- England
- U.S.

Providing Elaboration

Give Examples

During the drafting process, make sure you provide support for each of the statements you make about your subjects. Elaborate on your points by providing specific details and examples that clarify the similarities and differences between the subjects.

Provide Facts

Provide facts to give your readers a clear understanding of each subject under discussion.

EXAMPLE: Bike 3000 is suitable for the toughest terrain. It is tough enough to handle boulder-strewn trails and has special gearing for handling steep inclines. Advanced brakes help riders make quick stops on wet surfaces.

Cite Quotations and Figures

Use quotations and statistical or numerical figures to lend authority to the points you make in your comparison-and-contrast essay.

▲ **Critical Viewing** If you were thinking of purchasing a bike like the one shown, about what features would you want to know? **[Relate]**

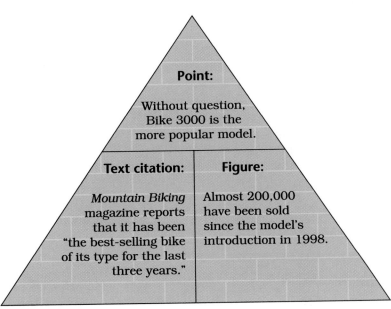

Point:

Without question, Bike 3000 is the more popular model.

Text citation:

Mountain Biking magazine reports that it has been "the best-selling bike of its type for the last three years."

Figure:

Almost 200,000 have been sold since the model's introduction in 1998.

Revising

Revising Your Overall Structure

Because your essay has two or more subjects, it's particularly important to make sure that its structure is sound. If the structure of the essay is disorganized, a reader may become confused about which subject you are discussing. You also need to ensure that your essay is balanced—that equal space is devoted to each subject.

▶ **REVISION STRATEGY**
Color-Coding by Subject

Using a highlighter of one color, go through your essay and mark each detail you have included about subject A. Then, use a highlighter of a second color to mark each detail you have included about subject B. Examine the essay. Is there a lot of one color and just a little of the other? If so, add more information about the other subject.

Also, check to be sure that your essay consistently follows either point-by-point or subject-by-subject organization. If the essay is well structured, your highlighted body paragraphs will form a pattern of color.

Student Work
IN PROGRESS

Name: *Emily Agy*
Pleasant Valley High School
Pleasant Valley, IA

Color-Coding to Check Structure

Emily highlighted information about England and the U.S. in different colors to make sure she had included sufficient details about both countries.

There are many differences when it comes to extracurricular school-sponsored activities. "Here there are all kinds of activities: football teams, field hockey teams, language clubs, etc. In England, we don't have extracurricular activities at school. If you want to play sports, you have to find the time to do it yourself...."

Revising Your Paragraphs

Once you've evaluated the balance and structure of your essay, analyze your writing at the paragraph level. You may want to reorganize some of your paragraphs to give your essay variety and to make it more interesting to read. Read the following examples to come up with ways to structure your paragraphs.

▶**REVISION STRATEGY**
Using TRI/PS/QA

TRI: *TRI* stands for Topic, Restatement, and Illustration.

Michael Jordan has had a serious impact on `Topic` the American economy. Some estimate that the "Jordan Effect" reached as high as $10 `Restatement` billion dollars over the course of his career. If that seems high, consider $165 million in basketball tickets, the $230 million worldwide `Illustration` gross of the movie he starred in, and almost $3 billion in Jordan-related merchandise.

PS: *PS* stands for Problem and Solution. In this kind of structure, both a problem and a solution are presented.

`PROBLEM`

A mountain bike must be able to withstand repeated bumps and jolts as it navigates the trails. Bike `SOLUTION` 3000 handles this requirement by incorporating a special frame geometry that disperses shocks more efficiently than conventional bikes.

QA: *QA* stands for Question and Answer. Using this organization, a paragraph poses and answers a question.

`QUESTION`

How did Tiger Woods gain so much acclaim, so quickly? The answer is a stunning string `ANSWER` of victories in both his amateur and professional careers.

Revising Your Sentences

Read your comparison-and-contrast essay carefully, examining the sentences you have written. Correct run-ons and fragments by joining or breaking up groups of words as needed. Also revise complete sentences to create variety within your essay. Make sure that your sentences flow smoothly and connect ideas.

Improve Connections Between Ideas

Review your draft, paying special attention to how well your ideas connect and flow together. If your sentences are choppy and unconnected, consider combining them. When combining sentences, use appropriate conjunctions to clearly indicate how the ideas within them are related.

▶**REVISION STRATEGY**
Using Conjunctions to Combine Sentences

Read your draft critically to make sure that your ideas flow smoothly and logically. Whenever you find a passage that contains short, choppy sentences, combine the sentences and use a conjunction within the sentence to indicate relationships. Use a coordinating conjunction to link ideas of equal importance. Use a subordinating conjunction to indicate that one idea within a sentence is dependent upon another.

Student Work
IN PROGRESS

Name: Emily Agy
Pleasant Valley High School
Pleasant Valley, IA

Adding Conjunctions to Connect
After reviewing her opening paragraph, Emily decided that her sentences were too short and choppy. She decided to add conjunctions to connect her ideas more smoothly.

It's one thing to move from one state to another, but To move from a different country to the United States must certainly be a challenge. Michael Johnson, a fifteen-year-old sophomore recently moved from Southend-on-Sea, England. Johnson was recently interviewed at a journalism club meeting where ~~students.~~ ~~During the interview,~~ he explained the differences between life in the United States and life in England.

Grammar in Your Writing
Conjunctions

A conjunction is a word used to connect other words or groups of words. In English, there are three main kinds of conjunctions: *coordinating conjunctions*, *correlative conjunctions*, and *subordinating conjunctions*.

Coordinating conjunctions connect similar kinds or groups of words. There are seven coordinating conjunctions: *and, but, or, nor, for, yet,* and *so.*

Examples:

The golfers and basketball players arrived at the tournament.

The carryall bag given out to students was sturdy yet lightweight.

Carry the picnic basket or the blanket outside.

Correlative conjunctions are used in pairs to connect similar words or groups of words. Examples of correlative conjunction pairs include *neither/nor, just as/so, both/and,* and *whether/or.*

Examples:

Neither thunder nor lightning had much of an effect on our sleepy cat.

Both Charles and Ed promised to help us get ready for the dance.

Just as bees fly to honey, so my car gravitates to potholes.

Subordinating conjunctions connect two complete ideas by placing one idea below the other in rank or importance. Commonly used subordinating conjunctions include *after, before, because, even if, since, so that, unless, until, when,* and *while.*

Examples:

He achieved a great deal of success because he practiced regularly.

We can go to the park today, even if it rains.

Now that the show is over, you can go home.

Find It in Your Reading Find an example of a coordinating conjunction and of a subordinating conjunction in a story you have read. Then, explain how the conjunctions help to show the relationships between the ideas being connected.

Find It in Your Writing As you revise your comparison-and-contrast essay, look for one example of each type of conjunction. Examine each conjunction to make sure it shows the relationship you intend. If you can't find any, challenge yourself to combine ideas with conjunctions.

For more on conjunctions, see Chapter 18.

Revising Your Word Choice
Add Transitions to Clarify Relationships

Transitions indicate relationships. You can improve the clarity of your writing by adding transitions that express the relationships between the ideas in your essay.

Common Transitions			
Time Relationships	Spatial Relationships	Comparison-and-Contrast Relationships	Logical Relationships
before; during after; first; second; last; next; then; when; at the same time; now; later; immediately; soon; recently	above; below; behind; in front of; alongside; next to; north; south; east; west; inside; outside; beneath; at the top of; at the bottom of	along with; together with; as well as; also; similarly; although; though; however; nevertheless; yet; but; on the other hand; in contrast	if; whether; unless; therefore; thus; hence; in fact; in essence; for example; for instance

▶ **REVISION STRATEGY**
Reading Aloud

Read aloud pairs of sentences in your draft. For example, read the first and second sentence, then the second and third sentence, and so on. Pause after each pair and ask: Would adding transitions clarify the relationship between the two sentences? If so, add a transition from the chart above. Reread the sentence to be sure that the transition works well.

Peer Review
Ask Questions

Work with a peer to revise your essay. Write down five questions about your essay that you would like your peer reviewer to answer. Then, exchange drafts and questions with your peer reviewer. Take your peer's comments into consideration as you prepare a final draft.

Sample Questions:

• What types of details would enhance my essay?

• Have I provided a balanced treatment of the two subjects?

• What aspects of the essay need improvement? Why?

🕐 **Timed Writing Hint**

Adapt the read-aloud strategy in an exam by reading silently to yourself. "Hear" how your sentence pairs sound and improve them when necessary.

9.5 Editing and Proofreading

Before sharing your comparison-and-contrast essay with others, proofread it carefully to correct errors in spelling, punctuation, and grammar.

Focusing on Punctuation

Because comparison-and-contrast essays discuss two or more subjects, they often contain compound sentences. Pay close attention to your punctuation of compound sentences to ensure that you have correctly used commas within them.

Technology Tip

Use the Find feature of your word-processing software to locate conjunctions like *and, but,* and *yet.* When each is found, examine the sentence to see if it is compound. If so, make sure that it has a comma before the conjunction.

Grammar in Your Writing
Punctuating Compound Sentences

A **compound sentence** consists of two or more independent clauses joined by a comma and a coordinating conjunction or by a semicolon. Use the following rules for properly punctuating compound sentences:

- Use a comma before the conjunction that joins the clauses of a compound sentence.

  Eighteen tourists remained on the island, **but** most were safely evacuated before the hurricane struck.

- Use a semicolon when no conjunction is used to join closely related independent clauses.

  The tour bus was forced to take a detour; mudslides had made the main road impassable.

Find It in Your Reading Find three examples of compound sentences in a short story. Explain the rules for punctuating them.

Find It in Your Writing As you proofread your comparison-and-contrast essay, check to be sure that you have punctuated all compound sentences correctly.

For more on punctuating compound sentences, see Chapter 28.

Publishing and Presenting

Consider the following possibilities for publishing and presenting your comparison-and-contrast essay:

Building Your Portfolio

1. **Presentation** Present your comparison-and-contrast essay to the class. Gather or create visual aids such photographs and charts, and decide on the order in which you'll present them. Rehearse your presentation to give it polish.
2. **Electronic Essay** Add to the details in your essay with digitized photographs, sound or video clips, or other multimedia elements. Share your essay with others by posting it on a Web site or uploading it onto a classroom computer.

Reflecting on Your Writing

Think back on your writing experience. Then, answer the following questions and save your responses in your portfolio.

- What surprises did you encounter while gathering details for your essay?
- If you could start over, would you choose the same subjects to compare and contrast? Why or why not?

🖥 Internet Tip

To see model essays scored with this rubric, go on-line:
PHSchool.com
Enter Web Code:
eek-1001

Rubric for Self-Assessment

Use the following criteria to evaluate your comparison-and-contrast essay:

	Score 4	Score 3	Score 2	Score 1
Audience and Purpose	Chooses details and language that engage audience and achieve purpose	Chooses details and language appropriate for audience and purpose	Chooses details that mostly suit audience and purpose	Chooses details inappropriate for audience and that do not fulfill any purpose
Organization	Clearly presents information in a consistent organization best suited to the topic	Presents information using an organization suited to the topic	Chooses an organization not suited to comparison and contrast	Shows a lack of organizational strategy
Elaboration	Elaborates several ideas, with facts, details, or examples; links all information to comparison and contrast	Elaborates most ideas with facts, details, or examples; links most information to comparison and contrast	Does not elaborate all ideas; does not link some details to comparison and contrast	Does not provide facts or examples to support a comparison and contrast
Use of Language	Demonstrates excellent sentence and vocabulary variety; includes very few mechanical errors	Demonstrates adequate sentence and vocabulary variety; includes few mechanical errors	Demonstrates repetitive use of sentence structure and vocabulary; includes many mechanical errors	Demonstrates poor use of language; generates confusion; includes many mechanical errors

Connected Assignment *Consumer Report*

When you want to compare and contrast several products or services, you can read a **consumer report.** In these reports, writers analyze different features of the products or services being discussed and come up with a recommendation. Consumer reports often take readers step by step through data such as user polls, expert opinions, and test results. They may use tables, graphs, or charts to show at a glance how the products or services compare and contrast.

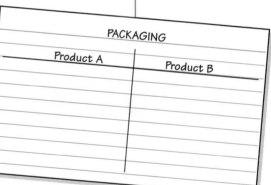

Write your own consumer report about a product or service you know well. Use the writing process tips outlined below to help you.

Prewriting Decide on two or more products or services to compare and contrast. To come up with an idea, think about products you are interested in buying or a service, such as car washes, that you have used.

Before you draft, collect details that describe the features of the products or services about which you are writing. Use a chart like this one to help you organize the information as you find it.

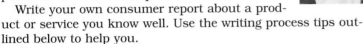

PACKAGING	
Product A	Product B

Drafting Open your draft with a general statement about the product type and a quick explanation of the features you will be examining. Refer to the chart often as you address each feature and evaluate the pros and cons of each product example. Close with a recommendation about which product or service you find superior.

Revising and Editing Check for consistency in your organization. For example, if have used point-by-point organization, don't switch to subject-by-subject organization later in the report. Confirm that all product names are accurate and correctly spelled. Strengthen your conclusion by correcting wordiness and adding persuasive modifiers.

Publishing and Presenting Make a neat copy of your consumer report, and post it for others to read. If time allows, collect consumer reports from your peers and assemble them into a binder for classmates to use as a reference.

Exposition
Cause-and-Effect Essay

Cause-and-Effect Relationships in Everyday Life

Identifying causes and effects is a part of daily life. Giving advice to a friend based on the effects you predict, fireproofing a potential fire hazard, and arguing about the best way to solve a problem—all these activities show an awareness of cause-and-effect relationships.

Cause-and-effect relationships are also explored in writing. Feature articles in your daily newspaper often describe causes and effects related to politics, crime, or the environment. History textbooks are primarily focused on causes and effects, as well. Even something as common as a recipe may describe a cause-and-effect process.

▲ **Critical Viewing**
When you look at this picture, what causes and effects come to mind? **[Relate]**

What Is a Cause-and-Effect Essay?

Exposition is writing that informs or explains. A **cause-and-effect essay** is a piece of exposition that describes the relationship between an event or circumstance and its causes. Good cause-and-effect essays contain

- a clearly stated topic that explains what cause-and-effect relationships will be explored.
- an effective and logical method of organization.
- details and examples that elaborate upon the writer's statements.
- transitions that smoothly and clearly connect the writer's ideas.

To preview the criteria on which your cause-and-effect essay may be evaluated, see the Rubric for Self-Assessment on page 136.

Writers in ACTION

Writer Rudolfo Anaya discusses the process of writing an expository essay:

"In expository writing you're guided by an idea that you want to develop. It may be a paragraph, it may be ten pages, but what you really have is a subject, and you want to convey it...."

Types of Cause-and-Effect Essays

Cause-and-effect relationships are explored in many types of writing, including the ones listed below:

- **Historical articles** explain how events in history contributed to or resulted in other events.
- **Process explanations** take readers step by step through a process, such as a math formula or a scientific technique.
- **Predictions** make educated guesses about future events based on knowledge of cause-and-effect relationships.

PREVIEW Student Work IN PROGRESS

In this chapter, you'll follow the progress of Jennifer Hoss, a student at Bel Air High School in El Paso, Texas, as she writes a cause-and-effect essay entitled "El Niño."

Prewriting

Choosing Your Topic

Choose a topic for your cause-and-effect essay that you find interesting and that centers around a cause-and-effect relationship.

Strategies for Choosing a Topic

1. **Sketch a Scene** Draw a scene from the world of nature. Review your sketch to find interesting details that make a good writing topic. For example, you might draw a field of dandelions and clover that has a pond in the middle of it. You might then decide to write about the effects of last year's drought on local flowers and crops.

2. **Make a List** List interesting events or scientific phenomena. After five minutes, circle the one you find most interesting. Then, write for another five minutes, listing any causes and effects that spring to mind when you think of that topic. Review what you wrote, and develop your topic into a cause-and-effect essay. If you find that your topic doesn't have a strong enough cause-and-effect relationship, continue the listing process until you find one that does.

3. **Scan a Newspaper** Scan a newspaper, looking for topics that you can link to causes or effects. Keep a list of the possible topics as you come across them. Then, review your list, and choose as a topic the item you find most interesting.

interactive Textbook

Get instant help! Make your list using the Essay Builder, accessible from the menu bar, on-line or on CD-ROM.

Student Work
IN PROGRESS

Name: *Jennifer Hoss*
Bel Air High School
El Paso, TX

Doing a Newspaper Scan to Find a Topic

Jennifer Hoss found her topic by flipping through a newspaper. She jotted down articles that explained causes and effects and chose the one she liked the best as her topic.

1. Academic scores rise dramatically
2. Indonesia elects a new president
3. Scientists analyze tissue from a twenty-five-thousand-year-old frozen woolly mammoth
4. El Niño crop failure blamed for high cost of chilies

TOPIC BANK

If you are having difficulty finding a specific topic for your cause-and-effect essay, use the following ideas:

1. **Influences of the Blues on Popular Music** Write an essay that reveals how blues instruments, blues singers, and recurring themes in blues songs affect music today.

2. **Causes of Changes in Rain Forests** In a cause-and-effect essay, explore the various factors that have led to the rain forest's acreage being decreased. You can find information about deforestation in current periodicals available at the library.

Responding to Fine Art

Rolling Power, Smith College Museum of Art

3. *Rolling Power* depicts a close-up view of the workings of a locomotive. Write a cause-and-effect essay, explaining how steam engines propel locomotives. As an alternative, explore the cause-and-effect relationship between the development of the railroad and patterns of settlement westward across the United States.

Responding to Literature

4. Read the technical article "Tides" by Joseph D. Exline and others. Using this selection as a model, research and write an essay in which you explain the causes of another natural phenomenon, such as the northern lights. You can find the article in *Prentice Hall Literature, Penguin Edition*, Grade 10.

Timed Writing Prompt

5. Write an essay in which you introduce a historical event and discuss its causes and effects. Identify at least two causes for the historical event you have chosen. Then, explain at least two effects that resulted from the historical event. Write this essay for a reader who knows nothing about the historical event you are discussing. **(40 minutes)**

Narrowing Your Topic

Once you have a general idea for a topic, work with the material until it is narrow enough to cover effectively within the scope of your essay. Cubing is one narrowing technique that you can use.

Use the Cubing Technique

Cubing lets you focus on details by helping you identify six perspectives or aspects of your topic. Answer the six questions, and decide to focus your essay on one or two of the perspectives or aspects you explored.

1. **Describe It** How would you describe your topic to someone who is unfamiliar with it?
2. **Associate It** What other situations or events does your topic bring to mind?
3. **Apply It** Why is your topic important? Why is it useful to explore?
4. **Analyze It** Where is it? When did it happen? Why might it happen again? Can anything stop it from happening?
5. **Compare or Contrast It** How does your topic compare and contrast with similar topics?
6. **Argue for or Against It** What are the positive and negative effects of your topic?

Considering Your Audience and Purpose

Before you gather details, identify your audience and your purpose. Your audience and purpose will affect your word choice, the details you include, and the way in which you present those details. For help identifying the types of details and style of language that will be most effective, devise a plan like the one that appears below.

Audience:	School Board
Purpose:	To explain effects of decreased music funding
Details:	Facts and statistics; cause-and-effect chart; examples
Style of Language:	Formal word choice; vivid persuasive language; tone of respect

Gathering Details

Before you draft, collect and organize details for your cause-and-effect essay. Following are two methods for collecting and organizing details:

Collect Note Cards

When you research a topic, it's important to keep note cards for each cause-and-effect idea and its source. Before you begin to draft your essay, collect note cards from at least three or four sources either at home or at the library. On each note card, record the quotation or the idea you want to include in your report. Mark the note card with a number that identifies its source and the page number(s) on which the information can be found.

As an alternative, photocopy source pages and highlight the information you use.

Chart Causes and Effects

On a sheet of paper, write the effect, or event, that is your subject. Then, use arrows and boxes to show events or conditions that are caused by or result from your topic. If one event has several different effects, use a separate arrow to point to each.

Technology Tip

If you find information on the Internet, print out the pages containing the information you plan to use. Make sure to print out or write down the Web address, too.

Student Work
IN PROGRESS

Name: Jennifer Hoss
Bel Air High School
El Paso, TX

Showing Causes and Effects

Jennifer prepared a cause-and-effect chart about the effects of El Niño.

Effects of El Niño

Violent weather → Chili crops died → Migrant workers unemployed

Chili crops died → Chili prices rise

Drafting

Shaping Your Writing

Now that you have gathered details on your topic, shape the structure of your essay. Choose a logical method of organization for your cause-and-effect essay.

Choose a Logical Organization

Chronological Organization Chronological, or time, organization is a logical choice for structuring a cause-and-effect essay. You can start either with the effect and go back through its causes one at a time, in chronological order, or you can start with the cause and proceed to describe its effects in time order.

▼ Critical Viewing
What effect has time had on the *Titanic*, shown in this recent photograph? **[Analyze]**

Effects Organized Chronologically:

After the *Titanic* sank, new marine regulations were put into effect. The tragedy of the *Titanic* caused mariners to firm up regulations about radio contact and lifeboats. Marine regulations instituted after the *Titanic* included these mandates: constant radio contact between vessels and sufficient lifeboats to hold all passengers.

Order-of-Importance Organization Order-of-importance organization allows you to build an argument or to present various causes or effects in the order of their relative importance. You can either begin with the most important detail and end with the least important detail or reverse it, beginning with the least important detail and ending with the most important detail.

Effects Organized in Order of Importance:

The *Titanic*'s voyage proved to be a disaster because of many causes. Chief among them was the failure of the crew to navigate around the iceberg. The resulting damage to the ship's hull made its sinking inevitable. . . .

Another contributing cause was the lack of adequate lifeboats and safety instruction. Because the *Titanic* was "unsinkable," the company that made the ship did not provide enough safety equipment to ensure the safety of passengers and crew.

The weather conditions certainly did not help. . . .

Providing Elaboration

Elaborate as you draft to add depth and detail to your cause-and-effect essay. Types of elaboration include examples, statistics, quotations, and other types of details that support your ideas. Use the following strategy to help you elaborate:

Use the SEE Technique for Elaboration

Use the SEE technique to layer, or give depth, to your writing as you draft. First, write a basic statement about your topic. Next, write a sentence that extends that statement. Finally, write a sentence that elaborates on the extension.

STATEMENT: **State the main idea of the paragraph.**

Exercise is beneficial to your health.

EXTENSION: **Restate the idea.**

People who exercise regularly live longer, fuller lives.

ELABORATION: **Add information that further explains or defines the main idea.**

For example, a person who works out for twenty minutes three times a week is often in far better shape than a person who has no regular routine.

Student Work
IN PROGRESS

Name: Jennifer Hoss
Bel Air High School
El Paso, TX

Using SEE to Elaborate
Using the SEE technique, Jennifer gave depth to her essay.

El Niño has since passed, but the world is still suffering from] Statement

its aftermath. Weather conditions, for example, have differed] Extension

from normal. Records from the past have shown that the

winters following El Niño have been some of the coldest and   ] Elaboration

fiercest in history.

Revising

Revising Your Overall Structure

As you look at the structure of your essay, make sure that the ideas you've presented appear in logical order and are clearly connected to each other.

Strengthen Your Introduction and Conclusion

In your introduction, clearly present the main idea of your cause-and-effect essay. You may also mention reasons for your choice of topic and give readers an idea about why it is interesting or important.

▶ **REVISION STRATEGY**
Circling to Identify Relationships

To make sure that your introduction and conclusion "match up," circle the main idea you present in your introduction. Then, find and circle in your conclusion a restatement of that main idea. If your conclusion does not contain such a restatement, either rewrite your introduction or rewrite your conclusion so that they work together effectively.

Following is an example of the circling strategy:

> **⏱ Timed Writing Hint**
> As you revise your timed writing, make sure that your introduction states your main idea in a clear and compelling way.

INTRODUCTION

The ancient Peruvian society was based upon agriculture. As a result, their need for social cooperation was great. For instance, crops needed to be gathered and stored so that all the people could eat them. Just as important were the division of labor among farming, home-building, child-rearing, and hunting. When the Incas conquered Peru's tribes, the Incas continued to support the existing social structure.

CONCLUSION

With a brilliant government strategy, the Incas maintained the social structures the conquered tribes already had in place and expanded them to include an empire. Because of the Incas' wise and thoughtful governing methods, they went on to rule a peaceful and prosperous society for more than a thousand years.

Revising Your Paragraphs

Review your paragraphs to be sure that each develops a single idea and that the paragraphs themselves flow together smoothly. Check to be sure that topical paragraphs—those that contain a topic sentence—are unified.

Strengthen the Unity of Paragraphs

Revise your topical paragraphs to make them unified—to make sure that each has a topic sentence and that the other sentences within the paragraph support or develop the main idea expressed in the topic sentence.

▶ **REVISION STRATEGY**
Color-Coding to Identify Related Details

Circle each topic sentence in every topical paragraph. (Functional paragraphs—those that perform a specific function—do not have topic sentences.) Then, using a pencil of a different color, circle the details that support the topic sentence. Examine sentences you have *not* circled. If they do not support the topic sentence, either rewrite or delete them.

Learn More

To learn more about unified paragraphs, see Chapter 3.

Student Work
IN PROGRESS

Name: *Jennifer Hoss*
Bel Air High School
El Paso, TX

Color-Coding to Identify Related Details
To make her writing more unified, Jennifer deleted an unrelated detail.

Because of adverse weather conditions brought on by El Niño, the Southwest's world-famous chili crops began to die. ~~The Southwest is in an area comprising New Mexico, Arizona, Texas, and California.~~ This in turn put many migrant workers, who harvest chili peppers, out of work and it raised the price of chili to much higher than it had been before. What was once affordable by the pound became a precious commodity. The Southwestern tradition of having a delicious red or green chili with every meal or as a staple ingredient was now not possible for some people until the prices fell.

Revising Your Sentences

Now that your paragraphs are unified, look even more close-ly at your writing. Within each sentence, check to see that the relationships are logical.

▶ **REVISION STRATEGY**
Clarifying Relationships

Within each sentence, make sure that the connections among words, phrases, and clauses are clear. Read each sentence carefully. If there is more than one thought within the sentence, you may have to add a transition to show how those thoughts are related. Some transitions indicate meaning or clarify the significance of a detail. For example, the phrase *not only* indicates that a detail is just one of many.

🕐 **Timed Writing Hint**

When you write quickly, you may neglect clear transi-tions. As you revise, add transition words as needed.

Student Work
IN PROGRESS

Name: *Jennifer Hoss*
Bel Air High School
El Paso, TX

Clarifying Relationships With Transitions
To make the relationships more clear, Jennifer added several transitions to her draft.

The phrase *not only* alerts readers that there is more than one effect being discussed.

By changing *and* to *but*, Jennifer clarifies the importance of the second detail in the sentence.

Because of adverse weather conditions the Southwest's world-famous chili crops began to die, and harvesting was delayed. This *not only* put many migrant workers out of work *but* and it also raised the price of chili to much higher amounts than it had been before. What was once affordable by the pound *now* became a precious commodity. The Southwestern tradition of having a delicious red or green chili with every meal or as a staple ingredient was put on the shelf for some people until the prices fell.

The word *now* was added to make the cause-and-effect relationship more clear.

Grammar in Your Writing
Transitional Phrases

A **phrase** is a group of words without a subject and verb. In your cause-and-effect essay, use transitional phrases to show connections between ideas. A phrase may appear at the beginning of the sentence, between the subject and the verb, or at the end of a sentence:

Beginning:
After lunch, we worked enthusiastically.

Between the Subject and Verb:
We, after eating lunch, worked enthusiastically.

End:
We worked enthusiastically after eating lunch.

There are many types of phrases that you can use as transitions, connecting ideas in your writing.

A **prepositional phrase** is a group of words made up of a preposition and a noun or pronoun, called the object of the preposition:

Inside the studio, the sound engineers began mixing the demo.

A **participial phrase** is a participle modified by an adverb or adverb phrase or accompanied by a complement. The entire phrase acts as an adjective:

Using a high-powered lens, Annette could just make out the letters.

An **infinitive phrase** is an infinitive with modifiers, complements, or a subject, all acting together as a single part of speech:

To avoid the iceberg, the captain had to steer hard to starboard.

Find It in Your Reading Read through a recent newspaper article. Identify three sentences that contain transitional phrases—phrases that connect ideas. Explain the ways in which those phrases help to clarify the relationships within the essay.

Find It in Your Writing Review your draft to identify where you have used phrases to show transitions. If you cannot identify six phrases, challenge yourself to add at least one more to your writing. Notice the improvement.

For more on phrases, see Chapter 20.

Revising Your Word Choice

Review Your Word Choice

If you use the same word or form of it several times within a passage, your writing can sound tedious and awkward. Learn to distinguish between useful repetition and careless repetition. Useful repetition helps to emphasize a point or to make a passage memorable. Careless repetition creates a dull impression on the reader.

USEFUL REPETITION: In the 1920's, people *flocked* to theaters to see plays; in the 1930's, they *flocked* to theaters to see movies.

CARELESS REPETITION: Because I have always loved the *theater,* I'm studying *theater* and *theater* arts in school.

▶ **REVISION STRATEGY**
Underlining Repeated Words and Forms of Words

Read through your draft, and underline repeated words or forms of words. Then, review your draft. If passages containing repetition are not intended, replace some of the repeated words with synonyms, words with the same meaning.

OVERUSED WORD: They *housed* the furniture for the *house* in a shed out back.

VARIED WORDS: They *stored* the furniture for the *house* in a shed out back.

OVERUSED WORD: We tried to *locate* a better *location* for our party.

VARIED WORDS: We tried to *find* a better *location* for our party.

Peer Review

"Say Back"

Work with a small group of peers to get feedback on your writing.
- Read your paper aloud to your peer editors twice.
- Have peers jot down two positive comments and three constructive comments for improvement.
- One by one, have your peers read aloud their comments to you.
- Take their comments into consideration as you prepare your final draft.

Grammar and Style Tip

If there is a thesaurus in your word-processing program, use it to locate alternative word choices.

10.5 Editing and Proofreading

Reread your cause-and-effect essay carefully, correcting any mistakes you find in spelling, punctuation, and grammar. Double-check statistics or other details you present as fact.

Focusing on Commonly Confused Words

Proofread your essay carefully. Make sure you've correctly used the following commonly confused words: *since, because, then,* and *than.*

Technology Tip

Use the Find feature of your word-processing program to locate the words *since, because, then,* and *than.* Once you've located those words, check to be sure your usage of them is correct.

Grammar in Your Writing
Using *Since, Because, Then,* and *Than* Correctly

As you proofread, make sure that you have used these words appropriately.

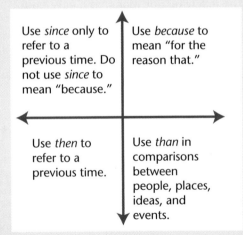

Use *since* only to refer to a previous time. Do not use *since* to mean "because."

Use *because* to mean "for the reason that."

Use *then* to refer to a previous time.

Use *than* in comparisons between people, places, ideas, and events.

Find It in Your Reading Review an essay you have written in which you correctly use the word *since.* Find the usage, and explain why your choice was correct.

Find It in Your Writing As you proofread your cause-and-effect essay, check to be sure you have used the words *since, because, then,* and *than* correctly. If you have not used any of those words, challenge yourself to add them to make clear connections between your ideas.

For more on word usage, see Chapter 26.

Publishing and Presenting

When you are finished writing your cause-and-effect essay, share it with others. Following are some ideas for sharing your writing:

Building Your Portfolio

1. **Presentation** Use your essay as the basis of a cause-and-effect presentation. Use photographs, charts, and diagrams as you explain the topic of your essay. Save the essay and visuals in your portfolio.

2. **E-mail** Share your essay electronically. Type the essay using word-processing software. Then, attach the file to an e-mail to a friend or relative.

Reflecting on Your Writing

Think back on your experience of writing a cause-and-effect essay. Then, respond to the following questions, and save your responses in your portfolio.

- During the process of writing, what did you learn about the subject you chose?

- Which strategy for writing a cause-and-effect essay might you recommend to someone as being most useful? Why?

Internet Tip

To see model essays scored with this rubric, go on-line:
PHSchool.com
Enter Web Code:
eek-1001

Rubric for Self-Assessment

Use the following criteria to evaluate your cause-and-effect essay:

	Score 4	Score 3	Score 2	Score 1
Audience and Purpose	Consistently targets an audience through word choice and details; clearly identifies purpose in thesis statement	Targets an audience through most word choice and details; identifies purpose in thesis statement	Misses target audience by including a wide range of word choice and details; presents no clear purpose	Addresses no specific audience or purpose
Organization	Presents a clear, consistent organizational strategy to show cause and effect	Presents a clear organizational strategy with occasional inconsistencies; shows cause and effect	Presents an inconsistent organizational strategy; creates illogical presentation of causes and effects	Demonstrates a lack of organizational strategy; creates a confusing presentation
Elaboration	Successfully links causes with effects; fully elaborates connections among ideas	Links causes with effects; elaborates connections among most ideas	Links some causes with some effects; elaborates connections among most ideas	Develops and elaborates no links between causes and effects
Use of Language	Chooses clear transitions to convey ideas; presents very few mechanical errors	Chooses transitions to convey ideas; presents few mechanical errors	Misses some opportunities for transitions to convey ideas; presents many mechanical errors	Demonstrates poor use of language; presents many mechanical errors

Connected Assignment *Documentary*

What Is a Documentary?

Documentaries are films that focus on real-life people and issues. Because they often deal with specific problems or issues, they usually demonstrate or track cause-and-effect relationships. An overarching narrative often ties all the pieces together and emphasizes cause-and-effect links.

The basis for a documentary is a script, written in stage format with stage directions and dialogue. In such a script, stage directions indicate the sequence of elements and camera shots along with any of the actors' movements.

Write your own documentary script. Use the following writing process guidelines:

▲ **Critical Viewing**
Judging from this photograph, does the person who's filming seem experienced? Explain why or why not. **[Make a Judgment]**

Prewriting Find a topic by thinking about your community and its history or problems. Look for trends that you can explain and new developments you can track to their results.

Research your topic at the library and through visits to locations. Conduct tape-recorded interviews, and take notes about your observations. Then, jot down your ideas for ways to present your findings visually. Also, look for existing visuals such as film clips. Generate index cards for each key idea, and note possible ways to express it. Then, focus on structuring the cause-and-effect relationship you want to show.

Drafting As you draft, bring your vision to life. Mix voice-over narration and still images (shots of letters or the outside of a building, for example) with live action scenes. When you're happy with the sequence and blend of visuals, write the narration in the dialogue portion of the script. Within the narrative, provide any necessary background information, identify people and places, and highlight cause-and-effect links.

Revising and Editing Mentally "view" your documentary as you read your script. Improve clarity by adding explanations, and strengthen connections by adding transitional sentences or phrases.

Publishing and Presenting Film your documentary, or a portion of it, and hold a screening for friends, peers, teachers, and relatives. Have a question-and-answer session following the screening.

Exposition

Problem-and-Solution Essay

Problem-and-Solution Essays in Everyday Life

Tackling difficult problems can help you develop powerful and effective strategies for daily life. As the poet Jean Toomer said, "We learn the rope of life by untying its knots." Writing about problems and solutions can help you find innovative solutions to your problems and allow you to share your discoveries with an audience. You might write a letter to a relative suggesting a way to resolve a family conflict or share your new solution to a school dilemma in a newspaper editorial.

▲ Critical Viewing
What problem might the people in this photograph be working together to solve? **[Speculate]**

What Is a Problem-and-Solution Essay?

Exposition is writing that explains or informs. A **problem-and-solution essay** is a specific type of exposition that identifies a problem and presents one or more potential solutions. An effective problem-and-solution essay

- clearly states a specific, real-life problem.
- identifies the most important aspects of the problem.
- presents one or more possible solutions.
- supports each solution with specific details and logical reasons.

To preview the criteria on which your problem-and-solution essay may be evaluated, see the Rubric for Self-Assessment on page 152.

Writers in
ACTION

Without challenges, life would become too predictable and even a bit boring. Author Marsha Sinetar acknowledges the importance of working on hard challenges:

"Rather than denying problems, focus inventively, intentionally on what solutions might look or feel like. . . . Our mind is meant to generate ideas that help us escape circumstantial traps—if we trust it to do so."

Types of Problem-and-Solution Essays

Problem-and-solution essays may address a wide variety of issues. Following are some of the specific types of issues they can address:

- **Consumer issues** include problems with products or services and how they can be remedied.
- **Local issues** may be problems facing your community, such as issues of school funding and library staffing.
- **Business issues** involve problems facing a company or business, such as budget shortages or schedule delays.

PREVIEW
Student Work
IN PROGRESS

Patrick Swan, of Muncie High School in Muncie, Indiana, realized that the parking situation at his school was out of control. Follow along as he uses prewriting, drafting, and revising techniques to develop an essay that analyzes the problem and proposes a solution.

Prewriting

Choosing Your Topic

Begin by identifying an important problem about which you feel strongly. Your essay will be more effective if you choose a significant and meaningful problem rather than a simple one that can be solved easily. Use these strategies to find a topic you would like to develop:

Strategies for Generating Topics

1. **Talk With a Peer** Talking with a partner can help you identify important problems in your school and community. You can also talk about state or national problems. Begin by working together to brainstorm for a list of problems. As you work, use a chart like the one below to gather ideas. When your chart is completed, choose the item you find most interesting to become the topic for your problem-and-solution essay.

School	City	Nation	World
Overcrowded classes Chaotic parking lot	Dangerous intersection at Elm and Watson Zoo closing	Highway safety Government corruption Campaign financing	International policies Diminishing resources World hunger

2. **Use Sentence Starters** Complete the sentence starters below to help you come up with a topic. Don't stop with one response. Try to come up with three or four endings for each sentence. Then, review your ideas to find a problem that is important to you.

   Possible Sentence Starters
   - The biggest problem facing students today is . . .
   - The world would be a much better place if we could solve the problem of . . .
   - I wish that we could eliminate the problem of . . .
   - One problem we could solve if we all work together is . . .

Try it out! Use the interactive Sentence Starters activity in **Section 11.2**, on-line or on CD-ROM.

TOPIC BANK

Consider these suggestions if you are having difficulty coming up with your own topic:

1. **Solution to a Math Problem** Write an essay in which you explain a complex math problem and its solution.

2. **Editorial Addressing a Local Issue** Choose a problem that faces your school or neighborhood, and write an editorial presenting a solution.

Responding to Fine Art

3. *Unloading the Cargo,* by Ralston Crawford, depicts the unloading of a ship's cargo. What sorts of problems might such a task involve overcoming? Write a problem-and-solution essay that describes one such problem and details the solution.

Unloading the Cargo, 1942, Ralston Crawford

Responding to Literature

4. In James Thurber's humorous story "The Dog That Bit People," the characters are confronted with a dog's behavior problems. Write a problem-and-solution essay proposing steps that could be taken to change the dog's behavior. You can find "The Dog That Bit People" in *Prentice Hall Literature, Penguin Edition,* Grade 10.

Timed Writing Prompt

5. Write a letter to the school board requesting a new facility for your school, such as an auditorium, a sports facility, or a science lab. Include clear examples of how your proposed facility would improve the school. **(40 minutes)**

Narrowing Your Topic

If your topic is broad, narrow it so that you can focus on presenting a solution to a single problem.

Use Looping to Narrow Your Topic

Looping can help you focus on key aspects of your topic. Begin by writing freely on your topic for about five minutes. Read what you have written, and circle the most interesting or important idea. Then, write about that idea for five minutes. Repeat this process until you arrive at a topic narrow enough to address thoroughly in your essay.

Problem: Pollution

> I think pollution is a big problem. Soon, we won't be able to enjoy the environment because it will be so polluted. It's not just the land, it's the water and air, too.

> Water Pollution: Acid rain is a problem. And oil spills in oceans. Even our local stream has suds in it. Lakes can get polluted, too.

> Miller Stream: The stream behind the school is unsafe because of phosphates dumped into it from local businesses.

Considering Your Audience and Purpose

The type of language you use will depend on the audience for your problem-and-solution essay. Some audiences, such as a group of friends, will relate best to informal language. Many other audiences, however, will respond better if you use formal language to communicate your ideas.

FORMAL LANGUAGE	INFORMAL LANGUAGE
The parking situation in the eastern lot is dangerous.	The parking lot is a mess.
The most effective solution to the problem of truancy is to make the issue of attendance important to students.	The best way to stop kids from cutting class is to make them feel that attendance is a big deal.

Timed Writing Hint

Pay close attention to all the details in a writing prompt. Read the prompt carefully twice to determine the purpose and the audience for your writing.

Gathering Information

To develop a successful essay, you need a strong set of facts, statistics, and other types of support. Most likely, you'll find it necessary to conduct research in the library or on the Internet to gather the material you need.

Gather Various Types of Details

As you gather details, look to find those that fully explain the problem you are proposing to solve and the steps or aspects of the solution.

- **Cite examples:** Give examples from research or real life to explain the problem and its history.
- **Interview:** Talk to people who have a deep knowledge of the problem or who have definite ideas on how to solve it.
- **Survey:** Create and distribute a survey that probes for ideas about the problem and possible solutions. Tabulate the responses, and cite the results in your essay.

Student Work IN PROGRESS

Name: *Patrick Swan*
Muncie Central High School
Muncie, IN

Collecting Details

Pat gathered details that will help him explain the problem and solution that form the heart of his essay.

Problem: "In our school, people without permits frequently take up parking spots, forcing people with permits to park illegally."—Phone interview with Principal Suding from Yorktown High School

Solution: Penalties for parking without a permit
  1. First offense: a warning
  2. Second offense: a detention
  3. Third offense: loss of parking privileges for duration of school year

11.3 *Drafting*

Shaping Your Writing

Start With the Problem

As inventor Charles Kettering once said, "A problem well stated is a problem half solved." Your problem-and-solution essay should begin with a detailed description of the problem. Make sure your audience understands all of the important aspects of your problem. Once the problem is clear, you can write about the solution or solutions you propose.

Using an Outline An outline can help you organize your ideas before you begin to draft. Look at the examples below. The first example shows how to organize an essay presenting a single solution to a problem. The second example shows how to organize an essay proposing more than one solution. Use the organization that fits your topic.

Interactive Textbook

Get instant help! To create your outline, use the Essay Builder, accessible from the menu bar, on-line or on CD-ROM.

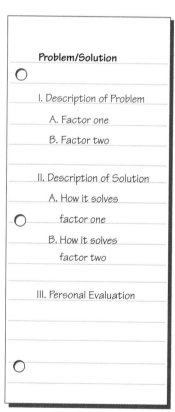

Problem/Solution

I. Description of Problem
   A. Factor one
   B. Factor two

II. Description of Solution
   A. How it solves
      factor one
   B. How it solves
      factor two

III. Personal Evaluation

Problem/Solution/Solution

I. Description of Problem
   A. Factor one
   B. Factor two

II. First Solution
   A. Advantages
   B. Disadvantages

III. Second Solution
   A. Advantages
   B. Disadvantages

IV. Personal Evaluation

Providing Elaboration

Following your outline, begin writing your first draft. Support each major point in your outline by adding facts and other details, expanding on ideas, and discussing important related concepts. This elaboration will help you convince readers of the soundness of your solution.

Expand on Your Outline

Support each major point in your essay by providing clear and relevant details. Doing so will help readers understand and accept the solution you are proposing.

Student Work
IN PROGRESS

Name: *Patrick Swan*
Muncie Central High School
Muncie, IN

Expanding on an Outline

Working from an outline, Pat expanded each point by giving specific examples. Notice how he elaborated one heading in the outline.

I. The parking lot is a mess

   A. Students park carelessly

   B. Unauthorized parking

   C. Damage to cars caused by vandalism and reckless driving

II. Parking Permits

   A. Students are accountable for their driving and parking

   B. Unauthorized parkers are easily identified

   C. Permits have worked at other schools

     1. Yorktown
     2. Delta

   D. Details of the plan

Unauthorized parking is another part of the problem. People who are not connected with the high school take advantage of the lot's central location. Commuters and shoppers take up spaces meant for students, teachers, and other school employees. This is not a new problem. According to former assistant principal James Suding, now principal at Yorktown High School, "Everyone from the community used to meet at Central and carpool. It's always been a mess there."

Revising

As you review your first draft, you will find many ways to improve your writing. You might begin by focusing on the overall structure to make sure the whole essay "hangs together." After that, look at each paragraph, sentence, and word to sharpen your work.

Revising Your Overall Structure

Solve the Problem

The success of a problem-and-solution essay depends on two things: You need to clearly define the problem, and you need to describe a specific and effective solution. The structure of your essay should make it easy to see how your solution answers every aspect of the problem.

▶ **REVISION STRATEGY**
Connecting Ideas

Use a highlighter to connect parts of the problem to related parts of the solution.

• Highlight or underline each problem or part of a problem and label it *P.*

• Highlight or underline each solution. Label it *S.* Connect related problems and solutions.

If you find a problem that has no matching solution, you need to expand your solutions. If you find a solution that doesn't fit part of the problem, it is probably unnecessary. You should consider cutting it.

▼ Critical Viewing
What sort of problems might someone encounter while wading this stream? **[Anayze]**

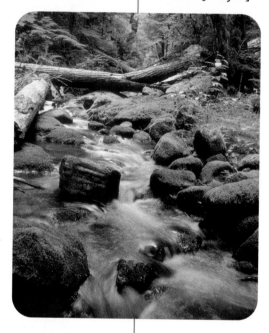

CONNECTING PROBLEMS TO SOLUTIONS

 P

 S

. . . A primary cause of the pollution is restaurants that use phosphates in their dishwashing liquids. Acid rain also contributes to the poor water quality. . . .

Requiring all local businesses to use phosphate-free detergents will greatly improve the water quality of Hawkins Stream. These detergents are slightly more expensive but clean equally well. . . .

Revising Your Paragraphs
Focus Each Paragraph on a Single Topic

Every paragraph in your problem-and-solution essay should develop a single idea or topic. You can test each paragraph by asking questions as you revise.

▶ **REVISION STRATEGY**
Questioning Your Paragraph Choices

Review your essay, and evaluate each paragraph as a separate unit. When you come to the end of a paragraph, pause to ask yourself why you grouped these sentences together.

- **Does the paragraph focus on one idea?** State the idea, and describe how each sentence expands on, supports, or clarifies that idea.

- **Does every sentence relate to the main idea?** If you find sentences on different topics, consider cutting them or moving them to other, more appropriate paragraphs.

- **Do two paragraphs discuss the same topic?** Consider combining the paragraphs to improve the flow of ideas.

🕐 **Timed Writing Hint**

When revising your essay in timed conditions, it is fine to add words and sentences neatly and to cross out sentences or words that you want to delete.

Student Work
IN PROGRESS

Name: *Patrick Swan*
Muncie Central High School
Muncie, IN

Focusing a Paragraph
Pat made several adjustments after considering the paragraphs in his problem-and-solution essay.

This solution has worked well at two local high schools. Both Yorktown and Delta high schools require students and faculty members to display parking permits. ~~The parking lots at these school are always filled to capacity.~~ The lots are patrolled periodically to identify cars without permits on display.

Administrators at both schools report that the permits have been popular and effective. Consequences have been created for students who fail to purchase a permit.

Revising Your Sentences
Fix Unnecessary Shifts in Tense

Your sentences should use verb tenses to indicate clearly when an event occurred. It is often best to stay with a single tense. For example, if you are writing about a problem in the past, make sure that all your verbs are in the past tense.

Mixed Tenses

The stream <u>has contained</u> high levels of dangerous chemicals. The surrounding ecosystem <u>will be</u> greatly affected. Fish living in the stream <u>suffered</u> because of the poor water quality. Birds that eat these fish <u>have gotten</u> sick, too.

Consistent Tense

The stream <u>contains</u> high levels of dangerous chemicals. The surrounding ecosystem <u>is</u> greatly affected. Fish living in the stream <u>suffer</u> because of the poor water quality. Birds that eat these fish <u>get</u> sick, too.

▶**REVISION STRATEGY**
Naming Each Tense

Read through your draft. Find each verb, and name the tense. If you find more than one verb tense in a sentence or paragraph, make sure that the tense shift is necessary. If it is not, revise accordingly.

Student Work
IN PROGRESS

Name: *Patrick Swan*
Muncie Central High School
Muncie, IN

Fixing Verb Tenses
Pat revised this paragraph to put each verb in the future tense.

Unauthorized parking will also be greatly reduced. Administrators ~~can~~ *will be able to*

recognize unauthorized cars because those cars ~~don't~~ *won't* have permits.

The plan ~~would also have helped~~ *will also help* our school identify potential suspects

in cases of damaged and vandalized automobiles.

Grammar in Your Writing
The Six Tenses of Verbs

There are six verb tenses. Each tense has a basic form, as shown in this chart.

Basic Forms

Present	I *look* for a solution.
Past	I *looked* for a solution yesterday.
Future	I *will look* for a solution tomorrow.
Present Perfect	I *have looked* for a solution before.
Past Perfect	I *had looked* for a solution until I almost gave up.
Future Perfect	I *will have looked* for a solution by the end of next week.

Each tense also has a progressive form, ending in *-ing*.

Progressive Forms

Present Progressive	I *am looking* for a solution.
Past Progressive	I *was looking* for a solution yesterday.
Future Progressive	I *will be looking* for a solution tomorrow.
Present Perfect Progressive	I *have been looking* for a solution since last week.
Past Perfect Progressive	I *had been looking* for a solution when I found the answer.
Future Perfect Progressive	I *will have been looking* for a solution for two weeks.

Find It in Your Reading Review a story you have read. Choose one paragraph, and identify the tense of each verb. Explain the reason for any shifts in tense that you find.

Find It in Your Writing Identify the tense of each verb in your draft. Highlight paragraphs that have more than one verb tense. Evaluate whether or not each shift in tense is necessary.

To learn more about verb tenses, see Chapter 22.

Revising Your Word Choice

Revise Your Word Choice to Create a Tone

The words you select help set the tone of your writing—the attitude toward your subject that you convey to your readers. Decide on a tone you would like to convey, and revise your choice of words to help you achieve that tone.

The following chart shows how an alteration in word choice can affect the tone of a piece of writing.

Optimistic Tone	Discovering an effective solution will be most challenging.
Pessimistic Tone	Reaching a workable solution will be extremely difficult.
Informal Tone	Getting at a decent answer will be really hard.

▶ **REVISION STRATEGY**
Highlighting Key Words

Changing just a few words can adjust or heighten the tone you want to develop. Highlight two or three key words in each paragraph, and brainstorm for ideas for words that might replace them. Weigh your choices carefully, and then make any desired changes.

▼ Critical Viewing
Do the students in the photograph seem to be working well together? Explain. **[Analyze]**

Peer Review

Key Questions

The actor Robert Redford has said that "problems can become opportunities when the right people come together." Revising your problem-and-solution essay with a partner is an excellent way to use teamwork to make effective changes. Have a partner or group read your problem-and-solution essay. Use these questions as a starting point for your discussion:

- How complete is the description of the problem?

- How well does the solution match the problem?

- Are there any important parts of the problem that are not discussed?

After listening to your classmates, consider using their suggestions to improve your work.

11.5 Editing and Proofreading

Because spelling and grammar errors can make your writing confusing and distract your readers' attention, make sure that your essay is error-free.

Focusing on *That* and *Which*

The words *that* and *which* are often misused, even by experienced writers. As you check your essay for errors, look to see whether you have used *that* and *which* correctly. Highlight each use of both words, and decide whether or not you have chosen the appropriate word.

Use the following information to help you determine whether your use of *that* and *which* is correct.

> **Speaking and Listening Tip**
>
> It is often helpful to read your writing aloud to check for errors. If you stumble over words while reading, look to see whether you have come across a typographical error or an error in punctuation.

Grammar in Your Writing
Restrictive and Nonrestrictive Clauses

Adjective clauses often begin with *that* or *which.* You can decide which word to use by deciding whether the clause is restrictive or nonrestrictive.

A **restrictive clause** contains information that is essential to the meaning of the noun it modifies. It can expand, limit, or define the noun. Begin a restrictive clause with *that:*

The essay that I wrote was published in the school newspaper.
I found a solution that was simple and effective.

A **nonrestrictive clause** contains information that is not essential to the meaning of the noun it modifies. Begin a nonrestrictive clause with *which.* Set off a nonrestrictive clause with commas:

The mayor's speech, which was about crime, was quite rousing.
"How to Stop Litter," which I wrote last year, won first prize in an essay contest.

Find It in Your Writing As you proofread, locate instances in which you used *that* and *which.* Then, check to be sure you've used those words correctly.

For more on restrictive and nonrestrictive clauses, see Chapter 20.

11.6 Publishing and Presenting

Once you have polished and completed your problem-and-solution essay, share your final draft with an audience. Your readers will enjoy learning about your solutions, and you will have the satisfaction of knowing that you have made a helpful proposal.

Building Your Portfolio

1. **Encourage Responses** Sponsor a group read-aloud of several problem-and-solution essays. Take time to discuss the proposed problems and solutions in each essay.

2. **Submit Your Essay** Send your essay to the editors of a magazine or Web site that accepts student writing. Use writers' directories to help you locate addresses.

Reflecting on Your Writing

Reflect on your writing experience by answering these questions. Save your responses in your portfolio.

- Which was more difficult to write about, the problem or the solution? Why?

- What strategies did you use to make sure that your solution was complete and effective?

 Internet Tip

To see model essays scored with this rubric, go on-line:
PHSchool.com
Enter Web Code:
eek-1001

Rubric for Self-Assessment

Use the following criteria to evaluate your problem-and-solution essay.

	Score 4	Score 3	Score 2	Score 1
Audience and Purpose	Contains language and details to engage audience and accomplishes purpose	Contains language and details appropriate for audience and that help contribute to purpose	Contains some language and details not suited for audience; contains some details that detract from purpose	Contains language and details that are not geared for a particular audience; has an unclear purpose
Organization	Is organized consistently, logically, and effectively	Has consistent organization	Has some organization, but its organization is not consistent	Is disorganized and confusing
Elaboration	Has a solution that is clearly laid out, along with details that support or explain	Has a solution that is supported with details	Has a stated solution, but it contains few details to support it	Has unclear solution, and no details are given to support it
Use of Language	Contains language that helps the writer achieve an effective tone; contains no errors in grammar, punctuation, or spelling	Contains language that creates a tone; contains few errors in grammar, punctuation, and spelling	Contains few examples of language that create tone; contains some errors in grammar, punctuation, and spelling	Demonstrates no attempt to create tone through word choice; contains many errors in grammar, punctuation, and spelling

Connected Assignment *Advice Column*

One way to solve a problem is to seek expert advice. You can often find expert advice in question-and-answer forums or in advice columns in magazines or newspapers. Topics may range from gardening to computer use to chess strategies to parenting. In such a column, one writer presents a problem and another writer responds with a proposed solution. Sometimes, however, the columnist presents both aspects after receiving an inquiring letter.

Write your own advice column, inventing the problem and coming up with a solution. Use the writing process skills outlined below to guide you.

Prewriting Make a T-chart of problems you've recently encountered. In the left-hand column, write down possible problems that an advice-seeker might have. In the right-hand column, jot down the solutions, or advice, you would give to address each problem.

Review your chart, and choose as a topic the advice you feel most confident about giving.

▲ Critical Viewing
Would you say the person in the photograph is posing a problem or presenting a solution? Why? **[Speculate]**

Problem	Solution
noise	ear plugs
	white-noise machine

Drafting Keep your audience—the advice-seeker and your readers—in mind as you draft your advice column. For example, you may want to adopt a friendly and persuasive tone as you present your solution. As you give advice, support it with examples, quotations, and other types of evidence.

Revising and Editing Review your advice column to ensure that both the problem and the solution are clearly stated. Add to or modify your language to create an upbeat and positive tone, especially in the advice portion.

Publishing and Presenting Share your advice column with others. Ask them whether or not they agree with the advice you have given.

Researching in Everyday Life

Our era has been called the Age of Information because there are so many different sources of information—from traditional print sources, like books and magazines, to multi-media sources, including film and video, CD-ROMs, and the Internet. You conduct research every time you tap into any information source. For example, you become a researcher when you look up a telephone number, talk to your doctor about nutrition, or read about the life of a favorite celebrity.

Research often serves as a foundation for writing. For an end-of-semester essay, for example, you might incorporate historical research. Later in life, you may find that researching skills help you to produce business reports, write historic plays, or re-create historic homes.

▲ **Critical Viewing**
What three research ideas does this photograph inspire? Why? **[Analyze]**

What Is Research Writing?

Research writing—writing based on information gathered from outside sources—gives you the power to become an expert on any subject. This focused study of a topic helps you to explore and connect ideas, make discoveries, and share your findings with an audience. Effective research writing

- focuses on a specific, narrow topic, which is usually summarized in a thesis statement.
- presents relevant information from a wide variety of sources.
- structures the information logically and effectively.
- identifies the sources from which the information was drawn.

To preview the criteria on which your research writing may be evaluated, see the Rubric for Self-Assessment on page 172.

Types of Research Writing

Besides the formal research report, there are many other specialized types of writing that depend on accurate and insightful research:

- **Multimedia presentations** support written information with a variety of media, including slide shows, videos, audio recordings, and fine art.
- **Statistical reports** explore a subject through numerical data.
- **Annotated bibliographies** are a compilation and evaluation of resources available about a specific subject.
- **Experiment journals** are a record of the process and results of an experiment.

Writers in
ACTION

Authors of all types of writing recognize the usefulness of research. Author N. Scott Momaday, for example, has the following to say about the importance of research:

"Research is absolutely essential to me as a writer. . . . In the case of The Way to Rainy Mountain, *I needed additional information. I needed to know about the history and the prehistory of the Kiowa people. And so I made the migration trip myself. . . . I saw firsthand the landscape that they had passed through, and I imagined —with the help of the stories—what it must have been like to come across this vast sea of plains."*

PREVIEW
Student Work
IN PROGRESS

While taking a class in photography, Michael S. Dougherty, a student at Central Bucks West High School in Doylestown, Pennsylvania, became interested in war photographers. In this chapter, you will see how he applied his curiosity about this subject to develop a strong piece of research writing. His completed report appears at the end of this chapter.

Prewriting

Choosing Your Topic

Choosing a subject for research writing is a matter of following your instincts and interests. Consider as a topic anything you would like to know more about, from antibiotics to zoology. These strategies can help you find topics to explore:

Strategies for Generating Topics

1. **Refer to a Map, Globe, or Atlas** A map, globe, or atlas can be a useful springboard to a world of research topics in geography, social studies, history, and other areas. Turn to a random page of an atlas or spin a globe of the world, and see where your finger lands; or open to a region you want to visit or know more about, and really inspect the surrounding terrain. Make a list of potential topics, and then evaluate your list. Choose one item as the topic for your research.

2. **Scan Headlines** A newspaper or magazine can provide many inspirations for subjects that connect to contemporary issues. Use a marker or self-sticking notes to indicate intriguing headlines or articles. Review your notes to find a topic you want to investigate in a research report.

3. **Make a Celebrity List** Biographical research can give you remarkable insights into the people you admire and respect. Make a list of celebrities about whom you would like to know more. You might organize your list into categories of accomplishment, such as athletes, actors, politicians, philanthropists, scientists, or philosophers. Review your list, and select the person you find most interesting to research. A sample listing of possible research subjects appears below:

Interactive Textbook

Try it out! Use the interactive Make a Celebrity List activity in **Section 12.2**, on-line or on CD-ROM.

Artists	Authors	Composers and Musicians
Diego Rivera	Michael Crichton	Duke Ellington
Henri Matisse	Mark Twain	Edith Piaf
Georgia O'Keeffe	Edith Wharton	Wolfgang Amadeus Mozart
Charles Schultz	George Eliot	George Gershwin
Mary Cassatt	John Updike	Elvis Presley
Jan van Eyck	Agatha Christie	Suzanne Vega
Camille Pissarro	Carl Sagan	Lyle Lovett
Henry Moore	Jamaica Kincaid	Paul McCartney

TOPIC BANK

Use these topics to help launch your research writing.

1. **Essay on a Historical Personality** Choose an influential historical personality, such as Genghis Khan, Joan of Arc, or Henry VIII. Begin by reading an encyclopedia entry to get a helpful overview, and choose one specific aspect of the person's life to research.

2. **Investigation of a Scientific Phenomenon** Select a unique occurrence on Earth or in space, such as fjords, coral atolls, or the aurora borealis. Browse through a science textbook to find a topic and some initial information. Use several additional sources to help you present a complete explanation for your audience.

Responding to Fine Art

3. List the historical conflicts that come to mind as you study the painting *Federal Brigade Commanded by General Winfield Scott* by Julian Scott. Choose one of these conflicts to research.

Federal Brigade Commanded by General Winfield Scott, Julian Scott, Smithsonian Institution

Responding to Literature

4. Read "The Marginal World" by Rachel Carson, a description of the ecology of the edge of the sea. Identify a topic she discusses that interests you and write a research report on it. The selection appears in *Prentice Hall Literature, Penguin Edition,* Grade 10.

Timed Writing Prompt

5. Write an essay about a topic that you would like to investigate. Identify three questions about the topic that you would like to answer through research. Then, discuss what resources you would use to conduct your research. **(45 minutes)**

Narrowing Your Topic

If your topic is not narrow enough to be covered fully within the space limitations of your essay, narrow it before you begin your research.

Use Research Clues to Narrow Your Topic

Use library or Internet sources for ideas on ways to divide subjects for a narrower focus.

- **Look at encyclopedia entries,** which often include subheadings and highlighted key words. Both of these features can help you identify narrower topics you might consider.

- **Read the table of contents** of books and the title and subheadings of magazine articles and Web pages to get ideas about different aspects of your topic.

- **Scan book indexes** to find groupings of related ideas.

Considering Your Audience and Purpose

As you gather details for your research report, choose words and details that will appeal to your audience and help you to accomplish your purpose for writing.

Use Formal Language

To reflect a serious tone, most writers of research reports use formal language. The features of formal language include sophisticated vocabulary, sentences with varied structures, and avoidance of slang and contractions. As you gather details about your topic, keep in mind that your details and word choice should be precise and formal.

▼ Critical Viewing
How is the scene in this illustration similar to and different from modern workday conditions? **[Compare and Contrast]**

Informal Language	Formal Language
Back in the 1850's and later, things changed a great deal for lots of women, especially in New England. Factories began to make the same stuff that women made at home. So the women didn't have any choice. They had to take factory jobs.	During the second half of the nineteenth century, the lives of many New England women changed dramatically. As factories began to compete with home industries, many women who had earned money by sewing and knitting at home were compelled to take factory jobs for the first time.

Gathering Information

Make a research plan to find the information you need from the wide array of sources available.

Perform Library Research

Historian Barbara Tuchman acknowledges, "To a historian, libraries are food, shelter, and even muse." Develop your library skills to help you use your library time effectively.

- Discover how your library is organized. Use the catalog to search for titles. Remember that books are organized by categories, so when you find a useful volume, be sure to explore the nearby titles as well.

- Use indexes like the *Readers' Guide to Periodical Literature* and bibliographies to find information about publications related to specific types of subjects.

- Many libraries today offer Internet access so that you can search for topics on the World Wide Web. Use key words to focus and speed your research.

To organize your library research plan, make a K-W-L Chart, filling in what you **k**now, what you **w**ant to know and what you **l**earned during your research.

Student Work
IN PROGRESS

Name: Michael S. Dougherty
Central Bucks West High School
Doylestown, PA

Guiding Research With a K-W-L Chart

After narrowing the subject of war photography to focus on one photographer, Robert Capa, Michael used a K-W-L chart to guide his library research.

Know	Want to Know	What I Learned
Robert Capa was a successful war photographer.	How did he get his start?	At the age of 18, he worked as a darkroom apprentice in Berlin.
Capa was often present during war battles.	How did he feel about being at battle scenes?	"It is not always easy to stand aside and be unable to do anything except record the suffering around one."

Take Organized Notes

One major challenge of conducting research is keeping track of all the information you discover. Use the following tips to organize your material.

Source cards list the publication information for each source you consult. When you find a source that you might use, make a source card for it and assign it a number.

Note cards list specific details for use in your writing, such as direct quotations or summaries of important facts.

Photocopy and highlight pages from sources you plan to use. Also, photocopy copyright information to use in your works-cited list.

Print copies of on-line source information for later reference. Be sure that the Web address can be clearly seen in the printout.

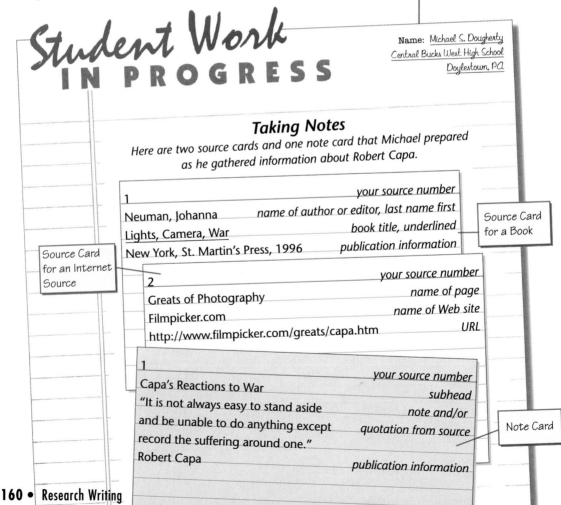

Student Work
IN PROGRESS

Name: Michael S. Dougherty
Central Bucks West High School
Doylestown, PA

Taking Notes

Here are two source cards and one note card that Michael prepared as he gathered information about Robert Capa.

1   your source number
Neuman, Johanna   name of author or editor, last name first
Lights, Camera, War   book title, underlined
New York, St. Martin's Press, 1996   publication information

Source Card for a Book

Source Card for an Internet Source

2   your source number
Greats of Photography   name of page
Filmpicker.com   name of Web site
http://www.filmpicker.com/greats/capa.htm   URL

1   your source number
Capa's Reactions to War   subhead
"It is not always easy to stand aside   note and/or
and be unable to do anything except   quotation from source
record the suffering around one."
Robert Capa   publication information

Note Card

Doing Investigative Research

Consider supplementing the information that you collect from published sources with your own investigative research. Conducting your own interviews, polls, and surveys can make your writing uniquely powerful: You can present facts and quotations that no one else can.

- **Interviews** Conduct an interview to get information directly from a primary source. Prepare for your interview by finding out about the subject you will interview. Familiarize yourself with the person's background so that you can ask informed questions. Be sure to compile a list of questions beforehand, but feel free to depart from your list when additional questions arise naturally.

Interview Tips

√ Prepare questions in advance.

√ Avoid asking "yes" and "no" questions.

√ Wait for answers. Don't interrupt the interviewee.

√ Ask permission to tape the interview.

- **Polls and Surveys** Use polls and surveys to gather information about public opinion. Write survey questions that are unbiased and easy to tabulate. Choose a random sample for your target group. Be careful when you interpret your poll results. Your group may not be representative of a larger population. For example, if you interview only seniors at your school, their opinions will not reflect those of all students in the school.

- **Experiments** Conduct experiments to test theories in science or social sciences. For example, to test a theory about student alertness, you might give different groups of students the same quick quiz early in the morning and late in the afternoon to see which group does better.

Whenever you conduct your own investigations, take careful notes using source cards and note cards. You may want to include information about your interviews or polls in your bibliography.

Research Tip

To write an effective survey, provide a limited number of responses. For example, ask people to rate their opinions using a 1–10 scale or to categorize their feelings according to terms like "strongly support," "support," "oppose," and "strongly oppose."

▼ **Critical Viewing**
What sort of research is the pictured student performing? Explain. [**Analyze**]

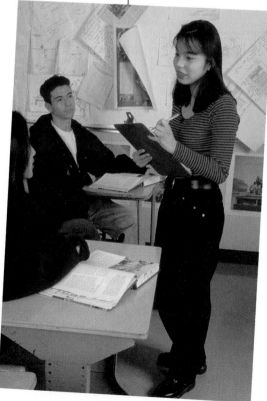

Drafting

Shaping Your Writing

Research writing needs an effective organization in order to communicate clearly with an audience.

Arrange Your Findings

Use your note cards or photocopied materials to identify major aspects of your topic. Gather related notes together, and consider their relationships. Arranging your notes on a table or adjusting their arrangement in a stack can help you try out different organizations.

Choose an Organizational Strategy

One of the most important decisions you will make as you draft is how to organize your information. A carefully planned structure can make the difference between powerful writing and confusing disorder. The chart below shows several common ways of organizing research writing. Choose a logical organization that matches the content and purpose of your writing.

Description	Uses
Chronological Order: Events are presented in time order.	Chronological order is useful for research reports on historical topics and for experiment journals. For example, if you were writing about a time in history, you could trace actual events.
Part-to-Whole Order: Aspects or parts of a larger topic are described one by one to build a complete picture.	Use this organization to examine the categories that make up a whole. For example, if you were writing about volcanoes, you could show how the location of volcanoes and volcanic eruptions have helped scientists learn about the Earth's interior.
Order of Importance: Details are presented from most important to least important or from least important to most important.	Order of importance can help you build an argument. To write about safety and skiing, you might begin with the least important or most obvious—wearing warm gloves—and end with the most important safety factor—avoiding restricted zones.

⏱ Timed Writing Hint

Pay close attention to the way a prompt is written. The prompt will often suggest which organizational strategy you should use.

Prepare an Outline

Prepare an outline to organize the details you have gathered. Begin by reviewing the notes or research materials you have photocopied and grouped. Then, use Roman numerals to indicate major sections of your report. Use capital letters to indicate subsections of each major section, and use Arabic numbers to indicate specifics you plan to discuss within each subsection. As you develop an outline, the entries at each level should be nearly equal in importance.

Your outline may be as broad or detailed as you like. Following are two types of outlines you may like to consider:

- A "sentence outline" can be used to help you rough out your ideas.

- A traditional outline will help you determine the major sections of your topic and will guide you as you write.

Student Work
IN PROGRESS

Name: Michael S. Dougherty
Central Bucks West High School
Doylestown, PA

Preparing an Outline

Michael created an outline to help him organize while drafting. His research report is organized chronologically.

I. Introduction: War Journalists

II. Birth and life in Hungary
   A. born Andrei Friedmann
   B. exiled due to activism

III. Germany
   A. darkroom apprentice
   B. first assignment: photographing Leon Trotsky
   C. left Germany because of Hitler's rise

IV. Paris
   A. Friedman invents Robert Capa to increase his prices
   B. An editor finds out
   C. Assumes the name Robert Capa

Providing Elaboration

Elaborate on Notes

As you draft, refer to your note cards or photocopies of source material to provide facts, statistics, and quotations you have discovered. In addition to citing your findings, also provide your own ideas, examples, and analyses as you weave together the information you found while researching. For example, if you give a statistic, also tell why you find the statistic interesting or significant.

Be sure to paraphrase the words of a source unless you plan to put the person's exact words within quotation marks. All source material, whether taken word for word or paraphrased, must be cited in your report.

Student Work
IN PROGRESS

Name: Michael S. Dougherty
Central Bucks West High School
Doylestown, PA

Elaborating on Notes

Michael referred to his notes as he drafted his report on Robert Capa. In addition to using the facts he found in his notes, Michael added his own insights to elaborate on what he found.

He was the sole photographer of the bloodiest landing, Omaha Beach, and took 106 photographs in what he considered to be an outstanding personal victory. Unfortunately, a darkroom assistant turned on too much heat while developing the pictures and destroyed all but eight. Despite such setbacks, Capa remained dedicated to photographing the war effort, making several other parachute landings as well (Stein 189).

> Although Michael paraphrased his source material, he was careful to include an in-text citation to credit the source's information.

Although his talents as a war journalist were outstanding, photographing the frightening images of war was never an easy task for Capa. As he once said, "It is not always easy to stand aside and be unable to do anything except record the suffering around one." Capa's humanity and compassion shine through his powerful photographs.

> Michael used what he found out about Capa to come up with this analysis.

12.4 *Revising*

Writer E. B. White once commented, "When you say something, make sure you have said it. The chances of your having said it are only fair." During revision, you have the opportunity to make sure that you have said what you wanted to say. You can make adjustments in your paper's organization, presentation of ideas, and language.

Revising Your Overall Structure

Create Unity

The first step in revising is to consider the "big picture." Your research writing needs to show unity, that is, a sense that the entire work relates to one specific subject. While you were drafting, your primary goal was to get the words down on paper. During revision, you take a close look at those words to make sure that you haven't strayed from your main idea, added empty padding to fill space, or used an illogical organization that is certain to baffle your audience.

▶ **REVISION STRATEGY**
Using Marginal Notes to Identify the Structure

Review the major sections and subsections in your report by writing notes about the main points of each paragraph. To make these notes stand out, work with a red pen or place self-sticking notes in the margins of your draft. After writing marginal comments or descriptions, read them from beginning to end to make sure that the flow makes sense. You might consider rearranging sections that flow awkwardly or cutting sections that stray from the central topic.

In the example at right, one unrelated section of a research paper about the Channel was deleted and another was moved to a more appropriate position.

Technology Tip

If you are working electronically, boldface any passages that are word-for-word quotations from a source. When you revise, you can quickly proofread those passages against the original source to check for accuracy.

THE ENGLISH CHANNEL TUNNEL

Earlier Attempts

About the English Channel

26 earlier, unsuccessful attempts to tunnel under the channel

~~Swimming the English Channel~~

Building the Chunnel

The project begins

Construction

The Chunnel tunnel opens in 1994

Effects of the Chunnel

Financing the building

Faster travel between London and Paris

Increased tourism

Revising Your Paragraphs

Every paragraph you write should have a clear organization that explains a single idea.

▶ **REVISION STRATEGY**
Coding to Identify the Structure

There are many different patterns you can use to organize your paragraphs. Three of the most common patterns are identified by the initials *TRI, PS,* and *QA*. Read through each paragraph in your research writing, and identify its structure. Revise paragraphs so that each is structured effectively.

T R I

When almost 100,000 people flooded to California in search of gold in 1848 and 1849, some cities grew almost instantly. }— Topic

These cities were known as "boom towns." }— Restatement

One city on the Yuba River had only two houses in September 1848. A year later, those two houses had expanded into a city of 1,000 inhabitants. }— Illustration

P S

Scientists are searching for new ways to handle epidemics that are spread by insects }— Problem

like mosquitoes. Spraying can often kill the insects, but it affects other animals and the environment as well. Intervention on the genetic level may offer the most promising solution. Soon, researchers might be able to generate mosquitoes that cannot carry specific germs. }— Solution

Q A

How did *gerrymandering* get its name? }— Question

Elbridge Gerry, an early Massachusetts governor, redivided election districts to strengthen his party. Artist Gilbert Stuart noticed that one of the new districts had the shape of a salamander. He drew a head, wings, and a tail onto the map. A newspaper editor added the caption "Gerrymander." }— Answer

🔎 **Learn More**

To learn more about writing effective paragraphs, see Chapter 3.

Revising Your Sentences

When most of the sentences within a written work are similar in length, type, or structure, it can have a numbing effect on the audience. Read through your draft carefully, and vary the length, type, and structure of your sentences to ensure that your writing is lively.

Invert Some Sentences for Variety

Most sentences contain a subject followed by a verb. To add variety to your sentences, you may want to invert the order of the subject and verb. As you do so, be careful not to introduce an error in subject-verb agreement.

▶ **REVISION STRATEGY**
Color-Coding to Identify Subject-Verb Patterns

First, circle the subjects and verbs in each sentence. Review your draft. If every sentence contains the traditional subject-verb order, invert a sentence to add variety to your writing.

Student Work
IN PROGRESS

Name: *Michael S. Dougherty*
Central Bucks West High School
Doylestown, PA

Color-Coding to Identify Patterns

While revising, Michael noticed that he always used a subject-verb pattern. He inverted a sentence in this paragraph to add variety to his writing.

Americans honor and respect the brave citizens who, over the years, have fought for their country. They have ensured the tranquillity of our people by bearing arms against the ever-changing threats to our nation's security. Often overlooked, however, are Scores of men and women who have gone into battle defenseless against enemy attacks are often overlooked however: wartime journalists. With only a camera or a pad and pencil in hand, they live a soldier's life while working a civilian job. Looking danger in the face, this unarmed crew records the dramatic details of war to inform people at home, as well as generations to come.

Grammar in Your Writing
Special Problems With Agreement

All sentences contain at least one subject and one verb. The subject and verb pairs should agree in number. In some instances, knowing how to make the subject and verb agree may not be immediately clear.

Inverted Sentences

When a verb precedes its subject in a sentence, the sentence is said to be inverted. A subject that comes after its verb must agree with it in number:

Under the boardwalk was a tiny crab.

There are no more seats left in the auditorium.

Collective Nouns

Collective nouns—such as *audience, class, couple, crowd, faculty, group,* and *team*—can be either singular or plural depending upon how they are used.

If a collective noun refers to a whole group, use a singular verb:

The army approaches the border.
The jury listens to the evidence.

If a collective noun refers to individual group members, use a plural verb:

The faculty discuss the proposal.
The jury are unable to reach a consensus.

Confusing Plurals

Some nouns are plural in form but singular in meaning. Many of these nouns name branches of knowledge: *ethics, mathematics, physics, politics, social studies.* Others name a single unit or idea: *measles, news, series.*

If a noun is plural in form but singular in meaning, use a singular verb:

Physics is an interesting subject.
The news today seems good.

Find It in Your Reading Review a story you have read. Within it, identify one collective noun and one noun that is plural in form but singular in meaning.

Find It in Your Writing Review the subject-verb agreement in your sentences, paying close attention to your use of collective nouns and plurals. Circle any subject-verb pairs that you want to reconsider. Discuss circled pairs with a peer reviewer.

To learn more about agreement, see Chapter 24.

Revising Your Word Choice
Delete Instances of Wordiness

Direct writing is more effective and interesting than writing that is weighed down with unnecessary words. Review your draft, and eliminate instances of wordiness.

WORDY: As a matter of fact, there are many qualities in Capa's photographs that are beautiful, despite the fact that they depict war.

CONCISE: Many of Capa's photographs are beautiful, even though they depict war.

▶ **REVISION STRATEGY**
Deleting Empty Words

This chart shows some common phrases that are often unnecessary. Read through your draft to locate the following phrases. If the phrase does not help connect ideas, delete it.

EMPTY WORDS AND PHRASES

as a matter of fact	in my opinion	to the extent that
as I said before	it is a fact that	the reason was that
by way of	it is also true that	there is/there are
despite the fact that	needless to say	the thing is
given the fact that	of course	the type of
indeed	on account of the fact that	what I mean is

Timed Writing Hint

When revising under timed conditions, it is fine to cross out empty words and rewrite sentences. Do so neatly so that your reader will not be confused.

Peer Review
Review With a K-W-L Chart

Determine how effectively your research writing meets your audience's needs by asking a peer reviewer or review team to complete a K-W-L chart as they review your work. Briefly describe the topic, and have your reviewers write what they **k**now about the topic and what they **w**ant to know. After reading your essay, reviewers complete the chart by adding what they **l**earned.

Use the charts to focus a group discussion. Then, incorporate appropriate suggestions from your peers as you revise your research writing.

12.5 *Editing* and *Proofreading*

Before you hand in your final draft, prepare a works-cited list, and proofread your draft to correct errors in spelling, grammar, and punctuation.

Preparing a Reference List

No research paper is complete without a reference list. Before you turn in your paper, compile a works-cited list on which you completely and accurately document the source material for your research paper. Check with your teacher to confirm the type of format your works-cited list should take.

Following is a list of style manuals you may want to consult as you put together your works-cited list:

- *Modern Language Association Handbook* (MLA)
- *American Psychological Association Handbook* (APA)
- *The Chicago Manual of Style* (CMS)

Focusing on Proofreading

Proofread to make sure all quoted passages, book titles, author names, and page references within parenthetical citations and on your works-cited page are correct. Also, check to be sure that your use of colons, commas, and other punctuation symbols conforms to a specific style of citation.

- Underline the titles of long written works and the titles of publications that are printed as a single work.
- Also, underline the titles of movies, TV and radio series, lengthy works of music, paintings, and sculptures.
- Use quotation marks around the titles of short works.
- Use quotation marks to set off titles of photographs.

Research writing often refers to titles of works, from books and articles to artworks and Internet sites. Check that you have capitalized and punctuated each title correctly.

Remember to capitalize the first, last, and key words in a title. Conjunctions and prepositions shorter than four letters are not considered key words.

Grammar in Your Writing
Citing Sources

In your research paper, be sure to credit the sources of information. To do this, include endnotes, footnotes, or internal citations within the text. Also, prepare a bibliography or works-cited list that will appear on the last page of your writing.

Footnotes and Endnotes When using footnotes and endnotes to provide internal documentation, include full details about the source and cite the page number. Indicate a footnote or an endnote by placing a number at the bottom of the page on which the information cited appears; for an endnote, place the documentation in numerical order on a page preceding the reference list.

> **Example footnote:** Bruce Goldfarb, *King of the Desert* (New York: Leland, 1999)

Parenthetical Documentation Using parenthetical references allows readers to learn about sources quickly and easily, without having to refer to a footnote. A parenthetical reference usually includes the author's last name and the page numbers from which the information is taken. The full publication information about each source to which you refer in parentheses will appear on your works-cited list.

> **Example:** Two thirds of employed actors appear only in commercials (Fleming 55).

Works-Cited List A works-cited list appears at the end of a piece of research writing and includes the publication information for any source used or quoted. Titles are usually arranged in alphabetical order by author's last name and are underscored or italicized. Your source cards will have all of the information you need to include on this list.

Bibliography Present your sources in a standardized format based on the type of resource referenced. Include the author's names, source title, place of publication, publisher, and date of publication.

> **Example entry:** Dryson, Edna. *Knowing a Thing or Two.* Chicago: Tower, 2000.

Find It in Your Reading Review a works-cited list. Explain why each title is underlined or set in quotation marks.

Find It in Your Writing Check the punctuation of the titles in your research writing. Make sure that you have used capitalization, underlining, and quotation marks correctly.

To learn more about punctuating cited sources, see Citing Sources and Preparing Manuscript on pp. 672–678.

Publishing and Presenting

Following are some ways to share your research writing:

Building Your Portfolio

1. **Class Anthology** Assemble an anthology of essays by combining your class's examples of research writing. Discuss the organization and title of the anthology, and work together to write an introduction or foreword explaining the project. Bind the anthology, and make it available to classmates.

2. **Internet Publication** Use the Internet to share your research writing. Send your finished draft to a friend or relative by e-mail, or submit your writing to a Web site that publishes student writing.

Reflecting on Your Writing

Think over your research writing experience. Then, answer the following questions, and record your responses in your portfolio.

• Where did you find the most useful information?

• Which writing strategies worked so well that you would like to try them again?

 Internet Tip

To see model research papers scored with this rubric, go on-line: PHSchool.com

Enter Web Code: eek-1001

Rubric for Self-Assessment

Evaluate your research writing using the following criteria.

	Score 4	Score 3	Score 2	Score 1
Audience and Purpose	Focuses on a clearly stated thesis, starting from a well-framed question; gives complete citations	Focuses on a clearly stated thesis; gives citations	Focuses mainly on the chosen topic; gives some citations	Presents information without a clear focus; few or no citations
Organization	Presents information in logical order, emphasizing details of central importance	Presents information in logical order	Presents information logically, but organization is poor in places	Presents information in a scattered, disorganized manner
Elaboration	Draws clear conclusions from information gathered from multiple sources	Draws conclusions from information gathered from multiple sources	Explains and interprets some information	Presents information with little or no interpretation or synthesis
Use of Language	Shows overall clarity and fluency; contains few mechanical errors	Shows good sentence variety; contains some errors in spelling, puncutation, or usage	Uses awkward or overly simple sentence structures; contains many mechanical errors	Contains incomplete thoughts and mechanical errors that make the writing confusing

12.7 Student Work
IN PROGRESS

FINAL DRAFT

Robert Capa

Michael S. Dougherty
Central Bucks West High School
Doylestown, Pennsylvania

Americans honor and respect the brave citizens who, over the years, have fought for their country. They have ensured the tranquillity of our people by bearing arms against the ever-changing threats to our nation's security. Often overlooked, however, are scores of men and women who have gone into battle defenseless against enemy attacks: wartime journalists. With only a camera or a pad and pencil in hand, they live a soldier's life while working a civilian job. Looking danger in the face, this unarmed crew records the dramatic details of war to inform people at home, as well as generations to come. The public certainly owes much to these brave and loyal workers. One of the most renowned of these war journalists was a photographer named Robert Capa, who dedicated his life to capturing the essence of war on film.

Capa was born Andrei Friedmann in Budapest, Hungary, in 1913. Little is known about his childhood, except that he did not have formal training in photography. Indeed, he taught himself everything that he learned in this field (Adato 98). While a high-school student in Hungary, he was exiled because of his political beliefs. Leaving his home country would have a strong influence on his life and career as a photographer.

In 1931, Friedmann got a job with a picture agency in Berlin, where he took his first assignment. He traveled to Copenhagen to photograph Russian Communist leader Leon Trotsky. Upon completing this assignment, he returned to Germany but was driven out by Hitler's menacing regime. Cast out from his second home, Friedmann found a new, more welcoming home in Paris, France.

While he was in Paris, Friedmann's career began to flourish, but not without an initial struggle. Even at the start of

Michael builds his opening paragraph to a thesis statement that describes the topic of his essay.

▼ **Critical Viewing**
What type of personality might you guess Capa to have had, based on this photograph? Explain. **[Speculate]**

his year in Paris, Friedmann was proud of the powerful images he was creating. However, he was dismayed that they were not selling for very much money, so he devised a plan that would benefit him and his wife financially. In order to sell prints for higher prices, Friedmann posed as the assistant to a completely fictitious American photographer named Robert Capa. For a while, he and his wife, who pretended to be the famous American's secretary, were making a substantial profit with this scheme. Unfortunately, in 1936, an editor recognized their fraud and threatened to expose them. Instead of abandoning the name, as the editor suggested, Friedmann decided to resolve the situation by adopting it. For the rest of his life, Andrei Friedmann was known as Robert Capa.

Michael clearly and effectively organizes his paper using chronological organization of details.

Later the same year, a conflict in Spain began to attract some of the world's attention away from the rising Nazi regime. Attracted by the limitless possibilities that war-field photography offered, Capa got a job with *Life* magazine and left France to cover the war. It was here that he developed a knack for war photography that made him famous. By shooting such remarkable images as "Death of a Loyalist Militiaman Frederico Borrell García, Cerro Muriano (Córdoba Front), 1936," Capa's reputation steadily grew until the European and American Press circles named him the "greatest war photographer in the world" (Emery 538).

Parenthetical documentation is used to name the sources of information. The full citation for the source appears at the end. The numbers indicate the page number.

In the following years, Robert Capa spent time covering China's war with Japan. He documented this war, but he was given his greatest opportunity when the Allied Forces declared war against Hitler's Axis Powers, which signaled the beginning of World War II.

As a Hungarian citizen based in America during this war, Capa suffered greatly. Because the Allies had declared war against the Axis, many Americans felt angry with Middle Europeans. Capa, a citizen of a country united with others against America, was categorized as an enemy alien. He was fired from his job at *Life* and found it difficult to make ends meet (Lande 251).

Michael uses formal language to share the facts and details he discovered during research.

Finally in 1943, Capa was hired to cover the war overseas for *Collier's* magazine. His first assignment was the North African invasion. Dodging bullets as he traveled across the countryside, Capa was always in the center of the action. He made many friends, but he was eventually fired from *Collier's* for pooling, or sharing, his pictures with them. Scrambling for a new assignment, Capa took a job once again for *Life*. He was assigned to fill in for a sick man who was scheduled to jump out of a plane with a squad of paratroopers. Although he was nervous, Capa showed his dedication to his job by hurling himself from the plane into the African canopy (Stein 188).

Michael italicized the titles of magazines. He proofread his writing carefully to make sure that it was free of distracting errors.

Capa's success was capped, however, when he was selected as one of four photographers who would make the D-Day landing in Normandy. He was the sole photographer of the bloodiest landing, Omaha Beach, and took 106 photographs in what he considered to be an outstanding personal victory (Neuman 85). Unfortunately, a darkroom assistant turned on too much heat while developing the pictures and destroyed all but eight. Despite such setbacks, Capa remained dedicated to photographing the war effort, making several other parachute landings as well (Stein 189).

Although his talents as a war journalist were outstanding, photographing the frightening images of war was never an easy task for Capa. As he once said, "It is not always easy to stand aside and be unable to do anything except record the suffering around one." Capa's humanity and compassion shine through his powerful photographs.

World War II eventually ended, but Capa's career moved forcefully ahead. After only three years, a conflict between the Israelis and Arabs broke out. Capa was one of the first men there and one of the first in Indochina to record fighting between the French and the Viet Minh.

Tragically, covering this event in 1954, Robert Capa was killed after stepping on a land mine. He had lived for forty years and covered four major wars. By capturing the horrifying and moving images of war, Robert Capa served America and its journalism well, eventually sacrificing his life for a profession he loved.

▲ **Critical Viewing** This photograph shows the Normandy invasion in action. If the invasion were to take place today, how would it be similar and different? Explain. **[Modify]**

Michael closes with a strong restatement of his opening thesis.

Works Cited

Adato, Allison. "The Double Life of a Legendary War Photographer." *Life*, March 1997: 98–103.

Emery, Edwin. *The Press and America: An Interpretive History of the Mass Media*. 3rd Edition. Englewood Cliffs, NJ: Prentice Hall, Inc., 1972.

Lande, Nathaniel. *Dispatches from the Front: News Accounts of American Wars*, 1776–1991. New York: Henry Holt and Company, 1995.

Neuman, Johanna. *Lights, Camera, War*. New York: St. Martin's Press, 1996.

Stein, M. L. *Under Fire: The Story of American War Correspondents*. New York: Julian Messner, 1968.

13 *Response to Literature*

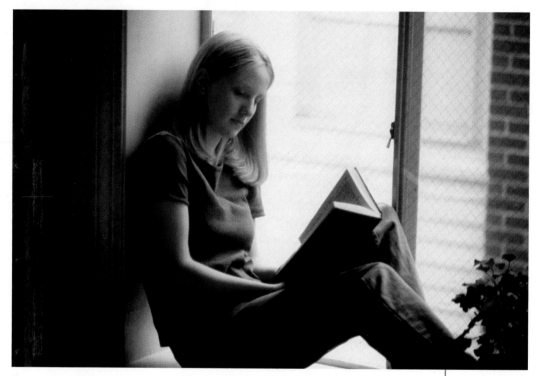

Responding to Literature in Everyday Life

You probably respond to literature in everyday life more often than you realize. For example, when you lend a book to a friend with a comment like "It's really funny," or when you summarize the plot of a favorite childhood story, you are responding to literature. Other ways of responding to literature in everyday life include silently identifying with a character in a book you're reading or sharing your views about a story or poem with a teacher or friend.

Responses to literature also appear in written form in everyday life. For example, your morning newspaper may contain a review of a new novel or collection of poetry. On-line, Web sites may be devoted to sharing readers' responses to a particular author's works or to a genre of literature.

▲ **Critical Viewing** What clues indicate that this student is enjoying what she is reading? Explain. **[Make a Judgment]**

What Is a Response to Literature?

A **response to literature** is a reader's reaction to any aspect of the literature he or she is reading. Some responses are formal and academic in tone; others are informal and more personal. Most responses to literature contain

- a reaction to a poem, story, essay, or other work of literature.
- references to or passages from works that support the writer's main points.
- personal and literary allusions, quotations, and other examples that support the writer's opinions.
- an effective and logical organization.
- a conclusion or evaluation that sums up the writer's response to the work.

To preview the criteria on which your response to literature may be evaluated, see the Rubric for Self-Assessment on page 190.

Types of Responses to Literature

Readers can respond to literature in various ways:

- **Journal entries** contain a reader's unique responses. They are generally informal and not shared with others.
- **Critical reviews** discuss various elements of a literary work—characters, plot, theme—and offer opinions about the work's effectiveness.
- **Literary analyses** examine various aspects of a work of literature. Often, an analysis compares the work with other works and offers an opinion of the work's literary importance.

PREVIEW
Student Work
IN PROGRESS

Follow the progress of Sheetal Wadera, a student at Hightower High School in Missouri City, Texas, as she drafts her response to Homer's *Odyssey*. Sheetal's completed response appears at the end of this chapter.

Prewriting

Choosing Your Topic

The best topic for a response to literature is a work about which you have strong ideas. Use the following strategies to come up with a topic for your response to literature:

Strategies for Generating Topics

1. **List** Begin by listing characters from literature whom you find interesting. These characters should belong to the stories and poetry about which you have the most to say. Review your list, and choose as a topic the character or work that you find most intriguing.

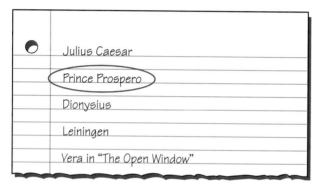

Julius Caesar

Prince Prospero

Dionysius

Leiningen

Vera in "The Open Window"

Get instant help! Make your list of characters using the Essay Builder, accessible from the menu bar, on-line or on CD-ROM.

2. **Review Your Journal** In your reading journal, you may have recorded quotes from literature or themes, plots, and imagery that intrigued you. Look through your journal, and put self-sticking notes on pages that contain interesting ideas. Revisit the pages you marked, and choose one entry for your response to literature.

3. **Browse a Bookshelf** Go to the library or to a bookstore, and browse through the bookshelves to get writing ideas. Jot down titles of literature that you have read, authors you like, and literature that you would like to read. Review your notes, and choose as a topic for your response to literature a book you have already read, a comparison of two works by the same author, or a review of a book that you found while browsing.

4. **Discuss With a Peer** Discuss with a peer the books and poems you have recently read. Notice the topics you discuss the longest: Those are probably the ones for which you have the most to say. Choose one of those discussion points to form the basis of your response to literature.

TOPIC BANK

If you are having difficulty choosing a topic for your response to literature, look at these suggestions:

1. **Critical Review** Write a review of the last work you read. Because it's fresh in your mind, this piece will be a good subject for you. Freewrite until you settle on a specific aspect of the work that interests you, such as character, theme, setting, or plot.

2. **Comparison and Contrast** Choose two poems by a favorite poet. Then, compare and contrast the elements the poems have in common—speaker, theme, imagery, or structure, for example.

Responding to Fine Art

3. Study the character and setting of *Children Dancing* by Robert Gwathmey. Then, write a response to the painting in which you explore your reactions to the mood and subject matter of the work.

Children Dancing, Robert Gwathmey, Butler Institute of American Art

Responding to Literature

4. Write an analysis of "The Masque of the Red Death" by Edgar Allan Poe. Discuss the central conflict in the story and the story's overall mood. Describe techniques the writer uses to create suspense and intensify the mood. You can find the story in *Prentice Hall Literature, Penguin Edition,* Grade 10.

🕐 Timed Writing Prompt

5. Write an essay in which you introduce your favorite book to your classmates. Clearly identify the book and its author. Then, discuss why the book was so compelling to you. Share the literary features—for example, the theme or the plot—that you found most interesting. Aim to convince your classmates that this is a book worth reading.
(45 minutes)

Narrowing Your Topic

Before you write your response to literature, narrow your topic so that you will be able to develop your ideas fully within the space limitations. Making a web is an effective way to narrow a response to literature.

Make a Web

Make a web like the one below, changing heads and categories as you see fit. Then, review your web, and choose as your narrowed topic one of the subtopics you wrote down.

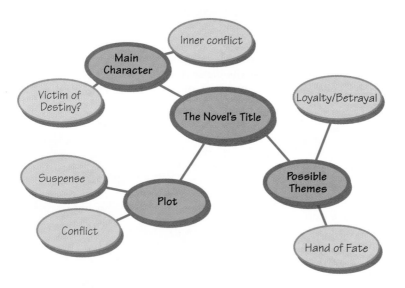

Considering Your Audience and Purpose

Responses to literature may be read by audiences of any age and may vary widely in their purpose. Choose details that will appeal to your audience and that will help you achieve your purpose.

Type of Response	Language and Details
Journal	Informal language: details that vary
Critical Review	Formal language: details that illustrate the work's strengths and weaknesses; excerpts from the work
Literary Analysis	Very formal language: details that prove your ideas about the work; excerpts from the work; excerpts from, or allusions to, other literary works

Timed Writing Hint

When writing under timed conditions, make a quick web to plan your essay.

Gathering Details

Once you have a narrowed topic, gather details to support your purpose and main idea and give depth to your writing.

Use Hexagonal Writing to Gather Details

One way to ensure that you have considered all the various aspects of a literary work is to use the technique of hexagonal writing. A hexagon is a six-sided geometrical figure. With hexagonal writing, you explore six aspects (one per side) of a work of literature.

Student Work
IN PROGRESS

Name: Sheetal Wadera
Hightower High School
Missouri City, TX

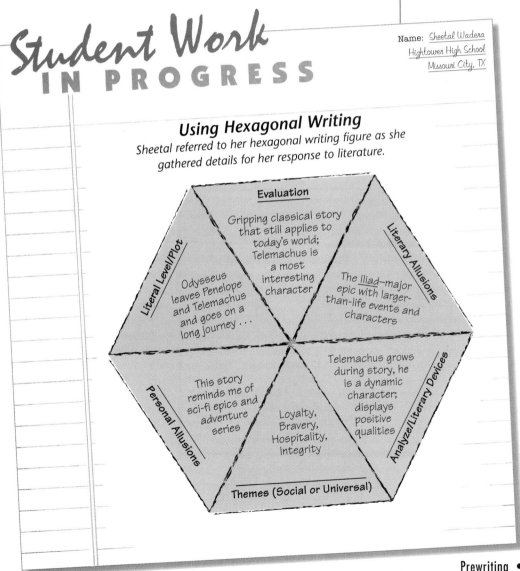

Using Hexagonal Writing
Sheetal referred to her hexagonal writing figure as she gathered details for her response to literature.

Evaluation
Gripping classical story that still applies to today's world; Telemachus is a most interesting character

Literal Level/Plot
Odysseus leaves Penelope and Telemachus and goes on a long journey . . .

Literary Allusions
The <u>Iliad</u>—major epic with larger-than-life events and characters

Personal Allusions
This story reminds me of sci-fi epics and adventure series

Themes (Social or Universal)
Loyalty, Bravery, Hospitality, Integrity

Analyze/Literary Devices
Telemachus grows during story, he is a dynamic character; displays positive qualities

Drafting

Shaping Your Writing

Take the details you have collected during prewriting, and organize them logically as you draft your response to literature. One way to do this is to develop a thesis statement and support it with details you've gathered.

Draft a Thesis Statement

The **thesis statement** is the main message of your essay, which you will support with various kinds of details. To come up with a thesis statement, review your notes, and answer the following:

Out of all that I have learned, the most important point I would like to make about [the work of literature] is ___?___ .

Then, use the following tips to draft your thesis statement:

- Write your thesis statement at the top of a sheet of paper.

- Refer to your prewriting notes, and list all the major details that help support your thesis statement.

- When the list is complete, decide on an organizational method that will present those details most effectively.

Thesis Statement: One theme of William Shakespeare's The Tragedy of Julius Caesar is loyalty.

Supporting Details:

1. Caesar's wife, Calpurnia, is loyal to him and warns him about his impending doom.

2. Caesar chooses to ignore his wife and trust Brutus; he believes that Brutus is his friend.

3. Brutus, however, helps to ambush and murder Caesar on the day he is to be crowned emperor. Just before his death, Caesar realizes that he has been betrayed.

The Tragedy of Julius Caesar appears in Prentice Hall Literature, Penguin Edition, Grade 10.

Providing Elaboration

Cite Passages From the Work

As you draft your response to literature, cite words, lines, or passages from the work to which you are responding. Doing so will help you make your points, as well as give your readers specific examples. Enclose cited passages within quotation marks, and indicate where the passage is in the literature. If you are citing a large passage of the work, indent your left and right margins, and type the excerpt in a separate paragraph. Quotation marks are not necessary when excerpts are set off this way.

Student Work
IN PROGRESS

Name: *Sheetal Wadera*
Hightower High School
Missouri City, TX

Citing Passages From Literature

Sheetal supported her main points by citing specific passages from the Odyssey.

In ancient Greek culture, women had few legal rights, and if their husbands passed away or went to war and never returned, they were expected to remarry. Because of this, Telemachus' house was constantly overrun with suitors who wished to court his mother. Although Telemachus wanted to get rid of the suitors, he did not possess the power to do so. "For he, too, was sitting there, unhappy among the suitors, a boy, daydreaming" (19–21).

In the course of the story, Telemachus makes many moral decisions that help the readers see that he truly knows the difference between right and wrong. A prime example of this is at the beginning of the epic, when Athena is talking to Telemachus about the obnoxious suitors, and she tells him, "You need not bear this insolence of theirs; you are a child no longer" (76–77).

Sheetal used quotations from the Odyssey to make her ideas clear for readers.

Drafting • **183**

Revising

Revising Your Overall Structure

Make Your Introduction and Conclusion Match

Review the overall structure of your response to literature to be sure that it is clear and effective. An effective essay usually contains an introduction, a body, and a conclusion. In your introduction, be sure you have presented the main message of your response. Your conclusion should restate that main idea and reveal additional insights you may have about your topic.

▶ **REVISION STRATEGY**
Underlining Details

Read through your introduction, and underline important points you make there, as well as questions you raise. Then, read your conclusion, and underline its important details. Review your introduction and conclusion to be sure that they match. If they do not, make necessary revisions.

Student Work
IN PROGRESS

Name: *Sheetal Wadera*
Hightower High School
Missouri City, TX

Underlining Details

Sheetal underlined important details in her introduction and conclusion to make sure that her response ended where she began. She decided to add a sentence to her introduction to make her overall intent more clear.

Introduction

The *Odyssey* mainly <u>focuses upon</u> the character of <u>Odysseus,</u> telling of his wartime adventures as an epic hero. Odysseus' son, <u>Telemachus, the secondary hero, also plays a vital role</u> in the *Odyssey*; the reader sees him grow from a young boy to a fully grown man, and this maturity comes from the fact that Telemachus has had to learn to fend for himself during his father's absence. ₍ₐ₎

In fact, tracing the growth of Telemachus during the *Odyssey* shows what qualities the ancient Greeks considered noble and admirable in a man.

Conclusion

All in all, <u>Telemachus is a very interesting character.</u> Not only do we see him as a young child, <u>but as time progresses,</u> as an intelligent young man. <u>He plays a vital role in the *Odyssey*.</u> His heroic actions, gestures, and thoughts make him a hero of great renown.

Revising Your Paragraphs

Polish Your Paragraphs

To be effective, a topical paragraph should have a single main idea that is supported by various types of information. An effective functional paragraph should perform a specific function, such as indicating a transition or emphasizing a point.

▶**REVISION STRATEGY**
Using a Checklist to Revise Paragraphs

Use these questions to help you analyze and revise the topical paragraphs in your response to literature. Complete the checklist, and revise your paragraphs accordingly.

1. Does the topic sentence clearly express the main idea of the paragraph?
2. Does the paragraph contain various types of support in the form of examples, quotations, and reasons?
3. Is any of the supporting information weak, repetitive, or inappropriate?
4. Does the supporting information pertain to the main idea of the paragraph?
5. Is the supporting information presented logically? Could the supporting information be organized more effectively?
6. Do transitions connect the ideas within your paragraph?

🖉 Learn More

To learn more about effective paragraphs, see Chapter 3.

EXAMPLE

~~In this story~~, the narrator ⟨*of "Axolotl"*⟩ reflects on his fascination with axolotls, which he defines as "the larval stage" (provided with gills) of a species of salamander. By the end of the first paragraph, ~~he~~ ⟨*the narrator*⟩ has summarized the whole plot: He saw some axolotls in an aquarium, he watched them ~~a lot~~, and thought a lot about them, and now he has become one. The plot sounds almost like a joke, like one of those cartoons in which a person and his or her pet start to look more and more alike. ~~I think Cortazar is making a point about how people become what they are.~~

This correction makes the main idea of the paragraph more clear.

This phrase was deleted to avoid unnecessary repetition.

This sentence belongs in another paragraph, because it deals with the story's theme, not with its plot.

Revising Your Sentences

Revise for Clarity

One of the problems that can occur when writing about literature is confusion about who or what is being discussed. This is especially true when you are discussing several characters, works, themes, or writers. Read through your draft, and make sure that each sentence has a clear subject.

▶ **REVISION STRATEGY**
Color-Coding Elements

Use a colored pen or highlighter to call out each character reference in your draft. Use a different color for each character. Then, locate personal pronouns that stand in for character names, and circle or highlight each using its appropriate color. If you experience confusion figuring out which color to use, the pronoun's antecedent is probably unclear. In that case, replace the pronoun with the proper noun.

Student Work
IN PROGRESS

Name: Sheetal Wadera
Hightower High School
Missouri City, TX

Color-Coding Characters to Check for Clarity

Sheetal used color-coding to make sure that each character reference was clear and that when she used personal pronouns, they had clear antecedents.

Unaware of his visitor's identity, Nestor invites Telemachus to join the feast of Poseidon, the blue-maned god. After the feast, he calls Telemachus and asks him who he is. The young prince [Telemachus] tells him that he is Odysseus' lost soldier and asks him [Nestor] if he knows anything about his lost father. "Nestor is full of praise for the lost soldier, and he quickly recognizes the heroic qualities of the son" (188–190). Nestor also praises Telemachus himself saying, "Your manner of speech couldn't be more like his; one would say No; no boy could speak so well" (191–192).

Grammar in Your Writing
Pronouns and Antecedents

In your response to literature, you may have used many **pronouns** to refer to characters or elements within the work. A pronoun is used in place of a noun. The noun the pronoun replaces is its **antecedent.**

Nouns and Pronouns

Robert	he him his
Marilyn and Robert	they them their
Marilyn	she her hers
clock	it it its

Fixing Unclear Pronouns

Because pronouns can be used in place of nouns, you can use them to help you avoid repeating a character or person's name over and over. However, when several characters are being discussed, it may be ambiguous or unclear to whom the pronoun refers. Ambiguous pronoun references can be fixed in two ways.

In the following example, the antecedent of *he* is unclear because two masculine nouns precede the masculine pronoun. The problem is eliminated by repeating Steve's name.

Unclear: Joe and Steve discussed the novel. They both enjoyed the characters and plot, but he didn't like the setting.

Clear: Joe and Steve discussed the novel. They both enjoyed the characters and plot, but Steve didn't like the setting.

In the next example, the antecedent is unclear because readers don't know whether Joe or Mike returned from vacation. The error is corrected by revising the sentence so that it is clear that Joe returned from vacation.

Unclear: Joe told Steve to read the book after he returned from vacation.

Clear: After Joe returned from vacation, he told Steve to read the book.

Find It in Your Reading   Review a novel you have read. Find three examples of pronouns, and identify their antecedents.

Find It in Your Writing   Identify three examples of pronouns that refer to characters in your response to literature. If you cannot find three examples, challenge yourself to add some. Use pronouns to avoid repetition of the characters' names.

For more on pronouns and antecedents, see Chapters 16 and 23.

Revising Your Word Choice

Review your draft to be sure that you've used words correctly. Also, check your word choice, making sure that any informal words were used intentionally.

Use Formal Language

In fiction writing and journal writing, you may use informal language—language that contains conversational expressions such as slang and idioms. In an academic report, however, you should use formal English.

EXAMPLES:

SLANG: There is no way I would discourage a friend from reading the *Odyssey*. It was **way cool.**

IDIOM: When I read the *Odyssey*, it was **a wake-up call.**

FORMAL: I would never discourage a friend from reading the *Odyssey*. It was excellent.

▶ **REVISION STRATEGY**
Reading and Replacing

Read through your draft, paying particular attention to the types of words you have chosen to convey your ideas. Rewrite contractions as full words, and replace slang and idioms with more formal word choices. Also, delete instances of informal phrases such as *like, you know,* and *kind of.*

Peer Review

Work with a peer to review the level of formality of the language in your response to literature. Following are two strategies for working with peers:

- Exchange papers with a partner, and review each other's language to make sure that the level is appropriate for an academic report. Make a list of informal expressions and contractions. Help replace these with formal language.

- Read your paper aloud to a small group, and ask them to stop you whenever they hear informal English. Discuss the language and possible revisions to use formal English.

Timed Writing Hint

When writing for an exam, it is wise to use formal, academic language unless a prompt asks for a conversational style.

▼ Critical Viewing
What sorts of mistakes are you likely to catch when reading a draft aloud? **[Generalize]**

13.5 Editing and Proofreading

Proofread your response to literature carefully, looking for any errors in grammar, spelling, and punctuation.

Focusing on Mechanics

In a response to literature, you will probably refer to the authors and titles of the works you are discussing. Make sure that you spell, capitalize, and style these names and titles correctly.

Grammar in Your Writing
Styling Titles of Poems, Stories, and Novels

Use the following rules for styling titles of literary works:

- Always capitalize the first and last words in the title, including articles and prepositions. Do not capitalize articles or prepositions with fewer than four letters, unless they are the first or last word of the title.
  Of Mice and Men   John Steinbeck
  "Through the Tunnel"   Doris Lessing

- The titles of short works—such as poems, songs, and short stories—are enclosed in quotation marks.
  "The Dog That Bit People"   James Thurber
  "After Apple-Picking"   Robert Frost

- The titles of long works—such as novels, plays, and epic poetry—are set in italics or underlined. Newspaper, magazine, movie, painting, and sculpture titles are also treated this way.
  the *Iliad*   Homer
  The New York Times
  Mona Lisa   Leonardo da Vinci

Find It in Your Reading Find a book title in a newspaper review. Tell why the title is styled as it is.

Find It in Your Writing As you proofread your response to literature, check to be sure that you have written and styled all titles correctly.

For more on styling titles, see Chapter 28.

13.6 Publishing and Presenting

Once you have completed your response to literature, share it with others.

Building Your Portfolio

1. **Student Newspaper or Web Site** You could publish in a student paper or on a student Web site a review of a work of literature that has deeply affected you. First, check with the editor for submission requirements and deadlines.

2. **Book Club** Share your critique of a work of literature with a small group that meets regularly to discuss books they are reading. Prepare organized notes to which you can refer as you speak.

Reflecting on Your Writing

Pause to think about what you experienced as you wrote your response to literature. Then, answer the following questions, and put a copy of your responses in your portfolio.

- In the process of writing, what did you learn about how you value literature?

- Which strategy for prewriting, drafting, revising, or editing would you recommend to a friend?

 Internet Tip

To see model essays scored with this rubric, go on-line:
PHSchool.com
Enter Web Code:
eek-1001

Rubric for Self-Assessment

Use these criteria as you evaluate your response to literature:

	Score 4	Score 3	Score 2	Score 1
Audience and Purpose	Presents sufficient background on the work(s); completely achieves purpose	Presents background on the work(s); achieves purpose	Presents some background on the work(s); partially achieves purpose	Presents little or no background on the work(s); does not achieve a purpose
Organization	Presents points in logical order, smoothly connecting them to the overall focus	Presents points in logical order and connects them to the overall focus	Organizes points poorly in places; connects some points to an overall focus	Presents information in a scattered, disorganized manner
Elaboration	Supports reactions and evaluations with elaborated reasons and well-chosen examples	Supports reactions and evaluations with specific reasons and examples	Supports some reactions and evaluations with reasons and examples	Offers little support for reactions and evaluations
Use of Language	Shows overall clarity and fluency; language is appropriate; makes few mechanical errors	Shows good sentence variety; language is mostly appropriate; makes some mechanical errors	Uses awkward or overly simple sentence structures and vague evaluative terms; makes many mechanical errors	Presents incomplete thoughts; makes mechanical errors that cause confusion

13.7 Student Work IN PROGRESS

FINAL DRAFT

Penelope at the loom and Telemachus, Museo Nazionale, Chiusi, Italy

◄ **Critical Viewing**
This urn displays an image of characters from Homer's *Odyssey*. Why might artists have chosen to decorate items such as urns with scenes from literature? **[Speculate]**

Telemachus
in Homer's Odyssey

Sheetal Wadera
Hightower High School
Missouri City, Texas

The *Odyssey* focuses mainly on the character of Odysseus, telling of his wartime travels and adventures as an epic hero. Odysseus' son, Telemachus, the secondary hero, also plays a vital role in the *Odyssey*; the reader sees him grow from a young boy to a fully grown man, and this maturity comes from the fact that Telemachus has had to learn to fend for himself during his father's absence. In fact, tracing the growth of Telemachus during the *Odyssey* shows what qualities the ancient Greeks considered noble and admirable in a man.

Sheetal reveals her thesis—the essay's main idea—in the final sentence of her introduction.

Telemachus' father, Odysseus, left home to go to war, leaving his very young son, Telemachus, and his beautiful wife, Penelope, behind. Since that fateful day, twenty years have passed, and young Telemachus has had to grow up and become sole protector of his mother and himself.

In ancient Greek culture, women had few legal rights, and if their husbands passed away or went to war and never returned, they were expected to remarry. Because of this custom, Telemachus' house was constantly overrun with suitors who wished to court his mother. Although Telemachus wanted to get rid of the suitors, he did not possess the power to do so. "For he, too, was sitting there, unhappy among the suitors, a boy, daydreaming" (19–21).

In this paragraph, Sheetal gives background information about Telemachus and his mother, Penelope.

Telemachus takes his first steps toward becoming a man—and developing positive character traits—when he first visits his father's old friend Nestor, king of Pylos and a hero of the Trojan War, to tell him of the suitors' rude comments. Unaware of his visitor's identity, Nestor invites Telemachus to join the feast of Poseidon, the blue-maned god. After the feast, Nestor calls Telemachus over and asks him who he is. Telemachus tells him that he is Odysseus' lost soldier and asks Nestor if he knows anything about his lost father. "Nestor is full of praise for the lost soldier, and he quickly recognizes the heroic qualities of the son" (188–190). Nestor also

Because this is an important event in the development of the character of Telemachus, Sheetal explains in detail what happened.

Ulysses and his son Telemachus, Kunsthistorisches Museum, Antikensammlung, Vienna, Austria

◀ **Critical Viewing**
Using details in this mosaic, decide which character is Odysseus (Ulysses) and which is Telemachus, his son. **[Analyze]**

praises Telemachus outright, saying, "Your manner of speech couldn't be more like his; one would say No; no boy could speak so well" (191–192). Nestor then tells Telemachus to visit Menelaus for further news.

Obedient and determined to learn more, Telemachus arrives at Menelaus' palace, which catches the eye with shining gems and precious metals such as gold, bronze, amber, silver, and ivory. The vision is more dazzling than anything Telemachus has seen before, and he immediately senses the power and wealth that Menelaus must have. Menelaus begins to tell his young visitor old war stories, and Telemachus finds Odysseus' name mentioned many times. Although this pleases Telemachus and reminds him of his father, the tribute brings tears to his eyes. At this instant, Menelaus and Helen (the lady whose elopement with the prince of Troy started the Trojan War) recognize their guest. "Never anywhere have I seen so great a likeness in man or woman, but it is truly strange! This boy must be the son of Odysseus, Telemachus . . ." (236–240)

This paragraph helps support Sheetal's thesis. It reveals further qualities of Telemachus' character.

Telemachus also displays hospitality on several occasions. The first time we see this is when Athena appears to have been waiting. "Straight to the door he came, irked with himself, to think a visitor had been kept there waiting" (26–27). In Greek culture, it was not unusual to invite visitors to feast without knowing anything about them. In fact, it was, on many occasions, expected. Much later in the story, Telemachus is visited by a stranger. Not realizing that the beggar is his father in disguise, Telemachus says, "Friend, sit down; we'll find another chair in our own hut" (1414–1415). In Greek epic poems, one can always spare a moment to help someone or feed someone.

Throughout this response to literature, Sheetal has used formal language appropriate for her audience and purpose.

In this paragraph, Sheetal cites examples from the text of the Odyssey *to support her main point— that Telemachus displays hospitality throughout the* Odyssey.

Perhaps the most important quality displayed by the maturing Telemachus, however, is his sense of loyalty—to the memory of his father and to his mother. For example, he doesn't force his mother to choose among the raucous suitors; he respects her desires and wishes. To his father, too, Telemachus displays touching faith and loyalty. Although he was an infant when Odysseus left, his son is proud of his father and eager to preserve his reputation.

Telemachus, as portrayed by Homer, embodies many qualities prized in Greek culture. As he grows, he shows initiative and develops a keen sense of kindness and loyalty. His heroic actions, gestures, and thoughts make him a hero in his own right—one who reflects many qualities considered ideal by ancient Greek culture, and indeed, by cultures far and wide.

In her conclusion, Sheetal restates her thesis and adds a further observation about connections among cultures.

Writing for Assessment

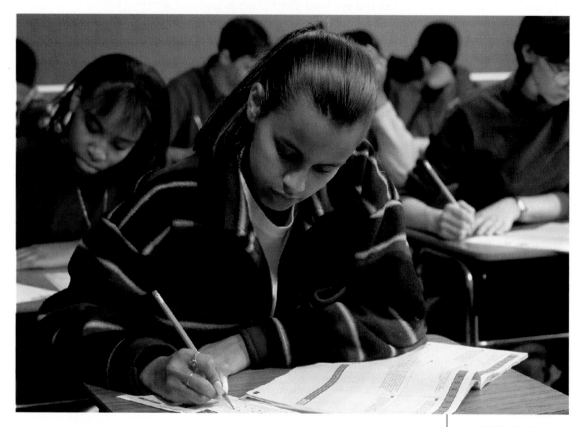

Assessment in School

Being evaluated is a part of life. For example, a music teacher may measure how much you have improved as a trombone player in the course of a year, or a track-and-field coach may assess your hurdling technique to help you prepares for an upcoming meet.

In class, evaluations help teachers assess how much students have learned and how well their students' progress compares with that of other students—in their own school and all over the nation. Teachers use various kinds of assessment tools, from pop quizzes to questions in class to essay assignments and special projects.

▲ Critical Viewing
What kind of test might these students be taking? How do you know? **[Analyze]**

What Is Assessment?

Assessment is evaluation. In life, people may be assessed by anyone, from parents to employers. In school, however, assessment is used to gauge the depth of students' knowledge, their ability to learn, and their problem-solving abilities.

Most educators who make assessments of students' work look for

- answers or responses that match the questions asked.
- clearly stated main points that are supported with details.
- writing that is organized logically and effectively.
- correct grammar, spelling, and punctuation.

To preview the criteria on which your essay may be evaluated, see the Rubric for Self-Assessment on page 203.

Writers in
ACTION

Emile-Auguste Chartier, renowned French philosopher, understood the importance of arriving at truths. He had the following to say about his methods:

"Every idea I get I have to deny. That's my way of testing it."

Types of Assessment

Many types of tests and essays allow teachers and other educators to assess their students' progress. Following are some assessment tools commonly used by educators:

- **Timed tests** assess students' familiarity with the tested topics.
- **Short-answer tests** require brief answers, ranging from a word or phrase to a few sentences for each question.
- **Analyses** are critical papers in which the structural components of a work are examined and evaluated.
- **Comparison-and-contrast essays** provide detailed information about the similarities and differences among two or more people, places, things, or ideas.
- **Personal essays** reveal the unique experiences and insights of the writer.

PREVIEW
Student Work
IN PROGRESS

Follow along as Tricia Bushnell, a student at Buena High School in Ventura, California, drafts and revises an essay about World War I for assessment.

Prewriting

Choosing Your Topic

You may be asked to write an essay to evaluate your understanding of a subject. In many cases, more than one essay question is provided, and you will be asked to choose one on which to write your essay. For help with choosing a topic for an essay test, follow these guidelines:

- **Skim the Questions** Quickly read the questions, and eliminate those about which you have limited knowledge. One quick way to measure your knowledge is to think of at least three details that you could use immediately in answering an essay question. If you cannot easily come up with three supporting points, choose another question to answer.

- **Look for Key Words** As you read through the essay questions, look for key words that reveal what your response must address. Key words can include *examine the causes, analyze, compare and contrast, distinguish between, identify,* and *evaluate.* Choose to answer the question that you feel most prepared to answer in full.

- **Identify the Format** Analyze the questions, and note the format your response will require. For example, a question may ask you to compare and contrast, trace the causes of something, or argue persuasively. If you feel especially confident with any one format over the others, choose to answer the question that requires that format.

TOPIC BANK

Following are some sample essay-test questions. If you plan to practice writing for assessment, choose one of these or ask your teacher to provide you with one.

1. Explain the conditions that must exist in order for a hurricane to occur.

2. Which American president governed most effectively? Give reasons to support your opinion.

3. If you had a motto in life, what would it be? Explain, using examples from experience, literature, and the media.

4. Define the concept of globalization, and give examples of it in action.

5. Discuss the causes of the bubonic plague epidemics in Europe and the effects the epidemics had on people's behavior and beliefs.

Narrowing Your Response

Narrow your response by identifying your main point. To do this, note specifically what the essay question is asking of you. For example, are you going to defend a position, show the causes of something, or make a prediction? For help narrowing your topic, use the strategies that follow.

Identify Key Words

Reread the question you're answering, and find key words within it that indicate the form your response should take. Key words may include *predict, trace, compare, analyze, evaluate, support,* and *criticize.*

Once you have identified exactly what the question is asking, stay within those limits to keep your topic narrow and focused.

Match Key Words to the Thesis

To narrow your topic, find the key words in an essay question, and write a thesis statement that answers the question. Use that thesis statement as a guide when you draft your essay. This will help you to keep your topic focused and to answer effectively and completely the question that is being asked.

Elizabeth Barrett Browning
1803–1861, Field Talfourd

Emily Dickinson, artist unknown

QUESTION: Who do you predict will have a more lasting reputation as a poet: Emily Dickinson or Elizabeth Barrett Browning? Why?

THESIS: I predict that Emily Dickinson will have a more lasting literary reputation because . . .

Considering Your Audience and Purpose

Before you begin drafting, take time to identify for whom you are writing and your purpose for writing. In most assessment situations, your audience and purpose are predetermined: You will write for evaluators and teachers, and your purpose will be to show them how well you understand your subject.

To impress your audience and achieve your purpose, choose details that support your main points and use a style of language that is formal and respectful.

▲ **Critical Viewing**
What similarities and differences can you identify between the styles of portraits shown here?
[Compare and Contrast]

Drafting

Shaping Your Writing
Choose an Organizational Method

Take time to organize your thoughts and to plan a structure for your essay. Doing so now will cut down on the amount of revision you will have to do later.

Comparison-and-Contrast Organization Use this method of organization to show how two or more subjects are alike and different. This organizational method can take two forms: subject by subject or point by point.

Chronological Organization Use chronological organization—time order—when you're asked to trace causes and effects, examine the history of something, or tell a personal story.

Nestorian Organization Use Nestorian organization when you want to build an argument or end your paper in the strongest possible way. In this method, you lead off with your second-most important point, and present the remaining points in increasing order of importance to end with your strongest observation.

Point-by-Point Organization	Subject-by-Subject Organization
Point A	Subject A
subject A	point A
subject B	point B
Point B	point C
subject A	Subject B
subject B	point A
	point B
	point C

NESTORIAN ORGANIZATION

Introduction

Second-most persuasive point

Third-most persuasive point

Remaining points, decreasing in importance

Most persuasive point

Conclusion

Providing Elaboration

As you draft, make your writing convincing and give it depth by providing supporting details. The supporting details you choose should define, restate, explain, or illustrate your main points.

Give Supporting Details

Examples may include illustrations, instances from real life, and allusions (references) to literary works or actual experiences.

Quotations may come from a well-known person or from a literary work.

Comparisons may be drawn from the past, the present, reality, or fiction. Comparisons help your readers understand vague or unfamiliar ideas.

Personal observations may include your opinions and experiences. You might also draw upon books you've read or movies you have seen.

Student Work
IN PROGRESS

Name: *Tricia Bushnell*
Buena High School
Ventura, CA

Elaborating With Supporting Details
Tricia used various kinds of details to support the main ideas presented in her essay.

German naval policy, on the other hand, did little to influence sympathy toward Germany. While Britain had been building ties with the United States, Germany had slowly been destroying any hope for them. With the sinking of the *Lusitania*, and later the *Arabian* and the *Sussex*, it became clear that Germany was not going to follow the previous standards of war.

> This sentence reinforces the topic sentence of the paragraph.

> This factual evidence further explains German naval policy.

14.3 Revising

Revise your writing as best you can, given the time allotted. Following are several strategies for revising your essay.

Revising Your Overall Structure

Make the Introduction and Conclusion Match

Review your essay to be sure your introduction and conclusion match. Your introduction should state your thesis or main idea and preview the contents of the essay. Your conclusion should reinforce the ideas presented in the introduction.

▶ **REVISION STRATEGY**
Listing Main Points

Read through your introduction, and list the main points you made there. Then, list the main points that you made in your conclusion. If the majority of the main points on your lists do not match, revise either the introduction or your conclusion so that they match more closely.

The following introduction and conclusion work well together. The introduction states the main points, and the conclusion reiterates them and gives readers more to think about.

Introduction
✓ 1. Superhighways changed how we live.
✓ 2. Cars promoted urban flight.
3. Suburbs became desirable places to live.

Conclusion
✓ 1. Cars and the development of highway systems had a huge impact on American life.
✓ 2. The rise of suburbs led to the fall of cities.
3. Will the coming of virtual offices promote flight to exurbs?

▲ Critical Viewing
What dominant impression is revealed in this photograph? **[Analyze]**

Revising Your Paragraphs

Develop and Build Your Argument or Thesis

Your essay should build an argument or develop your thesis, or main point. Make sure that the paragraphs in your essay work together, building to your conclusion.

▶ **REVISION STRATEGY**
Locating and Ranking Main Ideas

Reread each paragraph, and jot down its main idea. Then, review the main ideas, and assign them a ranking based on their relative importance. Review your list, and switch the order of paragraphs, if necessary, to build or develop your argument or thesis.

Revising Your Sentences

Create Sentence Variety

Review your draft to be sure that your sentences begin in a variety of ways.

▶ **REVISION STRATEGY**
Checking Sentence Beginnings

Read quickly through your draft, and look at the beginnings of your sentences. If more than three sentences in a row begin the same way, rewrite or combine some of them to break up the pattern and add interest and variety to your writing.

Revising Your Word Choice

▶ **REVISION STRATEGY**
Replacing or Deleting "Empty and Hedging Words"

Locate "empty words" and "hedging words" (words that take away from meaning) in your essay, and replace or delete them. The chart at right contains words and phrases you should eliminate from your essay:

Empty Words/ Hedging Words
by way of; despite the fact that; what I mean is; in my opinion; needless to say; to the extent that; there are; the reason was that; the thing is; almost; it seems; kind of; quite; rather; somewhat; sort of; tends; nearly

Student Work
IN PROGRESS

Name: *Tricia Bushnell*
Buena High School
Ventura, CA

Deleting Empty and Hedging Words
After closely examining her draft, Tricia deleted some words that added nothing.

Although President Wilson proclaimed neutrality at the start of the war, it soon became ~~somewhat~~ clear that the U.S.'s economic heart belonged to Britain and the Allies. Impeded by the British blockade, Americans, ~~needless to say,~~ found it substantially harder to trade with Germany.

Editing and Proofreading

Misspellings indicate sloppiness or carelessness on the writer's part. Be sure you correct misspellings before you hand in your essay.

Focusing on Spelling

For Open-Book and Nontimed Essays Use a dictionary to check the spellings of words about which you are unsure. If you are working electronically, use a spell-check feature to help you catch errors. Don't, however, rely on spell-checks to catch all typographical errors. A spell-check, for instance, will not catch the mistaken use of "he" for "the" or "you" for "your."

For Timed-Test Essays If you are aware of mistakes you often make in spelling, scan your writing for such mistakes now. Otherwise, check for common errors, such as misspellings in "*i* before *e* words" and homophones such as *to, too, two; its, it's;* and *there, they're,* and *their.*

Grammar in Your Writing
Spelling *ie* and *ei* Words

Use the traditional rule for spelling words with an *ie* or *ei* combination: "Use *i* before *e* except after *c* or when sounded like *a,* as in *neighbor* or *sleigh.*"

chief   ceiling   freight   tier

The most common exception to this rule involves words that contain the *sh* sound spelled with a *c.*

ancient   conscience

Following are some more exceptions to the rule:

either   foreign   heir   height   seize   neither   forfeit   their

Find It in Your Writing Read through your essay to be sure you've correctly spelled words containing either *ei* or *ie.*

To learn more about spelling rules, see Chapter 30.

14.5 *Publishing and Presenting*

Building Your Portfolio

1. **Portfolio** Save your completed essay in your portfolio. Attach a small note on which you describe when and where you took this test.

2. **Guidance Counselor** Give a copy of your writing for assessment to your guidance counselor for his or her review. Then, make an appointment with the counselor to discuss how to best take advantage of your writing skills.

Reflecting on Your Writing

Take a few moments to think about writing for assessment. Then, answer the following questions, and save your responses in your portfolio.

- Were you satisfied with the question you chose to answer? Why or why not?

- If you were to coach someone on how to write effectively for assessment, what points would you emphasize? Why?

 Internet Tip

To see essays scored with this rubric, go on-line:
PHSchool.com
Enter Web Code:
eek-1001

Rubric for Self-Assessment

Use the following criteria to evaluate your writing for assessment:

	Score 4	Score 3	Score 2	Score 1
Audience and Purpose	Uses appropriately formal tone; clearly addresses writing prompt	Uses mostly formal tone; adequately addresses prompt	Uses some informal tone; addresses writing prompt	Uses inappropriately informal tone; does not address writing prompt
Organization	Presents an effective, consistent organizational strategy	Presents a clear organizational strategy with few inconsistencies	Presents an inconsistent organizational strategy	Shows a lack of organizational strategy
Elaboration	Provides several ideas to support the thesis; elaborates each idea; links all information to support thesis	Provides several ideas to support the thesis; elaborates most ideas with facts, details, or examples; links most information to thesis	Provides some ideas to support the thesis; does not elaborate some ideas; does not link some details to thesis	Provides no thesis; does not elaborate ideas
Use of Language	Uses excellent sentence and vocabulary variety; includes very few errors	Uses adequate sentence and vocabulary variety; includes few errors	Uses repetitive sentence structure and vocabulary; includes many errors	Demonstrates poor use of language; generates confusion; includes many errors

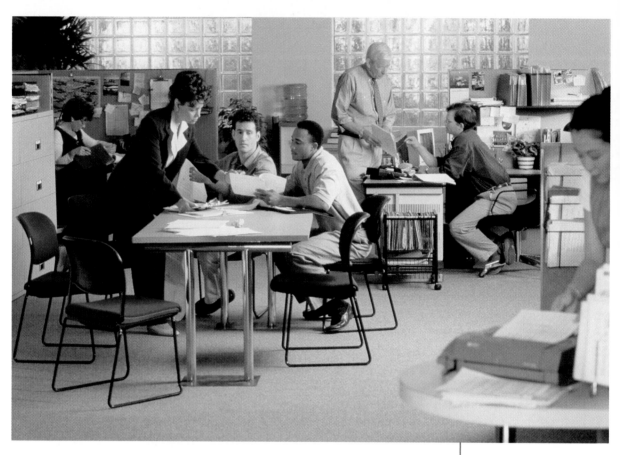

Workplace Writing in Everyday Life

When you complete a deposit slip at the bank or write a letter proposing your school as a site for a county competition, you are using workplace writing skills. Workplace writing helps people communicate with their classmates, co-workers, customers, or club members. It also carries messages from business to business and government to government. Effective workplace writing can inform consumers about their purchases, advise employees of changes in company policy, move time-linked information quickly, and even communicate important messages from one world leader to another.

▲ Critical Viewing
What clues in this photograph indicate that writing is an important workplace skill? **[Analyze]**

What Is Workplace Writing?

Workplace writing includes many different written products, all of which are fact-based and geared to communicate specific information in recognizable formats. Most pieces of workplace writing are informative or persuasive in nature. The ways we publish workplace writing are changing rapidly and now include the postal service, messengers, e-mail, interoffice memos, electronic bulletin boards, and more. Effective workplace writing

- gets a message across as clearly, directly, and briefly as possible within the chosen format.
- anticipates and answers any questions the readers might have.
- addresses manageable topics and stays focused on those topics.
- is neatly formatted and effectively organized.
- contains accurate information.

Writers in
ACTION

As you move into adult life and use workplace writing more and more frequently, remember these words spoken long ago by British author and dictionary writer Samuel Johnson:

"Knowledge is of two kinds. We know a subject ourselves, or we know where we can find information upon it."

There are many rules and conventions governing workplace writing. When you don't understand them or find them unfamiliar, ask!

Types of Workplace Writing

There are several basic forms of workplace writing that you may encounter over the next few years. Others you'll get to know when you enter the work force full time. Each type of workplace writing has its own purpose and audience:

- **Business letters** are written to communicate information on business topics of interest to the writer and recipients.
- **Meeting minutes** provide a written record of the issues, facts, and opinions addressed at a meeting for the benefit of those present and other interested parties.
- **Forms and applications** must be completed in many different situations in order to provide specific factual information requested by a business or corporation.

PREVIEW
Chapter Contents

In this chapter, you will become familiar with several examples of workplace writing, including a business letter, minutes of a meeting, and forms and applications. Writing techniques accompany the examples to guide you as you practice workplace writing.

Business Letter

What Is a Business Letter?

Business letters address every type of business issue in all fields and professions, from a letter of complaint to a letter congratulating a team of employees for a job well done. An effective business letter

- includes six parts: the heading, the inside address, the salutation, the body, the closing, and the signature.
- follows one of several acceptable forms: Each part of the letter begins at the left margin when you use a *block format*. In a *modified block format*, the heading, the closing, and the signature are indented to the center of the page.
- contains formal, polite language, regardless of its content.

> In the **heading,** include your own address and the date on which the letter is sent. Including a phone number or e-mail address is optional.

Model Business Letter

In this business letter, Sam Kendra inquires about counselor jobs at a local camp.

> In the **inside address,** include the name and title of the addressee, as well as the company or organization name.

> In the **salutation,** use the addressee's work title. If you do not have the name of a specific person within the company, use "To whom it may concern:"

> In the **body** of the letter, state your purpose and include important details.

> Depending on whom you are addressing and your purpose, decide on an appropriate **closing**. Options include "Sincerely," "Respectfully," "Regards," and "With regret."

3599 Parkview Drive
Marietta, GA 30060
(001) 376-5983

March 14, 20–

Jackson Ramirez, Director
Marietta Department of Parks and Recreation
800 Turner Road
Marietta, GA 30066

Dear Mr. Ramirez:

I am interested in working as a counselor in your summer camp program. I attended the camp myself as a young child and had a great time. My experiences at the camp taught me important lessons that I'd like to help other youngsters learn.

Please send me some information about becoming a Parks and Recreation counselor. What are the dates and hours that the camp will run? How many counselors will you be hiring, and when do you plan to begin the process?

I'm eager to work as a counselor and hope you will consider me for the job. Although I've never been a counselor, I have three younger brothers and sisters, so I'm used to organizing activities for young children. I love sports and nature.

I appreciate the time you will take to answer my questions and look forward to meeting you soon.

Sincerely,

Sam Kendra

Sam Kendra

TOPIC BANK

To write a business letter that communicates successfully, choose a situation with which you are familiar. If you're having trouble coming up with your own topic, consider these possibilities:

1. **Letter About a Pet** Suppose you've just gotten a pet—an animal that you never had before. Write a letter to a local pet store, pet owners' association, or veterinarian asking for information about how to care for your pet.

2. **Letter About Computers** Many schools are changing their technology systems to include more or different kinds of computers. To help them make successful choices, they may ask for student input. Write a letter to your local school board in which you identify ways that you use computers. Make at least one suggestion about the features school computers should have.

Prewriting Identify to whom you will be writing, and jot down his or her address, company name, business title, and business address. Then, take a few moments to think about why you are writing—what you hope to achieve by writing the letter. Also, take notes on the questions you have and how you would like the recipient of the letter to respond.

Drafting As you draft, follow the format—block or modified block—that you have chosen. Provide necessary details that clearly explain why you are writing. Remember to keep a positive and appreciative tone in letters that request something, but always remain polite even in letters of complaint.

Revising Carefully review your letter. Check to be sure that you clearly state your purpose in the opening lines. The paragraphs that follow should contain only necessary information; delete details that stray from your main point. Also, review your language to be sure that you have chosen formal language.

Editing and Proofreading Begin by checking your letter's format for correctness and consistency. Then, check to be sure that you have spelled names, addresses, titles, and phone numbers correctly.

Publishing Write, type, or word-process your letter on 8 1/2 x 11 inch paper. Keep the appearance of your letter conservative to focus the reader's attention on the content. Always sign a business letter to show that you stand behind its words. Mail your neatly folded letter in a properly addressed and stamped matching envelope.

Meeting Minutes

What Are Meeting Minutes?

Meeting minutes are a written record of a meeting—of the issues discussed, the opinions expressed, and any votes taken concerning group actions. Effective meeting minutes

- note the meeting's attendees, absentees, and date and time of the meeting.

- list and summarize issues discussed at the meeting and note action items—steps to take to resolve issues.

- contain factual information only.

> In the heading, identify the group members, the reason for the meeting, and the date of the meeting.

Model Meeting Minutes

Tracy Mueller published the following minutes of a meeting that she attended for her school newspaper.

> Meetings usually begin with ongoing, or "old" business such as reviewing the minutes of the previous meeting.

> Title each topic, briefly summarize the discussion and opinions presented, and then describe the action items and tell who is assigned to each.

> Use features such as bulleted lists, boldface, and underlining to help readers quickly find the information they need.

> Sign meeting minutes so that group members know whom to contact to have information clarified or corrected.

Monthly Editorial Meeting: November 8, 20--

Attended: Tuong Tran, John Applebee, Doreen Rigoletti, T. J. Bairos, Paul Nathan, Suzanne Wood, Tracy Mueller
Absent: Jennie Wu

Old Business

- <u>October Meeting Minutes:</u> Minutes of last month's meeting were read. Tuong corrected the chart of closing dates, noting that February's closing date is unusual because of President's Day.

- <u>New Camera Fund:</u> We need $50 more to buy a camera. T. J. suggested that we ask the school board to fund the remaining money. A motion was made and unanimously approved to make the request at the December board meeting. John will make the presentation.

Action Item: Prepare written presentation to board. (Paul and Doreen) Present proposal to board. (John)

New Business

- <u>December Issue:</u> Staff members discussed articles planned for December in order to choose a lead story. Tracy suggested the article on vacation activities for the lead. Tuong felt we should lead with the article on ways to help others during the holidays. Everyone agreed, including Tracy, that this was the best lead.

Action Item: Write and lay out lead story. (Doreen)

Next Meeting: December 2, 20-- (Remember that this meeting will be before school, due to after-school rehearsals for holiday events.)

Respectfully submitted,

Tracy Mueller

TOPIC BANK

When taking minutes of a meeting, come prepared with notepaper, some pens, and your attention. If you'd like to practice writing meeting notes and need some help getting started, consider these possibilities:

1. **Minutes of the Club Meeting** People form clubs to enjoy common interests, such as gardening or skiing. Attend the meeting of a club you belong to, or ask permission to visit the meeting of one you don't belong to. Record and write up minutes of the meeting.

2. **Minutes of a Family or Neighborhood Meeting** Discussions by family members and neighbors about how to handle common issues such as garbage collection or late-night noise are meetings, even if they are not formally labeled this way. Get permission to record meeting minutes at one of these gatherings.

Prewriting Gather and scan handouts offered at the meeting. Then, write down the names of people present. Use short sentences or phrases to jot down the issues addressed and the views expressed. List actions agreed to, and note the people to whom they are assigned. Organize your notes in a consistent way—using people's initials to indicate various speakers, for example. Keep any handouts after the meeting for later reference.

Drafting Prepare the minutes as soon as you can after the meeting. That way, your memory will be fresh. If there was a meeting agenda, follow its organization; if not, organize your notes chronologically. As you draft, use headings, boldface, or other type features to make your organization clear.

Revising First, reread your original notes against your draft to be sure that you have left nothing out. Then, review your draft for clarity. Delete cluttering details and revise emotionally biased words to reflect a neutral tone. Add or change organizational features, such as numbered lists and bulleting, to help readers locate information easily.

Editing and Proofreading Review the minutes, and correct any spelling and grammar errors you have made. If there are any inconsistencies in your formatting, correct them now.

Publishing Print out and distribute your meeting minutes before your group has its next meeting. If group members are on-line, you may prefer to send the meeting notes to group members via e-mail.

15.3 Forms and Applications

What Are Business Forms?

Forms are preprinted documents with spaces for the user to enter specific information. Some contain directions; others assume that users will follow the labels and common conventions. Two common forms in the workplace are *fax cover sheets* and *applications*. An effectively completed form

- is accurately and completely filled out.
- is written in blue or black ink.
- contains only information that is requested on the form.

> Using letterhead or otherwise heading the page with the sender's name immediately tells readers who is sending the fax.

Model Fax Cover Sheet

A fax (short for facsimile) *is a document that is electronically transmitted. Cover sheets tell whom the fax is for, whom it is from, and how long it is. The cover sheet should also list a phone number for the transmitter, in case the recipient has difficulty receiving or reading the fax.*

> A fax should contain the recipient's full name and title or the name of the company, to ensure that it gets delivered.

> Note the total page count (including the cover sheet) so that recipients can tell whether all the pages have been transmitted.

> Cover sheets are usually completed by hand. Neat handwriting is a must, especially as some clarity can be lost in transmission.

YOUNGS PRINTING
45 Hook Street • Utica, NY 11581
phone 315.555.3166 • fax 315.555.2244 e-mail:
young@nynet.com

Fax

FACSIMILE COVER SHEET

DATE: _10/25/20--_

TO: _Marci Conroy — c/o Hale High School_

FAX NUMBER: _315-555-5983_

FAX SOURCE TRANSMISSION NUMBER: _315-555-2244_

FROM: _Peter Dabbs_

TOTAL NUMBER OF PAGES (including this cover sheet): ___2___

REMARKS:

We'll be ready to print your newspaper by next Tuesday. I need to know how many copies you want so I can order the necessary paper stock. I've attached prices for different quantities. Call, fax, or e-mail me when you've settled on a number. Talk to you soon.

Thanks! Peter

Model Application

Many young people work part-time jobs to make money for school expenses or other needs. Often, potential employers will use a standard form like this one to gather basic information about job applicants.

APPLICATION FOR EMPLOYMENT

PRE-EMPLOYMENT QUESTIONNAIRE EQUAL OPPORTUNITY EMPLOYER

Kaleikini Video

Date _____ 6/8/--

Forms such as this one contain limited space in which to write. When filling out an application, print neatly in small letters.

Personal Information

NAME (LAST NAME FIRST) Hoskins, Jane		SOCIAL SECURITY NO. 145-01-2020		
PRESENT ADDRESS 705 Street	CITY Honolulu	STATE Hawaii	ZIP CODE 96813	
PERMANENT ADDRESS same	CITY	STATE	ZIP CODE	
PHONE NO. (001) 661-0947	REFERRED BY Lisa Du Plessis			

Labels like this one ask for specific information. Be sure to read each label carefully before filling in a space.

Employment Desired

POSITION sales clerk	DATE YOU CAN START 6/15/20--	SALARY DESIRED $7/hr.

ARE YOU EMPLOYED? ☐ Yes ☑ No	IF SO, MAY WE INQUIRE OF YOUR PRESENT EMPLOYER? ☐ Yes ☐ No

EVER APPLIED TO THIS COMPANY BEFORE? ☐ Yes ☑ No	WHERE	WHEN

When given several options, like this, use a check mark or an X to indicate the option that is correct or preferred.

Education

Name and Location of School		Years Attended	Did you graduate?	Subjects Studied
Grammar School	Mead Elementary	6	yes	general studies
High School	Honolulu High	2	expect to in 20--	

Former Employers

Date Month and Year	Name and Address of Employer	Salary	Position	Reason for Leaving
From 6/20/-- To 9/20/--	Honolulu Park & Rec 530 S. King Street	$6/hr.	counselor on summer arts program	summer ended
From 10/20/-- To 5/20/--	Anakua Street Theatre 5 Anakua Street	$6.50/hr.	usher candyseller	needed different hours

Because space is limited, use standard symbols and abbreviations, such as "$" and "hr."

PART

2

Grammar, Usage, and Mechanics

Delta, 1990, Paul Giovanopoulos, Louis K. Meisel Gallery, New York

Nouns, Pronouns, and Verbs

Every word you use can be classified as one of the eight *parts of speech*: nouns, pronouns, verbs, adjectives, adverbs, prepositions, conjunctions, and interjections.

Nouns, pronouns, and verbs form the heart of a sentence. Nouns are words that name people, places, and things. In writing about World War I, for instance, you might use nouns to name ships, planes, generals, countries, and so forth. Pronouns act as stand-ins for nouns. Instead of repeating the name each time, you may use the pronouns *he, she,* or *they.* Verbs tell something about nouns and pronouns, often by expressing some kind of action. For instance, you might write *Planes landed, and troops moved.* The words *landed* and *moved* are verbs.

The next three sections will explain these three important parts of speech.

▲ Critical Viewing
What nouns can you use to name the people, places, and things in this photo? [Identify, Relate]

Diagnostic Test

Directions: Write all answers on a separate sheet of paper.

Skill Check A. Identify the nouns in the following sentences. Label each *common* or *proper* and *concrete* or *abstract*. Circle any compound nouns.

1. World War I began as a local conflict between Austria-Hungary and Serbia.
2. The conflict escalated when war was declared on Russia.
3. Tension created by strong nationalism drew in other groups.
4. World War I eventually involved thirty-two nations.
5. On one side were the Allies; on the other side, the Central Powers.

Skill Check B. Identify each pronoun. Label it *personal, indefinite, reflexive, intensive, relative,* or *demonstrative.*

6. Many nations found themselves at war because of alliances they had made with other countries.
7. The war was precipitated by the assassination of Archduke Francis Ferdinand, who was heir to the Austrian throne.
8. Nationalism was one of the main factors in the war.
9. Germany, one of the primary aggressors, was itself once divided into many small principalities and kingdoms.
10. Those, however, had been united into one empire in 1871.

Skill Check C. Identify the verbs in the following sentences, and label them *action* or *linking, transitive* or *intransitive.*

11. Germany declared war on Russia on August 1, 1914.
12. The French mobilized on the same day.
13. A large-scale war appeared inevitable in Europe.
14 Concern in the United States grew as Germany employed submarine warfare.
15. American forces landed in France in 1917.

Skill Check D. Write the verb phrases in the following sentences, and underline each helping verb.

16. There had been many threats of war in Europe prior to World War I.
17. In one crisis, Germany had supported Morocco when it was agitating for independence from France.
18. This crisis was eventually settled by international conferences.
19. Austria-Hungary had annexed Bosnia and Herzegovina, and the Serbs had threatened to declare war.
20. Several diplomatic efforts had been made after the archduke was assassinated, but they had failed.

Nouns

The names people give to themselves and others, to the places where they live, and to the things that surround them are called *nouns*.

▶ **KEY CONCEPT** A **noun** is a word that names a person, place, thing, or idea. ■

Concrete and Abstract Nouns

Some nouns name things that can be perceived with the senses. Other nouns name qualities, characteristics, or ideas that are not known through the senses.

▶ **KEY CONCEPT** **Nouns** name things that can be seen and touched as well as those things that exist as concepts: ideas, qualities, and conditions. ■

The chart below shows examples of a variety of types of nouns.

CATEGORIES OF NOUNS			
People	Wilhelm	citizen	Aunt Jo
Places	beach	battlefield	Europe
Visible Things	hand	tree	lightning
Ideas	freedom	religion	friendship
Actions	decision	treatment	punishment
Conditions	health	dismay	happiness
Qualities	wisdom	strength	courage

Nouns that name people, places, or things that can be seen or recognized through any of the five senses are called *concrete nouns*. Nouns that name other things—such as ideas, actions, conditions, and qualities—are called *abstract nouns*.

Collective Nouns

Another special type of noun is used to name *groups* of people or things. Nouns of this type are called *collective nouns*.

COLLECTIVE NOUNS: community   army   team   flock
                  class   family   club   committee

Do not confuse collective nouns—nouns that name a collection of people or things acting as a unit—with plural nouns.

Theme: World War I
....
In this section, you will learn about nouns. The examples and exercises in this section are about World War I.
....
Cross-Curricular Connection:
Social Studies

GRAMMAR IN

LITERATURE

from **Swimming to Antarctica**
Lynne Cox

Notice the concrete nouns in the following excerpt.

I stared out the *window* at the brown crescent-shaped *beach*. There were snow-covered *hills* directly above the *beach*, and massive *glaciers* on either side.

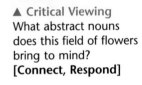

Compound Nouns

Some nouns—such as *Private Jones, son-in-law,* and *baseball*—consist of two or more words acting as a unit.

▶ **KEY CONCEPT** A **compound noun** is a noun that is made up of more than one word. ■

▲ **Critical Viewing**
What abstract nouns does this field of flowers bring to mind?
[Connect, Respond]

Notice the three ways in which compound nouns are formed:

TYPES OF COMPOUND NOUNS		
Separated	Hyphenated	Combined
fire engine soap opera	rock-and-roll jack-of-all-trades	toothbrush dishwasher

▶ **Exercise 1** Classifying Nouns Identify the nouns in the following sentences, labeling each *concrete* or *abstract*. Circle each compound noun. Underline each collective noun.
1. Prewar Europe was permeated by nationalism.
2. Political and economic rivalries existed between countries.
3. My class learned that European economic expansion was chiefly centered in Africa.
4. Feeling a military threat, each nation maintained a large army even in peacetime.
5. Archduke Ferdinand was the heir-presumptive to the Austro-Hungarian throne.

▶ **More Practice**

Grammar Exercise Workbook
• pp. 1–4
On-line Exercise Bank
• Section 16.1
Go on-line:
PHSchool.com
Enter Web Code:
eek-1002

▶ **Exercise 2** Writing With Nouns Write a paragraph using each of the following nouns: *soldiers, team, fund-raiser, general, bravery, victory, battlefield.*

Common and Proper Nouns

All nouns are either *common nouns* or *proper nouns*.

> **KEY CONCEPTS** A **common noun** names any one of a class of people, places, or things. A **proper noun** names a specific person, place, or thing. ■

Proper nouns always begin with capital letters.

Spelling Tip

Every proper noun begins with a capital letter. Consult a dictionary if you are unsure whether a noun is common or proper.

Common Nouns	Proper Nouns
novelist	Willa Cather, Erich Remarque
continent	North America, Africa
city	Paris, Berlin
planet	Mercury, Venus

Note About *Names of Family Members:* A noun used to describe a person's role in a family may be either common or proper, depending on how it is used. A name used simply to indicate a person's role is a common noun. A name used as a title before a personal name or as a name in direct address should be capitalized as a proper noun.

COMMON: My favorite person is my *uncle*.
PROPER: My favorite person is *Uncle* Barry.
DIRECT ADDRESS: Please, *Dad*, may I go out tonight?

> **Exercise 3** Distinguishing Between Common and Proper Nouns Identify each noun as *common* or *proper*. Supply a proper noun of the same category for each common noun. Supply a common noun of the same category for each proper noun.

1. town
2. war
3. continent
4. Wilhelm
5. League of Nations
6. England
7. country
8. general
9. battle
10. June

> **Exercise 4** Writing With Common and Proper Nouns Write a sentence using each of these words as a common noun. Then, write a sentence using each as part of a proper noun: *aunt, president, river, war, mountains.*

▼ Critical Viewing
Think of some proper nouns to explain where these soldiers might be. **[Speculate]**

Section Review

GRAMMAR EXERCISES 5–9

▶ **Exercise 5** Identifying Nouns
Identify the nouns in each sentence, and label them *concrete* or *abstract*.

1. The assassination of the Austrian archduke was a result of extreme nationalism.
2. Austria issued a declaration of war against the Serbs.
3. Soon, every major power in Europe was involved in the conflict.
4. To the east, the Russians achieved several victories against the Germans.
5. The reinforcement of the German Army enabled it to drive the enemy back to Russia by 1915.
6. No decision was achieved in the east, but Russia lost many men and supplies.
7. In December 1914, the Turks began an invasion of the Russian Caucasus region.
8. Russia sought the aid of the Allies to remove some of the Turkish pressure.
9 The Allied landings at Gallipoli were failures.
10. The United States maintained its neutrality until 1917.

▶ **Exercise 6** Recognizing Kinds of Nouns Identify the nouns in each sentence, labeling each *common* or *proper*. Also, indicate whether a noun is *collective* or *compound*.

1. In 1917, the Allies began an invasion of Greece and pressured the king to abdicate.
2. After King Constantine abdicated, the government of Greece declared war on the Central Powers.
3. Besides Greece, battles took place in other areas of the Balkans, in Italy, and in the Middle East.
4. After Russia and Romania made peace with the Central Powers, the outlook seemed ominous for the rest of the European community.
5. Allied progress in the Balkans led to the defeat of Bulgaria.
6. The Allied campaign in the Middle East also came to a successful conclusion in 1918.
7. The success of the Allied army led to the breakup of the Austro-Hungarian Empire.
8. The Czechs and the Slovaks formed a democratic state, the emperor abdicated, and an armistice was concluded.
9. The treaty of Versailles and other treaties changed the face of Europe.
10. People put their trust in the League of Nations to maintain peace.

▶ **Exercise 7** Find It in Your Reading
Read through a section of a history book about World War I. Find two examples of each of the following types of nouns: *abstract, concrete, common, proper, collective*, and *compound*.

▶ **Exercise 8** Find It in Your Writing
In a sample of your own writing, find five common nouns, one collective noun, and one compound noun. Name a proper noun that could replace each common noun. Explain whether replacing each common noun would or would not make your writing more clear.

▶ **Exercise 9** Writing Application
Write a brief account of an event that changed history in some way. Include at least two proper nouns, one compound noun, and one collective noun.

Pronouns

Repeating the same noun over and over in writing or speaking results in awkward, choppy sentences. You can avoid repeating the same noun by using substitutes called *pronouns*.

▶ **KEY CONCEPT** **Pronouns** are words that act as stand-ins for nouns or for words that take the place of nouns. ■

Antecedents of Pronouns

Pronouns get their meaning from the words they stand for. These words are called *antecedents*.

▶ **KEY CONCEPT** **Antecedents** are nouns (or words that take the place of nouns) for which pronouns stand. ■

In the following examples, the arrows point from the pronouns to their antecedents. In the first sentence, the pronouns *you* and *your* stand for the noun *Tom*. In the second sentence, the pronoun *it* stands for a group of words that takes the place of a noun, *Making chili for dinner.*

EXAMPLES: Tom, did *you* submit *your* article on New Mexico?

       Making chili for dinner was easy, and *it* was fun.

Antecedents usually come before their pronouns, as in the examples above. Sometimes, however, this pattern is reversed:

EXAMPLE: *That* is the best book I have ever read.

▶ **Exercise 10**   Identifying Pronouns and Antecedents
Identify each pronoun and its antecedent.
   (1) Taos in New Mexico is famous for its art colonies. (2) The area attracts artists who are drawn to its beauty. (3) The town was settled by Spaniards in the early seventeenth century, and they called it Don Fernando de Taos. (4) Native Americans and Spaniards traded their goods in town. (5) Author D. H. Lawrence did some of his writing there in the 1920's.

Theme: Tourist Attractions
····················
In this section, you will learn about pronouns. Examples and exercises in this section are about tourist attractions in various states.
····················
Cross-Curricular Connection: Social Studies

Get instant feedback! Exercise 10 is available on-line or on CD-ROM.

▶ **More Practice**

Grammar Exercise Workbook
• pp. 5–8
On-line Exercise Bank
• Section 16.2
  Go on-line:
  PHSchool.com
  Enter Web Code:
  eek-1002

Personal, Reflexive, and Intensive Pronouns

The pronouns that you use most often to refer to yourself, to other people, and to things are called *personal pronouns*. *Reflexive* and *intensive pronouns* are formed by adding *-self* or *-selves* to some of the personal pronouns.

Personal Pronouns

Personal pronouns are used more often than any other type of pronoun.

▶ **KEY CONCEPT** **Personal pronouns** refer to (1) the person speaking, (2) the person spoken to, or (3) the person, place, or thing spoken about. ■

◀ **Critical Viewing** What might you assume about the people who made this pottery? **[Infer, Support]**

First-person pronouns refer to the person who is speaking. *Second-person pronouns* refer to the person spoken to. *Third-person pronouns* refer to the person, place, or thing spoken about.

PERSONAL PRONOUNS		
	Singular	Plural
First Person	I, me, my, mine	we, us, our, ours
Second Person	you, your, yours	you, your, yours
Third Person	he, him, his, she, her, hers, it, its	they, them, their, theirs

In the first example below, the antecedent of the personal pronoun is the person speaking. In the second, the antecedent of the personal pronoun is the person being spoken to. In the last example, the antecedent of the personal pronoun is the thing spoken about.

FIRST PERSON: *My* name is not George.

SECOND PERSON: When *you* left for camp, *you* forgot *your* raincoat.

THIRD PERSON: Don't judge a book by *its* cover.

Reflexive and Intensive Pronouns

Pronouns that end in *-self* or *-selves* are either reflexive pronouns or intensive pronouns.

> **KEY CONCEPTS** A **reflexive pronoun** ends in *-self* or *-selves* and adds information to a sentence by pointing back to a noun or pronoun earlier in the sentence. An **intensive pronoun** ends in *-self* or *-selves* and simply adds emphasis to a noun or pronoun in the same sentence. ■

The reflexive and intensive pronouns are shown in the following chart.

REFLEXIVE AND INTENSIVE PRONOUNS		
	Singular	**Plural**
First Person	myself	ourselves
Second Person	yourself	yourselves
Third Person	himself, herself, itself	themselves

A reflexive pronoun always adds information to a sentence. It cannot be left out without changing the meaning. In the first example, *himself* tells whom Michael taught. In the second, *herself* tells for whom the jeans were bought.

REFLEXIVE: Michael taught *himself* to play the guitar.

Gloria bought *herself* a new pair of jeans.

An intensive pronoun emphasizes its antecedent but does not add information to a sentence. If an intensive pronoun is removed, a sentence will still have the same meaning.

Usually, an intensive pronoun immediately follows its antecedent, as shown in the first of the following examples. Sometimes, however, an intensive pronoun is located in another part of the sentence, as shown in the second example.

INTENSIVE: The President *himself* attended the gala opening.

We spliced the cable *ourselves*.

> **More Practice**
>
> Grammar Exercise Workbook
> • pp. 7–8
> **On-line Exercise Bank**
> • Section 16.2
> *Go on-line:*
> PHSchool.com
> *Enter Web Code:*
> eek-1002

GRAMMAR IN LITERATURE

from **Games at Twilight**
Anita Desai

The personal pronouns in this passage are highlighted in blue italics.

But Ravi would not let *them*. *He* tore himself out of *his* mother's grasp and pounded across the lawn into *their* midst, charging at *them* with *his* head lowered so that *they* scattered in surprise. "*I* won, *I* won, *I* won," he bawled, shaking *his* head so that the big tears flew. "Raghu didn't find *me*. . . ."

⊘ Learn More

To learn more about how to use pronouns correctly, see Chapter 23, "Pronoun Usage."

▶ **Exercise 11** Identifying Personal, Reflexive, and Intensive Pronouns
Identify each pronoun and label it *personal, reflexive,* or *intensive.*
1. Have you ever been to Houston?
2. Is Daniel himself making the plans?
3. Houston is a large city, but it is not the state's capital.
4. The city was named after Samuel Houston; he was the first president of Texas when it became independent.
5. Independence itself lasted less than ten years.
6. During Texas's time as a republic, Houston was its capital.
7. The city found itself growing rapidly.
8. Not only was Samuel Houston president of the Republic of Texas, he was among the first to represent the state when it was admitted to the Union.
9. The citizens of Houston are proud of their city, its symphony, and its Museum of Fine Arts.
10. Houston has many parks, among them Hermann Park.

▲ **Critical Viewing** How would you describe this scene in one sentence? What pronouns can replace the nouns you used? **[Assess]**

▶ **Exercise 12** Revising to Use Pronouns to Avoid Repetition
Revise this paragraph, replacing nouns with pronouns to avoid repetition. You might also combine some of the sentences.

Paul and Robert visited Houston last spring. Paul and Robert loved spending time in Houston. Paul's uncle Richard lives in Houston. The two boys stayed at Uncle Richard's house. Uncle Richard invited Paul and Robert to come back for another visit. Paul and Robert told Uncle Richard that next winter would be an ideal time.

Demonstrative, Relative, and Interrogative Pronouns

Three other kinds of pronouns—called *demonstrative, relative,* and *interrogative* pronouns—have very special uses.

▶ **KEY CONCEPT** **Demonstrative pronouns** direct attention to specific people, places, or things. ■

The following chart shows the four demonstrative pronouns.

DEMONSTRATIVE PRONOUNS	
Singular	Plural
this, that	**these, those**

Demonstrative pronouns may come before or after their antecedents:

BEFORE: *That* is the ranch I would like to own.

AFTER: I hope to visit Butte and Helena. *Those* are my first choices.

One of the demonstrative pronouns, *that,* can also be used as a *relative pronoun.*

▶ **KEY CONCEPT** A **relative pronoun** begins a subordinate clause and connects it to the rest of the sentence. ■

RELATIVE PRONOUNS
that   which   who   whom   whose

In the following sentences, relative pronouns connect a subordinate clause (shown in blue) to a word (shown in red).

EXAMPLE: He found the cattle *that* he had lost.

Carl, *whom* we all admire, rides well.

All relative pronouns except *that* can also be interrogative pronouns.

KEY CONCEPT An **interrogative pronoun** is used to begin a question. ∎

The following chart shows the five interrogative pronouns.

INTERROGATIVE PRONOUNS
what   which   who   whom   whose

In the following examples, notice that interrogative pronouns do not always have specific antecedents.

EXAMPLES: *What* did you say?

Which of the answers is best?
With *whom* did you wish to speak?
Mine is blue. *Whose* is red?

Exercise 13 Recognizing Demonstrative, Relative, and Interrogative Pronouns Identify the pronoun in each of the following sentences. Then, label each *demonstrative, relative,* or *interrogative.*

1. Butte, whose full name is Butte-Silver Bow, is in southwestern Montana.
2. The city is situated in an area that is rich in minerals.
3. What is the history of Butte?
4. Butte was settled by prospectors, who came to mine gold in the 1860's.
5. That was an activity later replaced by silver mining.
6. Was this later replaced by copper mining?
7. Gold, silver, and copper were the metals mined there; those brought prosperity to the area.
8. Which is more interesting: Butte's historic district or the Copper King Mansion?
9. The community, which was named after a nearby butte, was incorporated in 1897.
10. We learned about energy research, tourism, medicine, and mining; these have been most important to Butte's economy.

Exercise 14 Writing With Demonstrative, Relative, and Interrogative Pronouns Write an imaginary dialogue between you and a friend, discussing an interesting place that one of you has visited. Use at least four demonstrative pronouns, three relative pronouns, and three interrogative pronouns.

Spelling Tip

Do not confuse *who's* and *whose. Who's* is always a contraction of *who is* and should never be used as a pronoun.

▶ **More Practice**

Grammar Exercise Workbook
• pp. 9–10
On-line Exercise Bank
• Section 16.2
  Go on-line:
  PHSchool.com
  Enter Web Code:
  eek-1002

Interactive Textbook

Complete the exercises on-line! Exercises 13 and 14 are available on-line or on CD-ROM.

Indefinite Pronouns

Indefinite pronouns also often lack specific antecedents.

KEY CONCEPT **Indefinite pronouns** refer to people, places, or things, often without specifying which ones. ■

INDEFINITE PRONOUNS			
Singular		Plural	Singular or Plural
another anybody anyone anything each either everybody everyone everything little	much neither nobody no one nothing one other somebody someone something	both few many others several	all any more most none some

SPECIFIC ANTECEDENT: *Several* of the guests were late.
NO SPECIFIC ANTECEDENTS: *Everyone* ate *everything* offered.

In addition to functioning as pronouns, indefinite pronouns can also function as adjectives.

PRONOUN: *Few* are as famous as the Cleveland Orchestra.
ADJECTIVE: *Few* orchestras are as famous as this one.

Exercise 15 Recognizing Indefinite Pronouns Identify the indefinite pronouns in the following paragraph.

EXAMPLE: Did you eat any?
ANSWER: any

(1) Cleveland has several ways to attract visitors. (2) Everybody will enjoy the Rock and Roll Hall of Fame and Museum. (3) The museum is open for most of the year. (4) Something to remember is that admission is free on Wednesday evenings in the summer. (5) Anyone joining the museum receives unlimited free admission. (6) Many of the artists with exhibits at the museum do not allow their items to be photographed. (7) Not everyone likes rock-and-roll. (8) The Cleveland Ballet is popular with some. (9) More of the city's cultural institutions are found in University Circle. (10) Here are Cleveland's museums of art and natural history; each is worth a visit.

More Practice

Grammar Exercise Workbook
• pp. 11–12
On-line Exercise Bank
• Section 16.2
   Go on-line:
   PHSchool.com
   Enter Web Code:
   eek-1002

Get instant feedback! Exercise 15 is available on-line or on CD-ROM.

Section Review

GRAMMAR EXERCISES 16–22

► **Exercise 16** Identifying Pronouns and Antecedents Identify the pronoun and antecedent in each sentence. If a pronoun has no antecedent, write *none*.

1. Ithaca, which is in southcentral New York, is located on Cayuga Lake.
2. It was settled in 1789.
3. De Witt Clinton, the American statesman, made his home in Ithaca.
4. Residents of Ithaca find themselves surrounded by great natural beauty.
5. There are many cliffs and deep ravines, and their beauty is overwhelming.

► **Exercise 17** Identifying Personal, Reflexive, and Intensive Pronouns Identify the pronouns, and label each *personal*, *reflexive*, or *intensive*.

1. Taos, New Mexico, sits in the hills near its neighbor, Santa Fe.
2. The city itself has long been attractive to visitors from other states and countries.
3. They enjoy the beauty of the land and the spirit of the residents there.
4. At the Kit Carson Home and Museum, you can look at objects owned by Carson himself.
5. Literary buffs can occupy themselves at the D. H. Lawrence Ranch and Shrine.

► **Exercise 18** Recognizing Demonstrative, Relative, and Interrogative Pronouns Identify the pronouns in each sentence, and label them *demonstrative*, *relative*, or *interrogative*.

1. Visitors who come to Houston find a thriving city in southeast Texas.
2. These are often people interested in the history and culture of the area.
3. Which would you like to see: the ballet or the opera?

4. The Houston Grand Opera, whose home is in the Civic Center Complex, performs at the Gus Wortham Theater Center.
5. That is the theater of the Houston Ballet.

► **Exercise 19** Supplying Indefinite Pronouns Complete each sentence by adding an indefinite pronoun.

1. Has __?__ here visited Cleveland, Ohio?
2. __?__ of the attractions in Cleveland's park system include a zoo and an aquarium.
3. The Metropolitan Park System gives __?__ a chance to enjoy nature.
4. A __?__ of Cleveland's roads lead to Lake Erie.
5. Not __?__ can name __?__ of the Great Lakes.

► **Exercise 20** Find It in Your Reading Identify the reflexive pronoun in the excerpt from "Games at Twilight" on page 223. Then, find an example of this type of pronoun in another piece of literature.

► **Exercise 21** Find It in Your Writing In your own writing, find at least one example of each of these kinds of pronouns: *personal, demonstrative, relative, interrogative,* and *indefinite*. Then, replace at least two nouns with pronouns.

► **Exercise 22** Writing Application Write a short description of a city you would like to visit. Use at least two of each type of pronoun.

Action Verbs and Linking Verbs

Nouns are necessary to name all people, places, and things. To tell something about the nouns, *verbs* are also necessary.

> **KEY CONCEPT** A **verb** is a word that expresses time while showing an action, a condition, or the fact that something exists. ∎

Action Verbs

> **KEY CONCEPT** An **action verb** is a verb that tells what action someone or something is performing, has performed, or will perform. ∎

In the following examples, the verbs tell what actions have been or are being performed by Hank and the horse.

ACTION VERBS: Hank *painted* the toolshed.
The horse *waited* patiently.

GRAMMAR IN LITERATURE

from **How Much Land Does a Man Need?**

Leo Tolstoy
Translated by Louise and Aylmer Maude

The action verbs in this passage are highlighted in blue italics.

He *unfastened* his girdle and *tied* it tight below his stomach, *put* a little bag of bread into the breast of his coat, and, tying a flask of water to his girdle, he *drew* up the tops of his boots, *took* the spade from his man, and *stood* ready to start.

Theme: New Mexico

In this section, you will learn about verbs. The examples and exercises in this section are about New Mexico.

Cross-Curricular Connection: Social Studies

▼ Critical Viewing
What action verbs could you use in describing this picture? **[Describe]**

▶ **Exercise 23** Identifying Action Verbs Identify the action verb in each of the following sentences.

1. The earliest known inhabitants of New Mexico arrived around ten thousand years ago.
2. The Pueblo people inhabited adobe dwellings.
3. Nomadic Navajo and Apache peoples settled in New Mexico in the fifteenth century.
4. They attacked the Pueblo peoples, leading to four centuries of warfare.
5. Europeans learned about New Mexico in the late 1500's.

▶ **Exercise 24** Supplying Action Verbs On a separate sheet of paper, complete each sentence by supplying an action verb.

1. Spanish conquerers __?__ control of the land from the Native Americans.
2. The United States Army __?__ New Mexico in 1846 and claimed it for the United States.
3. The United States government __?__ the Arizona Territory from western New Mexico.
4. In 1863, the government __?__ the boundaries of New Mexico to their present position.
5. When people __?__ gold and silver, mining became a major industry.

Transitive and Intransitive Verbs

An action verb can be *transitive* or *intransitive*, depending on whether or not it transfers its action to another word in the sentence.

▶ **KEY CONCEPTS** A **transitive verb** takes an object. An **intransitive verb** does not direct its action to an object. ■

The word that receives the action of a transitive verb is called the *object* of the verb. The object is often a noun or pronoun.

Intransitive verbs do not have objects. The action is not directed toward any noun or pronoun in the sentence.

To find out whether a verb in a sentence is transitive or intransitive, ask *Whom?* or *What?* after the verb. If you can find an answer in the sentence, the verb is transitive. If there is no answer, the verb is intransitive

TRANSITIVE: Robert *polished* his saddle.
             Polished *what?* (saddle)

INTRANSITIVE: Linda *waited* for the wagon.
             Waited *what?* (*no answer*)

▶ **More Practice**

Grammar Exercise Workbook
• pp. 13–14
On-line Exercise Bank
• Section 16.3
Go on-line:
PHSchool.com
Enter Web Code:
eek-1002

Complete the exercises on-line! Exercises 23 and 24 are available on-line or on CD-ROM.

Most action verbs can be transitive or intransitive, depending on their use in the sentence. Some action verbs, however, can only be transitive, and others can only be intransitive.

TRANSITIVE
OR INTRANSITIVE: I *wrote* a letter from New Mexico.

The secretary *wrote* quickly.

ALWAYS TRANSITIVE: California grapes *rival* those of France.
ALWAYS INTRANSITIVE: She *winced* at the sound of his voice.

Consult a dictionary if you are uncertain about whether an action verb should have an object.

▶ **Exercise 25** Distinguishing Between Transitive and Intransitive Verbs Write the verb in each sentence. Then, label each *transitive* or *intransitive*. Finally, write the object of each transitive verb.

1. People call New Mexico the Land of Enchantment.
2. Tourists flock there for the beautiful scenery.
3. They also enjoy the state's unique culture.
4. The New Mexican landscape comprises four regions.
5. The Rocky Mountains extend southward into the state.
6. Western New Mexico contains part of the Colorado Plateau, a land of cliffs, canyons, and flat-topped hills.
7. Part of the Great Plains lies in the eastern part of the state's high peaks.
8. The basin and range region consists of wide valleys and high peaks.
9. The Rio Grande flows through New Mexico.
10. The Continental Divide crosses the state from north to south.

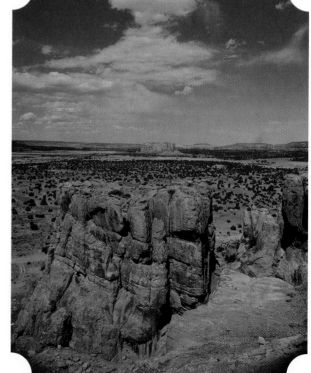

▶ **Critical Viewing** How would you describe this landscape? [**Analyze, Identify**]

Linking Verbs

Linking verbs link, or join, two or more words in a sentence.

More Practice

**Grammar Exercise
Workbook**
• pp. 15–16
On-line Exercise Bank
• Section 16.3
  Go on-line:
  PHSchool.com
  Enter Web Code:
  eek-1002

KEY CONCEPT A **linking verb** is a verb that connects a word or words at or near the beginning of a sentence with a word or words at or near the end. ∎

In the following examples, *was* connects the subject *Sam Houston* with the word *president,* and *is* connects the subject *calf* with the words *miserable and scared.* The verbs allow *president* and *miserable and scared* to help identify or describe the subjects.

LINKING VERBS: Sam Houston *was* president of Texas from 1841 to 1844.

The feverish calf *is* miserable and scared.

The above examples both use verbs that are forms of *be,* the most common linking verb. *Be* has many different forms, as shown in the following chart.

THE FORMS OF *BE*			
am	am being	can be	have been
are	are being	could be	has been
is	is being	may be	had been
was	was being	might be	could have been
were	were being	must be	may have been
		shall be	might have been
		should be	must have been
		will be	shall have been
		would be	should have been
			will have been
			would have been

Note About *Verbs Expressing Existence:* The forms of *be* do not always function as linking verbs. Instead, they express existence, usually by showing where something is located. The following examples show forms of *be* expressing existence.

EXAMPLES: Your shirt *is* in the closet.
             There *are* several mistakes in that article.

Twelve other verbs may also act as linking verbs. The verbs are shown in the chart on the next page.

OTHER LINKING VERBS					
appear	feel	look	seem	sound	taste
become	grow	remain	smell	stay	turn

These verbs also allow another word in the sentence to name or describe the subject of the sentence.

EXAMPLES: He *remained* a hermit for many years.

The music *sounded* tuneless to her.

Exercise 26 Recognizing Forms of *Be* Used as Linking Verbs Write each sentence, underlining the linking verb. Then, draw an arrow to show which words are linked by the verb. If the verb does not function as a linking verb, write *none*.

EXAMPLE: New Mexico <u>could have been</u> our home.

1. New Mexico was physically larger in the last century.
2. It is a land of magnificent and varied scenery.
3. The deserts have been there for thousands of years.
4. Irrigation would be impossible without reservoirs.
5. The landscape must have been very unfamiliar to European settlers.
6. Most rainfalls in New Mexico are brief and heavy.
7. The winters are drier than the summers.
8. The state is home to a wide variety of animal life.
9. Human impact has been a negative influence on some species.
10. The state will be the subject of interest long into future decades.

Exercise 27 Identifying Other Linking Verbs Write each sentence, underlining the linking verb. Then, draw an arrow to show which words are linked by the verb.

1. Despite the dry climate, agriculture remains economically important in the state.
2. Ranching seems more profitable than farming.
3. Overgrazing appeared ruinous to the grasslands.
4. As a result, the number of cattle became smaller.
5. With improved grazing practices, the outcome looks promising.

More Practice

Grammar Exercise Workbook
• pp. 17–18
On-line Exercise Bank
• Section 16.3
  Go on-line:
  PHSchool.com
  Enter Web Code:
  eek-1002

Get instant feedback! Exercises 26, 27, 28, and 29 are available on-line or on CD-ROM.

Linking Verb or Action Verb?

Most of the verbs in the chart on page 232 can be either linking verbs or action verbs. To see whether a verb is a linking verb, substitute *am, are,* or *is* for the verb. If the substitution makes sense and connects two words, then the original is a linking verb. Otherwise, the original is an action verb.

▶ **KEY CONCEPT** *Am, are,* or *is* will make sense when substituted for another linking verb in a sentence. ■

Notice how each of the verbs in these examples has been tested to see whether it is an action verb or a linking verb.

EXAMPLES: The breeze *felt* cool.
The breeze *is* cool? (linking)
Henry *felt* the sand.
Henry *is* the sand? (action)

▶ **Exercise 28** **Distinguishing Between Linking Verbs and Action Verbs** Identify each verb as either an action verb or a linking verb.
1. Reminders of the advanced cultures in New Mexico thousands of years ago remained today.
2. The Santa Fe Trail remained popular as a trading route between St. Louis and Santa Fe in the early 1880's.
3. Railroads appeared rapidly in New Mexico after the 1880's.
4. New Mexico sounds ideal for outdoor enthusiasts.
5. Chili peppers, which taste hot, are an important New Mexican crop.

▶ **Exercise 29** **Supplying Linking Verbs and Action Verbs** Complete each sentence with a form of one of the following verbs: *remain, feel, grow, look, sound, appear,* or *taste.* Label each verb *linking* or *action.*
1. New Mexicans ___?___ proud of their blend of cultures.
2. At Carlsbad Caverns National Park, tourists can ___?___ at the largest underground cave system in North America.
3. The echoes in the caves ___?___ eerie.
4. The New Mexican desert ___?___ beautiful at sunrise.
5. Have you ever ___?___ chili?

▼ Critical Viewing
What actions might the inhabitants of these dwellings perform? [Infer, Interpret]

Hands-on Grammar

Intransitive Verb Translator

Divide a sheet of paper into three columns. Label the first column *Subject,* the second column *Action Verb,* and the third column *What?* Then, fold the paper so the third column does not show. In the *Action Verb* column, list the following verbs: *traveled, blew, called, visited, wandered, waited, believed, asked,* and *helped.* In the *Subject* column, write a subject that makes sense with the verb. Read the sentence you have constructed.

Unfold the paper so that the third column shows. Add an object to each subject-verb combination. Before you add an object, the verb is intransitive. When you add an object, the verb becomes transitive. You may notice, however, that you cannot add an object to some of your subject-verb combinations because some verbs are always intransitive.

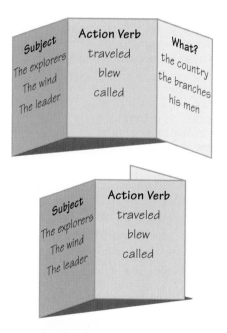

Find It in Your Reading Try this activity out with subject-verb combinations from an interesting piece of nonfiction that you read recently.

Find It in Your Writing Try the activity with subjects and verbs from a piece of your own writing.

Section 16.3

Section Review

GRAMMAR EXERCISES 30–36

Exercise 30 Identifying Transitive and Intransitive Action Verbs Identify the action verb in each sentence, and label it *transitive* or *intransitive*.

1. People often imagine New Mexico as a faraway, quiet place.
2. In fact, New Mexico has developed into a vital, vibrant, and diverse state.
3. Many interesting and unusual events have occurred in New Mexico.
4. For instance, the federal government selected Los Alamos as a site for nuclear research in 1942.
5. Some people wonder about supposed extraterrestrial landings in Roswell.

Exercise 31 Supplying Action Verbs Complete each sentence by supplying an action verb. Label the verb *transitive* or *intransitive*.

1. Taos, a small town, ___?___ national fame as an art center.
2. The Santa Fe Opera ___?___ outdoors during the summer.
3. Billy the Kid ___?___ from the Old Lincoln County Courthouse in 1881.
4. Sheriff Pat Garrett ___?___ Billy in Fort Summer, New Mexico.
5. To this day, many visitors ___?___ in the state's lakes and reservoirs.

Exercise 32 Recognizing Linking Verbs Write each sentence, underlining the linking verb. Draw an arrow showing which words are linked by the verb.

1. Santa Fe is the second-oldest city in the United States.
2. The Palace of the Governors is now the home of major museums.
3. This building had been the seat of government during the Spanish and Mexican occupations.
4. Native American and Hispanic cultures remain influential in New Mexico.
5. Native Americans seem eager to contribute to the social and economic affairs of the state.

Exercise 33 Distinguishing Between Linking Verbs and Action Verbs Complete each sentence with a form of one of the following verbs: *feel, grow, look, sound, taste, appear.* Then, label the verb *linking* or *action*.

1. Even a hot day in New Mexico ___?___ comfortable because the air is so dry.
2. Farmers in New Mexico ___?___ chili peppers, onions, and potatoes.
3. This chili ___?___ very hot and spicy.
4. When I ___?___ something spicy, I drink a big glass of water after it.
5. When the sun first ___?___, it shows off the colors of the landscape.

Exercise 34 Find It in Your Reading Choose ten verbs in a short story from your literature book. Label each action verb *transitive* or *intransitive*. Then, identify any linking verbs.

Exercise 35 Find It in Your Writing In your writing, find five examples of action verbs and five examples of linking verbs. Identify the words that are connected by the linking verbs.

Exercise 36 Writing Application Write ten sentences using these verbs, both as linking verbs and as action verbs.

taste, remain, stay, turn, become

Verb Phrases

One verb may consist of as many as four words. Acting as a unit, these words form a *verb phrase*.

> **KEY CONCEPTS** A **verb phrase** is made up of a main verb and one or more helping verbs. Any of the many forms of *be* as well as some other verbs can be used as helping verbs. ■

Below are other verbs besides *be* that can be used as helping verbs.

HELPING VERBS OTHER THAN *BE*			
do	have	shall	can
does	has	should	could
did	had	will	may
		would	might
			must

Remember that the verb *be* can also be the main verb in a sentence. Many of the helping verbs above can be used with *be.*

Helping verbs are sometimes called *auxiliary verbs* or *auxiliaries* because they help add meaning to other verbs. Notice how helping verbs change the meaning of the sentences in the following chart.

Without Helping Verbs	With Helping Verbs
I *talk* on the telephone.	I *will talk* on the telephone.
He *returned* that book.	He *should have returned* that book.

A verb and its helping verbs are sometimes interrupted by other words, especially in questions.

UNINTERRUPTED
VERB PHRASE: The groundhog *will see* its shadow.

INTERRUPTED
VERB PHRASES: The groundhog *will* probably not *see* its shadow.

Will the groundhog *see* its shadow?

Theme: Alcatraz Island

In this section, you will learn about verb phrases. The examples and exercises in this section are about the history of Alcatraz Island.

Cross-Curricular Connection: Social Studies

◀ **Critical Viewing** Why would Alcatraz Island (shown here) make an ideal spot for a prison? **[Analyze]**

Exercise 37 Recognizing Verb Phrases Identify the verb phrase or phrases in each sentence. Do not include any words that come between the helping verb and the main verb. Indicate which verb in each phrase is the helping verb.

1. During the Civil War, the Confederacy hoped that Colonel Johnston would somehow help them bring California into the Confederacy.
2. Confederate sympathizers could not have been more wrong about Colonel Johnston.
3. He had, in fact, been born in the South.
4. However, Johnston would still do what he felt to be his duty.
5. During the Civil War, Alcatraz Island was considered the chief Union defense post of San Francisco Bay.
6. Though Johnston had been arming it for defense, no one attacked the island.
7. A group of Confederates had planned to attack the island, but the scheme was ruined after one of them had foolishly bragged of the plan in a public place.
8. How might the success of this plan have affected the outcome of the Civil War?
9. The island's weapons were never used, and by the end of the war, they had become obsolete.
10. The island was then turned into a military prison, and many Confederate sympathizers were incarcerated there.

More Practice

Grammar Exercise Workbook
• pp. 19–20
On-line Exercise Bank
• Section 16.4
  Go on-line:
  PHSchool.com
  Enter Web Code:
  eek-1002

Get instant feedback! Exercise 37 is available on-line or on CD-ROM.

> **Exercise 38** Supplying Helping Verbs Add a helping verb to complete each sentence.
> 1. Alcatraz Island ___?___ become home to numerous colonies of birds.
> 2. The island's natural and manmade features ___?___ preserved by the National Park Service.
> 3. The name of the island ___?___ attributed to a Spanish explorer.
> 4. He might ___?___ called it *Isla de los Alcatraces* (Island of the Pelicans) because the birds were plentiful there.
> 5. *Alcatraz* ___?___ become the anglicized form of the original name.

More Practice

Grammar Exercise Workbook
• pp. 19–20
On-line Exercise Bank
• Section 16.4
   Go on-line:
   PHSchool.com
   Enter Web Code:
   eek-1002

> **Exercise 39** Writing Sentences With Verb Phrases Write a sentence in which you use each of the following verbs as the main verb in a verb phrase.
> 1. captured
> 2. imprisoned
> 3. isolated
> 4. preserved
> 5. visited

> **Exercise 40** Revising to Add Verb Phrases Revise the following paragraph so that each sentence contains a verb phrase.
> (1) Alcatraz Island is in the middle of San Francisco Bay. (2) In 1933, the federal government built a maximum security prison there. (3) Today, the prison is a tourist attraction. (4) The west coast's oldest operating lighthouse is also on the island. (5) Another feature of the island is the beautiful views of the bay that it provides.

▶ Critical Viewing What verb phrases might you use to describe what it was like to be imprisoned in these quarters in Alcatraz? [Describe]

Section 16.4 Section Review

GRAMMAR EXERCISES 41–45

Exercise 41 Supplying Helping Verbs Complete each sentence by adding a helping verb to fill each blank.

1. The army __?__ not anticipated the problems that the isolation of the island __?__ cause.
2. Prisoners __?__ work on the island, but the cost of transporting supplies __?__ becoming increasingly expensive.
3. The Great Depression __?__ contribute to the army's decision to close Alcatraz.
4. Most of the prisoners __?__ transferred to Fort Leavenworth or Fort Jay.
5. Tourists __?__ able to see the remains of Fortress Alcatraz and the disciplinary barracks.
6. The National Park Service __?__ working to make the island more accessible to tourists.
7. Visitors __?__ advised to purchase tickets well in advance.
8. The weather on the island __?__ change suddenly.
9. Tours to the island __?__ not begin until 9:30 A.M.
10. Sometimes the island __?__ closed because of adverse weather conditions.

Exercise 42 Identifying Verb Phrases Identify the verb phrase or phrases in each sentence. Do not include any words that interrupt the verb phrases.

1. Some visitors may find the quarter-mile walk from the dock to the cell-house difficult.
2. They can certainly ride the electric shuttle.
3. Eating and drinking are permitted only on the dock; bottled water may also be purchased there.
4. Visitors should know that tours may be sold out up to a week in advance.

5. Alcatraz has been part of the Golden Gate National Recreation Area since 1972 and has now become one of its most popular destinations.

Exercise 43 Find It in Your Reading Read the following excerpt from "Diamond Island: Alcatraz," by Darryl Babe Wilson. On a separate sheet of paper, write each verb phrase. Underline the helping verb(s) in each phrase.

There was a single letter in the mailbox. Somehow it seemed urgent. The address, although it was labored over, could hardly be deciphered—square childlike print that did not complete the almost individual letters. . . . Each word pressed heavily into the paper. I could not read it but I could feel the message. "Al traz" was in the first paragraph, broken and scattered, but there. At the very bottom of the final page—running out of space—he scrawled his name. The last letter of his name, *n*, did not fit: *Gibso*.

Exercise 44 Find It in Your Writing Identify the verb phrases in a piece of your own writing. Underline the helping verb(s) in each verb phrase.

Exercise 45 Writing Application Imagine that you had to stay on an isolated island by yourself for a week. Write a description of the things that you would like to take with you. Use at least five verb phrases in your writing. Underline the helping verbs.

Adjectives
and *Adverbs*

Nouns, pronouns, and verbs make simple communication possible. These three parts of speech can express essential ideas, such as *I need food.* For more descriptive and detailed communication, however, two other parts of speech are necessary: *adjectives* and *adverbs.*

Consider, for example, the incredible variety of birds that live in the world. Each species has unique features, abilities, and habits that make it different from every other species. Adjectives and adverbs give writers the ability to communicate these differences. In the sentence *Two majestic red-tailed hawks flew gracefully,* the adjectives *two, majestic,* and *red-tailed* provide important details about the hawks, while the adverb *gracefully* describes their action.

These two parts of speech that add description and detail to your written and spoken words are called *modifiers.* In this chapter, you will examine the ways adjectives and adverbs modify other words.

▲ **Critical Viewing**
Name three adjectives to describe the mother bird and two adverbs to describe how the baby birds are crying. **[Analyze]**

Diagnostic Test

Directions: Write all answers on a separate sheet of paper.

Skill Check A. Identify all adjectives, including articles, in each of the following sentences.

1. Ostriches are the largest birds in the world.
2. Mature males may attain a height of 8 feet.
3. The birds are characterized by long, thin necks and strong legs.
4. Ostriches also have short, stubby wings, but they cannot fly.
5. The soft, fluffy feathers of the male are black and white.

Skill Check B. List the proper and compound adjectives in the following sentences, and label each one *proper* or *compound*.

6. Ostriches live on the African continent.
7. They can be found in grassland areas below the Sahara.
8. Most American students have seen ostriches only in a zoo.
9. Ostriches are the fastest two-legged animals on the planet.
10. These overgrown birds can maintain speeds of 40 miles per hour for up to 30 minutes.

Skill Check C. Identify any nouns, pronouns, or verbs used as adjectives in the following sentences. Label each appropriately.

11. Foraging ostriches eat a variety of grasses and crawling insects.
12. Like other birds, ostriches do not have any teeth.
13. They swallow most selected foods whole.
14. Ostriches consume small stones to help them digest their stomach contents.
15. These birds must also remain near a water source, as they require two gallons of water per day.

Skill Check D. In each of the following sentences, identify the adverbs and the word each adverb modifies.

16. The zoologist held an ostrich egg gently in her hands.
17. The incredibly heavy egg weighed nearly 3 pounds.
18. Female ostriches normally lay ten perfectly white eggs each season.
19. Approximately fifty eggs may be concentrated into one centrally located nest.
20. The dominant male incubates the eggs nightly, and the females incubate them daily.

Skill Check E. Identify each underlined word below as either an *adjective* or an *adverb*.

21. The ostriches stood <u>close</u> to the nest to protect their eggs.
22. Incubation is a <u>daily</u> task for the ostriches.
23. The eggs will not hatch <u>early</u>.
24. The <u>ungainly</u> birds try to chase away predators.
25. The birds are formidable because they run so <u>fast</u>.

Adjectives

Whenever you want to create a clearer picture of a person, place, or thing, you are likely to use an *adjective*.

▶ **KEY CONCEPT** An **adjective** is a word used to describe a noun or pronoun or to give a noun or pronoun a more specific meaning. ■

The way an adjective describes a word or makes it more specific is called *modification*. Modification is the act of changing something slightly. An adjective modifies a noun or pronoun by adding information that answers any of four questions about the noun or pronoun:

▶ **KEY CONCEPT** Adjectives answer the question *What kind? Which one? How many?* or *How much?* about the nouns and pronouns they modify. ■

In the following chart, the examples show adjectives that answer the four questions noted about nouns or pronouns.

QUESTIONS THAT ADJECTIVES ANSWER	
What Kind?	
large hawk	*lost* boy
metallic gleam	*purple* feather
Which One?	
that bird	*any* number
other door	*last* opportunity
How Many?	
both swans	*some* falcons
five dollars	*frequent* interruptions
How Much?	
enough birdseed	*more* fun
less effort	*adequate* space

When an adjective modifies a noun, it usually comes before the noun. Occasionally, though, the adjective may follow the noun.

Theme: Birds

In this section, you will learn how adjectives are used to modify nouns and pronouns. The examples and exercises are about different species of birds.

Cross-Curricular Connection: Science

🖊 Spelling Tip

Suffixes such as *-ive, -ible,* and *-able* are often used to transform nouns into adjectives. For example, *response* becomes *responsive* or *responsible* and *reason* becomes *reasonable.*

▶ **KEY CONCEPT** An adjective may come before or after the noun it modifies. ■

BEFORE: The *large* condor is at the zoo.

AFTER: The condor at the zoo is *large*.

▶ **KEY CONCEPT** Two or more adjectives can modify one word. ■

EXAMPLE: *Several small, fuzzy* chicks were running around the farm.

Note About *a, an,* and *the*: Three adjectives—*a, an,* and *the*—are called *articles*. *The* is called a *definite article* because it refers to a specific noun. *A* and *an* are called *indefinite articles* because they refer to any one of a class of nouns. In the examples below, *the* refers to a specific zoo, while *an* refers to any apple.

DEFINITE: We will go to *the* zoo.

INDEFINITE: The parrot ate *an* apple.

▶ **Exercise 1** Recognizing Adjectives Write the adjectives, including articles, in each sentence below.

EXAMPLE: The swift parrot chased a small lizard.
ANSWER: The, swift, a, small

1. Parrots are found in the warm tropical areas of the planet.
2. A small number of species inhabit the cooler temperate regions.
3. The colorful birds have red, green, blue, and yellow plumage.
4. Parrots eat a wide variety of hearty seeds and nutritious fruits.
5. Parrots are monogamous, often remaining with a single mate for life.

▼ **Critical Viewing** Name three adjectives to describe either of the parakeets in this picture. What question does each adjective answer about the parakeet? **[Analyze, Connect]**

▶ **More Practice**
Grammar Exercise Workbook
• pp. 21–22
On-line Exercise Bank
• Section 17.1
Go on-line:
PHSchool.com
Enter Web Code:
eek-1002

Nouns Used as Adjectives

Many nouns can be used as adjectives. They become adjectives when they modify other nouns and answer one of two questions about the nouns they are modifying.

▶ **KEY CONCEPT** A noun used as an adjective answers the question *What kind?* or *Which one?* about a noun that follows it. ■

Noun	Adjective
pineapple	*pineapple* juice (*What kind* of juice?)
summer	*summer* habitat (*Which* habitat?)

Get instant feedback! Exercise 2 is available on-line or on CD-ROM.

▶ **Exercise 2** **Identifying Nouns Used as Adjectives** Write the noun used as an adjective in each sentence below.

EXAMPLE: The macaw perched on the top of the rock ledge.
ANSWER: rock

1. Macaws are large, noisy members of the parrot family.
2. The colorful macaws live in large flocks and roost along steep canyon walls.
3. They dig small nest holes in the relatively soft sandstone.
4. Major food sources for macaws are fruits and nuts.
5. Macaws perch among the tree branches while they eat.
6. Occasionally, they will also search the forest floor for food.
7. Because they live in the warm tropics of South America, the birds do not migrate to a winter territory.
8. Unfortunately, the macaw population is dwindling because of the actions of humans.
9. Cattle ranches are the biggest threat to the remaining habitat of the macaw.
10. The birds are also threatened by wildlife poachers.

▶ **More Practice**

Grammar Exercise Workbook
• pp. 23–24
On-line Exercise Bank
• Section 17.1
  Go on-line:
  PHSchool.com
  Enter Web Code:
  eek-1002

▶ **Critical Viewing** Each part of this parrot can be named by a noun. Can any of these nouns also act as adjectives to modify another noun? Give an example. **[Speculate, Identify]**

GRAMMAR IN LITERATURE

from **What Makes a Degas a Degas?**

Richard Mühlberger

Notice the different types of adjectives, including proper and compound, highlighted in blue italics in the following excerpt.

Degas placed a *cream-colored* umbrella in the middle of the painting above some of the figures in the carriage. Near it, balanced on the back of the driver's seat, is a *black* bulldog. . . .

. . . Throughout his life, the artist drew inspiration from the masterpieces in the Louvre in Paris, one of the *greatest* museums in the world. He also found ideas in *Japanese* prints.

Proper and Compound Adjectives

Two other types of adjectives are *proper adjectives* and *compound adjectives.*

Proper Adjectives Sometimes, proper nouns are used as adjectives or changed in form to become adjectives.

▶ **KEY CONCEPT** A **proper adjective** is a proper noun used as an adjective or an adjective formed from a proper noun. ■

Notice in the following chart that proper adjectives modify nouns by answering the questions *What kind?* or *Which one?*

Proper Nouns	Proper Adjectives
Vermont	*Vermont* cheddar (*What kind* of cheddar?)
Brahms	the *Brahms* symphony (*Which* symphony?)

Sometimes, proper nouns change their form when they are used as proper adjectives.

Proper Nouns	Proper Adjectives
Shakespeare	*Shakespearean* play (*What kind* of play?)
Germany	*German* tribes (*Which* tribes?)

Proper adjectives generally begin with a capital letter.

17.1

> **KEY CONCEPT** A **compound adjective** is an adjective that is made up of more than one word. ■

Most compound adjectives are hyphenated, but some are written as combined words.

Hyphenated	Combined
freeze-dried coffee *heavy-duty* boots	*farsighted* planner *underpaid* staff

If you are uncertain about the spelling of a compound adjective, consult a dictionary.

> **Exercise 3** Recognizing Proper and Compound Adjectives
Write only the proper and compound adjectives in each sentence below, and label each. (Note: Some may be compound proper adjectives.)

EXAMPLE: Flamingos can be found in the Brazilian forests.
ANSWER: Brazilian

1. The flamingo is the name for a family of long-legged birds.
2. Scientists are fascinated by these multicolored birds.
3. Flamingos are common throughout the world, and they can be found from the African savannas to the South American mountains.
4. They are characterized by a downward-turned bill, which is used to filter underwater organisms and vegetation.
5. The largest species, called the greater flamingo, inhabits the Caribbean region.
6. The Chilean flamingo is a variety that may be found in the lowland areas of Chile and Argentina on the South American mainland.
7. The lesser flamingo is the most common type, with a worldwide population of 4 million.
8. Flamingos fashion cone-shaped nests from mud, and they generally lay one off-white egg.
9. The newborn chicks are fed by the parents for months; however, they are self-sufficient after 30 days.
10. Flamingos make their North American homes in saltwater marshes and shallow freshwater ponds.

Grammar and Style Tip

Adjectives are an essential tool for writers because they add important details. However, writers should avoid using long strings of adjectives to describe every noun. The excessive use of adjectives may complicate your message or confuse your reader.

Pronouns Used as Adjectives

Just as nouns can be used as adjectives, so can certain pronouns. In fact, some personal pronouns, known as *possessive pronouns* or *possessive adjectives,* act as both pronouns *and* adjectives. Others act as either pronouns *or* adjectives.

▶ **KEY CONCEPT** A pronoun functions as an adjective if it modifies a noun. ■

Possessive Pronouns or Adjectives Seven personal pronouns are known as *possessive pronouns* or *possessive adjectives.* They are pronouns because they have antecedents. They are adjectives because they modify nouns and answer the question *Which one?*

POSSESSIVE PRONOUNS OR ADJECTIVES						
my	your	his	he	its	our	their

ANTECEDENT   WORD MODIFIED

The *flock* reached *its* winter feeding *grounds.*

Demonstrative Adjectives All four of the demonstrative pronouns can be used as adjectives. Unlike the personal pronouns above, they become demonstrative adjectives *instead of* pronouns. When they function as adjectives, they always come before the nouns they modify and never directly before a verb.

DEMONSTRATIVE ADJECTIVES	
this that these those	
Demonstrative Pronouns	Demonstrative Adjectives
Did the bird drop *this?*	Did the bird drop *this* feather?
Those are pretty birds.	*Those* birds are pretty.

Interrogative Adjectives Three of the interrogative pronouns become *interrogative adjectives* when they modify a noun.

INTERROGATIVE ADJECTIVES	
which what whose	
Interrogative Pronouns	Interrogative Adjectives
What happened? *Whose* is that?	*What* color is the egg? *Whose* pet is the canary?

Indefinite Adjectives Many indefinite pronouns become *indefinite adjectives* when they modify nouns. The charts below show whether they modify singular or plural nouns.

INDEFINITE ADJECTIVES		
Singular	Plural	Singular or Plural
another　　much each　　neither either　　one little	both few many several	all　　other any　　some more most

Indefinite Pronouns	Indefinite Adjectives
The parakeet ate *one*.	The parakeet ate *one* nut.
Few live in the Arctic.	*Few* birds live in the Arctic.
We saw *some* at the lake.	We saw *some* ducks at the lake.

Exercise 4 Distinguishing Between Pronouns and Adjectives Identify whether the underlined word in each sentence below functions as a *pronoun* or as an *adjective*. If it functions as an adjective, tell which word it modifies.

EXAMPLE:　We watched <u>that</u> toucan fly from the perch.
ANSWER:　adjective (modifies toucan)

1. On a recent trip to the zoo, <u>my</u> friends and I learned about toucans.
2. <u>Those</u> are brightly colored birds known for <u>their</u> large beaks.
3. <u>That</u> toucan's beak measures more than half of <u>its</u> body length.
4. <u>Our</u> tour guide said <u>some</u> toucans may grow to be 25 inches long.
5. <u>These</u> interesting birds inhabit the tropical forests of Central and South America.
6. Only <u>one</u> species, the toucanet, lives in the mountains.
7. <u>All</u> toucans have two forward-facing toes and two backward-facing toes.
8. A <u>few</u> people in the group asked <u>what</u> foods were eaten by toucans.
9. The tour guide said <u>most</u> toucans eat small fruits and berries, but <u>several</u> eat insects and small lizards.
10. We asked <u>which</u> of the zoo's <u>many</u> birds was <u>his</u> favorite.

More Practice

Grammar Exercise Workbook
• pp. 25–26
On-line Exercise Bank
• Section 17.1
Go on-line:
PHSchool.com
Enter Web Code:
eek-1002

Get instant feedback! Exercises 4 and 5 are available on-line or on CD-ROM.

Verbs Used as Adjectives

Many words that look like verbs can function as adjectives in sentences.

KEY CONCEPT Some verb forms, especially those ending in *-ing* and *-ed*, function as adjectives when they modify a noun. ■

Below are verbs used first as verbs and then as adjectives.

Verbs	Adjectives
The owl *was sitting* still.	The *sitting* owl was still.
The ice *melted* in the sun.	The *melted* ice was in the sun.

Exercise 5 Distinguishing Between Verbs and Adjectives Identify whether the underlined word in each sentence below functions as a *verb* or as an *adjective*. If it functions as an adjective, tell which word it modifies.

EXAMPLE: A <u>startled</u> peacock will make a lot of noise.
ANSWER: adjective (modifies peacock)

1. The peacock, a member of the pheasant family, is known for its brilliantly <u>colored</u> feathers.
2. Only the males are <u>endowed</u> with colorful blue, gold, and green plumage.
3. The <u>camouflaged</u> females, called peahens, have drab brown-and-green feathers.
4. <u>Competing</u> males display their ornate feathers to attract mates.
5. At night, peacocks usually <u>sleep</u> in high tree branches.
6. <u>Consuming</u> small snakes and lizards, they spend their days on the ground.
7. Until recently, scientists thought that these birds <u>inhabited</u> only the forests of Southeast Asia and India.
8. The Congo peacock is a rare species that occupies a very <u>confined</u> area in central Africa.
9. Because it had eluded scientists until 1936, this bird was considered a <u>living</u> mystery when it was discovered.
10. Today, the Congo peacock is a <u>protected</u> species.

▼ Critical Viewing
Use *singing* as a verb and then as an adjective in sentences about this bird. **[Connect]**

Hands-on Grammar

Turning Verbs Into Adjectives

To practice converting verb forms into adjectives, try this activity. Take several index cards, and cut out a long opening in each to create a box with two "wings," as in the model below. On one side of the card, write a verb phrase, such as *is crying, was shouting, has been forgotten*, or *was protected*. Flip the card over, and write just the participle form on the other side: *crying, shouting, forgotten, protected*.

Tape the edges of the wings of a card onto a piece of paper. In the opening, write an article and a noun spaced apart, so that a sentence such as *The child is crying* would appear. Now, bend the card to place *crying* between *the* and *child* to create the phrase *The crying child*. Create additional verb/adjective conversions. Then, extend the activity by writing a phrase after the verb form on both sides of the card. For example: Write *was shouting at his friend* on one side of a card and *shouting at his friend* on the flip side. This time, put the article and noun close together. Connecting this new card to *The child*, you can create an introductory adjective phrase such as *Shouting at his friend* to add to a longer sentence about the child.

Find It in Your Reading In your reading, find examples of sentences that contain verb forms used in introductory adjective phrases. Write the sentences on your paper, and underline the verb form acting as an adjective and the noun being modified.

Find It in Your Writing Look through samples of your own writing to find sentences in which you have used *-ing* and *-ed* forms of verbs. Rewrite the sentences, changing the verbs to adjectives and expanding the sentences.

Section 17.1 Section Review

GRAMMAR EXERCISES 6–11

Exercise 6 Recognizing Types of Adjectives Identify each underlined adjective below as *article*, *proper adjective*, *compound adjective*, *possessive adjective*, *indefinite adjective*, or *demonstrative adjective*.

1. <u>The</u> kiwi is a <u>strange-looking</u> bird that can be found only in <u>some</u> areas of New Zealand.
2. While kiwis are defenseless, <u>their</u> survival has been made possible because they have no natural predators on <u>this</u> <u>South Pacific</u> island.
3. Although <u>New Zealand</u> kiwis have small, stubby wings, they are <u>earth-bound</u> birds that cannot fly.
4. Long, <u>hairlike</u> feathers are <u>another</u> feature of <u>a</u> kiwi.
5. It is also the only <u>Asian</u> bird that locates food by <u>its</u> sense of smell.

Exercise 7 Recognizing Other Parts of Speech Used as Adjectives Identify any nouns, pronouns, or verbs used as adjectives in the following sentences. Write them on your paper, and label each. If none are used, write *none*.

1. The owl is a bird variety that is characterized by a large head, forward-facing eyes, and sharp claws.
2. The barn owl is the most common species in the United States.
3. The smallest species resides in the deserts of the Southwest.
4. In which places besides trees and abandoned buildings do owls make their homes?
5. The burrowing owl, for instance, may make its home in old rabbit holes.
6. Most owls are active after the evening stars have emerged.
7. They are the only birds whose eyes are located on the front of the face.
8. All owls also have excellent hearing abilities to assist their hunting efforts.
9. Rain deters hunting owls, since they cannot fly quietly with wet wing feathers.
10. Though many people dislike owls, these birds are our allies against rodents.

Exercise 8 Supplying Adjectives to Add Details Rewrite the paragraph below on your paper, supplying an adjective in each blank.

(1) The wild turkey is among the ___?___ birds in North America, much bigger than most other fowl. (2) Wild turkeys are found in ___?___ areas deep among the trees. (3) Males are ___?___ and ___?___ than females and are also more ___?___ . (4) The males can also be distinguished by the wattle, a ___?___ piece of ___?___ skin that hangs from the beak. (5) The skin of the head and neck of a wild turkey is usually ___?___ in color, but it may also be a brighter shade of ___?___ or ___?___ .

Exercise 9 Find It in Your Reading In the excerpt from "What Makes a Degas a Degas?" on page 245, identify the *compound adjective* and the *proper adjective*.

Exercise 10 Find It in Your Writing In your own writing, find at least one example of each of the following kinds of adjectives: *proper, compound, possessive,* and *demonstrative*. Copy the sentences, and label each type of adjective.

Exercise 11 Writing Application Write a description of your favorite bird. Be sure to use precise adjectives to bring the bird to life for your readers.

Adverbs

Like adjectives, *adverbs* are used to describe or add information about other words.

▶ **KEY CONCEPT** An **adverb** is a word that modifies a verb, an adjective, or another adverb. ■

Just as adjectives answer questions about nouns and pronouns, adverbs answer questions about words they modify.

▶ **KEY CONCEPT** An adverb answers one of four questions about the word it modifies: *Where? When? In what way?* or *To what extent?* ■

An adverb modifying a verb can answer any of the four questions. An adverb modifying an adjective or another adverb, however, will answer only one question: *To what extent?*

The chart below shows adverbs answering each of the four questions. Notice the positions of the adverbs. When an adverb modifies a verb or verb phrase, it may come *before* or *after* the verb or verb phrase. Frequently, it comes *within* the verb phrase. If an adverb modifies an adjective or another adverb, it generally comes *immediately before* the adjective or adverb.

Verbs	Adjectives
Where?	**When?**
slide *under* move *near* sit *there* slipped *between*	*often* asks sails *daily* should have answered *promptly* *soon* will depart
In What Way?	**To What Extent?**
reacted *positively* *silently* nodded left *quickly* *rudely* laughed was *cheerfully* humming	*widely* read *barely* walks researched *further* had *just* started must *not* have finished
Adverbs Modifying Adjectives	**Adverbs Modifying Adverbs**
To What Extent?	**To What Extent?**
very tall *somewhat* satisfied *frequently* absent *not* sad	*very* thoroughly *not* exactly *more* quickly *quite* definitely

Theme: Seashells

In this section, you will learn how adverbs are used to modify verbs, adjectives, and other adverbs. The examples and exercises are about different kinds of seashells.

Cross-Curricular Connection: Science

◀ Critical Viewing
Using this photo and
the information in
Exercise 12, describe
these cowries with
phrases containing
adverbs that answer
each of the four ques-
tions on page 252.
[Analyze]

▶ **Exercise 12** Recognizing Adverbs Identify the adverbs
in each sentence below. Then, tell which word each adverb
modifies.

EXAMPLE: The porpoise swam very rapidly.

ANSWER: very (modifies rapidly), rapidly (modifies swam)

1. Cowries are a very common variety of sea snails that are
   generally found in warm tropical waters.
2. They are mostly nocturnal animals, and they usually feed
   on algae.
3. A few species crawl slowly among corals and feed hungrily
   upon them.
4. These small creatures often have brilliantly colored shells.
5. For many years, cowry shells were used quite frequently by
   people in Africa, Asia, and Melanesia as a form of currency.

Nouns Used as Adverbs

A few words that are usually nouns can also act as adverbs.

▶ **KEY CONCEPT** Nouns used as adverbs answer the question *Where?* or *When?* about a verb. ■

Some of the nouns that can be used as adverbs are *home,*
yesterday, and *today.*

Nouns	Adverbs
The crab's *home* is under that rock.	The crab crawled *home.* (crawled *where?*)
The warm, summer *nights* cause the jellyfish to rise to the water's surface.	The jellyfish are active *nights.* (are active *when?*)

▶ **More Practice**
Grammar Exercise
Workbook
• pp. 27–28
On-line Exercise Bank
• Section 17.2
  Go on-line:
  PHSchool.com
  Enter Web Code:
  eek-1002

Get instant feedback!
Exercise 12 is available
on-line or on CD-ROM.

GRAMMAR IN
LITERATURE

from **Pride**
Dahlia Ravikovitch

The adverbs in this excerpt are printed in blue italics.

And *suddenly* the rock has an open wound.
I told you, when rocks break, it happens by surprise.
And people, *too*.

▶ **Exercise 13** Recognizing Nouns Used as Adverbs Identify two adverbs in each sentence below, and write them on your paper. Then, circle each noun used as an adverb.

EXAMPLE: Yesterday, I casually walked to the beach and collected seashells.

ANSWER: Yesterday, casually

1. Weekends, I like to take my little brother to a relatively unknown stretch of seashore.
2. We carefully search the beach for shells some mornings.
3. Most days, we are seldom disappointed.
4. Today, for example, we found a dozen shells nearby.
5. My brother always races home to show our parents the assortment of cowry, cone, and conch shells that we have found.
6. Afternoons, he thoroughly cleans any sand or other debris from the shells.
7. Both of us are eagerly awaiting our trip tomorrow.
8. Sundays, we generally have the whole beach to ourselves.
9. I fully enjoy being outside in the warm sea air.
10. Unfortunately, I have to work weekdays.

💡 Spelling Tip

To form adverbs from many words ending in *y*, change the *y* to *i* and then add the suffix *-ly*. For example, *happy* becomes *happily* and *lazy* becomes *lazily*.

Adverb or Adjective?

Sometimes, the same word can be either an adverb or an adjective, depending upon how it is used in a sentence.

▶ **KEY CONCEPT** Remember that an adverb modifies a verb, an adjective, or another adverb; an adjective modifies a noun or a pronoun. ■

Notice in the following examples that the adverb modifies a verb. The same word used as an adjective, on the other hand, modifies a noun.

ADVERB: The fish swam *straight* through the channel.

ADJECTIVE: The path was *straight*.

Generally, adverbs and adjectives have different forms. Many adverbs, in fact, are formed by adding *-ly* to an adjective.

Adjectives	Adverbs With *-ly* Endings
honest response	responded *honestly*
awkward movement	moved *awkwardly*

A few words ending in *-ly*, however, are adjectives.

ADJECTIVE: We found a *lovely* shell with *curly* edges.

▲ **Critical Viewing** If you used *lovely, hard,* and *underwater* in sentences about this turtle cone shell, would those words be adjectives or adverbs? Can any of them be both? **[Distinguish]**

⚙ **Grammar and Style Tip**

When using a word ending in *-ly* directly before a noun, check to make sure that it is an adjective.

Adverbs • **255**

▲ **Critical Viewing**
Write a sentence
containing *best*, in
which you reveal
your favorite type of
shell. In your sen-
tence, is *best* func-
tioning as an adjec-
tive or an adverb?
[Connect, Analyze]

▶ **Exercise 14** **Distinguishing Between Adverbs and
Adjectives** Identify each underlined word below as an *adverb*
or *adjective*.

EXAMPLE: The small fish eggs were <u>barely</u> visible.
ANSWER: adverb

1. Cone snails are an unusual variety of sea snails that have
   <u>hard</u>, elaborately colored shells.
2. These snails are <u>quite</u> effective hunters.
3. They may feed <u>daily</u> on live or dead fish.
4. They attack their prey with <u>deadly</u> accuracy.
5. Cone snails shoot poison-tipped darts <u>straight</u> at any fish
   that swims within range.
6. The unwitting fish may work <u>hard</u> to escape before the
   snail's venom immobilizes it.
7. These <u>lovely</u> mollusks live in the warm tropical waters
   between Australia and India.
8. Occasionally, their empty shells are found among the
   <u>stately</u> palms on South Pacific islands.
9. Some of the most visually stunning varieties are spotted
   <u>only</u> occasionally by lucky searchers.
10. This rare shell is the <u>only</u> shell of its kind at the auction.

▶ **More Practice**

Grammar Exercise
Workbook
• pp. 29–30
On-line Exercise Bank
• Section 17.2
  Go on-line:
  PHSchool.com
  Enter Web Code:
  eek-1002

Section Review

GRAMMAR EXERCISES 15–20

Exercise 15 Recognizing Adverbs
List the adverbs you find in each sentence below and the word each modifies.

1. The rarely studied nautilus is an extremely odd mollusk.
2. It is related most closely to squids and octopuses, but it really bears little resemblance to its relatives.
3. This unusual shellfish is entirely enclosed in a perfectly spiraled shell.
4. The nautilus also has approximately ninety tentacles that extend ominously from the opening of its shell.
5. During the day, these odd-looking shellfish usually hide quietly among the rocks on the ocean floor.
6. Nautiluses cautiously emerge after the sun has set.
7. They gradually begin to swim toward the surface and eventually reach the shallow waters of a coral reef.
8. Nautiluses feed ravenously upon crabs, which they capture easily.
9. At first light, they rapidly retreat to the relatively safe ocean floor.
10. The nautiluses' uniquely designed shells are highly prized by collectors.

Exercise 16 Supplying Nouns
Used as Adverbs Rewrite the sentences below on your paper, supplying a noun used as an adverb to fill each blank.

1. ___?___, I regularly dive along the coral reefs.
2. ___?___, I saw a very interesting mollusk called a giant clam.
3. The 4-foot-wide creature is active ___?___ and night.
4. The incredibly heavy shell was far too big to bring ___?___.
5. ___?___, I plan to dive down to the giant clam again to show it to my cousin.

Exercise 17 Distinguishing
Between Adverbs and Adjectives Label each underlined word below *adverb* or *adjective*.

1. Hermit crabs are most often found along the Atlantic coast of the United States.
2. Despite its name, many consider the hermit crab a friendly pet.
3. Because it lacks a hard shell, the young hermit crab is vulnerable to predators.
4. It works hard to insert its body into a discarded seashell, and then it carries the shell with it wherever it goes.
5. The crab cannot keep the same shell long, since it must move to a larger shell as it grows.

Exercise 18 Find It in Your
Reading In the excerpt from "Pride," on page 254, identify the words that the highlighted adverbs modify, and indicate whether each modified word is a *verb*, an *adjective*, or an *adverb*.

Exercise 19 Find It in Your
Writing Choose a piece of writing from your portfolio, and identify five adverbs. Are there places where you can add adverbs to create a clearer picture of the action for your readers?

Exercise 20 Writing Application
Write a short essay about something you collect or would like to collect. Include adverbs to add details to verbs, adjectives, and other adverbs.

Prepositions, Conjunctions, and Interjections

Prepositions, conjunctions, and interjections add meaning to sentences. Prepositions and conjunctions make connections and show special relationships between words. Interjections add emotion and expression to a sentence.

Whether you describe places, such as famous parks, or people, such as the Navajo, you will depend on these parts of speech to help you convey meaning effectively.

Learn how to use prepositions, conjunctions, and interjections correctly while exploring this chapter.

▲ Critical Viewing
Based on this photograph, how would you compare Central Park in New York City to other parks you've visited? What prepositions and conjunctions would you use in making these comparisons? [Compare]

Diagnostic Test

Directions: Write all answers on a separate sheet of paper.

Skill Check A. Write the prepositions in the following sentences.

1. Mr. Lee's favorite park in New York City is Van Cortlandt Park.
2. This 1,100-acre Bronx park is located next to Riverdale.
3. Miles of wooded trails wind within its boundaries.
4. Apart from the woods, visitors can play baseball, cricket, or golf or relax upon its rolling green fields.
5. Many enjoy the playgrounds instead of the hiking trails.

Skill Check B. Write the complete prepositional phrases. Underline the object or objects of each preposition.

6. The Wiechquaeskeck people once lived in the area of Van Cortlandt Park.
7. According to scientists, they built their permanent settlements there about 1,000 years ago.
8. They fished along the banks of Tibbets Brook.
9. Their crops were planted upon the present-day sites of the Parade Ground and Indian Field.
10. The park's lake didn't exist when Europeans arrived in America.

Skill Check C. Label underlined words *prepositions* or *adverbs*.

11. In 1639, the Dutch West India Company purchased much of the land <u>along</u> the lower Hudson Valley from Native Americans.
12. Travel <u>through</u> it was difficult, due to unrest in the area.
13. Jacobus Van Cortlandt bought the land in the 1690's, but the wealthy Philipse family had owned it <u>before</u>.
14. He looked <u>around</u> and decided to grow crops on his land.
15. Van Cortlandt began to grow grain and to mill <u>on</u> his property.

Skill Check D. Write the conjunctions, conjunctive adverbs, and interjections in the following sentences. If the word is a conjunction, label it *coordinating, correlative*, or *subordinating*.

16. The Van Cortlandts owned the land; subsequently, they built a home and dammed Tibbets Brook.
17. Yes, you can explore both the house and the man-made lake.
18. Say, let's go to the park today, or you may prefer the museum.
19. Because it was built in 1748, it's the oldest house in the Bronx.
20. Unless I'm mistaken, their estate became parkland in 1888.

Skill Check E. Label each underlined word *subordinating conjunction, preposition*, or *adverb*.

21. Have you explored Vault Hill <u>before</u>?
22. Frederick Van Cortlandt was buried here, and this has been the family burial ground ever <u>since</u>.
23. <u>When</u> the American Revolution began, City Clerk Augustus Van Cortlandt hid New York City records from the British here.
24. <u>After</u> a time, family remains were moved to Woodlawn Cemetery.
25. <u>After</u> we explore Vault Hill, let's visit an even older burial ground.

Prepositions

Prepositions add meaning to a sentence by showing the relationship between words.

▶ **KEY CONCEPT** A **preposition** is a word that relates a noun or pronoun that appears with it to another word in the sentence. ■

Words Used as Prepositions

A preposition can affect the entire meaning of a sentence.

▶ **KEY CONCEPT** The choice of preposition affects the way the other words in a sentence relate to each other. ■

Sixty of the words most often used as prepositions are listed in the following chart.

FREQUENTLY USED PREPOSITIONS				
aboard	before	despite	off	throughout
about	behind	down	on	till
above	below	during	onto	to
across	beneath	except	opposite	toward
after	beside	for	out	under
against	besides	from	outside	underneath
along	between	in	over	until
amid	beyond	inside	past	up
among	but	into	regarding	upon
around	by	like	round	with
at	concerning	near	since	within
barring	considering	of	through	without

Some prepositions consist of more than one word and are called *compound prepositions*.

COMPOUND PREPOSITIONS			
according to	because of	in place of	next to
ahead of	by means of	in regard to	on account of
apart from	in addition to	in spite of	out of
aside from	in back of	instead of	owing to
as of	in front of	in view of	prior to

Theme: City Parks

In this section, you will learn about prepositions. The examples and exercises in this section are about city parks.

Cross-Curricular Connection: Social Studies

▶ **More Practice**

Grammar Exercise Workbook
• pp. 31–32
On-line Exercise Bank
• Section 18.1

Go on-line:
PHSchool.com
Enter Web Code:
eek-1002

GRAMMAR IN LITERATURE

from **Mowing**
Robert Frost

The prepositions in this excerpt from a poem by Robert Frost are highlighted in blue italics.

There was never a sound *beside* the wood *but* one,
And that was my long scythe whispering *to* the ground.
What was it it whispered? I knew not well myself;
Perhaps it was something *about* the heat *of* the sun,
Something, perhaps, *about* the lack *of* sound—
And that was why it whispered and did not speak.

▲ **Critical Viewing**
What prepositions might you use in describing these two men? Why?
[Describe]

Notice how choosing different prepositions affects the relationship between words and gives each sentence a different meaning.

EXAMPLE:

We saw a squirrel $\left\{\begin{array}{l}\text{inside}\\\text{near}\\\text{within}\\\text{next to}\end{array}\right\}$ the *park.*

▶ **Exercise 1** Identifying Prepositions Identify the prepositions and compound prepositions in this paragraph.
(1) Central Park, one of America's first landscaped parks, was designed by Frederick Law Olmsted and Calvert Vaux. (2) Poor Irish and German immigrants occupied the land prior to the park's creation. (3) There was also a thriving African American community, Seneca Village, at Eighth Avenue and 82nd Street. (4) The park has been open since the late 1850's. (5) It remains extremely popular, owing to its wooded paths, baseball diamonds, green lawns, and, of course, the animals in its famous zoo.

▶ **Exercise 2** Revising to See How Prepositions Affect Meaning Revise the paragraph above, replacing the prepositions with other ones from the two facing lists. Explain how the changes in prepositions alter meaning.

⚙ Grammar and Style Tip

In your writing, use the correct preposition to clarify a relationship between separate things, such as location, direction, cause, or possession.

Prepositional Phrases

> **KEY CONCEPT** A **prepositional phrase** is a group of words that includes a preposition and a noun or pronoun, called the object of the preposition. ∎

EXAMPLE: We had a picnic in the(park.)

In the preceding example, *park* is the object of the preposition *in*.

PREPOSITIONAL PHRASES	
Prepositions	Objects of the Prepositions
for *throughout* *between*	*you* the *school* *you* and *me*

> **Exercise 3** Identifying Prepositional Phrases In each sentence, identify the prepositional phrase or phrases. Write each on a piece of paper, underline the preposition, and circle its object.
> 1. In 1868, San Francisco selected the roughly 1,000 acres of the Golden Gate Park.
> 2. Few were pleased by this selection because of its windy landscape.
> 3. When John McLaren became superintendent in 1890, the site was suffering from neglect and overuse.
> 4. Under his supervision, an international exposition was held during 1894; nothing was preserved from it except the Japanese Tea Garden and a museum.
> 5. It has been a popular setting for a variety of gatherings.

> **Exercise 4** Writing Sentences With Prepositional Phrases Use each phrase in a sentence about the picture.
> 1. over the roadway
> 2. to the sky
> 3. beyond the bridge
> 4. in the distance
> 5. under the bridge

More Practice
Grammar Exercise Workbook
• pp. 33–34
On-line Exercise Bank
• Section 18.1
  Go on-line:
  PHSchool.com
  Enter Web Code:
  eek-1002

▼ Critical Viewing The Golden Gate Bridge is in California. What other prepositional phrases can you use in sentences about this bridge? **[Apply]**

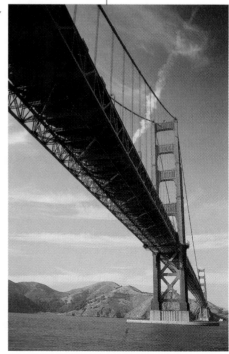

Preposition or Adverb?

Many of the words listed as prepositions in the charts on page 260 can also be adverbs.

▶ **KEY CONCEPT** Prepositions always have objects; adverbs do not. ■

If a word that can be used either as a preposition or as an adverb has an object, the word is acting as a preposition.

Prepositions	Adverbs
The smoke drifted *up* the chimney.	The dark, ugly smoke drifted *up*.
Flowers grew *along* the path.	Won't you come *along* with us?
The park is *near* our house.	We knew a park was *near*.

For a word to act as a preposition, it must have an object and be part of a prepositional phrase. In the preceding examples, notice that the adverb examples are not followed by nouns. They do not have objects.

EXAMPLE: People wandered through.
ANSWER: through (adverb)

▶ **Exercise 5** Distinguishing Between Prepositions and Adverbs Label underlined words *prepositions* or *adverbs*.
1. Hyde Park is located <u>near</u> Kensington Gardens in England.
2. Walk <u>in</u> and find a natural respite from urban London.
3. You will see horse riders trotting <u>around</u>.
4. <u>In</u> the past, the park was the hunting grounds of royalty.
5. Is the Achilles statue located <u>around</u> the park's center?

▶ **Exercise 6** Revising Sentences by Adding Objects Revise each sentence by adding an object to change the adverb to a preposition.
1. The park is near.
2. Will you walk in?
3. Stroll around and enjoy the scenery.
4. However, don't wander off.
5. The sign says "Keep off."

Section Review

GRAMMAR EXERCISES 7–12

▶ **Exercise 7** Identifying Prepositions and Prepositional Phrases Write each prepositional phrase. Then, underline each preposition and circle each object.

1. The famous Bois de Boulogne is located on the western edge of Paris.
2. It was created during the reign of Napoleon III.
3. The park was designed by Baron Georges-Eugène Haussmann.
4. According to many people, he greatly admired the large London parks, such as Hyde Park and Regents Park.
5. Napoleon wanted similar large parks for Parisians.

▶ **Exercise 8** Revising Prepositions and Prepositional Phrases Revise the following paragraph by replacing prepositions and prepositional phrases with ones that better convey the intended meaning.

(1) Have you strolled over another famous park, Boston Common? (2) It is the oldest public park from the United States. (3) The parkland was set outside in 1634. (4) It was first used for a military training ground and a cattle pasture. (5) Boston Common was enclosed on 1725, and its grounds were designed by famed architect Charles Bulfinch. (6) In the past, it was used in executions of pirates and other criminals. (7) In addition to this, the British Army camped there within the Revolution. (8) Under the park, you will see many magnificent statues and fountains. (9) A bandstand, tennis courts, and a cemetery are found among its borders. (10) In view of its historical significance, Boston Common is a fitting first stop at the famous Freedom Trail.

▶ **Exercise 9** Distinguishing Between Prepositions and Adverbs Identify each underlined word as *preposition* or *adverb*.

(1) Have you had a chance to walk around the Tuileries garden in Paris? (2) It is located near the center of the French capital. (3) The park stretches on a straight line from the Place de la Concorde to the Louvre. (4) Look around and you will see throngs of people admiring the toy boats in the square's fountain. (5) Hold on, I want to eat at one of the cafes within the Tuileries.

▶ **Exercise 10** Find It in Your Reading Identify the prepositions in this verse by Paul Simon. Then, rewrite the verse, replacing each preposition with a different one. Explain how the changes affect meaning.

> Lost in their overcoats,
> Waiting for the sunset.
> The sounds of the city
> Sifting through the trees,
> Settle like dust
> On the shoulders
> Of the old friends.

▶ **Exercise 11** Find It in Your Writing Identify at least ten prepositions in a piece of your own writing. Experiment with changing the prepositions. See if any of the changes would convey your intended meaning more clearly.

▶ **Exercise 12** Writing Application Imagine spending an afternoon boating in Central Park, as pictured on page 258. Write a description of your adventure using at least five prepositional phrases.

Conjunctions and Interjections

Section 18.2

The last two parts of speech you will learn about are *conjunctions* and *interjections*. You will use conjunctions more often than you will use interjections.

Different Kinds of Conjunctions

Unlike prepositions, which show relationships between words, conjunctions make direct connections between words.

KEY CONCEPT A **conjunction** is a word used to connect other words or groups of words. ■

Three main kinds of conjunctions connect words: *coordinating conjunctions, correlative conjunctions*, and *subordinating conjunctions*.

Coordinating Conjunctions The seven *coordinating conjunctions* connect similar words or groups of words.

COORDINATING CONJUNCTIONS						
and	but	for	nor	or	so	yet

EXAMPLES: Joaquin *and* I studied Navajo weaving and cloth making.

The loom broke, *yet* the weaver continued her work.

She hung the Navajo blanket on the wall *and* then stepped back to admire it.

She wrapped herself in the blanket, *for* it had become very cold in her room.

Correlative Conjunctions *Correlative conjunctions* are similar to coordinating conjunctions. They differ only in that correlative conjunctions are always used in pairs.

CORRELATIVE CONJUNCTIONS		
both . . . and	neither . . . nor	whether . . . or
either . . . or	not only . . . but also	

EXAMPLES: He made *neither* that blanket *nor* that rug.
Both gold *and* silver bracelets were considered.
Brenda purchased *either* a Navajo bracelet *or* a Navajo blanket.

Theme: Native Americans

In this section, you will learn about conjunctions and interjections. The examples and exercises in this section are about Native American culture and history.

Cross-Curricular Connection: Social Studies

More Practice

Grammar Exercise Workbook
• pp. 35–36
On-line Exercise Bank
• Section 18.2
Go on-line:
PHSchool.com
Enter Web Code:
eek-1002

Subordinating Conjunctions *Subordinating conjunctions* connect two complete ideas by making one of the ideas subordinate to, or less important than, the other.

FREQUENTLY USED SUBORDINATING CONJUNCTIONS			
after	because	now that	until
although	before	since	when
as	even if	so that	whenever
as if	even though	than	where
as long as	if	though	wherever
as soon as	in order that	till	while
as though	lest	unless	

The following example shows how a subordinating conjunction is used to connect related ideas.

                subord. idea   main idea

EXAMPLE: *Because* Carol practices, she is a good artist.

▶ **Exercise 13** **Identifying Conjunctions** Write the conjunction in each sentence. Then, label each *coordinating, correlative,* or *subordinating.*

1. Traditionally, Navajo men work as silversmiths, while the women are weavers.
2. Navajo silversmiths are among the most talented and creative in the world.
3. Even though they are immensely skilled in working silver, they are relatively new to the craft.
4. The Navajos had learned silversmithing from neighboring Mexicans before they were relocated by the government in 1864–1866, an event known as "The Long Walk."
5. In the late nineteenth century, Navajo fortunes improved, for traders recognized the market for the jewelry.
6. Trader Lorenzo Hubbell brought Mexican silversmiths to the reservation so even more Navajo men learned the craft.
7. These craftsmen would use not only Mexican but also United States coins for their raw material.
8. Whether it was a belt buckle, ring, necklace, or earring, the silversmiths' works were uniquely intricate.
9. While their silver work was already expert, the Navajos began adding their distinctive turquoise settings to jewelry in the late 1890's.
10. Neither the Navajo silversmiths nor the traders foresaw the great popularity of this jewelry.

▼ **Critical Viewing** What are two words you would use to describe this vase, and what conjunction would you use to connect the words? **[Describe]**

266 • Prepositions, Conjunctions, and Interjections

GRAMMAR IN LITERATURE

from **A Raisin in the Sun, Act I, Scene II**

Lorraine Hansberry

The conjunctions in the following excerpt are highlighted in blue italics.

MAMA. . . . In my time we was worried about not being lynched *and* getting to the North if we could *and* how to stay alive *and* still have a pinch of dignity too . . . Now here come you *and* Beneatha—talking 'bout things we ain't never even thought about hardly, me *and* your daddy. You ain't satisfied *or* proud of nothing we done.

Conjunction, Preposition, or Adverb?

After, before, since, till, and *until* can be subordinating conjunctions or prepositions. *After, before,* and *since* can also be adverbs. *When* and *where* can be subordinating conjunctions or adverbs. The part of speech of these words depends on their use within a sentence.

▶ **KEY CONCEPT** **Subordinating conjunctions** connect complete ideas. ■

The following examples show the word *before* used in three different ways.

SUBORDINATING CONJUNCTION:	She started to weave *before* she turned ten.
PREPOSITION:	The weaver starts work *before* sunrise.
ADVERB:	Have you ever watched a weaver make a blanket *before*?

▼ Critical Viewing
How does this picture connect to the examples shown on the left? **[Connect]**

▶ **Exercise 14** Identifying Words as Conjunctions, Prepositions, or Adverbs Label each underlined word *subordinating conjunction, preposition,* or *adverb.*

1. Navajo women have practiced the art of weaving <u>since</u> they learned the skill from Pueblo Indians in the 1800's.
2. As with silver, traders saw the potential value of Navajo-made cloth <u>when</u> setting up shops near the reservation.
3. Navajo cloths—such as blankets, belts, rugs, and bags—have been highly prized ever <u>since</u>.
4. The Navajos used pigments collected from local vegetation <u>until</u> they started weaving for a wider audience.
5. <u>Since</u> that time, they have begun to use commercially made dyes.

▶ **Exercise 15** Writing With Conjunctions, Prepositions, and Adverbs Write three sets of three sentences using *after, before,* and *until* as conjunctions, prepositions, and adverbs.

Conjunctive Adverbs

Some words act as both conjunctions and adverbs at the same time. These words are called *conjunctive adverbs.*

▶ **KEY CONCEPT** A **conjunctive adverb** is an adverb that acts as a conjunction to connect complete ideas. ■

FREQUENTLY USED CONJUNCTIVE ADVERBS		
accordingly	finally	nevertheless
again	furthermore	otherwise
also	however	then
besides	indeed	therefore
consequently	moreover	thus

Conjunctive adverbs are often used as transitions—words that serve as links between different ideas. In the following example, notice how conjunctive adverbs work to make transitions between related ideas.

EXAMPLES: They had never been on a reservation before. *Indeed,* they had never been far away from home.

It had rained during their visit; *consequently,* the outdoor Navajo art exhibit was canceled.

The conjunctive adverb is followed by a comma.

▶ **More Practice**

Grammar Exercise Workbook
• pp. 37–38
On-line Exercise Bank
• Section 18.2
Go on-line:
PHSchool.com
Enter Web Code:
eek-1002

Complete the exercises on-line! Exercises 14, 15, 16, and 17 are available on-line or on CD-ROM.

Exercise 16 Revising With Conjunctive Adverbs Revise
this paragraph, adding conjunctive adverbs to connect ideas.
(1) The Navajos live in a southwestern desert country of
mesas, cliffs, and canyons. This is reflected in the geometric
patterns they choose for their blankets and rugs. (2) They
changed their weaving styles after acquiring non-Navajo customers in the late nineteenth century. The years 1850 to 1880
are considered the "Classic Period" of weaving. (3) From the
1880's on, the Navajos adapted their weaving techniques and
traditions to satisfy tourist demands. These years are referred
to as the "Transitional Period." (4) Tourists preferred brighter
colors. Weavers began using commercial dyes in their works.
(5) Tourists also preferred rugs to blankets. Navajos began
producing more rugs.

More Practice

Grammar Exercise
Workbook
• pp. 39–40
On-line Exercise Bank
• Section 18.2
  Go on-line:
  PHSchool.com
  Enter Web Code:
  eek-1002

Interjections

Interjections are used mainly in speaking, not in writing.

KEY CONCEPT An **interjection** is a word that expresses
feeling or emotion and functions independently of a sentence. ■

Many feelings can be expressed by interjections, such as
ah, hey, oh, ouch, uh, well, or *wow.* These examples show
other interjections used to express different emotions.

| JOY: | *Hurray!* We won! | EXHAUSTION: | *Whew!* That was hard. |
| SURPRISE: | *Aha!* I found the sandpainting. | SORROW: | She knew, *alas,* the truth. |

Since interjections are independent from other words, they
are set off by exclamation marks or commas.

Exercise 17 Supplying Interjections For each sentence,
supply an interjection that suggests the specified emotion.

EXAMPLE: You spilled your milk on the rug. [dismay]
ANSWER: Oh, no! You spilled your milk on the rug.

1. I bought a Navajo blanket. [pleasure]
2. It was an imitation of a Navajo blanket. [anger]
3. Should I return it to the store? [hesitation]
4. The owner was a very large and threatening man. [fear]
5. He told me he would accept no returns. [acceptance]

**Grammar
and Style Tip**

Avoid interjections in
your formal writing
except in a special
situation such as a
direct quote.

Section Review

GRAMMAR EXERCISES 18–23

Exercise 18 Identifying **Conjunctions** Write the conjunctions in the following sentences. Then, label each *coordinating, correlative,* or *subordinating.*

1. Are you familiar with the Navajo art of sandpainting or drypainting?
2. Even though it has its roots in Navajo ceremonies, sandpainting is also a commercial art form.
3. Most scholars agree that the Navajos borrowed the idea of sandpainting and changed it to fit with their own ideas.
4. Because early sandpaintings were not permanent, there is little evidence to prove how this process occurred.
5. This sandpainting is both permanent and colorful.

Exercise 19 Identifying Different **Parts of Speech** Label the underlined words *conjunction, adverb, conjunctive adverb, preposition,* or *interjection.*

The first permanent sandpaintings were made in the late nineteenth century (1) in order that Navajo culture would be preserved. (2) Wow, did many Navajos object to this, but they were created anyway? (3) When they were published, interest in sandpaintings grew greater than (4) before. In 1915, Franc J. Newcomb, a trader's wife, befriended Hosteen Klah, a famous medicine man; (5) consequently, Newcomb amassed a large collection of sandpaintings drawn (6) both by her and by Navajos. (7) Now that it was filtering into non-Navajo land, artists began to use sandpainting motifs in permanent works. (8) Before this commercial use, however, the Navajos were careful to remove or alter certain designs. (9) However, despite their precautions, the acceptance of drypaintings as commercial art is still somewhat controversial, and (10) yes, many Navajos still do not approve.

Exercise 20 Revising With **Conjunctive Adverbs** Revise the following sentences using conjunctive adverbs.

1. The sandpainting is supervised by one person. Its construction is left to the most artistic.
2. Sandpaintings are difficult. Three to six men create one in about four hours.
3. It is made with colored pigments from rocks. The rocks must be collected and ground.
4. The paintings are made by sprinkling crushed rock over a floor of sand. Paintings for ceremonies are later destroyed.
5. Sandpaintings were created in Japan in the seventh century. They were created in England in the 1700's and 1800's.

Exercise 21 Find It in Your **Reading** Read the excerpt from *A Raisin in the Sun* on page 267. List the conjunctions, and label them by type.

Exercise 22 Find It in Your **Writing** Choose a writing sample from your portfolio. Find any conjunctions you have used. Challenge yourself to combine three to five sentences with similar ideas by connecting them using conjunctions.

Exercise 23 Writing Application Write five sentences based on the following emotions, each using an interjection and a conjunction.

1. outrage
2. sadness
3. disapproval
4. frustration
5. relief

Hands-on Grammar

Fill In the Blanks

Cut several pieces of construction paper into strips, each about an inch wide. Then, from a different-colored sheet of construction paper, cut several dozen squares about one inch by one inch. Next, write a sentence on each of the strips. Construct the sentences so that each contains one or more prepositions or conjunctions. Then, paste the squares over all of the prepositions and conjunctions.

Write prepositions and conjunctions on all of the remaining squares. Then, with a group of classmates, experiment with placing different squares in the various sentences. Discuss how the changes in the prepositions and conjunctions affect the meaning of the sentences.

When you've finished, write a few paragraphs summing up what you learned from the activity.

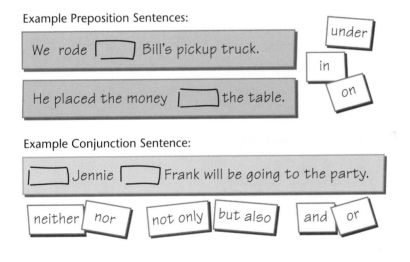

Example Preposition Sentences:

We rode [   ] Bill's pickup truck.

He placed the money [   ] the table.

under

in

on

Example Conjunction Sentence:

[   ] Jennie [   ] Frank will be going to the party.

neither   nor

not only   but also

and   or

Find It in Your Reading Try this activity with sentences from a nonfiction article that you have read recently.

Find It in Your Writing Try this activity with sentences from a piece of your own writing.

Basic Sentence Parts

◀ Critical Viewing
Who or what is
doing an action in
this photo? What is
the action? Combine
your answers into a
sentence. **[Analyze]**

The Ferris wheel is a popular attraction at carnivals. Its
simple rotating motion hides the fact that many gears and
other essential moving parts keep the wheel going around.
Similarly, you use sentences every time you speak or write,
yet you may not always think about their essential parts.

Like a Ferris wheel or any other device, a good sentence
functions well when its parts work together correctly. Knowing
how the parts of sentences work together will give you a better
understanding of how to communicate your ideas effectively.

Diagnostic Test

Directions: Write all answers on a separate sheet of paper.

Skill Check A. Write the complete subject and complete predicate in each sentence. Underline the simple subject once and the verb twice.

1. Fairs were an important part of commerce in the Middle Ages.
2. Buyers and sellers would trade commodities and merchandise.
3. Fairs improved and increased trade all over Europe.
4. Fairs for pleasure and commerce were often held together.
5. The largest fairs drew people from miles around.

Skill Check B. Write the subject of each sentence.

6. There are many fairs around the world.
7. When were these fairs established?
8. Take your brother to the fair.
9. Will Nancy be going with you?
10. Over the bridge lay the fairgrounds.

Skill Check C. Write each complement, and label it *direct object*, *indirect object*, or *objective complement*.

11. American engineer George Washington Gale Ferris invented the Ferris wheel.
12. After college, Ferris built bridges, railroads, and tunnels.
13. He eventually founded his own company.
14. He named it G.W.G. Ferris and Company.
15. Ferris showed the organizers of an 1893 exposition his plans for a 250-foot, steel-framed wheel ride.
16. The exposition organizers found his plans impressive.
17. They accepted Ferris's design.
18. Ferris promised them timely construction.
19. By selling stock in the project, he earned a profit of more than a million dollars.
20. The public considered Ferris's wheel a success.

Skill Check D. Write each complement, and label it *predicate nominative* or *predicate adjective*.

21. The most common type of fair in the United States was the agricultural fair.
22. The first United States fair, held in Massachusetts, was successful.
23. Some of the products on display were livestock, produce, and preserves.
24. The fair was quite profitable and popular among the local farmers.
25. Danbury, Connecticut, was the site of another famous fair.

Subjects and Predicates

When you are speaking to your friends, you may speak in partial sentences and still be understood. When you are writing, however, you should use complete sentences to express complete thoughts. Recognizing that every sentence must have two key parts will help you write clear, complete sentences.

Complete Subjects and Predicates

Every *sentence* that is grammatically correct consists of two parts: a *complete subject* and a *complete predicate.*

▶ **KEY CONCEPT** A **sentence** is a group of words with two main parts: a complete subject and a complete predicate. Together, these parts express a complete thought. ■

The complete subject includes a noun or pronoun that names the person, place, or thing that the sentence is about. The complete predicate includes a verb or verb phrase that tells something about the complete subject. The examples show that a complete subject or complete predicate may consist of only a single essential word (a noun or pronoun for the complete subject and a verb for the complete predicate). Often, however, a complete subject or complete predicate includes many other words that modify the essential words.

EXAMPLES: They | were celebrating in the streets.
COMPLETE SUBJECT | COMPLETE PREDICATE

The three clowns in the ring | tumbled.
COMPLETE SUBJECT | COMPLETE PREDICATE

▶ **Exercise 1** Recognizing Complete Subjects and Complete Predicates Make two columns as shown in the example. Then, write each complete subject in the first column and each complete predicate in the second column.

EXAMPLE: The fluffy squirrel chattered at us.
ANSWER:

Complete Subject	Complete Predicate
The fluffy squirrel	chattered at us.

1. Mardi Gras is celebrated in many countries.
2. The grand carnival marks the beginning of Lent.
3. Many Christians fast during Lent.
4. They indulge in merrymaking before this solemn time.
5. Food and drink are plentiful during Mardi Gras.

Theme: Carnivals

In this section, you will learn about the two main parts of sentences, subjects and predicates. The examples and exercises are about carnivals and celebrations.

Cross-Curricular Connection: Social Studies

▶ **More Practice**

Grammar Exercise Workbook
• pp. 41–42
On-line Exercise Bank
• Section 19.1
Go on-line:
PHSchool.com
Enter Web Code:
eek-1002

Interactive Textbook

Get instant feedback! Exercise 1 is available on-line or on CD-ROM.

Simple Subjects and Predicates

Every complete subject and complete predicate contains a word or group of words that is essential to the sentence.

▶ **KEY CONCEPTS** The **simple subject** is the essential noun, pronoun, or group of words acting as a noun that cannot be left out of the complete subject. The **simple predicate** is the essential verb or verb phrase that cannot be left out of the complete predicate. ■

In the following examples, notice that all the other words in the complete subject modify or add information to the *simple subject.* In the same way, all the other words in the complete predicate either modify the *simple predicate* or help it complete the meaning of the sentence.

	SIMPLE SUBJECT		SIMPLE PREDICATE	
EXAMPLES:	*Jugs* of sweet cider		*covered* the table.	
	COMPLETE SUBJECT		COMPLETE PREDICATE	

	SIMPLE SUBJECT		SIMPLE PREDICATE	
	Some *people*		*do* not *like* cider.	
	COMPLETE SUBJECT		COMPLETE PREDICATE	

Notice in the first example that the simple subject of the sentence is *jugs*, not *cider.* The object of a preposition can never be a simple subject. Notice also that in the next example, the verb phrase *do like* is split by an adverb, *not.*

Note About the Terms *Subject* and *Verb:* From this point on in this book, the word *subject* will refer to the simple subject and the word *verb* will refer to the simple predicate.

To find the subject of a sentence before the verb, ask, "What word is the sentence about?" Then, ask yourself, "What did the subject *do?*" The answer will be an action verb. If there is no answer to the second question, look for a linking verb.

EXAMPLE: The revelers marched happily through the park.
Subject: revelers *Question:* What did the revelers do? *Answer:* marched

If you find it easier to locate the verb before locating the subject, first look for an action verb or a linking verb. Then, ask *Who?* or *What?* before the verb. The answer will be the subject.

EXAMPLE: A colorful flag was hanging above the porch.
Verb: was hanging *Question:* What was hanging? *Answer:* flag

> **Exercise 2** Recognizing Simple Subjects and Simple Verbs
Write the simple subject and simple verb in each sentence.
Underline the subject once and the verb twice.

EXAMPLE: Ancient legends still fascinate us today.

ANSWER: <u>legends</u>   <u>fascinate</u>

1. Elaborate costumes abound at Mardi Gras celebrations.
2. Traditional celebrations of Mardi Gras last a full week.
3. *Mardi Gras* means "Fat Tuesday" in French.
4. The city of New Orleans is especially famous for its Mardi Gras festivities.
5. Spectacular fireworks end the carnival.

Compound Subjects and Verbs

The word *compound* describes a noun, adjective, or preposition with more than one part. *Airport*, for example, is a compound noun. *Compound* also describes subjects or verbs connected by conjunctions.

Compound Subjects The complete subject of a sentence may contain two or more subjects.

> **KEY CONCEPT** A **compound subject** is two or more subjects that have the same verb and are joined by a conjunction such as *and* or *or*. ■

In the next example, the parts of the *compound subject* are underlined once, and the verb is underlined twice.

EXAMPLE: <u>Clowns</u>, <u>balloons</u>, <u>pony rides</u>, and <u>face-painting</u> <u>were offered</u> at the carnival.

More Practice

Grammar Exercise Workbook
• pp. 45–46
On-line Exercise Bank
• Section 19.1
Go on-line:
PHSchool.com
Enter Web Code:
eek-1002

🌼 Grammar and Style Tip

Compound subjects joined with *and* take the plural form of a verb. Compound subjects joined with *or* take the form of the verb that agrees with the subject closest to the verb.

◀ **Critical Viewing**
Think of a series of actions a jester might do, and include them as compound verbs in a sentence. **[Connect]**

GRAMMAR IN
LITERATURE

from **The Dog That Bit People**
James Thurber

The compound verbs in the first sentence of this excerpt are highlighted in blue italics.

One morning when Muggs bit me slightly, more or less in passing, I *reached* down and *grabbed* his short stumpy tail and *hoisted* him into the air. It was a foolhardy thing to do and the last time I saw my mother, about six months ago, she said she didn't know what possessed me.

Compound Verbs Sentences may also contain two or more verbs in the complete predicate.

▶ **KEY CONCEPT** A **compound verb** is two or more verbs that have the same subject and are joined by a conjunction such as *and* or *or.* ■

In the following example, the compound verb has three parts.

EXAMPLE: The <u>star</u> <u>signed</u> autograph books, <u>smiled</u> at her fans, and then <u>departed</u> in a limousine.

Sentences may also have both compound subjects and compound verbs.

EXAMPLE: <u>Megan</u> and her <u>friends</u> <u>cheered</u> and <u>shouted</u>.

Note About *Compound Verbs:* When a compound verb consists of two or more verb phrases with the same helping verb, the helping verb is often used only with the first verb.

AWKWARD   The banjo <u>player</u> <u>was strumming</u> his banjo,
REPETITION: <u>was stomping</u> his feet, and <u>was singing</u> enthusiastically.

HELPING VERB   The banjo <u>player</u> <u>was strumming</u> his banjo,
NOT REPEATED: <u>stomping</u> his feet, and <u>singing</u> enthusiastically.

Exercise 3 Recognizing Compound Subjects and Compound Verbs Write the sentence. Then, underline the words that make up each compound subject once and each compound verb twice.

EXAMPLE: Harvest <u>festivals</u> <u>exist</u> in many cultures and <u>appear</u> in many varieties.

1. Flowers, fruits, and vegetables are often used to decorate homes.
2. Harvest festivals center around a happy event, feature a special crop, or honor heroes.
3. Families and friends gather together and celebrate with traditional foods and rituals.
4. New England colonists and neighboring Native Americans celebrated the first Thanksgiving Day and shared the bountiful harvest.
5. Community events and family observances provide an opportunity for reflection, celebrate heritage, and enrich culture.

Exercise 4 Revising Sentences by Forming Compound Subjects and Compound Predicates Revise each pair of sentences by combining information to form compound subjects or verbs.

EXAMPLE: After school, the band met. Then it practiced
REVISION: After school the band met and practiced.

1. Solar calendars determine the timing of some seasonal festivals. Lunar calendars determine the timing of other seasonal festivals.
2. Chinese New Year is set by the lunar calendar. It is celebrated for a whole month.
3. Boisterous parades and colorful costumes mark the celebration of Chinese New Year. Theatrical performances mark the celebration of Chinese New Year, too.
4. A Swiss festival celebrates the end of winter. At the same time, it welcomes the advent of spring.
5. The Swiss people burn straw dummies during Homstrom. They are saying goodbye to Old Man Winter.

More Practice

Grammar Exercise Workbook
• pp. 47–48
On-line Exercise Bank
• Section 19.1
   Go on-line:
   PHSchool.com
   Enter Web Code:
   eek-1002

Get instant feedback! Exercises 3 and 4 are available on-line or on CD-ROM.

Section 19.1 Section Review

GRAMMAR EXERCISES 5–10

Exercise 5 Identifying Complete and Simple Subjects and Predicates
Make two columns. Write each complete subject in the first column and each complete predicate in the second. Underline the simple subject once and the verb twice.

1. Important festivals of respect in many countries honor the dead.
2. Such festivals have long been observed.
3. Today, people continue age-old customs honoring national heroes.
4. In the Far East, festivals of the dead include family reunions and ceremonial meals at ancestral tombs.
5. Mexicans observe *El Dia de Los Muertos* (The Day of the Dead) with offerings of flowers, pottery, food, and toys.

Exercise 6 Recognizing Subjects and Predicates Write the subject and verb in each sentence, underlining the subjects once and the verbs twice. Some may be compound.

1. The most famous annual festival in Wales is the Royal National Eisteddfod.
2. The Eisteddfod honors the finest talent in Welsh literature and music.
3. Welsh language, literature, music, and culture are promoted at the festival.
4. The history of the Eisteddfod predates the Christian era.
5. The week-long ceremony revives ancient Welsh customs, offers cultural competitions, and gives Welsh poets and musicians an opportunity to perform.

Exercise 7 Revising Sentences by Creating Compound Subjects and Compound Predicates Revise each pair of sentences by combining information to form compound subjects or verbs.

1. Cultural festivals are popular all over the world. Commemorative days are also popular all over the world.
2. Kalevala Day in Finland honors the Finnish national epic, the *Kalevala*. It also recognizes the achievements of Finnish scholar Elias Lönnrot.
3. The Salzburg Music Festival is held in Austria each year. The festival celebrates the rich legacy of some of the world's finest composers.
4. Great food is a highlight of Hawaii's annual Aloha Festival. Native entertainment is also featured.
5. Film festivals, dance celebrations, and children's carnivals crowd the calendars of many nations. They attract tourists from around the world.

Exercise 8 Find It in Your Reading
Identify the simple subject and predicate of each sentence in this excerpt from "The Masque of the Red Death."

. . . [I]n this chamber only, the color of the windows failed to correspond with the decorations. The panes here were scarlet—a deep blood color.

Exercise 9 Find It in Your Writing
Look through your writing portfolio. Find examples of sentences with a compound subject or compound verb. Identify the complete subject and predicate in each sentence.

Exercise 10 Writing Application
Write a description of your favorite holiday or feast day. Tell how you celebrate the day, what food you eat, and what activities you enjoy. In each of your sentences, underline the simple subject once and the verb twice.

Hard-to-Find Subjects

In most English sentences, a subject is followed by a verb. This section will present sentences with subjects that are not so easily found.

Subjects in Orders and Directions

> **KEY CONCEPT** In sentences that give orders or directions, the subject is often understood to be *you*. ■

The following chart contrasts sentences with and without the understood *you*. The subjects are underlined once and the verbs twice. Notice in the last sentence that even when a person is addressed, the subject is still understood to be *you*.

Orders or Directions	With Understood *You* Added
Dust the furniture and then wax the floor.	[You] dust the furniture and then wax the floor.
Kim, give me an apple.	Kim, [you] give me an apple.

> **Exercise 11** Creating Sentences With Understood Subjects Use each verb in a sentence that gives an order or a direction. Add the understood subject in parentheses in each.

1. give
2. call
3. proofread
4. ask
5. train
6. ride
7. order
8. protect
9. tie
10. offer

Subjects in Inverted Sentences

In some sentences, the usual subject-verb order is *inverted*—that is, reversed. Sentences that may be inverted in English include questions and sentences beginning with *there* or *here*. In addition, some sentences are inverted for emphasis.

Subjects in Questions Questions are often inverted.

> **KEY CONCEPT** In questions, the subject often follows the verb. ■

An inverted question can begin with a verb, a helping verb, or one of the following words: *how, what, when, where, who, whose,* or *why.*

To find the subject in an inverted question, rephrase the question mentally as a statement. Then, the subject and verb will fall into the usual order.

In this section, you will learn how to locate hard-to-find subjects in sentences. The examples and exercises are about knights and castles.

Cross-Curricular Connection: Social Studies

Questions	Reworded as Statements
<u>Are</u> <u>we</u> ready?	<u>We</u> <u>are</u> ready.
<u>Do</u> <u>you</u> <u>like</u> castles?	<u>You</u> <u>do like</u> castles.
Where <u>was</u> the <u>car</u> <u>parked</u>?	The <u>car</u> <u>was parked</u> where.

Note About *Questions:* Some questions are not inverted. Those beginning with an interrogative adjective or pronoun may be in the usual subject-verb order.

EXAMPLES: Which <u>troubadour</u> <u>won</u> the prize this year?
Who <u>cares</u> about such nonsense?

▶ **Exercise 12** **Finding Subjects in Questions** Write each sentence, underlining the subject once and the verb twice.

EXAMPLE: Where <u>was</u> the <u>castle</u> <u>located</u>?

1. Who trained knights during the age of chivalry?
2. Where were the knights trained?
3. What were the requirements for knighthood?
4. Do knights still exist?
5. Was armor worn by all knights?
6. Which countries had a feudal system?
7. What are the dates of the Middle Ages?
8. Did you read about the Crusades?
9. How did gunpowder change knighthood?
10. Do knights fight in wars anymore?

Sentences Beginning With *There* or *Here* Two words that are often used to begin inverted sentences are *there* and *here.*

▶ **KEY CONCEPT** The subject of a sentence is never *there* or *here.* ■

When *there* or *here* begins a sentence, the subject usually follows the verb. As with inverted questions, mentally rephrase the sentence to find the subject.

Note About *Sentences Beginning With* There or Here: Some sentences beginning with *there* or *here* are not in inverted order, however. In such cases, the words *there* or *here* usually point out a specific location

EXAMPLES: There <u>you</u> <u>are</u>!
Here the <u>castle</u> <u>stands.</u>

More Practice

Grammar Exercise
Workbook
• pp. 49–50
On-line Exercise Bank
• Section 19.2
Go on-line:
PHSchool.com
Enter Web Code:
eek-1002

💡 **Spelling Tip**

Because English includes words borrowed from other languages, proper spelling is often a challenge. *Chivalry,* for instance, comes from the Old French word *chevalier,* which means "knight." When in doubt, look in a dictionary for the correct spelling of tricky words.

Sentences Beginning With *There* or *Here*	Reworded With Subjects Before Verbs
There <u>is</u> my old, battered <u>suitcase</u>.	My old, battered <u>suitcase</u> <u>is</u> there.
Here <u>is</u> the <u>museum</u>!	The <u>museum</u> <u>is</u> here.

In the sentences in the chart above, *there* and *here* are adverbs; they modify the verbs and tell *where*. Occasionally, *there* is merely used to help the sentence get started and does not modify the verb. When *there* is used in this way, it is not an adverb but an *expletive*.

EXAMPLES: There <u>is</u> no <u>bridge</u> across this river.
There <u>will be</u> a drastic <u>change</u> in the weather.

In sentences where *there* is an expletive, rephrasing to find the subject may not work. To find the subject in this situation, mentally drop *there* and ask *Who?* or *What?* before the verb.

Sentences With Expletive *There*	Questions for Finding Subjects
There <u>are</u> many <u>castles</u> in England.	*Question: What* are? *Answer:* castles
There <u>may</u> not <u>be</u> any logical <u>answer</u> to that question.	*Question: What* may be? *Answer:* answer

▶ **Exercise 13** **Finding Subjects in Sentences Beginning With *There* or *Here*** Write each sentence on your paper, underlining the subject once and the verb twice.

EXAMPLE: Here <u>is</u> my <u>book</u> about castles!

1. There are the turrets at the top.
2. Here is my favorite book on King Arthur.
3. There are many versions of the King Arthur legend.
4. There is no way of knowing the truth behind the legend.
5. There on the dresser is my copy of *Le Morte d'Arthur*.

▼ **Critical Viewing** Write three statements a tour guide might make about this castle. Start each with *there* or *here*. Underline each simple subject and verb. **[Analyze]**

GRAMMAR IN LITERATURE

from **Damon and Pythias**
Retold by William F. Russell

In the following excerpt, the subject-verb order is inverted both to supply emphasis and to recreate the style of older language.

Thus <u>did</u> <u>the two friends</u> of Syracuse, by the faithful love they bore to each other, <u>conquer</u> the hard heart of a tyrant king, and in the annals of true friendship there <u>are</u> no more honored <u>names</u> than those of Damon and Pythias—for no person can do more than be willing to lay down his life for the sake of his friend.

Inverted Order for Emphasis Sometimes, the subject-verb order is deliberately inverted to emphasize the word or words at the end of the sentence.

▶ **KEY CONCEPT** In some sentences, the subject is placed after the verb in order to receive greater emphasis. ■

Inverted subject-verb order directs attention to the subject at the end of the sentence and adds a sense of drama or surprise to the sentence. Rephrased in normal subject-verb order, the sentence is less dramatic.

Notice the different dramatic impact the sentence in the chart below makes when presented in inverted order instead of in normal subject-verb order.

Inverted Word Order for Emphasis	Reworded With Subject Before Verbs
Beneath the ruined temple <u>waited</u> the deadly <u>cobra</u>.	The deadly <u>cobra</u> <u>waited</u> beneath the ruined temple.

Exercise 14 Finding Subjects in Sentences Inverted for Emphasis Write the subject of each sentence.

EXAMPLE: Behind the bookcase was hidden a secret door.
ANSWER: door

1. At his master's side rode the brave young squire.
2. Outside the castle lurked the enemy.
3. Across the moat lay safety.
4. Atop the steep hillside stood the majestic castle.
5. Through the battlements came dangerous arrows.
6. From the castle ruled the noble monarch.
7. Uncomfortable was life in the castle.
8. Along the tops of the walls and towers walked the guards.
9. Above the castle flew the colorful flags.
10. With fairness governed the beloved king.

Exercise 15 Revising Sentences by Changing Subject-Verb Order Revise the following sentences, changing them from subject-verb order to inverted order or from inverted order to subject-verb order.

EXAMPLE: A trapdoor was hidden in the floor
REVISION: Hidden in the floor was a trapdoor.

1. In the clearing near the ancient castle waited three mounted knights.
2. One of the knights sat atop a majestic steed.
3. The armed knights raced toward the castle at break-neck speed.
4. A young, inexperienced squire was standing guard at the castle wall.
5. A bright moon shone above the castle.
6. Highlighted by the light of the full moon was the squire's face.
7. Filling his eyes was a look of total fear.
8. Serving as a barrier between the attackers and the castle was a drawbridge.
9. The crank that operated the drawbridge was near the squire's hand.
10. Three frustrated knights were there outside the castle walls.

▶ Critical Viewing Write three questions you might ask this knight about jousting. Identify the simple subject and verb in each question. [Analyze]

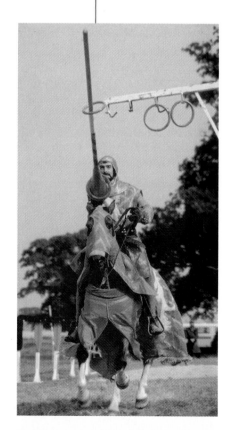

Hands-on Grammar

Inverted-Sentence Cards

In most sentences, the subject comes before the verb. Sentences can be inverted, however, to show emphasis or for dramatic effect. Explore the effect of subject-verb placement with the following activity.

On each of four index cards, write *subject*. On the reverse of each card, write one of these article/noun combinations: *the king, the queen, the knight, the squire.* Next, make four cards that say *verb* on one side and have a verb on the reverse. Use these verbs: *waits, stood, spoke, reads.* Finally, make a set of cards for the adverbs and adverb phrases: *impatiently, proudly, in the castle, at the door.*

Place each set of cards in a pile so that you can read the part of speech. Choose one card from each pile and line them up in the following order: *subject, verb, adverb (or adverb phrase),* Turn the cards over to read the sentence you have created. Then, turn the cards over again to read the part of speech. While the cards are still showing the part of speech, arrange them in the following order: *adverb (or adverb phrase), verb, subject.* Flip the cards to read the new sentence. Complete these steps with the rest of the cards in each pile. (Because the first word of the sentence depends on the arrangement of cards, none of the words on your cards are capitalized. Remember that if you were writing these sentences, you would capitalize the first word of each sentence.)

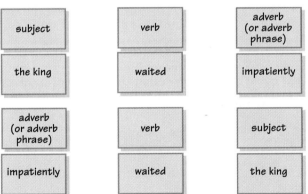

When you are finished, create a new set of cards and work with a partner to challenge each other to identify the subject in inverted sentences. Turn the cards over to check your answers. Create some inverted sentences that contain both adverbs and adverb phrases.

Find It in Your Reading Find an inverted sentences in a folk tale or a poem. Identify each part of the inverted sentence.

Find It in Your Writing Look through your portfolio to find a sentence that could be inverted for emphasis or effect. Identify the subject of the revised sentence.

Section Review

GRAMMAR EXERCISES 16–21

Exercise 16 Identifying Hard-to-Find Subjects Write the subject and verb in each sentence, underlining the subject once and the verb twice. If the subject is understood, write (*you*).

1. Do you know much about castles?
2. There were hundreds of castles built in Europe.
3. There are some still standing.
4. Where was the first castle built?
5. When was its construction completed?
6. Can you name all of the castles in Ireland?
7. Here is the article about feudalism.
8. There may not be enough information on-line.
9. Are you going to visit any castles?
10. Here we go!
11. Look at this painting of a medieval castle.
12. On the wall hung the knights' swords.
13. In the background wait the loyal squires.
14. Beneath the flapping flags strode the valiant knights.
15. On their shields appeared their crests.

Exercise 17 Rewriting Inverted Sentences to Locate Their Subjects Rewrite the following inverted sentences to put the subject before the verb. Then, underline the subject once and the verb twice.

1. Does a moat surround the castle?
2. Will our enemies use ladders to scale the walls of the castle?
3. There is the lowest wall of the castle.
4. Within the moat swim several deadly fish.
5. Here will we establish our best defense of the castle.

Exercise 18 Writing Orders, Directions, and Inverted Sentences Follow these instructions to write five sentences of your own. Underline the subject of each sentence. If the subject is understood, write (*you*).

1. Write a sentence addressing someone and giving the person an order.
2. Write a sentence that directs someone to do two things, one after the other.
3. Write a sentence that begins with *here*.
4. Write the first sentence of directions for building or cooking something.
5. Write a sentence with the order inverted for emphasis.

Exercise 19 Find It in Your Reading Identify the subject in each clause of this excerpt from "Morte d' Arthur."

Then spoke King Arthur, drawing thicker breath:/"Now see I by thine eyes that this is done./Speak out: What is it thou hast heard, or seen?"

Exercise 20 Find It in Your Writing In your writing portfolio, find a question and a sentence that begins with *there* or *here*. Label the subjects of the sentences. Also, challenge yourself to rewrite one of your sentences in inverted order.

Exercise 21 Writing Application Imagine that you are a knight. Write an advertisement seeking a squire to assist you. Include one sentence that gives directions, one that asks a question, and one that begins with *there* or *here*. Identify the subjects in your sentences.

Section 19.3

Direct Objects, Indirect Objects, and Objective Complements

In addition to a verb, a complete predicate may also have one or more *complements.*

> **KEY CONCEPT** A **complement** is a word or group of words that completes the meaning of the predicate of a sentence. ∎

This section presents three different kinds of complements used in sentences with action verbs: *direct objects, indirect objects,* and *objective complements.*

The Direct Object

Direct objects usually follow action verbs.

> **KEY CONCEPT** A **direct object** is a noun or pronoun that receives the action of a transitive action verb. ∎

To find a direct object, ask *Whom?* or *What?* after an action verb. In the following examples, subjects are underlined once, action verbs twice, and direct objects are boxed and labeled. Notice how the direct objects answer the questions *Whom?* and *What?*

EXAMPLES:

                                     DO

A <u>blanket</u> of snow <u><u>covered</u></u> the [pagoda].
Covered *what? Answer:* pagoda

                                     DO

The <u>woman</u> <u><u>is watching</u></u> the [children].
Watching *whom? Answer:* children

Only transitive action verbs direct their action toward someone or something—the direct object. Intransitive verbs have no direct objects.

TRANSITIVE:

                                  DO

The tidal <u>wave</u> <u><u>sank</u></u> the [ship].
Sank *what? Answer:* ship

INTRANSITIVE: The <u>wheels</u> <u><u>sank</u></u> into the mud.
Sank *what? Answer:* none

Direct Objects in Questions When a question follows the normal subject-verb order, you can still find the direct object by asking *Whom?* or *What?* after an action verb.

EXAMPLE: Who wrote that $\overset{\text{DO}}{\boxed{\text{story}}}$?

When a question is inverted, however, the direct object will sometimes appear near the beginning, before the verb. To find the direct object, reword the question as a statement in normal word order, as shown in the following examples.

INVERTED QUESTION: Which book did you read?

REWORDED AS   You <u>did read</u> which $\overset{\text{DO}}{\boxed{\text{book}}}$.
A STATEMENT:

Compound Direct Objects When an action verb directs action toward more than one direct object, the result is a compound direct object. If there is a compound direct object in a sentence, asking *Whom?* or *What?* after the verb will give you two or more answers.

EXAMPLE: The tourists visited Japanese $\overset{\text{DO}}{\boxed{\text{temples}}}$ and $\overset{\text{DO}}{\boxed{\text{shrines}}}$.

Exercise 22 **Identifying Direct Objects in Statements and Questions** List the direct object or compound direct object in each sentence below.

EXAMPLE: Japanese workers spend long hours on the job.
ANSWER: hours

1. Japan owes much of its economic success to its workers.
2. Japanese workers often express loyalty and respect toward their companies.
3. They take great pride in their companies' success.
4. They work longer hours and take fewer vacations than Western workers.
5. How do Japanese companies treat their employees?
6. Large companies often offer incentives to attract and keep workers.
7. Which benefits do workers appreciate most?
8. Many workers receive free housing or medical care.
9. These benefits keep the workers happy.
10. As a result, Japanese workers produce more goods than workers in most other countries do.

More Practice

Grammar Exercise Workbook
• pp. 51–54
On-line Exercise Bank
• Section 19.3
  Go on-line:
  PHSchool.com
  Enter Web Code:
  eek-1002

Get instant feedback! Exercises 22 and 23 are available on-line or on CD-ROM.

Direct Object or Object of a Preposition? A direct object is never the noun or pronoun at the end of a prepositional phrase. Do not confuse these two sentence parts.

EXAMPLES:

DO   PREP PHRASE

I photographed the woman with the children.
Photographed *whom*? *Answer*: woman

PREP PHRASE   PREP PHRASE

We walked with the children through the zoo.
Walked *what*? *Answer*: none

▶ **Exercise 23** Identifying Direct Objects and Objects of Prepositions On your paper, indicate whether the underlined word in each sentence is a *direct object* or *object of a preposition*.

EXAMPLE: A group of tourists stood outside the <u>pagoda</u>.

ANSWER: object of a preposition

1. Many Japanese pagodas are made of <u>wood</u>.
2. They are very vulnerable to <u>fire</u>.
3. Yet these pagodas can withstand earthquakes and <u>typhoons</u>.
4. Their interlocking construction makes <u>them</u> so strong.
5. A 1,300-year-old pagoda in Nara still shows no <u>sign</u> of weakness in its structure.

▼ **Critical Viewing**
Add a compound direct object to complete this sentence: *When I look at this pagoda, I see . . .* **[Identify]**

▶ **Exercise 24** Revising by Using Direct Objects Revise
each question and answer below to form a sentence that
includes a direct object or compound direct object. Underline
the direct object(s).

EXAMPLE: What does Japan have? A long coastline and
              mountainous terrain.

ANSWER: Japan has a long <u>coastline</u> and mountainous
              <u>terrain</u>.

1. Who did the Japanese educate at first? Only the members of
   the aristocracy
2. Who later assumed the responsibility for education? Buddhist
   priests
3. How did this change affect education? It made it available to
   a larger portion of society.
4. How long did the Japanese maintain this system? Until the
   1800's
5. What happened under Emperor Meiji in the late 1800's? A
   universal code for education was first adopted by the
   Japanese.

The Indirect Object

Sentences with direct objects may have *indirect objects,* too.

▶ **KEY CONCEPT** An **indirect object** is a noun or pronoun
that appears with a direct object and names the person or
thing that something is given to or done for. ■

To find an indirect object, first be certain that the sentence
has a direct object. Then, having found the direct object, ask
To or for whom? or *To or for what?* after the action verb.

EXAMPLES: *Liz* <u>promised</u> her ⌐IO⌐ ⌐DO⌐
                 Liz <u>promised</u> her [sister] a [book] about Japan.
                 Promised *to whom?*   *Answer:* sister

                 We <u>should give</u> Fred's [idea] a [chance].
                 Should give *to what?*   *Answer:* idea

Compound Indirect Objects When there is a compound
indirect object in a sentence, asking *To or for whom?* or *To or
for what?* after the verb will lead to two or more answers.

EXAMPLE: *Liz* <u>promised</u> her [sister] and [brother] a book.
                 Promised *to whom? Answer:* sister and brother

---

▶ **More Practice**

**Grammar Exercise
Workbook**
• pp. 51–54
On-line Exercise Bank
• Section 19.3
  Go on-line:
  PHSchool.com
  Enter Web Code:
  eek-1002

Complete the exer-
cises on-line! Exercises
24 and 25 are avail-
able on-line or on
CD-ROM.

Indirect Object or Direct Object? To avoid confusing an indirect object with a direct object, remember that an indirect object almost always comes between the verb and the direct object. In a sentence in normal subject-verb order, the pattern is always verb-indirect object-direct object.

EXAMPLE: Uncle Charlie handed the [IO bellhop] a [DO tip].

Asking the questions for direct and indirect objects will also help you distinguish between the two kinds of complements. In the above example, the question for direct objects—handed *what?*—gives the answer *tip.* The question for indirect objects—handed *to whom?*—leads to the indirect object *bellhop.*

Indirect Object or Object of a Preposition? Do not confuse an indirect object with an object of a preposition. An indirect object is never preceded by the word *to* or *for.* Moreover, it almost never follows the direct object. In the first example below, *friends* is the object of a preposition and is located after the direct object. In the second, there is no preposition and *friends* comes before the direct object.

EXAMPLES: Angela told the [DO news] [PREP PHRASE to her friends].

Angela told her [IO friends] the [DO news].

▲ Critical Viewing
Write a sentence about this performer using the word *audience* as an indirect object. What is the direct object of your sentence? **[Analyze]**

▶ **Exercise 25** **Recognizing Indirect Objects** Write each indirect object, including any compound indirect objects. If a sentence has no indirect object, write *none.*

EXAMPLE: They sent Mark and Elizabeth travel brochures.
ANSWER: Mark, Elizabeth

1. Mark's parents bought him plane tickets to Tokyo for his birthday.
2. He asked his boss for a leave of absence.
3. The company granted Mark eight weeks.
4. His friend lent him a suitcase large enough for his long journey.
5. As his plane lifted off, Mark felt a rush of excitement and nervousness.
6. While away, Mark wrote his parents a letter every week.
7. He told them about the culture and people of Japan.
8. A guide gave him a complete tour of the city.
9. Mark visited Tokyo's financial and commercial centers.
10. When Mark returned, he showed his friends pictures of Tokyo.

The Objective Complement

A third kind of complement, one that generally comes after a direct object, is called an *objective complement*.

KEY CONCEPT An **objective complement** is an adjective or noun that appears with a direct object and describes or renames it. ■

Objective complements do not occur often. They are used only with verbs such as *appoint, name, make, think,* or *call.*

An objective complement can be found only in a sentence that has a direct object. To determine whether a word is an objective complement, say the verb and the direct object and then ask *What?* The following examples illustrate the method you should use to locate objective complements.

EXAMPLES:

Ben called his dog Rover.
Called dog *what? Answer:* Rover

The beautician made Ann's hair short and curly.
Made hair *what? Answer:* short and curly

The objective complement in the last example is compound.

Exercise 26 Recognizing Objective Complements Write the objective complement in each sentence, including all parts of any compound objective complements.

EXAMPLE: Mr. Matsuto made his reply very short.
ANSWER: short

1. The Japanese consider the emperor the symbol of their nation.
2. They once thought their emperor sacred and inviolable.
3. Japan's 1947 constitution declared the emperor's position ceremonial.
4. The constitution named the prime minister head of state.
5. In 1989, Japan declared Akihito emperor.
6. The people considered his marriage to a commoner symbolic of Japan's democracy.
7. Japan's limited land and large population make the country densely populated.
8. Limited space makes housing development difficult.
9. In spite of the overcrowding, the Japanese find their homeland a paradise.
10. The Japanese call their country the "land of the rising sun."

Section 19.3 *Section Review*

GRAMMAR EXERCISES 27–32

▶ **Exercise 27** Recognizing Direct Objects Write the direct object in each sentence, including all parts of any compound direct objects.

(1) Japanese comprise 99 percent of the population of Japan. (2) The small remainder includes Koreans, Chinese, and Ainu. (3) The Ainu represent the aborigines of Japan. (4) They once inhabited the northernmost islands of Japan. (5) They possessed distinct biological characteristics. (6) After World War II, however, Japanese culture almost fully assimilated the Ainu. (7) Metropolitan areas now dominate the Japanese landscape. (8) Its people have created an industrialized urban society with relatively few resources. (9) Nearly all citizens speak Japanese. (10) In addition to speaking the official language, many Japanese also know some English.

▶ **Exercise 28** Recognizing Complements Used With Action Verbs Write and label each *direct object, indirect object*, and *objective complement.*

1. The Japanese named their country *Dia Nihon*, which means "origin of the sun."
2. The Treaty of Versailles made the Caroline Islands a part of Japan.
3. I showed my father the cities of Yokohama and Osaka on the map.
4. The rugged mountains and rocky soil of Japan make farming difficult.
5. Kirisawa wrote some of the Japanese ideogrammatic alphabet on the chalkboard for the class.
6. The University of Tokyo granted the foreign students a scholarship.
7. Our hosts offered us sushi for lunch.
8. At the Japanese festival, I ate blowfish.
9. The prime minister of Japan appoints legislators and cabinet members.
10. Frank sent me his book of Japanese architecture.

▶ **Exercise 29** Writing Sentences With Complements Complete each sentence by adding the complement(s) indicated in parentheses, plus needed modifiers.

1. Frances painted ___?___. (direct object)
2. The Japanese musician played ___?___. (compound direct object)
3. Anna's friend wrote ___?___. (indirect object and direct object)
4. Charlie bought ___?___. (compound indirect object and direct object)
5. Andrew considered ___?___. (direct object and objective complement)

▶ **Exercise 30** Find It in Your Reading In a newspaper, find an article about another country. Label any *direct objects, indirect objects*, and *objective complements* in the article.

▶ **Exercise 31** Find It in Your Writing In your own writing, find five direct objects and two indirect objects. Also, note whether you have used objective complements in any of your compositions.

▶ **Exercise 32** Writing Application Japan exports many products, such as automobiles and electronics, to the United States. Write a description of an item in your home that may have been imported from another country, and discuss how it works. Include and label two *direct objects*, one *indirect object*, and one *objective complement* in your description.

Subject Complements

In this section, you will see linking verbs followed by other kinds of complements, called *subject complements*.

▶ **KEY CONCEPT** A **subject complement** is a noun, pronoun, or adjective that appears with a linking verb and tells something about the subject of the sentence. ■

A subject complement will almost always be found *after* a linking verb. The two kinds of subject complements are known as *predicate nominatives* and *predicate adjectives*.

The Predicate Nominative

The word *nominative* comes from the Latin word *nomen* meaning "name." The words *noun* and *pronoun* are also derived from *nomen*. A *predicate nominative* names or identifies the subject of a sentence.

▶ **KEY CONCEPT** A **predicate nominative** is a noun or pronoun that appears with a linking verb and renames, identifies, or explains the subject of the sentence. ■

A subject and a predicate nominative are two different words for the same person, place, or thing. Acting as an equal sign, the linking verb joins these two parts and equates them.

In the examples, subjects are underlined once, linking verbs twice, and predicate nominatives are boxed and labeled.

EXAMPLES: That <u>painting</u> of the shoreline <u>is</u> a PN| masterpiece |.
(*Masterpiece* explains *painting*.)

The new <u>lifeguard</u> at the pool <u>will be</u> PN| Sue |.
(*Sue* renames *lifeguard*.)

Their first <u>choice</u> <u>was</u> PN| you |.
(*You* identifies *choice*.)

Like other sentence parts, predicate nominatives may be compound.

EXAMPLES: Most <u>people</u> at the beach <u>were</u> PN| sunbathers | or
PN| surfers |. (*Sunbathers* and *surfers* name *people*.)

The new <u>lifeguard</u> <u>may be</u> either PN| Sue | or PN| Celia |.
(*Sue* or *Celia* renames *lifeguard*.)

Theme: Beaches and Tides

In this section, you will learn about predicate nominatives and predicate adjectives. The examples and exercises are about beaches and tides.

Cross-Curricular Connection: Science

▶ **More Practice**

Grammar Exercise Workbook
• pp. 55–56
On-line Exercise Bank
• Section 19.4
Go on-line:
PHSchool.com
Enter Web Code:
eek-1002

GRAMMAR IN LITERATURE

from **In Commemoration: One Million Volumes**
Rudolfo A. Anaya

In the following excerpt, the predicate nominatives are shown in blue italics.

I was a librarian's *dream*. My tattered library card was my *ticket* into the same worlds my grandfather had known, worlds of magic that fed the imagination.

▶ **Exercise 33** **Recognizing Predicate Nominatives** Write the predicate nominative in each sentence, including all parts of any compound predicate nominatives.

EXAMPLE: This beach is a good site for fishing and an excellent place for diving.
ANSWER: site place

1. Beaches are strips of land bordering an ocean or another body of water.
2. Some of our favorite beaches are barrier beaches.
3. Barrier beaches are generally elongated islands or sandbars.
4. The beach at Coney Island, in New York, is a barrier beach.
5. Beaches along the islands of Hawaii are the main attraction for tourists.
6. Waves, tides, and the wind will always be a beach's worst enemy.
7. These elements are the primary cause of erosion.
8. Sand dunes are one result of winds and tides.
9. White sand on a beach is the product of coral and limestone deposits.
10. High tides and storms are cause for alarm for beach residents.

▼ **Critical Viewing** Complete this sentence: *This rocky coastline would be a great . . .* What is the predicate nominative in your sentence? **[Analyze]**

The Predicate Adjective

The other kind of subject complement is called a *predicate adjective*. With a linking verb, it describes the subject.

▶ **KEY CONCEPT** A **predicate adjective** is an adjective that appears with a linking verb and describes the subject of the sentence. ■

In each of the following examples, you can see that the linking verb joins the subject to a word that describes the subject. These descriptive words are predicate adjectives.

EXAMPLES: A trip to the beach <u>will be</u> fun.
                                                    P.A.

My sunburn <u>feels</u> hot and painful.
                                      P.A.

▶ **Exercise 34** **Recognizing Predicate Adjectives** Write the predicate adjective in each sentence, including all parts of any compound predicate adjectives.

1. In the cloudless sky, the moon appeared luminous.
2. The moon is closer to the Earth than the sun is.
3. Its gravitational pull on the Earth is stronger.
4. The Earth's oceans are responsive to the pull of the moon.
5. The gravitational pull of the moon is great and constant
6. Tides are higher at certain times of the day because of the moon's pull.
7. Marine life is plentiful at the edge of the sea.
8. These forms of life must be hardy and adaptable.
9. The fronds of sea-weed were smooth and gleaming.
10. The delicate shells on the shore looked unreal.

Interactive Textbook

Get instant feedback! Exercise 34 is available on-line or on CD-ROM.

▶ **More Practice**

Grammar Exercise Workbook
• pp. 55–56
On-line Exercise Bank
• Section 19.4
  Go on-line:
  PHSchool.com
  Enter Web Code:
  eek-1002

▶ **Critical Viewing** Write two sentences containing predicate adjectives to describe the beach and the sunset in this photograph. **[Analyze]**

Section 19.4 *Section Review*

GRAMMAR EXERCISES 35–40

▶ **Exercise 35** Recognizing Subject Complements Write and label the predicate nominatives or predicate adjectives in each sentence,

1. Shorelines are home to tidal pools.
2. The environments of tidal pools are unique and delicate.
3. The current is the source of a rich supply of nutrients along beaches.
4. Tidal pools are natural basins in sand.
5. Creatures in tidal pools are adaptable.
6. They are strange and beautiful forms of life.
7. Buffeting waves and frequent submersion are dangerous to them.
8. Suction-cup feet are the only protections of a starfish.
9. Rocks and boats are often host to marine animals like barnacles.
10. Seaweed is quite resilient.

▶ **Exercise 36** Supplying Subject Complements in Sentences Write a subject complement or compound subject complement to complete each sentence.

1. The waves that crashed on the shore were ___?___ .
2. The foam felt ___?___ and ___?___ .
3. The sun was a giant orange ___?___ in the sky.
4. Tides are a good ___?___ of energy.
5. A dam can be an essential ___?___ for capturing this energy.
6. Dams can be ___?___ , but they are worth the money.
7. The 50-foot tides in the Bay of Fundy in Canada are the ___?___ in the world.
8. Birds flying over the bay were ___?___ and ___?___ .
9. The beach is a good ___?___ to play or relax.
10. The most unusual thing I saw in the water was a ___?___ .

▶ **Exercise 37** Revising Sentences by Using Subject Complements Revise each sentence below so that it includes a predicate nominative or predicate adjective.

1. We took a refreshing morning walk along the beach.
2. We saw a rocky and craggy shoreline.
3. A distant boat seemed to be a tiny speck on the horizon.
4. Our dinner consisted of fresh fish and vegetables.
5. The beach at night has a mysterious quality.

▶ **Exercise 38** Find It in Your Reading Identify the predicate nominative and predicate adjective in this excerpt from *The Marginal World* by Rachel Carson.

. . . Water and air were pallid. Across the bay the moon was a luminous disc in the western sky, suspended above the dim line of the distant shore. . . .

▶ **Exercise 39** Find It in Your Writing Look through your writing portfolio. Find two examples of predicate nominatives and two examples of predicate adjectives. Label the complements, and underline the subject once and the linking verb twice in each sentence.

▶ **Exercise 40** Writing Application Write a description of a day at a beach or park. Include a predicate nominative, a compound predicate nominative, and two predicate adjectives in your description.

Phrases
and Clauses

Louvre Museum, Paris, France

The preceding chapters have described the simple building
blocks of grammar, including the various parts of speech
and the basic sentence parts. This chapter will focus on two
additional elements—phrases and clauses—that function in
specific ways in sentences.

A **phrase** is a group of words, without a subject and verb,
that functions in a sentence as one part of speech. A **clause** is
a group of words with its own subject and verb. Some clauses
can stand by themselves as complete sentences; others can
function only as parts of sentences.

Phrases and clauses add important pieces of information to
your writing. In a composition about France, for instance,
your phrases and clauses might add information about the
culture, social groups, politics, and economics of the country.

As you have seen in previous chapters, sentences are a
mixture of subjects, verbs, and modifiers that work together
to communicate an idea. In this chapter, you will learn how
various phrases and clauses can be incorporated into sentences
to enrich the quality of your writing.

▲ **Critical Viewing**
The glass pyramid
became part of the
Louvre in 1988.
What is its effect
placed in front of
the museum's
original buildings?
[Analyze]

Diagnostic Test

Directions: Write all answers on a separate sheet of paper.

Skill Check A. List the prepositional phrases, appositives, and appositive phrases in the following sentences, and label each. For each item that you list, identify the word it modifies or renames.

1. The Eiffel Tower, France's most recognizable structure, is a Paris landmark.
2. The tower was built for the Paris World's Fair of 1889.
3. Alexandre Gustave Eiffel, an engineer, was the tower's designer.
4. The tower is made of wrought iron and exceeds 984 feet in height.
5. The Eiffel Tower attracts thousands of visitors each year.

Skill Check B. Identify and label the infinitive phrase, gerund phrase, or participial phrase in each sentence. Identify the word modified by each participial phrase, and identify the function of each gerund and infinitive phrase.

6. Fontainebleau is a large chateau located southeast of Paris.
7. Constructing the chateau was the idea of King Francis I.
8. Many well-known artists were hired to decorate the ornate interior of the building.
9. Fontainebleau was looted during the French Revolution, but Napoleon managed to restore the palace to its former glory.
10. The republican government, assuming control of the chateau in 1871, made it a national monument.

Skill Check C. Write the subordinate clause in each sentence, and then tell whether it is an adjective, an adverb, or a noun clause. If a clause is elliptical, write the missing word or words.

11. Versailles is more famous than any other palace in Europe.
12. The enormous building, which has 1,300 rooms, was constructed on the site of a small hunting lodge.
13. Although more than 30,000 craftsmen labored on the palace, it still took longer than forty years to complete.
14. King Louis XIV, who ruled France for much of the seventeenth century, moved the royal court to Versailles in 1682.
15. Whoever visits the palace will be overwhelmed by the sheer size and beauty of the building.

Skill Check D. 16–20 For each adjective and adverb clause in Skill Check C, identify the word it modifies. Tell how each noun clause functions in its sentence.

Phrases

There are several kinds of *phrases*, among them prepositional phrases, appositive phrases, participial phrases, gerund phrases, and infinitive phrases. In this section, you will learn how phrases can be used to add meaning and variety to your sentences.

Prepositional Phrases

A **prepositional phrase** is a group of words made up of a preposition and a noun or pronoun, called the object of the preposition. *Over their heads, until dark,* and *after the baseball game* are all examples of prepositional phrases. Sometimes, a single prepositional phrase may have two or more objects joined by a conjunction. *Between the window and the wall* and *with the wind and freezing rain* are examples of prepositions followed by compound objects. (See Chapter 18 to review prepositions.)

In this section, you will learn how prepositional phrases modify other words by functioning either as adjectives or as adverbs within sentences.

Adjective Phrases

A prepositional phrase that acts as an adjective is called an *adjective phrase.*

▶ **KEY CONCEPT** An **adjective phrase** is a prepositional phrase that modifies a noun or pronoun by telling *what kind* or *which one.* ∎

The following chart contrasts adjectives with adjective phrases.

Adjectives	Adjective Phrases
A *beautiful* French painting hung in the palace.	A French painting *of great beauty* hung in the palace.
Mary took a *boxed* lunch.	Mary took lunch *in a box.*

A prepositional phrase that answers the question *What kind?* or *Which one?* will be an adjective phrase. In the first sentence on the right in the chart, for example, the question *What kind of painting?* is answered by *of great beauty.*

Adjective phrases usually modify nouns functioning as subjects, direct objects, indirect objects, or predicate nominatives.

Theme: France

In this section, you will learn to use prepositional, appositive, and verbal phrases. The examples and exercises in this section are about France.

Cross-Curricular Connection: Social Studies

🔁 **Learn More**

To review basic information about prepositions, turn to Chapter 18.

MODIFYING A SUBJECT: The mansion *across the road* has been abandoned.

MODIFYING A
DIRECT OBJECT: Let's take a picture *of the Eiffel Tower.*

MODIFYING AN
INDIRECT OBJECT: They gave the students *on the bus* a tour.

MODIFYING A
PREDICATE NOMINATIVE: France is a country *with many charms.*

A sentence may often have a series of two or more adjective phrases. When this happens, each succeeding phrase may modify the object of the preceding phrase.

EXAMPLE: We bought tickets *for the trip to Paris.*

The adjective phrase *for the trip* describes *tickets.* The adjective phrase *to Paris* modifies *trip.*
More than one adjective phrase may describe the same noun.

EXAMPLE: The painting *of the palace in the museum* is old.

Exercise 1 **Identifying Adjective Phrases** Write each sentence, underlining the adjective phrase or phrases in each. Then, draw an arrow from each phrase to the word it modifies.

EXAMPLE: France has miles of coastline.

ANSWER: France has miles of coastline.

1. France is the second-largest country in Europe.
2. The capital city of France is Paris.
3. Lyon, Toulouse, and Marseille are three other major cities in France.
4. The nickname of France is *L'Hexagone.*
5. The country borders two major bodies of water: the Atlantic Ocean and the Mediterranean Sea.
6. The Pyrenees Mountains along the southern border separate France and Spain.
7. One border country to the east of France is Switzerland.
8. North of France is the tiny principality of Luxembourg.
9. France controls a group of islands in the Pacific.
10. A rough estimate of the country's population is sixty million.

▶ **More Practice**

Grammar Exercise Workbook
• pp. 57–58
On-line Exercise Bank
• Section 20.1
   Go on-line:
   PHSchool.com
   Enter Web Code:
   eek-1002

Get instant feedback! Exercise 1 is available on-line or on CD-ROM.

Adverb Phrases

A prepositional phrase can also act as an adverb.

▶ **KEY CONCEPT** An **adverb phrase** is a prepositional phrase that modifies a verb, an adjective, or an adverb by pointing out *where, when, in what way,* or *to what extent.* ■

The following chart shows that adverb phrases function in a similar way to single-word adverbs.

Adverbs	Adverb Phrases
She ran *swiftly*.	She ran *with speed*.
They were happy *there*.	They were happy *at the French cafe*.

If a prepositional phrase is an adverb phrase, it will answer the question: *Where? When? In what way?* or *To what extent?* In the first example on the right in the chart, the question *Ran in what way?* is answered by *with speed,* an adverb phrase.

Unlike an adjective phrase, which almost always follows the word it modifies, an adverb phrase may either follow the word it modifies or be located elsewhere in the sentence.

EXAMPLES: An alpine village vanished *during the avalanche.*

During the avalanche, an alpine village vanished.

Like single-word adverbs, adverb phrases can modify verbs, adjectives, or adverbs.

MODIFYING
A VERB: The runner dashed *past the spectators.*

MODIFYING
AN ADJECTIVE: The Loire Valley is rich *in historical buildings.*

MODIFYING
AN ADVERB: The French exchange student arrived late *for class.*

Like adjective phrases, two or more adverb phrases may modify the same word.

EXAMPLE: *In the afternoon,* we walked *to Notre Dame.*

Many of the examples and exercises in this section contain names of French places and people, which may be unfamiliar or seem difficult to pronounce. Get together with a classmate who is studying French, and let him or her help you practice French pronunciation.

> **Exercise 2** Identifying Adverb Phrases Write each
sentence, underlining the adverb phrase or phrases in each.
Then, draw an arrow from each phrase to the word it modifies.

EXAMPLE: France is situated above the Iberian Peninsula.

ANSWER: France is situated <u>above the Iberian Peninsula</u>.

1. France's geography is marked by various natural formations.
2. Several large rivers cut across the country.
3. Without a doubt, the Seine River is the most important French river.
4. It flows through Paris and empties into the English Channel.
5. The Rhone, Loire, and Rhine rivers are also important to France.
6. Two impressive mountain ranges exist within French territory.
7. The French Alps rise majestically near France's southwestern boundary.
8. Europe's second-highest peak is located within this mountain range.
9. Cable cars carry skiers high up the mountain.
10. The Pyrenees Mountains stretch along the Spanish border.

> **More Practice**

Grammar Exercise Workbook
• pp. 57–58
On-line Exercise Bank
• Section 20.1
 Go on-line:
 PHSchool.com
 Enter Web Code:
 eek-1002

▲ **Critical Viewing**
In what ways might a winter-sports enthusiast react to skiing on Mont Blanc, the highest peak in the Alps? Use a prepositional phrase in your answer. [Infer]

Appositives and Appositive Phrases

The term *appositive* comes from a Latin verb meaning "to put near or next to."

Appositives

Using **appositives** in your writing is an easy way to give additional meaning to nouns and pronouns.

> **KEY CONCEPT** An **appositive** is a noun or pronoun placed next to another noun or pronoun to identify, rename, or explain it. ■

As the next chart shows, appositives generally follow immediately after the words they identify, rename, or explain.

APPOSITIVES

Some French villagers, the *old-timers*, prefer to travel the dirt roads.

Her greatest attribute, *charm*, was not enough.

Notice that commas are used because these appositives are *nonessential*. In other words, they could be omitted from the sentences without altering the basic meanings of the sentences.

Some appositives, however, are not set off by any punctuation because they are *essential* to the meaning of the sentence.

EXAMPLE: The artist *Monet* was a great French painter.

Note About Terms: Sometimes, the terms *nonrestrictive* and *restrictive* are used in place of *nonessential* and *essential*.

▶ **Exercise 3** Identifying Appositives Write the appositive in each sentence. Then, write the word each appositive renames.

EXAMPLE: Jacques, our guide, told us about French people.
ANSWER: guide (Jacques)

1. Sixty million people, France's population, are dispersed throughout the country.
2. Many rural people, farmers, are moving to urban areas.
3. Today, nearly one sixth of the population is located near Paris, the capital.
4. The most mountainous area, the southeast, has experienced a large decline in population in recent years.
5. France has a lower population growth rate than its neighbor Germany.

Appositive Phrases

When an appositive is accompanied by its own modifiers, it is called an *appositive phrase.*

▶ **KEY CONCEPT** An **appositive phrase** is a noun or pronoun with modifiers, placed next to a noun or pronoun to add information and details. ■

The modifiers within an appositive phrase can be adjectives, adjective phrases, or other groups of words functioning as adjectives.

▶ **More Practice**

Grammar Exercise Workbook
• pp. 59–60
On-line Exercise Bank
• Section 20.1
 Go on-line:
 PHSchool.com
 Enter Web Code:
 eek-1002

Get instant feedback! Exercise 3 is available on-line or on CD-ROM.

APPOSITIVE PHRASES

France was invaded during World War II, *the most terrible war the world has known.*

Amethyst, *a purple birthstone,* is the gem for February.

Fred explained numismatics, *the hobby of coin collecting.*

Appositives and appositive phrases may follow nouns or pronouns used in almost any role within a sentence.

WITH A SUBJECT:	Ernest Hemingway, *a famous author,* wrote in a terse style.
WITH A DIRECT OBJECT:	The chef prepared *escargots, a snail dish.*
WITH AN INDIRECT OBJECT:	I brought my brother, *a boy of six,* a souvenir from the Louvre.
WITH AN OBJECTIVE COMPLEMENT:	I chose the color purple, *an unusual color for a house.*
WITH A PREDICATE NOMINATIVE:	My favorite food was cassoulet, *a hearty stew.*
WITH THE OBJECT OF A PREPOSITION:	Store the onions in the cellar, *a cool, dry place.*

Appositives and appositive phrases may also be compound.

EXAMPLE:	Armand, both *his schoolmate* and *his confidant,* was always welcome in the house.

When appositives or appositive phrases are used to combine sentences, they help to eliminate unnecessary words. The following examples show how two sentences may be joined.

TWO SENTENCES:	Marseille is located on the Mediterranean Sea. The city is an important French seaport.
COMBINED:	Marseille, *an important French seaport,* is located on the Mediterranean Sea.

✹ Grammar ✹ and Style Tip

One good way to streamline your writing is to combine sentences using an appositive phrase. For instance, in the second example, the sentence could have started as two choppy sentences: The chef prepared *escargots. Escargots* is a snail dish.

20.1

> **Exercise 4** Combining Sentences With Appositive Phrases

Combine each pair of sentences by turning one of them into an appositive phrase.

EXAMPLE: Marie is a Sorbonne student. She is well educated.

ANSWER: Marie, a Sorbonne student, is well educated.

1. France's educational system is one of Europe's best. It is subsidized by the government.
2. Children are required to attend school until they reach early adulthood. That is generally sixteen years of age.
3. *Écoles* educate children six through ten years old. *Écoles* are French primary schools.
4. *Lycées* are attended by students between the ages of eleven and eighteen. *Lycées* are French secondary schools.
5. Jean-Luc attends a religious school, as do nearly one fifth of the students in France. Jean-Luc is a tenth grader.
6. A large number of French students take the *baccalauréat*. It is a difficult college-entrance exam.
7. After passing the test, students are eligible to attend college for free for one year. The year is their freshman year.
8. Students are given licenses after three years of study. The licenses are degrees similar to a bachelor's degree.
9. Some students choose alternative post-high-school paths. The paths may be technical schools or trade schools.
10. France also offers its most ambitious students the option to attend specialized institutions called *grandes écoles.* Those students are mainly business, science, and engineering majors.

> **More Practice**

Grammar Exercise Workbook
• pp. 59–60
On-line Exercise Bank
• Section 20.1
  Go on-line:
  PHSchool.com
  Enter Web Code:
  eek-1002

Complete the exercise on-line! Exercise 4 is available on-line or on CD-ROM.

The Panthéon, Paris

◀ **Critical Viewing**
The Panthéon contains the remains of illustrious French citizens—among them, writer Victor Hugo and scientist Marie Curie. How might this building serve to inspire the university students who pass by each day? Answer using an appositive phrase. **[Relate]**

Verbal Phrases

When a verb is used as a noun, an adjective, or an adverb, it is called a *verbal*. Although a verbal does not function as a verb, it still retains two characteristics of verbs: It can be modified in different ways, and it can have one or more complements. A verbal with modifiers or a complement is a *verbal phrase*.

Participles

Many of the adjectives you use are actually verbals known as *participles*.

KEY CONCEPT A **participle** is a form of a verb that can act as an adjective. ■

The most common kinds of participles are *present participles* and *past participles*. These two kinds of participles can be distinguished from each other by their endings. Present participles end in *-ing* (*frightening, entertaining*). Past participles usually end in *-ed* (*frightened, entertained*), but many have irregular endings such as *-t* or *-en* (*burst, written*).

The following chart shows participles modifying nouns within sentences.

Present Participles	Past Participles
Limping, the hiker favored his *aching* ankle.	*Confused*, Nan returned to her *interrupted* work.

Notice that participles answer the adjective question *What kind?* or *Which one?* about the nouns or pronouns that they modify.

EXAMPLES: Irma's *shining* eyes betrayed her excitement.
What kind of eyes? *Answer:* *shining* eyes
The *shattered* window needs replacement.
Which window? Answer: the *shattered* window

Note About *Being* and *Having*: Participles also have a present perfect form.

EXAMPLE: *Having decided*, Madeleine acted quickly.
Being greeted by his friends, François shakes hands all around.

⟲ Learn More

For information about irregular verb endings, turn to Chapter 22.

GRAMMAR IN
LITERATURE

from **Antigone**
Sophocles
Translated by Dudley Fitts and Robert Fitzgerald

Notice the highlighted past participles in this selection.

There's nothing in the world so demoralizing as money.
Down go your cities,
Homes *gone*, men *gone*, honest hearts *corrupted*,
Crookedness of all kinds, and all for money!

Exercise 5 Identifying Present and Past Participles Write the participle in each sentence. Then, label it *present* or *past*.
1. The established form of government in France is democracy.
2. The last adopted constitution of France was written in 1958.
3. According to the constitution, the people are represented by two large governing bodies.
4. The 577-member National Assembly is responsible for all proposed legislation.
5. The smaller group of elected officials, the Senate, must either ratify or veto the Assembly's legislation.

Exercise 6 Supplying Participles Complete each sentence by supplying the *present* or *past participle*, as indicated, of each word in parentheses.
1. The ___?___ Public elects a president to a seven-year term. (vote—present)
2. ___?___ elections determine the new members of the Assembly and the Senate. (stagger—past)
3. The ___?___ president must also select a Council of Ministers. (designate—past)
4. The prime minister holds one of the most ___?___ posts in the government. (tax—present)
5. The French president serves as the commander in chief of the country's ___?___ forces. (arm—past)

More Practice

Grammar Exercise Workbook
• pp. 61–66
On-line Exercise Bank
• Section 20.1
  Go on-line:
  PHSchool.com
  Enter Web Code:
  eek-1002

Get instant feedback! Exercises 5, 6, and 7 are available on-line or on CD-ROM.

Verb or Participle?

It is easy to confuse a participle acting as part of a verb phrase with a participle acting as an adjective because they share the endings -*ing* and -*ed*.

▶ **KEY CONCEPTS** A **verb** shows an action, a condition, or the fact that something exists. A **participle** acting as an adjective modifies a noun or a pronoun. ■

The following chart shows verbs and then participles as adjectives. Notice that as verbs, the words tell what someone or something does or did. The participles, however, describe someone or something.

Verbs	Participles
The dog is *snarling* at the plumber. (What is the dog doing?)	The *snarling* dog attacked the plumber. (*Which* dog?)
The mimes *delighted* their audience. (What did the mimes *do*?).	*Delighted,* the audience applauded. (*What kind* of audience?)

▶ **Exercise 7** **Distinguishing Between Verbs and Participles**
Identify each underlined word as a *verb* or *participle*. If it is a participle, write the word it modifies.

EXAMPLE: The French people have experienced <u>increasing</u> prosperity since the 1940's.

ANSWER: participle (prosperity)

1. Until World War II, France <u>based</u> its economy mainly on agriculture.
2. Today, the country has a very <u>diversified</u> economy.
3. France is a <u>leading</u> industrial power in the world.
4. It is a major producer of <u>advanced</u> electronics and other high-tech devices.
5. The government is <u>playing</u> an important role in the European Union.

▼ Critical Viewing Use a participle as an adjective in a sentence describing two features of the French countryside depicted in this photograph. **[Describe]**

Participial Phrases

Participles may be parts of *participial phrases.*

KEY CONCEPT A **participial phrase** is a participle modified by an adverb or adverb phrase or accompanied by a complement. The entire phrase acts as an adjective. ■

The following examples show different ways that participles may be expanded into phrases.

EXAMPLES: *Traveling quickly,* we saw much of the French countryside.

The tourist, *confused by the signs,* got lost.

Scanning the French dictionary, Ann found the words for "entrance" and "exit"—*entrée* and *sortie.*

Participial phrases are punctuated according to their use within a sentence. The following chart contrasts nonessential and essential participial phrases. In the sentences on the left, the participial phrases could be removed without altering the basic meaning of the sentence. However, if you remove the participial phrases from the sentences on the right, the meaning of the sentences will not be the same.

Nonessential Phrases	Essential Phrases
There is Craig, *standing by the bus stop.*	The boy *standing by the bus stop* is Craig.
Painted in 1497, the mural is Leonardo's masterpiece.	The mural *painted in 1497* is almost beyond repair.

In the first sentence on the left in the chart, *standing by the bus stop* merely adds information about *Craig,* who has already been identified. In a similar sentence on the right, however, the same phrase is essential for the identification of *boy,* because there could be many different boys in view. In the second sentence on the left, *painted in 1497* is an additional description of *mural.* In the sentence on the right, the phrase is essential. It identifies the mural that is being discussed.

Spelling Tip

Notice that many French words—even some commonly used in English—have accent marks. Watch for accents on words such as *résumé, café,* and *entrée* and on names such as *André* and *Renée.*

KEY CONCEPT Participial phrases can often be used to combine information from two sentences into one. ■

TWO
SENTENCES:
We were exhausted by the climb up Mont Blanc.
We rested by the side of the trail.

COMBINED:
Exhausted by the climb up Mont Blanc, we rested by the side of the trail.

Exercise 8 Recognizing Participial Phrases Write the participial phrase in each sentence. Then, write the word the participial phrase modifies. Finally, label the phrase *essential* or *nonessential.*

1. Pioneering in different fields, the French have been leaders in the scientific world.
2. The French government, having supported scientific research for more than 350 years, has made many advances possible.
3. In 1635, the Royal Garden became one of the first scientific research centers sponsored by a government.
4. King Louis XIV, known as the Sun King, founded the Royal Academy of Science.
5. Revered as the father of modern chemistry, Antoine Lavoisier gave much to science.

Exercise 9 Combining Sentences With Participial Phrases Combine each pair of sentences by turning one into a participial phrase.

1. Marie Curie helped found the field of nuclear chemistry. She did so studying radioactive elements.
2. French researchers have also achieved numerous medical breakthroughs. They have been striving to improve the quality of life.
3. During the eighteenth century, Marie François Xavier Bichat conducted research. It focused on the study of human anatomy.
4. Another French researcher, Louis Pasteur, invented several vaccines. He invented them for a world plagued by disease.
5. Pasteur devoted his life to scientific study. He made many other crucial discoveries.

More Practice

Grammar Exercise Workbook
• pp. 61–66
On-line Exercise Bank
• Section 20.1
Go on-line:
PHSchool.com
Enter Web Code:
eek-1002

▲ Critical Viewing Use a participial phrase in a sentence comparing one aspect of Marie Curie's laboratory with an aspect of a modern one. **[Compare and Contrast]**

Gerunds

Many nouns ending in *-ing* are actually verbals known as *gerunds*. Gerunds are not difficult to recognize once you realize that they always end in *-ing* and always function as nouns.

▶ **KEY CONCEPT** A **gerund** is a form of a verb that acts as a noun. ■

The following examples show some of the ways gerunds may be used as nouns.

GERUNDS	
Subject	*Eating* is my favorite pastime in France.
Direct Object	The French people make *visiting* a pleasure.
Indirect Object	Mr. Mendoza's lecture gave *traveling* a new dimension.
Predicate Nominative	One Frenchman's favorite activity is debating.
Object of a Preposition	Their well-behaved dog showed signs of careful *training*.
Appositive	Brady's profession, *advertising*, is very competitive.

▼ Critical Viewing Describe a structure in the United States that is as recognizable as the Eiffel Tower to people around the world. Use a gerund in your response. **[Relate]**

▶ **Exercise 10** **Identifying Gerunds** Write the gerund in each sentence. Label each one *subject*, *direct object*, *indirect object*, *predicate nominative*, *object of a preposition*, or *appositive*.

EXAMPLE: She gave fencing her best effort.
ANSWER: fencing (indirect object)

1. Nearly one third of the French population is involved in some type of athletic training.
2. This is remarkable, because the schools focus mainly on learning.
3. Jogging, running, and walking are practiced by hundreds of thousands of French people every day.
4. Rugged individual sports—climbing and hiking—are popular all over France.
5. Skiing is another widely enjoyed individual sport.

Verb, Participle, or Gerund?

Words ending in *-ing* may be either parts of verb phrases, participles acting as adjectives, or gerunds.

KEY CONCEPT Words ending in *-ing* that act as nouns are gerunds. They do not have helping verbs like verbs ending in *-ing*, nor do they act as adjectives, as participles do. ∎

The following chart shows the same word functioning in sentences as a verb, a participle, and a gerund.

Verb	Participle	Gerund
Kevin is yawning at his desk.	The yawning boy was very tired.	Yawning is contagious.

Exercise 11 Distinguishing Between Verbs, Participles, and Gerunds Identify each underlined word as a *verb*, *participle*, or *gerund*.

EXAMPLE: The French have been <u>increasing</u> the national literacy rate for the last fifty years.

ANSWER: verb

1. <u>Reading</u> is a popular pastime throughout France.
2. <u>Reading</u> newspapers and magazines, the commuter waited for the metro.
3. French people are <u>reading</u> more periodicals than ever.
4. Articles written in both English and French are strong <u>selling</u> points for many magazines.
5. <u>Selling</u> magazines is a difficult task in the competitive French market.
6. One of France's oldest newsmagazines, *L'Express* is <u>selling</u> well after many years of publication.
7. The <u>leading</u> daily newspapers include *Le Monde, Le Parisien,* and *Le Figaro.*
8. *The New York Times* and *The Washington Post* are <u>leading</u> the way for other English-language papers in France.
9. <u>Publishing</u> books is an ever-expanding industry in France.
10. Ironically, authors are <u>publishing</u> more comic books today than many other types of books.

▶ **More Practice**

Grammar Exercise Workbook
• pp. 67–68
On-line Exercise Bank
• Section 20.1
Go on-line:
PHSchool.com
Enter Web Code:
eek-1002

Get instant feedback! Exercises 10 and 11 are available on-line or on CD-ROM.

Gerund Phrases

Like participles, gerunds may be joined by other words to make *gerund phrases.*

▶ **KEY CONCEPT** A **gerund phrase** is a gerund with modifiers or a complement, all acting together as a noun. ■

The following examples show just a few of the ways that gerunds may be expanded into gerund phrases.

GERUND PHRASES	
With adjectives:	*His constant, angry ranting* made Napoleon difficult to tolerate.
With an adjective phrase:	*Arguing about grades* will get you nowhere.
With an adverb:	*Answering quickly* is not always a good idea.
With a prepositional phrase:	Many places in France prohibit *walking on the grass.*
With an object of a preposition:	Pierre was incapable of *reciting the poem.*
With indirect and direct objects:	The French teacher tried *giving her students praise.*

Note About *Gerunds* and *Possessive Pronouns:* Always use the possessive form of a personal pronoun in front of a gerund.

INCORRECT: We never listen to *him boasting.*

CORRECT: We never listen to *his boasting.*

▶ **Exercise 12** Identifying Gerund Phrases Write the gerund phrase or phrases in each sentence. Label each one *subject, direct object,* or *object of a preposition.*
1. Making movies is a big business in France.
2. An average year for the French film industry entails producing roughly 150 movies.
3. Only India and the United States are known for making more movies than France.
4. Viewing American movies is a popular French pastime, but the French try promoting their own films.
5. Government restrictions limit the showing of American films to one third of the nation's theaters.

Get instant feedback! Exercises 12 and 13 are available on-line or on CD-ROM.

▶ **More Practice**

Grammar Exercise Workbook
• pp. 60–70
On-line Exercise Bank
• Section 20.1
   Go on-line:
   PHSchool.com
   Enter Web Code:
   eek-1002

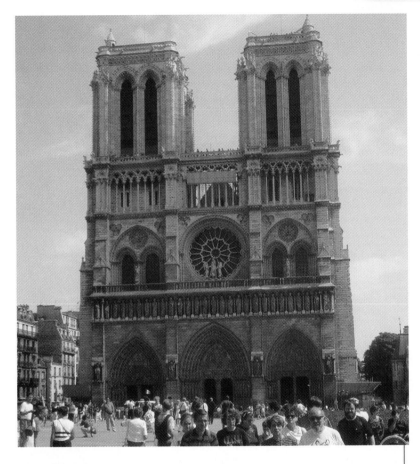

◄ Critical Viewing
What might be some
of the reasons for
the popularity of
Notre Dame, the
Gothic cathedral in
the middle of Paris?
Use at least one
gerund phrase in
your response.
[Speculate]

Exercise 13 Revising to Form Gerund Phrases Revise each sentence, changing the underlined words to a gerund phrase. You may have to add or change words to keep the meaning of the sentence.

EXAMPLE: Construction of *Notre Dame de Paris* began in 1163 <u>when the cornerstone was laid</u>.

ANSWER: Construction of *Notre Dame de Paris* began in 1163 with the laying of the cornerstone.

1. <u>To complete the cathedral</u> was no small task
2. <u>To gaze at Gothic architecture</u> makes our thoughts ascend.
3. Gothic architects and artisans worked <u>to craft</u> the rose windows of stained glass.
4. <u>To build it</u> took teams of workers eighty-seven years.
5. No expense was spared <u>to erect</u> a church that would reflect the prestige of Paris.

Infinitives

The third and last kind of verbal is the *infinitive*.

▶ **KEY CONCEPT** An **infinitive** is a form of a verb that generally appears with the word *to* and acts as a noun, an adjective, or an adverb. ■

The next chart shows examples of infinitives acting as nouns. When infinitives function as nouns in sentences, they can be used in almost as many ways as gerunds are.

INFINITIVES USED AS NOUNS	
Subject	To understand requires maturity and acceptance.
Direct Object	The peasants of France decided to rebel.
Predicate Nominative	The French soldier's only hope was to surrender.
Object of a Preposition	Our flight from Paris was about to leave.
Appositive	You have only one choice, to stay.

Unlike gerunds, infinitives can also act as adjectives and adverbs.

INFINITIVES USED AS MODIFIERS	
Adjective	The children showed a willingness *to cooperate*.
Adverb	During the war, the French people struggled *to resist*. Some people were unable *to fight*.

▶ **Exercise 14** Writing Sentences With Infinitives Write sentences on the subject of another country, using infinitives according to the instructions given.
1. Use *to visit* as an adverb.
2. Use *to watch* as a subject.
3. Use *to ride* as the object of a preposition.
4. Use *to eat* as a predicate nominative.
5. Use *to return* as an appositive.

▶ **More Practice**

Grammar Exercise Workbook
• pp. 71–72
On-line Exercise Bank
• Section 20.1
Go on-line:
PHSchool.com
Enter Web Code:
eek-1002

Exercise 15 Identifying Infinitives Write the infinitive in each sentence. Then, label each *subject, direct object, predicate nominative, object of a preposition, appositive, adjective,* or *adverb.*

EXAMPLE: Museums are my favorite places to visit.

ANSWER: to visit (adjective)

1. France has a large number of interesting museums to visit.
2. Almost every museum contains numerous priceless works of art for the visitor to admire.
3. Since many museums were in disrepair, the government decided in 1956 to renovate them.
4. To modernize was the ultimate goal of the government program.
5. Constructed originally as a fortress by King Philippe August, the Louvre was intended to defend Paris from its enemies.
6. To explore France's most important museum requires several full days.
7. Massive crowds during the 1980's left the museum with only one option, to expand.
8. American architect I. M. Pei was hired to design a new entrance.
9. To enter the Louvre through the enormous glass pyramid is a most awesome experience.
10. To economize, visitors can buy a three-day pass for the Louvre and other French museums.

🖥 **Internet Tip**

To learn more about the Louvre's history and collections, go to its official Web site at **http://www.louvre.fr/** Choose the **English** option.

◀ Critical Viewing
What features of this Louvre gallery make viewing its art an enjoyable experience for visitors? Use an infinitive phrase in your response. **[Evaluate]**

Prepositional Phrase or Infinitive?

The difference between a prepositional phrase and an infinitive is easy to recognize once you are aware of it.

> **KEY CONCEPTS** A prepositional phrase always ends with a noun or pronoun. An infinitive always ends with a verb. ■

Notice the difference between the prepositional phrase and the infinitive in the following chart.

Prepositional Phrase	Infinitive
The French soldier listened *to the command.*	A general's purpose in the army is *to command.*

Note About *Infinitives Without* To: Sometimes infinitives do not include the word *to.* When an infinitive follows one of the eight verbs listed here, the *to* is generally omitted.

dare	help	make	see
hear	let	please	watch

EXAMPLES: She doesn't dare *go* without permission.
Did you hear the French vocalist Edith Piaf *sing* on that old recording?

> **Exercise 16** Distinguishing Between Prepositional **Phrases and Infinitives** Write the infinitive or the prepositional phrase beginning with *to* in each sentence. Then, label each *prepositional phrase* or *infinitive.*

EXAMPLE: When I am in Paris, I like to drive.
ANSWER: to drive (infinitive)

1. To travel is very easy in France.
2. There are many different ways to tour.
3. In Paris, the subway is a good place to start.
4. The subway will take you to every part of the city.
5. You can travel easily from the fancy Sixteenth District to the Latin Quarter, where students hang out.
6. You will want to buy a book of tickets good for ten rides.
7. Outside of Paris, high-speed trains can take travelers to cities in several parts of the country.
8. These trains can accelerate to speeds of more than 200 miles per hour.
9. Travelers are also able to take high-speed trains as far as Amsterdam, Holland.
10. Trains to most European cities leave Paris often.

Infinitive Phrases

Infinitives also can be joined with other words to form phrases.

> **KEY CONCEPT** An **infinitive phrase** is an infinitive with modifiers, complements, or a subject, all acting together as a single part of speech. ■

INFINITIVE PHRASES	
With an adverb:	Jeffrey's entire family likes *to rise early*.
With adverb phrases:	*To skate on the ice* without falling was not easy for him.
With a direct object:	He hated *to leave the city of Lyon*.
With indirect and direct objects:	They promised *to show us the slides* from their trip to France.
With subject and complement:	I would like her *to determine her own goals*.

> **Exercise 17** Revising Sentences to Change Participles and Gerunds to Infinitives Rewrite each sentence, changing the participles and gerunds to infinitives.

EXAMPLE: One of my favorite activities is watching the French cooking show on Channel four.

ANSWER: One of my favorite activities is to watch the French cooking show on Channel four.

1. Eating in France is eating well.
2. Many French people prefer dining at home.
3. They browse among the small shops and markets, looking for the freshest ingredients.
4. Many French people learn cooking with herbs and spices.
5. Making a delicious meal with little money is a notable ability of French people.
6. Tempting travelers, each part of the country offers regional specialties.
7. Choosing among the wide variety of cooking styles in France is a difficult task.
8. The object of one style, *haute cuisine*, is preparing rich, elaborately presented meals.
9. The object of the style known as *nouvelle cuisine* is making light dishes without the heavy cream of *haute cuisine*.
10. The aim of all French cuisine is preparing food that is not only delectable but also attractively served.

More Practice

Grammar Exercise Workbook
• pp. 71–74
On-line Exercise Bank
• Section 20.1
Go on-line:
PHSchool.com
Enter Web Code:
eek-1002

Get instant feedback! Exercises 16 and 17 are available on-line or on CD-ROM.

GRAMMAR EXERCISES 18–27

Exercise 18 Identifying Adjective and Adverb Phrases Write the sentences, underlining each prepositional phrase. Identify each as either an *adjective phrase* or an *adverb phrase*.

1. Charlemagne was an influential figure in French history.
2. During the Middle Ages, he became the first true ruler of France.
3. In 771, Charlemagne inherited the territory of his father and brother.
4. He soon initiated a long series of wars against rival factions throughout western Europe.
5. Around this time, he also provided military aid to the Pope in Rome.
6. For a reward, the Pope gave Charlemagne the title of Holy Roman Emperor.
7. By the year 800, Charlemagne ruled over the majority of western Europe.
8. He founded his permanent capital of Aix-la-Chapelle in present-day western Germany.
9. Charlemagne imposed upon his subjects an intelligent system of laws and government.
10. He also established a number of crude educational centers among the monasteries under his control.

Exercise 19 Revising a Paragraph to Combine Sentences Using Appositives and Appositive Phrases Revise this paragraph, combining short sentences by using appositives and appositive phrases.

Joan of Arc was the national heroine of France. She saved the country from English rule during the Hundred Years' War. She was born in Domremy in 1412. Domremy was a small town in northeastern France. Joan believed she had a divine mission.

The mission was the liberation of France. Charles VII allowed her to lead his soldiers into battle against the English. Charles VII was the French king. After several important victories, Joan was captured by the Burgundians. The Burgundians were England's allies. The English executed Joan for the act of opposing the laws of the church. Such an act is called heresy.

Exercise 20 Supplying Participles Depending on the context of the sentence, supply either the present or past participle of the verb in parentheses. Then, label each participial phrase *essential* or *nonessential*.

1. The French author Voltaire is one of the most (admire) writers of the eighteenth century.
2. He was born with the (give) name François Marie Arouet in Paris in 1694.
3. (Serve) time in prison at age twenty-four, Arouet changed his name to Voltaire.
4. The young man was already a (respect) writer by this time.
5. (Achieve) popular and critical acclaim in 1718, the drama *Oedipe* is regarded as Voltaire's first major success.
6. In addition to being a writer, Voltaire was also an (aspire) philosopher.
7. (Rebel) against intolerance, censorship, and injustice, he founded a reformist group (call) the *Philosophes.*
8. This group of intellectuals attempted to change society by presenting (oppose) views of (accept) theories.
9. In all of his work, Voltaire offers his readers material (distinguish) by wit and intelligence.
10. The author of countless letters, plays, poems, and essays, he was clearly a master of the (write) word.

Exercise 21 Identifying Gerunds and Gerund Phrases Write the gerund or gerund phrase in each sentence. Identify the function of each as *subject, direct object, indirect object, predicate nominative, object of a preposition,* or *appositive.*

1. In 1642, the French king Louis XIV began the difficult task of ruling.
2. As he was only four years old, the running of France was left to his mother and her counselor until Louis was older.
3. After the death of his mother's counselor, Louis instituted a new policy: governing without a prime minister.
4. One of Louis's obsessions was expanding the power and influence of France.
5. Louis made conquering the Netherlands and defeating the English his priorities.

Exercise 22 Distinguishing Between Verbs, Participles, and Gerunds Identify each underlined word as *verb, participle,* or *gerund.*

1. <u>Conquering</u> Europe was the goal of French emperor Napoleon Bonaparte.
2. His <u>conquering</u> armies defeated the united forces of Europe in many battles.
3. French soldiers were <u>conquering</u> enemy armies for more than fifteen years.
4. After <u>attacking</u> Russia in 1812, Napoleon's army was forced to retreat.
5. In less than a year, France and allied European forces were <u>fighting</u> again.

Exercise 23 Writing Sentences With Verbal Phrases Write sentences about a political or military leader, using verbal phrases as instructed.

1. Use *leading* as a subject.
2. Use *inspired* as a predicate adjective.
3. Use *to continue* as a direct object.
4. Use *forgetting* as the object of the preposition *without.*
5. Use *to remember* as a subject.

Exercise 24 Identifying Infinitives and Infinitive Phrases Write the infinitive or infinitive phrase in each of the following sentences. Label each *subject, direct object, predicate nominative, object of a preposition, appositive, adjective,* or *adverb.*

1. Charles de Gaulle was to lead France through World War II and the difficult post-war years.
2. In the 1930's, De Gaulle thought the French army was unprepared for the war it was about to fight.
3. After the French government surrendered in 1940, De Gaulle felt he had but one choice, to escape.
4. He resolved to form a new French government in England.
5. For the remainder of the war, he continued to command the resistance groups and the Free French army.

Exercise 25 Find It in Your Reading In the excerpt from *Antigone* on page 308, name the word that each participle modifies.

Exercise 26 Find It in Your Writing In the compositions in your portfolio, find an example of an adjective and adverb phrase, an appositive, a participle, a gerund, and an infinitive. If you cannot find an item, challenge yourself to add it in an appropriate place in your writing.

Exercise 27 Writing Application Imagine that you are going to host a French exchange student. Write a brief letter telling the student about your school and town and what to bring to this country for the visit.

Clauses

Every clause contains a subject and a verb. However, not every clause can stand by itself as a complete thought.

KEY CONCEPT A **clause** is a group of words with its own subject and verb. ■

Independent and Subordinate Clauses

The two basic kinds of clauses are the *independent clause* and the *subordinate clause.*

KEY CONCEPT An **independent clause** can stand by itself as a complete sentence. ■

Independent clauses are used in several different ways.

STANDING ALONE:	That woman teaches Latin.
WITH ANOTHER INDEPENDENT CLAUSE:	Mudslides will engulf these hillside villas, *and some will be ruined.*
WITH A SUBORDINATE CLAUSE:	Brian asked to be excused from studying *because he was ill.*

KEY CONCEPT A **subordinate clause,** although it has a subject and verb, cannot stand by itself as a complete sentence; it can only be part of a sentence. ■

EXAMPLE: The woman *to whom I introduced you* teaches Latin.

This sentence contains the subordinate clause *to whom I introduced you,* which appears in the middle of an independent clause.

EXAMPLE: *Unless the rain stops soon,* mudslides will engulf these hillside villas.

In this sentence, the subordinate clause, *unless the rain stops soon,* precedes the independent clause.

EXAMPLE: Brian asked *that he be excused.*

Here, the subordinate clause follows the independent clause.

Like phrases, subordinate clauses can function as adjectives, adverbs, and nouns in sentences.

Theme: Ancient Rome

In this section, you will learn about adjective, adverb, and noun clauses. The examples and exercises in this section are about Ancient Rome.

Cross-Curricular Connection: Social Studies

ⓛ Learn More

To find out how different combinations of clauses determine different types of sentences, see Chapter 21.

▶ **Exercise 28** Recognizing Independent and Subordinate Clauses Write and label the independent and subordinate clauses in these sentences.

1. The luxury of baths, which we have come to associate with Rome, was imported from the East.
2. The earliest Roman literature, which contained translations from Greek classics, was based on Greek models.
3. Roman boys, who received better training than the girls did, were taught the Greek classics.
4. The Greeks were conquered by Rome, but culturally the Greeks were the conquerors.
5. Romans were proud of their civilization, although much of it was Greek in origin.

▲ Critical Viewing What might some of the figures on these ancient coins represent? Answer using a sentence with a subordinate clause. **[Speculate]**

Adjective Clauses

One way to add description and detail to a sentence is by using an *adjective clause.*

▶ **KEY CONCEPT** An **adjective clause** is a subordinate clause that modifies a noun or pronoun by telling *what kind* or *which one.* ■

Most often, adjective clauses begin with one of the relative pronouns: *that, which, who, whom,* or *whose.* Sometimes, however, adjective clauses may begin with a *relative adverb,* such as *before, since, when, where,* or *why.* All of these words relate the clause to the word it modifies.

▶ **KEY CONCEPT** An adjective clause begins with a relative pronoun or a relative adverb. ■

In the chart on the next page, the adjective clauses are italicized. Arrows indicate the noun or pronoun modified by each clause. These are adjective clauses because they answer the questions *What kind?* and *Which one?* Notice also that the first three clauses begin with relative pronouns and the last two begin with relative adverbs.

20.2

ADJECTIVE CLAUSES

Anyone *who reads about ancient Rome* will find it very interesting.

I finished reading the book *that you loaned me.*

We gave the story, *which we found fascinating,* a second read.

Spring is the time *when peepers make their shrill evening sound.*

Our trip to Italy ended with a visit to the town *where my parents were born.*

Like appositives and participial phrases, adjective clauses can often be used to combine information from two sentences into one. Using adjective clauses to combine sentences can indicate the relationship between ideas as well as add detail to a sentence.

TWO SENTENCES: This statue represents a Roman soldier. He is dressed for battle.

COMBINED: This statue represents a Roman soldier who is dressed for battle.

Adjective clauses, like appositive and participial phrases, are set off by punctuation only when they are not essential to the meaning of a sentence. The chart on the following page contrasts nonessential and essential adjective clauses.

Notice that in the sentences on the left, omitting the adjective clauses would not change the basic message. However, if you were to take away the adjective clauses on the right, the message would not be complete. (See Chapter 28 for more about punctuating adjective clauses.)

▶ Critical Viewing What elements of this sculpture suggest the subject's status as a soldier? Use a sentence with an adjective clause in your answer. [Analyze]

Nonessential Clauses	Essential Clauses
One of Dickens's best characters is Charles Darnay, *who appears in Dickens's novel about the French Revolution.*	The novel *that everyone must read by Monday afternoon* promises to be very exciting.
Jean McCurdy, *who studied three hours every evening for a month,* won the statewide competition.	A student *who studies regularly* usually finds test-taking easy.

In the sentences on the left, the commas indicate that the clauses give additional information. In the sentences on the right, the lack of commas shows that the clauses are needed to identify the words they modify. Read the contrasting sentences aloud. Notice that you naturally pause before and after the nonessential clauses and that your voice drops as you read them. Realizing this should help you recognize clauses in your own writing that need to be set off with commas.

Exercise 29 Identifying Adjective Clauses and the Words They Modify Write the adjective clause in each sentence. Then, write the word or words the adjective clause modifies. Finally, label the clause *nonessential* or *essential.*

EXAMPLE: The Roman Empire, which achieved greatness, had humble beginnings.

ANSWER: which achieved greatness; The Roman Empire (nonessential)

1. The Punic Wars, a name derived from the Latin word for *Phoenician,* were fought between Rome and Carthage.
2. The first war, which made Rome a naval power, ended in 241 B.C.
3. A second war that was fought between the two powers began in 218 B.C.
4. The Carthaginians, who were led by Hannibal, marched on Italy but failed to completely conquer the Romans.
5. The third Punic War, which resulted in ruin for Carthage, removed any serious threat to Rome's supremacy.
6. Slaves and gold that reached Rome from the new territories kindled the idea that conquest was profitable.
7. The city that began as a republic was becoming an empire.
8. The Romans conquered Gaul, now known as France.
9. The Greeks, who looked on the Romans as barbarians, were instrumental in shaping Roman culture.
10. The period of relative stability that Roman rule brought to its conquered territories was known as *pax romana* (Roman peace).

▶ **More Practice**

Grammar Exercise Workbook
• pp. 75–76
On-line Exercise Bank
• Section 20.2
Go on-line:
PHSchool.com
Enter Web Code:
eek-1002

Get instant feedback! Exercise 29 is available on-line or on CD-ROM.

Relative Pronouns

Relative pronouns function in two ways.

▶ **KEY CONCEPT** **Relative pronouns** connect adjective clauses to the words they modify and act as subjects, direct objects, objects of prepositions, or adjectives in the clauses. ■

To tell how a relative pronoun is used within a clause, separate the clause from the rest of the sentence, and find the subject and verb in the clause.

🌼 **Grammar** 🌼 and **Style Tip**

Although adding adjective and adverb clauses to your sentences can make your writing more interesting, be careful not to make your sentences too long. Too many long sentences can be just as distracting as too many short, choppy ones.

THE USES OF RELATIVE PRONOUNS WITHIN CLAUSES
As a Subject

A structure *that is built on a good foundation* is built to last.
    Clause: that is built on a good foundation.
    Subject: that   *Verb:* is built
    Use of relative pronoun: subject

As a Direct Object

My brother-in-law, *whom my sister met at college,* is a poet.
    Clause: whom my sister met at college
    Reworded clause: my sister met whom at college
    Subject: sister   *Verb:* met
    Use of relative pronoun: direct object

As an Object of a Preposition

This is the book *about which I read enthusiastic reviews.*
    Clause: about which I read enthusiastic reviews.
    Reworded clause: I read enthusiastic reviews about
                            which
    Subject: I   *Verb:* read
    Use of relative pronoun: object of a preposition

As an Adjective

The senator *whose opinion was in question* spoke to the press.
    Clause: whose opinion was in question
    Subject: opinion   *Verb:* was
    Use of relative pronoun: adjective

Note About *Understood Words:* Sometimes in writing and in speech, a relative pronoun is left out of an adjective clause. The missing word, though simply understood, still functions in the sentence.

EXAMPLES: The legendary heroes [*whom*] *we studied* were
            great men and women.
            The suggestions [*that*] *they made* were ignored.

Relative Adverbs

Unlike a relative pronoun, a relative adverb has only one use within a clause.

More Practice

Grammar Exercise
Workbook
• pp. 75–76
On-line Exercise Bank
• Section 20.2
  Go on-line:
  PHSchool.com
  Enter Web Code:
  eek-1002

KEY CONCEPT **Relative adverbs** connect adjective clauses to the words they modify and act as adverbs in the clauses. ∎

The following chart shows an adjective clause introduced by a relative adverb.

THE USE OF RELATIVE ADVERBS WITHIN CLAUSES

Pat yearned for the day *when she could walk without crutches.*

> *Clause:* when she could walk without crutches
> *Reworded clause:* she could walk when without crutches
> *Subject:* she   *Verb:* could walk
> *Use of relative adverb:* adverb

Exercise 30 **Recognizing the Uses of Relative Pronouns and Relative Adverbs** Write the adjective clause in each sentence, circling the relative pronoun or relative adverb. Then, label the use of the relative pronoun within the clause *subject, direct object, object of a preposition, adjective,* or *adverb.*

EXAMPLE: The first great ruler (that) we
            learned about was Julius
            Caesar.

ANSWER: that we learned about (object of
            a preposition)

1. Julius Caesar, about whom Shakespeare later wrote a play, was renowned as the conqueror of Gaul.
2. Rome, which was expanding quite rapidly, was undergoing a great deal of turmoil at home.
3. Julius Caesar, whose seven years in Gaul removed him from much of the intrigue, was a talented politician.
4. The army, which Caesar commanded ably, was devoted to him.
5. Julius Caesar claimed to be defending the republic at the moment when he and his army marched on Rome in 49 B.C.

▲ **Critical Viewing**
How well do you think this sculpture represents real human qualities? Answer using an adjective clause. **[Evaluate]**

Clauses • **327**

▶ **Exercise 31** Combining Sentences With Adjective Clauses
Turn each pair of sentences into a single sentence with an
adjective clause. Then, underline each adjective clause, and
draw an arrow from it to the word or words it modifies.
1. Caesar fought a civil war for four years after his march on
   Rome. He challenged those who might oppose him.
2. Julius Caesar was not a vicious conqueror. He made
   friends with his former enemies.
3. He was made dictator for life. This would be a position
   similar to that of a monarch.
4. Romans felt a monarchy would violate their ideals. They
   placed a high value on tradition.
5. Caesar's enemies united against him. They assassinated
   him in 44 B.C.

Adverb Clauses

Subordinate clauses can also act as adverbs.

▶ **KEY CONCEPT** **Subordinate adverb clauses** modify
verbs, adjectives, adverbs, or verbals by telling *where, when,
in what way, to what extent, under what condition*, or *why*. ■

▶ **KEY CONCEPT** All adverb clauses begin with subordinating conjunctions. ■

The following chart shows some of the most common subordinating conjunctions.

SUBORDINATING CONJUNCTIONS		
after	even though	unless
although	if	until
as	in order that	when
as if	since	whenever
as long as	so that	where
because	than	wherever
before	though	while

Recognizing these subordinating conjunctions will help you
identify adverb clauses. In the next chart, the adverb clauses
are italicized. Arrows point to the words modified by each
clause. The first answers the question *When?*, the second
adverb clause answers the question *Where?*, and so on. The last
two adverb clauses are different because they provide information that a single adverb cannot. The next-to-last adverb clause
answers the question *Under what condition?* The question *Why?*
is answered by the last adverb clause in the chart.

▶ **More Practice**

Grammar Exercise
Workbook
• pp. 75–76
On-line Exercise Bank
• Section 20.2
 Go on-line:
 PHSchool.com
 Enter Web Code:
 eek-1002

Complete the exercise
on-line! Exercise 31
is available on-line or
on CD-ROM.

ADVERB CLAUSES
Modifying a Verb
When you finish your book about Rome, you should then begin your report.
Modifying an Adjective
Tricia seemed happy *wherever she was*.
Modifying an Adverb
Faster *than the eye could follow*, the race car sped away.
Modifying a Participle
Laughing *until he gasped for breath*, Fred could not speak.
Modifying a Gerund
Driving a car *if you do not have a license* is illegal.
Modifying an Infinitive
We decided to remain in our seats *so that we could watch the movie again*.

▼ **Critical Viewing** Using an adverb clause, describe characteristics of this sculpture that are not unlike men's features today. **[Compare]**

Whether an adverb clause appears at the beginning, middle, or end of a sentence can sometimes affect the meaning.

EXAMPLES: *Before the year was over,* Caesar made plans to march into Rome.

Caesar made plans to march into Rome *before the year was over.*

Like adjective clauses, adverb clauses can be used to combine the information from two sentences into one. The combined sentence shows a close relationship between the ideas.

TWO SENTENCES: It was storming. They did not launch the attack.

COMBINED: *Because it was storming,* they did not launch the attack.

▶ **Exercise 32** Identifying Adverb Clauses and the Words
They Modify Write the adverb clause in each sentence. Then,
write the word or words each adverb clause modifies.

EXAMPLE: After Caesar was killed, his nephew Octavius
             gained power.

ANSWER: After Caesar was killed (gained)

1. Because he was Caesar's nephew, Octavius hunted
   Caesar's assassins after his death.
2. After he fought in Egypt and returned to Rome, he became
   emperor in all but name.
3. He was fortunate that the army had supported him.
4. Acting as if he himself were emperor, he was treated as
   one.
5. Since he was given the honorary title of Augustus, he has
   been known as Caesar Augustus.

🔲 **Research Tip**

Look for information
about Roman
emperors under
"Ancient Rome" or
under the names of
particular rulers:
"Julius Caesar,"
"Caesar Augustus,"
"Tiberius," "Nero,"
"Marcus Aurelius,"
and so on.

Elliptical Adverb Clauses

Sometimes, words are omitted in adverb clauses, especially
in those clauses that begin with *as* or *than* and are used to
express comparisons. Such clauses are said to be *elliptical*.

▶ **KEY CONCEPT** An **elliptical clause** is a clause in which
the verb or subject and verb are understood but not actually
stated. ■

Even though the subject or the subject and the verb have
been left out of an elliptical clause, they still function to make
the clause express a complete thought. In the following examples, the understood words have been added in brackets. The
sentences are alike except for the words *he* and *him*. In the
first sentence, *he* is a subject. In the second sentence, *him*
functions as a direct object. The use of each word is easy to
see when the omitted words are noted.

VERB UNDERSTOOD: She resembles their father more *than he*
                     [*does*].

SUBJECT AND VERB   She resembles their father more *than*
UNDERSTOOD: [*she resembles*] *him.*

When you read or write elliptical clauses, mentally include
the omitted words. Doing this should help clarify the meaning
you intend.

Exercise 33 Recognizing Elliptical Adverb Clauses Write each sentence, adding the missing words in any elliptical clause. Then, underline the complete adverb clause in each sentence, and circle the words you have added.

EXAMPLE: Roman emperors were treated more like gods than men.

ANSWER: Roman emperors were treated more like gods than (they were treated like) men.

1. Caesar Augustus was considered as divine as his uncle.
2. Rome's territories increased more under Augustus' rule than under his uncle's.
3. His successors expanded the empire even farther than he.
4. They depended on the army as much as Caesar Augustus.
5. The empire as we know it owes as much to his successors as to Caesar Augustus.

Exercise 34 Combining Sentences With Adverb Clauses Turn each pair of sentences into a single sentence with an adverb clause. Then, underline each adverb clause.

EXAMPLE: Rome was hard to rule. It was a large bureaucracy.

ANSWER: Rome was hard to rule because it was a large bureaucracy.

1. The nature and government of Rome resulted from Caesar Augustus. They evolved gradually.
2. Many emperors appointed their heirs. Control of the empire would be hereditary.
3. There were twelve emperors in the century following Augustus' death. Only four were related to him.
4. Augustus' line ended in A.D. 68. Nero, the last emperor related to him, died in A.D. 68.
5. The Senate might endorse or appoint a successor. Real power remained with the army.

Exercise 35 Writing Sentences With Adverb Clauses Write sentences about a historical era using adverb clauses, as indicated below.
1. Use *although* in a clause modifying a verb.
2. Use *if* in a clause modifying a gerund.
3. Use *as much as* in an elliptical clause.
4. Use *whenever* in a clause modifying an adjective.
5. Use *while* in a clause modifying a participle.

More Practice

Grammar Exercise Workbook
• pp. 77–78
On-line Exercise Bank
• Section 20.2
  Go on-line:
  PHSchool.com
  Enter Web Code:
  eek-1002

Interactive Textbook

Get instant feedback! Exercises 32, 33, 34, and 35 are available on-line or on CD-ROM.

Noun Clauses

Subordinate clauses can also act as nouns.

> **KEY CONCEPT** A **noun clause** is a subordinate clause that acts as a noun. ■

A *noun clause* acts in almost the same way as a single-word noun does in a sentence.

> **KEY CONCEPT** In a sentence, a noun clause may act as a subject, direct object, indirect object, predicate nominative, object of a preposition, or appositive. ■

The chart on the following page contains examples of the various functions of noun clauses.

Learn More

To review basic sentence parts, turn to Chapter 19.

GRAMMAR IN LITERATURE

from **Julius Caesar**

William Shakespeare

Act IV, Scene iii, Brutus' tent

In these lines, the noun clauses are highlighted in blue. In Brutus' last speech, notice that the word that, *introducing the noun clause, is understood.*

CASSIUS. *That you have wronged me* doth appear in this:
You have condemned and noted Lucius Pella
For taking bribes here of the Sardians;
Wherein my letters, praying on his side,
Because I knew the man, was slighted off.

BRUTUS. You wrong yourself to write in such a case.

CASSIUS. In such a time as this it is not meet
That every nice offense should bear his comment.

BRUTUS. Let me tell you, Cassius, *you yourself
Are much condemned to have an itching palm,
To sell and mart your offices for gold
To undeservers.*

Introductory Words

Noun clauses frequently begin with the words *that, which, who, whom,* or *whose,* the same words that are used to begin adjective clauses. *Whichever, whoever,* or *whomever* may also be used as introductory words in noun clauses. Other noun clauses begin with the words *how, if, what, whatever, where, when, whether,* or *why.*

KEY CONCEPT Introductory words may act as subjects, direct objects, objects of prepositions, adjectives, or adverbs in noun clauses, or they may simply introduce the clauses. ■

Note in this chart that the introductory word *that* in the last example has no function except to introduce the clause.

NOUN CLAUSES	
Subject	*Whoever is last* must pay a penalty.
Direct Object	Please invite *whomever you want.*
Indirect Object	His manner gave *whoever met him* a shock.
Predicate Nominative	Our problem is *whether we should stay here or leave.*
Object of a Preposition	Use the money for *whatever purpose you choose.*
Appositive	The occupied country rejected our plea *that orphans be cared for by the Red Cross.*

Exercise 36 Identifying Noun Clauses Write the noun clause in each sentence. Then, label the clause *subject, direct object, indirect object, predicate nominative, object of a preposition,* or *appositive.*

EXAMPLE: Whoever was Roman felt it a great honor.
ANSWER: Whoever was Roman (subject)

1. In the beginning, a Roman citizen was whoever was born in Rome.
2. Later, what was necessary was to be born in Roman territory.
3. Citizenship was available only to whoever was free-born.
4. Romans often made whomever they conquered slaves.
5. Romans often let conquered peoples do whatever they wanted as long as taxes were paid.

More Practice

Grammar Exercise Workbook
• pp. 78–79
On-line Exercise Bank
• Section 20.2
  Go on-line:
  PHSchool.com
  Enter Web Code:
  eek-1002

Get instant feedback! Exercise 36 is available on-line or on CD-ROM.

NOUN CLAUSES	
Direct object:	*Whatever he accomplished* would be satisfactory.
Adjective:	The little girl could not decide *which flavor of ice cream she would like.*
No function in clause:	The officials determined *that the polls had been rigged.*

Most words that begin noun clauses may also introduce adjective or adverb clauses. To decide whether a clause acts as a noun, look at the role of the clause in the sentence. In the following examples, all three subordinating clauses begin with *where*, but only the first is a noun clause because it functions in the sentence as a direct object.

NOUN CLAUSE: Caesar told his soldiers *where they would gather for battle.*

ADJECTIVE CLAUSE: They took the soldier to a tent *where a doctor examined his wound.*

ADVERB CLAUSE: She lives *where the weather is warm all year.*

Note About *Introductory Words:* The introductory word *that* is often omitted from a noun clause. In the following example, the understood word *that* is in brackets.

EXAMPLE: The secretary suggested [*that*] *you leave your name.*

▶ **Exercise 37** **Recognizing the Uses of Introductory Words** Write the introductory word from each noun clause in Exercise 36. Then, label the use of each within the clause *subject, direct object, object of a preposition, adjective, adverb,* or *a word with no function.*

EXAMPLE: Whoever was Roman felt it to be a great honor.
ANSWER: Whoever (subject)

▲ **Critical Viewing** Many aspects of present-day stadiums resemble the Roman Colosseum. Using a noun clause, describe one or two of them. **[Relate]**

Hands-on Grammar

Noun Clause Flip-and-Folds

Practice with a Noun Clause Flip-and-Folds to learn how to vary your sentences by using noun clauses in various positions. Begin with several narrow strips of paper about 4" long. On one strip, print WAS THAT WE WON THE CONTEST. On another strip, print IT WAS GOOD NEWS. On a third strip, print WE HEARD THE. Now begin making sentences. Put the first two strips together, beginning with IT WAS . . . ; cover up the WAS at the beginning of the second strip. You will have a sentence in which THAT WE WON THE CONTEST is an appositive.

> IT WAS GOOD NEWS | THAT WE WON THE CONTEST

Next, fold under IT WAS on the first strip, uncover WAS on the second strip, and use THE from the third strip. The noun clause is now a predicate noun.

> THE GOOD NEWS | WAS THAT WE WON THE CONTEST

Next, add WE HEARD THE to form these variations—one making the clause a direct object, and the other, again, an appositive:

> WE HEARD THAT WE WON THE CONTEST

> WE HEARD THE GOOD NEWS THAT WE WON THE CONTEST

Now, flip the two strips, fold under WAS on the noun clause strip, and fold under IT on the other strip. Note that the noun clause becomes the subject of the sentence.

> THAT WE WON THE CONTEST | WAS GOOD NEWS

When you have finished, make other strips to flip and fold. Try these sentence parts: WE KNOW / WE TALK ABOUT / WHO WON THE CONTEST / IT WAS OUR FRIEND / WHEN WE WON THE CONTEST. Add other sentence parts that you can flip and fold to make noun clauses. Be on the lookout for some constructions that may actually be adjective clauses.

Find It in Your Reading Find examples of noun clauses in a story or article. For each one, identify its function in the sentence.

Find It in Your Writing Review a piece of writing from your portfolio. Combine two pairs of sentences using noun clauses.

GRAMMAR EXERCISES 38–45

▶ **Exercise 38** Recognizing Independent and Subordinate Clauses Identify the independent and subordinate clause in each sentence.

1. The ruins of many of the Romans' great buildings are still standing.
2. Later civilizations used stones from the Roman ruins when they wanted to build.
3. This scavenging, which occurred in many countries, has reduced the available information about the Romans.
4. The ruins of the city itself, which are dotted throughout present-day Rome, are most amazing.
5. Ruins can also be found in other European cities that were once a part of the Roman Empire.

▶ **Exercise 39** Identifying Adjective Clauses, the Words They Modify, and Introductory Words Write the adjective clause in each sentence and the word the clause modifies. Circle each relative pronoun or adverb, and label its use *subject, direct object, object of a preposition, adjective,* or *adverb.* Finally, label the clause *essential* or *nonessential.*

1. Ancient Rome, which had a million inhabitants at its zenith, was the supreme city of the empire.
2. A Roman aqueduct that was built in Spain still carries water to the city of Segovia.
3. Romans, whose concerns were uniformity and tradition, built or added on to cities.
4. Each city had temples, baths, theaters, and a forum, which served as a meeting place.
5. The Romans, who were fond of their comforts, had indoor heating and plumbing.

6. The things that wealthy Romans took for granted fell into disuse for many centuries after the Romans' fall.
7. Virgil, whom later cultures respected, was perhaps the most famous Roman writer.
8. He is a writer about whom much has been said in praise.
9. Virgil moved to Rome when his father's farm was confiscated.
10. The poet, whose greatest work was the *Aeneid,* died before he could give it the final revision.

▶ **Exercise 40** Identifying Noun Clauses Write the noun clause in each sentence. Label the clause *subject, direct object, indirect object, predicate nominative, object of a preposition,* or *appositive.*

1. Historians observe that the Roman Empire was attacked by many tribes.
2. The British Isles were the site where invading barbarians wiped out most traces of the Romans.
3. One fact became clear: that the Roman bureaucracy could no longer support the empire.
4. Whoever wanted to avoid paying taxes moved to the country.
5. Whatever group invaded a particular area often assumed Roman administrative duties.
6. Roman armies often consisted of soldiers from whatever groups were living in a particular region.
7. Romans maintained whatever traditions they could.
8. Many people believed that the empire was still an entity.
9. Today's civilization owes whoever promoted Roman ideals a great debt.
10. We should remember one fact: that much of our language and culture comes from the Romans.

Exercise 41 Supplying Relative
Adverbs Supply a logical relative
adverb to complete each sentence. Then,
write the word or words it modifies.
Finally, add the missing words in the elliptical clauses.

1. In the third century A.D., the Romans
   encountered trouble __?__ they turned.
2. Barbarian tribes wanted to cross the
   frontier __?__ they could settle in
   Roman lands.
3. Trying appeasement __?__ they resort-
   ed to war, the Romans hoped to avoid
   fighting.
4. Refortifying towns __?__ they could be
   protected against raids was common.
5. Taxes had to be raised __?__ these
   defenses could be built.
6. Economic recession was soon widespread __?__ were the crushing taxes.
7. The Goths crossed into Roman territory earlier __?__ the Franks.
8. To repel the invaders, Romans collected more taxes __?__ before.
9. As a ruler, the emperor Aurelian was
   better __?__ others.
10. One of his successors, Diocletian,
    divided the empire so that it came to
    resemble two empires more __?__ one.

Exercise 42 Revising to Combine
Sentences Using Adjective and Adverb
Clauses Turn each pair of sentences into
one with an adjective or adverb clause.
Underline each clause, and indicate the
word or words it modifies.

1. Diocletian appointed a co-emperor.
   The co-emperor had the same powers
   as he did.
2. Diocletian laid more emphasis on the
   divine status of the emperor. He was
   less tolerant of Christianity.
3. Under Diocletian, the army increased
   in size. Conscription was reintroduced.

4. Later, Constantine gained control. He
   then reunited the divided empire
   under one ruler.
5. He ordered his soldiers to wear a
   Christian symbol on their shields. He
   wanted to see whether the God of the
   Christians would help him win a battle.
6. Tolerance of Christianity was promoted.
   Persecution was only a sporadic
   occurrence.
7. Christianity became officially protected. It was able to grow and develop
   within the empire.
8. Constantine built a new city called
   Constantinople. It then remained an
   imperial capital for a thousand years.
9. In A.D. 380, the emperor Theodosius
   came to power. He then forbade
   worship of the old pagan gods.
10. Constantinople and the East were
    progressing. The West was declining.

Exercise 43 Find It in Your
Reading In the excerpt from *Julius
Caesar* on page 332, identify the function
of the highlighted noun clause in each
sentence.

Exercise 44 Find It in Your
Writing Look through your writing
portfolio. Find an example of each of the
three types of subordinate clauses—adjective, adverb, and noun. If you cannot find
an example of a particular type of clause,
find a place where you can add such a
clause to a piece of writing.

Exercise 45 Writing Application
Choose a period in ancient history that
you would like to visit. Write a description
of what you think life would be like for you
in that time. Include at least one adjective
clause, one adverb clause, and one noun
clause.

When we first learn to talk, we start by speaking single words. Then, we begin grouping words together to form sentences. It is at this point that we are able to start communicating in a meaningful way. Putting words together into sentences—nouns or pronouns accompanied by verbs to express complete thoughts—is the first step toward being an effective communicator, both as a speaker and as a writer. In this chapter, you will learn basic sentence functions and structures—ways in which you can vary sentence structures to make your writing more clear and interesting—and some of the types of errors that can occur in your sentences.

▲ Critical Viewing
Write two sentences about this scene, one from the point of view of a passenger on the ship and one from the point of view of a penguin. **[Contrast]**

Diagnostic Test

Directions: Write all answers on a separate sheet of paper.

Skill Check A. Label each sentence *declarative, interrogative, imperative,* or *exclamatory.*

1. Have you ever wanted to visit Antarctica?
2. Make sure to dress as warmly as you can for that adventure.
3. What an amazing animal a penguin is!
4. How can the penguin survive in such a frigid environment?
5. Their bodies are well adapted to life in subfreezing temperatures.

Skill Check B. Combine these sentences using the method indicated.

6. Antarctica was not discovered until the early 1800's. This was mostly because of its remoteness. (turn a sentence into a phrase)
7. Captain James Cook was the first explorer to cross the Antarctic Circle. He was on a mission from the British navy. (join with a relative pronoun)
8. Cook circumnavigated Antarctica. He never actually sighted the continent. (join with a comma and a coordinating conjunction)
9. Cook studied deposits of rocks in icebergs at sea. Cook concluded that a barren southern continent existed. (use a compound verb)
10. Cook reported his findings. Explorers from several other countries began their own search for the southern continent. (join with subordinating conjunction)

Skill Check C. Rewrite the following sentences to be more direct or to vary their beginnings as indicated in parentheses.

11. A Russian expedition sailed around Antarctica and discovered some offshore islands in 1821. (prepositional phrase)
12. The first known landing on Antarctica was by John Davis, who was an American explorer and whose main interest was commerce. (appositive)
13. James Weddell, traveling farther south than any other explorer, discovered the sea that bears his name. (participial phrase)
14. It was in the 1840's, at which time Antarctica's status as a continent was finally established. (Be more direct.)
15. One determined explorer, James Ross, was an explorer from Britain who sailed into a gulf that is now called the Ross Sea. (Be more direct.)

Skill Check D. Label each of the following items *fragment, run-on,* or *misplaced modifier.* Then, rewrite the item so that it is correct.

16. Many expeditions in the late 1800's and early 1900's.
17. One scientific expedition became caught on the ice, its members spent the winter of 1897–1898 stranded there.
18. Ernest Shackleton led a British expedition before turning back because of exhausted supplies to within 97 miles of the South Pole.
19. The Norwegian Roald Amundsen and a party of four reached the South Pole using dogs to pull their sleds on December 14, 1911.
20. Arrived five weeks before a British expedition led by Robert Scott.

The Four Functions of a Sentence

Sentences can be classified according to what they do. The four types of sentences in English are *declarative, interrogative, imperative,* and *exclamatory.*

Declarative sentences are the most common type. They are used to "declare," or state facts.

▶ **KEY CONCEPT** A **declarative sentence** states an idea and ends with a period. ■

DECLARATIVE: Hot-air balloons are flown mainly for recreation. Recently, adventurers succeeded in flying around the world in a hot-air balloon.

Interrogative means "asking." An *interrogative sentence* is a question.

▶ **KEY CONCEPT** An **interrogative sentence** asks a question and ends with a question mark. ■

INTERROGATIVE: Have you ever flown in a hot-air balloon? Do you think you would enjoy the experience?

▶ **Exercise 1** Identifying Declarative and Interrogative Sentences Write each of the following sentences on your paper. Identify each as declarative or interrogative, and punctuate it correctly.
1. Have you ever been to a balloon festival
2. We went to one in Albuquerque last year
3. Although I had heard about such festivals, I wondered what I would see there
4. When we arrived, the balloons were still on the ground
5. Next year, do you think you might go

Theme: Balloons
In this section, you will learn about the four types of sentences. The examples and exercises are about balloons.

Cross-Curricular Connection: Science

▶ Critical Viewing Write a sentence comparing these festive balloons to the kinds of balloons used in a balloon festival. **[Compare and Contrast]**

The word *imperative* is related to the word *emperor*, a person who gives commands. *Imperative sentences* are like emperors: They give commands.

▶ **KEY CONCEPT** An **imperative sentence** gives an order or a direction and ends with either a period or an exclamation mark. ■

Most imperative sentences start with a verb. In this type of imperative sentence, the subject is understood to be *you*.

IMPERATIVE: Follow the directions carefully.
             Wait for me!

Notice the punctuation at the end of these examples. In the first sentence, the period suggests that a mild command is being given in an ordinary tone of voice. The exclamation mark at the end of the second sentence suggests a strong command, one given in a loud voice.

To *exclaim* means to "shout out." *Exclamatory sentences* are used to "shout out" emotions, such as happiness, fear, delight, and anger.

▶ **KEY CONCEPT** An **exclamatory sentence** conveys strong emotion and ends with an exclamation mark. ■

EXCLAMATORY: She's not going to make that balloon trip
              without me!
              I have been waiting for the opportunity all
              my life!

▶ **Exercise 2** Identifying Imperative and Exclamatory Sentences Write each of the following sentences on your paper. Add the correct punctuation to the end of each sentence. Label imperative sentences *I* and exclamatory sentences *E*.
 1. Tell me about the festival
 2. What an amazing sight it was
 3. I have never seen so many balloons
 4. Wait until next year
 5. Come with us, and you'll see what I mean

▶ **Exercise 3** Writing the Four Types of Sentences Write a paragraph to one of your friends encouraging him or her to participate in some type of adventure with you. Use each of the four types of sentences at least once. Identify each type you have used.

▶ **More Practice**

Grammar Exercise
Workbook
• pp. 81–84
On-line Exercise Bank
• Section 21.1
  Go on-line:
  PHSchool.com
  Enter Web Code:
  eek-1002

Complete the exercises on-line! Exercises 1, 2, and 3 are available on-line or on CD-ROM.

Section Review

GRAMMAR EXERCISES 4–9

Exercise 4 Classifying Sentences by Function Label each sentence *declarative, interrogative, imperative,* or *exclamatory.*

1. Did you know that the Four Corners Hot-Air Balloon Fiesta is held in late May?
2. What I didn't know is that the International Balloon Fiesta is held in October.
3. Last year's festival was fantastic!
4. Which festival did you attend?
5. When you go to next year's festival, take lots of pictures.
6. Have you ever gone up in a balloon?
7. Miranda said it was the most exciting experience she's ever had.
8. What a thrill that would be!
9. Let me know if you decide to do it.
10. Maybe I'll try it, too.

Exercise 5 Supplying Appropriate Punctuation for Sentences Punctuate each sentence according to its function.

1. The Montgolfier brothers were the first to experiment with hot-air balloons
2. When they began experimenting in the 1700's, no one else had yet been successful
3. Who do you think their first passengers were
4. Even if you don't know, take a guess
5. A duck, a rooster, and a sheep were the first passengers
6. That's crazy
7. Balloon flights soon became a fad in Europe
8. Which was more popular, the hot-air balloon or the hydrogen-gas balloon
9. Look at this picture of the Montgolfier brothers
10. How daring they were

Exercise 6 Writing Sentences to Fit Functions Write a sentence that revises or answers each of the sentences below. The sentence you write should have the function indicated in parentheses.

1. Who first experimented with hot-air balloons? (declarative)
2. Is that the most amazing thing you've ever heard? (exclamatory)
3. I hope to learn more about ballooning. (interrogative)
4. Jacques Alexandre Charles and the Roberts brothers launched the first hydrogen balloon. (interrogative)
5. Will you tell me more? (imperative)

Exercise 7 Find It in Your Reading Skim through a travel magazine to find at least two examples of each of the four types of sentences. You can find your examples in advertisements and in articles.

Exercise 8 Find It in Your Writing Review a short story or a piece of autobiographical writing from your portfolio. Find at least one example of each type of sentence. Check to see that you have punctuated each correctly.

Exercise 9 Writing Application Write a brief narrative about a group of people your age who take part in an unusual adventure, such as a ballooning expedition. You can include dialogue. Try to use each type of sentence at least twice in your story.

Section 21.2 *Sentence Combining*

Books written for very young readers present information in short, direct sentences. While this makes the book easy to read, it doesn't make it enjoyable or interesting to mature readers. Writing that is to be read by mature readers should include sentences of varying lengths and complexity to create a flow of ideas. One way to achieve sentence variety is to combine sentences—to express two or more related ideas or pieces of information in a single sentence.

EXAMPLE: We went to the South Pole.
             We met scientists.
             We went to the South Pole and met scientists.
             We met scientists at the South Pole.
             We met scientists when we went to the South Pole.

▶ **KEY CONCEPT** Sentences can be combined by using a compound subject, a compound verb, or a compound object. ■

EXAMPLE: Moira enjoyed learning about Antarctic exploration.
                       Tom enjoyed learning about Antarctic exploration.
COMPOUND SUBJECT: Moira and Tom enjoyed learning about Antarctic exploration.

EXAMPLE: Lisa raced her dog sled.
                       Lisa won a prize.
COMPOUND VERB: Lisa raced her dog sled and won a prize.

EXAMPLE: Scott rode the icebreaker.
                       Scott rode the snowmobile.
COMPOUND OBJECT: Scott rode the icebreaker and the snowmobile.

Theme: Antarctica

In this section, you will learn ways to combine sentences. The examples and exercises are about Antarctica and the South Pole.

Cross-Curricular Connection: Social Studies

◀ Critical Viewing Write a series of sentences describing this picture. Then, combine two sentences following one of the examples above. **[Describe]**

▶ **Exercise 10** Combining Sentences Using Compound Verbs, Subjects, and Objects Combine each pair of sentences in the way that makes the most sense. Identify what you have done to combine them.

EXAMPLE: Milly chopped ice with a pick. She also used an axe.

ANSWER: Milly chopped ice with a pick and an axe. (compound objects)

1. Sir Edmund Winterbottom was an explorer. So was his son, Cecil.
2. They wanted to go on an adventure together. They decided to visit the South Pole.
3. Their trip took months of preparation. Their trip took detailed planning.
4. Long underwear had to be purchased. Then, warm coats had to be bought.
5. They would travel to the southern tip of South America. They would fly from there to the American Antarctic outpost.
6. The Winterbottoms also needed a guide. They required transport across the ice.
7. Following months of preparation, they were ready to go. They were excited.
8. Sir Edmund packed a large bag. Cecil did, too.
9. Their guide met them at the outpost with provisions. He also met them with his dog-sled team.
10. Within minutes, they had their equipment packed. They were off!

▶ **KEY CONCEPT** Sentences can be combined by joining two independent clauses to form a compound sentence. ■

Use a compound sentence when combining ideas that are related but independent. Compound sentences are formed by joining two independent clauses either with a comma and a conjunction or with a semicolon.

EXAMPLE: The wind chilled the tundra. The snow battered my face.

COMPOUND   The wind chilled the tundra, and the snow
SENTENCE: battered my face.

EXAMPLE: The snowstorm lasted for hours. The wind and the snow mingled with the air.

COMPOUND   The snowstorm lasted for hours; the wind and
SENTENCE: the snow mingled with the air.

▶ **More Practice**

Grammar Exercise Workbook
• pp. 85–86
On-line Exercise Bank
• Section 21.2
  Go on-line:
  PHSchool.com
  Enter Web Code:
  eek-1002

Complete the exercises on-line! Exercises 10 and 11 are available on-line or on CD-ROM.

▶ **Exercise 11** Forming Compound Sentences by Joining
Independent Clauses Combine the following sentences using
the method given in parentheses.

EXAMPLE: (semicolon) The South Pole is very cold.
            Ice is everywhere.

ANSWER: The South Pole is very cold; ice is
            everywhere.

1. (semicolon) The South Pole is a point at the
   southern end of the Earth's axis. It rests in
   central Antarctica.
2. (comma and conjunction) It is often associated with the magnetic South Pole. They are
   1,600 miles apart.
3. (comma and conjunction) The magnetic poles
   change location with time, a phenomenon known
   as polar wandering. The direction of wandering has
   been observed to reverse.
4. (semicolon) Compasses do not work at the magnetic poles.
   The magnetic field at these poles is vertical.
5. (comma and conjunction) As for the South Pole, a
   Norwegian explorer named Roald Amundsen reached it
   first. He did so on December 14, 1911.
6. (comma and conjunction) Today, people actually live at the
   South Pole part of the year doing scientific research.
   Amundsen's feat was herculean for its day.
7. (semicolon) Antarctica is the coldest continent on Earth. It
   holds the record for the lowest temperature ever recorded:
   −128.6° F.
8. (semicolon) The interior of Antarctica is a windy polar desert. Average precipitation is less than two inches each year.
9. (comma and conjunction) Coastal areas of the Antarctic
   are milder. Precipitation in those regions averages up to
   eight inches per year.
10. (comma and conjunction) The precipitation that falls on
    the South Pole is always in the form of snow. It usually is
    the byproduct of cyclones.

▲ Critical Viewing
Write two separate
sentences describing
this penguin. Then,
combine the sen-
tences to form a
compound sentence.
[Describe]

▶ **KEY CONCEPT** Sentences can be combined by changing
one of them into a subordinate clause. ■

Use a compound sentence when you are combining sentences
to show the relationship between ideas. The subordinating conjunction will help readers understand the relationship.

EXAMPLE: We were frightened. We thought there
                             might be an avalanche.

COMBINED WITH   We were frightened because we
A SUBORDINATE CLAUSE: thought there might be an avalanche.

Sentence Combining • 345

▶ **Exercise 12** Combining Sentences Using Subordinating Clauses Using the subordinating conjunction or relative pronoun in parentheses, combine these pairs of sentences.

1. (although) Antarctica's total area in summer is about 5.5 million square miles. It does not always stay the same size.
2. (because) During the winter, Antarctica nearly doubles in size. A large amount of sea ice forms at its periphery.
3. (which) The true boundary of Antarctica is not the coastline of the continent but the Antarctic Convergence. It is a sharply defined zone at the southern ends of the Atlantic, Indian, and Pacific oceans.
4. (where) Colder waters flowing north from Antarctica mix with warmer waters moving south. The convergence is defined.
5. (because) A measurable physical difference in the ocean occurs at this point. The water surrounding the Antarctic continent is considered an ocean unto itself.
6. (even though) Antarctica has no native population. Scientific and support staffs reside there usually for no more than one year at a time.
7. (whose) The first person born in Antarctica was Emilio Palma. His father was an Argentine naval officer.
8. (which) Ninety-five percent of the surface of Antarctica is covered by ice. Antarctica contains 70 percent of Earth's freshwater supply.
9. (since) It has a thick ice cover. It has the highest average elevation of all the continents.
10. (although) The lowest point on the continent appears to be the Bentley Subglacial Trench, which is 8,200 feet below sea level and is covered by 9,840 feet of ice. Lower points may exist.

▶ **Exercise 13** Combining Sentences Using Subordinating Conjunctions or Relative Pronouns Using a subordinating conjunction or relative pronoun of your choice, combine the following pairs of sentences.

1. Seven nations—Argentina, Australia, Chile, France, Great Britain, New Zealand, and Norway—once declared territorial claims to parts of the Antarctic. The continent was uninhabited.
2. The Antarctic Treaty was signed in 1961. Their claims were renounced in the interests of international cooperation and scientific research.
3. Future economic development of the Antarctic landmass is unlikely. It is so icebound.
4. Extensive resources have yet to be harvested from the continental shelf. The technology is in development.
5. However, marine life in the Antarctic waters is being economically developed. It is plentiful.

▶ **More Practice**

Grammar Exercise Workbook
• pp. 85–86
On-line Exercise Bank
• Section 21.2
  Go on-line:
  PHSchool.com
  Enter Web Code:
  eek-1002

Get instant feedback! Exercises 12, 13, and 14 are available on-line or on CD-ROM.

▶ **KEY CONCEPT** Sentences can be combined by changing one of them into a phrase. ■

Change a sentence into a phrase when you are combining sentences in which one of the sentences just adds detail.

EXAMPLES: My dog-sled team races tomorrow. We race on the tundra of the Antarctic.
My dog-sled team races tomorrow on the tundra of the Antarctic.

My dog-sled team races tomorrow on the tundra of the Antarctic. The Antarctic is one of the most inhospitable places on Earth.
My dog-sled team races tomorrow on the tundra of the Antarctic, one of the most inhospitable places on Earth.

▶ **Exercise 14** **Combining Sentences With Phrases** Combine the following pairs of sentences by changing one to a phrase.

1. Antarctica was once a central, tropical region of Gondwanaland. Gondwanaland was an ancient supercontinent on Earth.
2. Gondwanaland broke apart many years ago. It broke from the force of shifts in the Earth's plates.
3. The supercontinent split to form the separate continents in the current Southern Hemisphere. It split during the late Mesozoic era.
4. Antarctica consists of two main geologic areas. These areas are East Antarctica and West Antarctica.
5. East Antarctica is covered by massive layers of ice. The ice is thousands of meters thick.
6. West Antarctica appears to be a continuation of the Andes Mountains. The Andes are in South America.
7. Glaciologists and geologists speculate that without its ice cover, West Antarctica would be an island archipelago. An island archipelago is a sea containing a large group of islands.
8. Despite its frozen landscape, West Antarctica is home to Mount Erebus. Erebus is a 12,448-foot volcano.
9. The two areas are separated by the Transantarctic Mountains. The mountain range is running across the entire continent.
10. Within these mountains are many coal deposits and fossil remains. The remains come from the time that Antarctica had a tropical climate.

▼ **Critical Viewing** Write a sentence about this photo in which you include the phrase *rising above the thick ice.* **[Describe]**

Hands-on Grammar

Folding in Phrases

You can practice what you have learned about combining sentences with phrases by doing the following activity.

Cut out several long, narrow strips from a legal size (8 1/2" by 14") piece of paper. On each strip, write one of the following pairs of related sentences:

Antarctica is a cold, white continent. It is covered almost entirely by ice and snow.

One animal that thrives in Antarctica is the southern elephant seal. It is the largest seal in the world.

Mount Erebus is Antarctica's most active volcano. It occasionally spurts volcanic rock over the island on which it sits.

In 1911, Norwegian explorer Roald Amundsen won the race to the South Pole. His victory was by a five-week margin.

Now combine the sentence pairs by folding over the paper to cover up the first few words of the second sentence that come before the phrase you want to connect to the first sentence. For example, by covering up *It is* on the second sentence of the first pair, you would be able to read: *Antarctica is a cold, white continent covered almost entirely by ice and snow.*

Read your combined sentences aloud to be sure they make sense. Then, write some new pairs of sentences of your own on additional strips of paper, and test your classmates' ability to combine them.

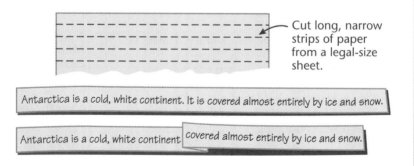

Cut long, narrow strips of paper from a legal-size sheet.

Antarctica is a cold, white continent. It is covered almost entirely by ice and snow.

Antarctica is a cold, white continent covered almost entirely by ice and snow.

Find It in Your Reading Select a long sentence from one of your textbooks. Split it into several shorter sentences that the writer may have combined.

Find It in Your Writing Look through your portfolio for paragraphs that contain several short sentences in a row. Combine the sentences using one of the ways you have learned in this chapter.

Section 21.2

Section Review

GRAMMAR EXERCISES 15–20

Exercise 15 Combining Sentences Using Compound Parts Combine each pair of sentences by creating a compound subject, verb, or object.

1. I watched a program about the South Pole. My dad saw it with me.
2. The show focused on exploration. It also highlighted elements of the climate.
3. The geography of Antarctica was mentioned. Also, its wildlife was discussed.
4. The program started on Monday. It concluded on Tuesday.
5. We found the program interesting. It was also intellectually stimulating.

Exercise 16 Combining Clauses and Phrases Combine each pair of sentences by creating a compound sentence, forming a complex sentence, or changing one sentence into a phrase.

1. The soil in the interior of Antarctica is very dry. The area receives only two inches of snow each year.
2. The soil is so dry. Some geologists call it a "polar desert."
3. Rainfall and snowfall are heavier in some areas. These areas are along the coasts.
4. Icy winds make the continent seem even colder. They blow across Antarctica throughout the year.
5. The largest ice shelf in Antarctica is the Ross Ice Shelf. It is the size of Texas.
6. Antarctica is isolated from the rest of the world. It has avoided problems found on other continents.
7. The ice there is the purest in the world. It is untainted by industrial pollution.
8. Residents obtain the water they need. They do this by melting ice and snow.
9. The climate is so cold. Few insects live on the mainland of Antarctica.
10. Few animals live on the mainland. The Antarctic Ocean abounds with wildlife.

Exercise 17 Revising a Paragraph by Combining Sentences Using phrases, combine pairs of sentences in the following passage.

Antarctica was not discovered until the early 1800's. This delay occurred because of its remoteness. The ancient Greeks first theorized about the existence of Antarctica. They were advanced in geography. They believed that the Southern Hemisphere must have large continents. These continents existed to balance those in the Northern Hemisphere. In 1772, British explorer James Cook sailed as far south as he could. Cook searched for the southern continent. Huge ice blocks prevented him from reaching Antarctica. He did spot many whales and seals. Groups of hunters arrived in the area. They arrived soon after Cook's voyage. Several hunters reached the continent. This occurred a few years later.

Exercise 18 Find It in Your Reading Select a long sentence from a story or textbook. Determine what ideas the writer has combined in the sentence and what method was used to combine ideas.

Exercise 19 Find It in Your Writing Revise a piece of writing from your portfolio. Combine at least five pairs of sentences, using different techniques.

Exercise 20 Writing Application Imagine that you were an early explorer of Antarctica. Write several short sentences from the journal you kept. Then, combine some of the sentences.

Varying Sentences

Vary your sentences to produce a rhythm, to achieve an effect, or to emphasize key points or connections among ideas. There are many ways that you can achieve sentence variety.

Vary Sentence Length

You have already learned that you can combine several short, choppy sentences to form a longer sentence. However, having too many long sentences in a row is as uninteresting as having too many short ones. When you want to emphasize a point or surprise a reader, insert a short, direct sentence to interrupt the flow of long sentences. Look at this example:

> The viola, which evolved from medieval fiddles, is first depicted in early sixteenth-century drawings and literature. Like most instruments of the Renaissance, it was built in a range of sizes. Played standing up, the largest violas were the specialties of Italian masters. <u>One such master was Antonio Stradivari.</u>

Some sentences contain only one idea and cannot be broken up. It may be possible, however, to state the idea in a shorter sentence. Other sentences contain two or more ideas and might be shortened by breaking up the ideas.

▶ **Exercise 21** **Making Simpler Sentences** In the following items, break up long sentences into two or more sentences or restate long sentences in a simpler, more direct way.

1. Plucked lutes include the banjo and guitar as well as the Arabic *oud,* from which the name of the European lute is derived.
2. The neck of a lute may be a short elongation of the body, as in the Chinese *pipa,* or it may be a separate element fastened to or piercing the body.
3. Frequently, the neck incorporates a fingerboard, which may have frets, against which the strings can be pressed to alter their sound.
4. The technique of bowing is not as old as that of plucking, and fiddles, or bowed lutes, such as the violin or viol, arrived in Europe from Asia only in the Middle Ages.
5. The violin and its relatives, at first associated with country dance music and considered inferior to the quieter, more sedate viol, became dominant during the 1700's.

Theme: Musical Instruments

In this section, you will learn ways to vary sentence lengths and beginnings to make your writing more interesting. The examples and exercises are about different musical instruments.

Cross-Curricular Connection: Music

▶ **More Practice**

Grammar Exercise Workbook
• pp. 87–88
On-line Exercise Bank
• Section 21.3

Go on-line:
PHSchool.com
Enter Web Code:
eek-1002

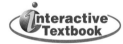

Complete the exercises on-line! Exercises 21 and 22 are available on-line or on CD-ROM.

GRAMMAR IN LITERATURE

from **The Bean Eaters**

Gwendolyn Brooks

The poet gives plain words an eloquent rhythm by varying the length of her sentences.

They eat beans mostly, this old yellow pair.
Dinner is a casual affair.
Plain chipware on a plain and creaking wood,
Tin flatware.

Two who are Mostly Good.
Two who have lived their day,
But keep on putting on their clothes
And putting things away.

▼ **Critical Viewing**
Write two sentences, one long and one short, to compare the sound of a violin to that of a guitar or a bass. **[Compare]**

> **Exercise 22** Revising a Paragraph to Improve Sentence Variety Rewrite this paragraph, breaking up long sentences into two or more simple sentences or restating long sentences more simply.

    Just as mechanical inventions served European music when the fully developed keyboard arose in the Middle Ages, so electrical engineers have offered twentieth-century musicians innovative ways of producing and controlling sounds. Since the 1930's, electric amplification has altered the technique of popular singers and instrumentalists. Electric organs have mostly influenced popular music, but since the mid-1960's, synthesizers have been important tools of composers of many music styles. Except in the manipulations of sound used in rock music, however, amplification, like broadcasting and recording, serves chiefly to disseminate music rather than to create it. With the electric guitar, such amplification replaced the sound box and stimulated new musical effects; the long-term implications of sound production cannot yet be predicted.

⚙ Grammar and Style Tip

One way to test how smoothly your sentences flow is to read them aloud. By reading your work aloud in a lively way, you will be able to identify when your sentence structure falls flat, grows boring, or does not provide the necessary interest for the subject matter. Reading your work aloud also helps you catch some of the common sentence errors discussed later in this chapter.

Varying Sentence Openers and Structures

Another way to produce sentence variety is to avoid starting each sentence in the same way. Consider these options:

START WITH A NOUN:	The piano is a difficult instrument to learn.
START WITH AN ADVERB:	Surprisingly, the piano is a difficult instrument to learn.
START WITH A PARTICIPLE:	Having played the piano, I know it is a difficult instrument to learn.
START WITH A PREPOSITIONAL PHRASE:	For many young musicians, the piano is difficult to learn.

You can also vary sentence beginnings by reversing the traditional subject-verb order.

EXAMPLES:

S   LV COMP
The pipers are here.

COMP LV   S
Here are the pipers.

S   V   ADV. PHRASE
The parade came around the corner.

ADV. PHRASE   V   S
Around the corner came the parade.

Exercise 23 Revising to Vary Sentence Openers Follow the instructions in parentheses to revise each sentence.
1. (Start with an adverb.) All drums are separately classified as part of the membranophone family of instruments.
2. (Start with a prepositional phrase.) A drum has one or two heads for sound resonance.
3. (Start with a participle.) The heads of a drum stretched across a frame are usually made of plastic or animal skin.
4. (Start with a prepositional phrase.) Cylindrical drums vary in size from huge basses to shallow snares.
5. (Start with an adverb.) The snare's intense, crisp sound surprisingly makes up for its lack in size.

Exercise 24 Revising to Invert Sentences Rewrite each sentence, reversing the traditional subject-verb order.
1. The orchestra enters from backstage.
2. The conductor is here.
3. Rehearsal is held in the auditorium.
4. The instruments remained silent before the concert.
5. The sound of a violin is beautiful.

More Practice

Grammar Exercise Workbook
• pp. 89–92
On-line Exercise Bank
• Section 21.3
  Go on-line:
  PHSchool.com
  Enter Web Code:
  eek-1002

Complete the exercises on-line! Exercises 23 and 24 are available on-line or on CD-ROM.

Section 21.3 *Section Review*

GRAMMAR EXERCISES 25–31

Exercise 25 Revising to Simplify Long Sentences In these items, break up long sentences into simple sentences or restate them more simply.

1. The xylophone, whose name comes from the Greek *xylon,* meaning "wood," is a percussion instrument consisting of a series of wooden bars that are struck with mallets to produce sounds.
2. Xylophones were developed in Southeast Asia by the fourteenth century, and they arrived and took root as folk instruments in Central Europe about 1500.
3. In Africa, where the xylophone was imported from Madagascar, its use spread throughout the continent; the xylophone became a prominent instrument in African music.
4. Africans who had been enslaved introduced the xylophone to Latin America, where it is known as a *marimba.*
5. By the nineteenth century, performers had popularized the xylophone in western Europe, and its first orchestral use was in *Danse Macabre* (1874) by the French composer Camille Saint-Saëns.

Exercise 26 Varying Sentence Openers Rewrite this sentence five times, each time beginning with one of the sentence parts listed below: *The members of the orchestra tuned their instruments.* (1) an adverb; (2) a prepositional phrase; (3) a participial phrase; (4) a different prepositional phrase; (5) a different adverb

Exercise 27 Revising Sentences by Inverting Subject-Verb Order Revise each sentence using an inverted structure.

1. The parade marches down the street.

2. The people along the curb are smiling and waving.
3. The brass instruments shine in the sun.
4. The shofar sounded low and mournful.
5. The orchestra is here.

Exercise 28 Revising Sentences in Several Ways Revise the paragraph below by varying sentence length, sentence beginnings, or word order.

A glass harmonica was invented by Benjamin Franklin. It is known as the Franklin harmonica and consists of a set of glass bowls, graduated in size to produce distinct pitches, and the bowls are fine-tuned by filling them with different amounts of water. The Franklin harmonica was popular in the early 1800's. Mozart and Beethoven were intrigued by the instrument. The pieces they wrote for the instrument are still performed occasionally.

Exercise 29 Find It in Your Reading Find a paragraph in a magazine article that illustrates strong sentence variety. Present your example to the class.

Exercise 30 Find It in Your Writing Make at least five revisions in a piece of your own writing to improve sentence variety.

Exercise 31 Writing Application Write a review of a concert by the school band or by your favorite band. Use sentences of different lengths, and vary the way your sentences begin or their subject-verb order to provide more interesting reading.

Avoiding Sentence Problems

Fragments, run-on sentences, and misplaced modifiers can all make your writing confusing. Being able to recognize the parts of sentences and different kinds of clauses and phrases can help you avoid certain errors in your writing.

Recognizing Fragments

Some groups of words, even though they have a capital at the beginning and a period at the end, are not complete sentences. They are *fragments*.

▶ **KEY CONCEPT** A **fragment** is a group of words that does not express a complete thought but is punctuated as if it were a sentence. ■

A fragment is only *part* of a sentence, but a sentence always has a subject *and* a verb. A fragment does not always have both parts. It can be a group of words with no subject. It can be a group of words that includes a possible subject but no verb. It can be a group of words with a possible subject and only part of a possible verb. It can even be a subordinate clause standing alone.

Theme: Instruments of the Orchestra

In this section, you will learn how to recognize and correct fragments, run-on sentences, and misplaced modifiers. The examples and exercises are about instruments in an orchestra.

Cross-Curricular Connection: Music

▼ Critical Viewing What happens if only part of an orchestra arrives for a concert? How does that compare to a sentence fragment? [Compare]

FRAGMENTS

To hear the orchestra play. *Subject*
Listened carefully and happily. *Subject*
The tuba in the marching band. *verb*
The parade coming around the bend. *verb*
When the band played. *Subject and verb*

You will usually be able to tell whether a group of words expresses a complete thought. One trick is to read the words aloud. This will help you hear whether or not some part is missing.

In the chart below, words have been added to the preceding fragments to make complete sentences. Read each italicized fragment; then read the sentence. Can you hear the difference? What part is missing in the fragment?

COMPLETED SENTENCES

We went *to hear the orchestra play.*
We *listened carefully and happily.*
I play *the tuba in the marching band.*
The parade was *coming around the bend.*
When the band played, I didn't recognize the song.

Each of the preceding examples needed one or more new parts. The first needed both a subject and a verb. The second needed only a subject. The third became complete when a subject and a verb were added. The fourth became complete when a helping verb was added. The final example needed a complete independent clause to go with the subordinate clause.

▶ **Exercise 32** Recognizing Sentence Fragments Write *F* for each item that is a fragment and *S* for complete sentences.
1. Consists of woodwind, brass, and percussion instruments.
2. Originally a section in ancient Greek theaters.
3. Located between the stage and the audience.
4. Dancers and instrumentalists used this area.
5. In a modern theater.
6. The part reserved for musicians called the orchestra pit.
7. The term *orchestra* now designates an area of seating in an auditorium.
8. The string section in four parts.
9. The double basses often duplicate the cello part an octave lower.
10. The number of instruments can vary.

Interactive Textbook

Get instant feedback! Exercise 32 is available on-line or on CD-ROM.

▶ **More Practice**

Grammar Exercise Workbook
• pp. 93–94
On-line Exercise Bank
• Section 21.4
Go on-line:
PHSchool.com
Enter Web Code:
eek-1002

Correcting Phrase Fragments

A phrase by itself is a fragment. It cannot stand alone because it does not have both a subject and a verb.

KEY CONCEPT A phrase should not be capitalized and punctuated as if it were a sentence. ■

Three types of phrases—prepositional, participial, and infinitive—are often mistaken for sentences. A *phrase fragment* can be changed into a sentence in either of two ways. The first way is to add the phrase fragment to a nearby sentence. This example shows a prepositional phrase following a sentence.

FRAGMENT: The musicians took their places. *On the stage.*

You can correct this fragment simply by attaching the phrase to the preceding sentence.

ADDED TO   The musicians took their places
NEARBY SENTENCE: *on the stage.*

You can correct other fragments simply by attaching them to the beginning of a sentence. The participial phrase fragment in the next example can easily be corrected in this way.

FRAGMENT: *Waiting for silence.* The conductor held
                   his baton in the air.

ADDED TO   *Waiting for silence,* the conductor held
NEARBY SENTENCE: his baton in the air.

Sometimes, however, you may not be able to correct a phrase fragment by adding it to a nearby sentence. Then, you will need to use the second way to change a phrase fragment into a sentence: Correct the fragment by adding to the phrase whatever is needed to make it a complete sentence. Often this method requires adding a subject or a verb.

CHANGING PHRASE FRAGMENTS INTO SENTENCES

Phrase Fragments	Complete Sentences
By the conductor.	The seating of an orchestra is determined *by the conductor.*
Listening to the opera.	*Listening to the opera,* I found myself swept away.
To play an instrument.	I would like *to play an instrument.*

Spelling Tip

The common and similar suffixes *-er* and *-or* are often mistaken for each other. For instance, the word *conductor* is sometimes mis-spelled as *conducter*. When you encounter such a word and are unsure which ending to use, look it up in a dictionary.

◄ **Critical Viewing**
The timpani is sometimes called a kettledrum. Explain why in a complete sentence. [**Make a Judgment**]

Exercise 33 Revising to Change Phrase Fragments Into Sentences Use each of the following phrase fragments in a sentence. You may use the phrase at the beginning, at the end, or in any other position in the sentence. Check to see that each of your sentences contains a subject and a verb.

EXAMPLE: Arriving at the music hall.

ANSWER: Arriving at the music hall, the performers tuned their instruments.

1. Accompanied by other musicians.
2. Into the night air.
3. To the left of the conductor.
4. Behind the strings section.
5. Playing the kettledrum.
6. Hearing the glockenspiel.
7. With a harp or piano.
8. Feeling the pounding of the bass drum.
9. Without brass instruments.
10. Reserving two orchestra seats.

More Practice

Grammar Exercise Workbook
• pp. 93–94
On-line Exercise Bank
• Section 21.4
  Go on-line:
  PHSchool.com
  Enter Web Code:
  eek-1002

Complete the exercise on-line! Exercise 33 is available on-line or on CD-ROM.

Correcting Clause Fragments

All clauses have subjects and verbs, but some cannot stand alone as sentences.

KEY CONCEPT A subordinate clause should not be capitalized and punctuated as if it were a sentence. ■

Subordinate clauses do not express complete thoughts. Although a subordinate adjective or adverb clause has a subject and a verb, it cannot stand by itself as a sentence. Like phrase fragments, *clause fragments* can usually be corrected in either of two ways:

1. Attach the fragment to a nearby sentence.

FRAGMENT:	The class enjoyed the concert. *That was held in the auditorium.*
ADDED TO A NEARBY SENTENCE:	The class enjoyed the concert *that was held in the auditorium.*

2. Add an independent clause to the fragment.

CHANGING CLAUSE FRAGMENTS INTO SENTENCES	
Clause Fragments	**Complete Sentences**
That we heard.	I bought a recording of the music *that we heard.* The music *that we heard* is now on CD.
When the orchestra played.	People got up to dance *when the orchestra played.* *When the orchestra played,* people got up to dance.

Exercise 34 Revising Clause Fragments to Form Sentences
Rewrite each fragment to make it a complete sentence.
1. Who directed the orchestra.
2. That was performed last week.
3. As the band played on.
4. That you like to hear.
5. That can be pleasing.
6. When the trombone player began.
7. That she described.
8. After we played a concert last week.
9. Who told me about the concert.
10. While the musicians tuned their instruments.

Correcting Run-on Sentences

Unlike a fragment, a *run-on sentence* is an overcrowded sentence—one that has too much information.

> ▶ **KEY CONCEPT** A **run-on** is two or more complete sentences that are not properly joined or separated. ■

Two Kinds of Run-on Sentences

There are two kinds of run-on sentences. One kind is made up of two sentences run together without any punctuation between them. This type of run-on is called a *fused sentence*. The other consists of two or more sentences separated only by a comma. This is called a *comma splice*.

RUN-ONS	
With No Punctuation	**With Only a Comma**
I go to concerts often Mozart is my favorite composer.	A clarinet has an almost cylindrical tube, an oboe has a conical pipe.

▼ **Critical Viewing** Write a sentence comparing the appearance or sound of these three instruments. Make sure your sentence is not a run-on. **[Compare]**

> ▶ **Exercise 35** Recognizing Run-on Sentences
On your paper write *S* if the item is a sentence and *RO* if the item is a run-on.

EXAMPLE: Bells vibrate at their rim gongs vibrate at their center. (RO)

1. Musical instruments around the world vary in purpose and design they can be made from natural or human-made materials.
2. Any tool that can expand the scope of musical sounds—such as clapping, stamping, whistling, and singing—is a musical instrument.
3. Sound arises from vibrations transmitted by waves to the ear, some vibrations are simply noise.
4. Regular vibrations produce tones that can be pleasing to the ear, the faster the vibrations, the higher the pitch that is perceived.
5. Some pipe organs encompass the full audible range of pitch, more than ten octaves most instruments have a much more limited range.

Correcting Run-on Sentences

Using End Marks Properly used, an end mark splits a run-on into two shorter but complete sentences. Which end mark you use depends upon the function of the sentence.

RUN-ON:
Many instruments were improved in the nineteenth century the piano was made with a cast-iron frame, which allowed a greater range of sounds.

CORRECTED SENTENCES:
Many instruments were improved in the nineteenth century. The piano was made with a cast-iron frame, which allowed a greater range of sounds.

RUN-ON:
Have you heard the new song, I heard it yesterday.

CORRECTED SENTENCES:
Have you heard the new song? I heard it yesterday.

Using Commas and Coordinating Conjunctions

Sometimes, the two parts of a run-on are related and should stay in the same sentence. In that case, the run-on can be changed into a compound sentence. Use a comma and a coordinating conjunction to combine two independent clauses into a compound sentence. To separate the two clauses properly, it is necessary to use both a comma and a coordinating conjunction. A comma by itself is not enough.

▲ Critical Viewing
Write two sentences about the sound of this instrument. Then, combine your sentences without forming a run-on. **[Describe]**

RUN-ON:
The oldest instrument family consists of idiophones, they are also the most widespread of instruments.

CORRECTED SENTENCE:
The oldest instrument family consists of idiophones, and they are also the most widespread of instruments.

RUN-ON:
I would like to play an instrument, I do not have musical ability.

CORRECTED SENTENCE:
I would like to play an instrument, but I do not have musical ability.

Using Semicolons You can sometimes use a semicolon to punctuate the two parts of a run-on when the ideas expressed in the two parts are closely related.

RUN-ON:
Idiophones range in complexity from hollowed logs to cast-bronze bells, the family dates back to the Stone Age.

CORRECTED SENTENCE:
Idiophones range in complexity from hollowed logs to cast-bronze bells; the family dates back to the Stone Age.

Exercise 36 Revising to Correct Run-ons Rewrite each of the following run-ons using any of the three methods described in this section.

1. Some instruments produce a tone with no identifiable pitch the triangle is one such instrument.
2. The greater the power of audio waves, the louder their sound, some electronically amplified music can reach a painful, ear-damaging intensity.
3. The tone color of the sound is influenced by the presence of the overtones in the sound wave, the perception of timbre is affected by the duration and location of the sound.
4. Musical sounds are caused by three components, the first component is the vibrating substance, such as a violin string, set into motion by bowing or striking.
5. The second component is the reflector, amplifier, or resonator connected to the vibrating substance, the third is the device that alters or varies the sound, such as a key, valve, or fret.

More Practice

Grammar Exercise
Workbook
• pp. 95–96
On-line Exercise Bank
• Section 21.4
   Go on-line:
   PHSchool.com
   Enter Web Code:
   eek-1002

Recognizing Misplaced Modifiers

Misplaced Modifiers A phrase or clause that acts as an adjective or adverb should be placed close to the word it modifies. Otherwise, the meaning of the sentence may be unclear. A modifier placed too far away from the word it modifies is called a *misplaced modifier.* Because they are misplaced, such phrases and clauses seem to modify the wrong word in a sentence.

MISPLACED
MODIFIER: Nancy marched in the parade *with a smile* on her face.

The misplaced modifier is the phrase *with a smile.* It sounds as though the parade has a smile. The sentence needs to be reworded to put the modifier closer to *Nancy.*

CORRECTED
SENTENCE: *With a smile* on her face, Nancy marched in the parade.

MISPLACED
MODIFIER: *Playing the trumpet,* the parade was enjoyable.

In this sentence, *playing the trumpet* should modify a person. Instead, it incorrectly modifies *parade.* The sentence needs to be rewritten to include the name of the musician.

CORRECTED
SENTENCE: *Playing the trumpet,* Elizabeth enjoyed the parade.

> **Exercise 37** Recognizing Misplaced Modifiers Some of
the sentences in the following exercise are correct, but most
of them contain a misplaced modifier. Read each sentence
carefully, and check the placement of the modifiers. If the
sentence is correct, write *C* on your paper. If the sentence
contains a misplaced modifier, write *MM*.

EXAMPLE: Touring extensively around the world, people
             love the Vienna Philharmonic Orchestra. (MM)

1. Zubin Mehta was born in Bombay, India, into a musical
   family.
2. His father from 1955 to 1959 served as associate concert-
   master of the Halle Orchestra in Manchester, England.
3. As a child, Mehta studied piano and violin.
4. In Vienna, Austria, Mehta left India and medical studies at
   age eighteen to study conducting.
5. At his musical studio in Vienna, Mehta studied with Hans
   Swarowsky.
6. Organized by the Royal Liverpool Orchestra, Mehta won
   the first conductor's competition.
7. Including a one-year engagement as assistant to the
   resident maestro, Mehta benefited from the prizes of the
   competition.
8. Working for a number of prominent orchestras, his career
   soon expanded.
9. Appointed music director for the Los Angeles Philharmonic
   and the Montreal Symphony, Mehta became the first conductor to head two major North American orchestras
   simultaneously.
10. Mehta replaced Pierre Boulez as music director of the New
    York Philharmonic, receiving much critical acclaim.

▲ **Critical Viewing**
Use the phrase
*looking up from
their music* in a sen-
tence about this
picture. Make sure
that the modifier
is not misplaced.
[Connect]

▶ **More Practice**

**Grammar Exercise
Workbook**
• pp. 97–98
On-line Exercise Bank
• Section 21.4
  Go on-line:
  PHSchool.com
  Enter Web Code:
  eek-1002

Get instant feedback!
Exercise 37 is available
on-line or on CD-ROM.

Revising Sentences
With Misplaced Modifiers

Among the most common misplaced modifiers are prepositional phrases, participial phrases, and adjective clauses. All
are corrected in the same way—by placing the modifier as
close as possible to the word it modifies.

First, consider a misplaced prepositional phrase. This error
usually occurs in a sentence with two or more prepositional
phrases in a row.

MISPLACED: *With their new instruments* in the auditorium, the
             orchestra practiced.

The misplaced modifier should be moved closer to *orchestra.*

CORRECTED: *With their new instruments*, the orchestra prac-
             ticed in the auditorium.

Participial phrases are sometimes used at the beginning of
sentences. When such a phrase is used this way, it must be
followed immediately by a word that it can logically modify.

MISPLACED: *Raising their bows*, the signal from the conductor
             was their cue.

Who or what is raising their bows? The sentence needs to be
rewritten to put a word such as *violinists* next to the modifier.

CORRECTED: *Raising their bows*, the violinists waited for the
             signal from the conductor.

A misplaced adjective clause should also be moved closer to
the word it modifies. In the following sentence, the clause is so
far away from *music* that it seems to modify *weeks* or *searching.* The sentence needs to be rearranged.

MISPLACED: I found the music after several weeks of

             searching *that the conductor recommended.*

CORRECTED: After several weeks of searching, I found the

             music *that the conductor recommended.*

Exercise 38 Revising Sentences to Correct Misplaced Modifiers Rewrite the sentences in the following exercise to eliminate the misplaced modifiers. In each rewritten sentence, underline the modifier that was misplaced in the original. Then, draw an arrow pointing from the modifier to the word it modifies.

EXAMPLE: Richard planned to meet Rachel before the concert at Radio City Music Hall at a restaurant.

ANSWER: Richard planned to meet Rachel <u>at a restaurant</u> before the concert at Radio City Music Hall.

1. Gustav Mahler was an Austrian composer and conductor whose works influenced many twentieth-century composers living in the nineteenth century.
2. After studying at the Vienna Conservatory, the assistant conductor at Bad Hall in Austria was named Mahler.
3. Mahler subsequently held posts in several European cities with opera companies.
4. Becoming artistic director of the Imperial Opera in Vienna, Vienna became a great operatic center because of Mahler.
5. Mahler moved to New York City, where he conducted the Metropolitan Opera and the New York Philharmonic, another city known for opera.
6. Mahler composed four numbered symphonies after years of conducting that included solo voices with or without chorus.
7. Mahler was the musical heir of Beethoven, Bruckner, and Wagner in his symphonies.
8. Achieving great fame, twentieth-century music was greatly influenced by Mahler.
9. Experimenting with the traditional system of keys and chords, most of his symphonies end in a key different from the initial key.
10. Leaving an unfinished tenth symphony, Mahler's death took place in Vienna in 1911.

More Practice

Grammar Exercise Workbook
• pp. 99–102
On-line Exercise Bank
• Section 21.4
  Go on-line:
  PHSchool.com
  Enter Web Code:
  eek-1002

Interactive Textbook

Complete the exercise on-line! Exercise 38 is available on-line or on CD-ROM.

▶ **Critical Viewing** Write a sentence about this picture that includes the participial phrase *holding a baton*. Make sure that the modifier is not misplaced. **[Connect]**

Section Review

GRAMMAR EXERCISES 39–44

▶ **Exercise 39** Revising Fragments to Form Sentences Change each of the following fragments into a sentence. Check to see that each of your sentences contains an independent clause.

1. The marching band fun to watch.
2. Before the music started.
3. When the opera starts.
4. With a piano solo.
5. The musicians starting to play.
6. Bagpipes and loudly playing drums.
7. Marching down Main Street.
8. To buy a saxophone.
9. After the open-air concert.
10. Three friends singing with the chorus.

▶ **Exercise 40** Revising to Eliminate Run-on Sentences Identify and eliminate run-ons from the following items. If a sentence is correct, write *correct*.

1. The score is the musical notation for a multipart composition, the music that is to be performed by each voice or instrument is written on a separate staff.
2. A full score shows the music for all of the instruments all of the staves are aligned one above another.
3. The individual musicians are given separate parts these parts show only the music for their particular instrument.
4. Until the early thirteenth century, all European music was circulated in complete scores, and performers read from these scores.
5. The use of these scores was abandoned in the thirteenth century, this was done for reasons of space.

▶ **Exercise 41** Revising a Paragraph to Eliminate Sentence Errors Revise the following paragraph, correcting any fragments, run-ons, or misplaced modifiers.

The piano is a stringed keyboard musical instrument, it is sometimes called the pianoforte. Predecessors of the piano, keyboard players performed on clavicords or harpsicords prior to the eighteenth century. By varying the touch of the fingers, the sound of the piano can be intensified. Unlike with earlier keyboard instruments. A harpsichord maker of Florence, Italy, the first piano was built by Bartolomeo Cristofori. Little did he know. That his invention would have such an impact on both concert and popular music. Today, pianos sit in concert halls and homes all around the world, millions of children and adults take piano lessons every day.

▶ **Exercise 42** Find It in Your Reading In this sentence from "Like the Sun" by R. K. Narayan, identify how the writer has avoided creating a run-on sentence.

Sekhar paused for a moment outside the headmaster's room to button up his coat; that was another subject the headmaster always sermonized about.

▶ **Exercise 43** Find It in Your Writing Carefully review a piece of your own writing for fragments, run-ons, or misplaced modifiers. Correct any errors you find.

▶ **Exercise 44** Writing Application Pick a musical instrument, and write a description of how the instrument sounds. Proofread your description carefully to make sure it contains no fragments, run-ons, or misplaced modifiers.

Verb Usage

Having a good command of the English language requires a thorough understanding of how to use verbs. Verbs can help you explain when actions occur and how the time of one action relates to the time of another. Some verbs follow predictable rules to show a change in tense or form. Others follow irregular patterns that you must memorize.

Just as the nations of Europe now use a standard currency to facilitate the exchange of goods and services, the rules of verb usage facilitate the exchange of information. By following these rules, you can communicate more effectively.

This chapter shows how verbs are formed and how they are used to indicate the time when an action occurs. It also illustrates how verbs are used to indicate who is performing an action.

▲ **Critical Viewing**
Think of the present and past tense forms of three verbs that describe actions you do with money. How do the two tenses vary in form?
[Connect, Contrast]

Diagnostic Test

Directions: Write all answers on a separate sheet of paper.

Skill Check A. Identify the tense of each verb in italics. Then, tell whether the form is *basic* or *progressive*.

1. My aunt and uncle *are running* a financial planning business.
2. They *have taught* many people how to save and use money well.
3. They *used* their own savings to start their business.
4. Next month, they *will hold* a financial planning seminar for teens.
5. I *have been studying* economics in school and plan to attend their seminar.
6. My aunt thinks most people *are relying* too heavily on credit.
7. My aunt and uncle *had done* the same thing when they were young.
8. They *had been struggling,* but now they are helping other people with similar problems.
9. Because I have been following their advice, they expect that my investments *will be growing* in the future.
10. By the time I graduate from high school, I *will have been employing* their system for four years.

Skill Check B. Write the four principal parts of the following verbs.

11. save
12. deposit
13. cost
14. spend
15. grow

Skill Check C. Choose the correct form of the verb in parentheses.

16. People have long (striven, strove) to earn or raise money.
17. People have also (did, done) many unusual things to earn money.
18. In dance marathons in the 1930's, people danced to win cash prizes until they (grown, grew) weak.
19. Others have (swam, swum) or have (ran, run) great distances to win money.
20. Whenever people's bank accounts have (shrank, shrunk), they have (hit, hitted) upon new schemes to raise money.

Skill Check D. Identify the verb in each sentence below as *active* or *passive.*

21. Mexicans call their currency the *peso.*
22. The currency of China is known by the Chinese as the *yuan.*
23. Banks often exchange one form of currency for another.
24. The *euro* now serves as the currency of numerous European nations.
25. The U.S. dollar has been used for many years as the prevailing currency of international trade.

Verb Tenses

In writing and speaking, the different *tenses* of verbs are used to express time.

▶ **KEY CONCEPT** A **tense** is a form of a verb that shows the time of an action or a condition. ■

The Six Tenses of Verbs

Verbs have six tenses, each of which can be expressed in two different forms—*basic* and *progressive*.

THE BASIC AND PROGRESSIVE FORMS OF THE SIX TENSES	
Present	She *writes* about U.S. currency for a living.
Past	She *wrote* an article about coin collecting last year.
Future	She *will write* a book about old coins next year.
Present Perfect	She *has written* for the best magazines.
Past Perfect	She *had written* her first article by the time she was eighteen.
Future Perfect	She *will have written* two books by July.
Present Progressive	She *is writing* a newsletter about rare coins now.
Past Progressive	She *was writing* her weekly column.
Future Progressive	She *will be writing* a new book soon.
Present Perfect Progressive	She *has been writing* for years.
Past Perfect Progressive	She *had been writing* speeches when her first book on coins was published.
Future Perfect Progressive	By the end of the year, she *will have been writing* about different forms of currency for a decade.

In this section, you will learn to recognize and use the six tenses of verbs in both their basic and progressive forms. The examples and exercises are about money around the world.

Cross-Curricular Connection: Social Studies

> **Exercise 1** Identifying Verb Tenses Using the chart on page 520, identify the tense of each verb in italics.

EXAMPLE: He *has been bartering* services for products.

ANSWER: present perfect progressive

1. Money *serves* as a convenient medium of exchange.
2. People *have used* money for many centuries.
3. Previously, people often *bartered* for goods and services.
4. This mode of exchange *had been serving* people for centuries when a simpler way of doing business was devised.
5. Soon, people *were using* shells and furs to make purchases.
6. Some cultures also *minted* coins from precious metals.
7. By the twentieth century, much of the world *had implemented* standard coins and paper money.
8. Today, we *are utilizing* a wide variety of means of exchange.
9. Imagine how we *will be buying* items in the year 3000.
10. By then, people *will have been conducting* business with one another for more than 4,000 years.

▲ **Critical Viewing** Write a series of sentences about the use of cash machines. Use three different verb tenses. **[Apply]**

> **More Practice**

Grammar Exercise Workbook
• pp. 107–112
On-line Exercise Bank
• Section 22.1
Go on-line:
PHSchool.com
Enter Web Code:
eek-1002

Get instant feedback! Exercise 1 is available on-line or on CD-ROM.

EXPRESSING TIME THROUGH VERB TENSES		
Past	Existing or happening in the past	James collected old Spanish doubloons.
Past Perfect	Existing or happening before a specific time in the past	James had collected stamps until then.
Present	Existing or happening now	James now collects U.S. silver dollars.
Present Perfect	Existing or happening sometime before now	He has collected that particular coin for several years.
Future	Existing or happening in the future	He will collect coins for a long time.
Future Perfect	Existing or happening before a specific time in the future	By the time he is sixty years old, he will have collected coins for most of his life.

Verb Tenses • **369**

Exercise 2 Identifying the Uses of Tense Identify the tense and time indicated by the italicized verb in each sentence.

EXAMPLE: People *have used* many metals to make coins.

ANSWER: present perfect; existing or happening some time before the present

1. American currency generally *has featured* pictures of past presidents.
2. George Washington's face *appears* on the quarter and the one-dollar bill.
3. The symbols and pictures that appear on coins and paper currency *have varied* from culture to culture.
4. The Greeks *were producing* coins with pictures of gods and goddesses on them in ancient times.
5. The ancient Romans *decorated* their coins with portraits of Roman emperors.

▼ Critical Viewing Which of the sentences in Exercise 2 do you think this coin illustrates? Why? [Connect]

Exercise 3 Writing Sentences in Different Tenses Rewrite each sentence, supplying the verb in the tense indicated.

EXAMPLE: Massachusetts (become—past) the first American colony to mint coins.

ANSWER: Massachusetts became the first American colony to mint coins.

1. At first, the British (try—past progressive) to prevent the American colonies from printing their own money.
2. The British government (hope—past perfect progressive) to make the colonists trade exclusively with England.
3. Despite the restrictions, the colonists (manage—past perfect) to purchase goods from foreign traders.
4. By 1690, the colony of Massachusetts (issue—past progressive) its own coins and paper money.
5. Our class (examine—future) several colonial coins during a field trip to a museum next week.

Get instant feedback! Exercises 2, 3, and 4 are available on-line or on CD-ROM.

Exercise 4 Revising Verb Tense Rewrite each sentence, correcting the tense of the italicized verb.
1. Until the twentieth century, coins used in the Islamic world *will contain* few pictures of people.
2. In the past, Islamic countries *adorn* their coins with inscriptions from the Koran, their holy book.
3. Today, in some countries, people *lobbied* to get new symbols and faces on their currency.
4. In the future, new faces *appear* on U.S. currency.
5. By 2300, people *had used* coins for nearly 3,000 years.

▶ **More Practice**

Grammar Exercise Workbook
• pp. 113–120
On-line Exercise Bank
• Section 22.1
  Go on-line:
  PHSchool.com
  Enter Web Code:
  eek-1002

The Four Principal Parts of Verbs

Tenses are formed from *principal parts* and helping verbs.

KEY CONCEPT A verb has four principal parts: the present, the present participle, the past, and the past participle. ■

The chart below lists the principal parts of two verbs.

THE FOUR PRINCIPAL VERB PARTS			
Present	Present Participle	Past	Past Participle
walk run	walking running	walked ran	walked run

The first principal part is used to form the present and future tenses. To form the present, an *-s* or *-es* is added whenever the subject is *he, she, it,* or a singular noun (*he walks, Paul runs*). To form the future tense, the helping verb *will* is added (*he will walk, Paul will run*).

The second principal part is used with various helping verbs to produce all six of the progressive forms (*he is walking, Paul was walking,* and so on).

The third principal part is used to form the past tense (*he walked, Paul ran*).

The fourth principal part is used with helping verbs for the three perfect tenses (*he has walked, Paul had run,* and so on).

Regular Verbs

Most of the verbs in the English language, including the verb *walk,* are regular.

KEY CONCEPT The past and past participle of a **regular verb** are formed by adding *-ed* or *-d* to the present form. ■

The past and past participle of regular verbs have the same form. In the chart at the top of the next page, *have* is in parentheses in front of the past participle to remind you that this verb form is a past participle only if it is used with a helping verb.

Notice that the final consonant is sometimes doubled to form the present participle (ski*pp*ing) as well as the past and the past participle (ski*pp*ed). Notice also that the final *e* may be dropped in forming the present participle (typing).

PRINCIPAL PARTS OF REGULAR VERBS			
Present	Present Participle	Past	Past Participle
wash	(is) washing	washed	(have) washed
help	(is) helping	helped	(have) helped
type	(is) typing	typed	(have) typed
print	(is) printing	printed	(have) printed
issue	(is) issuing	issued	(have) issued
plot	(is) plotting	plotted	(have) plotted

▶ **Exercise 5** Identifying Principal Parts of Regular Verbs
Identify the principal part used to form each verb in Exercise 2
on page 370. The first one is done as an example below.

EXAMPLE: American currency generally *has featured*
                    pictures of past presidents.

ANSWER: featured (past participle)

Irregular Verbs

Although most verbs are regular, a number of very common
verbs, such as *run,* are irregular.

▶ **KEY CONCEPT** The past and past participle of an **irregular
verb** are not formed by adding *-ed* or *-d* to the present form. ■

The past and the past participle of irregular verbs are
formed in various ways. Some common irregular verbs are
shown in the charts that follow. Whenever you are in doubt
about the principal parts of an irregular verb, use a dictionary
to check them.

THE FOUR PRINCIPAL PARTS OF IRREGULAR VERBS			
Present	Present Participle	Past	Past Participle
lay	laying	laid	(have) laid
bring	bringing	brought	(have) brought
begin	beginning	began	(have) begun
fly	flying	flew	(have) flown
cost	costing	cost	(have) cost
pay	paying	paid	(have) paid
lose	losing	lost	(have) lost
sell	selling	sold	(have) sold
spend	spending	spent	(have) spent

IRREGULAR VERBS WITH THE SAME PRESENT, PAST, AND PAST PARTICIPLE			
Present	Present Participle	Past	Past Participle
bid	bidding	bid	(have) bid
burst	bursting	burst	(have) burst
cost	costing	cost	(have) cost
cut	cutting	cut	(have) cut
hit	hitting	hit	(have) hit
hurt	hurting	hurt	(have) hurt
let	letting	let	(have) let
put	putting	put	(have) put
set	setting	set	(have) set
shut	shutting	shut	(have) shut
split	splitting	split	(have) split
spread	spreading	spread	(have) spread
thrust	thrusting	thrust	(have) thrust

⊛**Technology Tip**

The present participle can be used as a key word to locate information on the Internet. For instance, typing the word *flying* will lead you to Web sites that have information about flying airplanes and other related topics.

IRREGULAR VERBS WITH THE SAME PAST AND PAST PARTICIPLE			
Present	Present Participle	Past	Past Participle
bring	bringing	brought	(have) brought
build	building	built	(have) built
buy	buying	bought	(have) bought
catch	catching	caught	(have) caught
get	getting	got	(have) got *or* gotten
hang	hanging	hung	(have) hung
hold	holding	held	(have) held
keep	keeping	kept	(have) kept
lay	laying	laid	(have) laid
lead	leading	led	(have) led
leave	leaving	left	(have) left
lose	losing	lost	(have) lost
pay	paying	paid	(have) paid
sell	selling	sold	(have) sold
send	sending	sent	(have) sent
sit	sitting	sat	(have) sat
sleep	sleeping	slept	(have) slept
stand	standing	stood	(have) stood
stick	sticking	stuck	(have) stuck
strike	striking	struck	(have) struck
teach	teaching	taught	(have) taught
win	winning	won	(have) won
wring	wringing	wrung	(have) wrung

IRREGULAR VERBS THAT CHANGE IN OTHER WAYS			
Present	Present Participle	Past	Past Participle
arise	arising	arose	(have) arisen
began	beginning	began	(have) begun
blow	blowing	blew	(have) blown
break	breaking	broke	(have) broken
choose	choosing	chose	(have) chosen
come	coming	came	(have) come
do	doing	did	(have) done
draw	drawing	drew	(have) drawn
drink	drinking	drank	(have) drunk
drive	driving	drove	(have) driven
eat	eating	ate	(have) eaten
fall	falling	fell	(have) fallen
fly	flying	flew	(have) flown
freeze	freezing	froze	(have) frozen
give	giving	gave	(have) given
go	going	went	(have) gone
grow	growing	grew	(have) grown
know	knowing	knew	(have) known
lie	lying	lay	(have) lain
ride	riding	rode	(have) ridden
ring	ringing	rang	(have) rung
rise	rising	rose	(have) risen
run	running	ran	(have) run
see	seeing	saw	(have) seen
shake	shaking	shook	(have) shaken
shrink	shrinking	shrank	(have) shrunk
sing	singing	sang	(have) sung
sink	sinking	sank	(have) sunk
slay	slaying	slew	(have) slain
speak	speaking	spoke	(have) spoken
spring	springing	sprang	(have) sprung
steal	stealing	stole	(have) stolen
stride	striding	strode	(have) stridden
strive	striving	strove	(have) striven
swear	swearing	swore	(have) sworn
swim	swimming	swam	(have) swum
take	taking	took	(have) taken
tear	tearing	tore	(have) torn
throw	throwing	threw	(have) thrown
wear	wearing	wore	(have) worn
write	writing	wrote	(have) written

More Practice

Grammar Exercise Workbook
• pp. 113–120
On-line Exercise Bank
• Section 22.1
Go on-line:
PHSchool.com
Enter Web Code:
eek-1002

▶ **Exercise 6** Using the Principal Parts of Irregular Verbs
Choose the correct form of the verb in parentheses.

1. The Chinese emperor Shi Huangdi (holded, held) the reigns of power in China around 220 B.C.
2. He (seeked, sought) ways to strengthen his country.
3. To protect China's northern border, Shi Huangdi had (drew, drawn) up plans for a huge stone wall.
4. Then, he had (put, putted) 300,000 workers to the task of constructing the wall.
5. Once the wall had been (build, built), Shi Huangdi turned to the country's economy.

▶ **Exercise 7** Supplying the Correct
Principal Parts of Irregular Verbs Rewrite each sentence, supplying the correct principal part of the verb given in parentheses.

1. He ___?___ out an order requiring all Chinese to use the same currency, a round coin with a square hole in the middle. (send)
2. A common currency ___?___ it easier for one region of China to trade goods with another. (make)
3. Eight hundred years later, the Chinese ___?___ the first people to use paper money. (become)
4. When Marco Polo visited in the 1200's, he ___?___ that the Chinese were using paper money instead of coins. (see)
5. Polo had ___?___ to European leaders about this practice after he had returned to Italy. (speak)

▶ **Exercise 8** Revising to Correct the Use of Irregular Verbs
Revise this paragraph, correcting any errors in the use of irregular verbs.

The Chinese begun issuing paper money around A.D. 600. Even after they had heard about Chinese paper money from Marco Polo, Europeans remained unconvinced. They keeped wondering how a piece of paper could have value. It wasn't until the 1600's that banks in Europe choosed to issue paper bills, called bank notes, to their customers. When depositors took bank notes to their banks, they could be given gold or silver coins in exchange. The idea of government-issued paper money had not catched on until the 1800's.

▲ Critical Viewing
Use two different irregular verbs in describing this photograph of the Great Wall of China.
[Describe]

Conjugating the Tenses

With the principal parts of verbs and helping verbs, you can form all the tenses.

KEY CONCEPT A **conjugation** is a complete list of the singular and plural forms of a verb in a particular tense. ■

For each tense, there are three singular forms and three plural forms that correspond to the first-, second-, and third-person forms of personal pronouns.

To conjugate the six tenses in their basic forms, you need only three of the principal parts: the present, the past, and the past participle. To conjugate the six tenses in their progressive forms, you need the present participle and a form of the verb *be*.

CONJUGATION OF THE BASIC FORMS OF *PAY*		
	Singular	**Plural**
Present		
First Person Second Person Third Person	I pay you pay he, she, it pays	we pay you pay they pay
Past		
First Person Second Person Third Person	I paid you paid he, she, it paid	we paid you paid they paid
Future		
First Person Second Person Third Person	I will pay you will pay he, she, it will pay	we will pay you will pay they will pay
Present Perfect		
First Person Second Person Third Person	I have paid you have paid he, she, it has paid	we have paid you have paid they have paid
Past Perfect		
First Person Second Person Third Person	I had paid you had paid he, she, it had paid	we had paid you had paid they had paid
Future Perfect		
First Person Second Person Third Person	I will have paid you will have paid he, she, it will have paid	we will have paid you will have paid they will have paid

CONJUGATION OF THE PROGRESSIVE FORMS OF *PAY*

	Singular	Plural
Present Progressive		
First Person Second Person Third Person	I am paying you are paying he, she, it is paying	we are paying you are paying they are paying
Past Progressive		
First Person Second Person Third Person	I was paying you were paying he, she, it was paying	we were paying you were paying they were paying
Future Progressive		
First Person Second Person Third Person	I will be paying you will be paying he, she, it will be paying	we will be paying you will be paying they will be paying
Present Perfect Progressive		
First Person Second Person Third Person	I have been paying you have been paying he, she, it has been paying	we have been paying you have been paying they have been paying
Past Perfect Progressive		
First Person Second Person Third Person	I had been paying you had been paying he, she, it had been paying	we had been paying you had been paying they had been paying
Future Perfect Progressive		
First Person Second Person Third Person	I will have been paying you will have been paying he, she, it will have been paying	we will have been paying you will have been paying they will have been paying

Note About *Be:* The verb *be* is highly irregular. The following conjugation of the first two tenses lists the forms.

PRESENT: I am   we are
          you are   you are
          he, she, it is   they are

PAST: I was   we were
          you were   you were
          he, she, it was they were

▶ **Exercise 9** Conjugating the Basic Forms of Verbs
Conjugate the basic forms of the five verbs below.

EXAMPLE: spend (conjugated with *we*)

ANSWER: present: we spend   present perfect: we have
                                            spent

            past: we spent   past perfect: we had
                                            spent

            future: we will spend   future perfect: we will
                                            have spent

1. stop (conjugated with *she*)
2. cost (conjugated with *it*)
3. collect (conjugated with *they*)
4. sell (conjugated with *we*)
5. choose (conjugated with *I*)

▶ **Exercise 10** Conjugating the Progressive Forms of Verbs
Conjugate the progressive forms of the five verbs below.

EXAMPLE: spend (conjugated with *we*)

ANSWER: present progressive: we are spending
            past progressive: we were spending
            future progressive: we will be spending
            present perfect progressive: we have been spending
            past perfect progressive: we had been spending
            future perfect progressive: we will have been
            spending

1. study (conjugated with *they*)   4. forget (conjugated with *I*)
2. put (conjugated with *he*)   5. strive (conjugated with *we*)
3. lend (conjugated with *you*)

▶ **Exercise 11** Supplying the Correct Tense of Verbs On
your paper, write each sentence, using the indicated form for
each verb in parentheses.

1. Until recently, most coins (contain) precious metals like
   gold or silver. (past perfect)
2. However, the number of coins in circulation today greatly
   (exceed) the world's supply of precious metals. (present)
3. Making gold coins (become) impractical. (present perfect)
4. It is likely that the value of old silver and gold coins (rise)
   in the future. (future)
5. For that reason, more people than ever (seek) to collect old
   coins. (future progressive)

▲ **Critical Viewing**
How does this coin
compare with those
we use today? What
verb forms did you
use in making your
comparison?
[Compare]

**interactive
Textbook**

Get instant feed-
back! Exercises 9,
10, and 11 are avail-
able on-line
or on CD-ROM.

▶ **More Practice**

Grammar Exercise
Workbook
• pp. 113–120
On-line Exercise Bank
• Section 22.1

Go on-line:
PHSchool.com
Enter Web Code:
eek-1002

Hands-on Grammar

Top-Ten List of Irregular Verbs

Complete the following activity to prepare a reference that you can use to remind you how to conjugate irregular verbs that you find especially troublesome.

Brainstorm with classmates to come up with a list of irregular verbs that have at times caused problems in your writing. One of you should record the verbs on the chalkboard or on a piece of paper.

Review the list of verbs, and choose the ten that you find most difficult to conjugate. Then, make a folding chart like the one below, in which you list the present, past, future, present perfect, past perfect, future perfect, present progressive, past progressive, future progressive, present perfect progressive, past perfect progressive, and future perfect progressive tenses of each verb.

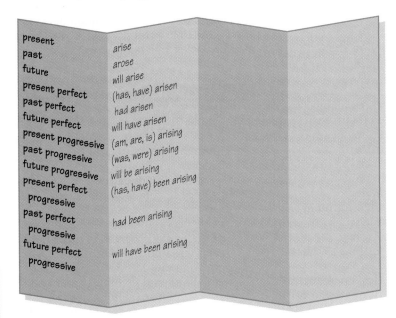

present	arise
past	arose
future	will arise
present perfect	(has, have) arisen
past perfect	had arisen
future perfect	will have arisen
present progressive	(am, are, is) arising
past progressive	(was, were) arising
future progressive	will be arising
present perfect progressive	(has, have) been arising
past perfect progressive	had been arising
future perfect progressive	will have been arising

Find It in Your Reading Scan through stories and essays you have read recently to help you come up with verbs to include on your list.

Find It in Your Writing Look through your portfolio to find examples of irregular verbs. Then, add them to your chart or, if necessary, compile a second chart.

Section Review

GRAMMAR EXERCISES 12–22

> **Exercise 12** Identifying Verb Tenses and Forms On your paper, label the tense and form of each verb in italics.

1. People *have been collecting* coins for hundreds of years.
2. People *call* coin collectors *numismatists*.
3. Coin collecting *has been rising* in popularity with the advent of the Internet.
4. Before being able to use the Internet, collectors often *had traveled* great distances to examine and buy coins.
5. Thanks to the Internet, numismatists can now *purchase* coins in faraway places with a click of a button.

> **Exercise 13** Identifying the Uses of Tense Label the tense and the time of the italicized verb in each sentence.

1. A second industry *has grown* alongside the development of national currencies.
2. Counterfeiting has been a major problem for banks and governments since the first coins and bills *were produced*.
3. Counterfeiters often *use* sophisticated methods to make fake money.
4. In some nations, counterfeit currency *had reduced* public confidence in the value of the country's currency.
5. By using new technology, the U.S. government *has thwarted* many recent attempts to counterfeit U.S. currency.
6. The government *changed* the design of the twenty-dollar bill to make it more difficult for counterfeiters to copy.
7. Many years ago, the U.S. government *had begun* to use special paper on which to print its money.
8. This unique paper *has* microscopic threads embedded in it.
9. It is certain that the world's governments *will use* new methods to deter counterfeiters in the future.

10. It is hoped that by the next millennium, governments *will have succeeded* in eradicating counterfeit currency.

> **Exercise 14** Revising to Correct Verb Tense Revise the following paragraph, correcting errors in verb tense.

A coin's condition influences its value. The value of coins changed with time. A rare penny that is worth thousands of dollars to collectors today is worth just one cent at one time. To help establish the value of a coin, numismatists establish five gradations to rank the condition of coins. It is possible that years from now, the change in your pocket has become valuable.

> **Exercise 15** Recognizing Principal Parts of Verbs Identify the principal part of each verb in italics.

1. Although most countries have their own currency, many *conduct* business using the U.S. dollar.
2. In the past, this situation *helped* to keep the value of the dollar stable.
3. At this very moment, people throughout the world *are making* business deals based on the U.S. dollar.
4. Improvements in international trade regulations and communication *have made* such transactions possible.
5. People *have bought* products from foreign businesses through the Internet without needing to convert currencies.

> **Exercise 16** Using the Principal Parts of Verbs Choose the principal part that is correct in each sentence on the next page.

1. Many books have been (wrote, written) on the value of money worldwide.
2. Writers have (gave, given) much thought to this topic.
3. Economists have long (knew, known) that the value of money fluctuates.
4. They have (threw, thrown) new light on that which gives money value.
5. For example, a dollar (buyed, bought) more in the 1920's than it does today.
6. Many of our grandparents have (saw, seen) prices double, triple, or even quadruple in their lifetimes.
7. Things that had (took, taken) five cents to purchase many years ago, now may cost several dollars.
8. In that sense, the value of a dollar has (shrank, shrunk) over the years.
9. As prices for goods have risen, the value of money has (fell, fallen).
10. All is not bad news, however. Along with rising prices, people's incomes have also (grew, grown).

▶ **Exercise 17** Supplying Correct Verb Forms Supply the correct principal part of the verb in parentheses.

1. Some economists have __?__ that coins and bills will slowly be replaced by other forms of currency. (claim)
2. Indeed, fewer people than ever before are __?__ cash today to purchase goods and services. (use)
3. These days, people routinely __?__ goods and services with credit cards, debit cards, and checks. (buy)
4. This __?__ not always __?__ the case. (be)
5. Until recently, people had __?__ most purchases with cash. (make)

▶ **Exercise 18** Revising to Correct the Use of Irregular Verbs Revise this passage, correcting errors in verb usage.

Today, many transactions occur without the exchange of coins or paper money.

This happen most often in wealthy countries when large amounts of money are involved. However, many employees are also payed by having funds deposited directly into their accounts. Experts speculate that in the future, very few people will be relying on cash to conduct business transactions. They speculate that once computer technology becomes common throughout the world, coins and paper money will have became obsolete. By 2010, we will have saw many changes.

▶ **Exercise 19** Conjugating the Basic and Progressive Forms of Verbs Conjugate the following verbs in both the basic and progressive forms.

1. earn (conjugate with *I*)
2. keep (conjugate with *you*)
3. go (conjugate with *they*)
4. tell (conjugate with *he*)
5. fly (conjugate with *we*)

▶ **Exercise 20** Find It in Your Reading Label the tense and form of each italicized verb in this excerpt from "Civil Peace" by Chinua Achebe.

. . . Jonathan *thought* he *heard* even more voices now than before and *groaned* heavily. His legs *were sagging* under him and his throat *felt* like sandpaper.

▶ **Exercise 21** Find It in Your Writing Choose a paragraph from one of your compositions. Circle each verb or verb phrase, and identify its tense and form.

▶ **Exercise 22** Writing Application In this section, you learned about the history of currency. Write about the history of something else that interests you. Use at least three different tenses. Circle each verb, and identify its tense.

Active and Passive Voice

In addition to using verbs to show the time that something happened, you can show whether the subject is performing or receiving the action. You can do this by changing the *voice* of a verb. You can show voice only with action verbs.

> **KEY CONCEPT** **Voice** is the form of a verb that shows whether the subject is performing the action. ■

There are two voices in English: *active* and *passive*.

> **KEY CONCEPTS** A verb is **active** if its subject performs the action. A verb is **passive** if its action is performed upon the subject. ■

Differences Between Active and Passive Voice

Any action verb, with or without a direct object, can be in the active voice. In these examples, the subject is doing the action.

ACTIVE VOICE: Ken *bought* a set of paints.
My sister *drives* to art school.

Most action verbs can also be used in the passive voice. A passive verb is made from a form of *be* and the past participle of a transitive verb (one that can have a direct object). In the first example below, Ken is still the performer; yet the word *Ken* is now the object of the preposition *by* and not the subject of the sentence. In the second example, *sister* is still the subject, but the person doing the action is not identified.

PASSIVE VOICE: A set of paints *was bought* by Ken.
My sister *was driven* to art school.

> **Exercise 23** **Distinguishing Between the Active and Passive Voices** Identify each verb or verb phrase as *active* or *passive*.
> 1. Many prominent nineteenth-century artists *lived* in France.
> 2. The Frenchman Auguste Rodin *is cherished* by art lovers.
> 3. Rodin's birthday, November 12, *is celebrated* by admirers.
> 4. Surprisingly, Rodin *did* not *grow* up in an artistic family.
> 5. His father *worked* as a police official.
> 6. Early success *was* not *experienced* by Rodin.
> 7. He *was denied* entrance to the finest art school in Paris.
> 8. Despite this setback, Rodin *persevered.*
> 9. He *pursued* sculpture on his own.
> 10. He also *worked* for other sculptors.

Theme: Artists

In this section, you will learn to recognize verbs in active or passive voice and practice rewriting sentences to use active voice verbs whenever possible. The examples and exercises are about artists and fine art.

Cross-Curricular Connection: Fine Art

Get instant feedback! Exercises 23 and 24 are available on-line or on CD-ROM.

> **More Practice**
> **Grammar Exercise Workbook**
> • pp. 121–124
> **On-line Exercise Bank**
> • Section 22.2
> *Go on-line:*
> PHSchool.com
> *Enter Web Code:*
> eek-1002

Using Voice Correctly

To write well, you must know when to use the active voice and when to use the passive voice. There are no firm rules, but here are some suggestions:

▶ **KEY CONCEPT** Use the active voice whenever possible. ■

Good writing is crisp and direct. Sentences with active verbs are less wordy and more direct than those with passive verbs. Notice that both sentences below report the same information, but the sentence in the active voice is shorter and more direct.

ACTIVE VOICE: Esteban *sketched* the bowl of apples.
PASSIVE VOICE: The bowl of apples *was sketched* by Esteban.

There are, of course, times when it is more appropriate to use the passive voice. Use the passive voice to point out the receiver of an action whenever the performer is not important or not easily identified.

▶ **KEY CONCEPT** Use the passive voice to emphasize the receiver of an action rather than the performer of an action. ■

Placing a word at or near the beginning of a sentence helps emphasize its importance. When you want to stress the importance of the receiver of an action, then it is proper to use the passive voice.

PASSIVE VOICE: Maria *was given* an art award by a museum official.
The damaged statue *was placed* downstairs.

▶ **Exercise 24** Revising Sentences in the Passive Voice Rewrite each sentence below, changing it from passive to active voice.
1. The art exhibit was seen by our whole family.
2. A review of the exhibit had been read by us before we went.
3. Tickets for the exhibit were purchased by my mother.
4. The Internet was used by her to make the purchase.
5. Each work in the exhibit was painted by an Impressionist artist.

▼ Critical Viewing
Think of two sentences concerning the creation of this painting, one in the active voice and one in the passive voice. Which sentence is shorter and more direct? [Connect, Contrast]

Tiberius and Agrippina, Peter Paul Rubens

Active and Passive Voice • **383**

GRAMMAR IN LITERATURE

from **The Masque of the Red Death**
Edgar Allan Poe

This passage by Edgar Allan Poe artfully combines active voice verbs (in blue italics) and a passive voice verb (in red italics) to convey the helplessness of revelers in the grip of impending doom.

And then the music *ceased*, as I have *told*; and the evolutions of the waltzers *were quieted*; and there was an uneasy cessation of all things as before. But now there were twelve strokes to be sounded by the bell of the clock; and thus it *happened*, perhaps, that more of thought *crept*, with more of time, into the meditations of the thoughtful among those who *reveled*.

▶ **Exercise 25** Revising to Use the Active Voice On your paper, rewrite the following paragraph, changing at least four uses of the passive voice to the active voice. If you have chosen to leave any sentence in the passive voice, explain your reason.

EXAMPLE: The sculpture was honored with a blue ribbon.

ANSWER: Keep in passive voice because performer of action is unidentified.

(1) The mid-twentieth century has been heralded by many art scholars as an exciting era for innovative art. (2) Jasper Johns, one of the most interesting artists of that era, worked in the United States in the 1950's. (3) Audiences and critics were thrilled by Johns's bold paintings. (4) Exploring a new direction, he painted such ordinary objects as numerals and the letters of the alphabet. (5) Thick layers of paint were used by Johns on his paintings. (6) The texture of his creations was intensified by this technique. (7) In the late 1950's, he incorporated actual objects into his paintings. (8) Objects like rulers and compasses were attached by him to his paintings. (9) Johns is considered by many art scholars to be one of the most influential American artists of the twentieth century. (10) Many of his works are exhibited in prominent art museums and galleries around the world.

▶ **More Practice**

Grammar Exercise Workbook
• pp. 121–124
On-line Exercise Bank
• Section 22.2
  Go on-line:
  PHSchool.com
  Enter Web Code:
  eek-1002

Complete the exercise on-line! Exercise 25 is available on-line or on CD-ROM.

Section 22.2 *Section Review*

GRAMMAR EXERCISES 26–31

Exercise 26 Distinguishing Between the Active and Passive Voices
On your paper, identify the voice of the verb in each of the following sentences.

1. In the 1960's, Andy Warhol was noticed by the art world for his silk-screen prints of ordinary objects.
2. Common objects, such as soup cans and soft-drink bottles, were often depicted in these prints.
3. This seemingly defiant approach to art defined the Pop Art movement.
4. Warhol also made silk-screen prints of famous celebrities.
5. Warhol's reputation as an innovator was established by these prints.

Exercise 27 Using the Passive and Active Voices
Identify the voice of the italicized verb in each sentence. Then, rewrite the sentence, changing the voice from active to passive or passive to active.

1. The works of Leonardo da Vinci *have inspired* viewers for hundreds of years.
2. Da Vinci *had been heralded* by his peers in Italy as a talented artist.
3. Modern critics *have praised* him as a superb painter, sculptor, architect, and scientist.
4. He *is remembered* best by art lovers for *The Last Supper* and the *Mona Lisa*.
5. *The Last Supper was painted* by Da Vinci on one wall of a dining hall of a monastery.
6. Many people *have described* the *Mona Lisa* as a masterpiece.
7. The work *depicts* a beautiful woman.
8. A sense of mystery *is captured* in the woman's smile.
9. The work also *displays* great technical mastery.
10. By the early 2000's, Da Vinci's works *will have been admired* by people for nearly five hundred years.

Exercise 28 Revising to Use the Active Voice
Rewrite this paragraph, changing several uses of the passive voice to the active voice. Explain why you have left any sentence in the passive voice.

(1) The fourteenth and fifteenth centuries are described by art historians as a time of revival in European art and culture. (2) This period has often been called the Renaissance, or "rebirth." (3) Prior to the Renaissance, European art had been marked by a long period of inactivity. (4) The sculptor Donatello is considered by critics and historians to be one of the greatest Renaissance artists. (5) A golden era in sculpture was signaled by Donatello's completion of a statue of David in 1435.

Exercise 29 Find It in Your Reading
Make a photocopy of a magazine article about one of the fine arts. Highlight all of the verbs in the active voice in one color and all of the verbs in the passive voice in another color.

Exercise 30 Find It in Your Writing
In a piece of your own writing, find at least five sentences in the passive voice. Rewrite these sentences in the active voice.

Exercise 31 Writing Application
Write a brief description of a work of art that you or one of your friends created. Use both active and passive voice verbs. Circle each verb, and identify its voice. Explain your use of the passive voice.

Pronoun Usage

At one time in the history of the English language, the forms of both nouns and pronouns were changed to indicate how they were being used in a sentence. Today, nouns change form only to show possession: A noun is made possessive by adding an apostrophe and an *s* (a *woman's* dress) or just an apostrophe (the two *boys'* gloves).

Pronouns in modern English still have different forms depending on how they are used in a sentence. This chapter will explain the various forms of pronouns and their uses.

The rules of proper pronoun usage have developed over time to help us communicate more effectively and efficiently. Whether you are writing about modern times or about America in the "Roaring Twenties," you need to use pronouns correctly in order to communicate.

▲ **Critical Viewing**
Describe the actions of both people in the picture, using such pronouns as *he, she, him, her, his, they,* and *their.*
[Analyze]

Diagnostic Test

Directions: Write all answers on a separate sheet of paper.

Skill Check A. Write the pronouns in each sentence, and identify the case for each as *nominative, objective,* or *possessive.*

1. They danced a popular dance from the 1920's.
2. The author dedicated his book on the Jazz Age to her.
3. We saw pictures of fancy dresses worn in the 1920's.
4. Grandfather remembers his best friend from way back then.
5. "The happiest people were we children," he recalled.

Skill Check B. Identify the case of each underlined pronoun in the following sentences, and tell how it is used in the sentence.

6. <u>Her</u> grandmother lived during the 1920's.
7. <u>She</u> is extremely happy that we are interested in <u>her</u> stories.
8. She enjoys telling <u>me</u> her stories.
9. The two biggest fans of the 1920's are she and <u>I</u>.
10. Talking to her fascinates <u>me</u>.

Skill Check C. Indicate the correct pronoun to complete the following sentences.

11. One of (me, my) favorite heroes of the 1920's is Charles Lindbergh.
12. (His, His') adventures were followed by people from all over the world.
13. His quest was known for (it's, its) difficulty.
14. Do you know where (you're, your) ancestors were in the 1920's?
15. I am sure that (their, they're) experiences are very interesting.

Skill Check D. Choose the correct pronoun in parentheses, and identify its function in the sentence or clause.

16. I know (who, whom) gave her the article about 1920's fashion.
17. She is not sure (who, whom) they are featuring next.
18. To (who, whom) did she lend her book?
19. Do you know (who, whom) made the first solo flight across the Atlantic Ocean?
20. Give it to (whoever, whomever) wrote this report on famous aviators.

Skill Check E. Choose the correct pronoun in parentheses. Then, write any words or phrases that are understood to precede or follow the pronoun.

21. I know more about the fads of the 1920's than (she, her).
22. The speaker knows less about the 1920's than (I, me).
23. The films of the 1920's are as familiar to his grandmother as (he, him).
24. No living silent film star is as respected as (she, her).
25. This collection of photographs from the 1920's is more precious to me than (they, them).

Case

Case is a term used to describe the different forms of nouns and pronouns.

> **KEY CONCEPT** **Case** is the form of a noun or a pronoun that indicates its use in a sentence. ■

The Three Cases

Both nouns and pronouns have three cases:

> **KEY CONCEPT** The three cases are the *nominative*, the *objective*, and the *possessive*. ■

The following chart shows the uses of each of these three cases.

Case	Use in Sentence
Nominative	Subject or Predicate Nominative
Objective	Direct Object, Indirect Object, Object of a Preposition, or Object of a Verbal
Possessive	To Show Ownership

Using the correct case of nouns is seldom a problem because the form changes only in the possessive case.

NOMINATIVE: The old *car* would not start.
OBJECTIVE: We could not start the old *car.*
POSSESSIVE: The old *car's* battery needed to be replaced.

In the first sentence, *car* is the subject. In the second sentence, *car* is the direct object. The form changes only in the *possessive* case, by adding an apostrophe and an *s*.

In contrast to nouns, personal pronouns have different forms for all three cases.

Nominative	Objective	Possessive
I	me	my, mine
you	you	your, yours
he, she, it	him, her, it	his, her, hers, its
we	us	our, ours
they	them	their, theirs

Theme:
Roaring Twenties
....
In this section, you will learn about the three cases of pronouns and their uses and forms. The examples and exercises in this section are about the Roaring Twenties.
....
Cross-Curricular Connection: Social Studies

GRAMMAR IN LITERATURE

from **Games at Twilight**
Anita Desai

Notice the pronouns in the nominative case (in red italics) and in the objective case (in blue italics) in this excerpt. How is each pronoun used?

Ravi had a frightening glimpse of *them* as Raghu combed the hedge of crotons and hibiscus, trampling delicate ferns underfoot as *he* did so. Ravi looked about *him* desperately, swallowing a small ball of snot in his fear.

▲ Critical Viewing
Write three sentences describing both the man holding the horse and the women in the carriage. Use *he, him, she, her, they,* or *them* in your sentences. **[Analyze]**

▶ **Exercise 1** Identifying Case Write the case of each underlined pronoun. Then, indicate its usage.

EXAMPLE: The reporter told the truth about <u>them</u>.
ANSWER: objective (object of a preposition)

1. <u>Our</u> ancestors lived through the 1920's, a remarkable period in history.
2. If <u>you</u> had been alive in the 1920's, you would have witnessed many exciting events.
3. The people of the 1920's saw <u>their</u> world change rapidly.
4. <u>They</u> enjoyed benefits brought about by advances in commerce and technology.
5. Many of <u>them</u> heard the world's first radio broadcast.
6. Other innovations in science and business amazed and excited <u>them</u>.
7. These advances brought about great prosperity for many Americans and <u>their</u> descendants.
8. Such advances in technology gave <u>them</u> a sense of optimism for the future.
9. The beneficiaries of their optimism are <u>we</u>.
10. Reading about events of the 1920's and studying <u>them</u> can offer many insights into modern times.

▶ **More Practice**

Grammar Exercise Workbook
• pp. 125–126
On-line Exercise Bank
• Section 23.1
  Go on-line:
  PHSchool.com
  Enter Web Code:
  eek-1002

The Nominative Case

There are two major uses of pronouns in the nominative case:

More Practice

Grammar Exercise
Workbook
• pp. 127–128
On-line Exercise Bank
• Section 23.1

Go on-line:
PHSchool.com
Enter Web Code:
eek-1002

▷ **KEY CONCEPT** Use the nominative case when a pronoun is used as the *subject* of a verb or as a *predicate nominative.* ∎

The chart below illustrates these two uses.

NOMINATIVE PRONOUNS	
Subject	*She* is the conductor of the band. *I* want to learn more about the music of the 1920's. *They* danced the Charleston while we sat.
Predicate Nominative	The famous historian is *she.* It is *I.* Our closest friends have always been *they.*

Nominative Pronouns in Compounds When using a compound subject or a compound predicate nominative, check the case by mentally removing the other part of the compound or by mentally inverting the sentence.

COMPOUND SUBJECT:	Marie and *I* watched a film about the 1920's. (*I* watched a film about the 1920's.) Beth and *he* will learn more about that time from his grandmother. (*He* will learn more about that time from his grandmother.)
COMPOUND PREDICATE NOMINATIVE:	The winners were Tim and *she.* (Tim and *she* were the winners.) The best dancers are Kay and *I.* (Kay and *I* are the best dancers.)

Nominative Pronouns With Appositives Appositives sometimes follow a pronoun in order to rename it or identify it. If a pronoun used as a subject or predicate nominative is followed by an appositive, the nominative case is still used.

SUBJECT:	*We* musicians love music of the 1920's.
PREDICATE NOMINATIVE:	The ones with the most spirit are *we* sophomores.

▶ **Exercise 2** Identifying Pronouns in the Nominative Case
Choose the nominative case pronoun that completes each sentence.
1. (We, Us) Americans have always enjoyed sports.
2. Fiercely devoted sports fans are (we, us).
3. My great-grandfather and (I, me) often talk about sports heroes from the 1920's.
4. My great-grandfather was obsessed with sports in the 1920's when (he, him) was a young boy.
5. (I, Me) have learned much about Babe Ruth and Red Grange from him.
6. His first heroes in baseball and football were (they, them).
7. My great-grandfather described a time when (he, him) saw Babe Ruth smack a home run.
8. His brother and (he, him) went to that game together.
9. He said that the most excited fans in the stadium were (they, them).
10. "(He, Him) and I almost caught that baseball," he recalled.

▶ **Exercise 3** Using Pronouns in the Nominative Case Write a nominative pronoun to complete each sentence. Then, identify how the pronoun is used in the sentence.
1. My friends and __?__ have been learning about the Roaring Twenties.
2. Did __?__ know that the Roaring Twenties closely followed World War I?
3. __?__ Americans were excited by the return of peace and improvements in our economy.
4. Many Americans supported the Republican party, and __?__ elected Warren G. Harding president in 1920.
5. It was __?__ who became the twenty-ninth president of the United States.

▼ **Critical Viewing**
Describe your impression of these two political leaders. Use *I, he,* and *they* in your sentences.
[Describe]

President
Warren G. Harding

Vice-President
Calvin Coolidge

▶ **Exercise 4** Revising to Correct Errors in Pronoun Usage
Revise the following sentences to correct errors in pronoun usage. If a sentence is correct, write *correct.*
1. I learned that him and his wife were from Ohio.
2. My friends and me are interested in learning more about Harding.
3. Harding appointed many friends to government positions. Some of they became involved in several scandals.
4. Harding served as president until August 1923, when he died of a heart attack in San Francisco, California.
5. Calvin Coolidge was vice president, so Harding's successor was he.

The Objective Case

The objective case is used with the objects of verbs and prepositions as well as with the objects of verbals.

▶ **KEY CONCEPT** Use the objective case when a pronoun is used as the object of any verb, preposition, or verbal. ■

The chart below illustrates the uses of objective pronouns.

OBJECTIVE PRONOUNS	
Use	Examples
Direct Object	I baked *them* yesterday. Our teacher praised *her.*
Indirect Object	Give *him* the good news. Alice gave *us* the poster from the 1920's.
Object of Preposition	Between *us*, there are no secrets. Walk beside *them.*
Object of Participle	Racing *her,* he crashed into an antique car. The girl chasing *them* was her sister.
Object of Gerund	Dad likes helping *me* with my homework. Warning *them* was my primary concern.
Object of Infinitive	To tell *them* clearly, he had to shout. He wants to ask *me* about my visit.

Objective Pronouns in Compounds Errors with objective case pronouns most often occur in compounds. To check yourself, mentally remove the other part of the compound.

EXAMPLES: Our history teacher praised John and *her.*
(Our history teacher praised *her.*)

The project was assigned to Charles and *him.*
(The project was assigned to *him.*)

Take special care to use the objective case after the preposition *between.*

INCORRECT: This matter is between *you* and *I.*

CORRECT: This matter is between *you* and *me.*

▶ **More Practice**

Grammar Exercise Workbook
• pp. 127–128
On-line Exercise Bank
• Section 23.1
Go on-line:
PHSchool.com
Enter Web Code:
eek-1002

▼ Critical Viewing
Write three sentences about this flapper. Use a pronoun in a different case in each sentence. **[Analyze]**

Objective Pronoun With Appositives
If an appositive appears after a pronoun used as an object, make sure that you use an objective pronoun.

DIRECT OBJECT: The musical entertained *us* girls.

INDIRECT OBJECT: The club gave *us* leaders an award.

OBJECT OF A   All of *us* history students were
PREPOSITION: nervous about the assignment.

▶ **Exercise 5** Identifying Pronouns in the Objective Case
Choose the pronoun in the objective case to complete each sentence. Then, identify how the pronoun is used in the sentence.

EXAMPLE: The orchestra plans to join (him, he) later.
ANSWER: him (object of infinitive)

1. To (we, us) historians, the 1920's is often known as the Roaring Twenties or the Jazz Age.
2. For Americans in the 1920's, the Jazz Age promised (they, them) great hope and excitement.
3. With stock holdings enriching (they, them), many Americans achieved wealth beyond their wildest dreams.
4. The independent, glamourous flappers of the 1920's are role models for some of (we, us) modern women.
5. Studying (they, them) holds special meaning for today's independent women.

▶ **Exercise 6** Supplying Pronouns in the Objective Case
Write an objective pronoun to complete each sentence. Then, identify how the pronoun is used in the sentence.

EXAMPLE: My parents gave ___?___ an antique watch for my birthday.
ANSWER: me (indirect object)

1. My aunt questioned my sisters and ___?___ about the 1920's.
2. She then gave ___?___ the novel *This Side of Paradise* (1920) by F. Scott Fitzgerald.
3. She enjoys suggesting books to ___?___.
4. Between my sisters and ___?___, we have read enough books to fill a small library.
5. It is easy to get my aunt to start talking; it is stopping ___?___ that is sometimes hard.

⊛ Technology Tip

The spell-check function on most word-processing programs will recognize *it's* and *its* as correctly spelled words. It is up to you to recognize that *it's* means *it is* or *it has* and that *its* shows ownership.

The Possessive Case

The possessive case of pronouns is used to show possession before nouns and before gerunds. Some possessive pronouns are also used by themselves.

KEY CONCEPT Use the possessive case before nouns to show ownership. ■

EXAMPLES: *My* report on the Roaring Twenties is almost done.
Their suggestions have been very helpful.

KEY CONCEPT Use the possessive case before gerunds. ■

EXAMPLES: *Your* asking questions made me focus.
I did not appreciate *his* writing in my book.

KEY CONCEPT Use certain possessive pronouns by themselves to indicate possession. ■

EXAMPLES: That book is *hers*, not *his*.
Is this movie poster *yours* or *mine*?

Sometimes, possessive pronouns are incorrectly spelled with an apostrophe. Spellings such as *your's, our's, their's,* and *her's* are incorrect. In addition, do not confuse the possessive pronouns *its, your,* and *their* (which do not contain apostrophes) with the contractions *it's, you're,* and *they're.*

POSSESSIVE PRONOUN: Which 1920's song is your favorite?

CONTRACTION: *You're* expected to dress up for the party.

Exercise 7 Using Pronouns in the Possessive Case Choose the correct word in parentheses.
1. Each era has (it's, its) distinct fashion trends.
2. Have you ever thought about how (your, you're) great-grandparents may have dressed in the 1920's?
3. Some clothing in the 1920's was similar to (ours, our's).
4. Flappers wore skirts that revealed (they're, their) knees.
5. Those long pearl necklaces were (hers, her's).
6. (They're, Their) choosing to dress that way was a clear break with tradition.
7. (Your, You're) going to enjoy our 1920's fashion show.
8. (Its, It's) scheduled for next Friday evening.
9. I found several suits from the 1920's; (they're, their) in the closet backstage.
10. Back then, men often wore (they're, their) hair parted in the middle.

▶ **More Practice**

Grammar Exercise Workbook
• pp. 129–130
On-line Exercise Bank
• Section 23.1
  Go on-line:
  PHSchool.com
  Enter Web Code:
  eek-1002

Get instant feedback! Exercise 7 is available on-line or on CD-ROM.

Section 23.1 Section Review

GRAMMAR EXERCISES 8–13

▶ **Exercise 8** Identifying Case Write the case of each of the underlined pronouns in the following sentences. Then, write its use.

1. Historians believe that studying the past will help <u>us</u> in the future.
2. In the 1920's, enterprising businessmen and <u>their</u> associates amassed fortunes.
3. Their investments in oil, railroads, and steel brought great wealth to <u>them</u>.
4. Their wealth won <u>them</u> status and fame.
5. The principal investors in the stock market were <u>they</u>.

▶ **Exercise 9** Identifying Pronouns in the Objective Case Choose the correct pronoun in parentheses to complete each sentence. Then, identify its case.

1. <u>They</u> used (their, they're) wealth to influence politicians.
2. (They, Their) having so much wealth and power made poor people jealous.
3. Bill and (me, I) read novels by some prominent writers of the 1920's.
4. The novelists wrote about rich people and sometimes criticized (they, them).
5. Our teacher said that (us, we) should learn more about the 1920's economy.

▶ **Exercise 10** Revising to Correct Pronoun Usage Revise this paragraph, correcting errors in pronoun usage.

(1) The people of the 1920's experienced many exciting events. A number of technological breakthroughs were witnessed by they. (2) Many of them thrilled at seeing new forms of entertainment. (3) Like the people of today, the people of the 1920's often spent they're Saturday afternoons at movie theaters. (4) On some of those Saturdays, them watched the films of Charlie Chaplin. (5) Its him who created the character of the little tramp with the funny walk. (6) People all around the world soon fell in love with he and his antics. (7) Two of the first international movie stars were him and Al Jolson. (8) Although Chaplin's early films did not feature dialogue, they were often accompanied by dramatic music. (9) Fortunately, Chaplin's films have survived to the present and still give many of we great enjoyment. (10) Watching them, your certain to laugh out loud.

▶ **Exercise 11** Find It in Your Reading In this passage from "A Visit to Grandmother" by William Melvin Kelley, identify at least one pronoun in each of the three cases, and tell how it is used.

She let him go, and fell back into her chair, grabbing the arms. Her hands were as dark as the wood, and seemed to become part of it.

▶ **Exercise 12** Find It in Your Writing In your portfolio, find five sentences containing pronouns in all three cases. Check that you have used the pronouns correctly. Write down each pronoun, its case, and its use in the sentence.

▶ **Exercise 13** Writing Application Imagine that you are interviewing a person who lived in the United States during the 1920's. Make a list of questions and responses from your interview. Try to use pronouns in all three cases in your transcript of the interview.

Special Problems With Pronouns

Choosing the correct form of a pronoun is not always a matter of choosing the form that sounds correct. For example, would it be correct to say, "I can run faster than her"? Though the sentence may sound correct to you, it is wrong because an objective pronoun (*her*) is used when a nominative pronoun (*she*) is needed. Several words are understood in the sentence, which reads, in full, "I can run faster than she (can run)."

This section will discuss two special pronoun problems: the proper uses of *who* and *whom* and the related forms *whoever* and *whomever*, as well as the use of pronouns in clauses where some words are omitted but understood.

Using *Who* and *Whom* Correctly

Knowing when to use *who* or *whom* and the related forms *whoever* and *whomever* is less confusing if you understand how the words are used.

KEY CONCEPT *Who* and *whoever* are nominative case pronouns. *Whom* and *whomever* are objective case pronouns. ■

The chart below shows the forms of these pronouns and their uses in sentences.

Case	Pronoun	Use in Sentence
Nominative	who, whoever	Subject or Predicate Nominative
Objective	whom, whomever	Direct Object, Object of a Verbal, or Object of a Preposition
Possessive	whose, whosever	To Show Ownership

The following pages focus on the nominative and objective pronouns, as the possessive case rarely causes problems.

Note About *Whose:* Do not confuse the contraction *who's*, which means "who is," with the possessive pronoun *whose*.

POSSESSIVE PRONOUN: *Whose* satellite went into orbit?

CONTRACTION: *Who's* our first contestant tonight?

Theme: Mars

In this section, you will learn about special problems with pronouns. The examples and exercises in this section are about Mars.

Cross-Curricular Connection: Science

The Nominative Case: *Who* and *Whoever* The nominative case is used for subjects and for predicate nominatives.

▶ **KEY CONCEPT** Use *who* or *whoever* for the subject of a verb. ■

EXAMPLES: *Who* is the person directing the Mars study?
I know *who* had the best science project.
He chose *whoever* volunteered for the space project.

In the last two sentences, *who* and *whoever* are the subjects of subordinate clauses. You can be sure you are using the correct case in a subordinate clause by determining the use of the pronoun. Consider the pronoun in the following sentence:

EXAMPLE: I will accept help from *whoever* will offer it.

The first step in checking the case of the pronoun is to isolate the subordinate clause. In this example, the subordinate clause is *whoever will offer it,* a noun clause acting as the object of the preposition *from.*
The next step is to see how the words in the subordinate clause are used. The verb in the clause is *will offer;* the direct object is *it. Whoever* is the correct pronoun because it acts as a subject and, therefore, must be in the nominative case.

▶ **KEY CONCEPT** Use *who* or *whoever* for a predicate nominative. ■

EXAMPLE: The culprit is *who?*

A problem may arise when the pronoun is the predicate nominative in a subordinate clause.

EXAMPLE: The police do not know *who* the culprit is.

To see whether the pronoun is correct, first isolate the subordinate clause (*who the culprit is*). Next, determine each word's use within the clause. Because this clause is inverted, put it into normal word order: *The culprit is who.* You can now see that the subject is *culprit,* the verb is *is,* and *who* is the predicate nominative of the linking verb. Because predicate nominatives require the nominative case, *who* is correct.

The planet Mars has a polar icecap.

▲ **Critical Viewing**
Write two questions about this picture using the word *who* or *whom* in each.
[Analyze]

The Objective Case: *Whom* and *Whomever* The objective case of these pronouns is used for direct objects of verbs, objects of verbals, and objects of prepositions.

> **KEY CONCEPT** Use *whom* and *whomever* for the direct object of a verb or the object of a verbal. ■

In this example, *whom* is the object of the infinitive *to see.* Check the pronoun's case by mentally rewording the sentence.

EXAMPLE: *Whom* did you expect to see?
(You did expect to see *whom*?)

Pronouns in the objective case also occur in the subordinate clauses of complex sentences.

EXAMPLES: We asked *whom* they chose to go into space.
You can select *whomever* you want.

To see whether the correct pronouns have been used, first isolate the subordinate clause (*whom they chose, whomever you want*). Next, put the clauses in normal word order: *they chose whom; you want whomever.* It now becomes clear that the subjects are *they* and *you* and that the correct direct objects are *whom* and *whomever.*

> **KEY CONCEPT** Use *whom* or *whomever* for the object of a preposition. ■

Whom is the object of a preposition in both examples below.

EXAMPLES: From *whom* did you receive the message?
Whom did you receive the message from?

If the pronoun is used to connect the clauses of a complete sentence, it is necessary to check the pronoun's case more carefully. Look at these two sentences with adjective clauses.

EXAMPLES: I spoke to the astronaut with *whom* we had dined.
I spoke to the astronaut *whom* we had dined with.

In the first sentence, the objective pronoun immediately follows its preposition, *with.* In the second sentence, the pronoun and the preposition are separated by many words. To check the case, isolate the subordinate clause: *whom we had dined with.* Next, put the clause in the normal word order: *We had dined with whom.* The clause has a subject (*we*), a verb (*had dined*), and a prepositional phrase (*with whom*). *Whom* is the correct pronoun because the objective case is required for the object of a preposition.

More Practice

Grammar Exercise Workbook
• pp. 131–132
On-line Exercise Bank
• Section 23.2
Go on-line:
PHSchool.com
Enter Web Code:
eek-1002

GRAMMAR IN LITERATURE

from **Making History With Vitamin C**

Penny Le Couteur and Jay Burreson

Notice the use of who *in the following excerpt.*

The word *scurvy* is said to be derived from Norse, the language of the seafaring Viking warriors *who*, starting in the ninth century, raided the Atlantic coast of Europe from their northern homelands in Scandinavia.

> **Exercise 14** Using *Who* and *Whom* Correctly in Questions and Clauses Choose the correct pronoun in each sentence, and identify the case of the pronoun.
> 1. (Who, Whom) has not wondered whether there is life on other planets?
> 2. From (who, whom) can we learn about plans to send a satellite to Mars?
> 3. The person most likely to be able to answer that question is (who, whom)?
> 4. If you could take a trip to Mars, (who's, whose) the person you would like most to accompany you?
> 5. Someday, such a trip may become possible. In the meantime, (whoever, whomever) is interested in Mars can learn more about it from books, magazines, and the Internet.

> **Exercise 15** Revising to Correct the Use of *Who* and *Whom* Revise the following sentences to correct errors in the use of *who* and *whom*. If a sentence is correct, write *correct*.
> 1. Cherie asked whomever she saw about the reddish planet in the sky.
> 2. Indeed, Mars is close enough to us that it is visible to whoever wants to search for it even without a telescope.
> 3. To who did you remark that it takes 687 Earth days for Mars to revolve around the sun?
> 4. Whom did you ask?
> 5. In whose book did you see a photograph of Mars?

▼ Critical Viewing Use *who* in a sentence about astronauts on Mars. Use *whom* in a sentence about the people watching them. [**Draw Conclusions**]

Use Pronouns Correctly in Elliptical Clauses

In an *elliptical clause*, some words are omitted because they are understood. Sentences with elliptical clauses are often used to draw comparisons. Such sentences are usually divided into two parts connected by *than* or *as: Fran is smarter than he,* or *Tom is as happy as I.* In selecting the case of the pronoun, you must know what the unstated words are.

▶ **KEY CONCEPT** In elliptical clauses beginning with *than* or *as,* use the form of the pronoun that you would use if the clause were fully stated. ■

The case of the pronoun depends upon whether the omitted words belong before or after the pronoun. In the examples below, the omitted words are supplied in brackets.

WORDS LEFT OUT AFTER PRONOUN:	Jo is as interested in space exploration as *he.*
	Jo is as interested in space exploration as he [is].
WORDS LEFT OUT BEFORE PRONOUN:	We gave Scott the same telescope as *her.*
	We gave Scott the same telescope as [we gave] her.

If the omitted words come *after* the pronoun, use a nominative pronoun because it is the subject of the omitted verb. If the omitted words come *before* the pronoun, use an objective pronoun because the pronoun will be an object, generally the direct object or indirect object of the omitted verb or the object of a preposition.

Often, the entire meaning of the sentence depends on the case of the pronoun. Compare, for example, the meaning of the following sentences when the nominative pronoun is changed to an objective pronoun.

WITH A NOMINATIVE PRONOUN:	Stan taught us more about the solar system than *she.*
	Stan taught us more about the solar system than she [did].
WITH AN OBJECTIVE PRONOUN:	Stan taught us more about the solar system than *her.*
	Stan taught us more about the solar system than [he taught] her.

Always follow the steps in the chart on the next page when you choose a pronoun in an elliptical clause.

⊙ Technology Tip

You can learn more about space exploration by visiting various government Web sites. Type *space program* or *NASA* into your browser.

CHOOSING A PRONOUN IN ELLIPTICAL CLAUSES

1. Consider the choices of pronouns: nominative or objective.
2. Mentally complete the elliptical clause.
3. Base your choice on what you find.

Exercise 16 Identifying the Correct Pronoun in Elliptical Clauses Rewrite each sentence, choosing one of the pronouns in parentheses and correctly completing the elliptical clause.

EXAMPLE: She is more knowledgeable about satellites than (I, me).

ANSWER: She is more knowledgeable about satellites than I am.

1. Astronauts who have traveled to outer space probably know more about Mars and the solar system than (we, us).
2. The desire to explore new frontiers is more pressing to them than (we, us).
3. Much of the exploration of Mars has been undertaken by machines that can travel far longer in outer space than (we, us) humans.
4. These machines are accurate and efficient; however, they aren't as expressive or emotional as (we, us) humans.
5. The desire to be an astronaut is much greater in (she, her) than (he, him).

Exercise 17 Using the Correct Pronoun in Elliptical Clauses Complete each sentence by choosing an appropriate pronoun and completing the elliptical clause.

EXAMPLE: Joanne writes more often than ___?___.

ANSWER: Joanne writes more often than I do.

1. Young children think about Mars more often than ___?___.
2. I wish I had as much imagination as ___?___.
3. The possibility of living on other planets seems more real to them than ___?___.
4. I don't think I'm nearly as imaginative as ___?___.
5. According to this science-fiction writer, problem-solving skills are more highly developed in Martians than ___?___.

More Practice

Grammar Exercise Workbook
• pp. 131–132
On-line Exercise Bank
• Section 23.2
Go on-line:
PHSchool.com
Enter Web Code:
eek-1002

Get instant feedback! Exercises 16 and 17 are available on-line or on CD-ROM.

Hands-on Grammar

Pronoun Fold-Over

Cut construction paper into strips that are each about an inch wide. Then, write sentences on each strip. Each sentence should contain half of a compound predicate. Leave a blank in each compound predicate where a pronoun would appear.

With a group of classmates, fold over each strip so that the first part of the compound predicate is hidden. Only the blank where the pronoun will appear should show. Hiding the first half of the compound predicate should help the members of your group identify which pronoun case to use to complete each sentence. Write down the pronouns in the blank spaces. Then, share your answers with classmates.

Use these sentences to create additional strips:

The only ones who attended were Bill and ___?___ .

The winners were Mrs. Simmons and ___?___ .

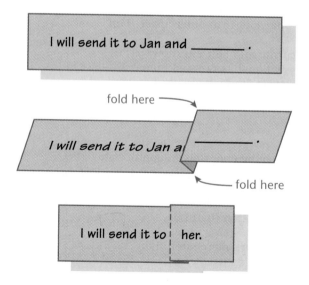

To extend this activity, create strips with sentences in which you leave out the first word of a compound subject.

Find It in Your Reading Find five sample sentences containing compound predicates or compound subjects in a work of narrative nonfiction. Include these sentences in the strips you make.

Find It in Your Writing Try the activity above with five sentences from a piece of your own writing.

Section 23.2

Section Review

GRAMMAR EXERCISES 18–23

Exercise 18 Using *Who* and *Whom* in Questions Choose the pronoun in parentheses that completes each question.

1. The first person to walk in space was (who, whom)?
2. From (who, whom) did we learn about the atmosphere on Mars?
3. Do you know (who, whom) is preparing a science project on Mars?
4. Is that the person (who, whom) I should interview?
5. With (who, whom) should I check my facts before I submit my paper?

Exercise 19 Using *Who* and *Whom* Correctly in Clauses Write the subordinate clause in each sentence. Then, identify how the form of *who* or *whom* is used.

1. I wonder (whose, who's) idea it was to name Mars after the Roman god of war.
2. The person was clearly someone (who, whom) knew a lot about mythology.
3. (Whoever, Whomever) gave Mars its name felt that the planet's red color was symbolic of blood and war.
4. No matter (who, whom) we asked, we could not find out how the names of Mars' moons were chosen.
5. I forget from (who, whom) we learned that Phobos and Deimos were sons of Ares, the Greek god of war.

Exercise 20 Using Pronouns Correctly in Elliptical Clauses Rewrite each sentence, choosing the correct pronoun and completing the elliptical clause.

1. Ancient people may have been more imaginative than (we, us).
2. Space was more a world of mystery for them than (you and I, you and me).

3. We modern people no longer believe, as (they, them), that Earth is the center of the universe.
4. We now know far more about outer space and the solar system than (they, them).
5. The concept of space exploration is far more familiar to us than (they, them).

Exercise 21 Find It in Your Reading Explain why the playwright used *who* instead of *whom* in this sentence from *Invasion From Mars* by Howard Koch.

. . . Incredible as it may seem, both the observations of science and the evidence of our eyes lead to the inescapable assumption that those strange beings who landed in the Jersey farmlands tonight are the vanguard of an invading army from the planet Mars.

Exercise 22 Find It in Your Writing Look through your portfolio and find at least five sentences in which you have used *who* or *whom*. Check to see that you used the pronouns correctly.

Exercise 23 Writing Application Imagine that you have met an alien life form. Write questions that you would ask. Use some of the following pronouns and phrases in your questions. Include at least two elliptical clauses in your questions.

1. more advanced than [pronoun]
2. whoever
3. as smart as [pronoun]
4. whom
5. than [pronoun]

Tornado Bahamas, Winslow Homer

When you speak, you automatically use words that agree with other words. You might say, for example, "The twister moves fast." You know you must add an *-s* to *move* when the subject is *twister* to make the verb agree with the subject.

Agreement is the match—the "fit"—between words or grammatical forms. Because grammatical agreement is not always obvious, you need to study some sentences more closely than others.

In the first section of this chapter, you will learn to make a subject agree with its verb. The second section focuses on agreement between pronouns and their antecedents.

▲ **Critical Viewing** Describe how you think the wind would sound and feel if you were in the scene depicted above. Use verbs that agree with the subjects in your sentences. **[Describe]**

Diagnostic Test

Directions: Write all answers on a separate sheet of paper.

Skill Check A. Choose the verb in parentheses that agrees with the subject of each sentence.

1. Thunderstorms (is, are) dangerous because of lightning.
2. If the right conditions (exists, exist), thunderstorms can become tornadoes.
3. Nebraska and Kansas, located in the region known as Tornado Alley, (has, have) been hit by many tornadoes.
4. A tornado in a southeastern state—such as Florida, South Carolina, or Georgia—(is, are) often caused by a hurricane.
5. A tornado or a hurricane (is, are) a frightening weather phenomenon.
6. Tornadoes occur when cold, dry polar air and warm, moist tropical air (meets, meet).
7. Each occurrence of a tornado (is, are) studied by a team of scientists.
8. The team (examines, examine) the atmospheric conditions and the damage caused by the tornado.
9. On the Internet, there (is, are) photos showing how tornadoes form.
10. Mathematics (is, are) important to scientists who must use formulas to determine the dimensions and speed of a tornado.
11. Two thirds of a town in Kansas (was, were) destroyed during one tornado.
12. Most of the damage could be fixed, but some buildings (was, were) damaged beyond repair.
13. Every one of the townspeople (has, have) been helping to rebuild.
14. Many (believes, believe) that within a year, much of the damage will be mended.
15. One hundred thousand dollars (is, are) the cost of the repairs.

Skill Check B. Choose the correct pronoun in each sentence.

16. John and Pam are studying earth science, a subject (you, they) need for a career in weather forecasting.
17. One of John's favorite teachers is (his, their) physics teacher.
18. Both John and Alfredo will be taking (his, their) tests today.
19. Every student feels (he or she, they) will do well on the test.
20. After I study for a test, I want to reward (me, myself).

Skill Check C. Revise the following sentences to correct problems in pronoun reference.

21. Alfredo told John he was sure he'd pass the test.
22. When the boys entered the classroom he each sat down.
23. On the test, they asked how tornadoes are formed.
24. Nearly every tornado gets their force from strong vertically spinning winds.
25. John and myself knew almost all the answers.

Subject and Verb Agreement

For a subject and verb to agree, both must be singular or both must be plural. In this section, you will learn how to distinguish between singular and plural subjects, how to make verbs agree with compound subjects, and how to deal with problems of agreement with special subjects.

Singular and Plural Subjects

When making a verb agree with its subject, you need to identify the subject and determine its number.

▶ **KEY CONCEPTS** A singular subject must have a singular verb. A plural subject must have a plural verb. ■

SINGULAR SUBJECT
AND VERB: Thunder usually follows lightning.

PLURAL SUBJECT
AND VERB: We are about to get our umbrellas.

▶ **Exercise 1** Making Verbs Agree With Their Subjects
Choose the verb in parentheses that agrees with the subject of each sentence.
1. Tornadoes (leaves, leave) a trail of destruction.
2. Meteorologists (uses, use) special instruments to measure the speed of tornado winds.
3. Tornado winds (races, race) at around 240 miles per hour.
4. In just a few minutes, a twister (roars, roar) past.
5. In that brief period, it (is, are) able to level buildings.

▶ **KEY CONCEPT** A phrase or clause that interrupts a subject and its verb does not affect subject-verb agreement. ■

EXAMPLES: The destruction of tornadoes is devastating.
             The community members who experience the devastation help each other.

In the first example, the singular subject *destruction* takes the singular verb *is*. Even though the plural noun *tornadoes* is closer to the verb, it is the object of a preposition and does not affect subject and verb agreement. In the second sentence, the plural subject *members* agrees with the plural verb *help* even though they are separated by an adjective clause that causes the singular noun *devastation* to be closer to the verb.

Theme: Wind

In this section, you will learn about subject and verb agreement. The examples and exercises in this section are about tornadoes and hurricanes.

Cross-Curricular Connection: Science

⚙ **Grammar and Style Tip**

Remember that in grammar, the concept of number refers to the two forms of a word: singular and plural. Singular words indicate one; plural words indicate more than one.

GRAMMAR IN LITERATURE

from **The Censors**
Luisa Valenzuela

The subjects and the verbs agree in the following excerpt. The subjects are printed in red and the verbs in blue.

He knows that *they examine, sniff, feel,* and *read* between the lines of each and every letter, and *check* its tiniest comma and most accidental stain. *He knows* that all *letters pass* from hand to hand and *go* through all sorts of tests in the huge censorship offices and that, in the end, very *few continue* on their way.

Exercise 2 Making Separated Subjects and Verbs Agree

Choose the verb in parentheses that agrees with the subject of each sentence.

1. A tornado occurring over a lake or an ocean (is, are) a waterspout.
2. A waterspout with winds of less than 50 miles per hour usually (lasts, last) longer than a tornado does.
3. A ship's crew members sailing on the ocean (fears, fear) waterspouts.
4. Water around waterspouts (churns, churn).
5. Small vessels caught in a storm (tosses, toss) violently from side to side.

Exercise 3 Correcting Subject and Verb Agreement

Revise the following passage, correcting all errors in subject-verb agreement. Not every sentence contains an error.

Scientists from the National Weather Service gathers weather information from all parts of the country. If the information indicates a tornado, a warning of severe weather conditions are issued. The movements of the tornado shows where it will strike. People living in that area evacuate. Putting storm cellars under homes also provide an excellent source of shelter. On hearing news of a tornado, members of a family heads for the shelter. Often, a supply of water and canned goods is kept there. When the powerful winds of the tornado passes, the people feel safe leaving the shelter. Usually, a broadcast on radio or TV announce the all-clear. What signs of the storm's fury remains?

More Practice

Grammar Exercise Workbook
• pp. 133–134
On-line Exercise Bank
• Section 24.1
  Go on-line:
  PHSchool.com
  Enter Web Code:
  eek-1002

Get instant feedback! Exercises 1, 2, and 3 are available on-line or on CD-ROM.

Compound Subjects

A compound subject has two or more subjects, usually joined by *or* or *and*. Use the following rules when making compound subjects agree with verbs.

Subjects Joined by *and* Only one rule applies to compound subjects connected by *and:* Whether the parts of the compound subject are all singular, all plural, or mixed, the verb is usually plural.

▶ **KEY CONCEPT** A compound subject joined by *and* is generally plural and must have a plural verb. ■

TWO SINGULAR SUBJECTS:	A <u>thunderstorm</u> and a <u>tornado</u> <u>hit</u> the town.
TWO PLURAL SUBJECTS:	<u>Thunderstorms</u> and <u>tornadoes</u> <u>appear</u> on the radar screen.
A SINGULAR SUBJECT AND A PLURAL SUBJECT:	Luckily, the <u>tornado</u> and the <u>thunderstorms</u> often <u>miss</u> our area.

There are two exceptions to this rule. If the parts of a compound subject are thought of as one item or the word *every* or *each* precedes the compound subject, then the verb is singular. Note the number of the subjects and verbs in the following examples:

EXAMPLES: The best <u>detection</u> and specialized tornado <u>equipment</u> <u>is</u> Doppler radar.
<u>Each tornado</u> and <u>thunderstorm</u> <u>demonstrates</u> nature's power.
<u>Every weather center</u> and <u>emergency network</u> in the United States <u>issues</u> warnings for severe weather.

Singular Subjects Joined by *or* or *nor* When both parts of a compound subject connected by *or* or *nor* are singular, a singular verb is required.

▶ **KEY CONCEPT** Two or more singular subjects joined by *or* or *nor* must have a singular verb. ■

EXAMPLE: A <u>tornado</u> or <u>hurricane</u> <u>causes</u> terrible damage.

▲ **Critical Viewing** Imagine that you are the person who took this picture. Write two sentences, one with a singular subject and one with a plural subject, that describe this situation. Make sure that each verb agrees with its subject. **[Speculate]**

Plural Subjects Joined by *or* or *nor* When both parts of a compound subject connected by *or* or *nor* are plural, a plural verb is required.

KEY CONCEPT Two or more plural subjects joined by *or* or *nor* must have a plural verb. ∎

EXAMPLE: Neither tornadoes nor hurricanes cause as many deaths as lightning storms.

Subjects of Mixed Number Joined by *or* or *nor* If one part of a compound subject is singular and the other is plural, the verb agrees with the subject that is closer to it.

KEY CONCEPT If one or more singular subjects are joined to one or more plural subjects by *or* or *nor*, the subject closest to the verb determines agreement. ∎

EXAMPLES: Neither David nor my parents are frightened by thunderstorms.
              Neither my parents nor David is frightened by thunderstorms.

Exercise 4 Choosing Verbs That Agree With Compound Subjects Choose the verb in parentheses that agrees with the subject of each sentence.

1. *Cyclone* and *typhoon* (is, are) other names for a type of storm that North Americans call a hurricane.
2. Meteorologists and other scientists (describes, describe) hurricanes as rotating storms from the tropical ocean.
3. Dull-red sunsets or a high barometric reading (predicts, predict) a potential hurricane brewing at sea.
4. In modern times, the radio or television (allows, allow) people to learn about a hurricane before it strikes.
5. Both strong winds and heavy rainfall (is, are) typical during hurricanes.
6. Late summer and early fall (is, are) hurricane season.
7. A moist, tropical region at high risk for hurricanes (is, are) the Caribbean Islands.
8. Neither Hurricane Andrew nor Hurricane Mitch (was, were) a mild hurricane.
9. Either Hurricane Camille or Hurricane Mitch (holds, hold) the record for the lowest barometric pressure ever recorded.
10. During one hurricane, four adults and a child (was, were) trapped in a building, but they were safely rescued in the end.

More Practice

Grammar Exercise Workbook
• pp. 135–136
On-line Exercise Bank
• Section 24.1
   Go on-line:
   PHSchool.com
   Enter Web Code:
   eek-1002

Get instant feedback! Exercise 4 is available on-line or on CD-ROM.

Confusing Subjects

Some kinds of subjects have special agreement problems:

Inverted Sentences Foremost among confusing subjects are the hard-to-find subjects that come after the verbs. A sentence in which the subject comes after the verb is said to be inverted. Subject and verb order is usually inverted in questions.

▶ **KEY CONCEPT** A verb must still agree in number with a subject that comes after it. ■

EXAMPLE: At the top of the hill <u>are</u> two light-
              ning <u>rods</u>.
              (Two lightning rods are at the top of
              the hill.)

Check to make sure the verb agrees with the subject by mentally rewording the sentence so that the subject comes first.

The words *there* and *here* often signal an inverted sentence. These words never function as the subject of the sentence.

EXAMPLES: There <u>are</u> the satellite <u>photos</u> of the hurricane.
              Here <u>is</u> the revised <u>information</u> on the storm.

Note About *There's* and *Here's*: Both of these contractions contain the singular verb *is*: *there is* and *here is*. They should not be used with plural verbs.

CORRECT: There<u>'s</u> only one <u>hurricane</u> expected this week.
          There <u>are</u> two <u>hurricanes</u> expected next week.

▶ **Exercise 5** Making Subjects and Verbs Agree in Inverted Sentences Choose the item in parentheses that agrees with the subject of each sentence.
1. (There's, There're) usually a series of warnings before a hurricane.
2. Causing the greatest losses (was, were) Hurricane Floyd.
3. On the radar (glows, glow) traces of a hurricane track.
4. Where on these radar screens (is, are) the eye of the hurricane?
5. Here (is, are) the flashlights and candles in case the lights go out during the storm.

▲ **Critical Viewing**
Write a sentence beginning with the word *there* that describes this photograph. **[Describe]**

▶ **More Practice**

Grammar Exercise Workbook
• pp. 137–138
On-line Exercise Bank
• Section 24.1
Go on-line:
PHSchool.com
Enter Web Code:
eek-1002

Subjects of Linking Verbs Subjects with linking verbs may also cause agreement problems.

▶ **KEY CONCEPT** A linking verb must agree with its subject, regardless of the number of its predicate nominative. ■

EXAMPLES: The strong <u>winds</u> <u>are</u> one reason we expect a tornado.
One <u>reason</u> we expect a tornado <u>is</u> the strong winds.

In the first example, the plural verb *are* agrees with the plural subject *winds*, although the predicate nominative *reason* is singular. In the next example, the singular subject *reason* takes the singular verb *is*, although the predicate nominative *winds* is plural.

Collective Nouns Collective nouns—such as *audience, class, club,* and *committee*—name groups of people or things.

▶ **KEY CONCEPTS** A collective noun takes a singular verb when the group it names acts as a single unit. A collective noun takes a plural verb when the group it names act as individuals with different viewpoints. ■

SINGULAR: The weather <u>club</u> <u>plans</u> to track the tornado.
PLURAL: The weather <u>club</u> <u>have</u> split the responsibilities of tracking the tornado.

Nouns That Look Like Plurals Some nouns that end in *-s* appear to be plural but are actually singular in meaning. For example, nouns that name branches of knowledge, such as *civics* and *economics,* and those that name single units, such as *molasses* or *mumps,* take a singular verb.

▶ **KEY CONCEPT** Use singular verbs to agree with nouns that are plural in form but singular in meaning. ■

SINGULAR: <u>Physics</u> <u>requires</u> skill in mathematics.
The <u>news</u> today <u>reports</u> good weather.

When words such as *ethics, politics,* and *acoustics* do not name branches of knowledge but indicate characteristics, their meanings are plural. Similarly, such words as *eyeglasses, pliers,* and *scissors,* though they name single items, generally take plural verbs.

PLURAL: The <u>acoustics</u> in the weather center <u>are</u> terrible.
The <u>scissors</u> <u>are</u> in the top drawer.

Indefinite Pronouns Some indefinite pronouns are always singular, some are always plural, and some may be either singular or plural. Prepositional phrases that interrupt the subject and verb do not affect agreement.

> **KEY CONCEPTS** Singular indefinite pronouns take singular verbs. Plural indefinite pronouns take plural verbs. ■

SINGULAR: anybody, anyone, anything, each, either, every, everybody, everyone, everything, neither, nobody, no one, nothing, somebody, someone, something

PLURAL: both, few, many, others, several

SINGULAR: <u>Everyone</u> on the rescue squad <u>has left</u> for the day.

PLURAL: <u>Many</u> of the houses <u>were damaged</u> during the storm.

> **KEY CONCEPT** The pronouns *all, any, more, most, none,* and *some* usually take a singular verb if the antecedent is singular, and a plural verb if it is plural. ■

SINGULAR: <u>Some</u> of the area <u>is ruined</u> due to the hurricane.

PLURAL: <u>Some</u> of the cars <u>are</u> beyond repair

> **Exercise 6** Making Verbs Agree With Indefinite Pronouns
Choose the item in parentheses that agrees with the subject of each sentence.
> 1. Everyone studying tornadoes (has, have) learned some amazing facts.
> 2. Using a computer program, each of us (was, were) assigned an imaginary tornado to track.
> 3. Many (finds, find) the assignment exciting and informative.
> 4. A few in the class (is, are) frightened by the strength of the twister.
> 5. Some of the students (researches, research) the effects of tornadoes in certain areas of the country.

Titles of Creative Works and Names of Organizations
Plural words in the title of a creative work or in the name of an organization do not affect subject-verb agreement.

> **KEY CONCEPT** A title or the name of an organization is singular and must have a singular verb. ■

EXAMPLES: <u>Dealing With Severe Weather Conditions</u> <u>is</u> a useful reference.
<u>Weather Services</u> <u>is</u> a helpful agency.

Amounts and Measurements Most amounts and measurements, although they appear to be plural, actually express single units or ideas

KEY CONCEPT A noun expressing an amount or measurement is usually singular and requires a singular verb. ■

EXAMPLES: Two hundred million dollars <u>is</u> the cost in property damage from the tornado.
Two miles <u>was</u> our distance from the tornado.
Three quarters of the town <u>was destroyed</u>.
Half of the trees <u>were uprooted</u>.

In the first three examples, the subjects take singular verbs. *Two hundred million dollars* is one sum of money; *two miles* is a single distance; and *three quarters* is one part of a town. In the last example, *half* refers to a number of individual trees and therefore takes a plural verb.

Exercise 7 Making Verbs Agree With Confusing Subjects
Choose the item in parentheses that agrees with the subject of each sentence.
1. Tornadoes (is, are) a good reason for extreme caution.
2. Each tornado (has, have) unique characteristics.
3. Most (looks, look) like a funnel.
4. Many (approaches, approach) without warning.
5. One sign of approaching turbulent weather (is, are) thunder clouds.
6. Experiencing the most tornadoes (is, are) the middle of the country.
7. Each year, a series of tornadoes (causes, cause) damage to the region of the United States known as Tornado Alley.
8. *Beware the Twisters* (is, are) a book about the destruction caused by tornadoes.
9. In 1968, three million dollars (was, were) the cost of the damage caused by a tornado that passed through Tracy, Minnesota.
10. All meteorologists in the agency (rates, rate) tornadoes.
11. Physics (is, are) a science meteorologists use to measure a tornado.
12. At the center of a tornado (appears, appear) areas of low pressure.
13. (There's, There are) lots of activity in the tornado's core.
14. Some areas of a tornado (is, are) illuminated by lightning.
15. The news occasionally (contains, contain) reports about people who have seen the core, or center, of a tornado.

More Practice

Grammar Exercise Workbook
• pp. 137–138
On-line Exercise Bank
• Section 24.1
Go on-line:
PHSchool.com
Enter Web Code:
eek-1002

interactive
Textbook

Get instant feedback! Exercises 6 and 7 are available on-line or on CD-ROM.

Hands-on Grammar

Inverted-Sentence Wheel

Practice inverting sentences and finding the subject.

1. Cut out a cardboard circle with a diameter of 5". Make four holes in it, as shown in the illustration. They should be about 1/4" from the edge of the circle.
2. Cut out four smaller cardboard circles—1" to 1-1/2" in diameter. Make a small hole in each circle.
3. Unfold four paper clips, as shown. Put the paper clips through the holes in the big circle, and then attach a small circle to the other end of each paper clip.
4. Tape a paper circle, 3-1/2" in diameter, to the middle of the large circle. That is the verb wheel.
5. On one of the small cardboard circles, write *two marbles*. Write *under the table* on the circle that is opposite. Then, write *the marble* on another small cardboard circle. On the opposite circle, write *under the table*. On the paper circle in the center, write the verbs *are* and *is* twice, as shown.
6. Turn the wheel so that a verb is upright. Then, read the sentence from top circle to bottom circle. Which is the subject? Spin the wheel so that the other verb is upright and read the sentence. Has the subject changed place in the sentence?

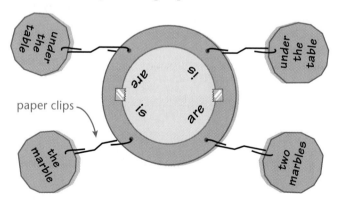

7. Illustrate the following sentences with your wheel:
   On the table is the vase.   *Cookie crumbs are under the table.*
   The vase is on the table.   *Under the table are cookie crumbs.*

Find It in Your Reading In a story or textbook that you are reading, find other examples of sentences with inverted word order. Illustrate those sentences on your wheel.

Find It in Your Writing Review a piece of writing from your portfolio. If you have used inverted word order in any of your sentences, check to be sure that the verb agrees with the subject.

Section
24.1

Section Review

GRAMMAR EXERCISES 8–15

▶ **Exercise 8** Making Subjects Agree With Their Verbs Choose the verb in parentheses that agrees with the subject of each sentence.

1. Rain during thunderstorms (falls, fall) quite rapidly.
2. Loud claps of thunder (shakes, shake) the house.
3. Lightning bolts (flashes, flash) across the sky.
4. Heavy rains or fast-melting snow (causes, cause) floods in many parts of the world.
5. Either too much rain or too much snow (makes, make) the level of rivers rise.
6. Rising rivers (means, mean) trouble.
7. Towns in the flood zone (is, are) in great danger.
8. A city or vacation spot located near the ocean (is, are) in danger of a tidal wave.
9. People (evacuates, evacuate) these areas before the storm hits.
10. Neither the Western Hemisphere nor the Eastern Hemisphere (is, are) immune to flooding.

▶ **Exercise 9** Choosing Verbs for Inverted Sentences and Indefinite Pronouns Choose the verb in parentheses that agrees with the subject of the sentence.

1. In the spring months (begins, begin) tornado season.
2. Most (occurs, occur) at this time of year due to weather patterns.
3. Often at the end of a hot, humid day (appears, appear) the thunderclouds.
4. Each cloud that produces tornadoes (is, are) different from regular clouds.
5. (Does, Do) people hear any thunder?
6. There (is, are) often rumbles of thunder before a tornado hits.

7. Each of the dark clouds (seems, seem) ready to burst.
8. At the bottom of the cloud (twists, twist) rounded cloud masses.
9. Everybody in the shelters (fears, fear) the powerful funnel.
10. Some of the most violent winds (uproots, uproot) trees and even overturn railroad cars.

▶ **Exercise 10** Choosing the Correct Linking Verb Choose the verb in parentheses that agrees with the subject of the sentence.

1. Severe weather conditions (is, are) a threat.
2. In Florida, one reason for building strong houses (is, are) hurricanes.
3. Hurricanes in early fall (is, are) a danger in the Southeast.
4. The responsibility of meteorologists (is, are) weather alerts.
5. These warnings (is, are) the key to saving lives during such storms.

▶ **Exercise 11** Making Verbs Agree With Confusing Subjects Choose the verb in parentheses that agrees with the subject of the sentence.

1. The news (includes, include) many stories of severe storms.
2. Tornadoes (represents, represent) one type of weather disaster.
3. In 1977, in the Midwest, there (was, were) millions of dollars of destruction from a tornado that lasted seven hours.
4. About 340 miles (was, were) the distance traveled by this tornado.
5. Most tornadoes (does, do) not last that long.

6. *Tornadoes* by Michael Allaby (is, are) a reference book on the subject.
7. Another natural disaster nearly everyone (fears, fear) is a tsunami.
8. A tsunami is a series of waves that (occurs, occur) in an ocean or other large body of water.
9. Most people in North America (calls, call) tsunamis *tidal waves.*
10. Earthquakes on the sea floor (is, are) a major cause of tsunamis.
11. About 12 to 23 inches (is, are) the height of the typical tsunami when it begins at sea.
12. As they approach the shore, some tsunamis (reaches, reach) a height of 100 feet.
13. There (was, were) several destructive tsunamis during the 1990's.
14. Sometimes, politics (causes, cause) a delay in aid to the regions that are affected by tsunamis.
15. Not one of the towns (has, have) received money to make repairs.

Exercise 12 **Revision Practice: Agreement** Copy the paragraph on a separate sheet of paper. Revise it to correct all errors in subject-verb agreement.

   Physics play an important role in predicting the weather. The science of weather studies and predictions are called meteorology. Both atmospheric occurrences and geographic location affects weather forecasts. Each of the weather forecasts depend on complex technology. Atmospheric pressure or wind require careful measurement. Twelve hours are the amount of advance time needed for short-range forecasts. For long-range predictions, mathematics create important numerical models. These models, along with a supercomputer, makes accurate forecasts possible. Neither the computers nor the math truly predict the weather. There's sometimes sudden changes in weather patterns.

Exercise 13 **Find It in Your Reading** Read the following excerpt from Pat Mora's poem "Uncoiling." Then, write all the verbs that agree with the subject, and indicate whether they are singular or plural.

   With thorns, she scratches
      on my window, tosses her hair
      dark with rain,
   snares lightning, cholla, hawks,
      butterfly
   swarms in the tangles.

Exercise 14 **Find It In Your Writing** Review a draft from your portfolio, written in the present tense. Underline each subject once and each verb twice. Make sure your subjects and verbs agree.

Exercise 15 **Writing Application** Use each of the items below as the subject of a sentence. Provide verbs for each sentence that agree with the subjects provided. Underline all the subjects once and all the verbs twice.

1. All of the trees
2. Thunder and lightning
3. All of the tornadoes
4. One of the houses
5. Two thirds of the town
6. Storms at sea
7. The path of most hurricanes
8. Spaghetti and meatballs
9. Rain or snow
10. Neither he nor she

Section 24.2 *Pronoun and Antecedent Agreement*

Antecedents are the nouns (or the words that take the place of nouns) for which pronouns stand. In this section, you will learn how to make a pronoun agree with its antecedent.

Agreement Between Personal Pronouns and Antecedents

The following rule is the basis for pronoun and antecedent agreement:

▶ **KEY CONCEPT** A personal pronoun must agree with its antecedent in number, person, and gender. ■

The grammatical number of a pronoun indicates whether it is *singular* or *plural*. *Person* indicates whether the pronoun is first person (the one speaking), second person (the one spoken to), or third person (the one spoken about). Some nouns and pronouns also indicate *gender*—masculine, feminine, or neuter.

In the following example, the pronoun *his* and the antecedent *Byron* are both singular, in the third person, and masculine.

EXAMPLE: *Byron* completed *his* trip to India.

Agreement in Number Making personal pronouns agree with their antecedents in number is usually a problem only when the antecedent is a compound.

▶ **KEY CONCEPT** Use a singular personal pronoun with two or more singular antecedents joined by *or* or *nor*. ■

EXAMPLE: Neither *Tim* nor *Ike* liked *his* flight to India.

▼ **Critical Viewing** The Taj Mahal was built by Shah Jahan as a mausoleum for his favorite wife. Write two sentences describing the Taj Mahal. Make sure that your personal pronouns agree with their antecedents. **[Describe]**

▶ **KEY CONCEPT** Use a plural personal pronoun with two or more antecedents joined by *and*. ■

EXAMPLE: *Darlene and Carol* liked *their* flights to India.

Agreement in Person and Number A personal pronoun and its antecedent will not agree if there is a shift in either person or number in the second part of the sentence.

▶ **KEY CONCEPT** When dealing with pronoun-antecedent agreement, take care not to shift either person or gender. ■

SHIFT IN PERSON: *Michelle* is studying Hindi, a language *you* will find useful while living in India.

CORRECT: *Michelle* is studying Hindi, a language *she* will find useful while living in India.

SHIFT IN NUMBER: Either *Tim* or *Ed* brought *their* map.
CORRECT: Either *Tim* or *Ed* brought *his* map.

Note About *Generic Masculine Pronouns:* Historically, a masculine pronoun (*he, his, him, himself*) has been used to refer to a singular antecedent whose gender is not specified. Today, however, many writers prefer to use both the masculine and feminine pronouns (*he or she, him or her, his or her, himself or herself*) instead of the generic masculine form. When using two pronouns becomes awkward, rewrite the sentence.

▶ **KEY CONCEPT** When gender is not specified, use both the masculine and the feminine pronouns or rewrite the sentence. ■

EXAMPLES: A *guest* might thank *his or her* host with a gift.
              Guests might thank *their* host with a gift.

▶ **Exercise 16** Supplying Personal Pronouns to Agree With Their Antecedents Choose the correct pronoun in each sentence.

EXAMPLE: Visitors to India need ___?___ passports.
ANSWER: their

1. Marge and Susan took ___?___ vacation in India last month.
2. Marge decided to spend ___?___ time touring Agra.
3. The Taj Mahal is well known for ___?___ beauty.
4. Neither Marge nor Susan forgot ___?___ camera.
5. Susan told me that both of them missed ___?___ families.

Interactive Textbook

Get instant feedback! Exercises 16 and 17 are available on-line or on CD-ROM.

▶ **More Practice**

Grammar Exercise Workbook
• pp. 139–140
On-line Exercise Bank
• Section 24.2
  Go on-line:
  PHSchool.com
  Enter Web Code:
  eek-1002

Agreement With Indefinite Pronouns

When you write a sentence with a personal pronoun that has an indefinite pronoun as its antecedent, make sure that the two pronouns agree. (See page 412 for indefinite pronouns.)

▶ **KEY CONCEPTS** Use a singular personal pronoun when the antecedent is a singular indefinite pronoun. Use a plural personal pronoun when the antecedent is a plural indefinite pronoun. ■

SINGULAR: *One* of the men rode *his* elephant.
PLURAL: *All* of the men rode *their* elephants.

With an indefinite pronoun that can be either singular or plural, agreement depends on the word to which the indefinite pronoun refers. In the first example below, the pronoun *some* refers to the singular noun *village*. In the second example, *some* refers to the plural noun *villagers*.

EXAMPLES: *Some* of the village had lost *its* charm.
               Some of the villagers expressed *their* displeasure.

▶ **Exercise 17** Making Personal Pronouns Agree With Indefinite Pronouns Choose the correct pronoun in each sentence.
1. Many visitors to India begin (his, their) vacations in Bombay.
2. All of the students enjoyed (his or her, their) visit to that city.
3. One of Bombay's best features is (its, their) pleasant climate.
4. Some of the city's appeal is (its, their) blend of old and new.
5. Both students knew (his, their) trip would be great.
6. Neither of them had developed (his or her, their) photographs of the city.
7. One of the girls finally let me see (her, their) pictures.
8. Every Indian city has (its, their) own charm.
9. Both Bombay and New Delhi face challenges because of (its, their) large populations.
10. However, either Bombay or New Delhi will delight and surprise (its, their) visitors.

▼ Critical Viewing
Write a sentence about this picture using this phrase: *Neither the boy nor his elephant . . .*
[Infer]

Using Reflexive Pronouns

Reflexive pronouns end in *-self* or *-selves* and refer to an antecedent earlier in the sentence.

KEY CONCEPT A reflexive pronoun must agree with an antecedent that is clearly stated. ■

POOR: The tour guide brought the good news to Peter and *myself*.

CORRECT: The tour guide brought the good news to Peter and *me*.

Exercise 18 Correcting Misuse of Reflexive Pronouns
Correct the sentences that misuse reflexive pronouns. If a sentence contains no error, write *correct*.
1. Karen and myself studied India in our social studies class.
2. Tom said that Paula and himself had learned about India.
3. It was Billy and myself who remembered that Gandhi was assassinated in 1948.
4. During the fight for independence, Gandhi wore simple garments he had spun himself.
5. The results were a surprise to the teachers and ourselves.

Four Special Problems in Pronoun Agreement

When you use personal pronouns, make sure that they have antecedents that are clearly defined. Problems can occur when the antecedent is unstated or unclear or when the personal pronoun refers to the wrong antecedent.

KEY CONCEPT A pronoun must agree with an antecedent that is either clearly stated or clearly understood. ■

VAGUE: The *movie* about India was disappointing because *they* never made the characters seem realistic.

CLEAR: The *movie* about India was disappointing because *it* never made the characters seem realistic.

CLEAR: The movie about India was disappointing because *the director* never made the characters seem realistic.

In the preceding example, the meaning of the sentence is vague because there is no antecedent for the pronoun *they*. The sentence can be made clear by replacing *they* with a personal pronoun or a noun that agrees with the antecedent *movie*.

More Practice

Grammar Exercise Workbook
• pp. 141–142
On-line Exercise Bank
• Section 24.2
  Go on-line:
  PHSchool.com
  Enter Web Code:
  eek-1002

Get instant feedback! Exercise 18 is available on-line or on CD-ROM.

▶**KEY CONCEPT** A personal pronoun should always refer to a single, obvious antecedent. ■

AMBIGUOUS: I put a postcard in the book, but I lost *it*.

CLEAR: I put a postcard in the book, but I lost the book.
I can't find the postcard that I put in the book.

In the first example, the pronoun *it* is ambiguous because *it* can refer to either *postcard* or, *book*.

▶**KEY CONCEPT** A personal pronoun should always be close enough to its antecedent to prevent confusion. ■

DISTANT: Charlie asked Ralph questions about the map of India. Ralph tried to help, but, even more confused, he asked the teacher.

CLEAR: Charlie asked Ralph questions about the map of India. Ralph tried to help him, but, even more confused, Charlie asked the teacher.

In the example above, the pronoun *he* is too far from its antecedent, *Charlie*. The passage is much clearer if the word *Charlie* is repeated. You could also reword the passage to move the pronoun closer to its antecedent.

▶**KEY CONCEPT** Use the personal pronoun *you* only when the reference is truly to the reader or the listener. ■

INCORRECT: During colonial rule in India, you weren't allowed the same privileges as many British citizens.

CORRECT: During colonial rule in India, Indian citizens weren't allowed the same privileges as many British citizens.

▲ **Critical Viewing**
Write two or three sentences describing some of the carving on this tenth-century Indian temple. Use *they* and *it* in your sentences and make sure that the antecedents are clear. **[Describe]**

Exercise 19 Recognizing Proper Usage Identify the sentence in each pair that better follows the conventions of English usage of pronouns. Explain your choices.

1. (A) The film we watched about India was informative because it explained Hinduism, Buddhism, Islam, and other religions.
   (B) The film we watched about India was informative because they explained Hinduism, Buddhism, Islam, and other religions.

2. (A) The next time it is shown, you should see it.
   (B) The next time they show it, you should see it.

3. (A) India has one of the largest Muslim populations in the world, even though they are a minority in it.
   (B) India has one of the largest Muslim populations in the world, even though Muslims are a minority there.

4. (A) Jane told Andrea that Indonesia has the largest Muslim population in the world, but Andrea wanted to confirm the information.
   (B) Jane told Andrea that Indonesia has the largest Muslim population in the world, but Andrea wanted to confirm it.

5. (A) Each of the students completed their assignment on the culture of India.
   (B) Each of the students completed his or her assignment on the culture of India.

Exercise 20 Correcting Special Problems in Pronoun Agreement Revise the following paragraph, correcting all errors in pronoun and antecedent agreement.

Mohandas K. Gandhi led Indians to independence from British rule. It made him famous. He promoted passive resistance, which you can use to change society. Sit-ins and boycotts are often involved in it. Gandhi was soon joined in his struggle by Jawaharlal Nehru. He was a much younger man. Gandhi taught passive resistance; he believed it would win them their freedom. When Gandhi became the leader of the Indian National Congress, he persuaded them that they needed to adopt his plan. Under this plan, one way you resisted British rule was by not paying your taxes. They also did not attend British schools or courts. Many of them gave up good jobs because they had to deal with the British. Gandhi and his followers believed passionately in the movement for independence, and they achieved it—especially when millions of Indians had joined it.

More Practice

Grammar Exercise Workbook
• pp. 143–144
On-line Exercise Bank
• Section 24.2
  Go on-line:
  PHSchool.com
  Enter Web Code:
  eek-1002

Interactive Textbook

Complete the exercises on-line! Exercises 19 and 20 are available on-line or on CD-ROM.

Section
24.2 **Section Review**

GRAMMAR EXERCISES 21–26

▶ **Exercise 21** **Supplying Personal Pronouns That Agree With Their Antecedents** Use an appropriate personal pronoun to complete each sentence.

1. We heard the ancient story of Rama from ___?___ Indian friend Ved.
2. Rama was loved by the people of the kingdom for ___?___ kind nature.
3. Sadly, Dasrath, Rama's father, had to send ___?___ son into exile.
4. While in exile, Rama worried about ___?___ wife Sitia.
5. Hanuman, a flying monkey general, found Sitia and told ___?___ that help was on the way.
6. Each region of India has ___?___ own fashions.
7. Some Indian women like colorful skirts that swirl as ___?___ walk.
8. An Indian may wear ___?___ traditional clothes every day.
9. Most women in India wear ___?___ saris every day.
10. Red is the color of joy and celebration, so brides usually wear ___?___.

▶ **Exercise 22** **Using Reflexive Pronouns Correctly** Rewrite each sentence, correcting the misused reflexive pronouns. If a sentence contains no error, write *correct.*

1. Ms. Shinh prepared ourselves and her other class to study Indian history.
2. Andy and myself reviewed the notes about the Indus valley.
3. Neither Anna nor Liz gave herself enough time to study.
4. This book on Sanskrit, India's ancient language, is meant for myself, not John.
5. Manita told the class that her sister and herself had come from New Delhi.

▶ **Exercise 23** **Revising to Eliminate Errors in Pronoun Agreement** Rewrite these sentences, correcting any vague pronoun-antecedent agreement.

1. During the 1700's, the British came to India to trade with the Indians, but they ended up ruling them.
2. The British built a railway system in India that linked parts of it.
3. The British told the Indians that the improvements were important to them.
4. In 1947, after years of protest, they finally won their freedom from them.
5. In 1950, India became a republic with a constitution; it is still in force.

▶ **Exercise 24** **Find It in Your Reading** Read this excerpt from Rabindranath Tagore's "The Cabuliwallah"; then, list each pronoun and its antecedent. List the narrator as the antecedent of "I."

I cannot tell what my daughter's feelings were at the sight of this man, but she began to call him loudly. Ah, I thought, he will come in, and my seventeenth chapter will never be finished!

▶ **Exercise 25** **Find It in Your Writing** Review a piece of your writing, and be sure that all the personal pronouns have clear antecedents. If you find pronouns with vague or missing antecedents, make the necessary revisions.

▶ **Exercise 26** **Writing Application** Write five sentences about a country you have studied. Include at least five pronouns, and provide clear antecedents.

▲ **Critical Viewing**
Compare the number of different types of musical instruments in the picture. Use the word *more* or *most* in your comparison. **[Identify]**

Adjectives and adverbs are important parts of speech that help writers make their sentences livelier, clearer, and more interesting and complete. What modifiers could a writer use to describe the sound of an unusual stringed instrument such as a sitar, a lute, or a hurdy-gurdy? The different sounds of these instruments make their music unique and colorful. Similarly, a carefully chosen adjective or adverb often turns an ordinary sentence into a superior one.

Modifiers are also important because they are used to make comparisons. For instance, if you wanted to compare the wide range of instruments in the world, you might use various forms of adjectives and adverbs to show similarities and differences in their sizes, shapes, and sounds.

In the first section of this chapter, you will learn rules for writing the forms of adjectives and adverbs used to make comparisons. In the second section, you will learn how to avoid a number of common usage problems involving comparisons.

Diagnostic Test

Directions: Write all answers on a separate sheet of paper.

Skill Check A. Identify the degree of each underlined modifier as *positive, comparative,* or *superlative.*

1. The sitar is the most prominent musical instrument in India.
2. It is more difficult to play than a guitar.
3. The earliest sitars were crafted more than 800 years ago.
4. It may take twenty years of practice to become a skillful sitar player.
5. My neighbor plays the instrument more competently than I do.

Skill Check B. Write the comparative and superlative form of each modifier.

6. rhythmic
7. loud
8. classical
9. quietly
10. far

Skill Check C. Write the appropriate form of the underlined modifier to complete each sentence.

11. The lute is more difficult to play than the mandolin, but the sitar is the __?__ of all to play.
12. The musical traditions of northern and southern India contain many similarities but even __?__ differences.
13. In general, Western musicians have taken little interest in Indian music and even __?__ in Korean music.
14. The untrained musicians played badly in the morning and even __?__ in the afternoon when they were tired.
15. Some scales are simple to play, and this one is the __?__ of all.

Skill Check D. Write the appropriate comparative or superlative degree of the modifiers in parentheses.

16 A hurdy-gurdy produces a (strong) sound than a lute.
17. Compared to the hurdy-gurdy and the lute, a sitar has the (distinctive) sound.
18. This pumpkin must be (dry) before it can be used to make a sitar.
19. The sitar has the (many) frets of all stringed instruments.
20. Of Sandra, Jacques, and me, I handle the instrument the (confidently).

Skill Check E. Rewrite each sentence, correcting the unbalanced or illogical comparison.

21. Ensembles of classical musicians are more common in India than amateur musicians.
22. The sitar's chords are more varied than the tambura.
23. The Yugoslavian tambura has a longer neck than any lute.
24. It resembles an Indian instrument more than any stringed instrument from Eastern Europe.
25. The Turks introduced this instrument in Yugoslavia, Greece, and everywhere in Europe.

Degrees of Comparison

Most adjectives and adverbs have three forms, called *degrees*, that are used to modify and make comparisons.

Recognizing Degrees of Comparison

Each of the three degrees of comparison has a name: the *positive*, the *comparative*, and the *superlative*.

▶ **KEY CONCEPT** Most adjectives and adverbs have three different forms to show degrees of comparison—the *positive*, the *comparative*, and the *superlative*. ■

There are different ways to form the *comparative* and *superlative* degrees of adjectives and adverbs. Notice, for example, how the forms of the adjectives and adverbs in the following chart are changed to show the degrees of comparison.

DEGREES OF ADJECTIVES		
Positive	Comparative	Superlative
simple impressive good	simpler more impressive better	simplest most impressive best
DEGREES OF ADVERBS		
soon impressively well	sooner more impressively better	soonest most impressively best

▶ **Exercise 1** Recognizing Degrees of Comparison Identify the degree of each underlined modifier.

EXAMPLE: Josef is the <u>best</u> player in the orchestra.
ANSWER: superlative

1. The accordion is a <u>small</u>, hand-held instrument.
2. It resembles an <u>earlier</u> German instrument, the handaoline.
3. Cyril Demian invented an <u>early</u> accordion in 1829.
4. The <u>oldest</u> accordions had only ten melody buttons.
5. Modern accordions have <u>more</u> melody and bass buttons.
6. These enable it to produce the <u>widest</u> range of notes.
7. The piano accordion is the <u>most familiar</u> type of accordion.
8. <u>Pianolike</u> keys are on the right side of the instrument.
9. Many people like the accordion <u>better</u> than the concertina.
10. The concertina has been used <u>most often</u> in folk music.

**Theme:
Unusual Musical
Instruments**

In this section, you will learn how to use adjectives and adverbs correctly to make comparisons. The examples and exercises in this section are about old or unusual musical instruments.

**Cross-Curricular
Connection:
Music**

▶ **More Practice**

Grammar Exercise Workbook
• pp. 145–146
On-line Exercise Bank
• Section 25.1
  Go on-line:
  PHSchool.com
  Enter Web Code:
  eek-1002

*i*nteractive
Textbook

Get instant feedback! Exercises 1 and 2 are available on-line or on CD-ROM.

Regular Forms

Modifiers can be either regular or irregular, depending on how their comparative and superlative degrees are formed. Two rules govern the formation of regular modifiers. The first rule applies to modifiers with one or two syllables.

▶ **KEY CONCEPTS** Use *-er* or *more* to form the comparative degree and *-est* or *most* to form the superlative degree of most one- and two-syllable modifiers. ■

The more common method for forming the comparative and superlative degrees of one- and two-syllable modifiers is to add *-er* and *-est* to the modifier rather than to use *more* and *most*.

EXAMPLES: loud   louder   loudest
            shiny   shinier   shiniest

More and *most* are used with one- and two-syllable modifiers when adding *-er* and *-est* would sound awkward.

EXAMPLES: famous   more famous   most famous

The comparative and superlative degrees of all adverbs that end in *-ly*, regardless of the number of syllables, are formed with *more* and *most*.

EXAMPLES: evenly   more evenly   most evenly

▶ **KEY CONCEPT** Use *more* and *most* to form the comparative and superlative degrees of all modifiers with three or more syllables. ■

EXAMPLES: difficult   more difficult   most difficult

Note About Comparisons With *Less* and *Least*: *Less* and *least*, the opposite of *more* and *most*, are also used to form the comparative and superlative degrees of most modifiers.

EXAMPLES: tall   less tall   least tall
            hopeless   less hopeless   least hopeless
            ambitious   less ambitious   least ambitious

▶ **Exercise 2** Writing Sentences Using Degrees of Comparison Write sentences using the modifiers and degrees given below. Use *less* or *least* in one or more sentences.

1. charming (comparative)
2. funny (comparative)
3. bold (superlative)
4. beautifully (superlative)
5. educated (comparative)

Grammar and Style Tip

When choosing the degree of a modifier, be careful to avoid excessive exaggerations, which may hurt your writing. Try not to use a superlative modifier when all you really need is one in the comparative degree.

▶ **Exercise 3** Supplying Comparative and Superlative
Modifiers Write each sentence on your paper. Use the form
that is specified in parentheses for the underlined modifier.

EXAMPLE: That is one of the <u>small</u> instruments I have ever
             seen. (superlative)

ANSWER: That is one of the smallest instruments I have
             ever seen.

1. Some types of bagpipes are <u>simple</u> than others.
   (comparative)
2. I learned that the Highland pipe can play <u>many</u> notes.
   (comparative)
3. The Irish *uilleann* pipe is the <u>complicated</u> version.
   (superlative)
4. As you may know, bagpipes are played <u>often</u> in Scotland
   (superlative)
5. Some Irish pipers play <u>expressively</u> than Scots pipers.
   (comparative)

Irregular Forms

The comparative and superlative degrees of a few commonly
used adjectives and adverbs are formed in unpredictable ways.

▶ **KEY CONCEPT** The irregular comparative and superlative
forms of certain adjectives and adverbs must be memorized. ■

Notice in the following chart that the form of some irregular
modifiers differs only in the positive degree. The modifiers
bad, badly, and *ill,* for example, all have the same comparative
and superlative degrees *(worse, worst).*

IRREGULAR MODIFIERS		
Positive	Comparative	Superlative
bad	worse	worst
badly	worse	worst
far (distance)	farther	farthest
far (extent)	further	furthest
good	better	best
ill	worse	worst
late	later	last *or* latest
little (amount)	less	least
many	more	most
much	more	most
well	better	best

More Practice

Grammar Exercise
Workbook
• pp. 147–148
On-line Exercise Bank
• Section 25.1
   Go on-line:
   PHSchool.com
   Enter Web Code:
   eek-1002

**interactive
Textbook**

Get instant feedback!
Exercises 3 and 4 are
available on-line or
on CD-ROM.

💡 **Spelling Tip**

Irregular modifiers
are not the only
modifiers with tricky
spelling changes.
Remember that some
regular modifiers are
changed in different
ways when adding
-er or *-est;* for example, *happy, happier,
happiest.*

▶ **KEY CONCEPTS** *Bad* is an adjective. Do not use it to modify an action verb. *Badly* is an adverb. Do not use it after a linking verb. ■

INCORRECT: Keith plays the bassoon *bad*.

CORRECT: Keith plays the bassoon *badly*.

INCORRECT: Keith feels *badly*.

CORRECT: Keith feels *bad*.

Note About *Good* and *Well*: Like *bad*, *good* is an adjective and cannot be used as an adverb after an action verb. It can, however, be used as an adjective after a linking verb.

INCORRECT: Jennifer plays the oboe *good*.

CORRECT: This oboe seems *good*.

Well is generally an adverb. Like *badly*, it can be used after an action verb.

CORRECT: Jennifer plays the oboe *well*.

When *well* is used to mean "healthy," it is an adjective. Thus, *well* can also be used after a linking verb.

CORRECT: Jennifer should be *well* soon.

▶ **Exercise 4** **Forming Comparative and Superlative Degrees of Irregular Modifiers** Write the appropriate form of the underlined modifier to complete each sentence.

EXAMPLE: My singing is <u>bad</u> today, but it was ___?___ yesterday.

ANSWER: worse

1. Your voice sounds <u>good</u>, but a kazoo makes it sound ___?___.
2. I play it <u>better</u> when I hum, but you say it is ___?___ when you talk into the kazoo.
3. Kazoos are used <u>little</u> as a children's toy, ___?___ in blues music, and ___?___ in a classical orchestra.
4. Usually it sounds <u>much</u> like buzzing, but sometimes it sounds ___?___ like quacking.
5. My harmonica-playing sounds <u>bad</u> and my kazoo-playing sounds ___?___, but my zobo playing is certainly the ___?___.

▲ **Critical Viewing** Compare this oboe to a flute in at least three different ways. Which modifiers would you use? **[Compare and Contrast]**

Degrees of Comparison • **429**

GRAMMAR IN LITERATURE

from **The American Idea**
Theodore H. White

Note the regular modifier in blue and the irregular modifier in red in the following passage. Both are in the superlative degree.

By the time Jefferson drafted his call, men were in the field fighting for those new-learned freedoms, killing and being killed by English soldiers, the *best*-trained troops in the world, supplied by the world's *greatest* navy.

▶ **Exercise 5** Supplying Irregular Modifiers Write an appropriate degree of an irregular modifier to complete each sentence. Use the chart on page 428 if you need help.

EXAMPLE: Suffering from a throbbing headache, the musician is not feeling __?__ today.

ANSWER: well

1. This store has the __?__ selection of antique instruments in the state.
2. I have been able to find __?__ nineteenth-century English woodwinds here than in a store in England.
3. The price I was quoted for a five-key clarinet was the __?__ of all the stores I visited.
4. Even though I had to travel __?__ to get here than to a local store, it was worth the trip.
5. This bassoon, made in 1880, has a __?__ sound than a modern bassoon.
6. I wish that I did not play the bassoon so __?__.
7. I have received __?__ training on the instrument than my sister.
8. She has been taking lessons for __?__ years than I.
9. She can play at least seven instruments very __?__.
10. Yet she is not the __?__ bit conceited.

▶ **More Practice**

Grammar Exercise Workbook
• pp. 147–148
On-line Exercise Bank
• Section 25.1
  Go on-line:
  PHSchool.com
  Enter Web Code:
  eek-1002

▼ **Critical Viewing** What qualities of this instrument make it seem older than a guitar? Use modifiers in your answers. **[Judge]**

Section 25.1 Section Review

GRAMMAR EXERCISES 6–12

▶ **Exercise 6** Recognizing Modifiers
Underline the modifier in these phrases.

1. most common lyre
2. played more skillfully
3. larger instrument
4. earliest versions
5. more decorated style

▶ **Exercise 7** Recognizing Degrees of Comparison Identify the degree of each underlined modifier.

1. You will have a <u>better</u> understanding of the Chinese *qin* if you know about zithers.
2. Zithers are among the <u>most common</u> stringed instruments in the world.
3. The *qin*'s strings are stretched over a <u>curved</u> board.
4. It features several melody strings and even <u>more numerous</u> accompaniment strings.
5. The *qin* is <u>more traditional</u> in China than a lute or a fiddle.

▶ **Exercise 8** Forming the Comparative and Superlative Degrees
Rewrite the underlined modifier in the degree indicated in parentheses.

1. The stronger the vibrations of the player's lips, the <u>loud</u> the sound from a horn. (comparative)
2. The <u>simple</u> type of horn is made from an animal horn. (superlative)
3. These instruments are <u>commonly</u> used in religious rituals. (superlative)
4. Horns made from shells are <u>little</u> used as musical instruments. (comparative)
5. Adding finger holes on the side gives it a <u>wide</u> range of notes. (comparative)

▶ **Exercise 9** Revising to Eliminate Errors in Modifiers Revise this paragraph, eliminating errors in forms and degrees of modifiers.

The *sheng* is one of the more old Chinese instruments. It is more popularist in China. It has a low pitch than the *chi*. Chinese instruments are used often in religious ceremonies than on other occasions. Archaeological digs have unearthed some of the better musical artifacts ever found.

▶ **Exercise 10** Find It in Your Reading Identify the degree of the underlined modifiers in this passage from R. K. Narayan's "Like the Sun."

. . . He felt very <u>unhappy</u> that he could not speak <u>more soothingly</u>. Truth, he reflected, required as much strength to give as to receive.

▶ **Exercise 11** Find It in Your Writing Look through your writing portfolio for examples of sentences containing modifiers in the comparative or superlative degree. You might also rewrite some of your sentences that contain positive modifiers so that they express comparisons.

▶ **Exercise 12** Writing Application
Write five sentences of your own using the modifier and degree given below.

1. deep (superlative)
2. talented (comparative)
3. musical (superlative)
4. well (positive)
5. highly (comparative)

Making Clear Comparisons

In this section, you will learn the correct uses of the comparative and superlative degrees. You will also learn how to change an illogical comparison into a logical comparison.

Using Comparative and Superlative Degrees

There are two simple rules that govern the use of the comparative and superlative degrees:

▶ **KEY CONCEPTS** Use the comparative degree to compare two people, places, or things. Use the superlative degree to compare three or more people, places, or things. ■

Notice in the examples below that specific numbers need not be mentioned. The context of the sentence indicates whether two or more than two things are being compared.

COMPARATIVE: Oil paintings are *more effective* than watercolors.
My sketch is *more detailed* than his.

SUPERLATIVE: We bought the *most expensive* painting of all.
This exhibit has the *largest* number of early works in the city.

Note About *Double Comparisons:* Do not add both *-er* and *more* or *-est* and *most* to a regular modifier. In addition, do not add any of these endings or words to an irregular modifier.

INCORRECT: That sailboat is *more faster* than the other.
John's technique is *more better* than mine.

CORRECT: That sailboat is *faster* than the other.
John's technique is *better* than mine.

▶ **Exercise 13** Supplying the Comparative and Superlative **Degrees** Write the appropriate comparative or superlative degree of the modifier in parentheses.

EXAMPLE: Alfred is the (young) of all the students.
ANSWER: youngest

1. Mary Cassatt was one of the (early) American Impressionists.
2. She used (bright) colors than many of her contemporaries.
3. Her revolutionary style in an art world dominated by men made it (difficult) for her to get her work displayed.
4. Mary Cassatt's (good) works are of families, especially mothers and daughters.
5. She lived (comfortably) in France than in the United States.

Theme: The Art of Mary Cassatt

In this section, you will learn the correct uses of the comparative and superlative degrees of adjectives and adverbs. The examples and exercises in this section are about the art of American painter Mary Cassatt.

Cross-Curricular Connection:
Art

interactive Textbook

Get instant feedback! Exercise 13 is available on-line or on CD-ROM.

▶ **More Practice**

Grammar Exercise Workbook
• pp. 149–150
On-line Exercise Bank
• Section 25.2
Go on-line:
PHSchool.com
Enter Web Code:
eek-1002

Making Logical Comparisons

Some comparisons are illogical—they do not make good sense. In order to write logical comparisons, you must make sure you do not mistakenly compare two unrelated items and that you do not unintentionally compare something with itself.

Balanced Comparisons Sometimes, when you are in a hurry, you may compare two or more unrelated items. It is then necessary to rephrase the sentence so that the comparison is properly balanced.

▶ **KEY CONCEPT** Make sure that your sentences compare only items of a similar kind. ■

Because an unbalanced comparison is illogical, it may be unintentionally humorous. The way the examples below are written, the paintings of an artist are being compared not to paintings but to another artist.

UNBALANCED: We prefer Auguste
Renoir's paintings to
Mary Cassatt.

CORRECT: We prefer Auguste
Renoir's paintings to
Mary Cassatt's.

UNBALANCED: Critics considered the
*paintings of
Mary Cassatt* to
be more emotional
than *James Whistler.*

CORRECT: Critics considered the
*paintings of
Mary Cassatt* to
be more emotional
than *those of James
Whistler.*

Child in a Straw Hat, Mary Cassatt

▶ **Critical Viewing** Write three statements about this painting that include the word *than*. **[Analyze]**

▶ **Exercise 14** **Making Balanced Comparisons** Rewrite each sentence, correcting the unbalanced comparison.

EXAMPLE: Cassatt's paintings were as detailed as Degas.
ANSWER: Cassatt's paintings were as detailed as Degas's.

1. Cassatt's later use of color was more vibrant than earlier.
2. Some of her works were more successful than her fellow painters.
3. Degas's friendship was more meaningful to her than Seurat.
4. Cassatt's earlier paintings were more relaxed than later.
5. An Impressionist's brush strokes are looser than an Expressionist.
6. Cassatt preferred outdoor light to a studio.
7. She posed her subjects more realistically than Picasso.
8. Her woodcuts were more influenced by Japanese art than France.
9. For Cassatt, Europe's artistic community was more accepting than America.
10. Americans' appreciation for modern art was less developed than Europeans.

Other and Else in Comparisons An illogical comparison can also be caused by failing to use the words *other* or *else*.

▶ **KEY CONCEPT** When comparing one within a group to the rest of the group, make sure that your sentence contains the word *other* or the word *else*. ■

Adding *other* or *else* in this type of comparison will prevent comparing something with itself. For instance, because Monet was an Impressionist, he cannot be compared to all Impressionists. He must be compared to all *other* Impressionists. Similarly, since Elizabeth works in the studio, she cannot be compared to *anyone* in the studio; she must be compared to *anyone else*.

ILLOGICAL: Monet's paintings became *more popular than those of any* Impressionist.

LOGICAL: Monet's paintings became *more popular than those of any other* Impressionist.

ILLOGICAL: Elizabeth has worked in the art studio *longer than anyone*.

LOGICAL: Elizabeth has worked in the art studio *longer than anyone else*.

Ballerine, Edgar Degas

▲ **Critical Viewing** What similarities do you see between this painting by Edgar Degas and the one by Mary Cassatt on page 433? **[Compare]**

 Spelling Tip

When making comparisons, don't confuse the word *than* with the word *then*. *Then* is an adverb that shows time. *Than* is a conjunction that links items in a comparison.

> **Exercise 15** Revising *Other* and *Else* in Comparisons

Revise each sentence, correcting the illogical comparison.

EXAMPLE: Richard is more talented than anyone in class.

ANSWER: Richard is more talented than anyone else in class.

1. Mary Cassatt produced more prints than any American artist of her time.
2. Her printmaking was more influenced by the art of Japan than that of any country.
3. When Cassatt and several artist friends attended an exhibition of Japanese prints in Paris, she was more impressed than anyone in the group.
4. Cassatt returned to the exhibit more often than anyone.
5. She began to concentrate on printmaking more than on any art form.

> **Exercise 16** Writing Clear Comparisons Rewrite each sentence on your paper, completing the comparison in a balanced and logical way.

EXAMPLE: Sherilyn's paintings of horses are more realistic than ___?___.

ANSWER: Sherilyn's paintings of horses are more realistic than Barry's.

1. For many people, yellow creates a happier feeling than any ___?___.
2. Many people prefer orange paint to blue because they feel orange is ___?___ than blue.
3. I have always considered green to be the ___?___ color of all.
4. Compared to green, black is a ___?___ and ___?___ color.
5. I believe purple is ___?___ than either red or blue.
6. I prefer the color ___?___ more than anyone ___?___ in ___?___.
7. The ___?___ color of all is ___?___.
8. If I were going to choose the ___?___ color of all for my room, it would be ___?___.
9. People who wear red clothes are ___?___ than people who wear black clothes.
10. I feel the ___?___ comfortable when I am wearing ___?___ clothes.

> **More Practice**

Grammar Exercise Workbook
• pp. 150–151
On-line Exercise Bank
• Section 25.2
Go on-line:
PHSchool.com
Enter Web Code:
eek-1002

▼ Critical Viewing
Make some comparisons of yellow to other colors. Use *-er, more, -est,* or *most* in your comparisons. **[Compare and Contrast]**

Hands-on Grammar

Comparison Flip Test

Use a Comparison Flip Test to learn when the word *other* is need-ed to complete a comparison. First, print this partial sentence across the middle of a sheet of paper: *I like* [leave 1-1/2" space] *better than . . .*

Next, cut out six 3" squares, and draw a 1" x 1-1/2" rectangle in from the middle of the left edge. On each rectangle, print a different category with the word *any*. Examples: *any city, any food, any sport,* and so on. Around the rectangle, print five examples of the category—five cities, five foods, and so on. Then, cut out the rectangles, turn them over, and print *any other* plus the category. (See illustration.)

Now, cut out six 1-1/4" squares. On one side of each, print one example of one of the categories: *Miami, pizza,* and so on. On the other side, print some-thing that is different from or opposite the category: *the country, plain water,* and so on. Then, do the flip test.

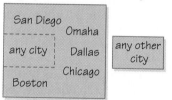

Place the 3" square at the end of your sentence, and fit the rectan-gle appropriate to the category in the cut-out section. Then, in the space between the words *I like* and *better than,* place the 1" square that corresponds to the category. If the item showing on the 1" square matches the category of items on the 3" square, you must flip the rectangle so that the *any other* side is facing up, because you are comparing something with others in the same category. If the item showing on the 1" square does not match the category, flip the rec-tangle so that the *any* side is facing up. Go on making comparisons by changing categories and flipping squares and rectangles to see when you need *any other* or when just *any* makes sense.

Find It in Your Reading Look in ads for "better than," "faster than," "more than," and so on, and see if the comparisons are correct.

Find It in Your Writing Review a piece of your writing to be sure your comparisons are logical and complete. Correct any that are not.

Section 25.2 Section Review

GRAMMAR EXERCISES 17–22

▶ **Exercise 17** Using Comparative and Superlative Forms Correctly
Choose the correct comparative or superlative form in each sentence.

1. Which painter do you like (better, best), Degas or Renoir?
2. Of all Impressionist painters, I consider Pissaro the (more, most) interesting.
3. Renoir was a (more intense, more intenser) artist than many of his peers.
4. However, the scenes he painted are often the (more, most) cheerful of all.
5. Of Degas, Cassatt, and Renoir, Degas was the (older, oldest).
6. He was also the (more, most) original of the three.
7. Of his paintings of horses and ballerinas, which do you prefer (more, most)?
8. Cassatt painted (slower, more slower) than Degas.
9. Of the work of all Impressionists, her paintings seem (more, most) peaceful.
10. Cassatt's paintings are much admired, but her prints are even more (famous, famouser).

▶ **Exercise 18** Supplying Correct Degrees of Modifiers Write the appropriate comparative or superlative degree of the modifier in parentheses.

1. Renoir focused on light (well) than many of the other Impressionists.
2. He used light to make skin, fabrics, and textures the (brilliant) parts of his paintings.
3. Renoir earned (much) money by painting portraits than by any other means.
4. His subjects are the (expressive) of all the Impressionists.
5. Renoir suffered for many years from arthritis, and at the end of his life it grew even (bad).

▶ **Exercise 19** Revising to Clarify Comparisons Revise each sentence to correct unbalanced or illogical comparisons.

1. Degas's focus was more on people than Renoir.
2. The techniques he used in painting ballet dancers were more sophisticated than his fellow painters.
3. His sketches of horse racing came earlier than dancers.
4. Cassatt was friendlier with Degas than anyone in the Impressionist group.
5. Cassatt's paintings were more inventive than any woman painter of her time.

▶ **Exercise 20** Find It in Your Reading In this excerpt from "What Makes a Degas a Degas?" is the author using a comparative or superlative modifier? What is he comparing?

The results of Degas's experiments could have been executed much more quickly had he used pastels instead of oils. What Degas wanted, however, was to make paint look spontaneous.

▶ **Exercise 21** Find It in Your Writing Look through your portfolio for examples of comparisons. Check to see that your comparisons are clear and logical.

▶ **Exercise 22** Writing Application Write a comparison of the work of two painters, musicians, or actors. Make sure that you use comparative and superlative modifiers correctly and that your comparisons are clear.

Miscellaneous Problems in *Usage*

Throughout history, women have achieved stunning success in many different fields. For example, Hildegard von Bingen delighted contemporaries with her writings and musical compositions in the twelfth century, and Amelia Earhart became a flying sensation in the twentieth century. These women strove for excellence in their chosen fields, and their successes inspire others.

Success in many fields requires, among other things, accurate and effective use of language. In this chapter, you will study some usage problems that have not been presented earlier. In the first section of this chapter, you will learn how to form negative sentences correctly. In the second section, you will study troublesome words and expressions.

▲ Critical Viewing
Marie Curie, pictured above, is renowned for her research in radioactivity. Use negative sentences to compare her laboratory to modern laboratories with which you are familiar.
[Distinguish]

Diagnostic Test

Directions: Write all answers on a separate sheet of paper.

Skill Check A. Choose the word in parentheses that makes each sentence negative without forming a double negative.

1. In earlier times, people assumed that women couldn't do (nothing, anything) outside the domestic sphere.
2. They thought women didn't have (no, any) leadership abilities.
3. It was also believed that women (had, hadn't) scarcely the strength or intelligence of their male counterparts.
4. Susan B. Anthony (was, wasn't) but one woman we remember for her achievements.
5. She (was, wasn't) hardly the only person to work for women's suffrage, but only Anthony is commemorated on U.S. currency.

Skill Check B. Choose the correct expression to complete each sentence.

6. Oftentimes, girls weren't (learned, taught) the same skills and lessons as boys.
7. Rather (than, then) science, math, or literature, girls studied cooking, sewing, and caring for the family.
8. (Being that, Because) they were often denied learning opportunities, their successes are that much more remarkable.
9. Women often had to make (their, there) own opportunities.
10. In ancient Egypt, Hatshepsut ruled as regent (due to, because of) her stepson's young age.
11. Within a few years, she had herself crowned pharaoh (so, so that) she could rule in her own right.
12. In more recent times, Marie Curie won an unprecedented (too, two) Nobel Prizes.
13. Her work, (which, who) dealt with radiation, advanced scientific research in the field of radioactivity.
14. Elizabeth I of England (adapted, adopted) to the requirements of sovereignty with strength and resolve.
15. (Beside, Besides) leading in peacetime, she also proved herself a strong leader in wartime.
16. In the twentieth century, Rosa Parks, an African American living in the South, refused to move (further, farther) back in the bus so that a white person could sit up front.
17. She inspired thousands and had a powerful (affect, effect) on the civil rights movement.
18. Eileen Collins (already, all ready) knew how to fly before she became an astronaut.
19. Harriet Tubman guided slaves (among, between) bondage in the South and freedom in the North.
20. (Them, Those) women, and many others, have inspired countless generations to strive to achieve their own dreams.

Negative Sentences

At one time, it was correct to use several negative words in one sentence. It was correct, for example, to say, "Father *didn't* tell *nobody nothing*." Today, however, only one negative word is used to make the entire sentence negative. The above sentence can be restated correctly in one of three ways: "Father *didn't* tell anybody anything," "Father told *nobody* anything," or "Father told *nothing* to anybody."

Recognizing Double Negatives

A **double negative** is the use of two negative words in a sentence when only one is needed.

▶ **KEY CONCEPT** Do not write sentences with double negatives. ∎

The following chart gives examples of double negatives and the two ways each can be corrected.

CORRECTING DOUBLE NEGATIVES	
Double Negatives	**Corrections**
She *couldn't* fix *nothing*.	She *couldn't* fix *anything*. She could fix *nothing*.
Ellen *didn't* have *no* training.	Ellen *didn't* have *any* training. Ellen had *no* training.
She *wouldn't* ask *no one* for help.	She *wouldn't* ask *anyone* for help. She asked *no one* for help.

▶ **Exercise 1** Avoiding Double Negatives Choose the word in parentheses that correctly completes each sentence.
1. No one (couldn't, could) tell Marie Curie that women were inferior in science.
2. She grew up in Poland, not (nowhere, anywhere) close to France, where she did her most famous work.
3. Marie wasn't as interested in (nothing, anything) as much as she was in radioactivity.
4. She and her husband won the 1903 Nobel Prize for Physics, but not without (no, some) help from Antoine Becquerel, who shared the award.
5. A woman hadn't (never, ever) before won a Nobel Prize.

💡 **Spelling Tip**

To make a helping verb negative, just add *n't* to the end of the verb or follow it with the word *not*. Watch out for some exceptions: *Can't* and *won't* lose some letters when put into the negative form, and *cannot* is spelled as one word.

More Practice

Grammar Exercise Workbook
• pp. 153–154
On-line Exercise Bank
• Section 26.1
Go on-line:
PHSchool.com
Enter Web Code:
eek-1002

Forming Negative Sentences Correctly

Negative sentences are formed correctly in one of three ways:

Using One Negative Word: The most common way to make a sentence negative is with a single negative word—such as *no, not, none, nothing, never, nobody,* or *nowhere*—or with the contraction *n't* added to a helping verb.

▶ **KEY CONCEPT** Do not use two negative words in the same clause. ■

Using two of these negative words in the same clause will create a double negative.

DOUBLE NEGATIVE: She *wouldn't never* learn that by herself.
CORRECT: She *wouldn't* ever learn that by herself.
She *would* never learn that by herself.

Using *But* in a Negative Sense: When *but* means "only," it usually acts as a negative.

▶ **KEY CONCEPT** Do not use *but* in its negative sense with another negative. ■

DOUBLE NEGATIVE: He *hadn't but* one hero.
CORRECT: He had *but* one hero.
He had *only* one hero.

Using *Barely, Hardly,* and *Scarcely*: These words have a negative sense and should not be used with other negative words.

▶ **KEY CONCEPT** Do not use *barely, hardly,* or *scarcely* with another negative. ■

DOUBLE NEGATIVE: She *hadn't barely* mastered the new language.
CORRECT: She had *barely* mastered the new language.

DOUBLE NEGATIVE: He *couldn't hardly* see beyond that hill.
CORRECT: He could *hardly* see beyond that hill.

DOUBLE NEGATIVE: It *hadn't scarcely* started to rain.
CORRECT: It had *scarcely* started to rain.

▲ **Critical Viewing**
Marie Curie is admired for her research in radioactivity, among other things. Write several sentences about a person whom you admire. Use the words *but, barely, hardly,* and *scarcely* in your sentences. **[Support]**

26.1

▶ **Exercise 2** Avoiding Problems With Negatives Choose the word in parentheses that makes each sentence negative without creating a double negative.

EXAMPLE: There (isn't, is) scarcely a more famous female aviator than Amelia Earhart.

ANSWER: is

1. Amelia Earhart hardly liked (anything, nothing) as much as flying.
2. Nobody (could, couldn't) keep her on the ground.
3. Before she became the first woman to break the speed record while crossing the Atlantic alone, some people thought women wouldn't (ever, never) be good pilots.
4. That (was, wasn't) but one aviation record that Earhart broke.
5. She disappeared during an attempt to fly around the world, and to this day no one (doesn't know, knows) for certain what happened on that last flight.

▶ **Exercise 3** Revising Sentences to Correct Double Negatives Rewrite each sentence, correcting the double negative.

EXAMPLE: Harriet Tubman didn't allow nothing to stop her from helping others.

ANSWER: Harriet Tubman allowed nothing to stop her from helping others.

1. Born into slavery, Harriet Tubman wasn't never supposed to enjoy the freedom of her white masters.
2. She didn't have no real childhood.
3. When still a young woman, she escaped to the North, but she didn't scarcely take any time to enjoy her new freedom.
4. Harriet didn't think nobody should be a slave.
5. She felt she didn't have but one choice: to return to the South to guide others to freedom.
6. No one wasn't able to stop her, and she never lost one person on her eighteen trips on the Underground Railroad.
7. She wouldn't let no one turn back once they had started.
8. Tubman didn't never stop fighting for freedom: During the Civil War, she served as a nurse, scout, and spy for the Union army.
9. She didn't hardly restrict herself to just one cause: She also fought for women's rights, raised money for schools for black people, and established a home for poor and elderly black people.
10. Harriet Tubman couldn't abide no injustices.

More Practice

Grammar Exercise Workbook
• pp. 153–154
On-line Exercise Bank
• Section 26.1
  Go on-line:
  PHSchool.com
  Enter Web Code:
  eek-1002

Complete the exercises on-line! Exercises 2 and 3 are available on-line or on CD-ROM.

Section 26.1 Section Review

GRAMMAR EXERCISES 4–9

▶ **Exercise 4** Avoiding Double Negatives Choose the word in parentheses that makes each sentence negative without forming a double negative.

1. In the 1840's, medical schools didn't want (nothing, anything) to do with female applicants.
2. Elizabeth Blackwell (would, wouldn't) never give up, however, and on her thirtieth try, she was accepted by Geneva College.
3. She (had, hadn't) barely gotten her degree when she traveled to Europe to gain practical experience in hospitals.
4. When she returned, no one in the medical community (would, wouldn't) trust her.
5. She wouldn't acknowledge (no, any) resistance and opened a hospital to serve poor women and children.

▶ **Exercise 5** Revising Sentences to Avoid Problems With Negatives Rewrite each sentence, correcting the double negative.

1. Aung San Suu Kyi didn't promote no violence in her struggle for freedom from the military government in Burma.
2. Her father, who was assassinated when Aung San Suu Kyi was only two, didn't want no one to live under oppression, and she continued his struggle.
3. While living in India, she didn't ignore none of the methods and teachings of Mohandas Gandhi, the nonviolent protest leader.
4. She couldn't hardly win a military battle, so she gave speeches, visited the people, and started a new political party based on democratic ideals.
5. The government couldn't do nothing to stem her popularity, so they placed her under house arrest for more than ten years.

▶ **Exercise 6** Revising a Paragraph to Correct Double Negatives Rewrite the following, correcting all double negatives.

When she wasn't barely a teenager, Joan of Arc heard the voices of saints. They told her that no one but she couldn't rid France of the invading English. First, she convinced the French king that she wasn't telling no lies when she claimed she could restore his kingdom. Charles VII believed he hadn't but one choice: to trust Joan. It didn't take scarcely ten days to break the English siege of Orleans. The English couldn't do nothing to defeat her. Joan wouldn't take no rest until Charles VII was crowned at Rheims. She didn't allow nobody to attack the king as she led him through enemy territory. In Paris, however, she couldn't do nothing to prevent her own capture. The English didn't want no more trouble from Joan, so they sentenced her to death.

▶ **Exercise 7** Find It in Your Reading Locate an article on a famous woman in a newspaper, a magazine, or one of your textbooks. Find at least two examples of negative sentences. Explain why the negatives are used correctly.

▶ **Exercise 8** Find It in Your Writing In your own writing, find five examples of negative words. Check to make sure that you have not included any sentences with double negatives.

▶ **Exercise 9** Writing Application Write about a woman whom you admire. Include three negative sentences. Be sure to avoid double negatives and to form all negative sentences correctly.

Common Usage Problems

This section presents an alphabetical list of forty-five usage problems that sometimes cause confusion in writing and speaking.

▶ **KEY CONCEPT** Study the items in this glossary, paying particular attention to similar meanings and spellings. ■

(1) a, an The article *a* is used before consonant sounds; *an* is used before vowel sounds. Words beginning with *h*, *o*, or *u* can have either a consonant sound or a vowel sound.

(2) accept, except *Accept* is a verb meaning "to receive." *Except* is a preposition meaning "other than" or "leaving out."

VERB: Settlers of the western frontier *accepted* the harsh realities of frontier life.
PREPOSITION: They easily found all the natural resources they needed *except* water and wood.

(3) adapt, adopt *Adapt* means "to change." *Adopt* means "to take as one's own."

EXAMPLES: Easterners quickly learned to *adapt.*
            Newcomers *adopted* the customs of neighbors.

(4) affect, effect *Affect*, almost always a verb, means "to influence." *Effect* may be used as a noun or as a verb. As a noun, it means "result." As a verb, it means "to bring about" or "to cause."

VERB: Natural disasters *affected* the farmers' success.
NOUN: Settlers knew the *effects* of nature and tried to combat them.
VERB: The tractor *effected* a drastic change in farming.

(5) ain't *Ain't* was originally a contraction of *am not*, but it is no longer considered standard English.

(6) all ready, already *All ready*, two separate words used as an adjective, is an expression meaning "ready." *Already*, an adverb, means "even now" or "by or before this time."

ADJECTIVE: The cowboys were *all ready* for the cattle drive.
ADVERB: Many of them had *already* driven cattle north.

Theme: Westward
Expansion
....
In this section, you
will learn about forty-
five common usage
problems. The exam-
ples and exercises in
this section are about
the people who took
part in the westward
expansion of the
United States during
the 1800's.
....
Cross-Curricular
Connection:
Social Studies

(7) all right, alright *Alright* is a nonstandard spelling. Make sure you use the two-word form.

NONSTANDARD: Business was *alright* if the town was located near some form of transportation.

CORRECT: Business was *all right* if the town was located near some form of transportation.

(8) all together, altogether *All together* means "together as a single group." *Altogether* means "completely" or "in all."

EXAMPLES: Cowhands had to work *all together* to transport cattle over long distances.
They would fail *altogether* if they worked alone.

(9) among, between Both of these words are prepositions. *Among* always implies three or more. *Between* is generally used only with two things.

EXAMPLES: Cows were branded so that the owners could pick out their cows from *among* a crowd.
Cowboys could transport the cows *between* the ranch and the railroad.

(10) anxious This adjective implies uneasiness, worry, or fear. Do not use it as a substitute for eager.

LESS ACCEPTABLE: The cowboys were *anxious* to reach the next town.

PREFERRED: The cowboys were *eager* to reach the next town.
The ranchers were *anxious* about cattle thieves.

(11) anywhere, everywhere, nowhere, somewhere Never end these adverbs with an -s.

NONSTANDARD: At first, ranchers didn't use fences, so cattle could wander *anywheres*.

CORRECT: At first, ranchers didn't use fences, so cattle could wander *anywhere*.

(12) as to *As to* is awkward. Replace it with *about*.

NONSTANDARD: Miners had no worries *as to* the land.
CORRECT: Miners had no worries *about* the land.

Technology Tip

If you are using the spell-check feature of a word-processing program, keep in mind that it will not pick up as errors words such as *all right, alright, all together*, and *altogether*.

(13) at Do not use *at* after *where*. Simply eliminate it.

NONSTANDARD: They didn't care *where* they were *at* as long as they found precious metals.

CORRECT: They didn't care *where* they were as long as they found precious metals.

(14) awhile, a while *Awhile* is an adverb that means "for a while." It is never preceded by a preposition. *A while* is an article and a noun, usually used after prepositions such as *for* or *after*.

ADVERB: The miners stayed *awhile* and worked the mine.

NOUN: After *a while*, a boom town would grow up to serve the needs of the miners.

(15) bad, badly *Bad* is an adjective that means "incorrect," "ill," or "undesirable." *Badly* is an adverb that means "in a bad way" or "poorly."

ADJECTIVE: Miners papered their walls with newspapers to insulate themselves from a *bad* winter.

ADVERB: Compared to today's insulation, the paper worked *badly*.

▲ **Critical Viewing**
Using the words *bad* and *badly*, write a movie scene using this photograph as inspiration.
[Speculate]

▶ **Exercise 10** Avoiding Usage Problems 1–15 Choose the correct expression to complete each sentence.
1. For (awhile, a while) ships and stagecoaches were the only means to deliver mail from the East to California.
2. In 1860, a California senator and a Missouri businessman (adapted, adopted) a plan to provide faster mail delivery.
3. The pony express delivered mail (among, between) St. Joseph, Missouri, and Sacramento, California.
4. At first, no one had any idea (as to, about) the exact time it would take a rider to travel from Missouri to California.
5. The service employed about eighty riders (altogether, all together) to deliver the mail.
6. Riders endured (bad, badly) weather and the threat of attacks by Indians.
7. After a rider covered at least 75 miles, he reached a station where another rider was (all ready, already) waiting.
8. The new rider would (accept, except) the leather saddlebag and continue along the route.
9. The fate of the pony express (ain't, isn't) a happy one.
10. The new transcontinental telegraph had a major (affect, effect) on the pony express, quickly shutting it down.

More Practice

Grammar Exercise Workbook
• pp. 155–156
On-line Exercise Bank
• Section 26.2
  Go on-line:
  PHSchool.com
  Enter Web Code:
  eek-1002

Get instant feedback! Exercise 10 is available on-line or on CD-ROM.

(16) because Do not use *because* after the word *reason*. Say "The reason . . . that" or reword the sentence.

NONSTANDARD: *The reason* miners moved so often is *because* they were always searching for a major strike.

CORRECT: *The reason* miners moved so often is *that* they were always searching for a major strike.
Miners moved so often *because* they were always searching for a major strike.

(17) being as, being that Do not use either expression. Use *because* or *since* instead.

(18) beside, besides *Beside* means "close to" or "at the side of." *Besides* means "in addition to."

EXAMPLES: Tombstone, Arizona, developed *beside* a mine.
Besides mines, towns were started near transportation centers and major shipping points.

(19) bring, take *Bring* means "to carry from a distant place to a nearer one." *Take* means the opposite: "to carry from a near place to a more distant place."

EXAMPLES: Cowboys would *bring* cattle over thousands of miles to a town with a train station.
The trains would then *take* the cattle to the East, where they would be sold for food.

(20) different from, different than *Different from* is preferred.

LESS ACCEPTABLE: A transportation town was *different than* a mining town because it was usually more permanent.

PREFERRED: A transportation town was *different from* a mining town because it was usually more permanent.

(21) doesn't, don't *Doesn't* is the correct verb form for third-person singular subjects. *Don't* is used with all other subjects.

NONSTANDARD: A town *don't* thrive without townspeople.
It *don't* seem very prosperous.
He *don't* want to stay if there is no work.

CORRECT: A town *doesn't* thrive without townspeople.
It *doesn't* seem very prosperous.
He *doesn't* want to stay if there is no work.

(22) done *Done*, the past participle of *do*, should always follow a helping verb.

NONSTANDARD: Merchants *done* the job of supplying farmers, miners, and cowhands.

CORRECT: Merchants *have done* the job of supplying farmers, miners, and cowhands.

(23) due to *Due to* means "caused by" and should be used only when the words *caused by* can logically be substituted.

NONSTANDARD: *Due to* the lack of natural resources, towns were often established in groups.

CORRECT: The establishment of towns in groups was *due to* the lack of natural resources.

(24) farther, further *Farther* refers to distance. *Further* means "to a greater degree or extent" or "additional."

EXAMPLES: The *farther* away a town was from transportation, the harder it was for people to get supplies.
The area around Virginia City, Nevada, was *further* developed to supply resources to the city.
Virginia City needed *further* support to survive.

(25) fewer, less *Fewer* is used with objects that can be counted. *Less* is used with qualities or quantities that cannot be counted.

EXAMPLES: *fewer* stagecoaches, *fewer* horses, *fewer* supplies
less land, *less* wood, *less* communication

(26) gone, went *Gone* is the past participle of *go*. It should be used as a verb only with a helping verb. *Went* is the past tense of *go* and is never used with a helping verb.

NONSTANDARD: Easterners *gone* west to find a better life.
They *could have went* to a major eastern city to make a better life for themselves.

CORRECT: Easterners *had gone* west hoping to find a better life.
Easterners *went* west to find a better life.
They *could have gone* to a major eastern city to make a better life for themselves.

(27) in, into *In* refers to position. *Into* suggests motion.

POSITION: People often traveled west *in* wagons.
MOTION: They loaded their supplies *into* a covered wagon.

✿ Grammar and Style Tip

Vary your vocabulary to make your writing more interesting. Explore new words and expressions, but always check for correct usage.

(28) irregardless Putting *ir-* on this word makes it a double negative. Use *regardless* instead.

NONSTANDARD: People settled in the West, *irregardless* of the dangers.

CORRECT: People settled in the West, *regardless* of the dangers.

(29) just When you use *just* to mean "no more than," place it right before the word or phrase it logically modifies.

LESS ACCEPTABLE: Since there was little wood, houses were *just* made of sod.

PREFERRED: Since there was little wood, houses were made of *just* sod.

(30) kind of, sort of These expressions should not be used to mean "rather" or "somewhat."

NONSTANDARD: Travel was *kind* of slow.

CORRECT: Travel was *rather* slow.

▼ Critical Viewing
Write a description of this painting, correctly using one of the two words listed in each of the usage problems 24–27. **[Interpret]**

▶ **Exercise 11** Avoiding Usage Problems 16–30 Choose the correct expression to complete each sentence.
1. Pony express riders carried the mail (irregardless, regardless) of bad weather, rough terrain, or danger.
2. They (gone, went) about 75 miles a day.
3. Teenagers (did, done) much of the riding.
4. They were chosen (due to, because of) their light weight.
5. Horses traveled (fewer, less) miles per day than the riders.
6. The mail was carried (in, into) special leather saddlebags.
7. (Beside, Besides) letters, pony express riders also carried small packages.
8. The mail traveled much (farther, further) in a day with the pony express than on a ship or stagecoach.
9. The service (just lasted, lasted just) a year and a half.
10. The reason it closed down is (that, because) the transcontinental telegraph service had opened for business two days earlier.

Grammar Exercise Workbook
• pp. 155–156
On-line Exercise Bank
• Section 26.2
Go on-line:
PHSchool.com
Enter Web Code:
eek-1002

Get instant feedback! Exercise 11 is available on-line or on CD-ROM.

(31) lay, lie *Lay* means "to put or set (something) down." Its principal parts—*lay, laying, laid,* and *laid*—are usually followed by a direct object. *Lie* means "to recline." Its principal parts—*lie, lying, lay,* and *lain*—are never followed by a direct object.

LAY: *Lay* the luggage on top of the stagecoach.
The driver is *laying* the bags in the back compartment.
The passengers *laid* their handbags on the seats.
The bags were jostled about and no longer rested where the driver had *laid* them.

LIE: Passengers had to sleep in the stagecoach and were not able to *lie* down.
The handbag is *lying* on the floor at her feet.
The child *lay* down across her parents' laps.
She had *lain* there throughout the night.

(32) learn, teach *Learn* means "to acquire knowledge." *Teach* means "to give knowledge to."

EXAMPLES: A person *learned* many different skills in order to survive in the West.
Settlers *taught* newcomers how to manage in the new terrain.

(33) leave, let *Leave* means "to allow to remain." *Let* means "to permit."

NONSTANDARD: Cowboys *leave* the cattle wander over great tracts of land.
They *let* calves with the mothers, even if the father belongs to a different herd.

CORRECT: Cowboys *let* the cattle wander over great tracts of land.
They *leave* calves with the mothers, even if the father belongs to a different herd.

(34) like *Like* is a preposition and should not be used in place of the conjunction *as*.

NONSTANDARD: Crime in the West was widespread, *like* it was in the East.

CORRECT: Crime in the West was widespread, *as* it was in the East.

(35) of Do not use the preposition *of* in place of the verb *have*. *Of* after *outside, inside, off,* or *atop* is also undesirable in formal writing. Simply eliminate it.

NONSTANDARD: A single sheriff would *of* watched over a group of towns.

CORRECT: A single sheriff would *have* watched over a group of towns.

LESS ACCEPTABLE: One judge held court *inside* of a restaurant.

PREFERRED: One judge held court *inside* a restaurant.

(36) only Be sure to place *only* in front of the word you mean to modify.

EXAMPLES: *Only* one cowboy wanted to go to town today. (No one else wanted to go to town.)
One cowboy *only* wanted to go to town. (He did not want to do anything else.)

(37) seen *Seen* is a past participle and can be used as a verb only with a helping verb.

NONSTANDARD: The judge *seen* a number of criminals.

CORRECT: The judge *has seen* a number of criminals.

Learn More

Your mastery of English usage is critical to your writing success. To develop the study skills to improve your usage, see Chapter 32.

(38) set, sit *Set* means "to put (something) in a certain place." Its principal parts—*set, setting, set,* and *set*—are usually followed by a direct object. *Sit* means "to be seated." Its principal parts—*sit, sitting, sat,* and *sat*—are never followed by a direct object.

SET: *Set* the tools in the barn.
He is *setting* the plow in the backyard.
His wife *set* the food on the table.
She had *set* the plates out earlier.

SIT: They brought a rocking chair from the East to *sit* in.
She is *sitting* in it right now.
She *sat* in it whenever they stopped.
Her mother had *sat* in that chair before her.

(39) so *So* is a coordinating conjunction. It should be avoided when you mean "so that."

LESS ACCEPTABLE: Townsfolk formed vigilante groups *so* they could enforce the law as they saw fit.

PREFERRED: Townsfolk formed vigilante groups *so that* they could enforce the law as they saw fit.

(40) than, then Use *than* in comparisons. *Then,* an adverb, usually refers to time.

EXAMPLES: The telegraph was faster *than* the pony express.
The transcontinental telegraph was installed, and *then* the pony express went out of business.

(41) that, which, who Use these relative pronouns correctly. *That* and *which* refer to things; *who* refers only to people.

EXAMPLES: The wagon *that* carried the food for a cattle drive was called the chuck wagon.
The person *who* took care of the extra horses on a cattle drive was called a wrangler.

(42) their, there, they're *Their,* a possessive pronoun, always modifies a noun. *There* can be used either as an expletive at the beginning of a sentence or as an adverb. *They're* is a contraction of *they are.*

PRONOUN: Farmers spent all *their* time working the land.

EXPLETIVE: *There* are many obstacles to a good harvest.

ADVERB: The fields over *there* will be planted tomorrow.

CONTRACTION: *They're* deciding what crops to plant this year.

(43) them Do not use *them* as a substitute for *those*.

NONSTANDARD: *Them* horses are extremely fast.
CORRECT: *Those* horses are extremely fast.

(44) to, too, two *To*, a preposition, begins a phrase or an infinitive. *Too*, an adverb, modifies adjectives and other adverbs. *Two* is a number.

PREPOSITION: *to* the homestead, *to* the miner
INFINITIVE: *to* dig, *to* plow
ADVERB: *too* dry, *too* quickly
NUMBER: *two* fields, *two* cows

(45) when, where Do not use *when* or *where* directly after a linking verb. Do not use *where* in place of *that*.

NONSTANDARD: A barn raising is *when* farmers could socialize with their neighbors.
   A general store is *where* they got supplies.
   He heard *where* the square dance was held after harvest time.
CORRECT: A barn raising allowed farmers to socialize with their neighbors.
   A farmer could get supplies at a general store.
   He heard *that* the square dance was held after harvest time.

Exercise 12 Revising a Paragraph to Correct Usage Problems 31–45 Rewrite the following paragraph, correcting the errors in usage. Not every sentence contains an error.

(1) Even though life in the West was difficult, settlers would leave some time to enjoy themselves. (2) Homesteaders often combined they're work and play. (3) They might travel too a neighbor's farm to help with harvesting a crop or husking corn. (4) A barn raising was when farmers could do some work and have some fun. (5) The men at a house or barn raising were divided into teams so the work would go faster and be more fun. (6) The teams would lie down the floor together and then each take responsibility for building a different wall. (7) This was a good way to learn newcomers some of the skills needed to survive in the West. (8) Women might set with their neighbors at a quilting bee. (9) Traveling vaudeville shows would set up outside of several towns each year. (10) One farmer seen the famous performers Buffalo Bill, Annie Oakley, Edwin Booth, and Laura Keene.

More Practice

Grammar Exercise Workbook
• pp. 155–156
On-line Exercise Bank
• Section 26.2
Go on-line:
PHSchool.com
Enter Web Code:
eek-1002

Get instant feedback! Exercise 12 is available on-line or on CD-ROM.

Hands-on Grammar

Illustrating Usage Problems on Index Cards

Work on common usage problems by creating illustrations that represent each word's proper usage. In the examples below, *in* and *into* are illustrated with paper airplanes and garbage cans showing that *in* refers to position and *into* suggests motion. *Bring* and *take* are illustrated with drawings and arrows showing that *bring* means "to carry from a distant place to a nearer one," while *take* means "to carry from a near place to a more distant one."

Each of the ten word pairs below represents a common usage problem. Using the common-usage glossary on pages 444–453, illustrate each word. Don't worry about making detailed drawings—just make sure they clearly illustrate the main difference between the proper usage of the two words. Use one index card for each word pair, and use the same side of the index card to illustrate both words.

After you have completed your illustrations, practice the correct usage of each word. Working with a partner, take turns selecting index cards at random, studying the illustrations, and forming sentences that use each word correctly. Refer to the common-usage problems glossary to check your answers.

1. among, between
2. fewer, less
3. lay, lie
4. beside, besides
5. leave, let
6. that, which, who
7. set, sit
8. learn, teach
9. accept, except
10. farther, further

Find It in Your Reading In textbooks or magazines, find examples of the words above used correctly in sentences. Write the example sentences on the backs of the appropriate index cards.

Find It in Your Writing Look through pieces of writing in your writing portfolio for examples of the words above used correctly in sentences. Write the example sentences on the back of the appropriate index cards. If you cannot find examples of any of the words, challenge yourself to write new sentences on the backs of the cards using the words correctly.

Section Review

GRAMMAR EXERCISES 13–19

▶ **Exercise 13** Supplying *a* or *an*
Correctly Complete each expression
with *a* or *an*.

1. occurrence
2. usual amount
3. heirloom
4. urban outfit
5. hard-packed trail

▶ **Exercise 14** Avoiding Usage
Problems Choose the correct expression to complete each sentence.

1. Life in the West favored those who could (adapt, adopt) to many jobs.
2. A well-rounded man could (except, accept) any kind of job to survive.
3. If he were paid (bad, badly) at one occupation, he could move on to another.
4. He could move about freely (like, as) the birds did.
5. George Jackson, (who, which) is credited with discovering gold in the Rockies, also worked as a roustabout, farmhand, miner, and businessman.
6. Buffalo Bill Cody is a famous jack-of-all-trades, (too, two).
7. After his father died when Bill was eleven, he worked for (awhile, a while) as a messenger for a freight company.
8 (Being as, Because) war broke out in 1861, Bill joined the Union army.
9. In 1872, Bill embarked on a career very (different from, different than) any of his previous occupations.
10. As a showman, he traveled much (further, farther) than ever before.

▶ **Exercise 15** Revising Sentences
to Correct Usage Errors Rewrite each sentence, correcting the error in usage.

1. The life of a cowboy was kind of lonely.
2. On long cattle drives, cowboys spent all day setting in the saddle.

3. They had to keep the cattle altogether for the entire ride.
4. On these drives, cowboys laid down under the stars to go to sleep.
5. At home on the range, cowboys just didn't watch over the cattle.
6. They also would of had to do repairs.
7. The installation of fences effected relations with the ranchers' neighbors.
8. Tension between cattle ranchers and farmers was all ready strained.
9. Everyone was anxious to help.
10. Range wars erupted everywheres across the West.

▶ **Exercise 16** Writing Sentences
Using Troublesome Words Correctly
use each word in an original sentence.

1. accept
2. further
3. like
4. which
5. altogether
6. just
7. awhile
8. lay
9. set
10. effect

▶ **Exercise 17** Find It in Your
Reading In a newspaper, find five
examples of words discussed in this section. Explain why each is used correctly.

▶ **Exercise 18** Find It in Your Writing
In your own writing, find three examples of words discussed in this section.
Check to make sure that your usage of the words is correct. If not, revise your work.

▶ **Exercise 19** Writing Application
Write an essay telling what you would
and would not like about life in the Old
West. Be sure to avoid all the usage errors
described in this section.

Chapter 27 Capitalization

▲ **Critical Viewing**
In what ways would you use capitalization if you were writing a description of this mountain? **[Describe]**

Although you wouldn't remember it, you probably started using capital letters when you learned the alphabet. Without your realizing it, capital letters most likely continue to catch your attention when you look at advertisements, headlines, and road signs, among other things. Capital letters also serve an important role in writing. Through capitalization, writers indicate important words or signal a new thought.

Many rules govern the use of capitalization. This chapter will introduce you to the most widely accepted rules, showing you when and where to capitalize letters in your writing.

Diagnostic Test

Directions: Write all answers on a separate sheet of paper.

Skill Check A. Copy each of the underlined words below, and tell whether it is a *proper noun* or a *proper adjective.*

1. the <u>Swiss</u> countryside
2. the <u>Rocky Mountains</u>
3. <u>Yellowstone National Park</u>
4. the <u>Australian</u> continent
5. explorer <u>David Livingstone</u>

Skill Check B. Write the words that should be capitalized in each of the following sentences.

6. the himalayas of asia are the highest mountain range in the world.
7. they are located between the indus river and the brahmaputra river.
8. these majestic mountains were formed millions of years ago when the indian subcontinent collided with the eurasian landmass.
9. the majority of the greatest peaks can be found in the countries of tibet, nepal, and india.
10. the tallest himalayan peak is mt. everest, which is situated approximately 80 miles from nepal's capital of kathmandu.
11. it was named for sir george everest, a british surveyor who was the first to establish its location and height.
12. the enormous mountain was successfully scaled in 1953 by members of an expedition led by col. john hunt of great britain.
13. on may 29, 1953, edmund hillary of new zealand and a nepalese guide, tenzing norgay, were the first men to stand on the summit.
14. since that time, everest has been climbed by several international teams, including the italians, the japanese, and, in 1963, an american expedition.
15. for more information on this region of the world, read the books *geography of the himalayas* and *in exile from the land of snows.*

Skill Check C. Proofread the following paragraph, and correct all errors in capitalization.

Few people can claim to have stood on top of the world—And only one man can claim to have been there first. That person is sir Edmund Hillary. although he shares the glory of his achievement with his climbing partner, tenzing norgay, hillary was the first person to reach the Summit of mount Everest in nepal, 29,028 feet above Sea Level—the highest spot on earth. Hillary has said of himself, "i've moved from being a child who dreamed a lot and read a lot of books about adventure, to actually getting involved in things like mountaineering. . . ." These are humble words for a man who has climbed the swiss alps and conquered eleven different peaks of more than 20,000 Feet in the himalayas of tibet and nepal.

Using Capitals for First Words

Capital letters work as a visual clue to the reader by making certain words stand out more prominently on a page.

Sentences

Always signal the start of a new idea by capitalizing the first word in a sentence.

▶ **KEY CONCEPT** Capitalize the first word in declarative, interrogative, imperative, and exclamatory sentences. ■

Note that each of the following sentences is complete. Each contains both a subject and a verb and makes sense by itself.

DECLARATIVE: Alberto visited the Grand Canyon last summer.
INTERROGATIVE: Did you mail the monthly bills?
IMPERATIVE: Get a stamp out of the drawer.
EXCLAMATORY: This letter says I've won a trip to Niagara Falls!

▶ **KEY CONCEPT** Capitalize the first word in interjections and incomplete questions. ■

EXAMPLES: Fantastic! Ouch! Darn!

EXAMPLES: When? For Maria? How much?

▶ **KEY CONCEPT** Capitalize the first word of a complete sentence following a colon. If a list follows a colon, it is not a complete sentence and, therefore, no capital letter is used. ■

SENTENCE
FOLLOWING COLON: We saw what was in the valley: It was a beautiful waterfall.
LIST FOLLOWING COLON: The mail carrier delivered our mail: two letters, a package, and a card.

Quotations

▶ **KEY CONCEPT** Capitalize the first word in a quotation if the quotation is a complete sentence. ■

EXAMPLE: "Mountains are earth's undecaying monuments."
—Nathaniel Hawthorne

Theme: Geography
In this chapter, you will learn about capitalization. The exercises and examples are about geography.

Cross-Curricular Connection: Geography

Even when the quotation appears with a "he said/she said" expression, a capital letter is still used to begin the quotation.

EXAMPLE: "It's awfully hot in the canyon," the man said.

If a "he said/she said" expression occurs in the middle of quoted material that is one continuous sentence, only the first word of the quotation gets a capital letter.

EXAMPLE: "If you visit her," Liz said, "please tell me."

If a "he said/she said" expression sits between two complete sentences, both sentences receive capital letters.

EXAMPLE: "Our family vacations are great fun!" Arleen exclaimed. "We are going camping this year."

When a portion of a quotation that is not a complete sentence is contained within a longer sentence, do not capitalize the first word of the quoted part of the sentence.

EXAMPLE: Mark Twain, who saw pony express riders in action, said that a rider was "usually a little bit of a man."

If the quoted fragment shifts to the beginning of the sentence, the first word should then be capitalized.

EXAMPLE: "Usually a little bit of a man" is the way Mark Twain described a Pony Express rider.

▲ Critical Viewing
What are three different capitalization rules that you might use in writing about this waterfall? [Connect]

Poetry

▶ KEY CONCEPT Capitalize the first word in each line of most poetry even if the line does not begin a new sentence. ∎

EXAMPLE: Falling upon earth,
            Pure water spills
            From the cup   —Bashō

I and O

These words always require capitalization.

▶ KEY CONCEPT Capitalize *I* and *O* throughout a sentence. ∎

EXAMPLES: "Eureka! I have found it."—Archimedes
            "O Romeo, Romeo! Wherefore art thou Romeo?"
                                            —Shakespeare

27

Exercise 1 Using Capitals for First Words Copy the following items, adding the missing capitals. Some items may require more than one capital letter.

1. central Australia is home to Ayers Rock.
2. my teacher said, "surprisingly, Ayers Rock is the largest single rock formation in the world."
3. wow! the red sandstone monolith rises 1,143 feet above the surrounding terrain.
4. seventy million years ago, the rock appeared much different from the way it does today: it was a small island surrounded by an inland sea.
5. did you know that Ayers Rock is called Uluru by the aboriginal people of Australia?

Exercise 2 Writing a Postcard Using Capital Letters for First Words Imagine that you are on a trip to Australia or another distant tourist destination. Write a postcard to a friend, describing some of your experiences. Use each of the rules for capitalizing first words at least once in your postcard.

More Practice

Grammar Exercise Workbook
• pp. 157–158
On-line Exercise Bank
• Chapter 27
Go on-line:
PHSchool.com
Enter Web Code:
eek-1002

▼ Critical Viewing If you were to write a few sentences describing the Australian landscape shown here, what would you write? What capitalization rules would you use? **[Describe]**

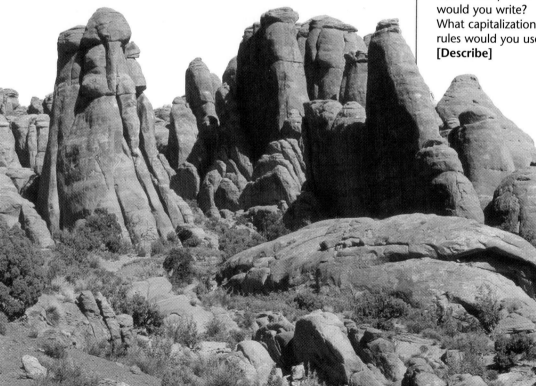

460 • *Capitalization*

Using Capitals for Proper Nouns

A **proper noun** is a noun that names a specific person, place, or thing.

▶ **KEY CONCEPT** Capitalize all proper nouns, including each part of a person's name. ■

The given or first name, the initials standing for a name, and the surname or last name all receive capital letters.

EXAMPLES: Chester Worth, Maria A. Lopez

If a surname begins with *Mc, O',* or *St.,* the letter following it is capitalized.

EXAMPLES: McGregor, O'Mara, St. John

The capitalization of names beginning with *de, D', la, le, Mac, van,* or *von* will vary.

EXAMPLES: De Mello, de Mello

▶ **KEY CONCEPT** Capitalize the proper names of animals. ■

EXAMPLES: Rin-Tin-Tin, Sylvester, Fido

▶ **KEY CONCEPT** Capitalize geographical names. ■

Capitalize the names of streets, towns, cities, counties, states, provinces, countries, continents, valleys, mountains, rivers, and oceans. If a place can be found on a map, you should normally capitalize it.

EXAMPLES: Strokes Avenue, Galapagos Islands, Red Sea

The sun and the moon are not capitalized.
When a compass point is used simply to show direction, it is not capitalized. A specific location is capitalized.

EXAMPLES: We headed northwest.
My cousin lives in the Southwest.

▶ **Exercise 3** Capitalizing Names Write the names below on a separate sheet of paper, inserting capital letters where appropriate.

1. sydney, australia
2. hawaiian islands
3. the pacific northwest
4. mr. ed
5. lassie

▶ **KEY CONCEPT** Capitalize the names of monuments, buildings, and meeting rooms. ■

The following chart shows examples of monuments, buildings, and meeting rooms:

SPECIFIC PLACES	
Monuments and Memorials	Washington Monument, Lincoln Memorial
Buildings	Smithsonian Institution, Superdome, the Actors' Conservatory Theater
School and Meeting Rooms	Room 20B, Laboratory C, Oval Office

Do not capitalize the words *theater, hotel,* and *university* unless they are part of a proper name.

EXAMPLES: The theater is one of the oldest buildings in town.
              The Fallon House Theater is in an old ghost town.

The word *room* is capitalized only if it refers to a specific room and is combined with a name, letter, or number.

EXAMPLE: The geology exam will be given in Room 46.

▶ **KEY CONCEPT** Capitalize the names of specific events and periods of time. ■

SPECIAL EVENTS AND TIMES	
Historic Events	Stone Age
Historic Periods	War of 1812
Documents	Gettysburg Address, Homestead Act
Days and Months	Monday, April
Holidays and Religious Days	Labor Day, Good Friday
Special Events	Kentucky Derby

▶ **KEY CONCEPT** Do not capitalize the seasons. ■

EXAMPLE: We felt a winter chill in the air as we reached the mountaintop.

> **KEY CONCEPT** Capitalize the names of various organizations, government bodies, political parties, nationalities, and languages. ■

SPECIFIC GROUPS AND LANGUAGES	
Clubs	Rotary Club, Lynbrook Speech Club, Lions Club
Organizations	League of Women Voters, American Cancer Society, United Farm Workers
Institutions	University of Miami, Marymount General Hospital
Businesses	Fresh Food Corporation, Unlimited Knowledge, Inc.
Government Bodies	Senate of the United States, Houses of Parliament, Department of Defense
Political Parties	Republicans, Whigs
Nationalities	American, French, Russian, Mexican
Languages	English, Spanish, French, Yiddish

> **KEY CONCEPT** Capitalize references to religions, deities, and religious scriptures. ■

Each religion has a set of words referring to the important and sacred beliefs it holds. The major religious groups to which you are likely to refer in your writing include Christianity, Judaism, Buddhism, Islam, Confucianism, and Hinduism.

CHRISTIANITY: God, Lord, Father, Son, Holy Spirit, Bible, books of the Bible (Exodus, Kings, Romans)

JUDAISM: God, Lord, Prophets (Moses, Abraham), Torah, Talmud

EASTERN RELIGIONS: Buddhism (Buddha, Tripitaka); Islam (Allah, Koran); Hinduism (Brahma, Vedas)

This list is not complete. Other religious references that you encounter must also be capitalized. These include any pronoun references made to the deity in Christian or Jewish writings.

When writing about mythological gods and goddesses, capitalize the proper names of gods and goddesses, but do not capitalize the words *god* and *goddess.*

EXAMPLES: the god Pluto, the goddess Athena

▶ **KEY CONCEPT** Capitalize the names of awards. ■

Notice in the following examples that the word *the* is not capitalized.

EXAMPLES: the Kevin E. Morris Scholarship; the Nobel Peace Prize; the Academy Awards; the Oscar; Eagle Scout

▶ **KEY CONCEPT** Capitalize the names of specific types of air, sea, space, and land craft. ■

When capitalizing the names of air, sea, space, and land craft, do not capitalize the word *the* preceding a name unless the word is part of the official name.

AIR: Boeing 747   SPACE: *Sputnik I*
SEA: *Lusitania*   LAND: the Model T

More Practice

Grammar Exercise Workbook
• pp. 159–160
On-line Exercise Bank
• Chapter 27
Go on-line:
PHSchool.com
Enter Web Code:
eek-1002

Get instant feedback! Exercises 4, 5, and 6 are available on-line or on CD-ROM.

▶ **Exercise 4** Using Capitals in Sentences With Proper Nouns
Copy the following sentences, adding the missing capitals.
1. The sahara stretches 3,200 miles across the northern portion of africa.
2. The desert begins at the atlantic ocean and extends to the red sea.
3. The northern edge of the desert terminates in the atlas mountains, a dramatic scene that has been photographed from satellites such as landsat.
4. During the ice age, north africa was a land of shallow lakes and rich vegetation.
5. By the time of the roman empire, the region had completely turned to desert.

▲ Critical Viewing What proper nouns might apply to this picture? **[Speculate]**

▶ **Exercise 5** Proofreading to Correct Errors in the Capitalization of Proper Nouns Rewrite this paragraph, adding or eliminating capital letters where appropriate.
(1) The Sahara is the largest desert in the World. (2) The Desert covers large sections of several countries, including morocco, algeria, tunisia, libya, and egypt. (3) Although the desert is generally flat, the snow-capped mount Tahat rises above the swirling sands of the central sahara. (4) A small group of Nomadic muslims, people called bedouins, travel throughout the desert. (5) The majority of the Desert Population, however, is confined to cities, such as luxor, ghat, and reggane.

Using Capitals for Proper Adjectives

A proper noun used as an adjective or an adjective formed from a proper noun is called a *proper adjective.*

> **KEY CONCEPT** Capitalize most proper adjectives. ■

EXAMPLES: Swiss government, American people, Gothic style

Proper adjectives used in popular expressions are exceptions.

EXAMPLES: french fries, venetian blinds

Adjectives referring to culture or climate that derive from capitalized terms for regions are also generally lowercase.

EXAMPLES: arctic wind (but *the Arctic*), western pioneers (but *the West*)

> **KEY CONCEPT** Capitalize brand names used as adjectives. ■

EXAMPLES: Timetrue watches, Hercules luggage

> **KEY CONCEPT** Do not capitalize prefixes attached to proper adjectives unless the prefix refers to a nationality. ■

EXAMPLES: pre-Mayan architecture, Indo-European

> **KEY CONCEPT** In a hyphenated adjective, capitalize only the proper adjective. ■

EXAMPLE: Spanish-speaking Americans

> **Exercise 6** **Using Capital Letters for Proper Adjectives** Copy the sentences and add any missing capitals.
> 1. The european continent is dominated by the massive peaks of the Alps.
> 2. They were formed millions of years ago as a result of a collision between the eurasian and african landmasses, which forced the rock to rise.
> 3. Today, the Alps exist within the borders of France, Switzerland, Italy, and Austria.
> 4. french-speaking, german-speaking, and italian-speaking peoples inhabit the area.
> 5. The tallest of the Alps are taller than the tallest of the Rocky Mountains of the american West.

Grammar and Style Tip

Sometimes, proper nouns can function as proper adjectives: a *New Zealand* citizen, the *Niagara Falls* area.

▼ Critical Viewing What is a proper adjective you might use in describing this ship? **[Describe]**

Using Capitals for Titles

Capital letters are used to indicate titles of people and works of art and literature.

Titles of People Titles used before names and in direct address require capitalization.

▶ **KEY CONCEPT** Capitalize a person's title when it is used with the person's name or when it is used in direct address in place of a person's name. ■

TITLE:	Professor Scott gave an interesting lecture.
IN PLACE OF A NAME:	Your lecture, Professor, was very interesting.
GENERAL REFERENCE:	My history professor is late.

The titles of government officials may require capitalization in certain cases.

▶ **KEY CONCEPT** Capitalize titles of government officials when they are followed by a proper name or when used in direct address. ■

In the United States, titles such as supervisor, mayor, governor, congressman, congresswoman, senator, judge, and ambassador are used for different government officials. Officials of other countries also have titles. All of these are capitalized when they are used before a proper name or in direct address. General references, however, usually omit the capital.

PRECEDING A PROPER NAME:	Mayor Martin Hanley will speak.
IN DIRECT ADDRESS:	Will you speak tonight, Mayor?
IN A GENERAL REFERENCE:	The mayor works on the budget.

▶ **Critical Viewing** This illustration depicts a former justice of the Supreme Court, Thurgood Marshall. How would you use capitals when writing his name and title? **[Connect]**

▶ **KEY CONCEPT** Capitalize titles of certain high government officials if they refer to the incumbent even when the titles are not followed by a proper name or used in direct address. ■

EXAMPLES: The President returned from his trip early.
He will meet with the Queen of England today.
The Supreme Court of the United States has
eight justices and a Chief Justice.

▶ **KEY CONCEPT** Capitalize important words in compound titles, but not prefixes and suffixes added to the title. ■

EXAMPLES: Lieutenant Governor, ex-Senator Jorgenson

▶ **KEY CONCEPT** Capitalize titles showing family relationships when they refer to a specific person unless they are preceded by a possessive noun or pronoun. ■

EXAMPLES: Did Uncle John find this stone in the cave?
Anne's uncle climbed Mount Everest.

▶ **KEY CONCEPT** Capitalize abbreviations of titles before and after names. ■

The most common abbreviations found before and after names include *Mr., Mrs., Ms., Jr.,* and *Sr.*

EXAMPLES: Mr. Kevin Peterson, Jr.,   Mrs. Ann Sikorski

▶ **Exercise 7** **Using Capitals for Titles of People** Copy the sentences below that need capitals, adding the missing capitals. If a sentence does not need additional capitalization, write *correct*.

1. While exploring northeastern Wyoming in 1875, a team of surveyors led by colonel Richard Dodge discovered an unusual rock formation, which they named Devil's Tower.
2. Several years after its discovery, senator Francis Warren campaigned to protect it.
3. In 1906, president Theodore Roosevelt, jr., designated Devil's Tower as the first national monument.
4. A popular destination for rock climbers, Devil's Tower was first scaled in 1893 by mr. William Rogers and mr. Willard Ripley.
5. In the 1990's, secretary of the interior Bruce Babbitt banned rock climbing at the site during June.

▶ **More Practice**

Grammar Exercise Workbook
• pp. 161–162
On-line Exercise Bank
• Chapter 27
Go on-line:
PHSchool.com
Enter Web Code:
eek-1002

Get instant feedback! Exercise 7 is available on-line or on CD-ROM.

KEY CONCEPT Capitalize the first word and all other key words in the titles of books, periodicals, poems, stories, plays, paintings, and other works of art. ■

BOOK: *Heart of Darkness*
PERIODICAL: *Better Homes and Gardens*
POEM: "Flower in the Crannied Wall"
STORY: "A Visit to Grandmother"
PLAY: *How to Succeed in Business Without Really Trying*
PAINTING: *The Artist's Daughter With a Cat*
SONG: "This Land Is Your Land"

As you look at the preceding examples, there are a number of things to notice. First, articles—the words *a*, *an*, and *the*—are capitalized only when they are the first word of the title. Second, conjunctions and prepositions shorter than four letters are capitalized only when they are the first word in the title. Third, adjectives, nouns, pronouns, verbs, and adverbs are all considered key words and are always capitalized. When capitalizing a subtitle, the same rule is used.

EXAMPLE: *Language: A Reflection of People and Culture*

KEY CONCEPT Capitalize titles of courses when the courses are language courses or when the courses are followed by a number. ■

WITH CAPITALS: Latin II, English, California History 1A
WITHOUT CAPITALS: mathematics, history, home economics

Exercise 8 **Capitalizing Titles of Things** Write the following titles, adding the missing capitals. Underline the titles that are printed in italics.

EXAMPLE: Play: *fiddler on the roof*
ANSWER: <u>Fiddler on the Roof</u>

1. class: psychology 101
2. newspaper: *the new york times*
3. painting: *starry night*
4. statue: *the thinker*
5. story: "the lottery"

More Practice

Grammar Exercise Workbook
• pp. 161–162
On-line Exercise Bank
• Chapter 27
Go on-line:
PHSchool.com
Enter Web Code:
eek-1002

Interactive Textbook

Get instant feedback! Exercise 8 is available on-line or on CD-ROM.

Hands-on Grammar

Capitalization Card

Create a capitalization reference card that you can keep in your notebook, and refer to it any time you are unsure of a capitalization rule. Start by reviewing the chapter and noting all of the different types of items that are capitalized. Then, draw lines on a piece of paper to divide it into squares. Draw as many squares as you need to cover each of the types of items that are capitalized. Use both sides of the card. Categories might include countries, cities, and corporations.

List the categories in alphabetical order in the boxes you've created. Add examples beneath each of the categories. Once you've finished, keep the card you have created in your notebook.

BOOK TITLES All Creatures Great and Small	BUILDING NAMES Space Needle	BUSINESSES Prentice Hall
CITIES Miami, Florida	CLUBS Rotary Club	COUNTRIES England

Find It in Your Reading Look through your history book to find examples of words that fit into the various categories. Then, as you continue reading in various subjects, add other examples you come across.

Find It in Your Writing Consult your capitalization card whenever you are working on a piece of writing and are unsure about a capitalization rule.

Punctuation

MOONLIGHT SONATA

LUDWIG VAN BEETHOVEN

1st Movement
Op. 27, No. 2

Adagio sostenuto
sempre **PP**

Moonlight Sonata
Piano Masterpiece

Instantly custom printed at:

by

a product of

▲ **Critical Viewing**
How is the musical
notation in this piece
like punctuation in a
sentence? **[Compare]**

When Beethoven wrote the "Moonlight Sonata" more than
150 years ago, he included in his music not only the notes he
wanted played but also *how* he wanted them played. Through
the use of accepted music notation, he left precise instructions on the tempo, the mood he wanted to convey, the loud-
ness and softness, and the rests. By following Beethoven's
instructions, today's musicians are able to play that piece
almost exactly as Beethoven played it himself.

Just as a composer must do more than set down notes on
paper, a writer must do more than set down words on paper.
Just as a composer must tell musicians how to play the
music, so a writer must tell readers how the words are to be
read. To give the reader this information, a writer uses a set of
standard marks called *punctuation.*

Diagnostic Test

Directions: Write all answers on a separate sheet of paper.

Skill Check A. Write the following sentences, using proper end marks to punctuate them.

1. Did Beethoven write the "Moonlight Sonata" in 1801
2. Oh Wasn't it called the Piano Sonata No 14
3. It is only sixteen minutes long
4. What a great figure-skating performance was choreographed to that sonata
5. Play the "Moonlight Sonata" on the piano

Skill Check B. Write the following sentences, inserting commas where necessary.

6. When I was in third grade I first heard the song "Moondance."
7. My mother thinks "Blue Moon" "Moon River" and "It's Only a Paper Moon" are better songs.
8. "Obviously when we bought the album" said Larry "we knew there would be many famous songs."
9. I hope the album will arrive in Albany New York before June 21 2001.
10. I wanted to share my favorite song "Shine On Harvest Moon" with them.

Skill Check C. Write the following sentences, inserting colons and semicolons where necessary.

11. Van Gogh painted my two favorite pieces *Starry Night* and *Sunflowers.*
12. *The Night Sky* is not very realistic nevertheless it is beautiful.
13. *The Sleeping Gypsy* is dominated by a few subjects the lion, the gypsy, and the moon.
14. Michelle's birthstone is a diamond Debra's is an opal.
15. Warning If taken internally, consult a physician immediately.

Skill Check D. Write the following sentences, inserting quotation marks where necessary.

16. Have you ever been to the Prado? he asked.
17. It is filled with wonderful Spanish art, he continued.
18. Goya, Velázquez, and El Greco he said are all there.
19. Perhaps you should take me there, I suggested.
20. Have you read The Road Not Taken by Robert Frost?

Skill Check E. Write the following sentences, inserting apostrophes, hyphens, and dashes where necessary.

21. My favorite book growing up I still like to read it every now and then! was *Goodnight Moon.*
22. I scored twenty five points in my last basketball game.
23. Have you ever spent much time with a two year old?
24. It is my oldest sisters favorite movie.
25. Really, I havent seen it yet.

End Marks

Just as every sentence must begin with a capital letter, so it must end with an end mark. The three end marks are the *period* [.], the *question mark* [?], and the *exclamation mark* [!]. These marks clearly indicate to a reader that he or she has arrived at the end of a thought. End marks also indicate the emotion or tone of a sentence. In this section, you will have the opportunity to review the more common uses of end marks and to study some of their other functions.

Basic Uses of End Marks

The period has three basic uses:

▶ **KEY CONCEPT** Use a period to end a declarative sentence, a mild imperative, and an indirect question. ■

A *declarative sentence* is a statement of fact or opinion.

STATEMENT OF FACT: The moon is a satellite of the Earth.
STATEMENT OF OPINION: The moon looks pretty tonight.

An *imperative* gives a direction or command. An imperative often begins with a verb.

MILD IMPERATIVE: Look through the telescope.

Some declarative sentences include an *indirect question*.

DIRECT QUESTION: Is the moon smaller than the Earth?
INDIRECT QUESTION: I asked whether the moon was smaller than the Earth.

◀ **Critical Viewing**
This is a view of the Earth from the moon. Imagine that you are standing on the moon, and write two exclamatory sentences about the view. **[Speculate]**

KEY CONCEPT Use a question mark to end a direct question, an incomplete question, or a statement intended as a question. ■

A *direct question* demands an answer; it stands as a direct request. All direct questions must end with a question mark.

DIRECT QUESTIONS: Did you see the full moon?
                         How far away is the moon?

In some cases, only a portion of the question is written out and the rest is simply understood. When this occurs, place a question mark at the end of the incomplete question.

INCOMPLETE QUESTIONS: Where? What color? How much?

Sometimes, a question is phrased as if it were a declarative sentence. Use a question mark to show that the sentence is a question.

STATEMENTS INTENDED   You saw that?
AS QUESTIONS: The Earth has one satellite?

Because some sentences express a great amount of emotion, another end mark was developed—the exclamation mark.

KEY CONCEPT Use an exclamation mark [!] to end an exclamatory sentence, a forceful imperative sentence, or an interjection expressing strong emotion. ■

An *exclamatory sentence* shows strong emphasis or emotion. Use an exclamation mark at the end of an exclamatory sentence.

EXCLAMATORY SENTENCES: A man landed on the moon!
                         That shuttle cost millions of dollars!

A strongly worded imperative that demonstrates forcefulness or strong emotion will also take an exclamation mark.

STRONG IMPERATIVE: Don't touch those wires!

Strong interjections should also be followed by an exclamation mark.

STRONG INTERJECTIONS: Breathtaking! Ouch! Oh!

Sometimes, a strong interjection may appear before a short exclamatory sentence. If this occurs, you may use either a comma or an exclamation mark after the interjection.

WITH A COMMA: Goodness, that thunder was loud!
WITH AN
EXCLAMATION MARK: Goodness! That thunder was loud!

End Marks • 473

> **Exercise 1** Using the Period, Question Mark, and Exclamation Mark Copy the following items, adding the necessary periods or question marks.

1. The moon's diameter is about one fourth the size of the Earth's
2. Is it true that there is no atmosphere on the moon
3. The moon travels around the Earth at approximately 2,300 miles per hour
4. That is really fast
5. The pull of gravity is only one-sixth that of the Earth's
6. Did you see the footage on television of Neil Armstrong's moon landing
7. You can see only half the moon's entire surface at any one time
8. Is there a new moon tonight
9. Look There's a full moon
10. When the moon is full, it is farther away from the sun than it is when it is a new moon

Other Uses of End Marks

> **KEY CONCEPT** Most abbreviations end with a period. ■

ABBREVIATIONS WITH PERIODS:	Mrs.	Jr.	Ave.	Capt.	Wash.
	M.D.	R.N.	A.M.	ft.	

ABBREVIATIONS WITHOUT PERIODS:	FBI	FL	kg	L

> **KEY CONCEPT** Use a period after numbers and letters in outlines. ■

EXAMPLE:
    I. Our Solar System
      A. Earth
        1. moon
      B. Pluto
        1. Charon

> **Exercise 2** Proofreading for End Marks Proofread the following sentences, inserting end marks where necessary.

1. When I was ten, I was 4 ft 9 in tall
2. Did they arrive at 9:00 A.M. or P.M.
3. Mr Roth is our band teacher
4. We have a holiday in honor of Martin Luther King, Jr
5. Watch out, Capt Reid, that coffee cup is leaking

Learn More

For an abbreviations reference, see Abbreviations on pages 686–689.

Interactive Textbook

Get instant feedback! Exercises 1 and 2 are available on-line or on CD-ROM.

More Practice

Grammar Exercise Workbook
• pp. 163–164
On-line Exercise Bank
• Section 28.1
Go on-line:
PHSchool.com
Enter Web Code:
eek-1002

Section Review

GRAMMAR EXERCISES 3–7

▶ **Exercise 3** Using End Marks Copy all of the following sentences, adding all necessary end marks.

1. Early observers thought that the dark spots on the moon were oceans
2. This is why they are called *mares*, the Latin word for "sea"
3. Are there oceans on the moon
4. No, there are not
5. The moon is so bright tonight
6. There are mountains and craters on the moon
7. The highest ranges have peaks almost as tall as the Himalayas
8. What is the origin of the moon's craters
9. Some craters show signs of being volcanic in origin
10. Most resulted from impacts with meteorites or asteroids

▶ **Exercise 4** Proofreading to Correct End Marks On a separate sheet of paper, copy the following passage. Proofread the passage, correcting and adding end marks as needed.

In the mid-twentieth century, people began to travel in space On April 12, 1961, a cosmonaut from the USSR made a single orbit around the Earth Alan B Shepherd completed a 300-mile flight, but John H Glenn, Jr was the first person from the United States to orbit the Earth. Glenn orbited the Earth on Feb 20, 1962 Wow That must have been a thrill

Since then, many spaceflights have been launched from the John F Kennedy Space Center in Florida Who would have believed how far the technology would advance. Today, astronauts from the United States and cosmonauts from the former Soviet Union often work together on research Have you ever seen a picture of the space station in which they work It's quite a feat of engineering

▶ **Exercise 5** Find It in Your Reading
Read the following from "Leiningen Versus the Ants." Tell why you think the writer uses an exclamation mark.

The Brazilian rose heavily to his feet. "I've done my best," he gasped. "Your obstinacy endangers not only yourself, but the lives of your four hundred workers. You don't know these ants!"

▶ **Exercise 6** Find It in Your Writing
Look through your portfolio. Find examples of sentences that you have ended with a period, a question mark, or an exclamation mark. Explain why you used each mark.

▶ **Exercise 7** Writing Application
Write sentences of your own using the following directions.

1. Write a question about schoolwork, and then rephrase it as an indirect question.
2. Write a declarative sentence about something you like.
3. Rewrite your declarative sentence so that it can end with an exclamation mark.
4. Write a strong imperative you have heard from your teacher.
5. Write a statement intended as a question to get information from a friend about a book he or she has read.

Commas

The comma [,] tells the reader to take a short pause before continuing the sentence.

The comma is used more than any other internal punctuation mark. As a result, many errors are made in its use. This section presents rules to help you use the comma correctly— to separate basic elements and to set off added elements in sentences.

Commas With Compound Sentences

A compound sentence is two or more independent clauses joined by one of the following coordinating conjunctions: *and, but, for, nor, or, so,* or *yet.* A comma is needed to separate the independent clauses.

> **KEY CONCEPT** Use a comma before the conjunction to separate two independent clauses in a compound sentence. ■

Always check to make sure that you have written two complete sentences joined by a coordinating conjunction before you insert a comma.

EXAMPLES: We read about Mexico, and then we wrote our report on it.

Storm clouds were gathering overhead, so we brought the lawn chairs inside.

The most common error that writers make with this rule is to insert a comma automatically when they see a conjunction. Remember, however, that coordinating conjunctions can also join compound subjects, compound verbs, prepositional phrases, and clauses. When they are used in one of these ways, no comma is required.

COMPOUND SUBJECT:	The parents and the teachers meet tonight.
COMPOUND VERB:	Tourists swim and play sports when they visit Mexico.
TWO PREPOSITIONAL PHRASES:	I hit the golf ball into the water and then into a sand trap.
TWO SUBORDINATE CLAUSES:	My brothers enjoy books only if they are relatively short and only if they offer a lot of action.

Theme: Mexico
In this section, you will learn about the various uses of commas. The examples and exercises are about Mexico.

Cross-Curricular Connection: Social Studies

Exercise 8 Using Commas in Compound Sentences If a comma is needed in one of the following sentences, write the word before the comma, the comma, and the conjunction following the comma. If no comma is needed, write *correct.*

EXAMPLE: I practice my Spanish daily but I still make
             mistakes.
ANSWER: daily, but

1. Mexico's full name is the United Mexican States and it is known as *Estados Unidos Mexicanos* in Spanish.
2. The capital is Mexico City and it is also Mexico's largest city.
3. The United States is to Mexico's north and Belize and Guatemala are to its south.
4. The Tropic of Cancer goes through Mexico so the area to the south can be extremely hot.
5. In parts of the country, the temperature can go as high as 120 degrees Fahrenheit yet as low as 32 degrees Fahrenheit.
6. Some southern parts of Mexico can receive up to sixty inches of rain a year but most of the country is much drier.
7. It is hotter in Monterey than in Mexico City but not much hotter.
8. The wide temperature range gives Mexico an extremely varied plant life but rainfall affects it, too.
9. The north is desertlike but cacti grow there and yucca and mesquite as well.
10. Wolves are found in the north and in the mountain forests, along with bears and jaguars.

More Practice

Grammar Exercise Workbook
• pp. 165–170
On-line Exercise Bank
• Section 28.2
  Go on-line:
  PHSchool.com
  Enter Web Code:
  eek-1002

interactive **Textbook**

Get instant feedback! Exercise 8 is available on-line or on CD-ROM.

◀ Critical Viewing
Make a statement about the contrast between rural and urban areas of Mexico. Use two independent clauses. Identify where you would place the comma. Then, revise the sentence so that a comma is not required. **[Analyze]**

Commas With Series and Adjectives

Series Whenever a series of words, phrases, or clauses occurs in a sentence, you will need to insert commas.

> ▶ **KEY CONCEPT** Use commas to separate three or more words, phrases, or clauses in a series. ■

WORDS:	I read the articles, extracts, and books for my final exam.
PREPOSITIONAL PHRASES:	Mexico had been ruled by the Spanish, by the Mexicans, and by the French.
CLAUSES:	The bank filled quickly with people who transferred their accounts, who cashed checks, and who opened safe-deposit boxes.

Some writers omit the last comma in a series. This is permissible as long as the writer follows a consistent pattern. In your own work, however, you will find that the full use of commas generally works better. This is especially true in those cases where the last comma is needed to prevent confusion.

CONFUSING:	Streams of people, honking geese and souvenir vendors swarmed outside the hotel.
ALWAYS CLEAR:	Streams of people, honking geese, and souvenir vendors swarmed outside the hotel.

Commas are not needed when all the items in a series have already been separated by conjunctions (usually *and* or *or*).

EXAMPLE:	I cut and chopped and diced onions until I cried.

Commas should also be avoided within pairs of items that are used together so frequently that they are thought of as a single item. Notice in the following example that commas separate the pairs but not the items in the pairs.

EXAMPLE:	I asked for ham and eggs, coffee and cream, and bread and butter.

Grammar and Style Tip

When showing a contrast, use opposing series of adjectives to create parallel structure.

GRAMMAR IN LITERATURE

from **Morte d'Arthur**
Alfred, Lord Tennyson

In the following passage, commas are used to separate the names of guests at a Christmas celebration listed as items in a series.

> At Francis Allen's on the Christmas eve—
> The game of forfeits done—the girls all kissed
> Beneath the sacred bush and passed away—
> The parson Holmes, the poet Everard Hall,
> The host, and I sat round the wassail bowl, . . .

Adjectives Use commas to divide adjectives of equal rank. Such adjectives are called *coordinate adjectives*.

> **KEY CONCEPT** Use commas to separate **coordinate adjectives**—adjectives of equal rank. ■

To determine whether adjectives in a sentence are of equal rank, ask yourself two questions: First, can you put an *and* between the adjectives and still have the sentence retain its exact meaning? Second, can you switch the adjectives and still have a sentence that sounds grammatically correct? If the answer to the two test questions is yes, you have adjectives of equal rank and a comma should be placed between them.

EXAMPLES: The country's wild, beautiful scenery is an attraction for tourists.

She left detailed, precise instructions for the substitute.

In these examples, *wild* and *beautiful* and *detailed* and *precise* qualify as coordinate adjectives.

> **KEY CONCEPT** Do not use commas to separate **cumulative adjectives**—adjectives that must stay in a specific order. ■

EXAMPLES: Colonial Mexico had rigid social classes.

In a few short hours, we will be finished.

Try putting an *and* between these adjectives or changing their order. The sentences do not make sense. These adjectives must stay in the order in which they are written. Therefore, no comma is used to separate them.

28.2

Exercise 9 Separating Items in a Series Copy each sentence that needs commas, adding the necessary commas. For sentences that need no commas, write *correct*.

EXAMPLE: Mexican cooking uses tomatoes chilies and lots of spices.

ANSWER: Mexican cooking uses tomatoes, chilies, and lots of spices.

1. Reptiles found in Mexico include turtles iguanas rattlesnakes and lizards.
2. Both sea and game birds are numerous.
3. Corn cotton fruits wheat beans coffee tomatoes and rice are grown in Mexico.
4. Natural resources in Mexico include petroleum silver copper gold lead and zinc.
5. Plant and animal life vary with climatic zone altitude and precipitation.
6. Mexican culture is a mixture of Native American North American and Spanish influences.
7. Native American groups included the Maya the Aztec and the Toltec.
8. Evidence suggests that a hunting people existed in 13,000 B.C. that crop cultivation developed around 8000 B.C. and that the first major civilization in Mexico was the Olmec.
9. The Aztecs reached the height of their power by the fifteenth century and were intellectually and artistically advanced.
10. The Spaniards heard of the Aztecs' wealth wanted to take their gold and sent a large invading army in 1519.

Exercise 10 Using Commas With Adjectives For each of the following phrases, write *cumulative* if the adjectives are cumulative and require no comma. If the adjectives are equal in rank, write the adjectives, inserting the comma.

EXAMPLE: a vivid beautiful scene

ANSWER: a vivid, beautiful scene

1. spicy hot food
2. several distinct cultural groups
3. rigid social classes
4. hot humid climate
5. earliest advanced civilizations
6. small native minority
7. bleak arid landscape
8. rich complex history
9. varied native fauna
10. distinctive regional character

More Practice

Grammar Exercise Workbook
• pp. 165–166
On-line Exercise Bank
• Section 28.2
  Go on-line:
  PHSchool.com
  Enter Web Code:
  eek-1002

*i*nteractive Textbook

Get instant feedback! Exercises 9, 10, and 11 are available on-line or on CD-ROM.

Commas After Introductory Material

> **KEY CONCEPT** Use a comma after an introductory word, phrase, or clause. ■

KINDS OF INTRODUCTORY MATERIAL		
Words	Introductory Words	No, I will not go to Mexico with you.
	Nouns of Direct Address	Cindy, could you hold this picture of Mexico?
	Common Expressions	Of course, we can get that printed for you.
	Introductory Adverbs	Obviously, the student had tried. Hurriedly, she hid the present she had wrapped.
Phrases	Prepositional Phrases	In the deep recesses of the couch, I found the watch I had lost.
	Participial Phrases	Jumping over the fence, the horse caught its back hoof.
	Infinitive Phrases	To get to the appointment on time, the man left early.
Clauses	Adverb Clauses	When the steaks were medium rare, we took them off the grill.

> **Exercise 11** Proofreading for Commas After Introductory Material Copy the following passage on a separate sheet of paper. Add commas after introductory material as needed.

When the Spaniards decided to conquer Mexico they appointed Hernán Cortés to lead the army. Soon after landing in Mexico Cortés found someone who could speak Aztec. Having learned of discord in the Aztec Empire Cortés convinced some natives to join him. At the time that all of this was happening Montezuma was the leader of the Aztec Empire. During his march to the Aztec capital Cortés was in communication with Montezuma. Reaching the capital in November of 1519 Cortés took Montezuma hostage. In the following year Cortés had to return to the coast of Mexico. In his absence his deputy mistreated and killed many Aztecs. After Cortés returned from the coast a battle was fought in which Montezuma was killed. Taking the capital in 1521 the Spaniards ultimately ended Aztec power.

> **More Practice**
>
> Grammar Exercise Workbook
> • pp. 167–168
> On-line Exercise Bank
> • Section 28.2
> *Go on-line:*
> PHSchool.com
> *Enter Web Code:*
> eek-1002

Commas With Parenthetical and Nonessential Expressions

Commas are often used within a sentence to set off parenthetical and nonessential expressions.

Parenthetical Expressions A parenthetical expression is a word or phrase that interrupts the general flow of a sentence. Study the following list of common parenthetical expressions.

NOUN OF DIRECT ADDRESS:	Don, Mrs. Burke, my son, sweetheart
CONJUNCTIVE ADVERBS:	also, besides, furthermore, however, indeed, instead, moreover, nevertheless, otherwise, therefore, thus
COMMON EXPRESSIONS:	by the way, I feel, in my opinion, in the first place, of course, on the other hand,
CONTRASTING EXPRESSIONS:	not that one, not there, not mine

▲ **Critical Viewing**
In a sentence about the condition of these ruins, include a parenthetical comment about the grass. [**Describe**]

 KEY CONCEPT Use commas to set off parenthetical expressions. ■

Two commas are used to enclose the entire parenthetical expression when the expression is located in the middle of the sentence.

NOUN OF DIRECT ADDRESS:	We will go, Marge, as soon as your father arrives.
CONJUNCTIVE ADVERB:	The boys, therefore, decided to go to Acapulco.
COMMON EXPRESSION:	The flowers, in my opinion, have never looked healthier.
CONTRASTING EXPRESSIONS:	It was here, not there, that we found the answer.

If one of these expressions is used at the end of the sentence, however, only one comma is necessary.

EXAMPLE: We will go as soon as your father arrives, Marge.

Essential and Nonessential Expressions Because commas are used only with nonessential expressions, writers must learn to distinguish between essential and nonessential material. (The terms *restrictive* and *nonrestrictive* are some-times used to refer to the same types of expressions.)

An *essential* expression is a word, phrase, or clause that provides essential information in a sentence: information that cannot be removed without changing the meaning of the sentence. In the following example, the clause following *boy* tells *which* boy the writer means. Thus, it provides essential information in the sentence.

KEY CONCEPT Do not use commas to set off essential expressions. ■

EXAMPLES: The boy who is holding the book is going to Mexico.

The famous dramatist Ben Jonson wrote these comedies.

Because the clauses in the sentences above are essential expressions, they are not set off with commas.

Nonessential expressions provide additional, but not essen-tial, information in a sentence. If you remove nonessential material from a sentence, the remaining sentence will still contain all the necessary information required by the reader.

EXAMPLES: Joe Warren, who is holding the book, is going to Mexico.

Ben Jonson, a famous dramatist, wrote these comedies.

In the first example, the boy is specifically named, and the information contained in the clause provides only an addition-al fact. Thus, this clause is nonessential.

Once you have decided whether or not an expression is essential, you can apply this rule:

KEY CONCEPT Use commas to set off nonessential expressions. ■

When applying this rule, be alert for three types of word groups: appositives, participial phrases, and adjective clauses. They often serve as either essential or nonessential expres-sions. Check them carefully to avoid committing comma errors. Study the chart on the next page until you feel confi-dent that you can tell the difference between essential expres-sions and nonessential expressions.

(?) **Learn More**

To learn more about essential and nonessential expressions, see Chapter 20.

ESSENTIAL AND NONESSENTIAL EXPRESSIONS		
Appositive	Essential	My friend Joanne went to the University of Indiana.
	Nonessential	Joanne, my friend, went to the University of Indiana.
Participial Phrase	Essential	The teacher wearing a blue dress took the students on the field trip.
	Nonessential	Mrs. Goff, wearing the blue dress, took the students on the field trip.
Adjective Clause	Essential	The hotel that we enjoyed the most had three swimming pools and lighted tennis courts.
	Nonessential	The Royal Tahitian Hotel, which was our favorite, had three swimming pools and lighted tennis courts.

▶ **Exercise 12** Setting Off Parenthetical Expressions

Copy each of the following sentences, inserting any commas necessary to set off parenthetical expressions. If no change is necessary, write *correct*.

EXAMPLE: The Spanish conquest of Mexico was in fact quite complex.

ANSWER: The Spanish conquest of Mexico was, in fact, quite complex.

1. The first Spanish viceroy of Mexico Antonio de Mendoza was appointed in 1535.
2. This appointment it appears established a Spanish colonial government in Mexico for almost three hundred years.
3. Moreover the Spaniards had sixty-one viceroys in Mexico.
4. Mexico you know was called New Spain then.
5. A series of expeditions adding land to Spain's territory increased the power of Spain in the Americas.
6. New Spain included present-day Texas and New Mexico and California.
7. The viceregal system was not in fact always a fair one.
8. Native Americans who were supposed to be free were treated like slaves.
9. The most powerful institution in colonial Mexico was in all probability the Roman Catholic Church.
10. The people who occupied positions of power were from the Spanish-born minority who enjoyed power out of proportion to their numbers.

▶ **More Practice**

Grammar Exercise Workbook
• pp. 167–168
On-line Exercise Bank
• Section 28.2
Go on-line:
PHSchool.com
Enter Web Code:
eek-1002

Get instant feedback! Exercises 12 and 13 are available on-line or on CD-ROM.

▶ **Exercise 13** Distinguishing Between Essential and Nonessential Expressions If one of the following sentences contains an essential expression needing no additional commas, write *essential*. If the sentence contains a nonessential expression, copy the sentence and add the necessary commas.

EXAMPLE: Those who tried to institute reforms sometimes succeeded but more often failed.

ANSWER: essential

(1) Spain attempted reforms which proved largely ineffectual to help the condition of Native Americans. (2) Their failure due to the fact that distance made enforcement difficult kept the Native Americans in misery. (3) The inefficiency and corruption that were so prevalent in the colonial government greatly disturbed Spain. (4) Spain tried reforms in the eighteenth century that could not eliminate the problem. (5) Resentment of the Mexican-born population which was inflamed by European ideas of freedom continued to grow. (6) The most immediate and perhaps most important cause of the Mexican War for Independence was the occupation of Spain by Napoleon. (7) Independence which took more than ten years to achieve was formally proclaimed in August 1821. (8) Peace long missing in Mexico did not last long. (9) Mexico a country that was not used to democracy continued to have problems. (10) Antonio Lopez de Santa Anna who was elected president in 1833 was to have an impact on both Mexico and the United States.

GRAMMAR IN LITERATURE

from **Arthur Becomes King of Britain**

T. H. White

In the following sentence, notice that the phrase which he did not read *is nonessential and the phrase* on the pommel *is essential. The writer sets off the nonessential phrase (highlighted in blue italics) with commas.*

He saw the golden letters, *which he did not read,* and the jewels on the pommel, flashing in the lovely light.

Other Uses of the Comma

Commas are used in the following situations:

With Locations Whenever you are citing a specific place, check to see whether a comma is required.

> **KEY CONCEPT** When a geographical name is made up of two or more parts, use a comma after each item. ■

EXAMPLES: I traveled from Taos, New Mexico, to Tijuana, Mexico.
This cheese was shipped from Montigny, Moselle, France, by my friend Robert.

With Dates Dates containing numbers require commas.

> **KEY CONCEPT** When a date is made up of two or more parts, use a comma after each item except in the case of a month followed by a day or a month followed by a year. ■

EXAMPLES: On Friday, April 17, we will have a special meeting.
We will discuss the class trip to Monterey on November 11, 2001.
February 1980 was one of the wettest months on record.

If the parts of a date have already been joined by prepositions, no comma is needed.

EXAMPLE: The city's new mass-transit system ran its first train on June 11 of 1974.

With Titles Use a comma with titles that follow a name.

> **KEY CONCEPT** When a name is followed by one or more titles, use a comma after the name and after each title. ■

EXAMPLE: I noticed that Jeremy McGuire, Sr., is a partner in this firm.

A similar rule applies with some business abbreviations:

EXAMPLE: She worked for Heller and Ramirez, Inc., for a year.

With Addresses Addresses consisting of two or more parts need commas to separate the parts.

KEY CONCEPT Use a comma after each item in an address made up of two or more parts. ■

EXAMPLE: Katie Wedel's new address is 160 11th Street, Anytown, Missouri 63131.

If this address were on an envelope, most of the commas would be omitted.

```
Mahoney
260 Broadway                    ┌──────┐
Anytown, NY 10960               │ stamp │
                                └──────┘

              Katie Wedel
              160 11th Street
              Anytown, MO 63131
```

Avoid using commas if prepositions join parts of an address.

EXAMPLE: Katie Wedel lives on 11th Street in Anytown.

With Salutations and Closings You will need to use commas in the openings and closings of many letters.

KEY CONCEPT Use a comma after the salutation in a personal letter and after the closing in all letters. ■

SALUTATIONS: Dear Rupert,   Dear Aunt Dolly,
CLOSINGS: Sincerely,   In appreciation,

▶ Critical Viewing What punctuation is used on this sign? In what situation would a comma be required with this street name? **[Apply]**

With Numbers Certain numbers also need commas.

▶ **KEY CONCEPT** With numbers of more than three digits, use a comma after every third digit from the right. ■

Learn More

For a more detailed explanation of punctuating quotations, see Section 28.4.

EXAMPLES: The projected complex would house 1,245 people.
             The company has sold 498,362,719 jelly beans.

There are several exceptions to this rule: ZIP Codes, phone numbers, page numbers, serial numbers, years, and house numbers do not have commas.

ZIP CODE:	26413
TELEPHONE NUMBER:	(612) 555-3702
PAGE NUMBER:	page 1047
HOUSE NUMBER:	18364 Lamson Road
SERIAL NUMBER:	173 55 2007

With Omissions Sometimes, you will purposely omit a word or phrase from a sentence; this omission results in an elliptical sentence. For clarity, you should insert a comma where the words have been left out.

▶ **KEY CONCEPT** Use a comma to indicate the words left out of an elliptical sentence. ■

In the following example, the omitted word is clearly understood. The comma serves as a visual clue to the reader that an omission exists.

EXAMPLE: The man walked quickly and the woman, slowly.

With Direct Quotations Commas also set off direct quotations.

▶ **KEY CONCEPT** Use commas to set off a direct quotation from the rest of the sentence. ■

EXAMPLES: The guest asked, "Do you know of any nearby grocery stores that are open all night?"
             "If you don't mind a little drive," the host said, "you will find one about three miles down the road."
             "Oh, that will be perfect," the guest replied.

For Clarity You will occasionally run across a sentence structure that may be confusing without a comma. By inserting a comma, you can reduce the confusion and prevent misreading.

▶ **KEY CONCEPT** Use a comma to prevent a sentence from being misunderstood. ■

UNCLEAR:	She studied French and Mayan art.
CLEAR:	She studied French, as well as Mayan art.

Note About the *Careless Use of Commas:* Generally, you should not use a comma unless you have a rule clearly in mind. Study the following examples of the careless overuse of commas, and avoid such use in your own writing.

MISUSED WITH ADJECTIVE AND NOUN:	The Mexican, Aztecs came from farther north.
CORRECT:	The Mexican Aztecs came from farther north.
MISUSED WITH COMPOUND SUBJECT:	We watched as the man, and woman executed some fancy dance steps.
CORRECT:	We watched as the man and woman executed some fancy dance steps.
MISUSED WITH COMPOUND VERBS:	The dancers leaped, and twirled around the stage.
CORRECT:	The dancers leaped and twirled around the stage.
MISUSED WITH PREPOSITIONAL PHRASES:	The dancers bowed to the audience, and to the conductor.
CORRECT:	The dancers bowed to the audience and to the conductor.
MISUSED WITH SUBORDINATE CLAUSES:	I won't forget that you gave me the ticket, and that I thoroughly enjoyed the performance.
CORRECT:	I won't forget that you gave me the ticket and that I thoroughly the performance.

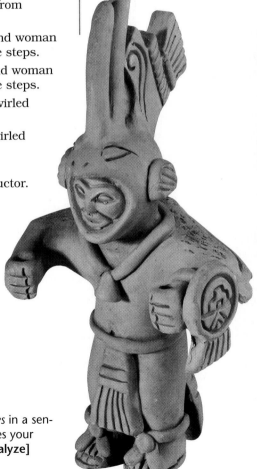

▶ **Critical Viewing** Use the verbs *wears* and *dances* in a sentence about this sculpture of an Aztec warrior. Does your sentence require a comma? Why or why not? **[Analyze]**

Exercise 14 Using Commas in Other Situations Copy the following sentences, adding the necessary commas.

1. On April 21 1836 the Mexicans were defeated by Texans.
2. The Texans' victory occurred at San Jacinto Texas.
3. America had territorial ambitions in Texas and California so in 1846 they declared war on Mexico.
4. United States troops occupied northern Mexico and in 1847 Mexico City.
5. In February of 1848 a large part of Mexican territory became part of the United States.
6. This loss occurred on February 2 1848.
7. "Santa Anna" according to the encyclopedia "was compelled to resign after the war."
8. Again Mexico suffered internal dissension and in 1854 a revolution.
9. June 1863 saw French troops reach Mexico and cause the current government officials to flee.
10. Porfirio Díaz a general was dictator of Mexico from 1877 to 1911.

Exercise 15 Correcting the Careless Use of Commas
Some of the commas have been used incorrectly in the following sentences. Rewrite each sentence, removing any incorrect commas. Write *correct* if the sentence requires no additions or alterations.

EXAMPLE: I knew that I was right, and that Chichén Itzá was Mayan.

ANSWER: I knew that I was right and that Chichén Itzá was Mayan.

1. Díaz led a rebellion in 1871, and in 1877, to become leader of Mexico.
2. He fought, and struggled to gain power.
3. He rebelled against President Juárez, and against his successor, Tejada.
4. After ruling for over thirty years, he lost power to Francisco Madero.
5. Emiliano Zapata, and Pancho Villa refused to recognize Madero's authority.
6. Madero's assassination, rival leaders, and foreign intervention all contributed to turmoil in Mexico.
7. Finally, things began to improve in the twenties.
8. Mexico, and the United States, began to work more closely.
9. Leaders searched for ways to improve Mexico's economic prosperity, and the prosperity of all its citizens.
10. The country, like all countries, still has problems, but it is struggling to solve them.

More Practice

Grammar Exercise Workbook
• pp. 169–170
On-line Exercise Bank
• Section 28.2
  Go on-line:
  PHSchool.com
  Enter Web Code:
  eek-1002

Get instant feedback!
Exercises 14 and 15 are available on-line or on CD-ROM.

Section 28.2 Section Review

GRAMMAR EXERCISES 16–24

Exercise 16 Using Commas in Compound Sentences If a comma is needed in one of these sentences, write the word before the comma, the comma, and the word after the comma. If no comma is needed, write *correct.*

1. Mexico is a federal republic and it has jurisdiction over several islands.
2. The Sierra Madre contains the highest peaks in Mexico and it is a volcanic range.
3. Mexico is not exempt from earthquakes nor are they always mild.
4. A serious earthquake struck and killed more that 7,000 people in 1985.
5. The country is also prone to hurricanes and these can be quite devastating.

Exercise 17 Separating Items in a Series Copy each sentence that needs commas, inserting them as required. If no comma is needed, write *correct.*

1. Mexico can be roughly divided into the *tierra caliente tierra templada* and *tierra fría.*
2. In English, this means "the hot land" "the temperate land" and "the cold land."
3. The climate is governed by latitude and elevation.
4. The country includes coastal plains a central plateau and volcanic peaks.
5. Some of Mexico's rivers are the Grijalva the Usumacinta and the Conchos.

Exercise 18 Proofreading for Commas With Series, Adjectives, and Introductory Material Copy the following passage on a separate sheet of paper. Add or delete commas as needed.

When people think of Mexico today they think of its tourist attractions. These attractions include ancient ruins beautiful beaches rural villages and exciting urban areas. Obviously there is much to see in Mexico.

In order to reach Acapulco you must travel quite far south. Historically it is both a good harbor port and a tourist resort. Tourists flock to Acapulco to relax to enjoy the sun and to visit the interesting historical sites.

Exercise 19 Setting Off Parenthetical Expressions Copy each of the following sentences, inserting commas as necessary.

1. Mexico City the capital is also the cultural center of the country.
2. Octavio Paz a Mexican writer won the prestigious Nobel Prize for Literature in 1990.
3. Mayans and Aztecs in fact were highly advanced in art and science.
4. Mayans it is said excelled at painting and sculpture.
5. Mexican folk arts such as weaving and pottery are world renowned.

Exercise 20 Distinguishing Between Essential and Nonessential Expressions If a sentence contains an essential expression needing no commas, write *essential.* If it contains a nonessential expression, insert the commas where needed.

1. Mexico City is home to several museums that display the country's past.
2. The National Museum of Anthropology which is in Mexico City is devoted to Mayan and other artifacts.
3. The museum that is in Chapultepec Castle is concerned with Mexico's history since the Spanish conquest.

4. Another museum that has an important archaeological collection is in Yucatan.
5. Mexico is a country whose cultural glory is not all in the past.
6. Some Mexican actors who have achieved world fame are Cantinflas and Dolores Del Rio.
7. Architecture so popular with Native Americans is still a flourishing art.
8. A group of dancers that specializes in Mexican folk dances tours the world.
9. Some folk dances which predate the Spanish conquest still survive today.
10. Mexico where sports are popular has hosted the Olympic Games and the World Cup.

▶ **Exercise 21** Other Uses of Commas Remove incorrectly used commas or add them where necessary.

1. Mexico's area is approximately 756066 square miles.
2. I told my pen pal that my address is 23 Deer Park Lane Omaha Nebraska 27103.
3. She said "I will write to you very soon."
4. He studied Aztec, and Mayan culture.
5. Spanish, and other languages, are spoken in Mexico.
6. Some of Mexico's peaks are almost 19000 feet high.
7. Mayans were famous for their architecture and for their sculpture.
8. Europeans are the smallest minorities in Mexico.
9. Mexico, and the United States share a common border.
10. He is going to Acapulco Mexico for his vacation this year.

▶ **Exercise 22** Find It in Your Reading Explain the reason for each of the commas in the following excerpt from "Work That Counts" by Ernesto Ruelas Inzunza.

. . . At eight this morning, as Jeros and I climbed the observation tower, about forty-five Swainson's hawks were just taking off from the nearby canyon where they had spent the night. Shortly afterward, we saw hundreds of them turning circles in the thermal columns of hot air, effortlessly gaining altitude. By eleven, the Swainson's had joined smaller numbers of broad-winged hawks and turkey vultures, forming long streams of migrants. Such large flocks, totaling more than 20,000 birds at times, can take up to thirty minutes to pass overhead. Resembling myriad moving organisms in a plankton sample, the raptors filled our binoculars' field of view. We watched the avian river continue north until it disappeared.

▶ **Exercise 23** Find It in Your Writing In your portfolio, look for examples of cumulative and coordinate adjectives. Make sure that you have used commas correctly in each example.

▶ **Exercise 24** Writing Application Write five sentences of your own using the following instructions.

1. Use at least three adjectives to describe your best friend.
2. Write a compound sentence with two independent clauses, each containing information about a place you would like to visit.
3. Write a sentence listing at least three things you like about the place where you live.
4. Write your address as it would appear on an envelope and in a sentence.
5. Write a sentence about a movie you have seen in which a character uses the expression *by the way*.

Section 28.3

Semicolons and Colons

The semicolon [;] is a punctuation mark that serves as the happy medium between the comma and the period. It signals the reader to pause longer than for a comma but to pause without the finality of a period. The colon [:] is used primarily to point ahead to additional information. It directs the reader to look farther.

The first part of this section will cover the rules that govern the use of semicolons. The second part will present the ways in which you can use colons.

Using the Semicolon

The semicolon is used to separate independent clauses that have a close relationship to each other. A semicolon is also used to separate independent clauses or items in a series that already contain a number of commas.

Using the Semicolon With Independent Clauses
Semicolons are most often used between independent clauses.

▷ **KEY CONCEPT** Use a *semicolon* to join independent clauses that are not already joined by the conjunction *and, but, for, nor, or, so,* or *yet.* ∎

Two sentences joined by a conjunction need a comma before the conjunction.

EXAMPLE: My mother works in a school, but she does not teach.

Because the semicolon is stronger than the comma, it replaces both the comma and the conjunction. Notice in the following example that the second independent clause of two clauses joined by a semicolon starts with a lowercase letter. Do not use a capital following a semicolon unless the word following a semicolon would call for a capital in any position.

EXAMPLE: My mother works in a school; she does not teach.

Do not use a semicolon to join unrelated independent clauses. Use a semicolon to join only those that are closely related.

INCORRECT: My aunt and uncle have five children; it will snow today.

CORRECT: My aunt and uncle have five children; they have two boys and three girls.

Theme: Friends and Relations
In this section, you will learn about semicolons and colons. The examples and exercises are about friends, relatives, neighbors, and acquaintances.
Cross-Curricular Connection: Social Studies

Sometimes, the independent clauses will share a similar structure as well as a similar meaning.

EXAMPLE: Before today, my uncle was out of work; tomorrow, he starts a new job.

Notice that both sentences center around a shared subject—work. The sentences are also similar to each other in structure. This is a situation in which to use a semicolon.

Occasionally, independent clauses may set up a contrast:

EXAMPLE: My sister excels at art; I can barely draw a straight line.

So far, the discussion has concentrated on using a semicolon to join two independent clauses. However, if there are more than two independent clauses, you can still use semicolons:

EXAMPLE: Joe's grandparents were not born in this country; they emigrated here from Italy; they settled comfortably in Boston.

Independent clauses also need a semicolon when they are joined by a conjunctive adverb or a transitional expression.

KEY CONCEPT Use a semicolon to join independent clauses separated by either a conjunctive adverb or a transitional expression. ■

Conjunctive adverbs are adverbs used as conjunctions to connect independent clauses. Common conjunctive adverbs are *accordingly, also, besides, consequently, furthermore, however, indeed, instead, namely, nevertheless, otherwise, similarly, therefore,* and *thus.* Transitional expressions are expressions that connect one independent clause with another. Transitional expressions include *as a result, at this time, first, for instance, in fact, on the other hand, second,* and *that is.*

CONJUNCTIVE ADVERB: A cloudless blue sky dawned that morning; nevertheless, rain was expected.

TRANSITIONAL EXPRESSION: We needed to fit the whole family around the dinner table; as a result, Dad pulled out the extra leaf.

Because words used as conjunctive adverbs and transitions can also interrupt one continuous sentence, use a semicolon only when there is an independent clause on each side of the conjunctive adverb or transitional expression.

INCORRECT: The team was; consequently, disqualified.
CORRECT: The team was, consequently, disqualified.

Using the Semicolon to Avoid Confusion The semicolon can also be used to avoid confusion in sentences that contain other internal punctuation; for example, two independent clauses that contain their own internal punctuation.

▶ **KEY CONCEPT** Use semicolons to avoid confusion when independent clauses already contain commas. ■

When a sentence consists of two independent clauses joined by a coordinating conjunction, the tendency is to place a comma before the conjunction. However, when one or both of the sentences also contain commas, a semicolon may be used before the conjunction to prevent confusion.

EXAMPLE: My cousins borrowed my favorite album, a recording of a jazz concert; but they returned it safely.

The semicolon also helps avoid confusion in a series of items containing their own internal punctuation. A series generally has several items separated only by commas.

▼ **Critical Viewing** Do you think the boys in the picture are friends or relatives? Explain your answer. **[Speculate]**

Snap the Whip, Winslow Homer

▶ **KEY CONCEPT** Use a semicolon between items in a series if the items themselves contain commas. ■

EXAMPLE: We visited the Averills, who live in Wisconsin; the Wilsons, friends in Michigan; and the Garcias, former neighbors now living in North Dakota.

You will use the semicolon in a series most commonly when the items contain either nonessential appositives, participial phrases, or adjective clauses.

APPOSITIVES: I sent notes to Mr. Nielson, my science teacher; Mrs. Jensen, my history instructor; and Mrs. Seltz, my coach.

PARTICIPIAL PHRASES: I developed a terrible headache from listening to my cat, meowing at the door; my dog, howling at the neighbors; and my sister, babbling on the phone.

ADJECTIVE CLAUSES: The car that I bought has spare tires, which are brand new; a stereo, which has just been installed; and a great engine, which has been newly tuned.

Notice that commas are used to separate the nonessential material from the word or words to which they refer or that they modify. The semicolons separate the complete items in the series.

▶ **Exercise 25** Using the Semicolon With Independent Clauses Decide where a semicolon is needed in each of the following sentences. Write the word that goes before the semicolon, the semicolon, and the word that goes after it.

EXAMPLE: I once had a red yo-yo my sister had a green one.
ANSWER: yo-yo; my

1. Genealogy is the history of the descent of a family from an ancestor the family tree gives information about the family.
2. The earliest known ancestor is placed at the top of a family tree direct descent can be traced easily.
3. Genealogy is a very popular pastime it can also be a challenging profession.
4. Genealogy is useful in the validation of wills it can ensure the fair distribution of property if a dispute occurs.
5. One practical use of genealogy is found in the medical field physicians can search genealogical records for family histories of unusual diseases.

▶ **More Practice**

Grammar Exercise Workbook
• pp. 171–172
On-line Exercise Bank
• Section 28.3
   Go on-line:
   PHSchool.com
   Enter Web Code:
   eek-1002

Get instant feedback! Exercises 25 and 26 are available on-line or on CD-ROM.

GRAMMAR IN
LITERATURE

from **A Connecticut Yankee in King Arthur's Court**
Mark Twain

Twain uses a semicolon before the conjunction to avoid confusion. Because this sentence contains two independent clauses with internal punctuation,

You shall remain king over all your dominions, and receive all the glories and honors that belong to the kingship; but you shall appoint me your perpetual minister and executive, and give me for my services one percent of such actual increase of revenue over and above its present amount as I may succeed in creating for the state.

▼ Critical Viewing How do semicolons prevent words from becoming as jumbled as these birthday candles? **[Connect]**

▶ **Exercise 26** Using Semicolons With Internal Punctuation

Copy each sentence, adding semicolons where they are needed to avoid confusion. Also, add necessary commas.

EXAMPLE: For my mother's birthday I baked cookies which were made with raisins muffins which were made with dates and a cake.

ANSWER: For my mother's birthday, I baked cookies, which were made with raisins; muffins, which were made with dates; and a cake.

1. Jane heard loud poorly played piano music the shouts of her sisters Mary Tina and Carol and the television announcer's voice.
2. The dinner table laden with food looked inviting and the happy hungry family sat down eagerly to the birthday dinner.
3. On the table were turkey which was made with gravy noodles which were cooked in butter and ham which was baked with honey and five vegetables.
4. Jane's family had invited several neighbors—Mr. Jensen who lived next door Laura Wilson Jane's friend and Mr. and Mrs. Wilson Laura's parents.
5. Air travel was a topic of conversation among Mr. Jensen an airline pilot Laura a model-plane enthusiast and Mr. and Mrs. Wilson airline customer-service agents.

Using the Colon

The colon acts mainly as an introductory device. It is also used in several special situations.

Using Colons as Introductory Devices To use the colon correctly as an introductory device, you must be familiar with the different items it can introduce.

> **KEY CONCEPT** Use a colon before a list of items following an independent clause. ■

EXAMPLE: We must bring the following items to the family reunion: potato salad, a grill, and a blanket.

As shown in this example, the independent clause before a list often includes a phrase such as *the following* or *the following items.* You should familiarize yourself with these phrases, because they often indicate the need for a colon. Of course, you should not depend on these phrases alone to signal the need for a colon. The most important point to consider is whether or not an independent clause precedes the list. If it does, use a colon.

EXAMPLE: I bought my father several gifts: a shirt, a tie, and a pair of shoes.

Colons can also be used to introduce certain quotations:

> **KEY CONCEPT** Use a colon to introduce a quotation that is formal or lengthy or a quotation that does not contain a "he said/she said" expression. ■

Often, a formal quotation requiring a colon will consist of more than one sentence. However, your best guideline for inserting a colon should be the formality of the quotation. The more formal the quotation, the more likely you will need a colon. Do not use a colon to introduce a casual quoted remark or dialogue, even if more than one sentence is used.

COLON: The speaker began with these words: "I have never been so honored in all my life."

COMMA: As Ann left the room, she called, "I really must hurry. I don't want to be late."

▲ **Critical Viewing** Finish this statement: *The gift in the box might be one of the following items . . .* Where will you place the colon? Where will you use commas? **[Speculate]**

EXAMPLES: Dad walked angrily to the door and then turned: "Your excuses are weak. You have gone too far this time."

Teresa stood up slowly: "I think I'll go home. It's been a long day."

A colon can also serve as an introductory device for a sentence that either amplifies or summarizes what has preceded it:

▶**KEY CONCEPT** Use a colon to introduce a sentence that summarizes or explains the sentence before it. ∎

EXAMPLES: The garage attendant provided me with one piece of advice: He said to check my water level often until I could get my car in for the needed repairs.

His tuna casserole lacked a rather vital ingredient: He forgot the tuna!

Notice that a capital letter follows the colon because the words following make a complete sentence.

▶**KEY CONCEPT** Use a colon to introduce a formal appositive that follows an independent clause. ∎

Using a colon, instead of a comma, to introduce an appositive that follows an independent clause gives additional emphasis to the appositive.

EXAMPLE: I missed one important paragraph lesson: writing the topic sentence.

When you are using colons in sentences, always check to be sure that an independent clause comes before the colon.

INCORRECT: We decided to: see an old movie.
CORRECT: We decided to see an old movie: *An American in Paris.*

INCORRECT: Our tour took us by: the rose gardens, the Japanese park, and the hanging gardens.
CORRECT: Our tour took us by some beautiful spots: the rose gardens, the Japanese park, and the hanging gardens.

Although an independent clause must precede a colon, it is not necessary that the words following the colon be an independent clause. An appositive composed of a word or short phrase may, for example, follow a colon.

EXAMPLES: From the jeep, I looked out over the dry grass and saw the king of beasts: a lion.

I have the best friend in the world: my sister.

You could successfully argue that a comma would also be appropriate where the colon is inserted. However, the colon provides a slightly more dramatic effect.

Special Uses of the Colon The colon has several specialized functions that you will probably encounter in your reading and writing:

Among the special situations that require the use of a colon are references to time, volume and page numbers, chapters and verses in the Bible, book subtitles, business letter salutations, and labels that are used to introduce important ideas. Study the examples that are given in the following chart; it shows how the colon is used in each of these special situations.

SPECIAL SITUATIONS REQUIRING COLONS	
Numerals Giving the Time	5:22 A.M. 7:49 P.M.
References to Periodicals (Volume Number: Page Number)	*Forbes* 4:8
Biblical References (Chapter Number: Verse Number)	Genesis 1:5
Subtitles for Books and Magazines	*Fixing Hamburger: One Hundred Ways to Prepare Delicious Meals*
Salutations in Business Letters	Dear Mr. Biggs: Ladies: Dear Sir:
Labels Used to Signal Important Ideas	**Warning:** Cigarette smoking can be hazardous to your health. Note: This letter must be postmarked no later than the tenth of this month.

▶ **Exercise 27** Understanding the Use of the Colon Copy the following sentences, adding colons where necessary. Capitalize the first word if a complete sentence follows the colon.

1. I have one project for myself this summer to chart my family tree.
2. To begin, I will need some important information my mother's maiden name, my grandparents' dates of birth and marriage, and the year the family came to America.
3. Before long, I will have found just what I need my grandfather's birth certificate.
4. It is time to do the research off to City Hall!
5. My grandmother gave me sound advice "know your roots."
6. My sister scorned the advice and my project "why do all that work?"
7. There is a simple explanation for my sister's attitude she is too young to understand.
8. I have found all of the papers I need birth and death certificates, marriage licenses, and immigration records.
9. I made a startling discovery my great-grandparents were born in China!
10. I am proud of my work this summer the genealogical search for my ancestry.

▶ **Exercise 28** Using Colons for Special Writing Situations Copy each of the following items, adding the necessary colons. Underline any titles that appear in italics.

1. My family tree is entitled "The Gens One Hundred Years and Growing."
2. I used an interesting book for my research, *Finding Your Roots Tracing Your Family History.*
3. There was also a helpful article in *Time* 147 34.
4. I began my research at 8 30 A.M. today.
5. I carefully hurried past a sign that read "Warning Stairs may be slippery."

▶ Critical Viewing In a sentence about this picture, use a colon to set off a list of interesting features of this building on Ellis Island. **[Describe]**

More Practice

Grammar Exercise Workbook
• pp. 173–174
On-line Exercise Bank
• Section 28.3
  Go on-line:
  PHSchool.com
  Enter Web Code:
  eek-1002

Hands-on Grammar

Semicolon Connections

Often, the choice between using a conjunction or a semicolon to connect clauses is a stylistic one. Explore the effects of each choice with the following activity.

Write the following sentence on a strip of colored paper. Cut on either side of the subordinating conjunction. Turn over the piece you have cut, and write a large semicolon on the other side of the piece. Next, flip the card to read the sentence with the subordinating conjunction; then, with the semicolon. Determine which version gives an indication of the relationship between events.

We left because we were tired.

We left | ; | we were tired

Write and cut sentence strips using the conjunctions *therefore, if, after, unless, as,* and *where.* (For this activity, place the subordinate clause at the end of the sentence rather than at the beginning.) Discuss with a partner how the meaning of the sentence is affected when you change the conjunction to a semicolon.

Next, complete sentence strips for compound sentences that contain coordinating conjunctions. Cut the coordinating conjunctions out to make flip sections with semicolons on the other side. (Keep the comma that precedes the conjunction with the conjunction rather than with the sentence.) Again, discuss with a partner when a semicolon is more effective and when the comma and conjunction are more effective.

The evidence is clear, and it cannot be denied

The evidence is clear | ; | it cannot be denied

Find It in Your Reading Look for compound and complex sentences in a short story. Use the Semicolon Connections activity to evaluate the author's choice of conjunction or semicolon.

Find It in Your Writing Look for compound and complex sentences in your writing. Identify one place where you have used a semicolon to connect clauses. If you cannot find one, challenge yourself to revise at least one sentence to include one.

Section 28.3 Section Review

GRAMMAR EXERCISES 29–33

Exercise 29 Using Semicolons and Colons Correctly Copy each of the following sentences, adding semicolons and colons where necessary.

1. Many Americans wish to discover their roots most families can be traced back to the time of their arrival.
2. Tracing the family's country of origin is usually difficult it can also become expensive.
3. My mother gave me a book, *Tracing Your Irish Ancestors A Few Simple Steps.*
4. She would like me to learn more about the place our family came from County Kerry in Ireland.
5. Genealogical research in Britain and Ireland is relatively easy records are well kept and accessible.
6. Other records may have been lost language is often a barrier.
7. We will be visiting relatives in Ireland next summer It is a place I can't wait to see!
8. I know exactly where to start my research the library.
9. The library opens at 10 00 Saturday morning.
10. It closes at 3 00 P.M.

Exercise 30 Revising to Combine Sentences With Semicolons and Colons On a separate sheet of paper, revise the following paragraph. Use semicolons and colons as appropriate to combine clauses or to set off lists.

Genealogy is a major hobby around the world. Its popularity is increasing in the United States. The great surge in interest here started in the 1930's. Then, it increased somewhat after World War II. People engage in genealogical research for a variety of reasons. Some are curious. Some hope to establish a legal right to property, which may require proof of family connections. Some seek membership in lineage societies, which are becoming increasingly popular.

On a family tree are listed the names of relatives. The relatives listed include the following parents, grandparents, great-grandparents and so on. Information is recorded for each person on the tree. The information usually recorded is as follows date and place of birth, marriage, death, and names of children.

Exercise 31 Find It in Your Reading Read the following excerpt from "The Way to Rainy Mountain," and tell why the author used a semicolon in this case.

. . . They could find no buffalo; they had to hang an old hide from the sacred tree.

Exercise 32 Find It in Your Writing In a selection in your writing portfolio, find two related independent clauses that are linked by a comma and coordinating conjunction. Rewrite the sentence so that the clauses are joined by a semicolon instead.

Exercise 33 Writing Application Interview an older member of your family. In a detailed, well-developed essay, tell an interesting story about your family or describe one of your family's time-honored traditions. If you use direct quotations, remember to punctuate your work correctly. Use at least three semicolons and three colons in your essay.

Quotation Marks and Underlining

Writers try to provide support for their ideas and arguments. Direct quotations can provide that support. They can also make short stories and novels more interesting. Learn the rules for the use of quotation marks. This section will discuss the use of underlining as well as quotation marks to indicate different types of titles, names, and words.

Direct Quotations

This section will take a close look at direct quotations to help clarify any uncertainties you may have regarding the way to punctuate them.

▶ **KEY CONCEPT** A direct quotation represents a person's exact speech or thoughts and is enclosed in quotation marks [" "]. ■

DIRECT QUOTATION: "High school is closer to the core of the American experience than anything else I can think of."—Kurt Vonnegut, Jr.

Do not confuse direct quotations with indirect ones.

▶ **KEY CONCEPT** An indirect quotation reports only the general meaning of what a person said or thought and does not require quotation marks. ■

INDIRECT QUOTATION: Kurt Vonnegut, Jr., wrote that being in high school was a true part of the American experience.

An indirect quotation rephrases someone else's words. The words are not the exact words of the speaker. In a direct quotation, the words of the speaker are quoted exactly.

All direct quotations must be indicated by quotation marks. There are various ways a writer may present a direct quotation. One way is to quote an uninterrupted sentence. Another way is to present a quoted phrase within an otherwise complete sentence. Writers may also use an introductory, concluding, or interrupting expression with a quotation.

To enclose a sentence that is an uninterrupted direct quotation, double quotation marks [" "] are placed around the quoted material. Of course, each complete sentence of any quotation begins with a capital letter.

EXAMPLE: "The past is but the beginning of a beginning."
—H. G. Wells

**Theme:
Science Fiction**

In this section, you will learn about using quotation marks, italics, and underlining. Many of the examples and exercises are about science fiction.

**Cross-Curricular
Connection:
Literature**

Sometimes, you will insert only a quoted phrase into a
sentence. You must set off this fragment with quotation marks
also. Notice in the following examples that the first word of a
phrase or fragment is capitalized only when it falls at the
beginning of a sentence or when it would be capitalized
regardless of its position in a sentence.

EXAMPLES: In writing about history, H. G. Wells called it
"a race between education and catastrophe."

"A race between education and catastrophe"
is the way H. G. Wells referred to history.

Generally, you will wish to add a "he said/she said"
expression to a quotation to show who is speaking. Use the
following rule for a "he said/she said" expression that comes
before the quotation.

▶ **KEY CONCEPT** Use a comma or colon after an
introductory expression. ■

INTRODUCTORY H. G. Wells wrote, "The past is
EXPRESSION: but the beginning of a beginning."

If you do not use a "he said/she said" expression in your
introduction to a quotation or if the introductory phrase
takes a more formal tone, use a colon instead of a
comma before the quotation.

EXAMPLE: The professor held up a
book: "Today, we will
discuss Jules Verne's
work *Around the
World in Eighty Days.*"

▶ **KEY CONCEPT** Use a comma, a
question mark, or an exclamation
mark after a quotation followed by
a concluding expression. ■

CONCLUDING "The past is but the beginning
EXPRESSION: of a beginning," wrote Wells.

▲▼ **Critical Viewing**
Use these pictures to
illustrate a scientific
principle. **[Connect]**

When a direct quotation is interrupted by a "he said/she said" expression, quotation marks enclose both parts of the quotation.

KEY CONCEPT Use a comma after part of a quoted sentence followed by an interrupting expression. Use another comma after the expression. ■

INTERRUPTING
EXPRESSION:

"The past," wrote Wells, "is but the beginning of a beginning."

Two quoted sentences may also be interrupted.

KEY CONCEPT Use a comma, question mark, or exclamation mark after a quoted sentence that comes before an interrupting expression. Use a period after the expression. ■

EXAMPLE:

"What does writing teach?" Ray Bradbury asked. "First and foremost, it reminds us that we are alive."

Exercise 34 Indicating Direct Quotations Copy each sentence that needs quotation marks, adding the necessary marks. If no quotation marks are needed, write *correct*.

EXAMPLE:

Mary Shelley wrote I beheld the wretch—the miserable monster whom I had created.

ANSWER:

Mary Shelley wrote, "I beheld the wretch—the miserable monster whom I had created."

1. Mr. Phileas Fogg lived, in 1872, at No. 7, Saville Row, Burlington Gardens.—Jules Verne
2. Verne wrote that Phileas Fogg was an Englishman.
3. One of his questions was Was Phileas Fogg rich?
4. You are a Frenchman, I believe, asked Phileas Fogg, and your name is John?
5. Then, the new servant responded, Jean, if monsieur pleases.
6. Mr. Fogg told him that the name Passepartout was preferable.
7. He must have traveled everywhere, at least in the spirit.—Jules Verne
8. You are well recommended to me; I hear a good report of you, said Phileas Fogg.
9. Then, Fogg told Passepartout that his watch was four minutes slow.
10. I have a natural aptness for going out of one business into another, confided Jean Passepartout.

Grammar and Style Tip

Vary the way you indicate the speaker of a quotation. Sometimes, introduce the quotation with an indication of the speaker; sometimes, indicate the speaker following the quotation; and sometimes, interrupt the quotation.

▶ **Exercise 35** Indicating and Capitalizing Quotations Copy the following sentences, making the necessary corrections in punctuation and capitalization. In two of the sentences, the quote has been underlined so that you can identify it.

EXAMPLE: space—the final frontier announced Captain Kirk these are the voyages of the starship *Enterprise*.

ANSWER: "Space—the final frontier," announced Captain Kirk. "These are the voyages of the starship *Enterprise*."

1. the year 1866 was marked by a strange event begins Verne's *20,000 Leagues Under the Sea*.
2. sea-going ships have been encountering an 'enormous thing' Verne continues a long spindle-shaped object.
3. this was described as infinitely larger and quicker than a whale.
4. but it did exist said Verne's narrator there was now no denying the fact.
5. some characters in the book said that they would not believe it existed unless they had seen it . . . with their own scientific eyes.
6. as for dismissing it as a myth wrote Verne this was no longer possible.
7. the monster came into fashion in all the big cities said the narrator.
8. it was sung about in cafes continued the narrator jeered at in the newspapers, acted out in the theaters.
9. the 'monster subject' inflamed people's minds.—Jules Verne
10. after some encounters with ships, the narrator said the problem took on a different complexion.

▶ **More Practice**

**Grammar Exercise
Workbook**
• pp. 175–176
**On-line
Exercise Bank**
• Section 28.4

Go on-line:
PHSchool.com
Enter Web Code:
eek-1002

▼ **Critical Viewing**
With a partner, exchange two or three sentences about this picture. Write down what was said. Use capitals and quotation marks as needed. **[Apply]**

Other Punctuation Marks With Quotation Marks

Whether to place punctuation inside or outside the quotation marks presents a problem for some writers. Four basic rules, once learned, will help clear up most of the confusion.

KEY CONCEPT Always place a comma or a period inside the final quotation mark. ■

EXAMPLES: "I enjoy Jack Finney's work," said Elaine.

"The future," C. S. Lewis believed, "is something which everyone reaches at the rate of sixty minutes an hour."

Note in the second example that the quotation is split, but this makes no difference in the placement of the comma. It still goes inside the quotation marks.

KEY CONCEPT Always place a semicolon or colon outside the final quotation mark. ■

EXAMPLES: One repair person said, "I can't do it for less than eighty dollars"; another indicated he could fix it for half that price!

She listed the ingredients for "an absolutely heavenly salad": spinach, mushrooms, hard-boiled eggs, and bacon.

KEY CONCEPT Place a question mark or exclamation mark inside the final quotation mark if the end mark is part of the quotation. ■

EXAMPLES: The reader asked, "How will the story end?"

The TV announcer exclaimed, "You just won the $10,000 jackpot!"

▶ **KEY CONCEPT** Place a question mark or an exclamation mark outside the final quotation mark if the end mark is not part of the quotation. ∎

EXAMPLES: Did you hear that speaker when he said, "Just use your imagination to write science fiction"?

I was thrilled when they said, "And for president, Debbie Schmidt"!

With question marks and exclamation marks, only one mark is needed. In the following, the quotation is a question and the sentence is a statement. No period, however, is needed.

EXAMPLE: My mother asked, "Did you feed the animals?"

▶ **Exercise 36** Adding Other Punctuation Marks Copy the following sentences, adding any needed commas, colons, semi-colons, or end marks.

EXAMPLE: The young child shouted gleefully, "I believe in time travel"

ANSWER: The young child shouted gleefully, "I believe in time travel!"

1. Was it in *The Time Machine* that H. G. Wells wrote, "The Time Traveller, for so it will be convenient to speak of him"
2. He asked, "You have all heard what they have to say about this Fourth Dimension"
3. "The thing the Time Traveller held in his hand was a glittering metallic framework," wrote Wells, "scarcely larger than a small clock, and very delicately made"
4. The Time Traveller said "It is my plan for a machine to travel through time"
5. The Psychologist in *The Time Machine* exclaimed, "Of all the wild, extravagant theories"
6. The narrator said, "I am absolutely certain there was no trickery" then the time machine vanished.
7. Then, the Medical Man asked, "Do you seriously believe that that machine has travelled into time"
8. "Into the future or the past," responded the Time Traveller, "I don't, for certain, know which"
9. Did you believe it when the Time Traveller said, "I intend to explore time"
10. The characters agreed, "None of us quite knew how to take it"

▶ **More Practice**

Grammar Exercise Workbook
• pp. 177–180
On-line Exercise Bank
• Section 28.4
  Go on-line:
  PHSchool.com
  Enter Web Code:
  eek-1002

ⁱnteractive Textbook

Get instant feedback! Exercise 36 is available on-line or on CD-ROM.

Exercise 37 Adding Quotation Marks and Other Punctuation Marks Copy the following sentences, adding the necessary quotation marks and punctuation.

EXAMPLE: Did you say Let's meet after the first showing of *Somewhere in Time*?

ANSWER: Did you say, "Let's meet after the first showing of *Somewhere in Time*"?

1. Does Mary Shelley's *Frankenstein* begin I am by birth a Genevese
2. So soon as the dazzling light vanished says the narrator the oak had disappeared
3. He acknowledges that Destiny was too potent
4. Her immutable laws had decreed my utter and terrible destruction said the Monster
5. He added It is with considerable difficulty that I remember the original era of my being
6. Did you realize who spoke the lines A strange multiplicity of sensations seized me
7. I saw, felt, heard, and smelt all at the same time continued the Monster
8. By degrees he said I remember, a stronger light pressed upon my nerves
9. Upon spotting the village, he exclaimed How miraculous did this appear
10. The teacher asked Do you know who the Monster is

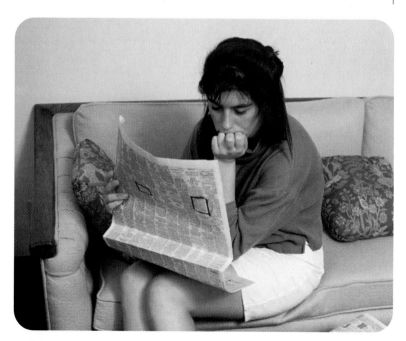

◄ **Critical Viewing** What information might this girl be reading that would surprise or amaze someone from the nineteenth century? **[Deduce]**

Quotation Marks in Special Situations

Several special situations may occur when you write direct quotations. These include dialogues, quotations of more than one paragraph, and quotations within other quoted material.

First, consider the use of quotation marks when writing a dialogue—a direct conversation between two or more people. Use quotation marks to enclose the directly quoted conversation, and begin a new paragraph for each change of speaker.

▶ **KEY CONCEPT** When writing dialogue, begin a new paragraph with each change of speaker. ■

EXAMPLE: The station attendant shouted from behind the hood, "You're a quart low on oil, Mrs. Lowell. Would you like me to put some in for you?"
"Yes, thank you," she replied.
"What kind of oil do you use in the car?"

In cases where one quotation consists of several paragraphs of quoted material, remember the following rule:

▶ **KEY CONCEPT** For quotations longer than a paragraph, put quotation marks at the beginning of each paragraph and at the end of the final paragraph. ■

EXAMPLE: "Experts are noticing a change in the types of food Americans are buying. More fast foods, such as TV dinners and canned meals, are being purchased by food shoppers.
"Many people who used to spend a great deal of time preparing meals now work outside their homes. Researchers conclude that this is the reason more fast foods are being purchased.
"People need well-balanced meals. They now buy meals that can be prepared quickly. Thus, people today must spend more time at work and less time in the kitchen."

Occasionally, you may need to indicate a quotation contained within another quotation.

▶ **KEY CONCEPT** Use single quotation marks for a quotation within a quotation. ■

EXAMPLE: The fund-raiser concluded, saying, "As we try to raise money for this worthy cause, let us not forget that old English proverb that says, 'Where there's a will, there's a way.' "

GRAMMAR IN
LITERATURE

from **Arthur Becomes King of Britain**
T. H. White

Notice how the dialogue in the following passage is punctuated. How can you tell who is speaking?

"Sir," said Sir Ector, "I will ask no more of you but that you will make my son, your foster-brother, Sir Kay, seneschal of all your lands."

Kay was kneeling down too, and it was more than the Wart could bear.

"Oh, do stop," he cried.

Exercise 38 **Proofreading for Punctuation and Capitalization** The following dialogue has no paragraphing, quotation marks, capitalization, or punctuation. Each number indicates a new speaker. Copy the dialogue, starting new paragraphs and adding the necessary quotation marks, capitalization, and punctuation.

(1) science fiction is not a modern invention said the speaker these subjects have been written about since ancient times what is the oldest example of science fiction that you can recall (2) tara raised her hand and said *the twilight zone* is pretty old (3) yes agreed the speaker can anyone think of any books (4) i used to read jules verne's books like *from the earth to the moon* said michael (5) jules verne wrote a great deal of early science fiction said the speaker enthusiastically other books were *journey to the center of the earth* and *off on a comet* (6) what about *star trek* said someone (7) yes *star wars* is my favorite another voice exclaimed (8) one at a time said the speaker attempting to control the crowd these are all great examples they are all similar because they are about the future and scientific and technological developments (9) another speaker added science fiction began in ancient times and still continues today ray bradbury said the whole history of mankind is nothing but science fiction he also said that science fiction is a combination of our dreams and our accomplishments (10) how do you feel about science fiction do you enjoy it asked tara

Underlining and Other Uses of Quotation Marks

In printed material, italics and quotation marks are used to set some titles, names, and words apart from the rest of the text. In handwritten or typed material, italics are not available, so underlining is used instead. Quotation marks, on the other hand, are used in both printed and handwritten materials.

This section gives rules for using underlining and quotation marks as well as rules for titles and names that require neither.

Underlining You should use underlining in your writing or typing to highlight titles of long written works and other major artistic works. You will also need to indicate certain names and foreign expressions by underlining them. In addition, you can use underlining to indicate words you want to emphasize.

▶ **KEY CONCEPT** Underline or italicize the titles of long written works and the titles of publications that are published as a single work. ■

Following are examples of titles you should underline:

TITLES OF WRITTEN WORKS THAT ARE UNDERLINED	
Titles of Books	<u>Dune</u> by Frank Herbert
Titles of Plays	<u>A Raisin in the Sun</u> by Lorraine Hansberry <u>The Man Who Came to Dinner</u> by Moss Hart
Titles of Periodicals	<u>Galaxy Science Fiction</u> <u>Journal of American History</u>
Titles of Newspapers	<u>The New York Times</u> the Palm Beach <u>Post</u> the Chicago <u>Sun-Times</u>
Titles of Long Poems	<u>Idylls of the King</u> by Alfred, Lord Tennyson <u>Gilgamesh</u>

Notes About *Newspaper Titles:* The portion of the title that should be underlined will vary from newspaper to newspaper. *The New York Times* should always be fully capitalized and underlined. Other papers, however, can usually be treated in one of two ways: *The Los Angeles Times* or the Los Angeles *Times*. Unless you know the true name of a paper, choose one of these two forms and use it consistently.

Many media presentations and pieces of artwork also require underlining.

▶ **KEY CONCEPT** Underline the titles of movies, television and radio series, paintings, sculpture, and lengthy works of music. ■

MOVIE:	<u>It's a Wonderful Life</u>, dir. Frank Capra
SERIES:	<u>NOVA</u>, PBS
PAINTING:	<u>The River</u>, Claude Monet
SCULPTURE:	<u>The Minute Man,</u> Daniel Chester French
MUSIC:	<u>The Water Music,</u> George Friedrich Handel

▼ Critical Viewing
In a research paper about Charles Lindbergh and this plane, how would you set off the name of the plane? **[Apply]**

▶ **KEY CONCEPT** Underline the names of individual air, sea, space, and land craft. ■

AIR:	the <u>Spirit of St. Louis</u>
SEA:	the S.S. <u>Seagallant</u>
SPACE:	<u>Millenium Falcon</u>
LAND:	the <u>De Witt Clinton</u>

If a *the* precedes the name, do not underline or capitalize it because it is not considered part of the official name. Note also that a specific name given to a group of vehicles (for example, the Explorer spaceships) is capitalized but not underlined.

▶ **KEY CONCEPT** Underline foreign words not yet accepted into English. ■

EXAMPLES: It is <u>verboten</u> to leave the building without permission. (German: forbidden)

Everyone said that the <u>coq au vin</u> was delicious. (French: chicken cooked in wine)

Because the process of accepting words and phrases into the English language is a continuous one, you cannot always be certain whether a phrase is still considered foreign. Check those doubtful phrases in the dictionary. If the word or phrase is not in the dictionary, you can generally consider it foreign. If it is in the dictionary, it will either be labeled with the name of the foreign language, in which case you should underline it, or it will be given standard treatment as an English word, in which case you should not underline it.

Certain other words need underlining because they are being used in a special way.

▶ **KEY CONCEPT** Underline numbers, symbols, letters, and words used to name themselves. ■

NUMBERS:	When I say the number <u>three</u>, you start running.
SYMBOLS:	Is that an <u>!</u> at the end of that sentence?
LETTERS:	Is that first letter a <u>G</u> or an <u>S</u>?
WORDS:	She wrote the word <u>fluid</u>, but she meant <u>fluent</u>.

⚙ Grammar ⚙ and Style Tip

In much formal writing, numbers are written out as words. In newspaper articles—especially sports articles—numerals are often used. When you are writing, use one method of presentation for numbers. Do not switch back and forth between numerals and spelled-out words

> **KEY CONCEPT** Underline words that you wish to stress. ∎

EXAMPLE: We will need a <u>minimum</u> of six dollars for the trip.

Although the underlining of the word in this example clarifies the meaning of the sentence, do not overdo underlining for emphasis. In most cases, you should rely on precise word selection to convey your meaning and emphasis.

> **Exercise 39** Underlining Titles, Names, and Words Write and underline titles, names, or words that require underlining. If a sentence needs no correction, write *correct*.

1. The movie Planet of the Apes was released in 1968.
2. Reviews were published in The New York Times and many other papers.
3. The Planet of the Apes soundtrack was by Jerry Goldsmith.
4. Charlton Heston wrote about starring in the movie in An Actor's Life.
5. He had a small role in the sequel Beneath the Planet of the Apes.
6. Rod Serling, creator of The Twilight Zone series, wrote the screenplay for Planet of the Apes.
7. We thought we could see the movie in Radio City Music Hall.
8. The magazine Starlog has published many articles about the series.
9. The word apes was used to include the many species in the movies.
10. The surprise ending of the first movie was greeted as a true coup de théâtre.

Quotation Marks With Titles

Quotation marks are used to set off certain titles.

> **KEY CONCEPT** Use quotation marks around the titles of short written works. ∎

SHORT STORY:	"Nightfall" by Isaac Asimov
CHAPTER FROM A BOOK:	"Five Days in a Mine" from *Kids With Courage*
SHORT POEM:	"Mowing" by Robert Frost
ESSAY TITLE:	"Style" by Maya Angelou
ARTICLE TITLE:	"How to Organize Your Life"

> **More Practice**

Grammar Exercise Workbook
• pp. 179–180
On-line Exercise Bank
• Section 28.4
  Go on-line:
  PHSchool.com
  Enter Web Code:
  eek-1002

interactive Textbook

Get instant feedback! Exercises 39 and 40 are available on-line or on CD-ROM.

Technology Tip

When writing about a particular work, use the search feature of a word-processing program to help you find every instance of the title. Make sure that you have correctly used quotation marks or underlining to set off the title.

▶ **KEY CONCEPT** Use quotation marks around the titles of songs, episodes in a series, and parts of a long musical composition. ■

EPISODE:	"The Iran File" from *60 Minutes*
SONG TITLE:	"Swing Low, Sweet Chariot"
PART OF A LONG MUSICAL COMPOSITION:	"E.T. Phone Home" from *E.T., The Extra Terrestrial* soundtrack

Occasionally, you may refer to a title of one long work contained in a larger work. Singly, each title would require underlining; when used together, another rule applies:

▶ **KEY CONCEPT** Use quotation marks around the title of a work that is mentioned as part of a collection. ■

EXAMPLE: "Plato" from *Great Books of the Western World*

▶ **Exercise 40** **Using Quotation Marks With Titles** From each of the following sentences, copy the title and enclose it in quotation marks.

EXAMPLE: The story Euphio Effect is about the addictive quality of television.
ANSWER: "Euphio Effect"

1. The short poem Ozymandias by Shelley addresses some science-fiction themes.
2. Swift wrote science fiction and essays like A Modest Proposal.
3. Edgar Allan Poe ventured into science fiction with stories like The Tell-Tale Heart.
4. Bradbury's short story There Will Come Soft Rains was set thirty-five years into the future.
5. The Day the World Ended is the opening chapter of one of Kurt Vonnegut's books.

▲ **Critical Viewing** What type of musical composition might this orchestra be playing? Would you use underlining or quotation marks when writing the title of such a work? **[Speculate]**

Titles Without Underlining or Quotation Marks

Some titles require neither underlining nor quotation marks.

KEY CONCEPT Do not underline or place in quotation marks the names of the Bible, its books, divisions, or versions or other holy scriptures, such as the Koran. ∎

EXAMPLE: He received a Bible as a gift.

KEY CONCEPT Do not underline or place in quotation marks the titles of government charters, alliances, treaties, acts, statutes, or reports. ∎

EXAMPLES: the Declaration of Independence
Civil Rights Act

Exercise 41 **Punctuating Different Types of Titles** Copy the titles, enclosing them in quotation marks or underlining them. If neither quotation marks nor underlining is needed, write *correct*.

1. I listened to the Binary Sunset track on the Star Wars: A New Hope soundtrack.
2. A different soundtrack also includes music from Close Encounters of the Third Kind.
3. Here They Come! is an exciting piece from Star Wars.
4. Shadows of the Empire is a book set between the movies The Empire Strikes Back and Return of the Jedi.
5. Han Solo and The Princess is a short romantic composition by John Williams.
6. My essay Leia Through the Trilogy will have to be revised after the release of the first trilogy.
7. Nick submitted the poem A Jedi Knight to Amazing Stories for publication.
8. It was the source of the chapter My Time With Yoda in the book we are trying to write.
9. I thought we could model it after a long poem like Byron's The Prisoner of Chillon.
10. He thought a short poem like Poe's Dream Within a Dream was more inspiring.

More Practice

Grammar Exercise Workbook
• pp. 179–180
On-line Exercise Bank
• Section 28.4
  Go on-line:
  PHSchool.com
  Enter Web Code:
  eek-1002

Get instant feedback! Exercise 41 is available on-line or on CD-ROM.

Section
28.4 Section Review

GRAMMAR EXERCISES 42–47

Exercise 42 Punctuating
Quotations Copy the following sentences, adding the appropriate quotation marks and other punctuation marks. Quoted phrases are underlined.

1. I thought C. S. Lewis wrote only children's books said Ryan
2. In a letter about *The Lion, the Witch, and the Wardrobe,* Lewis wrote Let us suppose that there were a land like Narnia
3. A frequent question is Why is my set of Narnia books numbered in the wrong order
4. So perhaps it does not matter very much in which order anyone reads them—C. S. Lewis
5. He wrote many scholarly essays about a variety of topics the teacher explained

Exercise 43 Punctuating
Different Types of Titles Copy the titles, enclosing them in quotation marks or underlining them.

1. Kurt Vonnegut's book Welcome to the Monkey House includes the short story A Long Walk to Forever.
2. Some of the stories were originally published in magazines like The Atlantic Monthly or The Magazine of Fantasy and Science Fiction.
3. In 1970, he wrote a play called Happy Birthday, Wanda June.
4. The New York Times called Vonnegut "a laughing prophet of doom."
5. In his novel Cat's Cradle, the chapter called Nice, Nice, Very Nice introduces the reader to one of Bokonon's songs.

Exercise 44 Using Quotation
Marks and Underlining Copy the following sentences, adding the appropriate quotation marks and properly punctuating any titles. The quoted phrase is underlined.

1. Roger Ebert writes E.T. is a movie full of surprises
2. It is a variation of the story The Wizard of Oz.
3. During the movie, E.T. watches an episode of Tom and Jerry and reads the Buck Rogers comic strip.
4. He also watches an old science-fiction movie called This Island Earth.
5. During the movie, Gertie hears the bedtime story Peter Pan.

Exercise 45 Find It in Your
Reading Look through several movie, music, and book reviews to find examples of different kinds of titles and how they are set off. Then, look in these reviews for direct quotations and how they are punctuated. Copy the titles and quotations on a separate sheet of paper. Note the source of each.

Exercise 46 Find It in Your
Writing Find a selection in your portfolio that has quoted material in it. Make sure that you have punctuated correctly with quotation marks.

Exercise 47 Writing Application
Write a brief descriptive paragraph about your favorite science-fiction story. Include a quotation from one of your favorite characters. Be sure to properly punctuate your titles and quotations.

Dashes, Parentheses, and Hyphens

Commas, dashes, and parentheses all perform a similar function—that of separating certain words, phrases, and clauses from the rest of the sentence. To use these marks effectively, a writer must become acquainted with their different qualities. The comma is the most common mark and, therefore, draws the least attention to itself. The dash sets off material more dramatically. Parentheses set off technical or explanatory material clearly from the rest of the sentence.

This section will focus on the uses of the dash, parentheses, and hyphens, giving you rules to follow in using them.

Dashes

The dash, a long horizontal mark made above the writing line [—], functions to set off material in three basic ways:

▶ **KEY CONCEPT** Use dashes to indicate an abrupt change of thought, a dramatic interrupting idea, or a summary statement. ■

In the following chart, examples illustrate the three basic uses of the dash.

USES OF THE DASH	
To indicate an abrupt change of thought:	I cannot believe how many free throws my brother missed—oh, I don't even want to think about it!
To set off interrupting ideas dramatically:	The slam dunk—which must be the most spectacular shot in basketball—makes a great addition to any highlight film. Next Saturday—do you have to work that day?—we want you to play basketball with us.
To set off a summary statement:	Point guard, shooting guard, small forward, power forward, and center—deciding which of these positions to play took me a full five minutes. To see his jersey hanging from the rafters—this was his greatest dream.

It may help you to know that words such as *all, these, this,* and *that* frequently begin a summary sentence preceded by a dash.

Theme: Basketball

In this section, you will learn about using dashes, parentheses, and hyphens. The examples and exercises are about basketball, past and present.

Cross-Curricular Connection: Physical Education

Although nonessential appositives and modifiers are usually set off with commas, dashes are sometimes used.

KEY CONCEPT Use dashes to set off a nonessential appositive or modifier when it is long, when it is already punctuated, or when you want to be dramatic. ■

APPOSITIVE: The cause of her happiness—winning the lead in the school play—pleased her parents.

MODIFIER: The drum major—who wore a white hat, a gold cape, and blue boots—led the band at the game.

Notice how the examples in the following charts each meet at least one of the three criteria in the rule.

Grammar and Style Tip

Use dashes sparingly. As an alternative to commas, they can add emphasis and variety to your writing. If overused, however, they will lose their impact.

USING DASHES WITH NONESSENTIAL APPOSITIVES	
Reasons for Use	**Examples**
Length	The selfish player—an egomaniac more concerned with his own statistics than his team—will not pass the ball.
Internal Punctuation	Some of the players on the team—for example, Karen, Susan, and Maria—always play well under pressure.
Strong Emphasis	The upsets—three games against superior teams—were totally unexpected.

Nonessential modifiers are generally set off only when they have internal punctuation or when strong emphasis is desired.

USING DASHES WITH NONESSENTIAL MODIFIERS	
Internal Punctuation	The coach—who, for some reason known only to himself, decided to take the star player out of the game—has no fans.
Strong Emphasis	Lara's three-point shot—which she has mastered so well that even a professional could take lessons from her—is helping us beat formidable teams.

You may recall that a parenthetical expression consists of words or phrases that are inserted into a sentence but have no essential grammatical relationship to it. Parenthetical expressions are often enclosed by dashes.

KEY CONCEPT Use dashes to set off a parenthetical expression when it is long, already punctuated, or especially dramatic. ■

Short parenthetical expressions do not need dashes.

EXAMPLE: I will, I think, go.

If the parenthetical expression is long or contains its own punctuation, you may want to set it off with dashes:

EXAMPLE: Their amazing winning streak—they won by two points Monday, by one point yesterday, and by one point today—cannot last long.

Use dashes if the parenthetical expression is a question or an exclamation:

EXAMPLE: After Karen hit the improbable shot at the buzzer—can you believe the ball swooshed in?—the fans carried her away on their shoulders.

Enclose a parenthetical expression in dashes if you want it to stand out from the rest of the sentence:

EXAMPLE: At the first practice of the season—the coach actually told us that we would hate every minute of every practice—he made us run for two hours.

Although the dash has many uses, be careful not to overuse it. Using an occasional dash adds sentence variety and interest; putting dashes in too often will make your thoughts seem confused and disjointed.

Exercise 48 **Using the Dash** On your paper, copy the following sentences, adding one or two dashes in each.

1. The rules of basketball I don't even want to think how many there are! have changed over the years.
2. Basketball enjoyed by people all over the world was invented in 1891 by James Naismith in Springfield, Massachusetts.
3. To create a game suited for indoor play this was Naismith's goal.
4. Naismith thought his game such a fantastic game would be appropriate for indoor play in the wintertime.
5. Many star basketball players for example, Dr. J, Oscar Robertson, and Michael Jordan often practiced a skill until they could execute it flawlessly.

More Practice

Grammar Exercise Workbook
• pp. 181–182
On-line Exercise Bank
• Section 28.5
  Go on-line:
  PHSchool.com
  Enter Web Code:
  eek-1002

Get instant feedback! Exercise 48 is available on-line or on CD-ROM.

Parentheses

Parentheses set off supplementary material not essential to the understanding of the sentence. Though not as dramatic as the dash, parentheses are the strongest separator you can use.

Rules for Using Parentheses The following rules will help you determine when using parentheses is appropriate:

▶ **KEY CONCEPT** Use parentheses to set off asides and explanations only when the material is not essential or when it consists of one or more sentences. ■

Note that you can take out all the material in parentheses in the following examples without altering the meaning:

EXAMPLES: The coaches will look at each player's skills (passing, shooting, and rebounding) when deciding which players to recruit for the all-star team. Nancy perfected her passing (only after years of practice) and will now start as her team's point guard.

We will pick up the new uniforms tomorrow. (The salesperson promised that she would have them ready.) By tomorrow night, we should be wearing our new jerseys.

▶ **KEY CONCEPT** Use parentheses to set off numerical explanations such as dates of a person's birth and death and around numbers and letters marking a series. ■

EXAMPLES: James Naismith invented the game of basketball at the request of Luther H. Gulick (1865–1918), who was his employer.

One half of the team's members (6) caught the flu just before the championship game.

You need to raise at least twenty thousand dollars ($20,000) to send the team to play the exhibition game in China.

Go to the sporting goods store and pick up these items: (1) basketball, (2) water bottle, (3) towels, and (4) bandages.

Who played in the NBA first: (a) Larry Bird, (b) Nate Archibald, or (c) Shaquille O'Neal?

▼ Critical Viewing
Use a parenthetical comment about a nonessential element in a statement about this picture. **[Describe]**

In following these rules, be careful not to overuse parentheses. As with the dash, overuse can lead to choppy, unclear prose—something every good writer wants to avoid.

Capitalizing and Punctuating With Parentheses

Several guidelines will help you punctuate and capitalize the material in parentheses.

KEY CONCEPT When a phrase or declarative sentence interrupts another sentence, do not use an initial capital or end mark inside the parentheses. ■

EXAMPLE: A frankfurter (my grandmother tasted one for the first time last summer) provides a delicious snack at a basketball game.

However, if the sentence is exclamatory or interrogative, the rule changes.

KEY CONCEPT When a question or exclamation interrupts another sentence, use both an initial capital and an end mark inside the parentheses. ■

EXAMPLE: College basketball games (These have featured some remarkable personalities!) reach millions of viewers every March through television.

There is another rule for sentences between sentences:

KEY CONCEPT With any sentence that falls between two complete sentences, use both an initial capital and an end mark inside the parentheses. ■

EXAMPLE: We drove to the high-school basketball championship. (It took more than five hours.) The high level of play surpassed our expectations.

Apply this rule for commas, semicolons, colons, and end marks:

KEY CONCEPT In a sentence that includes parentheses, place any punctuation belonging to the main sentence after the parenthesis. ■

EXAMPLES: Our shooting guard had an amazing season (averaging 45 points per game)!

The powerful center set several scoring records (22, to be exact), and he helped his team capture three championship titles.

More Practice

Grammar Exercise Workbook
• pp. 183–184
On-line Exercise Bank
• Section 28.5
Go on-line:
PHSchool.com
Enter Web Code:
eek-1002

> **Exercise 49** Using Parentheses On your paper, copy the following sentences, adding the necessary parentheses.

EXAMPLE: Pete Maravich Have you ever seen him play? displayed remarkable passing skills.

ANSWER: Pete Maravich (Have you ever seen him play?) displayed remarkable passing skills.

1. Michael Jeffrey Jordan Wasn't he the greatest basketball player ever? was born on February 17, 1963, in Brooklyn, New York.
2. After a stellar high-school career it must have been spectacular Jordan earned an athletic scholarship to attend the University of North Carolina.
3. Jordan He had such an amazing career! played the guard position at the University of North Carolina.
4. When did Jordan first win a college championship: a 1982, b 1983, or c 1984?
5. Jordan left college after his junior year. He was that good! He then began his career as a professional basketball player.

> **Exercise 50** Using Capitals and Punctuation With Parentheses On your paper, copy each sentence, making the necessary changes in capitalization and punctuation. If no corrections are needed, write *correct*.

EXAMPLE: When I finished the workout (what a tough one it was) I took a shower.

ANSWER: When I finished the workout (What a tough one it was!), I took a shower.

1. Shooting (do you know how to shoot a jump shot?) is one of the most important skills in basketball.
2. You can improve your jump shot (It's one of basketball's most effective offensive weapons!) only by practicing.
3. The jump shot (It's the most commonly used shot in competitive basketball today) takes much practice to perfect.
4. Your shooting form (So much depends on your mechanics.) is extremely important.
5. Maybe you can become a better shooter (you'd better hope so!) with practice.

▼ Critical Viewing
Add a parenthetical statement to the following sentence: *One of the players is my neighbor.* [Apply]

Hyphens

The hyphen is often mistaken for the dash. You should note that the hyphen is shorter than the dash.

Hyphens are used to divide certain numbers and parts of words, to join some compound words, and to divide words at the ends of lines. This section will focus on the rules governing the appropriate use of the hyphen.

With Numbers Some numbers written out as words require hyphens to separate the parts of the number:

KEY CONCEPT Use a hyphen when writing out the compound numbers *twenty-one* through *ninety-nine*. ■

EXAMPLE: The star of the team scored *forty-seven* points!

KEY CONCEPT Use a hyphen with fractions used as adjectives. ■

EXAMPLE: The recipe calls for *one-half* cup of mushrooms.

In the preceding example, the fraction functions as an adjective. If it were used as a noun, the hyphen would then be omitted.

EXAMPLE: *Three fourths* of the junior varsity team came to the practice.

With Word Parts Some word parts require the use of a hyphen:

KEY CONCEPT Use a hyphen after a prefix that is followed by a proper noun or an adjective. ■

EXAMPLE: The school's basketball season started in *mid-September.*

KEY CONCEPT Use a hyphen in words with the prefixes *all-, ex-,* and *self-,* and in words with the suffix *-elect.* ■

EXAMPLES: all-star   self-addressed
          ex-teacher   senator-elect

Always check to make sure that a complete word joins the prefix or suffix. When these prefixes and suffixes combine with only part of a word, no hyphen is needed.

INCORRECT: ex-ecutive
CORRECT: executive

With Compound Words Hyphens are used with some compound words:

> **KEY CONCEPT** Use a hyphen to connect two or more words that are used as one word unless the dictionary gives a contrary spelling. ■

The use of hyphens in compound words is a matter of changing style. The dictionary should always be your authority on this matter. Three examples, hyphenated in most dictionaries, follow.

EXAMPLES: merry-go-round   crow's-feet   off-season

> **KEY CONCEPT** Use a hyphen to connect a compound modifier that comes before a noun. ■

EXAMPLES: The clouds cast a *grayish-blue* tint on the water.
             The *well-prepared* team played with confidence.

If a compound modifier comes after the noun, however, the hyphen is dropped.

BEFORE: We got the pizza from an *all-night* deli.
AFTER: A deli open *all night* delivered the pizza.

If, however, the dictionary shows the compound modifier with a hyphen, the word remains hyphenated regardless of its position in the sentence.

EXAMPLES: We water-skied behind a *jet-propelled* boat.
             Our ski boat was *jet-propelled.*

> **KEY CONCEPT** Do not use hyphens with compound modifiers that include words ending in *-ly* or with compound proper adjectives or compound proper nouns acting as adjectives. ■

INCORRECT: The *badly-damaged* car sat in the body shop.
CORRECT: The *badly damaged* car sat in the body shop.
INCORRECT: The *North-American* continent has many mountains.
CORRECT: The *North American* continent has many mountains.

⚡ Spelling Tip

Most words that end in *ball*—for example, *baseball, basketball, football,* and *volleyball*—describe a particular sport. They are spelled without a hyphen or a space.

For Clarity Certain letter combinations may cause a reader to misread a passage. Inserting a hyphen can prevent this.

KEY CONCEPT Use a hyphen within a word when a combination of letters might otherwise be confusing. ■

EXAMPLES:
co-op   versus   coop
re-lay   versus   relay

Unusual combinations of words can also be made clearer with hyphens.

KEY CONCEPT Use a hyphen between words to keep the reader from combining them erroneously. ■

EXAMPLES:
a new *car-buyer*   versus   a *new-car* buyer
three-point margins   versus   three *point-margins*

Exercise 51 Using Hyphens in Numbers, Word Parts, and Words On your paper, rewrite the sentences, adding necessary hyphens. Use a dictionary when in doubt. If no hyphen is needed, write *correct.*

EXAMPLE: The politician congratulated the senator elect.
ANSWER: The politician congratulated the senator-elect.

1. The history of basketball is filled with many all star players.
2. Some players have been self proclaimed stars; some have been legitimate stars.
3. Many players have become famous because of their offensive ability.
4. Moses Malone—a powerful center with a body like a tank—became famous because of his mind boggling rebounding.
5. Although he was not an ex marine, he often appeared to possess the posture of a soldier.
6. He displayed awe inspiring prowess when going after rebounds.
7. He routinely grabbed twenty six or twenty seven rebounds in a game when others felt lucky to grab ten.
8. He quickly set all time rebounding records.
9. Moreover, from the beginning of his career, he displayed the self assurance of a veteran.
10. Not surprisingly, he won numerous fans, including thousands from the non English speaking world.

More Practice

Grammar Exercise Workbook
• pp. 185–186
On-line Exercise Bank
• Section 28.5
Go on-line:
PHSchool.com
Enter Web Code:
eek-1002

Interactive Textbook

Get instant feedback! Exercises 51 and 52 are available on-line or on CD-ROM.

Exercise 52 **Using Hyphens to Avoid Ambiguity** On your paper, copy the sentences, adding hyphens to make each sentence clear.

EXAMPLE: We had to relay the wood floor.

ANSWER: We had to re-lay the wood floor.

1. The coaches who attended the awards ceremony were dressed so neatly that it was obvious that they had repressed their suits for the event.
2. The organizers decided to repair presenters and coaches.
3. Unfortunately, one of the coaches could not resign a promising point guard for his team.
4. The point guard was semi literate and had failed his classes.
5. Another coach was elated about a twelve year old boy he had spotted playing at a local playground.
6. The boy was apparently a selftaught basketball prodigy who played as if he were nineteen years old.
7. When I asked him how to prepare for next season, he gave me a selfhelp book on strength training.
8. The coauthor of the book is a famous sportswriter from the Midwest.
9. The writer claims that basketball is considered to be a semiinfectious disease in her state.
10. After I left the ceremony, I could not reenter the arena because I no longer had my standing room ticket.

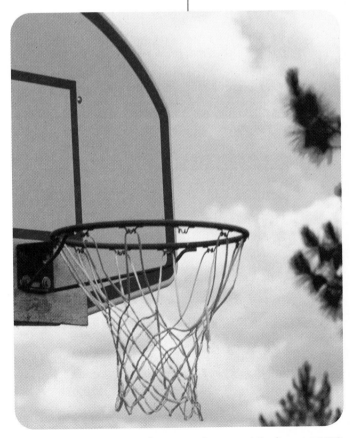

▶ **Critical Viewing** What hyphenated words might you use in a written description of this picture? **[Connect]**

Using Hyphens at the Ends of Lines

"To divide or not to divide?" This question comes up again and again when a writer reaches the end of a line of writing. In such a situation, you must decide whether to put one last word on the line, drop the word down to the next line, or divide it. The decision should be based on certain rules. The most important rule is the one regarding syllables.

KEY CONCEPT If a word must be divided, always divide it between syllables. ■

If you are in doubt about how to divide a word into syllables, check a dictionary. It will show, for example, that the word *intricately* has four syllables, *in tri cate ly*, and it can be divided as in the following example:

EXAMPLE: The coach's plan was a model of intri-
             cately plotted teamwork.

Always place the hyphen at the end of the first line—never at the start of the next line.

INCORRECT: The fans and players will continue to sup
             -port this coach as long as he wins.
CORRECT: The fans and players will continue to sup-
             port this coach as long as he wins.

Prefixes and suffixes provide a natural place for division.

KEY CONCEPT If a word contains word parts, it can almost always be divided between the prefix and the root or the root and the suffix. ■

PREFIX: ex-tend   out-side   mis-fortune
SUFFIX: hope-less four-some   fif-teen

If the suffix is composed of only two letters, however, avoid dividing the word between the root and suffix.

▶ Critical Viewing Identify three multisyllable words based on this picture. Between what letters in each word could you use a hyphen at the end of a line? [Apply]

In addition to avoiding a two-letter suffix, there are a number of other words that should not be divided. Be on the lookout for one-syllable words that sound like two-syllable words or look as if they are long enough to be two syllables. Do not divide them.

INCORRECT: lod-ge   clo-thes   thro-ugh
CORRECT: lodge   clothes   through

Each of these examples consists of only one syllable; therefore, dividing them is inappropriate. You will also need to watch divisions that result in a single letter standing alone.

▶**KEY CONCEPT** Avoid dividing a word so that a single letter stands alone. ■

INCORRECT: stead-y   a-ble   e-vict
CORRECT: steady   able   evict

▶**KEY CONCEPT** Avoid dividing proper nouns and proper adjectives. ■

The following divisions have traditionally been considered undesirable.

INCORRECT: We recently hired Sylvia Rodri-
                guez.
                I just finished eating a Mexi-
                can banana.

You may occasionally need to divide a word that already contains a hyphen.

▶**KEY CONCEPT** Divide a hyphenated word only after the hyphen. ■

If you use the word *apple-pie* as an adjective, you would hyphenate it. When dividing the word at the end of a line, divide it only at the hyphen.

INCORRECT: Plans for a strong team appeared to be in ap-
                ple-pie order.
CORRECT: Plans for a strong team appeared to be in apple-
                pie order.

Spelling Tip

The spell-check feature in most word-processing programs will not recognize uncommon family names and may highlight them as incorrect. Double-check your spelling of proper nouns.

▶ **KEY CONCEPT** Avoid dividing a word so that part of the word is on one page and the remainder is on the next page. ■

Often, chopping up a word in this way will confuse your readers or cause them to lose their train of thought.

▶ **Exercise 53** Using Hyphens to Divide Words In the sentences below, if a word has been divided correctly, write *correct*. If not, divide the word correctly or write it as one word if it cannot be divided.

EXAMPLE: Have you given much tho-
                 ught to this problem?
ANSWER: Have you given much thought to this problem?

1. Do you want to play basketball with my team-
   mates?
2. We play basketball ever-
   y Saturday morning.
3. The star of our team (Did you know we had a star?) is my sister-in-law.
4. Do you know how much of the world's population enjoys playing basketball?
5. Millions of people enjoy watching or playing basketball.
6. Some people like to play basketball indoors; others like playing outdoors.
7. Basketball has long been dominated by powerful centers.
8. Wilt Chamberlain was one of basketball's most dominant centers.
9. Did you and your friends know that Wilt Chamberlain once scored 100 points in a professional game?
10. He did so against the New York Knicker-
    bockers in 1962.

▶ **Exercise 54** Using Hyphens in Written Work On a piece of looseleaf paper with the margins marked, copy a paragraph from your social studies textbook. Use the margin guidelines to keep the margins of your report even. Break words as necessary to stay within the margin guidelines.

▶ **More Practice**

Grammar Exercise
Workbook
• pp. 185–186
On-line Exercise Bank
• Section 28.5
  Go on-line:
  PHSchool.com
  Enter Web Code:
  eek-1002

Complete the exercises on-line!
Exercises 53 and 54 are available on-line or on CD-ROM.

Section 28.5 Section Review

GRAMMAR EXERCISES 55–60

▶ **Exercise 55** **Using the Dash** On your paper, copy the following sentences, adding one or two dashes in each.

1. Basketball which has long been thought to be an urban game is extremely popular in the suburbs.
2. Modern players are much more muscular it's rare to see a lanky player anymore than players from the past.
3. This does not mean that basketball is a game only for giants thank goodness!
4. People of average height less than six feet tall have had basketball careers.
5. Tyrone "Muggsy" Bogues who enjoyed a stellar career at Wake Forest University in the late 1980's and went on to play professionally stands just five feet three inches tall.

▶ **Exercise 56** **Using Parentheses** On your paper, rewrite the following sentences using the necessary parentheses and capitalization.

1. Earvin Johnson did you know that he was called Magic Johnson? was one of the best point guards in basketball.
2. Johnson My dad saw him play was born in 1959 in Lansing, Michigan.
3. He starred as the point guard perhaps the most important position on the team of the Michigan State team.
4. By the time he retired in 1991, he had won numerous All-Star honors 12.
5. When did Magic Johnson first lead his professional team to a world championship: a 1980, b 1981, or c 1982?

▶ **Exercise 57** **Using Hyphens in Numbers, Word Parts, and Words** Rewrite the sentences that need hyphens. Use a dictionary when in doubt. If no hyphen is needed, write *correct.*

1. Wilt Chamberlain was one of the most intimidating players in basketball.
2. He was a perennial allstar during his long professional basketball career.
3. An ex high school standout, he enjoyed a stellar college career at the University of Kansas.
4. Chamberlain played for three seasons with the University of Kansas team— that university had well trained teams.
5. During his long career, he demon strated great self discipline.

▶ **Exercise 58** **Find It in Your Reading** Explain the use of hyphens in the excerpt from "Rare Air: Michael on Michael."

. . . And teams played me one-on-one at North Carolina. They never double-teamed me.

▶ **Exercise 59** **Find It in Your Writing** Look through your portfolio. Find examples of hyphens, parentheses, and dashes you have used. Explain why you used each mark.

▶ **Exercise 60** **Writing Application** Imagine that a talent scout has come to watch you play a sport. Write five sentences that you would want to say following the game. Use the guidelines below.

1. Use ex-teacher in a question.
2. Use the word second-class in a sentence about the sport.
3. Use a dash to set off a statement.
4. Use parentheses to set off an interrupting idea.
5. Use the dash to indicate an abrupt change of thought.

Section 28.6 — *Apostrophes*

Insects comprise the largest class of animals on the planet. They are social animals, and they are extremely organized. So, too, are the rules governing apostrophes.

Though the apostrophe ['] is classified as a punctuation mark and not as a letter, its misuse can result in the misspelling of many words. The apostrophe serves two purposes: to show possession and to indicate missing letters. In most cases, you must place the apostrophe between the letters of the word, not before or after it. Thus, misplacement of the apostrophe leads to spelling errors. This section will provide you with rules so that you can use the apostrophe correctly.

Theme: Bugs

In this section, you will learn about the use of apostrophes. The exercises and examples are about insects and other bugs.

Cross-Curricular Connection: Science

GRAMMAR IN LITERATURE

from **Tepeyac**
Sandra Cisneros

Some of the apostrophes in this excerpt indicate possession. These words are highlighted in blue italics. The apostrophe in the red italic word indicates the missing letters in a contraction.

I take *Abuelito's* hand, fat and dimpled in the center like a valentine, and we walk past the basilica, . . . Past the very same spot where long ago Juan Diego brought down from the *cerro* the miracle that has drawn everyone, . . . past La *Muñeca's* mother watering her famous dahlias . . . .
   Who *would've* guessed, after all this time, it is me who will remember when everything else is forgotten, . . .

Apostrophes With Possessive Nouns

An apostrophe must be used to indicate possession or ownership with nouns.

With Singular Nouns As shown in the examples, the following rule applies to most singular nouns:

KEY CONCEPT Add an apostrophe and *s* to show the possessive case of most singular nouns. ■

EXAMPLES: The wing of the *insect* becomes the *insect's* wing.

The sections of the *ant* become the *ant's* sections.

The mandibles of the *cockroach* become the *cockroach's* mandibles.

The legs of the *centipede* become the *centipede's* legs.

The eye of the *fly* becomes the *fly's* eye.

The forelegs of a *mantis* become a *mantis's* forelegs.

When a singular noun ends in *s*, as in the last example, you can still follow this style in most cases. Ancient and classical names are the exception.

EXAMPLE: Zeus' thunderbolt.

With Plural Nouns Showing possession with plural nouns ending in *s* or *es* calls for a different rule:

KEY CONCEPT Add an apostrophe to show the possessive case of plural nouns ending in *s* or *es*. ■

EXAMPLES: The wings of the *bees* become the *bees'* wings.
The tracks of the *caterpillars* become the *caterpillars'* tracks.
The larvae of the *moths* become the *moths'* larvae.

▲ **Critical Viewing**
In a complete sentence that contains the possessive of *insect*, identify and describe three features of this insect. **[Describe]**

Not all plural nouns end in *s* or *es*, however. Another rule will help you form the possessive case of these nouns:

KEY CONCEPT Add an apostrophe and *s* to show the possessive case of plural nouns that do not end in *s* or *es*. ■

EXAMPLES: The books of the *men* become the *men's* books.

The songs of the *people* become the *people's* songs.

With Compound Nouns Sometimes, you will find that a noun showing ownership consists of several words.

KEY CONCEPT Add an apostrophe and *s* (or just an apostrophe if the word is a plural ending in *s*) to the last word of a compound noun to form the possessive. ■

This rule refers to names of businesses and organizations, names with titles, and hyphenated compound nouns.

APOSTROPHES WITH COMPOUND NOUNS	
Businesses and Organizations	The Good Earth's menu the Lions Clubs' motto
Names With Titles	the Secretary of Defense's visit Edward VIII's abdication
Hyphenated Compound Nouns Used to Describe People	my father-in-law's glasses the secretary-treasurer's pen

With Expressions Involving Time and Amounts If you use possessive expressions involving time or amounts, you will need to use an apostrophe.

KEY CONCEPT To form possessives involving time or amounts, use an apostrophe and *s* or just an apostrophe if the possessive is a plural ending in *s*. ■

TIME: a day's journey   six years' time
AMOUNT: one quarter's worth   fifty cents' worth

To Show Joint and Individual Ownership When two nouns are involved, take care to show ownership accurately.

> **KEY CONCEPT** To show joint ownership, make the final noun possessive. ■

EXAMPLES: Roger and Jeremy's ant farms
              (They share the same ant farms.)

              the husband and wife's car
              (They share one car.)

> **KEY CONCEPT** To show individual ownership, make each noun possessive. ■

EXAMPLES: Roger's and Jeremy's ant farms
              (Each has his own ant farm.)

              the husband's and wife's cars
              (Each owns a separate car.)

Checking Your Use of the Rules Often, confusion results over the application of the various rules because writers forget to determine whether they are writing about a singular noun or a plural noun. First, determine whether the owner is singular or plural. Then, consider the word before the apostrophe you are going to add. If you place the apostrophe correctly, the letters to the left of the apostrophe should spell out the owner's complete name. Look at the checking technique in this chart:

CHECKING THE USE OF APOSTROPHES		
Incorrect	Explanation	Correction
Jame's car	The owner is not *Jame*, but *James*.	James's car
one boys' book	The owner is not *boys*, but *boy*.	one boy's book
two girl's lunches	The owner is not *girl*, but *girls*.	two girls' lunches

Exercise 61 Using Apostrophes With Single-Word Possessive Nouns Copy the underlined nouns, which may be singular or plural, putting them into the possessive form when necessary. For sentences that do not require possessive forms, just write the underlined word.

EXAMPLE: Insects sizes can vary tremendously.
ANSWER: Insects'

1. The insects class is the largest in the world.
2. The class distribution is all over the world.
3. Insects outnumber all other animal species.
4. Some moths wingspans can be twelve inches.
5. A stick insect length can also be twelve inches.

Exercise 62 Using Apostrophes With Compound Nouns Copy the underlined nouns, putting them into the possessive form.

EXAMPLE: I share my sister-in-law fear of insects.
ANSWER: sister-in-law's

1. Life-cycle lengths vary from insect to insect.
2. The seventeen-year locust maturation period is from thirteen to seventeen years.
3. The jaws function in an insect is to crush food.
4. Some insects live in a highly organized society, with the leader role being taken by the queen.
5. My entomological society rules for membership are strict.

Exercise 63 Using Apostrophes to Show Joint and Individual Ownership From each of the following sentences, copy the underlined words, changing them to show joint or individual ownership as the instructions indicate.

1. Plant and insect relationships are often necessary to the plant. (joint)
2. Bee and ant organizations are quite complex. (individual)
3. Wasps and termites social interactions are also quite unique. (individual)
4. Some wasps and flies maturation period is a matter of days. (individual)
5. Certain insects live by one of two methods; parasitism and predation features are quite different. (individual)

More Practice

Grammar Exercise Workbook
• pp. 187–188
On-line Exercise Bank
• Section 28.6
Go on-line:
PHSchool.com
Enter Web Code:
eek-1002

interactive Textbook

Get instant feedback! Exercises 61, 62, and 63 are available on-line or on CD-ROM.

Apostrophes With Pronouns

Some pronouns showing ownership require an apostrophe:

▶ **KEY CONCEPT** Use an apostrophe and *s* with indefinite pronouns to show possession. ∎

EXAMPLES:　　another's　　nobody's　　one's
　　　　　　　anyone's　　someone's　everybody's

If you form a two-word indefinite pronoun, add the apostrophe and the -*s* to the last word only.

EXAMPLES:　　nobody else's　　one another's

Possessive personal pronouns do not need an apostrophe.

▶ **KEY CONCEPT** Do not use an apostrophe with the possessive forms of personal pronouns. ∎

With the words *yours, his, hers, theirs, its, ours,* and *whose,* no apostrophe is necessary. These already show ownership.

EXAMPLES:　　Looking at the butterfly collections, I decided
　　　　　　　yours far outdistanced the other entries.
　　　　　　　Its beautiful colors drew everyone's notice.

Pay special attention to the possessive forms *whose* and *its* because they are easily confused with the contractions *who's* and *it's.* Just remember that *whose* and *its* show possession.

PRONOUNS:　　*Whose* wallet is this?

　　　　　　　Its chimes rang out clearly.

Who's and *it's,* on the other hand, are contractions of the words *who is* and *it is.* They both require apostrophes to indicate the missing letters.

CONTRACTIONS:　　*Who's* responsible for naming insects?

　　　　　　　　It's up to whoever discovers a new species to name it.

▼ **Critical Viewing**
What possessive pronoun would you use to refer to the colony of these insects? **[Apply]**

More Practice

Grammar Exercise
Workbook
• pp. 187–188
On-line Exercise Bank
• Section 28.6
  Go on-line:
  PHSchool.com
  Enter Web Code:
  eek-1002

> **Exercise 64** Proofreading for Correct Use of Apostrophes

On a separate sheet of paper, rewrite each sentence. Correct
any errors in the use of apostrophes.

EXAMPLE: That hive is her's.
ANSWER: That hive is hers.

1. A parasite finds it's nourishment in other living creatures.
2. A social hierarchy is usually led by a queen, and all the
   offspring are her's.
3. Workers are usually male, and their's is the responsibility
   to keep the society going.
4. Some ants take over others colonies and use them for
   workers.
5. The eyes of an insect are on its head.
6. Some insect societies are almost as complex as our's.
7. My fear of insects is greater than yours.
8. I thought this was your ant farm, but it must be someone's else.
9. An insect has a nervous system who's center is a nerve
   cord running from the head to the abdomen.
10. An insect's heart is not as complicated as your's or mine's.

▼ Critical Viewing
Identify two
possessive nouns
suggested by
this picture. What
possessive pronouns
could take the place
of these nouns?
[Apply]

Apostrophes With Contractions

The meaning of a contraction is implied by its name. It is a word contracted in size by the removal of some letter or letters and the insertion of an apostrophe to indicate the missing letters. This leads to the following basic rule for contractions:

▶ **KEY CONCEPT** Use an apostrophe in a contraction to indicate the position of the missing letter or letters. ■

Contractions With Verbs Verbs are often used in a contracted form. Look at the following chart, noticing how often these verb contractions are used in common speech patterns.

COMMON CONTRACTIONS WITH VERBS		
Verbs with *not*	are not = aren't do not = don't	was not = wasn't were not = weren't
Pronouns with *will*	I will = I'll you will = you'll	she will = she'll they will = they'll
Pronouns and nouns with the verb *be*	I am = I'm you are = you're	who is = who's Mark is = Mark's
Pronouns with *would*	I would = I'd he would = he'd	we would = we'd they would = they'd

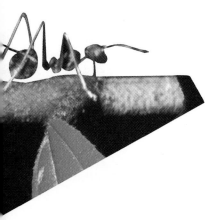

One special contraction changes letters as well as drops them: *Will not* becomes *won't* in the contracted form.

Try to avoid most verb contractions in formal writing. They tend to make your style more informal than you may wish.

INFORMAL: He's promised that he'll hide the beetle if we're still afraid of it.

FORMAL: He has promised that he will hide the beetle if we are still afraid of it.

Contractions With Years In writing about years, insert an apostrophe in places where a number is left out.

EXAMPLES: Decathlon Champion of '75

the snowstorm of '03

Contractions With o', d', and l' These letters followed by the apostrophe make up the abbreviated form of the words *of the* or *the* as spelled in several different languages.

EXAMPLES: o'clock   d'Angelo
                O'Sullivan l'Abbé

    As you can see, these letters and apostrophes are combined most often with surnames.

Contractions With Dialogue When writing dialogue, you may want to keep the flavor of the speaker's individual speaking style. Therefore, use any contractions the speaker might use. You may also want to include a regional dialect or a foreign accent. Because speech often includes pronunciations with omitted letters, you should insert apostrophes to show those changes.

EXAMPLES: C'mon—aren't you comin' fishin'?
                'Tis a fine spring morn we're havin'.
                That li'l ant is aworkin' hard!

    As with most punctuation, overuse reduces the effectiveness and impact, so watch the overuse of the apostrophe with contractions—even in dialogue.

Exercise 65 **Apostrophes With Contractions** If a contraction is underlined in the following paragraph, write the original two words. If two words are underlined, write the contraction they would form.

EXAMPLE: <u>Aren't</u> people who study insects called entomologists?

ANSWER: Are not

    (1) Insects <u>do not</u> have lungs but a network of tubes to carry air through the body. (2) They are invertebrates, which means that they <u>haven't</u> got a backbone. (3) <u>They've</u> been found on land and in most types of water. (4) Insect predators <u>cannot</u> live without feeding on other insects. (5) Most species <u>don't</u> grow in the same way people do. (6) <u>They are</u> able to reach adulthood by metamorphosis. (7) Insects that are scavengers <u>will not</u> eat living plants or animals. (8) Some parasitic insects are so small that you <u>would not</u> be able to see them without a microscope. (9) An <u>insect's</u> often distinguished by its three body parts. (10) My friend studies insects and says that <u>it's</u> an interesting field.

More Practice

Grammar Exercise Workbook
• pp. 189–190
On-line Exercise Bank
• Section 28.6
   Go on-line:
   PHSchool.com
   Enter Web Code:
   eek-1002

Get instant feedback! Exercises 65 and 66 are available on-line or on CD-ROM.

Special Uses of the Apostrophe

An apostrophe is also used to show the plural of numbers, symbols, letters, and words used to name themselves.

▶ **KEY CONCEPT** Use an apostrophe and *s* to write the plurals of numbers, symbols, letters, and words used to name themselves. ■

EXAMPLES: There are two *8*'s in that number.
You need two more *?*'s.
Her *b*'s and *d*'s all look the same.
A's and *an*'s cause confusion.

▶ **Exercise 66** Using the Apostrophe in Special Cases Copy the following sentences, adding an apostrophe and an *s* to numbers, symbols, letters, and words whenever necessary. Underline all items in italics.

EXAMPLE: On my last report card, I got all *A* and *B*.
ANSWER: On my last report card, I got all *A*'s and *B*'s.

1. On my two papers on insects, I got *95*.
2. I might get *100* on my next papers.
3. I spelled beetle with too many *e*.
4. I must have written twenty *entomology* in that paper.
5. People in their *20* generally have a lot of energy.
6. Europeans put an extra line in their *7* to show that they are different from their *1*.
7. Insect abdomens are segmented into *10* or *11*.
8. Insect legs are usually arranged in *2*.
9. Is it all right to use *&* in my paper, or should I spell out the word?
10. She is allergic to bees, so she has two *Rx* in case she gets a bee sting.

▶ Critical Viewing Describe the appearance of this bug. What possessive noun did you use? [Apply]

Academic and Workplace Skills

Speaking, Listening, Viewing, and Representing

Speaking, listening, viewing, and representing are all unique forms of communication used for conveying and receiving information. Speaking and listening both use language to represent ideas. Therefore, understanding language is the key to developing good speaking and listening skills.

Forms of viewing and representing also use language to convey information, but always in combination with visual representations. Learning how to interpret these visual representations and seeing how they work with language to present meaning is the first step in improving your viewing and representing skills.

All together, speaking, listening, viewing, and representing are the building blocks of communication and of one's view of the world.

▲ **Critical Viewing**
Which of these students is speaking? Which is listening most attentively? Explain your choices. **[Infer]**

Speaking *and* Listening Skills

In school, good speaking and listening skills are essential for success. Learning how to take part in group discussions and how to give a well-prepared oral presentation are two activities that require good speaking skills.

Critical listening skills are important also. Learning how to become a critical listener will enable you to understand and evaluate the most important points in a speaker's message.

Speaking in a Group Discussion

In school, you will most likely participate in a number of *group discussions,* or informal meetings used to openly discuss ideas. These group discussions will focus on subjects you are studying or activities being planned. To get the most from a group discussion, you have to learn to participate in it.

Communicating Effectively Effective communication means thinking before speaking. Plan the points you want to make and how you will express them. Organize these points in a logical order. Think of examples or supporting facts to illustrate your points. Also, remember to speak clearly, pronouncing words slowly and carefully.

Asking Questions Get in the habit of asking questions. Asking questions can help you clarify your understanding of another speaker's ideas. Questions can also be used to call attention to possible errors in the speaker's points or areas of confusion.

Making Relevant Contributions The information or ideas you choose to contribute should be related to the topic being discussed. When you do contribute, clearly show how your ideas are connected to the topic.

> **Exercise 1** Policy Discussion With three to five other students, hold a fifteen-minute group discussion about the benefits and drawbacks of a particular school policy. After the discussion, write a brief journal entry about how you used the strategies above as you participated.

> **More Practice**
> Academic and Workplace Skills Activity Book
> • p. 1

Speaking in Public

Giving a presentation in front of an audience is *public speaking.* By learning more about speeches and speechmaking, you can improve your public-speaking skills.

Understanding Different Types of Speeches

There are four kinds of speeches: informative, persuasive, entertaining, and extemporaneous. To make your speech more effective, use language—informal, standard, or technical—that suits your purpose and is appropriate for the audience.

▶ **KEY CONCEPT** Choose the kind of speech you will give and the language you will use by thinking about your purpose and what your audience is like. ■

- An **informative speech** explains an idea, a process, or an object. Facts must be presented in a clear, organized way. Also, in an informative speech, technical language may be used to more accurately describe the topic.

- A **persuasive speech** is usually spoken in standard English; it tries to make the audience agree with the speaker's position or to take some action. Opinions need to be supported by statements or facts.

- An **entertaining speech**, spoken both in standard and informal language, offers the audience an enjoyable experience. Entertaining passages may be included in other kinds of speeches to offer variety or to provide emphasis.

- An **extemporaneous speech** is an informal speech given to suit an occasion, event, or audience and does not rely on a prepared manuscript but on the speaker's knowledge and ability to improvise.

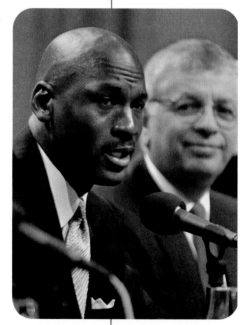

▲ Critical Viewing
Do you think this athlete is giving a prepared speech or an extemporaneous speech? Explain.
[Deduce]

▶ **Exercise 2** Listing Speech Topics and Audiences List two possible topics and the intended audience for each of the four types of speeches discussed on this page.

Preparing and Presenting a Speech

Once you know what kind of speech you will give and have chosen an appropriate topic, you will need to gather and organize information and practice your speech before you present it.

▶ **KEY CONCEPT** To prepare your speech, research your topic, cite reliable sources, and organize your thesis. ■

Gather Valid Proof From Reliable Sources Research the subject using the library or other reliable sources to find valid proof, or conclusive evidence, to support your claims. Research is especially important when preparing an informative or persuasive speech.

Use Appropriate Appeals to Support Your Arguments The evidence you use to support your claims should be appropriate to your topic. For example, if you are writing a persuasive speech on the benefits of a healthy diet, it would be appropriate to research and cite evidence from nutritional experts, but not from the founder of a fast-food chain.

Present a Clear Thesis To help you organize and develop your thesis, make an outline. Begin your outline with any necessary background material. Arrange information in a rational sequence. Include logical points to support your message. Then, transfer this information to index cards to which you can refer while presenting your speech.

▶ **KEY CONCEPT** When presenting your speech, use rhetorical forms of language and verbal and nonverbal strategies. ■

Use Rhetorical Strategies Let the audience know your important points by repeating key words and phrases. Keep your speech lively and interesting by using active verbs and colorful adjectives. Create a sense of rhythm in your speech through the use of parallel phrases or parallel series of words.

Use Verbal and Nonverbal Strategies Vary the pitch of your voice and the rate at which you speak, and use movements, gestures, and facial expressions to emphasize key points of your message.

▶ **Exercise 3** Presenting a Persuasive Speech Prepare a persuasive speech on a topic that interests you. Follow the steps on this page to prepare and present your speech to your classmates.

Technology Tip

Practice your speech by recording it on an audio- or videotape. Play it back to analyze how you sound and look. Use the evaluation tips on page 550 to discover ways to improve your speech and delivery.

More Practice

Academic and Workplace Skills Activity Book
• p. 2

Evaluating a Presentation or Performance Evaluate works by your peers. These include presentations, such as original essays or narratives. They also include performances, such as interpretations of poetry and individual or group performances of scripts. The main purpose of the evaluation is to determine which techniques and skills were successful and which need more work. A secondary purpose is to apply the successful techniques and skills to improve your own presentations and performances.

KEY CONCEPT An effective speaker uses verbal and nonverbal techniques to gain and hold an audience's attention. ■

> **TIPS FOR EVALUATING A SPEECH**
>
> - Did the speaker introduce the topic clearly?
> - Did the speaker support main ideas with appropriate details?
> - Did the speaker establish eye contact?
> - Did the speaker's gestures and movements reinforce the message?
> - Did the speaker project loudly enough?
> - Did the speaker vary voice, pitch, and speaking rate?
> - Did the speaker pronounce all words clearly and correctly?

Improving Your Own Presentations and Performances When you evaluate another speaker's presentation or delivery, you identify the reasons you, as a listener, did or did not find the presentation effective. Keep these reasons in mind as you practice your next presentation. If you found your attention wandering because the speaker never varied his or her position or made eye contact, then be sure to vary your position as you speak and to make eye contact with your audience.

Exercise 4 Evaluating a Presentation or Performance
Use the suggestions on this page to evaluate a presentation or performance given in class. Comment on the skills that the person used effectively, and give specific examples of how the skills were used. Be tactful in pointing out any problems the speaker displayed. Give your completed evaluation to the person.

Research Tip

Ask your librarian for help in finding information on giving presentations, such as speeches or dramatic performances. Also, look for presentations and performances on audio- and videotape, and study the techniques used by the presenters or performers.

Listening Critically

There's a lot more to listening than just hearing words. Listening involves active participation. Listening critically involves evaluating and making judgments about what you hear.

▶ **KEY CONCEPT** A critical listener takes an active role in the information he or she hears. ■

Learning the Listening Process One reason to become a better listener is to acquire new ideas and information on which to build your knowledge. Understanding the listening process will bring you one step closer to becoming a critical listener.

Focus Your Attention Give the speaker your undivided attention so you can fully understand the information you hear. If you are planning to attend a formal presentation or speech on a particular topic, acquire more information about the topic before attending. This will increase your interest and make it easier for you to focus your attention.

Interpret the Information When you are listening to a speaker, you have to analyze what you are hearing. Some information will be more important than other information. It is up to you to be selective in what you will try to remember. Use the following suggestions to guide you:

- Listen for words and phrases that are emphasized or repeated.

- Test your understanding of important statements by rephrasing them in your own words.

- Take notes and summarize ideas in writing.

- Be alert to nonverbal signals, such as tone of voice, gestures, and facial expressions. Often, body language is as important a part of the communication process as verbal language.

- Find a meaningful pattern in which to combine present and past information.

Respond to the Speaker's Message After the speaker has finished speaking, respond to the information you heard. Think about whether you feel the speaker has made valid points and supported them well. Jot down questions you still have after listening. If possible, ask questions to clarify the speaker's message.

▶ **Exercise 5** Using the Listening Process Apply the listening strategies on this page to a lecture by your teacher or a presentation or a performance by one of your peers.

◉ Technology Tip

To improve your ability to interpret information, listen to tape recordings of classroom lectures. Ask your teachers for permission before taping. Practice your listening skills, using the techniques on this page, while you play the tapes at home.

▶ **More Practice**

Academic and Workplace Skills Activity Book
- p. 3

Using Different Types of Listening Part of being a critical listener is knowing how to adjust your listening according to the situation. There are four main types of listening: *critical, empathic, appreciative,* and *reflective.*

Types of Listening		
Type	**How to Listen**	**Situation**
Critical	Listen for facts and supporting details to understand and evaluate the speaker's message.	Informative or persuasive essays, class discussions, announcements
Empathic	Imagine yourself in the other person's position, and try to understand what he or she is thinking.	Conversations with friends or family
Appreciative	Identify and analyze aesthetic or artistic elements, such as character development, rhyme, imagery, and descriptive language.	Oral presentations of a poem or short story and dramatic performances
Reflective	Ask questions to get information, and use or reflect on the speaker's responses to form new questions.	Class or group discussions

Asking Different Types of Questions Use different types of questions to get the information you want to know.

- An **open-ended** question allows the person you are asking to make choices about the kinds of information used in the response. Use follow-up questions to clarify specific points. An example of an open-ended question is "Why are you the best candidate for class president?"

- A **closed** question leads to a specific response and must be answered with a yes or a no. Sometimes, you may want to explore the reasons for the answer by asking an open-ended follow-up question.

- A **fact** question is aimed at getting a particular piece of information and must be answered with facts: "How many votes did you receive in the election?" Follow-up questions may help you pinpoint the source of information.

> **Exercise 6** Using Different Types of Listening For one week, keep a "listening log." Jot down examples of ways you have used each of the types of listening. Remember that you may use more than one type of listening for the same situation.

> **Exercise 7** Using Different Types of Questions Work with a classmate on this exercise. Have your classmate choose a topic in which he or she is interested and knowledgeable. Then, ask two open-ended, two closed, and two fact questions to learn about that topic. Record the person's responses, and then switch roles.

Evaluating Your Listening Improve your listening skills by evaluating them. Use the following strategies to guide you:

Rephrase and Repeat Statements Test your understanding of the speaker's statements by rephrasing and then repeating them. If necessary, ask questions to improve your paraphrase.

Compare and Contrast Interpretations Compare your interpretation of a speaker's message with that of a classmate's. Before discussing with your classmate, jot down a brief summary of the speech or presentation and any questions you have. Then, compare your notes with your partner's.

Research Points of Interest or Contention Use the library or other references to learn more about the topic or to check questionable facts in the speaker's presentation.

> **Exercise 8** Evaluating Your Listening Skills Working with another classmate, use the skills listed above to evaluate how well you listen to a lecture by a teacher, a presentation by a classmate, or a story told by one of your friends. Afterward, write an evaluation describing how well you listened and the areas in which you need to improve.

Technology Tip

Practice your critical listening skills by listening to campaign speeches at school and in local elections and by listening to commentary on current events on television.

Viewing Skills

Visual representation is an important and effective way to communicate. Television programs, textbooks, Web sites, and works of art are common types of media that use images to add to your view of the world. In this section, you will learn how to interpret information from visual sources.

Interpreting Maps and Graphs

Finding information in maps and graphs involves understanding the features contained within them.

▶ **KEY CONCEPT** Determine your purpose for reading the map or graph, and then find the information to fulfill this purpose. ■

Maps A *map* can show climate, population density, changes over historical periods, battles in a war, the relative heights of landforms, or weather patterns, among many other types of information. To interpret a map, (1) determine the type and purpose of the map; (2) read the title, captions, and labels, and examine the distance scale and other symbols; (3) relate the information on the map to any written information accompanying it.

Research Tip

Browse through atlases to see the many uses that maps have. Note the features of each map and the various symbols used to communicate information.

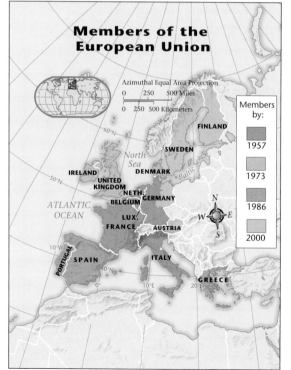

◀ **Critical Viewing**
What is the purpose of this map? **[Analyze]**

Graphs

Graphs present numerical information in visual form and compare two or more sets of related information. Study the following three types of commonly used graphs.

Line Graph A *line graph* shows changes over a period of time. A line connects points, which appear as dots at intersections on the graph. Each dot represents a number or a quantity of something. To interpret a line graph, (1) read the labels to see what the data represent and the time interval for which the data are being recorded, (2) read both the horizontal axis (left-to-right line) and the vertical axis (bottom-to-top line) that make up the two axes of the graph, and (3) compare and contrast the data.

Bar Graph A *bar graph* compares and contrasts quantities. The height or length of each bar shows what numbers it represents. To interpret a bar graph, (1) match the label of each bar on the horizontal axis to the number that the bar reaches on the vertical axis, (2) note the labels to see what each bar represents and why the two bars are being compared, and (3) compare and contrast the data.

◄▲ Critical Viewing
What can you learn about Siberia from these two graphs? [Synthesize]

Pie Graph A *pie graph* shows the relationship of parts to a whole. The graph is a circle that represents 100 percent of something. Each part stands for a portion, or percentage, of the whole. To interpret a pie graph, (1) look at the numbers that go with each part, (2) match the parts to the key to see what each represents, and (3) use the numbers and parts to make comparisons.

THE LABOR FORCE IN SELECTED WESTERN EUROPEAN COUNTRIES

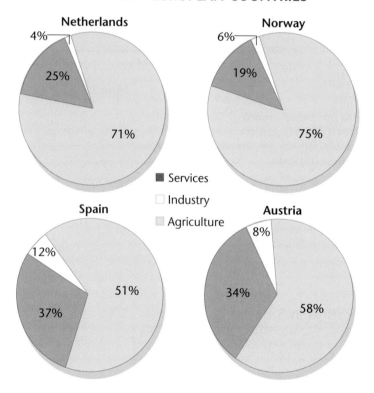

◄ **Critical Viewing**
Which country has the largest agricultural labor force? **[Identify]**

> **Exercise 9** Reading Information Visually Use the tips you have just read to interpret the map and the graphs in this section. Write an explanation of the information presented in each. Then, decide what conclusions can be drawn from them.

> **More Practice**
Academic and Workplace Skills Activity Book
• pp. 4–5

Viewing Information Media Critically

To be an informed consumer of information, it is important that you learn to critically evaluate what you see and hear in the media. Applying critical viewing skills to the various forms of news media will help you to understand events and issues and to formulate your own opinions.

KEY CONCEPT Learn to identify and evaluate the different kinds of information found in nonprint media. ▪

Recognizing Kinds of Information Media Much of the information you receive comes to you from visual media, particularly television. The quality and relevance of this information depends on the type of program being viewed.

The following chart describes several forms of nonprint information media.

NONPRINT INFORMATION MEDIA			
Form of News Media	Topic(s)	Coverage and Content	Point of View
Nightly News	Current events or news	Brief summaries illustrated by video footage	Presents information objectively
Documentary	One topic of social interest	Story shown through narration and video footage	Expresses controversial opinions
Interview	Topics of social interest	Conversation of questions and answers	Presents opinions of interviewee
Television Newsmagazine	Covers a variety of topics	Feature with hosts and footage, meant to entertain and inform	Emphasizes stories that grab a viewer's attention
Commercial	Products, people, and ideas	Short message of images and slogans	Presents information to sell something or to persuade

Evaluating and Critiquing Persuasive Techniques

When you view any form of media, you should be aware of persuasive techniques used to misrepresent information and possibly distort your understanding of a message or an event.

Glittering generalities are lofty, broad statements that seek to appeal to a wide audience. The statement, "The best is yet to come if we all do our part" "glitters" with positive words and ideas, but it offers no real insight. Note glittering generalities, and examine them to find out what they really mean.

Bandwagon appeals are statements that use a form of peer pressure as their support. A bandwagon appeal suggests that you should take a certain action or think in a certain way because many others do.

Symbols are images that stand for or embody the qualities of another thing. For example, an advertisement for a car may include symbols of wealth, power, and prestige in addition to showing the actual car. Including these symbols suggests that the car is also a symbol of these qualities and that owning the car will make you feel wealthy, powerful, and important.

Deconstructing Information From the Media First, determine the kind of media program you are watching. Then, use your knowledge of persuasive techniques combined with the following strategies to deconstruct—break down into pieces—the images and language of the media you are viewing.

- Be aware of the purpose and limitations of the program you are watching. Find out who wrote or sponsored the program.
- Separate **facts** (proven statements) from **opinions** (beliefs). Use resources to check questionable information.
- Watch for **bias**—presenting a subject from one point of view.
- Note the kinds of images shown and their emotional impact.
- View the complete program before reaching your own conclusions about issues, people, and information.

▶ **Exercise 10** Identifying Persuasive Techniques in Advertisements Find examples of glittering generalities, bandwagon appeals, and symbols in advertising. Choose your examples from electronic and print media. Write a brief explanation of the persuasive technique used in each advertisement.

⟲ Learn More

For more information about methods of persuasion, see Chapter 7. For information on how advertisements persuade, see Chapter 8.

▶ **More Practice**

Academic and Workplace Skills Activity Book
• p. 6

Interpreting Fine Art

Paintings, drawings, sculpture, and photographs are all examples of fine art. To enrich your understanding and enjoyment of these works, you must interpret the various elements that make up the artwork.

▶KEY CONCEPT In works of art, meaning is communicated through elements of design. ■

Interpreting Elements of Design To help you interpret a work of art, consider the following questions:

- Does the work present definable objects or is it abstract—not showing any particular objects?
- What shapes, lines, and colors do you see?
- What mood, theme, or message does the work convey?
- Which areas are darkest, and which are lightest? What does the contrast of light and dark areas suggest?
- How do all the individual elements work together to create a feeling or an idea?

▶Exercise 11 **Responding to Fine Art** Interpret the painting *Dancers, Pink and Green,* by Edgar Degas, by answering the questions listed above. Write your answers in a notebook, along with any other observations. Share your impressions in an open discussion with your classmates.

Dancers, Pink and Green, Edgar Degas, Metropolitan Museum of Art

🖱 Research Tip

Spend some time in the library viewing books and slides of fine art. Which artists and works of art do you prefer? Make notes in your journal about why they appeal to you.

💿 Technology Tip

Great art museums are waiting for you on the Internet. Enter the name of the museum in a search engine to find the URL (address) of the museum's Web site.

Representing Skills

Graphic organizers, multimedia presentations, and perform-ances are ways in which you can express yourself to the world. In this section, you will learn how to prepare your own visual representations.

Creating Visual Aids

For large amounts of information or complex ideas, it is help-ful to organize the material into a visual aid, such as a graphic organizer, map, or diagram. These visual aids can also help you present information to others and to organize and remember information when you study.

▶ **KEY CONCEPT** Graphic organizers make information easier to comprehend and remember. ■

Use these strategies to construct your own visual aid:

- **Use Text Descriptions** Note the headings and subheadings that are used to organize the text. You can use headings to develop a concept map or an idea web, which will present these categories in visual form.

- **Determine the Text Structure** Consider the structure of the text when you choose a visual aid to display the infor-mation. For texts that show comparison and contrast, a Venn diagram may be the best choice. A flowchart is a good way to display cause-and-effect relationships. Problems and solutions can be shown in charts or diagrams. Main ideas and supporting details lend themselves to an outline. Chronological events can be represented on a timeline.

- **Identify Your Purpose** Is the purpose of the visual aid to help you study or to present information to others? Your answer will determine what information to include and which visual aid to use. Visual aids used for studying can be simple webs, charts, tables, or outlines. Visual aids used for presentations should be designed with an audience in mind. They should be appealing to the viewer and easy to understand.

- **Study Effective Graphics** Notice the effective use of graph-ics in textbooks, newspapers, and magazines. How are these graphics used to support the information in the text? For example, a graph may show information to support a view-point or to prove an argument.

⊘ Learn More

For more information about text structures, see the following "Exposition" chapters: "Comparison and Contrast," Chapter 9; "Cause and Effect," Chapter 10; "Problem and Solution," Chapter 11.

Following are descriptions of various types of visual aids and examples of how they are used.

Charts, Graphs, and Tables These visual aids can be used to present survey statistics, results of experiments or research, and other complex information. A table outlining a feudal society, for example, would show the people occupying the highest ranks (kings, emperors, and lesser rulers) at the top and those of lower ranks (merchants, peasants, and craftsmen) at the bottom.

Diagrams, Maps, and Illustrations These drawings show the features of an object, place, or process. For example, you might make a drawing, like the one below, of how a volcano erupts.

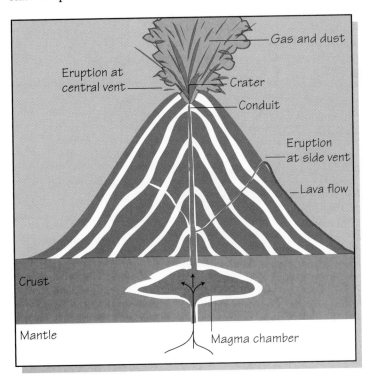

⊛ Technology Tip

Explore the table, graph, and graphics features on a computer, including changing text into graph and table form, merging text and pictures, and drawing capabilities.

▶ **Exercise 12** Creating Visual Aids From Textbooks Choose a chapter from your math, science, or social studies textbook. Make a graphic organizer to represent a concept or group of facts in the chapter. Explain why you chose that particular type of visual aid and how it helps to clarify the information.

▶ **More Practice**

Academic and Workplace Skills Activity Book
• p. 8

Using Formatting

There are many formatting techniques on most word processors that can aid you in making visual representations like the flyer shown here. Remember that the features you use should match the purpose of the text.

- Type styles have different effects on the viewer. Letters and characters can be italic (slanted), bold (dark type), or a combination of the two. They can also be shadowed or outlined and printed in a range of colors.

- Different effects can be produced by indenting and spacing the text. Information can be presented in bulleted lists or, when information has to appear in a certain order, numbered lists.

- Parts of the text can be shaded or colored for effect or to call attention to the information. Borders can be added to make information stand out or for decoration.

- Graphics can be added to attract the viewers and to give them an idea of what kind of information they can expect to read.

Have Rake, Will Travel
Buried in Autumn Leaves?

HARD-WORKING, DEPENDABLE
HIGH-SCHOOL STUDENT WILL RAKE YOUR LAWN

- Have own rake and leaf blower
- Will rake leaves from lawn and shrubbery
- Will bag leaves and take them to curb
- Reasonable rates
- Satisfaction guaranteed
- Available most weekdays 3:15 P.M. – 6:30 P.M. and weekends

*Call or e-mail
Tom Wilson*
Tel. 101-555-3377 or
twilson@rakeleaves.com

Exercise 13 Using Formatting to Design a Brochure
Use the tips on formatting and design to prepare a flyer or brochure that promotes a school sport or club. When your flyer is complete, ask a classmate to evaluate your use of various formatting and design features.

Technology Tip

Consult the software manual, Help feature, or toolbar to explore the possibilities for formatting, using the software on your computer.

Working With Multimedia

Some kinds of information are most effectively presented with sounds and visuals. When preparing a multimedia presentation, consider using an overhead projector, a slide projector, a videotape player, or an audiocassette player. These can enhance your presentation with still images, moving images, recorded voices, music, graphic organizers, and art.

Giving a Multimedia Presentation Although almost any kind of media can be used in a multimedia presentation, you should consider the topic, the audience, and the available equipment before you choose which media to use.

Use the following suggestions to help you prepare and give a multimedia presentation:

- Outline your oral report, and decide which parts will be more effective if presented through visual and aural media.
- Choose forms of media that suit your topic. If your topic is American life during World War II, you might play popular music of that time as a background and show slides of women workers in defense industries to illustrate the changes in society resulting from the war.
- Use media selections evenly throughout your presentation, not just at the beginning or end.
- Make sure all visual images can be seen by the entire audience. Small images can be photocopied and enlarged before being shown on an overhead projector.
- Rehearse your presentation with the multimedia equipment. Become familiar with making adjustments to the equipment.
- Before the presentation, double-check your equipment to make sure everything is in working condition.
- Have a backup plan in case your equipment fails. You might have copies of illustrations or graphic organizers to give to the audience.

> **Exercise 14** Preparing and Giving a Multimedia Presentation Look through some of your past speeches and reports. Choose one, and prepare a plan for enhancing it with multimedia selections. Outline your presentation, including the media you will use and the order of presentation. Practice a few times, and then present it to your classmates.

Technology Tip

Use a search engine to find Web sites with graphics you can print or download and use in your multimedia presentation.

More Practice

Academic and Workplace Skills Activity Book
• p. 10

Producing a Video

Video cameras allow individuals to record their experiences and express their ideas through the medium of film. In addition to operating the camera, video artists must learn to edit the tape to produce the effects they want.

> **KEY CONCEPT** A video can inform, entertain, persuade, or serve all three purposes. ■

Making a Video The process of making a video is similar to making a film, although on a smaller scale. First, you must write out a story or list of scenes meant to convey a message. This document is the beginning of a *shooting script.* Include descriptions of settings, narration or dialogue between characters, and costumes and props needed. Decide on *camera angles*, or positions, for each shot or sequence of shots.

Use the shooting script to make a *storyboard* that illustrates a clear sequence of events. A storyboard looks like a cartoon strip, with each important shot planned and illustrated.

Select locations for shooting, and get permission to use them. Cast the roles, and rehearse. Write out a shooting schedule listing each scene, when and where it will be shot, and who is in it. Film the scenes, and store the video in a safe place.

Edit the video to produce the effect you want. You might cut to make action happen more quickly, to move from one location to another, or to insert flashbacks or new material. You may also decide to reshoot some scenes.

Tips for Videotaping

- Hold the camera steady. Learn to use all the features of the equipment.

- Use shooting techniques such as **panning** (moving the camera to the left or right), **zooming** (adjusting from a distant to a close view or from a close view to a distant one), **fading** (increasing or decreasing image intensity), and **cutting** (moving directly from one shot to another).

- Be sure to shoot enough film. It is always easier to cut than to reshoot.

> **Exercise 15** Producing a Video Produce a five-minute documentary or story video. You may work with a partner. Write out a shooting script. On your storyboard, plan the scenes you will shoot. Then, select locations, cast actors, rehearse, and film your video. After editing, present your video to your classmates.

> **More Practice**
>
> Academic and Workplace Skills Activity Book
> • p. 11

Performing or Interpreting

In an oral interpretation, the performer communicates his or her personal conception of a written work.

KEY CONCEPT Performers use voice and gestures and their own personal insights to communicate the meaning of a text. ■

Preparing a Performance or Interpretation It is best to choose a poem or story that has personal meaning for you and that you think the audience will appreciate. Write the text out and highlight the ideas and phrases you wish to emphasize. Decide on the mood you wish to achieve. Experiment with different ways of reading the text aloud to achieve the desired effect. Use tone of voice and pitch to express emotions. Use gestures and other body language to convey meaning and mood. Set the scene through background music, props, and costumes, if appropriate. Rehearse in front of a mirror and then before friends and family. Ask for their feedback to improve your performance.

Exercise 16 Interpreting a Poem Choose a poem you would like to interpret for an audience. Make notes on key words and ideas and the emotions and meanings you wish to convey. Practice reading the poem aloud and get feedback from listeners. Then, interpret the poem for your class.

More Practice

Academic and Workplace Skills Activity Book
• p. 12

Reflecting on Your Speaking, Listening, Viewing, and Representing

Review the skills covered in this chapter. Write a journal entry evaluating your experiences using these skills. Use the following questions as a starting point:

• How might effective speaking and listening benefit me in the different areas of my life—school, work, hobbies, friends, and family?

• How have I improved my ability to critically evaluate information from the media?

• What have I learned from producing visual presentations and/or interpreting literature through performing?

Chapter
30 *Vocabulary*
and *Spelling*

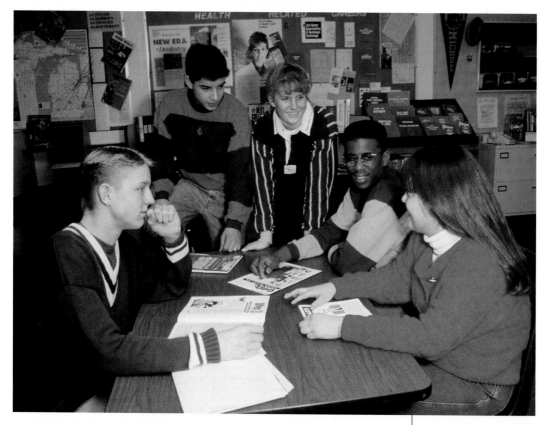

You encounter new words in many ways. You see new words in textbooks or in the reading you do for pleasure. In addition, you hear new words in conversations, in the classroom, and on radio and television.

Learning different ways to expand your vocabulary and improve your spelling are some of the most useful skills you can acquire. No matter how large your vocabulary is, you can always increase your knowledge of word meanings and spellings. The best way to build these skills is to work on remembering and using new words. This task requires some patience, but it is not as difficult as you may think—and the rewards of being able to read, write, and speak more successfully are well worth the effort.

▲ **Critical Viewing**
Is working in a group such as this one helpful in building vocabulary? Why or why not? **[Infer]**

Developing Your Vocabulary

In today's era of communication, words are a fundamental tool. The more words you have to choose from, the more ideas and feelings you can express. Trying to write or speak with a limited vocabulary is like trying to paint a picture with a limited number of colors.

To increase your vocabulary, you must first have a desire to expand your knowledge of word meanings, as well as a commitment to studying new words. Following are a number of helpful techniques that you can use:

Reading, Listening, and Discussing

Most of the words that we use every day we learned when we were children, just by keeping our eyes and ears open.

▶ **KEY CONCEPT** The most common ways to increase your vocabulary are listening, reading, and taking part in conversations. ■

Hearing and Using New Words There was a time when you did not know even the simplest words. You had to learn the meaning of *mother* and *father*, *run* and *walk*, *hot* and *cold*, *in* and *out*. First, you heard the words spoken. Then, you learned to repeat them. Eventually, you were able to put the new words together and use them in conversation.

Listening and discussing are still excellent ways to expand your vocabulary. When you talk to other people, follow discussions in class, watch television, hear literature on audiocassettes, or listen to the radio, be alert to unfamiliar words. Find out the meaning by using a dictionary or by asking. (Never be embarrassed to ask what a word means; it shows that you are listening and that you want to learn.) Whenever possible, try to use the new words in conversation.

Reading Extensively In general, people use a wider variety of words when they write than when they speak. Therefore, you can expand your vocabulary by reading even more than you can by listening.

The more you read, the more you will be introduced to new words. You will also encounter familiar words used in new, unfamiliar ways. To expand your vocabulary, try to read as extensively as possible: A wide variety of sources and subjects means a wide variety of words. Textbooks, newspapers, magazines, novels, and articles on the Internet can all be rich sources of vocabulary.

Recognizing Context Clues

When you come across an unfamiliar word, you may be able to guess its meaning by examining its context. The context of a word is determined by the other words in the sentence or the passage surrounding it.

A knowledge of the different types of context clues can help you use them effectively.

> **KEY CONCEPT** Use context clues to determine the meaning of unfamiliar words. ■

TYPES OF CONTEXT CLUES	
Clue	**Example**
Key words in the sentence that give the word's meaning	*Mountains* and *tall* buildings scare me because I have <u>acrophobia</u>. (Italicized words suggest height. <u>Acrophobia</u> must mean "fear of high places.")
Comparisons; contrasts; synonyms; antonyms	One cat is *courageous* and *loves* adventure; the other is <u>timorous</u> and hides under the sofa. (<u>Timorous</u> must mean "fearful.")
Words or phrases that follow a word closely and rename or define it	<u>Bonsai</u>, *the art of growing trees in small pots*, is well known in Japan. (The italicized phrase provides the correct meaning.)

> **Exercise 1** Recognizing Context Clues Use context clues to determine the meaning of each underlined word. Check your answers in a dictionary.
> 1. Gloria's <u>animosity</u> could be seen in her unfriendly expression and hostile tone of voice.
> 2. After his eight-mile run, Mel was <u>voracious</u> and ate everything in the refrigerator.
> 3. The newcomer appeared to be <u>morose</u>, but later her spirits lifted.
> 4. Sitting for a long time watching a lot of television can reduce your energy, resulting in a feeling of <u>lethargy</u>.
> 5. Moving not a muscle, the actor playing the victim was able to remain <u>inert</u>.

🔍 Research Tip

Find a current newsmagazine, and select five unfamiliar words. Guess their meanings according to their context, and check your answers in a dictionary.

> **More Practice**
>
> Academic and Workplace Skills Activity Book
> • pp. 13–14

Denotation and Connotation

Context can help you determine a word's exact meaning. Knowing the denotations and connotations of a word can help you discriminate between different shades of meaning.

▷ **KEY CONCEPTS** The **denotation** of a word is its literal definition. Its **connotations** include the ideas, images, and feelings that are associated with the word. ■

A definition of *dictator* is "a ruler with absolute power and authority." That is the denotation of the word. However, what comes into your mind when you hear the word *dictator*? You may think of ideas such as injustice and cruelty. You may picture specific images, such as an iron fist or a specific historic figure, such as Joseph Stalin. You may even feel emotions, such as fear and anger. All of these are connotations associated with the word *dictator*. As you strengthen your vocabulary, be aware of both positive and negative connotations of the words you use.

▷ **Exercise 2** Discriminating Between Denotation and Connotation Read each pair of sentences below. For each pair, write a sentence explaining the different connotations of the underlined words. Use a dictionary to help you.

1. John was <u>unaware</u> of the recent events in Asia.
   John was <u>ignorant</u> of the recent events in Asia.
2. The <u>slim</u> model walked gracefully down the ramp.
   The <u>skinny</u> model walked gracefully down the ramp.
3. The <u>uninvited</u> guests arrived at three o'clock.
   The <u>unexpected</u> guests arrived at three o'clock.
4. That store carries a lot of <u>cheap</u> clothing.
   That store carries a lot of <u>inexpensive</u> clothing.
5. The fans <u>crowded</u> around their favorite movie star.
   The fans <u>swarmed</u> around their favorite movie star.

▼ Critical Viewing
Write two sentences describing this picture. In one, use words with a positive connotation; in the other, try to be neutral. **[Interpret]**

Recognizing Related Words

Discovering how words relate to other words is a good way to increase your vocabulary.

Technology Tip

Do an on-line search, and find five new pairs of homophones. Add any unfamiliar words to your notebook.

KEY CONCEPTS **Synonyms** are words that are similar in meaning. **Antonyms** are words that are opposite in meaning. **Homophones** are words that sound alike but have different meanings and spellings. ■

Synonyms It is often easier to remember a one-word synonym for a word than to remember a long dictionary definition. For example, you may be able to remember the word *attain* by remembering its synonym, *achieve.*

Antonyms Remembering antonyms in pairs may help you to recall each word's meaning. For example, *happy* is the antonym of *sad.*

Homophones Knowing that certain words sound alike but have different meanings and spellings can help you use their correct forms in writing. For example, make sure that you know the difference between the homophones *stationery* (writing material) and *stationary* (not moving).

Exercise 3 Recognizing Related Words Using a dictionary, identify each pair as either *synonyms, antonyms,* or *homophones.*
1. lead/led
2. rustic/refined
3. raze/raise
4. whether/weather
5. irk/annoy
6. insurrection/revolt
7. defer/delay
8. random/deliberate
9. ample/plentiful
10. vertical/horizontal

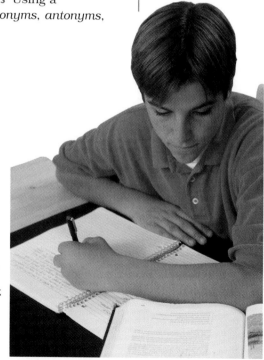

▶ **Critical Viewing** What subject do you think this student is studying? How will writing vocabulary words in a notebook help him expand his vocabulary? **[Infer]**

Using Related Words in Analogies

Working with analogies strengthens your vocabulary by increasing your understanding of connections between word meanings. Analogies are often found on standardized tests.

▶ **KEY CONCEPT** An **analogy** is some similarity between things that are otherwise unlike. Analogy problems present pairs of words that have some relationship to each other. ■

Look at the following analogy, and see whether you can find the pair of words whose relationship is the most similar to the capitalized pair:

EXAMPLE: HINGES : DOOR ::
a. roof : chimney
b. rock : atom
c. keyboard : organ
The answer is *c*.

The key to solving analogies is to understand what the relationship is between the capitalized words. In this example, the relationship between the capitalized words is *part to whole*—*hinges* are part of a *door*. A *roof* is not a part of a *chimney*. A *rock* is not a part of an *atom*. (Although an *atom* is part of a *rock*, the words appear in a different order from the capitalized pair.) A *keyboard*, however, is a part of an *organ*.

There are other common analogy relationships. They include *type* (crocodile : reptile), *defining characteristic* (white : snow), *instrument* (knife : cut), *degree* (afraid : terrified), *sequence* (summer : autumn), and *proximity* (sidewalk : street).

▶ **Exercise 4** Working With Analogies First, identify the analogy relationship expressed in the capitalized pair. Then, choose the lettered pair that best expresses this relationship.
1. INTRODUCTION : SPEECH ::
   a. preface : book b. speaker : audience c. scene : act
2. HUMOR : COMEDIAN ::
   a. finish line : runner b. intelligence : genius c. lecture : teacher
3. PAINTER : STUDIO ::
   a. sculpture : painting   b. judge : court c. writer : essay
4. GEOMETRY : MATHEMATICS ::
   a. botany : science b. shape : number c. theorem : equation
5. NEARBY : ADJOINING ::
   a. ocean : shore b. perpendicular : parallel   c. noisy : stentorious

▶ **More Practice**

Academic and Workplace Skills Activity Book
• pp. 15–16

Studying Words Systematically

Using Resource Materials

Two of the most valuable resource tools are a dictionary and a thesaurus. A dictionary is most helpful when you are reading; a thesaurus is most useful when you are writing.

KEY CONCEPTS Use a dictionary to find the meaning, spelling, pronunciation, and origin of words. Use a thesaurus to expand the meaning of words. ■

Using a Dictionary It is a good idea to keep an unabridged (complete) dictionary nearby.

• Study the pronunciation given in parentheses after the word.

• Become aware of the part of speech (*n.*, *v.*, *adj.*). The meaning of a word can change depending upon its usage.

Using a Thesaurus A thesaurus gives a list of words similar in meaning to the one you know. (For example, if you look up *give* in a thesaurus, you might find *grant*, *contribute*, *tip*, *remit*, *fork over*, and *donate*.) Be sure to check a dictionary to see whether your substitute has the correct connotation.

Learning About Etymologies Understanding word origins can help you understand words even if you have never seen them before. The English language adopts words from a variety of sources.

• English borrows or adopts words from other languages, especially Latin and Greek. (Examples: *Drama* is a Greek word. *Tycoon* is borrowed from China and Japan.)

• Words can change meaning over time and through usage. (Example: The word *dear* used to mean "expensive.")

• Words can be invented, or coined, to serve new purposes. (Example: The words *paperbacks* and *quiz* are coined.)

• Words can be shortened. (Example: The word *flu* is short for *influenza*.)

Exercise 5 Using Vocabulary Reference Aids Look up each of the following words in the references indicated. Compare and contrast the information found in each source.
1. streak (dictionary, science textbook glossary)
2. annex (social studies textbook glossary, dictionary)
3. durability (dictionary, thesaurus)
4. grow (science textbook glossary, on-line thesaurus)

🖱 Research Tip

Find five unfamiliar words. Look them up in a thesaurus. Then, look them up in a dictionary to determine differences in their meanings. Add the new words to your notebook.

More Practice

Academic and Workplace Skills Activity Book
• pp. 17–18

Remembering Vocabulary Words

To make a word part of your vocabulary, study its definition, use it in your writing and speaking, and review it to make sure that you really understand its meaning.

KEY CONCEPT Use one or more review techniques to remember the meanings of new words. ■

Using a Vocabulary Notebook Keep a notebook for vocabulary words. Divide your page into three columns: the *words* you want to learn; hints or *bridge words* that help you remember their meanings; and their *definitions*. Test yourself by covering either the second or third column.

VOCABULARY NOTEBOOK

Word	Bridge	Definition
ornithology	oriole	study of birds
oscillate	pendulum	swing back and forth
effervescent	soda	bubbly

Making Flashcards On the front of an index card, write a *word* you want to remember and the *bridge word*. On the back, write the *definition*. Test yourself by flipping through the cards. Enter any difficult words in your vocabulary notebook. As you master the meanings, remove these cards and add new ones.

Using a Tape Recorder Record your vocabulary words. Leave a ten-second space after each word, followed by the definition and a short sentence using the word. Replay the tape. Fill in the blank space with the definition and a sentence. Replay the tape until you can give the information easily.

▶ **Exercise 6** Adding New Words to Your Vocabulary
Identify five difficult words from one of your textbooks. Enter the words and their definitions in your vocabulary notebook. Study the words using one of the above methods. Then, test yourself by using each word in a sentence. Check your answers and correct them.

Studying Word Parts and Origins

In addition to learning new words, you can improve your vocabulary by learning about *word structure*, or the parts that make up a word.

The three word parts that can combine to form a word are a root (such as *-duc-* in pro*duc*tion), a prefix (such as *pro-* in *pro*duction), and a suffix (such as *-tion* in produc*tion*). Many of these word parts come to us from Latin, Greek, and Anglo-Saxon languages.

Recognizing Word Roots

The **root** of a word contains its basic meaning. Learning to recognize the most common word roots in English is the foundation of developing your vocabulary.

▶ **KEY CONCEPT** The **root** of a word carries the basic meaning of the word. ■

In some words, especially shorter words, the root may stand alone. In either case, knowing roots can help you figure out the meanings of unfamiliar words.

Roots have come into the English language from many sources, especially from Latin and Greek. (In the chart below, Latin and Greek roots are identified by the letters *L* and *G*). In the first column below, additional spellings of the roots are indicated in parentheses.

TEN COMMON ROOTS		
Root and Origin	**Meaning**	**Examples**
-cap- (-capt-, -cept-, -ceipt-) [L.]	to take, seize	*cap*able, *capt*ivate, ac*cept*, re*ceipt*
-chor- (-cho-) [Gr.]	to dance, sing	*chor*eography, *cho*ir
-duc- (-duce-, -duct-) [L.]	to lead	pro*duc*e, re*duc*e, con*duct*
-fer- [L.]	to bring, carry	trans*fer*, in*fer*ence
-graph- [Gr.]	to write	auto*graph*
-path- [Gr.]	to feel, suffer	sym*path*y, anti*path*y
-phil- [Gr.]	to love	*phil*osophy
-puls- (-pel-) [L.]	to drive	*puls*ate, pro*pel*
-tend- (-tens-, -tent-) [L.]	to stretch	dis*tend*, ex*tens*ion, ex*tent*
-vid- (-vis-) L.	to see	e*vid*ent, *vis*ion

> **Exercise 7** Using Roots to Define Words Using the chart on the previous page, select the definition that matches the word. Consult a dictionary if necessary.

1. pathos
2. reception
3. telegraph
4. impulse
5. tendency

    a. a system for sending messages
    b. a driving force
    c. an inclination to act in a particular way
    d. arousing pity or sorrow
    e. a social function for receiving guests

> **Exercise 8** Finding Common Roots Look up each pair of words below in a dictionary, paying close attention to the word's root, shown in italics. Then, write the basic meaning of the root shared by each pair of words.

1. *spec*imen, in*spect*
2. con*vene*, in*vent*or
3. *ten*ure, de*tain*
4. pro*ceed*, suc*cess*
5. con*vert*, di*vers*ion

Using Prefixes

A **prefix** is one or more syllables at the beginning of a word.

> **KEY CONCEPT** The *prefix* appears before the word root and adds to its meaning. ■

Learning Prefixes Learn the meanings and origins of the prefixes below. Additional spellings are given in parentheses. The abbreviations *L*, *Gr*, and *AS* mean Latin, Greek, and Anglo-Saxon, the origins from which the prefixes have come. Notice that some prefixes take more than one form—as shown in parentheses—but still have the same meaning.

TEN COMMON PREFIXES		
Prefix and Origin	**Meaning**	**Examples**
ad- (ac-, af-, al-, ap-, as-, at-) [L.]	to, toward	*ad*join, *af*fix, *ac*knowledge
com- (co-, col-, con-, cor-) [L.]	with, together	*col*laborate, *cor*respond
dis- (di-, dif-) [L.]	away, apart	*dis*connect, *dif*fuse
epi- [Gr.]	on, outside, among	*epi*taph, *epi*center
ex- (e-, ec-, ef-) [L.]	forth, from, out	*ec*centric, *ef*fluent
in- (il-, im-, ir-) [L.]	in, into, on, toward	*in*dent, *ir*rigate
mis- [AS]	wrongly	*mis*calculate
mono- [Gr.]	one, alone	*mono*tonous
non- [L.]	not	*non*essential
syn- [Gr.]	together with	*syn*chronize

> **More Practice**
>
> Academic and Workplace Skills Activity Book
> • pp.19–20

💡 Spelling Tip

Don't confuse the prefix *ante-*, meaning "before," with the prefix *anti-*, meaning "against."

> **Exercise 9** Defining Words With Prefixes Using your knowledge of prefixes, figure out the meaning of each word below. Then, check your answers in a dictionary.

1. *ap*point
2. *con*tribute
3. *epi*dermis
4. *di*vert
5. *e*migrate
6. *mis*place
7. *il*luminate
8. *mono*cle
9. *syn*thesize
10. *non*sense

> **Exercise 10** Defining Prefixes and Prefix Origins Using a dictionary, write the definition of each prefix and its origin. Then, provide an example of a word using each prefix.

1. ab- (a-, abs-)
2. in- (il-, im-, ir-)
3. inter-
4. non-
5. un-

Understanding Suffixes

A **suffix** is a syllable or group of syllables added to the end of a word root to form a new word. Note that a suffix often alters the part of speech.

> **KEY CONCEPT** The *suffix* is added to the end of the root and can change its meaning or part of speech. ■

Learning Suffixes Suffixes are unique in that they can change both word forms and parts of speech. In the first column, additional spellings are in parentheses. Note: *L, Gr,* and *AS* mean Latin, Greek, and Anglo-Saxon.

TEN COMMON SUFFIXES

Suffix and Origin	Meaning and Examples	Part of Speech
-able (-ible) [L.]	capable of being: *reliable*	adjective
-ate [L.]	to make: *activate*	verb
-fy [L.]	to cause, become: *clarify*	verb
-ist [Gr.]	a skilled person: *violinist*	noun
-ize (-ise) [Gr.]	to make: *improvise*	verb
-less [AS.]	without: *ageless*	adjective
-ly [AS.]	in a certain way: *hourly, harshly*	adjective or adverb
-ness [AS.]	state of: *laziness*	noun
-or [L.]	quality of: *error*	noun
-tion (-ion,-sion, -ation) [L.]	the action of; state of being: *action*	noun

⊚ Technology Tip

Search for an on-line Web site that provides more information on Latin, Greek, and Anglo-Saxon suffixes. Find five new words, and add them and their definitions to your vocabulary notebook.

▶ **Exercise 11** Defining Suffixes For each suffix, write its definition and origin. Use a dictionary to assist you.

1. -esque
2. -ism
3. -ous (-ious)
4. -ity
5. -or
6. -ant (-ent)
7. -ful
8. -ment
9. -ance (-ence)
10. -ade

▶ **More Practice**

Academic and Workplace Skills Activity Book
• p. 21

▶ **Exercise 12** Using Suffixes to Form Words Add the correct suffix to each underlined word to form a new word that will complete each sentence below. In your notebook, write each new word and its part of speech.

1. A person who <u>conforms</u> is usually called a ___?___.
2. People who are unable to <u>help</u> themselves are considered to be ___?___.
3. When you cause something to become <u>active</u>, you ___?___ it.
4. To cause an activity to become <u>legal</u> is to ___?___ it.
5. When someone gives the <u>glory</u> to someone else, they ___?___ that person.
6. One who <u>mediates</u> a controversy between people or groups is called a ___?___.
7. The quality of loving one's country like a <u>patriot</u> is called ___?___.
8. If you give a lot of <u>thought</u> to other people's feelings, you are said to be ___?___.
9. An action intended to <u>punish</u> someone is called a ___?___.
10. If it is possible to <u>break</u> something, that item should be considered ___?___.

◀ Critical Viewing Think of some words with suffixes that this photograph calls to mind. **[Interpret]**

Improving Your Spelling

When it comes to spelling, English is one of the most difficult languages in the world. In some languages, such as
Italian or French, spelling tends to follow a few basic rules. In
English, however, there are many exceptions to almost every
spelling rule. As a result, the same sound might be spelled in
different ways. For example, the words *so, hoe, dough, flow,
sew,* and *beau* all rhyme. In addition, the same combination
of letters might be pronounced different ways, as in the words
dough, rough, through, and *bough.*

Despite this difficulty, it is important to learn to spell
correctly. Careless spelling tends to indicate either that you
do not know how to spell or that your writing is careless.
Someone reading your writing may be less than favorably
impressed, and the value of your efforts to communicate is
diminished. By using a strategy that includes practice and
some simple rules, you can improve your spelling and thereby
have a positive effect on all of your writing.

Keeping a Spelling Notebook

You can reduce spelling errors if you keep track of and
study words that are especially difficult for you. The best
place to do this is in a special section of your notebook.

KEY CONCEPT Make a personal spelling list of difficult
words; enter it in your notebook; and keep it up to date. ∎

Setting Up Your Spelling Notebook Prepare a page
with four columns. In the first column, record the incorrectly
spelled words as you wrote them. In the second column,
record the correct spelling. In the third column, enter the
dates when you practiced the word. In the fourth column,
write hints that help you remember the correct spelling.

PERSONAL SPELLING LIST			
Misspelled Words	Correct Spelling	Practice Dates	Memory Aids
artic	arctic	4/11	no art in arctic
seperate	separate	4/11, 4/18	separate means apart and both have two A's.

> **Exercise 13** Selecting Words for a Personal Spelling List
Look over all of the writing you have done in the last month.
Record any of your misspelled words on your list.

Studying Problem Words

Some words may be difficult for you to spell because you
seldom use them. Others you may repeatedly misspell. A systematic study can help you correct both kinds of mistakes.

> **KEY CONCEPT** To study problem words, use several
steps: Look, say, listen, write, and repeat.■

STEPS FOR REVIEWING PROBLEM WORDS

1. *Look* at each word carefully to notice the arrangement or
   pattern of the letters. Try to see the word in your mind.
2. *Pronounce* each syllable of the word to yourself.
3. *Write* the word, and check its spelling in a dictionary.
4. *Review* your list until you can write each word correctly.

> **Exercise 14** Working With Problem Words In each of
the following sentences, select the word in parentheses that
is spelled correctly. After you complete the exercise, add to
your spelling notebook the correct spellings of any words you
spelled incorrectly.
1. The (pronunciation, pronunciation) of some words is
   difficult.
2. The thunder and (lightening,
   lightning) terrified us.
3. The (personnel, personal) office
   has job information.
4. I hate to fill out (questionnaires,
   questionaires).
5. Who is (responsible, respons-
   able) for this messy room?
6. The (defendant, defendent)
   might be innocent or guilty.
7. Can you draw (parallel, paralel)
   lines without a ruler?
8. What kind of (mileage, milage)
   does your car get?
9. Your (appearance, appearence)
   will affect your job search.
10. The hotel can (accommodate,
    accomodate) 250 guests.

> **More Practice**
Academic and
Workplace Skills
Activity Book
• pp. 22–23

▼ Critical Viewing
Identify two words
associated with this
picture that might
cause spelling difficul-
ties. Explain why.
[Connect]

Developing Memory Aids

You may find the correct spelling of some words especially difficult to learn. This is often true of words that do not follow any set rules. However, many of these words can be mastered by using memory aids.

KEY CONCEPT Creating and using memory aids can help you remember the correct spelling of words that you find especially difficult to learn. ■

Using Words Within Words as a Memory Aid One useful memory aid is to look for a shorter, more familiar word within the harder one. Then, use both words to compose a sentence that you will be able to remember:

EXAMPLES: bulletin   Watch for the *bullet* in the *bullet*in.
            vegetables   Did you *get* the ve*get*ables from the market?
            friend   You will be my fri*end* to the *end*.

Using Association as a Memory Aid Associate the trickiest part of the problem word with a related word that you already know how to spell.

EXAMPLES: cellar   A cell*ar* is often d*ar*k. (Both words contain *ar*.)
            medicine   This medic*ine* will help you feel f*ine* (both words end in *ine*.)
            clientele   Clien*tele* means a group of customers. Customers often order what they want on the *tele*phone. (Both words contain *tele*.)

Exercise 15 Developing Memory Aids Create memory aids for the ten words listed below. Then, choose five difficult words from your own spelling notebook, and find a memory aid for each one. Write the hints in your notebook to help you remember the correct spelling.

1. restaurant
2. raspberry
3. cushion
4. sophomore
5. cinnamon
6. tortoise
7. rehearse
8. comedy
9. environment
10. oyster

Research Tip

Choose five words from a dictionary that would be difficult words for you to spell. Add them to your notebook, and develop a memory aid for each one.

More Practice

Academic and Workplace Skills Activity Book
• pp. 24–25

Applying Spelling Rules

The spellings of some words must be learned by memorization. However, the correct spelling of other words can be learned without too much difficulty by using spelling rules. For example, some words follow certain rules about how to form plurals, how to add prefixes and suffixes, or when to use *ie* or *ei*.

Plural Forms

The plural form of a noun is the form that indicates "more than one." Plural forms can be either *regular* or *irregular*.

Regular Plurals As a general rule, you can just add *-s* to the end of a word to form a regular plural. With certain regular plurals, however, you may have to choose whether to add *-s* or *-es*. Occasionally, you may also have to change a letter or two in the singular form of the word.

1. Form the plurals of words ending in *s*, *ss*, *x*, *z*, *sh*, or *ch* by adding *-es* to the base word:

   circus + *-es* = circuses   mass + *-es* = masses
   fox + *-es* = foxes   fizz + *-es* = fizzes
   dish + *-es* = dishes   finch + *-es* = finches

2. Form the plurals of words ending in *y* or *o* preceded by a vowel by adding *-s* to the base word:

   donkey + *-s* = donkeys   toy + *-s* = toys
   trolley + *-s* = trolleys   birthday + *-s* = birthdays
   stereo + *-s* = stereos   studio + *-s* = studios

3. To form the plurals of words ending in *y* preceded by a consonant, change the *y* to *i* and add *-es*. For most words ending in *o* preceded by a consonant, add *-es*. (Exceptions to this rule are musical terms ending in *o*; form these plurals by simply adding *-s*.):

   baby + *-es* = babies   fly + *-es* = flies
   veto + *-es* = vetoes   hero + *-es* = heroes
   cello + *-s* = cellos   alto + *-s* = altos

4. To form the plurals of some words ending in *f* or *fe*, change the *f* or *fe* to *v* and add *-es*. For words ending in *ff*, always add *-s*:

   knife + *-es* = knives   shelf + *-es* = shelves
   half + *-es* = halves   elf + *-es* = elves
   gulf + *-s* = gulfs   proof + *-s* = proofs
   chef + *-s* = chefs   tariff + *-s* = tariffs

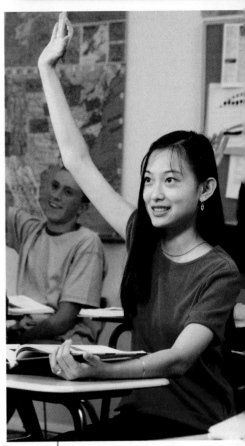

▲ **Critical Viewing**
Think of some ways that you can study spelling rules with other students. **[Support]**

Irregular Plurals Irregular plurals are not formed according to the rules on the previous page. If you are unsure of how to form a plural, check a dictionary. You will usually find the spelling of an irregular plural listed right after the pronunciation of the word. If no plural form is given in the dictionary, add -s or -es to the singular form. Below is a list of common irregular plurals:

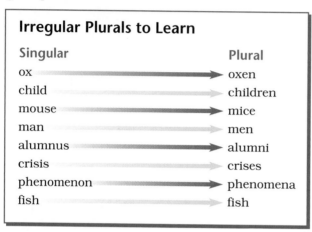

Irregular Plurals to Learn

Singular	Plural
ox	oxen
child	children
mouse	mice
man	men
alumnus	alumni
crisis	crises
phenomenon	phenomena
fish	fish

Forming the Plurals of Compound Words: To form the plural of a compound word that is written as two or more separate or hyphenated words, make the word that is being modified plural by adding -s or -es to the singular form. For example, *rule of order* becomes *rules of order*, and *mother-in-law* becomes *mothers-in-law*.

Exercise 16 Forming Plurals Write the plural for each of the nouns listed below. Consult a dictionary if you need to confirm your answers.

1. ox
2. loaf
3. tax
4. chief
5. cry
6. deer
7. alley
8. stew
9. class
10. jelly
11. sheaf
12. goose
13. crisis
14. block
15. hunch
16. belief
17. brush
18. potato
19. volcano
20. heart

Prefixes and Suffixes

A prefix is one or more syllables added at the beginning of a word to form a new word. A suffix is one or more syllables added to the end of a word.

> **KEY CONCEPTS** Adding a prefix to a word does not affect the spelling of the original word. Adding a suffix often involves a spelling change in the word. ■

Adding Prefixes When a prefix is added to a word, the spelling of the word root remains the same.

- This rule also pertains to words with double letters (*dis-* + satisfy = dissatisfy).
- A prefix may change to aid pronunciation when it is added, but the root stays the same (*ad-* becomes *al-* before *locate* to form *allocate*; *in-* becomes *ir-* before *reverent* to form *irreverent*).

> **Exercise 17** Spelling Words With Prefixes Form words by combining roots with prefixes. You may have to change the form of the prefix. Check a dictionary.

1. *ad-* + portion
2. *de-* + activate
3. *com-* + respond
4. *in-* + migrate
5. *ex-* + fervescent
6. *pre-* + eminent
7. *co-* + operate
8. *mis-* + speak
9. *ad-* + fluent
10. *un-* + necessary

> **More Practice**
>
> Academic and Workplace Skills Activity Book
> - pp. 24–25

Adding Suffixes Some words require spelling changes when adding suffixes. The following three lists summarize the major kinds of spelling changes that can take place when a suffix is added.

Spelling Changes in Words Ending in *y*: Use the following rules for spelling changes of words ending in *y*, paying careful attention to the rules' exceptions:

1. When adding a suffix to words that end in *y* and are preceded by a consonant, change *y* to *i*. Most suffixes beginning with *i* are the exception to the rule.

   rely + *-able* = reliable
   rely + *-ing* = relying
   friendly + *-ness* = friendliness
   fly + *-ing* = flying

2. For words that end in *y* and are preceded by a vowel, make no change when adding most suffixes. A few short words are the exceptions.

   joy + *-ous* = joyous
   day + *-ly* = daily
   employ + *-ment* = employment
   pay + *-ed* = paid

Spelling Changes in Words Ending in *e*: Use the following rules for spelling changes of words ending in *e*, paying careful attention to the rules' exceptions:

1. For words ending in *e*, drop the *e* when adding a suffix beginning with a vowel. The major exceptions to this rule are (1) words ending in *ce* or *ge* with suffixes beginning with *a* or *o*, (2) words ending in *ee*, and (3) a few special words.

   love + -*able* = lovable   thrive + -*ing* = thriving
   manage + -*able* = manageable   sane + -*ity* = sanity
   agree + -*able* = agreeable   see + -*ing* = seeing
   dye + -*ing* = dyeing   be + -*ing* = being

2. For words ending in *e*, make no change when adding a suffix beginning with a consonant. A few special words are the exceptions.

   peace + -*ful* = peaceful   brave + -*ly* = bravely
   argue + -*ment* = argument   true + -*ly* = truly

Doubling the Final Consonant Before Suffixes: Use the following rules for cases in which a final consonant may or may not change, paying careful attention to the rules' exceptions:

1. For words ending consonant + vowel + consonant in a stressed syllable, double the final consonant when adding a suffix beginning with a vowel. The major exceptions to this rule are (1) words ending in *x* or *w* and (2) words in which the stress changes after the suffix is added.

   mud + -*y* = mud´dy   submit + -*ed* = submit´ted
   mix + -*ing* = mixing   row + -*ing* = rowing
   refer´ + -*ence* = ref´erence   confer´ + -*ence* = con´ference

2. For words ending consonant + vowel + consonant in an unstressed syllable, make no change when adding a suffix beginning with a vowel. There are no major exceptions to this rule.

   angel + -*ic* = angelic   final + -*ize* = finalize
   hammer + -*ed* = hammered   person + -*al* = personal

▲ **Critical Viewing**
Identify three adverbs that describe how these crew members are rowing. Which rules, if any, apply to the suffixes at the ends of the adverbs? **[Apply]**

Exercise 18 Spelling Words With Suffixes Using the rules given above, write the correct spelling for the words below. Check your answers in a dictionary.

1. fascinate + -*ion*
2. lucky + -*ly*
3. lobby + -*ist*
4. swim + -*er*
5. cease + -*less*
6. control + -*able*
7. confer + -*ence*
8. courage + -*ous*
9. alphabet + -*ic*
10. apply + -*ance*

Spelling *ie* and *ei* Words and Words Ending in *-cede*, *-ceed*, and *-sede*

Words containing *ie* and *ei*, and words with the endings *-cede*, *-ceed*, and *-sede* often prove troublesome to spell.

For most words containing *ie* or *ei*, you can use the traditional rule: "Place *i* before *e* except after *c* or when sounded like *a*, as in *neighbor* or *weigh*." For words that are exceptions to this rule as well as for words ending in *-cede*, *-ceed*, and *-sede*, it is often best to memorize the correct spellings.

ie and ei Words The *ie* and *ei* rule applies to many words, but like most rules, it has exceptions.

Exceptions for ie words: *counterfeit, either, foreign, forfeit, heifer, height, heir, leisure, neither, seismology, seize, seizure, sheik, sleight, sovereign, their, weird*

Exceptions for ei words: *ancient, conscience, efficient, financier, sufficient*

> **Exercise 19** Spelling *ie* and *ei* Words Fill in the blanks by inserting the missing letters. Check your work in a dictionary.
>
> 1. ach __?__ ve
> 2. bel __?__ f
> 3. dec __?__ ve
> 4. sl __?__ gh
> 5. s __?__ zure
> 6. rec __?__ pt
> 7. effic __?__ nt
> 8. h __?__ ress
> 9. r __?__ gn
> 10. rel __?__ ve

More Practice

Academic and
Workplace Skills
Activity Book
• pp. 26–27

Words Ending in *-cede*, *-ceed*, and *-sede* The best way to handle words that end with these suffixes is to memorize the correct spelling. The words ending in *-cede* are *accede, concede, intercede, precede, recede, secede*. The three words endings in *-ceed* are *exceed, proceed, succeed*, and the only word ending in *-sede* is *supersede*.

> **Exercise 20** Working With Words Ending in *-cede*, *-ceed*, or *-sede* Complete the word for each sentence below by filling in the blanks with *-cede*, *-ceed*, or *-sede*.
>
> 1. No repairs can be done until the waters re __?__ .
> 2. To reach the drive-in, pro __?__ down Elm Avenue.
> 3. The senator refuses to con __?__ defeat.
> 4. We would like to ac __?__ to your proposal if we can.
> 5. The new regulations super __?__ the old ones.

Other Confusing Endings

In certain instances, suffixes may sound alike.

KEY CONCEPT Learn to distinguish between similar word endings that can cause errors. ■

COMMON WORDS ENDING IN *-able* and *-ible*

acceptable	memorable	accessible	eligible
believable	peaceable	digestible	incredible

COMMON WORDS ENDING IN *-ance* and *-ence*

acquaintance	radiance	convenience	patience
appearance	resonance	correspondence	presence

COMMON WORDS ENDING IN *-sy*

autopsy	curtsy	epilepsy	hypocrisy
biopsy	ecstasy	fantasy	idiosyncrasy

COMMON WORDS ENDING IN *-efy*

liquefy	putrefy	rarefy	stupefy

COMMON WORDS ENDING IN *-uous*, *-eous*, and *-ious*

ambiguous	gorgeous	conscious
continuous	courteous	contagious

Exercise 21 Writing Words With Confusing Endings Fill in the blanks below. Consult a dictionary if necessary.

1. court __?__ s
2. caut __?__ s
3. convert __?__ ble
4. unforgett __?__
5. liqu __?__ fy
6. irresist __?__ ble
7. hypocr __?__ y
8. correspond __?__ ce
9. stren __?__ s
10. gorg __?__ s

Proofreading Carefully

Often, spelling errors are merely the result of writing quickly to try to get your thoughts down on paper. Get into the habit of proofreading everything you write, to eliminate careless errors.

KEY CONCEPT Review everything you write, and proofread for spelling errors. ■

There are a number of different proofreading skills. To discover the proofreading methods that work best for you, use a variety or combination of strategies.

Learn More

For more information on commonly misspelled words, see the Commonly Misspelled Words list at the back of this book.

PROOFREADING STRATEGIES

- Proofread your work by slowly reading it aloud or silently to yourself.

- Proofread only one line at a time. Use a ruler or other device to focus on the line you are proofreading and to cover up the lines you are not proofreading.

- Read backward, from the last word to the first. This forces you to focus only on the words themselves.

- Consult a dictionary when you come across a word that you suspect is spelled incorrectly.

- Check the spelling of proper nouns.

▶ **Exercise 22** **Proofreading Carefully** Find the misspelled word, and correct it. Use a dictionary if necessary.

1. He is quite cheerfull about the unpleasant task.
2. We need your assistence for several moments.
3. Although there were several qualified contestants, they were all farely certain of the outcome.
4. She has the abilety to do several things equally well.
5. After all that work, a peice of pie would taste delicious.
6. The exhausted speaker aksed for a glass of water.
7. The monkys ran around the cage, begging for bananas.
8. Our friends incisted that we spend a few more hours and stay for dinner.
9. The package arrived on Wensday; we found that strange because we expected it on Friday.
10. Although many people don't realize it, penguins exhist only in the Southern Hemisphere.

▶ **More Practice**

Academic and Workplace Skills Activity Book
- p. 28

Reflecting on Your Vocabulary, Spelling, and Proofreading Skills

Ask yourself the following questions to think about the way you learn vocabulary and spelling words:

- Do I have more trouble with pronunciations or meanings?

- Which types of spelling words are hardest for me?

- What kinds of errors do I usually make?

Reading Skills

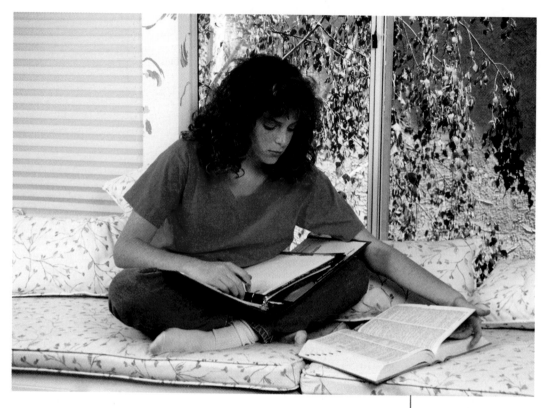

There are no other skills that are more essential to your success in life than reading skills. Throughout your years in school and throughout your life, you will read a wide variety of materials—from textbooks to newspapers to pamphlets to novels to road signs. It is important for you to be able to read all of these materials with a high level of comprehension and retention. In this chapter, you will learn skills and strategies that will help you increase your level of comprehension and become a more effective and efficient reader.

▲ Critical Viewing
What type of reading
do you think this girl
is doing? On what
do you base your
answer? [Speculate]

Reading Methods and Tools

The way in which you approach reading can vary widely, depending on the nature of the piece of writing. However, there are certain skills and strategies that you can apply to virtually anything you read.

Reading Textbooks

At least 80 percent of the reading you do for school involves textbooks. If you are able to get the most out of the textbooks you read, you will almost certainly improve your performance in school.

KEY CONCEPT Use study aids when reading textbooks to help you understand what you are reading and to remember it better later. ■

Textbook Sections The material in a textbook is structured so that you can read it and learn it easily. Unlike most other books, textbooks include reading aids to help you make the best use of the books. Following are descriptions of these special sections:

Table of Contents This section shows how the book is organized by listing units and chapters with their page numbers. It offers a quick overview of the book.

Front of the Book

Preface or Introduction Located before or after the table of contents, these features state the author's purpose in writing the book and may give suggestions for using the book.

Front of the Book

Index This section alphabetically lists all topics covered in the book and the pages on which they can be found, making it possible to locate information quickly.

Glossary The glossary lists in alphabetical order all the specialized words and terms used in the book and defines them clearly.

Back of the Book

Appendix This feature can include such things as charts, lists, documents, or other material related to the subject of the book. An appendix can serve as an immediate reference source.

Back of the Book

Bibliography A bibliography lists books and articles that the author has used or referred to in writing the book. Many of the entries may be useful for follow-up study or for research projects.

Back of the Book

Textbook Features

Textbooks also have a number of other features designed to help you find and review material:

Titles, Headings, and Subheadings These divide the material into manageable segments. They are printed in large, boldfaced type, often in different colors. Main topics have larger headings, and subtopics have smaller ones. By scanning the headings, you can get a quick idea of the topics being covered. You can then focus on topics with which you are having difficulty or on those that your teacher has identified as being important.

Overviews The chapters in textbooks often begin with an overview, objectives, outline, or a summary of what will be covered. These features help you to preview and review what is being covered.

Questions and Exercises Most textbooks include questions or exercises at the ends of sections or chapters. Previewing the questions and exercises before you read will help you focus your reading on the most important concepts and details. After reading, answer the questions to check your understanding.

Pictures, Captions, and Graphics Pictures can add to your understanding of the ideas in the text. Look for captions that explain the content of the pictures and connect them to the reading. Use graphics, such as maps and charts, to help you understand complex concepts.

> **KEY CONCEPT** Use titles, headings, and subheadings; overviews; questions and exercises; pictures, captions, and graphics to help you thoroughly comprehend the material. ■

> **Exercise 1** Examining a Textbook Choose one of your textbooks, and use it to answer the following questions:
> 1. Use the table of contents to identify the organization.
> 2. If there is a preface, does it explain the author's purpose in writing the book? If so, what is the purpose?
> 3. What are two specific terms found in the index?
> 4. Use the glossary to find the definitions of the two terms you found in the index.
> 5. If there is an appendix, what information does it contain?
> 6. Explain the format of any questions and exercises.
> 7. Find a chart, and explain the concept it conveys.
> 8. Identify at least three pictures you find useful, and explain why you think the publisher chose them.
> 9. What features appear at the beginning of each chapter?
> 10. Identify at least three different levels of headings.

Using Reading Strategies

Strong readers use various reading strategies to help them comprehend and critically examine what they're reading. In addition, they vary their reading style according to the content.

Vary Your Reading Style

▶ **KEY CONCEPT** Adjust your reading style to suit your purpose in reading. ■

Skimming Skimming a text means to look it over quickly to get a sense, or a general idea, of its contents. Look for highlighted or bold type, headings, and topic sentences. Use skimming to preview, review, and locate information.

Scanning Scanning involves looking through a text to find specific information. Look for words related to your topic or purpose for reading. Use scanning to research, review, and find information.

Close Reading Close reading refers to reading carefully to take in all of the main ideas and to understand the relationships among those ideas. Use this technique whenever you are reading material in your textbooks for the first time.

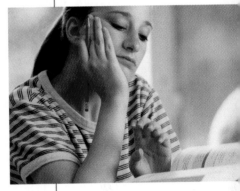

▲ Critical Viewing Based on her posture, what type of reading style do you think this girl is using? Why? **[Analyze]**

▶ **Exercise 2** Varying Your Reading Style Choose a nonfiction book. Skim it in its entirety. Write down what you have learned. Then, scan it until you come across an interesting section. Read that section closely, and take detailed notes.

Use Question-Answer Relationships (QARs)

Understanding how questions are written can help you to answer them. There are four general types of questions. Learning to identify these types will help you to answer questions more easily. You can also improve your reading skills by asking and answering these types of questions as you read:

1. **Right There** This type of question deals with answers that are right there in the text, usually in one or two paragraphs or sentences.
2. **Think and Search** The answer to this type of question is in the text, but you need to think about the question's answer and then search for evidence to support it.
3. **Author and You** These questions call on you to consider what the author says and connect it to what you know.
4. **On Your Own** The answers to these questions are not in the text. They require you to draw on your experiences.

Use the SQ4R Method

To get the most out of your textbook, use the SQ4R method, a guided reading approach that involves these six skills:

1. **Survey** Preview the material you are going to read, focusing on chapter titles, headings, overviews, summaries, objectives, and questions or exercises.
2. **Question** Write down a question about each heading.
3. **Read** As you read, search for the answers to the questions that you have posed.
4. **Recite** Orally or mentally, recite the questions and their answers.
5. **Record** Take notes to further reinforce information in your mind. Include a list of main ideas and major details.
6. **Review** Review the material on a regular basis.

> **KEY CONCEPT** Use the SQ4R method to guide your reading and to help you recall information later. ■

Technology Tip

Use the SQ4R method when you visit new Web pages for research purposes. The notes that you record will guide you and save you time when you return to the Web page for more information.

THE SQ4R METHOD

> **Exercise 3** Using the SQ4R Method Use the SQ4R method to study a chapter in one of your textbooks. Then, write a brief review of the ways in which using SQ4R helped. Note information that you might have missed if you had not been using SQ4R, and explain how the overall use of SQ4R affected your understanding of the material.

Outlining What You Read

An **outline** is a structured list of information. The information is arranged according to main ideas, major details, and supporting details. Outlines are an excellent study tool that can help you prepare for tests and quizzes on information in your textbooks.

▶ **KEY CONCEPT** Make an outline as you read to keep track of important information and ideas. ■

Follow these steps to make an outline:

- Use Roman numerals for main ideas. Use capital letters for major details. Use Arabic numerals for supporting details.

- Use indentation to indicate importance. Main ideas begin at the left. Items begin farther to the right as they become less important.

- Never place a single item under any main idea. Always place two or more items or none at all.

The example below illustrates a formal outline on the magician Jean-Eugène Robert-Houdin:

SAMPLE OUTLINE

I. The magician Robert-Houdin ———————— Main idea
   A. Robert-Houdin in 1880's ——————— Major detail
      1. Developed rules for performing tricks ┐
                               ├ Supporting details
      2. Created many new tricks ————┘
   B. Tools of the magician ———————— Major detail
      1. Skill with hands ┐
      2. Secret devices │
                         ├ Supporting details
      3. Misdirects people's attention │
      4. Encourages false conclusions ┘

▶ **Exercise 4** Making an Outline Using an assigned chapter of a textbook, make an outline of one section. Give your outline at least two main ideas. Then, test the effectiveness of your outline by sharing it with a schoolmate who has not read the chapter. See whether the schoolmate can answer the chapter review questions using the outline alone. If not, you may have left some key concepts out of your outline.

Using Graphic Organizers

Graphic organizers are an effective reading aid. They can help you sort out main topics and key details as well as identify relationships among the details. When choosing what organizer to use, consider the type of organization the author uses.

Analyze Chronological Order

When the events in a piece you are reading are presented in chronological order, or the order in which the events occur, you will probably find a **timeline** most effective. Use the top of the timeline to name the event, and use the bottom to indicate the elapsed time. Look at the sample below.

TIMELINE

Event 1   Event 2   Event 3   Event 4   Event 5

Time intervals (years, months, days, minutes)

Chart Main Points and Subtopics

When a piece of writing is divided clearly into main points and subtopics, you will probably want to use a **cluster diagram,** also known as a **web.** Begin by writing your topic in the center of a sheet of paper. Circle that topic. Then, write down any subtopics, and draw circles around them, making the circles large enough to add supporting details. Link the related ideas to the main topic with lines, and list the supporting details.

CLUSTER DIAGRAM

Analyze Comparison-and-Contrast Structure

Writers often make comparisons between two or more subjects. A **Venn diagram** is probably the most effective graphic organizer to help you sort out the details of such comparisons. In addition, a Venn diagram can help you make comparisons between two or more pieces of writing—a task that you will often be asked to do in school or on standardized tests.

To make a Venn diagram, draw overlapping circles. In the overlapping sections of the circles, write the subjects' shared characteristics. In the other sections of the circles, write their differences. Note that the Venn diagram below would be used for three subjects.

VENN DIAGRAM (3 Subjects)

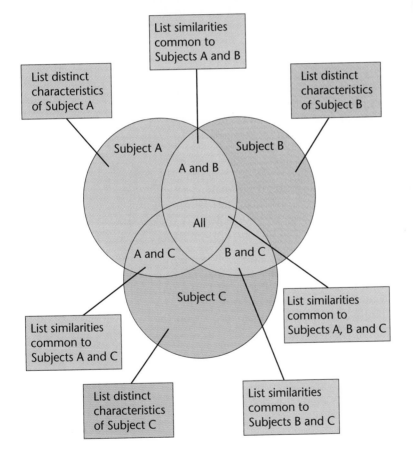

Research Tip

Discover more types of graphic organizers and variations on cluster diagrams and Venn diagrams by reviewing your textbooks. Note how information is organized and relationships are shown on the graphic organizers that you find. Use them to guide you as you create your own.

▶ **Exercise 5** Using Graphic Organizers Read a chapter from one of your textbooks or a work of literature. Then, use a Venn diagram, a timeline, or a cluster diagram to organize information from the text.

Reading Nonfiction Critically

Over the course of your life, you'll probably read more non-fiction than any other type of writing. Nonfiction refers to writing that has a basis in fact. Newspaper reports, reference books, and history texts are all examples of nonfiction.

Analyzing and Evaluating Nonfiction

When you read nonfiction, it is important not only to grasp the writer's main ideas and key points, but to evaluate critically the accuracy and reliability of what you read. Use a variety of reading strategies to examine, evaluate, and form judgments about what you read.

Make Inferences Nonfiction writers are generally more direct than fiction writers in making their key points. However, that doesn't mean that some information isn't left out of a typical nonfiction work. To grasp ideas that are either only hinted at or left out, you need to make inferences, or draw conclusions, based on the information the author *does* provide.

Make Generalizations When a writer provides a related set of facts and details on one topic, you can often make generalizations about that topic. For example, if an author tells numerous stories about people who experienced hardships settling in a new land, you might make the generalization that many people who came to the land faced similar hardships.

Recognize the Author's Purpose or Bias A writer's purpose, or reason for writing, can influence the choice of details and presentation of material. In addition, writers often present an issue with their own bias—their outlook on an issue or topic. Try to identify a writer's purpose, and be on the lookout for details that suggest bias.

Evaluate the Strength of the Evidence and the Writer's Credibility Check to see that a writer thoroughly supports the points with facts, examples, and details. Also, check to see that a writer has expertise or has done thorough research on the topic.

Recognize Persuasive Techniques Be on the lookout for appeals to your emotions. Make sure a writer offers sound evidence before accepting his or her position.

Judge the Writer's Work When you read many works by the same writer, try to draw some overall conclusions about the quality of his or her work.

 Internet Tip

Treat the information you find on the Internet the same way you would treat any nonfiction book: Critically analyze and evaluate the material using the strategies presented on this page.

Distinguishing Fact From Opinion

Don't just assume that every piece of nonfiction you read is reliable. Often, information that is presented as being the truth is simply the writer's opinion.

▶ **KEY CONCEPT** To help you evaluate the reliability of what you read, be careful to distinguish facts from opinions. ■

A statement of fact can be verified, or proved true, by experimentation, records, or personal observation. A statement of opinion cannot be proved true; before it can be accepted, it must be validated, or supported, with satisfactory sources or facts. An opinion may be based on facts, but an opinion is *not* a fact.

FACT: To put a satellite in space, a rocket must travel fast enough to escape the Earth's gravity.

OPINION (feeling): Space travel is too dangerous.

OPINION (judgment): A mechanical flaw in a spacecraft could threaten an astronaut's life.

OPINION (prediction): In the next decade, humans will colonize the moon.

Verify facts and validate opinions to determine whether the material you are reading is reliable.

▶ **Exercise 6** Analyzing Fact and Opinion Statements First, identify each of the following statements as *fact* or *opinion*. Then, analyze whether each fact statement is *true* or *false*, and analyze whether each opinion statement is *valid* or *invalid*.

1. Abraham Lincoln was the greatest president the United States has ever had.
2. Our team is sure to win the baseball game next week.
3. The blue whale is the largest animal ever to inhabit Earth.
4. The Supreme Court has eleven justices.
5. We will have snow tomorrow because a cold front is approaching.

▶ **Exercise 7** Analyzing Facts and Opinions in a Magazine Look through a newsmagazine. Write down five examples of facts. Then, find at least two examples of opinions. Tell whether the opinions are backed by facts.

▼ Critical Viewing Based on her expression, do you think this girl agrees or disagrees with what she is reading? [Infer]

Applying Modes of Reasoning

When you read critically, you draw conclusions about what you read. These conclusions need to be sound and logical.

> ▶ **KEY CONCEPT** Think logically to draw valid conclusions. ■

Inductive and Deductive Reasoning

When you think logically, you use *reasoning* to lead to or support a conclusion. Two main forms of reasoning are *inductive* and *deductive*.

Inductive Reasoning Inductive reasoning involves drawing an overall conclusion, or making a generalization, from a set of specific facts. A valid generalization is a statement supported by evidence that holds true in a large number of cases. The more evidence you have, the more reliable your generalization will be.

Deductive Reasoning When you use deductive reasoning, you move from the general to the specific. For example, if you learn that everyone who works at a certain company has excellent health benefits, then you can deduce that someone you know who works there has excellent health benefits.

> **🖱 Research Tip**
>
> To understand the use of generalizations, research the published results of polls and surveys. Note the conclusions drawn from the results, and determine whether the generalizations are hasty or valid.

Logical Fallacies

A logical fallacy occurs when the rules of logic are not followed. Two types of logical fallacies are hasty generalizations and circular reasoning.

Hasty Generalization A hasty generalization is a statement that is made about a large number of cases or a whole group on the basis of a few examples, without taking into account exceptions or qualifying factors. Look at this example:

VALID: Every homeroom in our school has more girls than boys, so there are more girls than boys in our school.

HASTY: There are fifteen girls and ten boys in my homeroom, so there must be more girls than boys in our school.

Circular Reasoning Circular reasoning, also called *begging the question*, occurs when a person restates a general statement as if it were a fact without supplying supporting evidence.

Other Forms of Reasoning

Analogies An analogy is a comparison between two unlike things that are in some way similar. A *complete analogy* is one that names the specific ways in which two things are similar. An *incomplete analogy* is one that simply states one thing is like another without offering the specifics.

COMPLETE: The cell is like a factory—it processes raw materials, produces energy, and discharges wastes.

INCOMPLETE: The human body is like a machine.

The first analogy is complete because it compares particular functions that actually are similar. The second is incomplete because it fails to acknowledge ways in which the body is *not* like a machine.

RECOGNIZE COMPLETE/INCOMPLETE ANALOGIES

1. How are the two things being compared essentially different?
2. How are the two things alike? Is the comparison logical?
3. What is the truth that the comparison tries to show?

Cause and Effect A cause-and-effect sequence is one in which something is caused by one or more events that occurred before it. When one event happens immediately after another, people sometimes conclude that the first event caused the second event. An unrelated sequence is one in which the first event did not cause the second event. In many cases, events can occur one after the other *without* signifying a cause-and-effect relationship.

▶ **Exercise 8** Analyzing Forms of Reasoning First, identify the form of reasoning (inference, generalization, analogy, or cause and effect) used in each of the following statements. Then, tell whether each conclusion is valid or invalid.
1. If you leave the lights of a car turned on, the battery will run down.
2. The atom is like a miniature solar system.
3. The two meals I got on the plane were not good, so all airline food must be terrible.
4. Luis has been elected class president for the past three years, so he must be a real leader.
5. When the available supply of a product increases, the price usually goes down.

Identifying an Author's Purpose and Evaluating Language Use

Identify an Author's Purpose

To read critically, you must also determine why the material was written. Is the author trying to inform you, persuade you, or simply entertain you?

IDENTIFYING AN AUTHOR'S PURPOSE IN WRITING	
Purpose	**Informational Clues**
To inform:	Series of factual statements that are verified by records or personal observation
To instruct:	Sequential development of an idea or a process
To offer an opinion:	Presentation of an issue with a predominant point of view backed up by valid authority
To sell:	Persuasion designed to sell an idea or a product
To entertain:	Narration of an event in a humorous way; often used to lighten a serious topic

Evaluate the Use of Language

Learning to understand and evaluate the various ways in which words are used is an important part of becoming a critical reader.

Connotation and Denotation As you read critically, you must be sensitive to the author's tone, or attitude toward the topic. Tone can be expressed using words with *connotative*, or implied, meanings that differ from the *denotative*, or literal, meanings. Connotations can affect a person emotionally and cause a particular response to the material. The following three statements are similar, yet each gives a different impression of the event described.

DENOTATION: The speaker walked quickly up to the lectern.

CONNOTATION: The speaker strode confidently up to the lectern.

CONNOTATION: The speaker stumbled clumsily up to the lectern.

Irony Irony refers to a contrast between perception and reality; between what is said and what is actually meant.

Understatement When an idea is played down or treated casually, it is considered to be an understatement.

Inflated Language and Jargon Inflated language refers to writing that sounds very scholarly or is filled with scientific or technical terms or overly long phrases. One type of inflated language is called jargon. Jargon is the specialized vocabulary used by people in a particular field. In its place, it is useful, but jargon is often misused to impress the reader or to conceal meaning.

Euphemism A euphemism is a word or phrase used to replace words that may be considered offensive.

Slanting Slanting is the writing of a passage so that it leans toward one point of view. Choosing words with either positive or negative connotations is one type of slanting. Another type of slanting is presenting only one side of an issue by leaving out important facts that would support another point of view.

SLANTED STATEMENT:	Management offered the union a salary increase of only 7 percent.
MORE BALANCED STATEMENT:	Management offered a 7-percent salary increase plus an expanded benefits package, including profit sharing.

> **Exercise 9** Applying Critical Reading Skills Analyze this passage for statements of fact and opinion, forms of reasoning, author's purpose, and use of language.

Nowadays, it is impossible to drive down any street for more than a few minutes without passing at least one jogger, clad in colorful shorts and expensive running shoes, and usually panting or even gasping for air. The death from a heart attack of Jim Fixx, a fellow slave to the exercise mania, seems not to have deterred these fanatical amateur athletes. Millions of dollars are spent each year in fashionable exercise salons run by sharp entrepreneurs. If you could manage to stop one of the victims long enough to ask why he is putting himself through such torture, he would probably mumble something about the heart being a muscle that needs exercise. There is no medical evidence for this. It is true that exercise is a good thing, but overexercising is too much of a good thing. In fact, victims of the physical fitness craze may actually be harming themselves. Doctors report seeing many more injuries to joints, muscles, and tendons. And, of course, there is always the risk of a heart attack during violent exercise.

> **Speaking and Listening Tip**
>
> A speaker's tone of voice or facial expression is often a clue that he or she is using irony or understatement.

▼ **Critical Viewing** What types of connotations might the words have in a description of this runner? **[Speculate]**

Reading Literary Writing

Although you will most often read literature for pleasure, you will get more out of what you read if you apply the strategies that follow. The reading strategies on this page can be applied to any type of literature. On the pages that follow, you'll find specific strategies for reading short stories and novels, drama, poetry, and epics and legends.

Analyzing and Evaluating Fiction

Establish a Purpose for Reading Before you begin, establish a purpose for reading to focus your thoughts. For example, you might read simply for enjoyment, or you might read to learn something about the exotic setting of a novel, or you might read to learn lessons you can apply to your life.

Ask Questions As you read, ask questions: *Why* did the character do this? *When* are the events taking place? *What* are the consequences of these events? Look for answers to these questions as you work your way through the piece.

Reread or Read Ahead When you are unsure what is happening or if the meaning of a sentence or a paragraph is unclear, reread it. At times, you may also find it helpful to read ahead to find more information and to make connections.

Make Personal Connections You will increase your understanding and enjoyment if you connect the characters and events to your own experiences. Consider what you would do and how you would feel if you were taking part in the action.

Read Aloud Read aloud to hear the sounds of the words. This technique is especially effective for poetry, in which sound is just as important as meaning.

Analyze When you analyze, you try to determine the meaning behind events and the characters' actions. Works of literature usually convey a theme, or a central message about life. Most themes are conveyed indirectly, so you may need to do some analyzing to grasp the message.

Respond As you read, think about how the characters and events make you feel, and explore the associations that they bring to mind. When you have finished reading, take some time to reflect and to consider what the work means to you. This may help you decide whether to read other works by that author.

Research Tip

Published literary criticisms reflect one writer's or a group of writers' critical readings of a work of literature. Review several books that contain literary criticisms to see how professional writers apply the critical thinking skills you are learning to use.

Reading Fiction

Following are some strategies for reading fiction:

Predict As you read, ask yourself what might happen next. Base your predictions on what you know about the characters and setting as well as on clues the author provides.

Connect to Your Own Experiences To help you understand how the characters feel, compare their experiences to those you've had in your own life.

Envision the Setting and the Action Use details from the story to create a picture in your mind, as if you were watching the story unfold on the big screen. You might even use a chart like this one to list important details of a scene and to identify the importance of the scene to the story.

🔍 Research Tip

You can view film versions of stories, novels, epics, and legends for an understanding of historical context. Be aware, however, that the historical information you see may not be completely accurate and may reflect the filmmakers' interpretations.

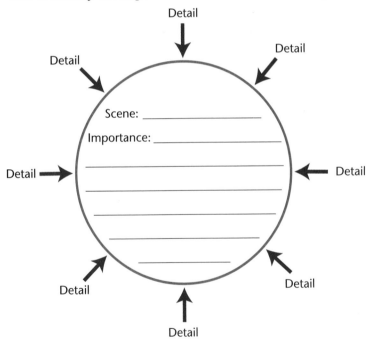

Scene: _____

Importance: _____

Draw Inferences and Conclusions Writers don't always tell you everything directly. Sometimes, you have to make inferences, or draw conclusions, by considering the underlying meaning of details that the writer includes or doesn't include.

▶ **Exercise 10** **Reading Short Stories** Read a short story. Apply all of the strategies above. When you have finished, write a brief explanation of how you used each strategy.

Reading Drama

The key difference between dramas and other forms of literature is that dramas are meant to be performed. As a result, the story unfolds and the characters are revealed through dialogue and action—there are no long passages of description and no direct revelations about how characters feel. Stage directions indicate when and how the actors move and sometimes suggest lighting and sound effects.

Envision the Action Remember that dramas are meant to be performed rather than read. As you read, try to envision how the play would look if it were being performed on stage. Use the stage directions to help you see in your mind the action taking place and to visualize the costumes.

Connect the Play to Its Historical Context
Sometimes, the time in which a play is set can have a dramatic impact on how the characters act and can shape the message the play conveys. Look in the stage directions for information about the time in which the play is set.

Summarize Most dramas are broken into acts or scenes. Pause between acts or scenes to review in your mind the action that has taken place. Make a chart like the one below. List the act, and identify the scenes, characters, and conflict. Then, briefly summarize the events.

```
Act I: _____

    Scene I: _____

        Characters: _____

        Conflict: _____
```

> **Exercise 11** Reading Drama Read the first act of a play in your textbook or in another collection. Explain the play's setting, including its historical context. Tell how the stage directions and characters' comments and actions enabled you to envision the scene. Then, summarize the conflict and the events that occurred in the act.

Technology Tip

You can find performances of many plays on videotape. Once you have finished reading a play, try to find a recorded performance. Watch the video, and compare and contrast the impact of watching it with that of reading it.

Reading Poetry

Reading poetry is unlike reading other types of literature because it is a very distinctive kind of writing—it differs in its appearance, its use of language, and its sound. Poets' imaginative use of language can sometimes make a poem seem complex or hard to understand. Using specific strategies can help you to understand and appreciate poetry.

Identify the Speaker When you read a poem, you are hearing the voice of the poem's speaker. The speaker is not necessarily the poet, although it can be. The speaker may be a character created by the poet. Determine who you think is "telling" the poem, and try to determine his or her perspective on the situation in the poem.

Envision Images Use your senses to experience the pleasures of a poem. For instance, *see* the image of a storm scattering red autumn leaves and *hear* the sound of the wind howling.

Read According to Punctuation Keep in mind that even if a poem is shaped to fit a particular rhythm and rhyme, a poem's words are usually put together and punctuated as sentences. When you read a poem, don't stop at the end of each line unless a punctuation mark stops you.

Listen to the Poem One of the things that distinguishes poetry from prose is its sound. Poetry is meant to be read aloud; by doing so, you will hear the music of the poet's words.

Exercise 12 Reading Poetry Select a poem from your textbook. Read the poem aloud, according to its punctuation, and listen to its sound. Then, write a brief description of the poem in which you identify the speaker, describe three images or figures of speech, and describe the poem's sound.

Speaking and Listening Tip

To appreciate how listening to poetry differs from reading it, attend a local poetry reading. If this isn't possible, find recordings of poetry. Compare and contrast the effect of listening to a poem with the effect of reading one.

Reading From Varied Sources

Today, there are more sources of reading material than ever before. Not only can you read books, magazines, newspapers, and other forms of printed material, but you can also read an almost unlimited amount of material on the Internet. The following are just a few of the sources from which you can choose. When selecting a source, consider your purpose for reading, along with any time constraints with which you're faced.

Read Diaries, Letters, and Journals Diaries, letters, and journals are a great source for firsthand accounts of historical events. Use them to discover how it felt to be part of an event in which you are interested or as primary source material in a research paper. As you read, remember that diaries and journals present a single perspective—the writer's—of the events. To find a balanced point of view, look at several diaries and journals.

Read Newspapers Newspapers are probably the best source for up-to-date information on issues and events. When you are writing a research paper on a historical event, you may want to use newspapers to capture the way information about the event was presented to people at that time. You will also want to use newspapers when you are writing about current events. Beyond school, you'll probably continue to use newspapers as a means of keeping up with current events. Although newspapers are one of the most objective sources, be on the lookout for any words or choices of details that suggest a bias.

Read Speeches Transcripts of speeches can be another excellent source for learning about historical or current events. Keep in mind that a speech that you are reading was originally written to be presented orally to an audience. Also, consider that a speech presents a single point of view—that of the speaker. Many speeches, such as political speeches, have a persuasive purpose. As a result, speakers often carefully choose words and details to achieve a specific effect. Try to avoid being swayed by appeals to emotion or charged language. Instead, see how effectively the speaker has backed up his or her key points with facts, statistics, and other types of support.

▼ **Critical Viewing** This painting shows Patrick Henry delivering his famous "Give Me Liberty or Give Me Death" speech. What can you tell about his delivery based on the painting? **[Analyze]**

"GIVE ME LIBERTY, OR GIVE ME DEATH!"
PATRICK HENRY delivering his great speech on the Rights of the Colonies, before the Virginia Assembly, convened at Richmond March 23rd 1775, concluding with the above sentiment, which became the war cry of the Revolution.

Read Electronic Texts The main type of electronic texts that you will encounter are Web pages. There is an incredible amount of information on the Web, and the amount is growing every day. Some of the information is reliable and objective; some is biased or targeted toward a specific audience. When you read material on the Internet, do so with a critical eye. Determine the purpose behind the material. Often, you will discover that the material has a persuasive purpose. Check whether any points made in a text on the Web are thoroughly supported by facts and details. Also, evaluate the credibility of the source.

Exercise 13 Reading Varied Sources Find at least one example of each of the sources mentioned on these pages. Read the material carefully. Then, write a brief summary of each piece. Follow your summary with an evaluation of the reliability of the material. How well has the author supported his or her main points? Is the author credible? Why or why not? Would you recommend the material to others? Explain.

Reflecting on Your Reading

After a week of applying reading skills and strategies for both nonfiction and fiction works, think about the experience of using them. Use these questions to direct your reflection:

- Which sections of the books that I read did I find most useful?

- How has varying my reading style affected my reading time?

- Which graphic organizers have I used to process and understand information from my reading?

- How do the steps of the SQ4R method help me obtain more complete information and understanding?

- How have critical reading skills helped me to analyze and evaluate the material I read?

- Which strategies for reading fiction did I find most useful? Which strategies did I find most difficult to use?

Jot down your responses and ideas in a journal or notebook. If you like, compare your thoughts and ideas with those of a partner.

Chapter 32

Study, Reference, and Test-Taking Skills

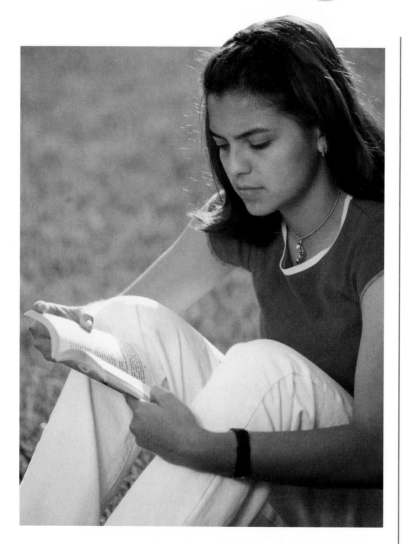

◀ Critical Viewing
What type of school-
work would and
would not be appro-
priate to do in the
setting shown here?
Why? [Analyze]

Learning how to improve your study, reference, and test-taking skills will make your schoolwork easier and prove to be a valuable asset throughout your education. The first two sections of this chapter will show you how to improve your general study habits and how to research specific information in printed and electronic forms. The final section will discuss strategies that you can use to improve your performance on tests.

Basic Study Skills

As with most other things, the more you think out and plan how you study, the more effective your studying will be. Develop a systematic approach to studying that includes how and where you study and how you record what you learn.

Developing a Study Plan

Good study habits begin with a strong study plan. The purpose of a study plan is to help you make the best use of the time available to you for doing your assignments. Your study plan should include setting up a study area, establishing a study schedule, and keeping a study notebook.

KEY CONCEPT Use a *three point study plan* to manage your time and keep track of your assignments. ■

Technology Tip

You can use a software time-management program to help you set up and keep track of your study schedule.

USING A STUDY PLAN

STUDY AREA
1. Set up a well-lit study area free from distractions.
2. Equip the area with work materials: pens, paper, ruler, dictionary.

STUDY NOTEBOOK
1. List assignments and include their due dates.
2. List long-term assignments in steps.
3. Check off assignments as you complete them.

STUDY SCHEDULE
1. Block out periods of time in which you have fixed activities.
2. Plan to study 2–3 hours a day, in 30–45 minute periods.
3. Study your hardest subject first.

Exercise 1 Evaluating Your Study Plan Identify which area of your study plan you need to improve most: setting up a study area, making a study schedule, or keeping a study notebook. Work to improve that skill for one week, and then evaluate your progress.

Taking Notes

Notes are an important study tool. Not only will you need them to study, but the very act of writing information down helps you retain it. Divide your notebook by subject, and take notes on what you learn in class and read in your textbooks.

KEY CONCEPT Keep an organized notebook in which you take notes while listening or reading. ■

Modified Outline Because there is not enough time to write everything down, you should take notes on only the most important information. One of the fastest ways to take notes is by using a *modified outline form*, in which you list main ideas at the margin, indent to show major details, and indent further for supporting details, if necessary.

PASSAGE:

Silicon Chips are engraved with hundreds of electronic circuits. These chips are small enough to pass through the eye of a needle, yet they can store 64,000 pieces of information. They are already at work in the digital watch, the pocket calculator, and the microwave oven.

SAMPLE MODIFIED OUTLINE

Silicon Chips)——————— Main idea
1. Engraved with hundreds of)—— Major details
    electronic circuits   )
2. Extremely small,
    yet store 64,000 pieces of information
3. Used in digital watches,
    calculators, microwave ovens

Summaries A summary is an excellent tool to help you review material. It is a restatement of key ideas in your own words. Written summaries are usually arranged in paragraphs. You can use a summary to capture main ideas from a piece you've just read or a lecture you've just heard. You can also summarize a modified outline you've developed.

Exercise 2 Developing a Modified Outline and a Summary Develop a modified outline and a summary of a chapter from one of your textbooks.

Technology Tip

If you have steady access to a computer and are a strong keyboardist, you may want to record and store some of your notes on computer. Make sure that you back up your notes on a separate disk and that you keep a hard copy.

Reference Skills

The recent revolution in electronic media has made more kinds of information available than ever before. Virtually every kind of printed reference now has an electronic equivalent, either on CD-ROM or on-line or both. At public or school libraries, you can often find all these sources: fiction and non-fiction books, audiocassettes, videocassettes, periodicals (newspapers, magazines, and scholarly journals), reference works in printed and electronic form, information on microfilm, and computer access to the Internet.

Finding Library Resources

Some library resources *circulate*—that is, you can borrow them for a fixed period of time. Others are for *reference* only and must be used at the library. Some materials are displayed on *open stacks,* or shelves, where you get them yourself; others are stored on *closed stacks* open only to library staff, who will bring you the material when you request it.

Using the Library Catalog The catalog shows whether the library owns a work. Use the catalog to help you find works by specific authors or on particular subjects. The catalog also clarifies whether a book is fiction or nonfiction and gives call numbers of nonfiction works so that you can locate them on the shelves.

▶ **KEY CONCEPT** Use the library catalog— in *card, printed,* or *electronic* form—to find important information about the materials that a library stocks. ■

Card Catalog Each work in a library has an *author card* and *title card*; each nonfiction book also has at least one *subject card.* Cards are filed alphabetically in small drawers, with author cards alphabetized by last names and title cards alphabetized by the first words of the titles, excluding *A, An,* or *The.*

CARD CATALOG (AUTHOR CARD)	
306.209C Collins, Gail	call number / author
Scorpion Tongues	title
New York:	city of publication
William Morrow, 1998	publisher, / publication date
322 p; index	number of pages / index
United States—Politics	subject

Electronic Catalog Most libraries now keep an electronic catalog, an on-line database or a CD-ROM that you access from special library computer terminals. Usually, you can find a book's catalog entry by typing in its title, key words in the title, its author's name, or (for nonfiction) an appropriate subject. Electronic catalogs usually indicate whether the book is available or has been checked out. Often, the catalog will also indicate whether the book is available from other local libraries through an inter-library loan system.

Printed Catalog A printed catalog is a booklet that lists each work alphabetically by author, by title, and (for nonfiction) by subject.

> **Technology Tip**
>
> Some electronic catalogs can be accessed remotely through the Internet. Ask your librarian if this option is available.

▶ **Exercise 3** Using the Library Catalog Visit your school or local library, and use the catalog to answer these questions.
1. What kind of catalog does the library use?
2. Who wrote *The Red Badge of Courage*? Is this book fiction or nonfiction?
3. What are the titles, subjects, and call numbers of three nonfiction books by Annie Dillard?
4. What are the titles, authors, and call numbers of three books about nutrition published since 1998?
5. What are the titles, authors, and call numbers of two nonfiction books about space exploration?

▼ Critical Viewing
How do the stacks at this library compare with those at your own library? **[Compare]**

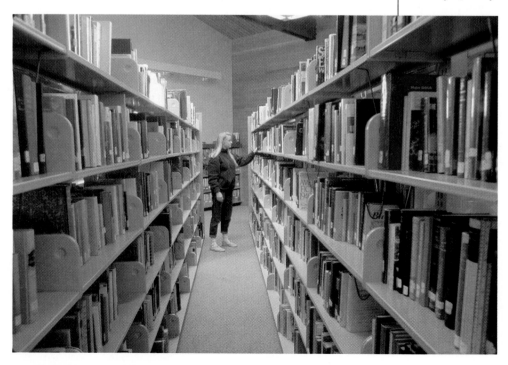

Finding Books on Library Shelves Libraries generally separate fiction (made-up stories) from nonfiction (factual material). Nonfiction includes two smaller groups often shelved separately: biographies (real-life people's stories) and reference works (works to which you refer for information and which must be used at the library).

KEY CONCEPT Find fiction arranged alphabetically by authors' last names and nonfiction arranged by call number. ■

Fiction Books of fiction are shelved in a special section alphabetized by authors' last names. In the library catalog and on its spine, the book may be labeled *F* or *FIC*, followed by one or more letters of the author's last name; for example, *FIC Cis* may appear on a novel by Sandra Cisneros.

KEY CONCEPT Find nonfiction on the shelves by using the call numbers. ■

Nonfiction Works of nonfiction are assigned number-letter codes, called *call numbers*, based on their content. The call numbers are placed on the spine of each book, and the books are arranged in number-letter order on the shelves—for example, 216.1, 216.2, 216.41A, 216.41G, 216.42B, 217.1. To find a nonfiction book, look it up in the library catalog to learn its call number and then follow number-letter order to locate the book on the shelf.

Most public libraries assign call numbers according to the **Dewey Decimal System,** which divides all knowledge into ten main groups numbered from 000 to 999. The following chart shows the number spans for these ten content areas.

MAIN CLASSES OF THE DEWEY DECIMAL SYSTEM	
Number	Subject
000–099	General Works (encyclopedias, periodicals, etc.)
100–199	Philosophy
200–299	Religion
300–399	Social Sciences
400–499	Languages
500–599	Science
600–699	Technology (applied science)
700–799	Arts and Leisure
800–899	Literature
900–999	History

Special Sections In the Dewey Decimal System, *biographies* are often not assigned call numbers but instead are shelved in a special section alphabetized by the last names of their subjects (the people they are about). In the library catalog and on the book's spine, a biography may be labeled *B* or *BIO*, followed by one or more letters of the subject's last name; for example, *BIO Ein* may appear on a biography of Albert Einstein.

Reference works usually have their own special section—and an *R* or *REF* before their call numbers. Many libraries also have special sections for young-adult books (often labeled *YA*) and children's books (usually labeled *J* or *JUV* for *juvenile*).

The **Library of Congress System,** unlike the Dewey Decimal System, is organized letter-number. In the Library of Congress System, the call numbers begin with letters. The main classes are designated by a single letter; combinations of two letters designate the subclasses. The letter designations are followed by a numerical notation, from 1 to 9999, which can be further subdivided:

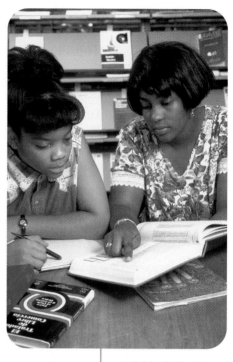

▲ Critical Viewing
What type of assistance do you imagine that the librarian is providing for the girl in this photograph?
[Speculate]

MAIN CLASS:	H	Social Sciences
SUBCLASS:	HF	Commerce, Marketing, Advertising
DIVISION:	5717	Business Communication

> **Exercise 4** **Finding Fiction and Nonfiction** In your notebook, answer the following questions.
> 1. To find fiction by Ralph Ellison on a library shelf, would you look before or after fiction by George Eliot?
> 2. For a nonfiction work with call number 310.3R, would you look before or after of a work with call number 310.2J?
> 3. For a book with call number R032.1B, would you look in the reference, biography, or fiction section?
> 4. Arrange this fiction in the order that you would find them on library shelves: *Moby-Dick* by Herman Melville, *The Bluest Eye* by Toni Morrison, *Ethan Frome* by Edith Wharton, and *The Joy Luck Club* by Amy Tan.
> 5. Arrange these call numbers in the order that you would find them on library shelves: 519.3B, 518.1P, 518.6C, 518.1K, 519.6A. What is the general subject or content area of books with these call numbers?

Using Periodicals and Periodical Indexes

A *periodical* is a newspaper, magazine, or similar publication issued at regular intervals. Such publications are good sources of up-to-date information. To find out which periodicals a library carries, look up the title in the card catalog.

Periodical Indexes To find which periodicals contain articles on a particular subject, consult a periodical index. Issued regularly in printed or electronic form, these indexes contain *citations* that tell you where and when an article was published. They also may contain *abstracts*, or brief summaries, of the articles. In addition, many electronic indexes provide the *full text*, or complete article, for some articles cited.

> **KEY CONCEPT** Use articles from periodicals for up-to-date information and periodical indexes to locate the articles. ■

Some indexes—such as the *Readers' Guide to Periodical Literature*—cover articles from many periodicals; others, such as *The New York Times Index*, cover articles from only one publication. Look at this sample *Readers' Guide* entry.

SAMPLE READERS' GUIDE ENTRY

subject heading ——————[HORSEMANSHIP

See also

cross-references ——————[Polo
Rodeos

subheading ⌐ **Competition**   article topic clarified in brackets
title of article ⌐ A show of hooves [pony club rally].

illustrated

author ⌐ J.B. Banks   *National Geographic World* v288 no 4
name of periodical ⌐   volume and number

pages ——————[p. 12–15   date   ⌐ Ag 1999

Technology Tip

Many newspapers and magazines now have free Internet Web sites where you can read current editions at no cost.

Research Tip

Find citations in an electronic index by typing in the subject, the author's name, or a key word in the title of the article. Find citations in printed indexes by looking up the subject or author.

> **Exercise 5** **Using Periodicals** Visit a school or local library to answer these questions.
> 1. What daily newspapers does the library carry?
> 2. Find an article in a current magazine that provides information you could use in an essay.
> 3. Use a periodical index to find four citations for articles on women in sports. Also, list the subjects you looked under.
> 4. Use a periodical index to find an article on a subject you are studying. Read the article, and share your findings.
> 5. Using a periodical index, find an article about someone you admire. Read the article, and then write a summary.

Using Dictionaries

A *dictionary* is a collection of words and their meanings, along with other information about words, such as their parts of speech and pronunciations.

> **KEY CONCEPT** Use a dictionary to find information about words, such as spelling, pronunciation, and parts of speech. ∎

English-Language Dictionaries An *unabridged* dictionary of the English language attempts to cover all the words in the language, including those no longer in use, and gives detailed information on each word's history. An *abridged* English-language dictionary, which is shortened for everyday use, is the kind of dictionary that most people have in their homes and offices.

Specialized Dictionaries These dictionaries are limited to words of a particular type (for example, slang) or words in a particular field (for example, legal or literary terms). They also include *foreign-language dictionaries*, which are two-part dictionaries that give English equivalents of words in a particular foreign language and vice versa.

Dictionary Organization Dictionaries are available in both printed and electronic form. In printed dictionaries, entry words are arranged in *alphabetical order*. To speed your search for a word, use the **thumb index,** a series of right-hand notches that makes it easier to thumb alphabetically through a dictionary. Each notch, labeled *A*, *B*, *C*, and so on, shows the section of entries for words that start with that particular letter.

Also use the **guide words,** two large words at the top of each dictionary page that show the first and last entry words on the page. All other entry words on the page fall alphabetically between these two guide words. For instance, if the guide words are *rider* and *rift*, the words *ridge* and *rife* will also be on that page; however, the word *right* will not be there.

In **electronic dictionaries,** you usually find a word simply by typing the word and having the dictionary search the dictionary database.

Dictionary Entries Dictionary entries contain a wealth of information about words and their use. Here is an example:

DICTIONARY ENTRY

Pronunciation ──────────── Inflected Forms ──────

Primary Stress ───────────── Part of Speech ─┐

Word Entry ─┐ **pret·ty** (prit′ē; *often* purt′ē) *adj.* **-ti·er, -ti·est**

Syllabification ─┤ [ME. *prati* < OE. *prættig,* crafty < *prætt,* a

Etymology ──────── craft, trick] **1.** Pleasing or attractive in a
dainty, delicate or graceful way rather than
through striking beauty, elegance, grandeur,
or stateliness **2.** *a)* fine; good; nice: often

Numbered ───── used ironically *[a pretty fix]* b) adroit; skillful

Definitions *[a pretty move]* **3.** [Archaic] elegant **4.** [Archaic

Usage Label ── or Scot.] brave; bold; gallant **5.** [Colloq.]

Part of Speech considerable; quite large *[a pretty price]* —adv.
1. fairly; somewhat *[pretty sure]*: sometimes,
by hyperbole, quite or very *[pretty angry]* **2.**
[Colloq.] prettily *[to talk pretty]* —**n.,** pl. **-ties**
pretty persons or things —*vt.* **-tied,**
-ty·ing to make pretty (usually with *up*)
—**SYN.** SEE BEAUTIFUL —sitting pretty [Slang]

Derived ───── in a favorable position —**pret′ti·ly** *adv.*

Words —**pret′ti·ness** *n.* —**pret′ty·ish** *adj.*

Entry Word With Syllabification The word being defined appears in dark print at the start of the entry. From it you can confirm the word's spelling and usually learn how to break it into syllables (if the word has more than one syllable). Dashes, dots, or spaces usually show the syllables.

Pronunciation Usually appearing in parentheses or brackets immediately following the entry word, the pronunciation shows how to say the word and uses accent marks (′) to show which syllable or syllables to stress. To understand the symbols in the pronunciation, you need to consult the dictionary's *pronunciation key.* When you consult the key that follows the pronunciation of *pretty,* you see that the *e* sounds like the *i* in *is* and the *y* sounds like the first *e* in *even.*

Part-of-Speech Label The dictionary uses abbreviations to show how a word functions in a sentence—as a noun (*n*), a transitive verb (*vt*), an intransitive verb (*vi*), an adjective (*adj*), an adverb (*adv*), or another part of speech.

Plurals and Inflected Forms The dictionary shows irregularly formed plurals and verb tenses and will show inflected forms, such as comparative and superlative modifiers, if there is anything unusual about their spellings.

Etymology Information about the word's origin and history also appears in brackets, parentheses, or slashes near the start or end of the entry. It often uses abbreviations for languages, all explained in the dictionary's key to abbreviations and symbols (at the front of most printed dictionaries).

Definition and Example The meanings of the entry word are numbered if there is more than one, and sometimes examples are included to illustrate their uses in phrases or sentences.

Usage and Field Labels Some definitions have labels showing how or where they are used. For instance, definitions labeled *Archaic (Arch)*, *Obsolete (Obs)*, or *Rare* are not widely used today. Those labeled *Colloquial (Colloq)* or *Slang* are not considered standard English. Those labeled *British (Brit)* or *Scottish (Scot)* are not much used in America. Those labeled with particular field names—*Electronics (Elec)*, for example, or *Music*—are not much used outside their field. American dictionaries also use a symbol (such as a star) to show whether a particular word or definition is mainly used in America.

Idioms and Derived Words The end of an entry may list and define *idioms*, or expressions, in which the entry word appears. It may also list *derived words*—words formed from the entry word—along with their part of speech.

> **Exercise 6** Understanding Dictionary Entries Use a dictionary to answer these questions.
>   1. Which of these words is NOT spelled correctly?
>   **a.** accommodate **b.** definite **c.** hypocrasy **d.** rendezvous
>   2. In the word *phlegmatic*, which syllable is stressed?
>   3. What is the origin of the word *algebra*?
>   4. Identify two meanings of the word *parade*.
>   5. Is there an adverb derived from *nasty*? If so, what is it?

Using a Thesaurus

A *thesaurus* is a specialized dictionary providing extensive lists of *synonyms*, or words with similar meanings, and often some *antonyms*, or words with opposite meanings.

KEY CONCEPT A thesaurus is one of the most useful writing tools, because it can help you to avoid the repetition of words and to make your language as precise as possible. ■

In a thesaurus, words may be arranged alphabetically or they may be grouped by theme. When the arrangement is thematic, you first have to look up the word in the index to find out in which thematic grouping its synonyms will appear. When the thesaurus is arranged alphabetically by word, you simply look up the word as you would in any dictionary.

Technology Tip

Many of the word-processing programs provide an on-line thesaurus. To use this feature, simply enter a word and you will be given a list of synonyms.

THESAURUS ENTRY

Part of Speech ——————————— Synonyms grouped by shared part of speech
Entry Word ———————

MELODY—*n.* melody, euphony, mellifluence,
Synonyms —— air, tune, carillon, measure, lay, song, chime, aria, run, chant.

Part of Speech for related forms of word — *adj.* melodious, melodic.
Synonyms for related forms — euphonious; sweet, mellow, mellifluous, mellifluent, sweet-sounding, dulcet; lyric, songful; clear, silvery, silver-tongued, full-toned, deep-toned, rich, resonant, ringing.

Cross-references to other entries — See also HARMONY, MUSIC, SINGING, SOUND, SWEETNESS. *Antonym*—See
Cross-reference to antonym — HARSH.

Exercise 7 Using a Thesaurus Use a thesaurus to find appropriate synonyms for the words in italics. For each sentence, explain whether the synonym you have identified is more effective than the original word.

1. After two workers left, the shop advertised for new *workers*.
2. The manager *managed* the search.
3. He *ran* several interviews over a two-week period.
4. The last applicant seemed very *brainy*.
5. The manager was also pleased by her *pleasant* manner.

Using Other Reference Works

Most libraries have all kinds of useful *reference works*, or resources to which you refer for information instead of reading them in their entirety. Such works are usually found in the reference section of the library. Most libraries will not allow you to check out reference works, so you must look at them while on site.

> **KEY CONCEPT** Reference works are a good source for learning general information about a topic or as a starting point for a research project. ∎

SOME GENERAL ENCYCLOPEDIAS	SOME SPECIALIZED ENCYCLOPEDIAS
Encyclopædia Britannica *The World Book Encyclopedia* *Grolier's Multimedia Encyclopedia* *Compton's Pictured Encyclopedia*	*Van Nostrand's Scientific Encyclopedia* *Health Reference Center Encyclopedia of the Arts* *Grove's Dictionary of Music & Musicians* *The Baseball Encyclopedia*

Encyclopedias An *encyclopedia* is a collection of articles on different subjects. Encyclopedias list articles alphabetically by subject and usually span several volumes, with letters on the spine showing which subjects each volume contains; for example, a volume labeled *Ma to Mi* may contain an article on Maine but not Montana. Not all topics have their own article, but an alphabetical index, usually in a separate volume, tells you in which articles particular topics are covered.

A *general encyclopedia* collects articles offering basic information on a great many subjects. A *specialized encyclopedia* collects more complex or detailed articles in a particular field.

Almanacs These annual publications (updated more frequently in some electronic versions) offer factual information on a wide range of subjects, including history, geography, government, weather, science, industry, sports, and entertainment. In printed almanacs, the index may be in the back or the front.

🔋 Research Tip

Encyclopedias can help you gather background information to get started on a research project. However, they should not be one of your main sources of information. Instead, you should rely on nonfiction books, interviews, and reliable Internet resources.

Biographical References These works provide brief life histories of famous people, usually listed alphabetically by last name. Some biographical references, such as *Current Biography* or *Webster's Biographical Dictionary*, cover people from many walks of life; others, such as *Contemporary Authors* or *The International Who's Who of Women*, cover people in specific fields or areas.

Literary Indexes The library catalog lists books and other full-length publications, but to find a shorter work, you need to consult a literary index. A *literary index* tells you in which *anthologies*, or collections, shorter works of literature are found. Examples include *Granger's Guide to Poetry, Poem Finder*, the *Short Story Index*, the *Play Index*, and the *Essay Index*.

Books of Quotations Looking for a snappy quotation to use in a report? Trying to learn who first said an oft-quoted remark? You can perform either task with a *book of quotations*, which lists famous remarks and tells you who said them and where. Examples include *Bartlett's Book of Quotations, The Oxford Dictionary of Quotations*, and *Gale's Quotations*.

Atlases and Electronic Map Collections *Atlases* or *electronic map collections* contain maps and geographical information based on them. They also may include statistics about population, climate, agriculture, industry, natural resources, and so forth. In printed atlases, maps often have a numbered and lettered grid; to find a particular place on a map, you look it up in an alphabetical list called a *gazetteer*, which refers you to the area on the grid that the place appears.

▼ **Critical Viewing** What type of reference book would you use to find out what type of flowers these are and to gather information about them? **[Connect]**

▶ **Exercise 8** Using Other Reference Works Use printed or electronic reference works to find answers to these questions. Indicate the type of reference you used.

1. In what year was the city of Wichita, Kansas, founded?
2. What is Elizabeth Blackwell's claim to fame?
3. What is the highest dam in the United States?
4. Which countries border Mexico?
5. Find a quotation about nature from any work by Ralph Waldo Emerson. Include the name of the work.

Using the Internet and Other Media Resources

Find and Evaluate Information on the Internet

Through the Internet, you can access a virtually unlimited amount of information without ever leaving your desk. Because so much information is available, however, it is easy to get lost on the Web. For this reason, it is essential to know how to find information quickly on the Web and to critically evaluate the information you do find.

KEY CONCEPT The Internet provides a wealth of information on just about any topic. However, the information must be critically evaluated. ■

Locating Appropriate Web Sites The information on the Web is offered through thousands of individual Web sites, each of which has its own address, or URL (Universal Resource Locator). These sites usually consist of several Web pages of text, graphics, and sometimes audio or video displays. Use these tips to help you find appropriate sites:

- If you know a reliable Web site and its address (URL), simply type the address into your Web browser.

- If you don't know a particular Web site, use an Internet search engine to find the information. Use general search engines to search for a key term. Use other search engines to search in specific fields or categories.

- Also, consult reference librarians familiar with the Internet or Internet coverage in established library journals (such as *Booklist* and *The Library Journal*) for information on useful, reliable reference Web sites.

Evaluating Web Sites Since almost anyone can create a Web site, not every Web site provides useful or reliable information. Once you find a Web site, evaluate its reliability by considering the following:

- Identify who set up the site. Is the organization or individual who set it up an authority on the topics covered?

- Be on the lookout for **bias,** the presentation of a single point of view on a topic. If a site does represent a single position on a topic, it is essential that all of the arguments that are presented are backed up by facts and examples.

- Check to see that the information is up to date. What clues can you find that suggest when the site was last updated?

- Compare the information presented on the topic to information presented on other related sites.

Technology Tip

You often can print a Web page or download it onto a disk. On a home computer, you can also highlight and copy text and paste it into a file in your word-processing program.

> **Exercise 9** Using the Internet On a library, school, or home computer, use the Internet to do this research:
> 1. Go to the U.S. Postal Service Web site, **www.usps.gov**, to learn the ZIP Code for 146 K St., Washington, D.C.
> 2. Find the official Web site for the Metropolitan Museum of Art in New York City and from it find the museum hours.
> 3. Choose a topic for a science paper. List names and URLs of four Web sites that you think can help you.
> 4. Find the text of the poem "To Helen" by Edgar Allan Poe. Be sure to record the name and URL.
> 5. From a reliable source, find out about Lyme disease and how to prevent it. Record source information.

Use Other Media Resources

In addition to the Internet, there are a wide range of other media resources that you can use for research. These include videos, CD-ROMs, and electronic databases. You can probably find many of these resources at your local or school library.

Video Resources Videos, such as the ones below, can be an excellent reference tool and a key part of a multimedia report.

- **News Programs** provide up-to-date information on key events and issues and can offer insights into how people responded to major events at the time they happened.

- **Documentaries** can offer in-depth information on a wide range of specific topics.

CD-ROM References Most of the print references mentioned earlier in this chapter are also available on CD-ROM. For example, there are a wide range of CD-ROM encyclopedias that provide text information, photographs, video, and audio. In addition, there are CD-ROM atlases and map programs that you can use to find information about geographical regions. To use a CD-ROM reference, you simply need to type in key words and the program will take you to your topic.

Electronic Databases Electronic databases provide large collections of data on specific topics. The databases allow you to sort and examine the information in a variety of ways. You can usually find the sort feature of a database in the menu bar. To conduct a search, type in one or more key words.

> **Exercise 10** Using Media Resources Choose a topic that interests you. Conduct research on that topic, using two different media resources. Present your findings to the class.

Technology Tip

Electronic maps often have "zoom in" and other features in which you simply click the mouse to enlarge or change the area shown.

Technology Tip

Remember that in electronic database searches, one wrong letter can result in failure. Be sure to type carefully and spell everything correctly. If you aren't sure of a spelling, try several variations.

Test-Taking Skills

In this section, you will learn some strategies to improve your performance on tests and to deal with the different kinds of questions they often contain.

Taking Tests

Objective tests are those in which each question has a single correct answer. To prepare for such tests, carefully study the material that the test will cover. Be sure to arrive at the test on time, well rested, and with all the equipment you were told to bring—pencils, pens, and so on.

▶ **KEY CONCEPT** When taking a test, divide your time into three steps—previewing, answering, and proofreading. ■

PREVIEW THE TEST

1. Put your name on each sheet of paper you will hand in.
2. Look over the entire test to get an overview of the types of questions and how they are arranged.
3. Find out whether you lose points for incorrect answers. If you do, do not guess at answers.
4. Decide how much time you must spend on each section of the test.
5. Plan to devote the most time to questions that are hardest or worth the most points.

ANSWER THE QUESTIONS

1. Answer the easy questions first. Put a check next to harder questions, and come back to them later.
2. If permitted, use scratch paper to jot down your ideas.
3. Read each question at least *twice* before answering.
4. Supply the single best answer, giving only one answer to a question unless the instructions say otherwise.
5. Answer all questions on the test unless you are told not to guess or there is a penalty for wrong guesses.
6. Do not change your first answer without a good reason.

PROOFREAD YOUR ANSWERS

1. Check that you have followed directions completely.
2. Reread test questions and answers. Make sure that you have answered all of the questions.

Answering Different Kinds of Questions

Although the content of tests varies greatly, the types of questions that appear on these tests are fairly similar. This section will inform you about different types of test questions and specific strategies for answering them.

KEY CONCEPT Improve your test scores by learning about different kinds of questions and the strategies for answering them. ■

True-or-False Questions True-or-false questions ask you to identify whether or not a statement is accurate.

- If a statement seems true, be sure that it is all true.
- Pay special attention to the word *not*, which often changes the whole meaning of a statement.
- Take note of the generalizing words *all, always, never, no, none,* and *only.* They often make a statement false.
- Take note of the qualifying words *generally, much, many, most, often, sometimes,* and *usually.* They often make a statement true.

Multiple-Choice Questions This kind of question asks you to choose from four or five possible responses.

- Try to answer the question before reading the choices. If your answer is one of the choices, select that choice.
- Eliminate obviously incorrect answers, crossing them out if you are allowed to write on the test paper.

Matching Questions Matching questions require that you match items in one group with items in another.

- Count each group to see whether any items will be left over.
- Read all the items before you start matching.
- Match the items you know first, and then match the others. If you can write on the paper, cross out items as you use them.

Fill-in Questions A fill-in question asks you to supply an answer in your own words. The answer may complete a statement or it may simply answer a question.

- Read the question or incomplete statement carefully.
- If you are completing a statement, look for context clues that may signal the answer. Pay special attention if the word *an* appears right before the missing word, which indicates that the missing word begins with a vowel sound.

Analogies An *analogy* is a special type of multiple-choice question that often appears on vocabulary and reading tests. Analogy items usually provide a pair of words and ask you to choose another pair that expresses a similar relationship.

EXAMPLE: FURNITURE : CHAIR ::

a. food : meat   **c.** daisy : flower
b. wall : window   **d.** olive : green

In the preceding example, the answer is *a*. The relationship between the pairs of words is *kind*. A chair is a *kind* of furniture, and meat is a *kind* of food. Notice that the sequence of the words matters. The following chart lists common analogy relationships:

⊘ **Learn More**

Having a strong vocabulary will help you answer analogy questions. For more on developing your vocabulary skills, see Chapter 30.

COMMON ANALOGY RELATIONSHIPS	
Relationship	**Example**
Shared quality (synonyms)	impetuous : rash
Lack of a quality (antonyms)	enthusiasm : boredom
Degree (greater to lesser / lesser to greater)	guffaw : giggle / whisper : scream
Part to whole / Whole to part	drawer : desk / house : room
Kind (specific to general / general to specific)	salamander : lizard / dog : poodle
Sequence	arrest : trial
Location or proximity	knee : calf
Device	wrench : plumber

Short-Answer Questions Short-answer questions call on you to write one or more sentences in which you provide certain information. Before you respond to a short-answer question, look carefully at the question. Identify key words, such as *explain, compare,* and *identify.* When you answer the question, provide only the information called for through the key words. Be as direct and concise as possible.

Essay Questions On many standardized tests and tests you take in school, you will be called on to write one or more essays. Sometimes, you are given a choice of prompts to which you can respond. In other instances, you are given only a single prompt. Look for key words in the prompt or prompts to determine exactly what information you are being asked to provide. Take a few minutes to gather facts, examples, and other types of details you can include in your essay. Devote most of your time to drafting your essay. However, try to allow a little time to make revisions in your work.

▶ **Exercise 11** Completing Analogies For each item, choose the letter of the pair of words that expresses the relationship most like the relationship of the words in capital letters. Also, indicate the type of relationship.

1. MANGO : FRUIT ::
   a. vegetable : corn **b.** peas : beans **c.** zucchini : vegetable
2. JOY : ECSTASY ::
   a. admiration : love **b.** life : hope **c.** happiness : sorrow
3. FOREWORD : EPILOGUE ::
   a. appetizer : dessert **b.** team : spirit **c.** introduction : book
4. THERMOSTAT : HEAT ::
   a. watt : light **b.** scale : weight **c.** temperature : thermometer
5. CONCEIT : MODESTY ::
   a. anger : fury **b.** vitality : sloth **c.** kindness : virtue

▶ **Exercise 12** Understanding the Various Types of Test Questions Using a subject you are studying in one of your classes, prepare an objective test on the material. Write five true-or-false questions, five multiple-choice questions, five matching questions, and five fill-in questions. Exchange papers with another student, and take that student's test, writing your answers on a separate sheet of paper. Exchange again, and grade the test.

Reflecting on Your Study, Reference, and Test-Taking Skills

Consider the methods you have learned for improving study skills, the reference works available for improving your research skills, and the strategies for improving your test-taking skills. Answer the following questions in a journal entry:

- What changes should I make in my study area or schedule?
- What changes should I make to take notes effectively?
- Which reference materials seem the most useful to me?
- Which reference materials do I feel I need to learn more about?
- How can I budget my time more effectively when taking tests?
- What new strategies should I adopt for different kinds of test questions?

Workplace Skills and Competencies

Many skills that make you a successful student also help to make you a valuable employee when you begin a career. In addition to writing and speaking effectively, listening attentively, and reading carefully, you will benefit from knowing how to communicate well with others and how to accomplish tasks efficiently and creatively.

This chapter will help you improve skills you already have and develop new ones in several important areas. You will learn strategies for effective interaction, goal setting, and problem solving. In addition, you will learn how to manage your time and money wisely and how to apply math and computer skills to the workplace.

▲ Critical Viewing
Identify a career that requires the computer and interpersonal skills these students are demonstrating. [Connect]

Working With People

Whether you pursue a career as a salesperson, researcher, contractor, or train conductor, you will be expected to interact effectively with people. The way you speak and interact with supervisors, co-workers, clients, or the general public will influence their impression of you and the company you represent. This section will help you to further develop skills needed for communicating in one-on-one and group situations.

Learn to Communicate One on One

In the workplace, you may need to interact in one-on-one situations involving people you know only on a professional level or people you don't know at all. The first of these one-on-one situations is the job or college interview: Performing effectively during an interview can help you get into the college of your choice, land a job, or advance in the workplace.

Interviewing Interviews are the most formal type of one-on-one communication. In addition to sharing information about training, strengths, weaknesses, and interests, interview candidates must also present a positive first impression.

> ▶ **KEY CONCEPT** A job or college interview requires preparation, professional conduct, and follow-up work. ■

Keys to a Successful Interview

Before the Interview

- Bring copies of your résumé and names of references with you.
- Review the key points of your background and experience so you will be prepared to answer questions.
- Research the employer or college, and prepare questions that demonstrate your knowledge and interest.
- Dress neatly.

During the Interview

- Be respectful and polite at all times.
- Listen carefully, and respond directly to each question.
- Smile, and maintain eye contact.
- Thank the interviewer for his or her time, and ask when a decision will be made.

After the Interview

- Send a follow-up letter, restating your interest and thanking the interviewer for his or her time.
- When the deadline for a decision arrives, call to check your status.

▶ Speaking and Listening Tip

Use your experiences outside of school to practice professionalism. Request information from store clerks and telephone operators as if you were in a work environment. Discuss with a partner how communicating in this way affects the way people respond to you.

Interacting Successfully In school or in the workplace, you will have conferences with others to discuss your performance and your plans for the future. In addition, you may have meetings with colleagues to get a job done. Whether you need to organize a project, solve an unexpected problem, or deal with customers, your ability to interact respectfully may mean the difference between success and failure.

KEY CONCEPT To interact effectively in school and work situations, treat others with respect, listen carefully, and do not hesitate to communicate your thoughts and concerns. ■

> **More Practice**
> Academic and Workplace Skills Activity Book
> • p. 54

Guidelines for Successful Interaction

- **Be sensitive to verbal or nonverbal messages** you receive from other people. Know when you need to be serious and when you can be casual or humorous.
- **Listen carefully,** and ask questions if necessary.
- **Find common ground**—similar interests or experiences that connect you to the other person.
- **Respect differences,** and accept that others may have different backgrounds, abilities, and opinions.
- **Use language that is appropriate** in tone, style, and complexity for your audience. For example, you may use slang with friends but not with an employer.
- **Avoid finger pointing;** instead, look for a positive resolution to problems rather than a person to blame.

Exercise 1 **Interviewing for a Position** With another student, choose a job you would like to pursue. Then, for a group, role-play a job interview for that position. The interviewer should ask questions to prompt the interviewee to describe his or her qualifications. After the role-play is over, ask the group to point out the strengths and weaknesses you demonstrated as a candidate.

Exercise 2 **Interacting With Others in Various Situations** With other students, role-play the following situations. In each case, discuss what you learned from the experience.
1. Two students: a new student asks a coach about joining a team in midseason.
2. Four students: a salesperson is helping a customer who cannot make a decision; others are growing impatient as they wait for assistance.
3. Two students: an employee asks a supervisor for a raise.

▼ Critical Viewing Are these students having a positive or a negative interaction? On what do you base your answer? **[Deduce]**

Learning Teamwork

Team efforts are critical to success in many arenas outside of sports. For example, you may use teamwork to develop a group project with fellow students, participate in a town committee, or work on a job-based project team. Group interaction requires basic communication skills and the ability to anticipate or avoid conflicts among the many personalities involved. To work successfully as a team, members must be willing to listen and be respectful of one another's opinions and roles.

Conducting Meetings and Group Discussions Effective meetings or group discussions will help a team work well together. Participants can take specific roles to keep the group focused. Ideally, these roles should be rotated each meeting:

- A **facilitator** guides the discussion and encourages the interaction of all group members.
- A **note-taker** records key points and distributes meeting minutes or notes after the meeting.
- A **timekeeper** keeps track of the time allotted to a topic.

> **KEY CONCEPT** For a group to work effectively, all members must be organized, focused on the task at hand, and aware of their responsibilities. ∎

The following chart shows some of the other ground rules for an effective meeting:

GROUND RULES FOR A MEETING OR DISCUSSION

- ☑ Establish a time limit, and begin and end on time.
- ☑ Assign roles, including facilitator, timekeeper, and note-taker.
- ☑ Use a flip chart to record key points.
- ☑ When trying to make plans or find solutions, allow time for brainstorming—the free exchange of ideas.
- ☑ Make sure everyone participates.

> **Exercise 3** Using Group Roles Working with five classmates, choose a group facilitator, a timekeeper, and a note-taker. Then, begin a fifteen-minute discussion about the impact on students of one of the following areas: volunteering, the Internet, after-school jobs, or sports. Have the rest of the class evaluate your teamwork.

⚜ Challenge

Often, the group establishes an *agenda* that lists the order of the topics being discussed. If new issues or questions are raised during the discussion that cannot be solved during the allotted time, all of the people involved should plan to meet again.

Participating Effectively Assuming roles and setting ground rules are good first steps toward running an effective meeting or discussion. However, the success of a meeting or discussion ultimately rests on the effective participation of each group member. To participate effectively in these situations, be prepared to make suggestions, be open to the ideas of others, and give and accept constructive criticism.

> **KEY CONCEPT** A good participant contributes ideas and constructive criticism and allows others to do the same. ■

▲ **Critical Viewing**
What details of this photograph suggest that the students shown are meeting informally?
[Interpret]

TIPS FOR EFFECTIVE PARTICIPATION

Listen respectfully to all viewpoints.

Share your perspective, and encourage others to do so.

Focus on the topic, and help others to focus on it as well.

Give and receive criticism gracefully.

> **Exercise 4** Conducting a Meeting Form a committee with a group of classmates. Assign roles, and set an agenda for a meeting in which you will identify a goal you would all like to see accomplished, such as building a new park in your community. Then, work together at your meeting to lay out plans for how this goal might be accomplished. When your meeting is complete, list contributions each group member made to the plan.

> **Exercise 5** Analyzing a Group Discussion Using the tips outlined above, evaluate a televised round-table discussion. In your notebook, describe what you have witnessed. Refer to the strategies for effective participation to explain how the group did or did not work well together.

Moving Toward Goals

Thoughtful planning is a key to success in school, the workplace, and other areas of life. When you plan and set goals, you give yourself a better chance of achieving them.

▶ **KEY CONCEPT** Goals should be specific and include a clear timeline for completion. ■

Personal and Professional Goals

Some goals are *personal*—for example, making a sports team or improving your reading speed. Other goals are *professional*, because they focus on accomplishments in school or your work life. Getting into college, finishing a project on time, and earning a promotion are professional goals.

Because goals can conflict with each other, it is useful to identify all the goals you are working to achieve. You can then decide which are most important. You'll find that your priorities can shift over time. For example, when schoolwork includes final exams, you may let your academic goals override some of the other goals you are working to achieve.

Setting and Achieving Goals A vague goal like "exercising more" is hard to track. Set a specific goal, such as "exercising twice a week," and then make an action plan to outline the steps for achieving it. Assign a time for completion, and be ready to adjust your goals if necessary. A chart such as the one below can help you track your progress.

GOALS CHART

GOAL	STEPS NEEDED TO ACHIEVE IT	PROGRESS
A. ____	1. _____	_____
	2. _____	_____
	3. _____	_____
B. ____	1. _____	_____
	2. _____	_____
	3. _____	_____

▶ **Exercise 6** Developing a Goals Chart Develop a goals chart. Include at least one personal and one professional goal, and chart your progress as you work toward achieving them.

▶ **Exercise 7** Devising an Action Plan Devise an action plan for earning money to buy a new stereo system. Include the steps needed to achieve the goal, the time frame for completing each step, and the resources required for each step.

📖 Research Tip

To help plan your career goals, investigate fields of interest at the career center of a local college.

▶ **More Practice**

Academic and Workplace Skills Activity Book
• p. 55

Solving Problems and Thinking Creatively

Learn More

For more instruction about problem-and-solution writing, see Chapter 11.

As you work to achieve your personal and professional goals, you are bound to meet unexpected problems. Knowing how to face these problems calmly and devise workable solutions can help you stay on track to meet the goals you have set. To master this skill, you need a strategy for outlining problems and analyzing their solutions. For particularly difficult problems, you must also learn to think creatively to generate a number of possible solutions with which to work.

Learning to Solve Problems Most problems can be solved by using a systematic strategy that will allow you to analyze the problem and define a solution more clearly.

> **KEY CONCEPT** Solving a problem requires a thorough understanding of what's wrong, a number of possible solutions, and a careful review of each one. ■

Use the following steps to solve problems more efficiently, minimize setbacks, and move forward.

STEPS IN PROBLEM SOLVING

> **Exercise 8** Solving Problems Using the steps outlined above, identify at least two possible solutions for one of the following problems. Then, choose the best solution.
> 1. A student can't master a concept in math class.
> 2. A store manager realizes she may be losing business because cashier lines are too long on weekends.
> 3. A baby can choke on the small pieces of some of his older brother's games, but the older boy enjoys playing with these games.

Thinking Creatively You can use creative thinking to come up with possible solutions for a difficult problem. All you have to do is open your mind to ideas that are new, different, and sometimes unconventional.

> **KEY CONCEPT** Creative thinking requires openness to unusual approaches from which to draw new ideas. ■

If a star pitcher was slated to appear in the championship game but also wanted to go to a friend's birthday celebration scheduled for the same time, creative thinking might help. While standard problem solving might encourage the athlete to split time between both events, creative thinking might generate a more appealing idea: The athlete could videotape a message and ask his friend to wait until the party to play the tape.

CREATIVE THINKING SUGGESTIONS

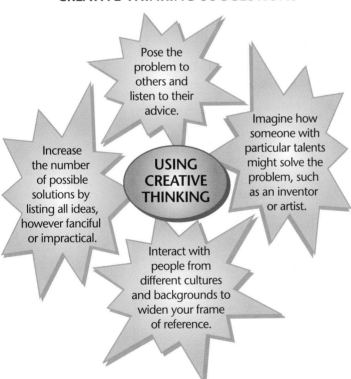

Pose the problem to others and listen to their advice.

Imagine how someone with particular talents might solve the problem, such as an inventor or artist.

Increase the number of possible solutions by listing all ideas, however fanciful or impractical.

USING CREATIVE THINKING

Interact with people from different cultures and backgrounds to widen your frame of reference.

> **Exercise 9** **Using Creative Thinking** Use creative thinking to offer two more suggestions to the problems identified in Exercise 8.

Managing Time

Although different careers require different abilities, most work situations present workers with tasks that need to be completed according to tight deadlines. In addition to the major projects you are assigned to complete, you often have to address unexpected problems and emergencies. In that case, your ability to manage your time effectively will play a critical role in determining your success.

Managing Your Time Proper time management takes planning and the ability to decide which of your goals and activities are most important. Budgeting your time well helps ensure that important projects are accomplished, time is free for other activities, and hasty decisions are prevented.

> **KEY CONCEPT** Manage your time effectively by keeping a calendar marked with appointments and key events, preparing daily or weekly "to-do" lists, prioritizing your tasks, and breaking up large tasks into manageable portions. ■

SAMPLE CALENDAR AND TO-DO LIST

To-Do List

1. Practice reading lines from play

2. Buy birthday present

3. Renew membership at gym

4. Write e-mail to my pen pal

Mon _9:30 Meeting with_
teacher

Tues _____

Wed _3:00–5:00 Drama_
auditions

Thur _7:00–10:00 Baby-sit_

Fri _____

Sat _7:30 Katie's birthday_
party

Sun _____

> **Exercise 10** **Managing Your Time** Record your schedule for a week. Include a daily to-do list, with activities and appointments ranked according to importance. At the end of the week, evaluate how effectively this system worked for you.

Managing Money

The strategies of money management are simple: Spend less than you make to allow for the unexpected; treat your savings account like a bill to be paid rather than a place to put "extra" money; and plan your expenditures. Setting and sticking to a budget ensures that you will have money for what you need and want.

🖒 Research Tip

You can find easy-to-understand guides to managing your time and money at your local library.

▶**KEY CONCEPT** To manage money wisely, track your spending, set financial goals, and make a plan to meet these goals. ∎

Developing a Budget A budget helps you manage money efficiently by tracking *credit,* or incoming money (in black), and noting *debits,* or expenses (in red). When a budget is balanced, credit and debit are equal. If debit exceeds credit, the budgeter must make choices about cutting spending or increasing income. When credit exceeds debit, the budget reveals a savings or a profit. Look at this example:

SAMPLE BUDGET

STUDENT GOVERNMENT MONTHLY BUDGET			
	INCOME	REGULAR EXPENSES	PROJECTED EXPENSES
Snack sale	200.00		
Alumni donations	50.00		
Savings for class gift		20.00	
Purchase of snacks for sale		75.00	25.00
Security deposit on tickets and chairs for dance			100.00
Total	250.00	95.00	125.00

▶**Exercise 11** Managing a Budget Develop a budget for someone who earns $200 a month, spends $10–20 per week on entertainment, $5 per week on snack foods, $20 per month on gifts, and puts $50 per month in a savings account.
1. How long will it take this person to save $400 without using money from the savings account?
2. Make a recommendation for cutting expenses.

▶**More Practice**

Academic and Workplace Skills Activity Book
• pp. 57–58

Applying Math Skills

Although there are many ways to apply your math skills to everyday life, this section addresses three of the most common ways: those used in the workplace, in shopping, and in the analysis of statistics.

▶ **KEY CONCEPT** Math skills are necessary to manage money properly, to make wise purchases, and to evaluate certain types of information. ■

Following are three areas in which math will prove useful:
1. **Succeeding in the Workplace** You may need to use your math skills while at work. For example, contractors often set rates based on the materials they need plus a fee for the hours they will work. Office managers often need to balance a budget, buy supplies, and calculate payroll. Whatever job you do, a knowledge of your own pay rate will help you determine your ability to afford items you may want to purchase.
2. **Making Wise Purchases** When you are faced with multiple choices in a competitive market, use unit prices to calculate the most economical buys. For example, when you do the math, you may see that a "buy one, get one free" sale doesn't offer the bargain you had originally imagined.
3. **Analyzing Statistics** Business reports, daily newspapers, and other sources of information often use statistics to support certain points of view. Knowing how to weigh the value of those numbers helps you to make informed judgments.

▼ Critical Viewing How can a knowledge of math skills help you as you consider purchasing CDs? **[Connect]**

▶ **Exercise 12** Using Math Skills to Decide Whether or Not to Accept a Job
A neighbor has offered you and a friend $350 to paint her house. From your past painting experience, you realize that it will take five eight-hour days to complete the job, six gallons of paint at $25 per gallon, and the purchase of $50 in painting materials.
1. What is the total cost of supplies?
2. What is your hourly wage on this job?
3. Identify one other factor that might influence your decision.
4. Would you accept this job? Explain your answer.

Applying Computer Skills

With computers common in many workplaces, employers in a variety of fields expect new workers to have computer skills. Consider improving your skills to increase your opportunities in the workplace.

More Practice

Academic and
Workplace Skills
Activity Book
• pp. 59–60

KEY CONCEPT A knowledge of your computer means the ability to enter information accurately, format text, use a variety of software, and access Internet information. ∎

Following are a few ways to make the most of a computer:

1. **Practice your keyboarding skills.** Being an accurate and quick keyboarder gives you more time to focus on other tasks. A good typing speed is 45 words per minute, but remember that accuracy is more important than speed.
2. **Learn how to format.** You can use fonts, bullets, and other features to organize and emphasize information. Consider learning a variety of programs to help you apply your skills in any working environment.
3. **Use the thesaurus and spell-check tools.** To make your work professional and accurate, get in the habit of using a word processor's language functions. For example, with a click of a mouse, you can find just the right word or catch errors you may have missed while proofreading.
4. **Learn to use the Internet.** With a teacher's guidance, discover the wealth of information available at your fingertips.

Exercise 13 Working With Computers Complete these activities:

1. Find an application that creates charts or graphs, and use the computers Help menu to create one.
2. Conduct interviews to find out how computers enhance the workplace of several people you know.

Reflecting on Your Workplace Skills and Competencies

To reflect on your workplace skills and competencies, consider the job you most want to pursue. Then, jot down your responses to these questions:

• What skills are most important in the job or career you want to pursue?

• What skills should you improve? Why?

Test Preparation Handbook

Preparing for the New SAT® and the ACT®

The new SAT® and the ACT® are standardized tests. They are designed to help colleges compare the abilities of prospective students from all over the world. As a tenth grader, you may feel that college is in the distant future. However, if you are serious about attending college, chances are you will take the new SAT®, the ACT®, or both. Now is the perfect time to begin preparing for these tests.

This Test Preparation Handbook will focus on the Writing Section of the new SAT® and the Writing Test of the ACT®. Colleges use the results of the writing sections to find out if students are prepared for the kind of writing expected of them in college.

The Writing Section

The writing sections on both the new SAT® and the ACT® include a timed essay. On the new SAT®, students are given twenty-five minutes to write an essay in response to a prompt. On the ACT®, students are given thirty minutes to do so. This Test Preparation Handbook introduces you to the structure of both new SAT® and ACT® prompts. By studying this section carefully, you can prepare effectively for this part of the exams.

In addition to the twenty-five-minute timed essay, the new SAT®'s Writing Section contains three types of multiple-choice questions on grammar and usage. This Test Preparation Handbook will introduce you to each type of grammar and usage question that appears on the new SAT®. It will also be helpful to those preparing for the ACT®, because the same topics are addressed in the English Section of that exam.

CONTENTS

Reading Comprehension 642–647

Grammar 648–662
  Faulty Subject-Verb Agreement 648
  Faulty Verb Tense 649
  Faulty Pronoun Case 650
  Faulty Pronoun-Antecedent
  Agreement 652
  Shifts in Pronoun Person 653
  Faulty Parallelism 654
  Faulty Word Choice 655
  Mixed Constructions 656
  Sentence Fragments 657
  Faulty Punctuation: Comma Use 658

  Faulty Punctuation: Semicolon Use 659
  Paragraph Structure 660
  Transitions Within a Paragraph 662

Writing 663–671
  Introduction to the New SAT®
  and ACT® Writing Tests 663
  Planning the Persuasive Essay 664
  Supporting an Argument With
  Examples 665
  The ACT® Writing Test 666
  The New SAT® Essay 668
  Proofreading in Five Minutes 670
  Reflecting on Test Preparation 671

Reading Comprehension Questions

Both the new SAT® and the ACT® test your ability to understand what you read. Although reading comprehension is not a part of the writing sections of either exam, this section will introduce you to the types of reading comprehension questions you are likely to encounter on the new SAT® and ACT®. Reading Comprehension questions typically test three reading skills:

- Vocabulary in Context: These questions test your ability to understand what a word means from the way it is used in a sentence or passage.

- Finding Information in the Text: These questions test your ability to understand the basic information stated in a text.

- Extended Reasoning: These questions test your ability to infer meaning from a text. You should expect questions that ask about the passage's main idea and details, the author's logic and attitude, and the implications of the author's statements.

The following section contains one example of each type of reading passage presented on the new SAT®. These include the following passages:

Short passages	These passages can be as short as one hundred words and are followed by two questions.
Long passages	These passages can be as long as eight hundred words and are followed by as many as thirteen questions.
Paired passages	These pairs consist of two passages and are followed by questions that ask about each passage, as well as questions that ask you to compare and contrast the paired passages.

Please note that on the new SAT® or the ACT®, these passages will be followed by at least two questions. In this Test Preparation Handbook, only one question for each reading passage will be presented along with steps to answer the question. It is a good idea to practice further by completing reading comprehension questions from old SAT® or ACT® tests. Your teacher can help you to identify books that contain practice tests. Finally, another excellent way to prepare for the Reading Comprehension section of these exams, and for college, is to read widely and often.

Reading Comprehension

Long Passage

The passage below tells about the reign of Queen Elizabeth I of England.

 STRATEGY **Vocabulary in Context:** When you encounter an unfamiliar word in a test passage, make inferences about its meaning by looking for context clues in the surrounding words.

▷ **Sample Test Question**

Directions: Read the passage carefully. Then, answer the question.

Queen Elizabeth I

1   When Queen Elizabeth I ascended the throne, the English people were deeply divided in terms of religion. Years earlier, Elizabeth's father, King Henry VIII, had established the Church of England with himself as its head.

5   He required the English people to join the Church of England, rather than remain in the Catholic Church. This directive created great unrest throughout England, which was almost entirely Catholic at the time.

     Elizabeth took a humane and compassionate view of her
10   divided people. She was willing to allow individuals a share of privacy in their religious convictions as long as they showed outward obedience to her as queen. She is famous for saying, "I will not make windows into men's souls," by which she meant that she was unwilling to invade the
15   privacy of her subjects. Her main concern was for peace and order within her realm.

     Elizabeth's strategy for dealing with difficult situations was often to delay in addressing them. Some of her contemporaries criticized this approach, for it seemed to
20   lack the decisiveness necessary in a leader. However, this technique actually revealed a keen understanding of how power works. For as long as she delayed in making a decision, she held power over the people vying for each side of an argument. By delaying her decision, she delayed
25   losing the loyalty of the people on the other side of the argument. Often enough, the situation resolved itself before she addressed it. When that happened, Elizabeth won because she had not sided with one group over another. As a result, she successfully <u>retained</u> the loyalty of
30   both sides. Through this strategy of indecision, Elizabeth remained in power through extremely turbulent times.

QUESTION: The word *retained* (line 29) most nearly means

   A   lost

   B   ignored

   C   sought

   D   kept

   E   relinquished

S T E P S

1. **Carefully read the passage to be sure you understand its general meaning.** Then, read the question. Reread the sentence containing the target word *retained*. Use the context clues, such as *successfully* and *loyalty of both sides,* to help you think about what the word might mean. From these context clues, you can tell that the word *retained* has a positive meaning in the sentence.

2. **Find context clues in the sentences surrounding the target word.** Reread the sentences before and after the sentence containing the target word. Notice that these sentences tell us that Elizabeth resisted choosing sides in an argument and that this technique helped her to avoid losing the loyalty of one group of people by siding with another party. This context helps the reader to understand that *she successfully retained the loyalty of both sides* means that she avoided losing the loyalty of a group of people. Therefore, *retain* must mean something along the lines of "kept."

3. **Review the answer choices.** If you are unsure about which answer choice to select, substitute each answer choice for *retain* in the sentence. Choices A, B, and E do not make sense within the sentence or the passage. Choice C, *sought,* is incorrect because Elizabeth's approach was a passive one and the word *sought* suggests a more active pursuit of the loyalty of both sides than the passage suggests. Choice D, *kept,* most nearly defines the target word because it makes sense within the context of the sentence. The passage tells us that Elizabeth was concerned with losing the loyalty of one of the sides in an argument. Therefore, it makes sense that her strategy allowed her to successfully *retain* or *keep* the loyalty of both sides. The answer to the question is choice D.

Reading Comprehension

Paired Reading Passages

The passages below come from two novels. In both passages, an important male character is introduced. The first passage is from the novel *Pride and Prejudice* by Jane Austen. The second passage is from the novel *Wuthering Heights* by Emily Brontë.

 New SAT® PREP ACT® **STRATEGY** **Make Inferences:** If the answer to a question is not plainly stated in a selection, look beyond the details and information to understand the suggestions and implications of the author's words.

> ### Sample Test Question

Directions: Read both passages. Then, answer the question based on what is stated or implied in the paired passages.

Passage 1

> Mr. Bingley had soon made himself acquainted with all the principal people in the room; he was lively and unreserved, danced every dance, was angry that the ball closed so early, and talked of giving one himself at Netherfield. Such amiable qualities must speak for themselves.

Passage 2

> His figure was enveloped in a riding cloak, fur collared and steel clasped; its details were not apparent, but I traced the general points of middle height and considerable breadth of chest. He had a dark face, with stern features and a heavy brow; his eyes and gathered eyebrows looked ireful and thwarted just now; he was past youth, but had not reached middle-age; perhaps he might be thirty-five. I felt no fear of him, and but little shyness. Had he been a handsome, heroic-looking young gentleman, I should not have dared to stand thus questioning him against his will, and offering my services unasked. I had hardly ever seen a handsome youth; never in my life spoken to one.

QUESTION: Both passages support which general statement?

    A   People form judgments about others based on their behavior and appearance.

    B   Physical attractiveness tends to make a person intimidating and unapproachable.

    C   Social interactions are structured by a complicated set of rules one must follow.

    D   Many people who appear mean-spirited are kind, once you get to know them.

    E   Cowardly people often mask their insecurity by acting confident and outspoken.

S T E P S

1. **Carefully read the passages to be sure you understand the general meaning of each passage.** As you read the second passage, think about the ways in which the second passage is similar to and different from the first.

2. **Read the question.** With the question in mind, reread the passages. As you reread the passages, ask yourself what the two passages have in common. Passage 1 describes the activities of Mr. Bingley at a ball. Passage 2 describes the narrator's reactions to a man he has met for the first time. Both passages depict the forming of an impression of a person.

3. **Review the answer choices.** Look for an answer choice that reflects an implication of *both* passages. Choice B may appear correct, but this idea is only present in Passage 2. Likewise, choice C is only implied by Passage 1. Choices D and E are inferences that are not supported by either passage. On the other hand, choice A contains an inference that could be drawn from both passages, *People form instant judgments about others based on outward appearances.* Therefore, the answer to the question is choice A.

Reading Comprehension

Short Passage

The passage below describes how immigrant children growing up at the turn of the century entertained themselves.

 STRATEGY **Find the Main Idea:** To identify the main idea of a passage, read the passage carefully to make sure you understand its general meaning. Then, pay special attention to its first and last sentences. These sentences often communicate the main idea of a selection.

▷ **Sample Test Question**

Directions: Read the passage carefully. Then, answer the question shown.

Children's Play Long Ago

Long before television and video games, children played games using simple, everyday objects. In the early 1900's, immigrant children who were growing up in America's crowded cities were especially resourceful. A ball, a stick, some bottle caps, and a piece of chalk were all that were needed for a summer of fun.

While the boys played in the streets, the girls claimed the sidewalks. Hopscotch and jumping rope were great favorites. Games that involved clapping and rhyming were delightfully simple. They required no more equipment than a good memory and a fast pair of hands. The idea that expensive equipment or special skills were necessary in order to have fun would never have occurred to the immigrant children who grew up on the city streets of America!

QUESTION: The author would most likely agree with which one of the following statements?

    A   An earlier generation of children missed out because they were born before the invention of television and video games.

    B   It is remarkable how creative and resourceful the immigrant children of the early 1900's were.

    C   Immigrant children were unfortunate because they grew up in crowded cities at the beginning of the twentieth century.

    D   The games of immigrant children were hard to learn.

    E   Today, immigrant children do not live in overcrowded cities.

STEPS

1. **Carefully read the passage to be sure you understand its general meaning.** Then, read the question. This type of question is really testing your ability to make an inference based on your understanding of the author's main idea.

2. **Pay attention to the first sentence of the passage.** Notice that the first sentence of the passage states that children from long ago played games using simple objects. The other sentences in the first paragraph reinforce this main idea.

3. **Pay attention to the last sentence of the passage.** Notice that it echoes the first paragraph's main idea and extends it by adding that children long ago could not have imagined requiring anything fancy in order to have fun. The rest of the second paragraph supports the point made in the final sentence. Now that you have identified the main idea of each paragraph, you can determine the main idea of the passage: Children long ago used simple objects and their imaginations to entertain themselves.

4. **Review the answer choices.** Look for the choice that reflects an understanding of the author's *overall* message. Choices A and C suggest that the author feels sorry for the children mentioned in the selection. There is nothing in the passage to support this idea, so choices A and C are incorrect. Choices D and E reflect inferences that are not clearly supported by the text. Choice B, *It is remarkable how creative and resourceful the immigrant children of the early 1900's* were, is correct. The author would agree with this statement because it reflects the main idea of his writing. Therefore, the answer to the question is choice B.

Reflecting on Reading Comprehension

Now that you have worked through the Reading Comprehension section, answer the following questions about your reading and test-taking skills.

- Which types of strategies or questions were you already familiar with?

- Which types of strategies or questions did you find challenging?

Once you have identified areas that you need to work on further, ask your teacher for help in finding materials that can help you improve your skills.

Grammar

The new SAT® and the ACT® include multiple-choice grammar questions. These questions typically feature sentences and paragraphs that require corrections or revisions. Many students find grammar difficult. However, by focusing on the grammar and usage rules that are most often tested, you can prepare yourself to succeed on these types of questions.

Some people can spot grammar and usage errors easily. These people can spot errors because they *hear* the errors as they read. This technique does not work for everyone. If you have a tendency to make grammar and usage errors, it is best to use a systematic approach for answering these questions. This section introduces a step-by-step process for answering common multiple-choice grammar questions.

Faulty Subject-Verb Agreement

▶ **RULE**   A singular subject must have a singular verb. A plural subject must have a plural verb.

▶ **Sample Test Question**

Directions: Read the sentence carefully. Identify the sentence error from the underlined options. If there is no error, select choice E.

<u>When</u> the theater <u>lights flickered</u>, the audience
    A   B
<u>were reminded</u> of the <u>impending start</u> of the performance.
     C   D
<u>No error</u>
   E

QUESTION: What is the error in the sentence?
- **A**   When
- **B**   lights flickered
- **C**   were reminded
- **D**   impending start
- **E**   No error

STEPS

1. **Read the sentence carefully.** Focus your attention on the underlined words or phrases.

A Word to the Wise
Agreement
When a verb and a subject are in agreement, they are in harmony. A subject and a verb must agree in order to make sense together.

TIP: Be careful with subjects that are indefinite pronouns. *Each, either, everyone, someone,* and *no one* are always singular subjects. *Few, both, many,* and *several* are always plural subjects.

2. **Ask yourself: "Does any underlined word or phrase sound wrong?"** If one word or phrase definitely sounds wrong to you, you have probably identified the error in the sentence.

3. **If no words or phrases sound wrong to you, ask yourself: "Does any underlined word or phrase violate a grammar or usage rule that I have learned?"**

4. **Identify the subject of the sentence.** The subject is *audience*. Notice that the word *audience* is a collective noun. A collective noun is always singular. It must be paired with a singular verb in a sentence.

5. **Identify the verb in the sentence.** The verb in the sentence is *were reminded*, which is plural.

6. **Check for subject-verb agreement.** The subject, *audience*, is singular, but the verb, *were reminded*, is plural. Therefore, the subject and verb do not agree in this sentence. In order for the verb to agree with the subject, it should be written in singular form: *was reminded*.

7. **Review the answer choices.** The verb, *were reminded*, is the error in the sentence. Therefore, the answer to the question is choice C.

Faulty Verb Tense

RULE The tense of a verb shows the time an action takes place. Verb tense must make sense within the context of its sentence.

▷ **Sample Test Question**

Directions: Read the sentence carefully. Identify the sentence error from the underlined options. If there is no error, select choice E.

The Royal Library at Alexandria will have educated generations
      A   B
of scholars before it was mysteriously destroyed. No error
   C   D   E

QUESTION: What is the error in the sentence?

- **A** The Royal Library
- **B** will have educated
- **C** scholars
- **D** mysteriously
- **E** No error

FOR REVIEW

To review subject-verb agreement in greater depth, see Chapter 24, Section 1.

A Word to the Wise
Verb

The word *verb* comes from the Latin word *verbum*, which means "word."

Grammar

STEPS

1. **Read the sentence carefully.** Focus your attention on the underlined words or phrases.

2. **Ask yourself: "Does any underlined word or phrase sound wrong?"** If one word or phrase definitely sounds wrong to you, you have probably identified the error in the sentence.

3. **If no words or phrases sound wrong to you, ask yourself: "Does any underlined word or phrase violate a grammar or usage rule that I have learned?"** Notice that there are two verbs in the sentence. The first verb, *will have educated*, is in the future perfect tense. The second verb, *was destroyed*, is in the past tense.

4. **Check that the tense of the verbs makes sense within the structure of the sentence.** The words *before it was mysteriously destroyed* make it clear that the library no longer exists. It is impossible that the library *will have educated* people if it *was destroyed* long ago. Therefore, the use of the future perfect tense, *will have educated*, does not make sense in the sentence.

5. **Review the answer choices.** The verb *will have educated* is the error in the sentence. The verb should be *had educated*. Therefore, the answer to the question is choice B.

> **FOR REVIEW**
> To review verb tenses in greater depth, see Chapter 22, Section 1.

Faulty Pronoun Case

▶ **RULE**   Case is the form of a noun or pronoun that indicates its use in a sentence. A pronoun must be in the correct case for its function in a sentence.

▶ **Sample Test Question**

Directions: Read the sentence carefully. Identify the sentence error from the underlined options. If there is no error, select choice E.

> <u>After hearing</u> the lecture by the environmentalist,
>   **A**
> <u>several teachers and us</u> organized a <u>recycling</u> program
>   **B**   **C**
> <u>at our school</u>. <u>No error</u>
>   **D**   **E**

A Word to the Wise
Case

Case is the form of a noun or pronoun that indicates its use in a sentence. The three cases of nouns and pronouns are the nominative, the objective, and the possessive.

QUESTION: What is the error in the sentence?

- **A**   After hearing
- **B**   several teachers and us
- **C**   recycling
- **D**   at our school
- **E**   No error

S T E P S

1. **Read the sentence carefully.** Focus your attention on the underlined words or phrases.

2. **Ask yourself: "Does any underlined word or phrase sound wrong?"** If one word or phrase definitely sounds wrong to you, you have probably identified the error in the sentence.

3. **If no words or phrases sound wrong to you, ask yourself: "Does any underlined word or phrase violate a grammar or usage rule that I have learned?"** Notice that the subject of the sentence, *several teachers and us,* seems awkward.

4. **Check the pronoun case in the subject of the sentence.** Notice that the pronoun *us* is in the objective case. As part of the compound subject of the sentence, *us* should be in the nominative case, that is, *we.* Although awkward-sounding, the subject would be grammatically correct if written *several teachers and we.* (It would, however, be more elegant to write *we organized a recycling program with several teachers.*) The error in the sentence is the faulty pronoun case, *us.* Therefore, the answer to the question is choice B.

FOR REVIEW

To learn about pronoun case in greater depth, see Chapter 23, Section 1.

Grammar

Faulty Pronoun-Antecedent Agreement

> **RULE** A pronoun must agree with its antecedent in person, number, and gender.

> **Sample Test Question**

Directions: Read the sentence carefully. Identify the sentence error from the underlined options. If there is no error, select choice E.

<u>Surprisingly</u>, neither the director <u>nor the actor</u> had
    A   B

<u>previously</u> won an award <u>for their work</u>. <u>No error</u>
    C   D   E

QUESTION: What is the error in the sentence?

  A   Surprisingly,

  B   nor the actor

  C   previously

  D   for their work

  E   No error

S T E P S

1. **Read the sentence carefully.** Focus your attention on the underlined words or phrases.
2. **Ask yourself: "Does any underlined word or phrase sound wrong?"** If one word or phrase definitely sounds wrong to you, you have probably identified the error in the sentence.
3. **If no words or phrases sound wrong to you, ask yourself: "Does any underlined word or phrase violate a grammar or usage rule that I have learned?"** Notice that the subject of the sentence is *neither the director nor the actor*. This construction makes the subject singular.
4. **Identify any pronouns in the sentence.** The pronoun in the sentence is *their*. It refers to the antecedent, *neither the director nor the actor*.
5. **Check for pronoun-antecedent agreement.** The antecedent is singular. Therefore, the pronoun that refers to it must also be singular. However, the pronoun *their* is plural. This pronoun is an error.
6. **Review the answer choices.** The faulty pronoun case represented by the use of *their* is the error in the sentence. Therefore, the answer to the question is choice D.

A Word to the Wise
Antecedent

The word *antecedent* comes from the Latin words *ante,* which means "before," and *cedere,* which means "to go." Therefore, *antecedent* means "that which comes before." An antecedent is a noun that comes before a pronoun. The pronoun refers to it and must match it in person, number, and gender.

TIP: If a sentence doesn't sound right to you, check to see if the awkwardness is caused by faulty pronoun-antecedent agreement. Remember to check the words that link two or more antecedents.

> **FOR REVIEW**

To learn about pronoun-antecedent agreement in greater depth, see Chapter 24, Section 2.

Shifts in Pronoun Person

> **RULE** When using a pronoun to refer to an antecedent more than once in a sentence, use the same pronoun. A shift in pronoun person creates confusion.

> **Sample Test Question**

Directions: Read the sentence carefully. Identify the sentence error from the underlined option. If there is no error, select choice E.

<u>When the seniors</u> took their class trip <u>to Quebec,</u> they discovered that
　　A　　　　　　　　　　　　　　　　B

<u>you needed</u> extra time <u>to pass through customs.</u> <u>No error</u>
　　C　　　　　　　　　　　D　　　　　　　　E

QUESTION: What is the error in the sentence?

A　When the seniors

B　to Quebec

C　you needed

D　to pass through customs

E　No error

STEPS

1. **Read the sentence carefully.** Focus your attention on the underlined words or phrases.
2. **Ask yourself: "Does any underlined word or phrase sound wrong?"** If one word or phrase definitely sounds wrong to you, you have probably identified the error in the sentence.
3. **If no words or phrases sound wrong to you, ask yourself: "Does any underlined word or phrase violate a grammar or usage rule that I have learned?"**
4. **Identify the subject of the sentence.** The subject of the sentence is *the seniors.*
5. **Identify the pronouns in the sentence.** There are three: *their, they,* and *you.* Notice that they all refer to the antecedent *the seniors.*
6. **Check for pronoun-antecedent agreement.** The pronouns *their* and *they* correctly refer to *the seniors.* However, the pronoun *you* is incorrectly used. Because the pronoun refers to the seniors, the pronoun should be *they.*
7. **Review the answer choices.** The error in the sentence is the choice of the pronoun *you.* Therefore, the answer to the question is choice C.

TIP: If a sentence sounds correct to you, look closely at the pronouns used. Errors in pronoun-antecedent agreement are common in everyday spoken language and may not stand out when you hear a sentence in your mind.

FOR REVIEW

To learn about pronoun choice in greater depth, see Chapter 24, Section 2.

Grammar

Faulty Parallelism

> **RULE**   When one thing is compared to another in a sentence, both items should be grammatically parallel or equivalent, that is, equal in structure.

> **Sample Test Question**

Directions: Read the sentence carefully. Identify the sentence error from the underlined options. If there is no error, select choice E.

<u>My music teacher</u> told me <u>that she</u> enjoys
     A   B

<u>Ludwig van Beethoven's</u> symphonies <u>more than Joseph</u>
        C   D

<u>Haydn.</u> <u>No error</u>
        E

QUESTION: What is the error in the sentence?

A   My music teacher

B   that she

C   Ludwig van Beethoven's

D   more than Joseph Haydn

E   No error

S T E P S

1. **Read the sentence carefully.** Focus your attention on the underlined words or phrases.
2. **Ask yourself: "Does any underlined word or phrase sound wrong?"** If one word or phrase definitely sounds wrong to you, you have probably identified the error in the sentence.
3. **If no words or phrases sound wrong to you, ask yourself: "Does any underlined word or phrase violate a grammar or usage rule that I have learned?"** Notice that the sentence compares *Ludwig van Beethoven's symphonies* to *Joseph Haydn.* A comparison must be made between two grammatically equal elements. It is illogical to compare the music of Beethoven to the person of Joseph Haydn. In order to be grammatical, the sentence should compare *Ludwig van Beethoven's symphonies* to *the symphonies of Joseph Haydn.*
4. **Review the answer choices.** The error in the sentence is the unparallel comparison. Therefore, the answer to the question is choice D.

A Word to the Wise
Parallel

The word *parallel* means "having comparable or identically structured parts." It comes from the Greek roots *-para-*, which means "beside," and *-allos-*, which means "one another."

FOR REVIEW

To learn about comparisons in greater depth, see Chapter 25, Section 2.

Faulty Word Choice

> **RULE** Words that are spelled similarly or sound alike can be easily confused. Such words often have very different meanings.

> **Sample Test Question**

Directions: Read the sentence carefully. Decide whether it is correct or whether it needs to be revised. If no revision is necessary, select choice E.

Harvey was surprised that such an imminent scholar could be so verbose and pretentious.

QUESTION: What is the correct way to rewrite the sentence?

A Pretentious and verbose though he was, Harvey was surprised that such an imminent scholar could be.

B Harvey was surprised that such an eminent scholar could make such an obvious mistake.

C Such an imminent scholar should not be so verbose or pretentious, thought Harvey with something like surprise.

D Harvey was surprised that such an eminent scholar could be so verbose and pretentious.

E No revision necessary

S T E P S

1. **Read the sentence carefully.**
2. **Ask yourself: "Does the sentence sound wrong?"**
3. **Notice that this sentence has three difficult vocabulary words: *imminent*, *verbose*, and *pretentious*.** Using a knowledge of roots, you can tell that *verbose* might mean "wordy" and *pretentious* might mean "someone who likes to pretend." *Imminent* looks and sounds like *eminent*, which means "of high rank." However, *imminent* means "coming soon." *Eminent* fits the context of the sentence perfectly but *imminent* does not.
4. **Review the answer choices.** Choices A and C misuse the word *imminent*. Choice B replaces the word *imminent* with *eminent* but changes the meaning of the second half of the sentence. Choice D replaces *imminent* with *eminent*. Therefore, choice D is the answer to this question.

TIP: If you are not sure that a word is being used correctly in a sentence, try replacing it with its definition. If the new sentence does not make sense, then you have found an error.

> **FOR REVIEW**
> To learn about word choice in greater depth, see Chapter 10, Section 4.

Grammar

Mixed Constructions

> **RULE** Every word in a sentence has a role to play, such as subject, verb, conjunction, or modifier. A single word cannot play more than one role in a sentence. Run-on sentences can sometimes be mixed constructions.

> **Sample Test Question**

Directions: Read the sentence carefully. Decide whether the underlined portion is correct or needs to be revised.

In 2003, New Hampshire lost <u>the Old Man of the Mountain crumbled from the side of Cannon Mountain.</u>

QUESTION: What is the correct way to write the underlined words?

A   the Old Man of the Mountain when it crumbled from the side of Cannon Mountain.

B   the Old Man of the Mountain. Because it crumbled from the side of Cannon Mountain.

C   the Old Man of the Mountain crumbling from the side of Cannon Mountain.

D   crumbled from the side of Cannon Mountain.

E   No revision necessary

S T E P S

1. **Read the sentence carefully.** Focus your attention on the underlined words or phrases.

2. **Ask yourself: "Does any underlined word or phrase sound wrong?"** If one word or phrase definitely sounds wrong to you, you have probably identified the error in the sentence. Notice that the author seems to have started a new sentence *(the Old Man of the Mountain crumbled from the side of Cannon Mountain)* halfway through writing another sentence *(In 2003, New Hampshire lost)*.

3. **Ask yourself: "Does any underlined word or phrase violate a grammar or usage rule that I have learned?"** The sentence is confusing because there is no conjunction to make the connection clear between the first part of the sentence and the second. As a result, this sentence is a mixed construction.

4. **Review the answer choices.** Choice B divides the sentence into two sentences; however, the second sentence is a fragment. Choice C has the same mixed construction error as the sample sentence, with a different verb tense. Choice D places two verbs, *lost* and *crumbled* next to each other, which does not make sense. Choice A divides the sentence into an independent clause and a subordinate clause by adding *when it*. Therefore, the answer to the question is choice A.

Sentence Fragments

▶ **RULE**   A sentence fragment is a group of words with end punctuation that either does not have a subject or a verb or does not express a complete thought. Sentence fragments are a common error.

▶ **Sample Test Question**

Directions: Read the sentences carefully. Decide whether the underlined portion is correct or needs to be revised.

Joshua Tree National Park is one of the best places to see spring <u>flowers in bloom. Even though it is located</u> in the California desert.

QUESTION: What is the correct way to write the underlined words?

A	flowers in bloom. Happily, located
B	flowers in bloom, even though it is located
C	flowers in bloom, when it is located
D	flowers in bloom. Regardless of whether it is located
E	No revision necessary

S T E P S

1. **Read the sentence carefully.** Focus your attention on the underlined words or phrases.
2. **Ask yourself: "Does any underlined word or phrase sound wrong?"** If one word or phrase definitely sounds wrong to you, you have probably identified the error in the sentence.
3. **If no words or phrases sound wrong to you, ask yourself: "Does any underlined word or phrase violate a grammar or usage rule that I have learned?"**

FOR REVIEW

To review sentence structure in greater depth, see Chapter 21, Section 4.

A Word to the Wise
Fragment

The word *fragment* comes from the Latin *fragere*, meaning "to break." A fragment is a broken piece of something.

Grammar

4. **Notice that "Even though it is located in the California desert" is not a sentence.** It is a sentence fragment.

5. **Review the answer choices.** Identify the answer choice that correctly joins the sentence fragment to the preceding sentence. Choices A and D simply reproduce a sentence fragment. Choice C does not make sense. Choice B correctly uses a comma before the conjunction *even though* to join the fragment to the preceding sentence. This solution is both grammatically correct and logical. Therefore, the answer to the question is choice B.

FOR REVIEW

Sentence fragments are often subordinate clauses. To review subordinate clauses in greater depth, see Chapter 20, Section 2.

Faulty Punctuation: Comma Use

> **RULE** A comma must be used before a conjunction to separate two clauses in a compound sentence.

> **Sample Test Question**

Directions: Read the sentence carefully. Decide whether the underlined portion is correct or needs to be revised.

You may think that all doctors practice <u>medicine but any person with a Ph.D.</u> may use the title "Doctor."

QUESTION: What is the correct way to write the underlined words?

A medicine: but any person with a Ph.D.

B medicine; but any person with a Ph.D.

C medicine but, any person with a Ph.D.

D medicine, but any person with a Ph.D.

E No revision necessary

A Word to the Wise
Conjunction

The word *conjunction* comes from the Latin word *conjunctio,* which means "joining." A conjunction is a word that joins ideas within a sentence. Some examples of conjunctions are *and, but, as,* and *because.*

STEPS

1. **Read the sentence carefully.** Focus your attention on the underlined words or phrases.

2. **Ask yourself: "Does any part of the sentence look or sound wrong?"** If one word or phrase definitely sounds wrong to you, you have probably identified the error in the sentence.

3. **If no words or phrases sound wrong to you, ask yourself: "Does any underlined word or phrase violate a grammar or usage rule that I have learned?"** Notice that the sentence is a compound sentence. The conjunction *but* correctly joins the two clauses within the sentence.

4. **Check the punctuation of the sentence.** A comma should be placed before a conjunction to join the two clauses. This sentence does not contain a comma before the conjunction *but*. This omission is the error in the sentence.

5. **Review the answer choices.** Choices A and B can be eliminated as correct choices because they do not use a comma before the conjunction. Choice C places a comma *after* the conjunction, which is incorrect. Choice D correctly places a comma before the conjunction. Therefore, the answer to the question is choice D.

FOR REVIEW

To learn about comma use in greater depth, see Chapter 28, Section 2.

Faulty Punctuation: Semicolon Use

▶ **RULE**   A semicolon can be used to connect two independent clauses that are similar or contrasting in meaning.

▶ **Sample Test Question**

Directions: Read the sentence carefully. Decide whether the underlined portion is correct or needs to be revised.

You can drive all the way to mile zero on <u>U.S. Highway 1, the road ends</u> in Key West, Florida.

QUESTION: What is the correct way to write the underlined words?

A	U.S. Highway 1? The road ends
B	U.S. Highway 1 the road ends
C	U.S. Highway 1; the road ends
D	U.S. Highway 1 "the road ends
E	No revision necessary

S T E P S

1. **Read the sentence carefully.** Focus your attention on the underlined words or phrases.

2. **Ask yourself: "Does any underlined word or phrase look or sound wrong?"** If one word or phrase definitely sounds wrong to you, you have probably identified the error in the sentence.

3. **If no words or phrases sound wrong to you, ask yourself: "Does any underlined word or phrase violate a grammar or usage rule that I have learned?"**

Grammar

4. **Notice that the sentence contains two independent clauses.** The sentence incorrectly joins the independent clauses *You can drive all the way to mile zero on U.S. Highway 1* and *the road ends in Key West, Florida* with a comma. The comma should be replaced with a semicolon in order to make the sentence correct.

5. **Review the answer choices.** Look for the choice that correctly joins the independent clauses with a semicolon. Choices A incorrectly adds a question mark to the end of the first independent clause. Since there is nothing in the way the clause is written to suggest that it is a question, choice A is incorrect and can be eliminated. Choice B uses no punctuation at all between the clauses, which is incorrect. Choice D uses a quotation mark, which is also incorrect. Choice C places a semicolon *between the two clauses.* Therefore, the answer to the question is choice C.

FOR REVIEW

To learn about semicolon use in greater depth, see Chapter 28, Section 3.

Paragraph Structure

▶ **RULE**   A paragraph should consist of a topic sentence and supporting sentences. Each sentence should follow logically from the last.

TIP: When evaluating paragraphs, identify the topic sentence and look for sentences that do not support it.

▶ **Sample Test Question**

Directions: Read the passage carefully. Then, answer the question that follows.

> **(1)** Elmer Samuel Imes changed the scientific community's view of quantum theory. **(2)** Imes's research showed that quantum theory could be used to solve many important problems. **(3)** Other scientists finally understood that quantum theory was valid. **(4)** The scientific community owes a great deal to Elmer Samuel Imes's contribution.

QUESTION: In context, what is the best revision to the underlined portion of sentence 3 (reproduced below)?

<u>Other scientists finally understood</u> that quantum theory was valid.

    A   At the time, scientists knew

    B   Scientists other than Imes generally understood

    C   In fact, other scientists finally understood

    D   Because of Imes's work, other scientists finally understood

    E   No revision necessary

S T E P S

1. **Read the paragraph carefully.** Then, read the question. Focus your attention on the underlined words or phrases. Ask yourself if this portion of the sentence needs to be revised in order to make its relevance to the topic sentence clearer.

2. **Identify the topic sentence of the paragraph.** The topic sentence in this paragraph is *Elmer Samuel Imes changed the scientific community's view of quantum theory.*

3. **Ask yourself if sentence 3 follows logically from sentence 2.** Notice that there seems to be a gap in logic between the two sentences. The relationship between Imes's research and other scientists finally understanding the validity of quantum theory is unclear.

4. **Review the answer choices.** Choices A, B, and C do not revise the sentence in such a way as to explain *why* the scientists understood. Choice D uses the phrase *Because of Imes's work* to make the cause-and-effect relationship between two sentences clear. Therefore, the answer to the question is choice D.

> **FOR REVIEW**
>
> To review paragraph development and structure in greater depth, see Chapter 3, Section 2.

Grammar

Transitions Within a Paragraph

▷ **RULE** Transition words and transitional phrases make the connections between sentences clear. They also improve the flow of a paragraph.

▷ **Sample Test Question**

Directions: Read the passage carefully. Then, answer the question below.

> **(1)** Emily Dickinson used unusual techniques in her poetry. **(2)** She did not follow the standard rules of punctuation. **(3)** Dickinson used dashes to separate ideas in many of her poems.

QUESTION: In context, which is the best revision to the underlined portion of sentence 3 (reproduced below)?

<u>Dickinson used dashes to separate ideas</u> in many of her poems.

    A   You will also find that she used dashes

    B   However, Dickinson used dashes to separate ideas

    C   Separate ideas she did with the use of dashes

    D   For example, Dickinson used dashes to separate ideas

    E   No revision necessary

S T E P S

1. **Read the paragraph carefully.** Then, read the question. Focus your attention on the underlined words or phrases. Notice that while it is it reasonably clear that sentence 3 states an example of a practice explained in sentence 2, the flow of the paragraph is rather awkward.

2. **Review the answer choices for the best revision.** A transition is needed in order to make the connection between sentences 2 and 3 clearer. Choice A does not have a transition, so it can be eliminated. Choice B contains the transition *however,* which does not make sense within the context of the paragraph. Choice C does not have a transition and rephrases the sentence in an oddly formal style that does not fit with the rest of the paragraph. Choice D uses a transitional phrase, *For example,* to indicate that what follows is an example of something described in the preceding sentence. Therefore, the answer to the question is choice D.

A Word to the Wise
Transition

The word *transition* comes from the Latin word *transitio,* meaning "change." A transition signals a change from one thought or idea to another.

TIP: Review common transitional words and phrases by category:

    Causes: *Since, if, because, as soon as,* and *until*

    Effects: *Therefore, consequently, as a result, subsequently,* and *then.*

FOR REVIEW

To review transition words in greater depth, see Chapter 3, Section 2.

Writing

Introduction to the New SAT® and ACT® Writing Tests

This section will introduce you to the demands of the new SAT® essay and the ACT® essay respectively. You will read a sample prompt for each test and a student essay written for each prompt. By studying each prompt and essay, you can become familiar with what is expected of you on the essay section of either test.

The first thing to notice is that both tests require you to write a *point-of-view* or *persuasive* essay. In this type of essay, you are presented with an issue and asked to present your opinion on it. Your point of view must be clearly stated. Furthermore, you must support your argument with examples from current events, history, science, literature, and your own experience. The aim of the essay is to persuade the reader that your point of view is sound, logical, and wise. For this reason, it is always a good idea to show that you can see the other side of the issue you are discussing. When you acknowledge a point of view opposite to your own, you show maturity and the ability to reason and judge. You also strengthen your argument by showing that it is the result of careful consideration.

> **New SAT® PREP ACT®**
>
> **TIP:** The ACT® and the new SAT® have different time limits. The ACT® has a thirty-minute time limit for the essay while the SAT® has a twenty-five minute time limit.

The Ingredients of a Persuasive Essay

Look at the table shown. It lists the ingredients of a successful persuasive or point-of-view essay.

Every point of view essay must contain . . .	Strategies
a clear position on the issue.	Read and reread the essay prompt. Be sure you understand what the prompt means. Then, decide your position on the issue.
three examples to support your position.	While outlining your essay, come up with at least three examples to support your position. If possible, vary the sources of your examples. For example, use one example from your personal life, another from a book you've read, and another from history.
a counterexample.	Think of one argument that someone might use if they were arguing against your position. Discuss your position with regard to this argument. Show why you find this argument weak compared to your own point of view.
clear transitions.	Make the logic of your essay clear by using transition words or phrases that show the relationship between one idea and another. Transition words include *therefore, for this reason, however,* and *in conclusion.*
a strong conclusion.	Wrap up your essay with a strong, confident closing statement.

Writing

Planning the Persuasive Essay

 STRATEGY Spend five minutes planning the essay before you begin to write. Make sure your outline includes at least three examples to support your argument.

STEPS

1. **Read the prompt and the assignment twice carefully.** Make sure you understand the issue presented in the prompt.

2. **Consider both sides of the argument.** To get started thinking critically, imagine what a person might say to prove each side of the issue. Use a graphic organizer like this one to capture your ideas.

PRO	CON
1.	1.
2.	2.
3.	3.

3. **Choose your position on the issue.** Review the chart you've completed and decide which side of the argument you will develop in your essay.

4. **Support your argument with at least three examples.** A strong essay will support each main point with an example.

5. **Include a counterexample in your outline.** Jot down the strongest argument you would make if you had to argue against the position you have chosen. In your essay, you will acknowledge the strength of this counterexample, but explain why it is not persuasive enough to make you choose the opposing point of view on the issue.

6. **Consult your outline as you write your essay.** Use it as a checklist to make sure you cover your main points and examples.

TIP: If you are given thirty minutes to complete an essay, plan to spend

- five minutes planning.
- fifteen minutes drafting.
- five minutes revising and editing.
- five minutes proofreading.

FOR REVIEW

To review planning a point-of-view essay, see Chapter 7, Section 2.

Supporting an Argument With Examples

STRATEGY It is best to draw from a wide range of examples to support your position in a persuasive essay.

Essay prompts often ask students to support their position with examples. It is wise to pay attention to the *kinds* of examples a prompt calls for. If a prompt asks you to draw examples from a range of sources, do not draw all of your examples from one type of source. Instead, draw one example from your reading, one example from your studies (for example, history or science), and one example from your personal experience and observations.

Many students are unsure about what types of examples they can draw from a particular source. Look at the chart shown to learn more about the kinds of examples you might use in an essay.

If a prompt asks for examples from . . .	Follow this strategy for identifying strong examples.
your reading	Use your knowledge of literature to cite examples of plot lines and characters that are relevant. For example, if you are writing an essay about the individual's responsibility to society, you might cite a novel about a character who ignores his responsibility to society and what happens to him.
your studies	Use your knowledge of history or science to cite examples that are relevant. For example, if you are writing an essay about the individual's responsibility to society, you might cite the ideas in Thomas Paine's *The Rights of Man*.
your own experience	Use events that have happened to you or your family to cite relevant examples. For example, for an essay about the individual's responsibility to society, you might write about your own experience dealing with obligations to society.
your observations	Use insights into the topic from events or people you have observed. You might address your observations about social trends or about things happening in your neighborhood.

Writing

The ACT® Writing Test

> **RULE** A persuasive essay presents the writer's point of view on an issue and supports this view with convincing arguments, examples, or details. It may even encourage readers to take action.

Directions: You have thirty minutes to write an essay on the topic assigned below.

Sample Writing Prompt

Many historians argue that it is irrelevant to study the personal lives of historic figures. They claim that one should focus on how these men and women changed the course of history. Other historians argue that learning about the private lives of historic figures gives us a richer understanding of their accomplishments and motivations. What value, if any, is there in learning about the personal lives of historic figures?

Assignment: In your essay, take a position on this question. You may write about either one of the two points of view given, or you may present a different point of view on this question. Use specific reasons and examples to support your position.

Studying a Model ACT® Essay

Here are some steps to follow to learn from a model essay.
- **Read the prompt and the assignment carefully.** Make sure you understand the issue at hand.
- **Read the model essay.** Decide whether the student does a good job of persuading you, the reader, that his point of view is valid and well thought out.
- **Read the call-outs.** Find out what an examiner might notice about the essay.

Writing the ACT® Essay

S T E P S

1. **After you have read the model essay, try out the prompt on this page yourself.** Give yourself thirty minutes to respond to the prompt.
2. **Make a short outline of what you will write.** Take time to think your plan through carefully as it will drive your essay. This step should take no longer than five minutes.
3. **As you draft, follow your outline to stay on task.**
4. **Allow for five minutes to proofread your essay.** Use the technique on page 670 to proofread your essay.
5. **Once the essay is complete, use the criteria on this page to judge your essay.**

TIP: The ACT® Writing Test is optional. It features a persuasive essay that must be completed within thirty minutes. If you take this exam, you will be asked to write an essay explaining your point of view on an issue.

How to succeed on the ACT® Writing Test

1. State a clear position on the issue.
2. Focus on the topic throughout the essay.
3. Support your position with examples.
4. Show logical reasoning through a well-organized essay.
5. Use standard written English.

FOR REVIEW
To review writing persuasive essays in greater depth, see Chapter 7.

Model Essay

The personal lives of historic figures are of no importance. They may be interesting, in the way that gossip is interesting. However, gossip—talking about people behind their backs—is not a worthwhile activity. In the same way, talking or reading or writing about the personal lives of historic figures is trivial. The fact that someone had a happy or unhappy life doesn't meaningfully add to the historic nature of his or her accomplishments.

Take Benjamin Franklin, for example. He apparently had an unhappy marriage. Does this change his involvement in the writing of the Constitution? Or in the writing and printing of *Poor Richard's Almanac*? Or his ambassadorship to France? It does not. Much has been made about Franklin's poor background. However, Franklin accomplished great things regardless of his difficult start in life. It is more interesting to focus on the impact of what he achieved than to get bogged down in his personal life story.

Sometimes the details of a historic figure's life story are used to make him or her seem more admirable. For example, Abraham Lincoln's poor family background has been used to make him seem more extraordinary. The truth is that what makes Lincoln's achievements admirable is that they are truly historical. By that I mean that his actions changed the course of history. So they are admirable on their own; we don't need to add his personal story to make them admirable.

In other instances, the details of a historic figure's life story are used to make a historic figure seem less admirable. For example, historians have researched many aspects of President Kennedy's life story that detract from his reputation. Many books have been written on this subject. However, this information does not change how Kennedy governed the nation. What made Kennedy a great president were the actions that he took as our leader. The choices he made in his private life are separate from that.

There are occasions when I can understand why a historic figure's personal life might be relevant to his or her professional life. For example, Thomas Jefferson, who was largely responsible for our Constitution (which declares all men to be free), had slaves. This is a major and disturbing contradiction. In this case, I can see some value in learning more about Jefferson's personal life. But even in this context, I think the crucial historical fact is that Jefferson's constitution got it right even if his personal life was misguided. And because the constitution contains the principle of freedom for all, it eventually helped ensure that all men and women were free in the United States.

In conclusion, I believe that historic figures ought to be judged for the actions they took that changed the course of history. Their personal lives only provide an interesting, but ultimately unimportant, insight into those public actions.

Strong and clear position on the issue.

The student writes an engaging concluding sentence that elaborates on the main idea of the first paragraph.

The student supports his argument with a reference to a historical figure.

The student further supports his argument by including another example from history.

The essay acknowledges the other side of the issue and introduces the counterexample of Thomas Jefferson.

The student effectively uses his counterexample to reinforce his original argument.

The student ends this polished essay with a concise concluding paragraph in which he powerfully sums up his argument.

Writing

The New SAT® Essay

The new SAT® essay must be completed in twenty-five minutes. The writing prompt presents an issue. You must develop a position on the issue and write a short essay that develops and supports your point of view.

> **RULE** A persuasive essay opens with a statement of the writer's point of view on a topic, provides reasons why this point of view is valid, and supports these reasons with examples or details. The intent of a persuasive essay is to use a sound argument to convince the reader that the writer's point of view about a topic is valid or correct.

Directions: You have twenty-five minutes to write an essay on this issue. Think carefully about the issue presented in the following excerpt and assignment below.

To write the new SAT® essay successfully, your essay should

- develop a point of view on the issue.
- use logical reasoning and appropriate examples.
- be well-organized and focused.
- demonstrate good language skills and appropriate vocabulary.
- use a variety of sentence lengths.
- have relatively few errors of grammar, punctuation, or spelling.

Sample Writing Prompt

Increasingly, people seem to be reluctant to fulfill their obligations as members of society. More and more people tend to live their lives as though their convenience is more important than any other consideration.

Assignment: Does the existence of society depend upon people's willingness to occasionally place society's best interests before their individual concerns?

Model Essay

A society is a network of people bound to one another by their relationships and shared interests. In order for a society to function, there has to be cooperation between members. That means that occasionally the members of a society must place the needs of society before their own concerns.

Members of a society can address their personal concerns a lot of the time. For example, weekends offer free time. Some of the time, however, members of a society must honor their obligations to one another. Whether or not they want to, they must work together to help society function. They must put the needs of society before their own needs.

Even children must put their own wishes aside. Most children would prefer not to go to school. They'd rather stay home and play. However, children must go to school because that's the way the next generation of the society will be prepared to contribute to society when they are older. Adults must go to work so that they can earn money and take care of their families, pay taxes, and provide services that help other members of society. We don't get to do what we want all the time, but we do get the benefit of being a member of a community or a society.

The essay opens by stating a clear point of view that directly addresses the prompt.

The student illustrates her point with a strong example from her observations.

When people opt out of some of these expectations, by not paying taxes or by not voting or by not going to work, society suffers. I have noticed this play out in my own experience. At our school, the PTA is barely active. The purpose of the PTA is to support the school in various ways. However, if parents don't contribute their time and energy, the school is deprived of resources and assets. That is the situation at my school, where we had to cancel our annual trip to Washington, D.C., due to lack of funds. In this way, the individual choices of members of society have a large impact.

There is no clearer example of this problem than in the statistics regarding voting. Just half of eligible voters vote for the President of the United States. That means that half of the population doesn't care about the future of the country. It also means that their own needs and wishes are not reflected by the leadership of the country. With so little participation in the voting process, it is little wonder that there are so many problems in society. Voting for effective leaders is one of the best ways to deal with major social problems. But if people cannot even be bothered to vote, then that is perhaps the biggest social problem of all because it means that half the population is not serious about improving their nation and society.

To conclude, society depends entirely on the cooperation of individuals. People must be willing to look beyond their own concerns and act for the greater good.

> The student supports her point with a strong example from her experience.

> The student includes an example from current events to strengthen her argument.

> The student closes the essay with a strong and polished statement that reiterates her main point.

Studying the Model Essay

Here are some steps to follow in order to learn from the model essay.

- **Read the prompt and the assignment carefully.** Make sure you understand the issue at hand.

- **Read the sample essay.** Decide whether the student does a good job of persuading you, the reader, that her point of view is valid and well thought out.

- **Read the call-outs.** Find out what an examiner might notice about the essay. Pay attention to the elements of the essay that are noted, such as clear and strong introductions and conclusions and the use of many types of examples.

Writing

Writing the SAT® Essay

STEPS

1. **Now that you have read a model essay, try out the prompt on page 668 yourself.** Give yourself twenty-five minutes to respond to the prompt.

2. **Make a short outline of what you will write.** Take time to think your plan through carefully as it will drive your essay. This step should take no longer than five minutes.

3. **As you draft, follow your outline to be sure you stay on task.** Allow about about thirteen minutes for drafting and two minutes for revising your essay.

4. **Allow for five minutes to proofread your essay.** Use the technique below to proofread your essay in five minutes or less.

5. **Once the essay is completed, use the criteria on page 663 to evaluate your essay.**

FOR REVIEW

To review writing persuasive essays in greater depth, see Chapter 7.

Proofreading in Five Minutes

 STRATEGY On a timed essay, spend five minutes proofreading your essay. Since you don't have a lot of time, use the acronym *CUSP* to remember to check the following elements:

C = Capitalization: check that every sentence begins with a capital letter and that proper nouns begin with capital letters. Make sure that no words begin with capital letters unnecessarily.

U = Usage: check that your grammar and word choice are correct.

S = Spelling: check that all words are correctly spelled.

P = Punctuation: check that there are no missing or unnecessary punctuation marks.

Finally, check that your essay is neatly presented. If your writing is illegible, try to make it clearer. Check that any inserted words or sentences are neatly indicated.

Reflecting on Test Preparation

Now that you have reached the end of the Test Preparation Handbook, take some time to think about what aspects of test preparation were most challenging for you. Use these tips to get your ideas started.

1. Quickly flip through the pages of the Test Preparation Handbook and jot down reading, grammar, and writing topics that represent a challenge for you.

2. Once you have identified a particular problem area or areas, work through the textbook chapter on the topic. Then, review the Test Preparation Handbook so that you can learn strategies for answering questions on those topics in exams.

3. Ask your teacher for help in building your skills and accessing old standardized tests that you can use for practice.

As a tenth grader, you have a good amount of time to prepare for success on the new SAT® or the ACT®. Use this time wisely so that you can do your very best on these tests.

Citing Sources and Preparing Manuscript

The presentation of your written work is important. Your work should be neat, clean, and easy to read. Follow your teacher's directions for placing your name and class, along with the title and date of your work, on the paper.

For handwritten work:

- Use cursive handwriting or manuscript printing, according to the style your teacher prefers. The penmanship reference below shows the accepted formation of letters in cursive writing.
- Write or print neatly.
- Write on one side of lined $8\frac{1}{2}$" x 11" paper with a clean edge. (Do not use pages torn from a spiral notebook.)
- Indent the first line of each paragraph.

- Leave a margin, as indicated by the guidelines on the lined paper. Write in a size appropriate for the lines provided. Do not write so large that the letters from one line bump into the ones above and below. Do not write so small that the writing is difficult to read.
- Write in blue or black ink.
- Number the pages in the upper right corner.
- You should not cross out words on your final draft. Recopy instead. If your paper is long, your teacher may allow you to make one or two small changes by neatly crossing out the text to be deleted and using a caret [^] to indicate replacement text. Alternatively, you might make one or two corrections neatly with correction fluid. If you find yourself making more than three corrections, consider recopying the work.

PENMANSHIP REFERENCE

For word-processed or typed documents:

- Choose a standard, easy-to-read font.
- Type or print on one side of unlined $8\frac{1}{2}$" x 11" paper.
- Set the margins for the side, top, and bottom of your paper at approximately one inch. Most word-processing programs have a default setting that is appropriate.
- Double-space the document.
- Indent the first line of each paragraph.
- Number the pages in the upper right corner. Many word-processing programs have a header feature that will do this for you automatically.

- If you discover one or two errors after you have typed or printed, use correction fluid if your teacher allows such corrections. If you have more than three errors in an electronic file, consider making the corrections to the file and reprinting the document. If you have typed a long document, your teacher may allow you to make a few corrections by hand. If you have several errors, however, consider retyping the document.

For research papers:

Follow your teacher's directions for formatting formal research papers. Most papers will have the following features:

- Title page
- Table of Contents or Outline
- Works-Cited List

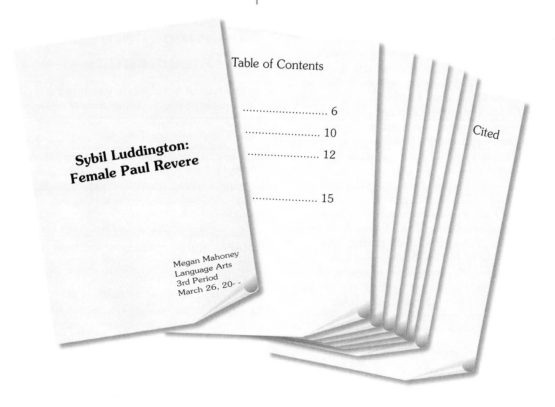

Table of Contents

.... 6

.... 10

.... 12

.... 15

Sybil Luddington:
Female Paul Revere

Megan Mahoney
Language Arts
3rd Period
March 26, 20- -

Cited

Incorporating Ideas From Research

Below are three common methods of incorporating the ideas of other writers into your work. Choose the most appropriate style by analyzing your needs in each case. In all cases, you must credit your source.

- **Direct Quotation:** Use quotation marks to indicate the exact words.
- **Paraphrase:** To share ideas without a direct quotation, state the ideas in your own words. While you haven't copied word-for-word, you still need to credit your source.
- **Summary:** To provide information about a large body of work—such as a speech, an editorial, or a chapter of a book—identify the writer's main idea.

Avoiding Plagiarism

Whether you are presenting a formal research paper or an opinion paper on a current event, you must be careful to give credit for any ideas or opinions that are not your own. Presenting someone else's ideas, research, or opinion as your own—even if you have rephrased it in different words—is *plagiarism*, the equivalent of academic stealing, or fraud.

You can avoid plagiarism by synthesizing what you learn: Read from several sources and let the ideas of experts help you draw your own conclusions and form your own opinions. Ultimately, however, note your own reactions to the ideas presented.

When you choose to use someone else's ideas or work to support your view, credit the source of the material. Give bibliographic information to cite your sources of the following information:

- Statistics
- Direct quotations
- Indirectly quoted statements of opinions
- Conclusions presented by an expert
- Facts available in only one or two sources

Crediting Sources

When you credit a source, you acknowledge where you found your information and you give your readers the details necessary for locating the source themselves. Within the body of the paper, you provide a short citation, a footnote number linked to a footnote, or an endnote number linked to an endnote reference. These brief references show the page numbers on which you found the information. To make your paper more formal, prepare a reference list at the end of the paper to provide full bibliographic information on your sources. These are two common types of reference lists:

- A **bibliography** provides a listing of all the resources you consulted during your research.
- A **works-cited list** indicates the works you have referenced in your paper.

Choosing a Format for Documentation

The type of information you provide and the format in which you provide it depend on what your teacher prefers. These are the most commonly used styles:

- **Modern Language Association (MLA) Style** This is the style used for most papers at the middle-school and high-school level and for most language arts papers.
- **American Psychological Association (APA) Style** This is used for most papers in the social sciences and for most college-level papers.
- ***Chicago Manual of Style* (CMS) Style** This is preferred by some teachers.

On the following pages, you'll find sample citation formats for the most commonly cited materials. Each format calls for standard bibliographic information. The difference is in the order of the material presented in each entry and the punctuation required.

MLA Style for Listing Sources

Book with one author	Pyles, Thomas. *The Origins and Development of the English Language.* 2nd ed. New York: Harcourt Brace Jovanovich, Inc., 1971.
Book with two or three authors	McCrum, Robert, William Cran, and Robert MacNeil. *The Story of English.* New York: Penguin Books, 1987.
Book with an editor	Truth, Sojourner. *Narrative of Sojourner Truth.* Ed. Margaret Washington. New York: Vintage Books, 1993.
Book with more than three authors or editors	Donald, Robert B., et al. *Writing Clear Essays.* Upper Saddle River, NJ: Prentice-Hall, Inc., 1996.
A single work from an anthology	Hawthorne, Nathaniel. "Young Goodman Brown." *Literature: An Introduction to Reading and Writing.* Ed. Edgar V. Roberts and Henry E. Jacobs. Upper Saddle River, NJ: Prentice-Hall, Inc., 1998. 376–385. [Indicate pages for the entire selection.]
Introduction in a published edition	Washington, Margaret. Introduction. *Narrative of Sojourner Truth.* By Sojourner Truth. Ed. Washington. New York: Vintage Books, 1993. v–xi.
Signed article in a weekly magazine	Wallace, Charles. "A Vodacious Deal." *Time* 14 Feb. 2000: 63.
Signed article in a monthly magazine	Gustaitis, Joseph. "The Sticky History of Chewing Gum." *American History* Oct. 1998: 30–38.
Unsigned editorial or story	"Selective Silence." Editorial. *Wall Street Journal* 11 Feb. 2000: A14. [If the editorial or story is signed, begin with the author's name.]
Signed pamphlet	[Treat the pamphlet as though it were a book.]
Pamphlet with no author, publisher, or date	*Are You at Risk of Heart Attack?* n.p. n.d. [n.p. n.d. indicates that there is no known publisher or date]
Filmstrips, slide programs, videocassettes, DVDs, and other audiovisual media	*The Diary of Anne Frank.* Dir. George Stevens. Perf. Millie Perkins, Shelley Winters, Joseph Schildkraut, Lou Jacobi, and Richard Beymer. 1959. DVD. Twentieth Century Fox, 2004.
Radio or television program transcript	"Washington's Crossing of the Delaware." Host Liane Hansen. Guest David Hackett Fischer. *Weekend Edition Sunday.* Natl. Public Radio. WNYC, New York City. 23 Dec. 2003. Transcript.
Internet	"Fun Facts About Gum." NACGM site. National Association of Chewing Gum Manufacturers. 19 Dec. 1999. <http://www.nacgm.org/consumer/funfacts.html>. [Indicate the date of last update if known and the date you accessed the information. Content and addresses at Web sites change frequently.]
Newspaper	Thurow, Roger. "South Africans Who Fought for Sanctions Now Scrap for Investors." *Wall Street Journal* 11 Feb. 2000: A1+ [For a multipage article that does not appear on consecutive pages, write only the first page number on which it appears, followed by a plus sign.]
Personal interview	Smith, Jane. Personal interview. 10 Feb. 2000.
CD (with multiple publishers)	Simms, James, ed. *Romeo and Juliet.* By William Shakespeare. CD-ROM. Oxford: Attica Cybernetics Ltd.; London: BBC Education; London: HarperCollins Publishers, 1995.
Article from an encyclopedia	Askeland, Donald R. "Welding." *World Book Encyclopedia.* 1991 ed.

APA Style for Listing Sources

The list of citations for APA is referred to as a Reference List and not a bibliography.

Book with one author	Pyles, T. (1971). *The Origins and Development of the English Language* (2nd ed.). New York: Harcourt Brace Jovanovich, Inc.
Book with two or three authors	McCrum, R., Cran, W., & MacNeil, R. (1987). *The Story of English.* New York: Penguin Books.
Book with an editor	Truth, S. (1993). *Narrative of Sojourner Truth* (M. Washington, Ed.). New York: Vintage Books.
Book with more than three authors or editors	Donald, R. B., Morrow, B. R., Wargetz, L. G., & Werner, K. (1996). *Writing Clear Essays.* Upper Saddle River, New Jersey: Prentice-Hall, Inc. [With six or more authors, abbreviate second and following authors as "et al."]
A single work from an anthology	Hawthorne, N. (1998) Young Goodman Brown. In E. V. Roberts, & H. E. Jacobs (Eds.), *Literature: An Introduction to Reading and Writing* (pp. 376–385). Upper Saddle River, New Jersey: Prentice-Hall, Inc.
Introduction to a work included in a published edition	[No style is offered under this heading.]
Signed article in a weekly magazine	Wallace, C. (2000, February 14). A vodacious deal. *Time, 155,* 63. [The volume number appears in italics before the page number.]
Signed article in a monthly magazine	Gustaitis, J. (1998, October). The sticky history of chewing gum. *American History, 33,* 30–38.
Unsigned editorial or story	Selective Silence. (2000, February 11). *Wall Street Journal,* p. A14.
Signed pamphlet	Pearson Education. (2000). *LifeCare* (2nd ed.) [Pamphlet]. Smith, John: Author.
Pamphlet with no author, publisher, or date	[No style is offered under this heading.]
Filmstrips, slide programs, and videotape	Stevens, G. (Producer & Director). (1959). *The Diary of Anne Frank.* [Videotape]. (Available from Twentieth Century Fox) [If the producer and the director are two different people, list the producer first and then the director, with an ampersand (&) between them.]
Radio or television program transcript	Broderick, D. (1999, May 23). The First Immortal Generation. (R. Williams, Radio Host). *Ockham's Razor.* New York: National Public Radio.
Internet	National Association of Chewing Gum Manufacturers. Available: http://www.nacgm.org/consumer/funfacts.html [References to Websites should begin with the author's last name, if available. Indicate the site name and the available path or URL address.]
Newspaper	Thurow, R. (2000, February 11). South Africans who fought for sanctions now scrap for investors. *Wall Street Journal,* pp. A1, A4.
Personal interview	[APA states that, since interviews (and other personal communications) do not provide "recoverable data," they should only be cited in text.]
CD (with multiple publishers)	[No style is offered under this heading.]
Article from an encyclopedia	Askeland, D. R. (1991). Welding. In *World Book Encyclopedia.* (Vol. 21 pp. 190–191). Chicago: World Book, Inc.

CMS Style for Listing Sources

The following chart shows the CMS author-date method of documentation.

Book with one author	Pyles, Thomas. *The Origins and Development of the English Language,* 2nd ed. New York: Harcourt Brace Jovanovich, Inc., 1971.
Book with two or three authors	McCrum, Robert, William Cran, and Robert MacNeil. *The Story of English.* New York: Penguin Books, 1987.
Book with an editor	Truth, Sojourner. *Narrative of Sojourner Truth.* Edited by Margaret Washington. New York: Vintage Books, 1993.
Book with more than three authors or editors	Donald, Robert B., et al. *Writing Clear Essays.* Upper Saddle River, New Jersey: Prentice-Hall, Inc., 1996.
A single work from an anthology	Hawthorne, Nathaniel. "Young Goodman Brown." In *Literature: An Introduction to Reading and Writing.* Ed. Edgar V. Roberts and Henry E. Jacobs. 376–385. Upper Saddle River, New Jersey: Prentice-Hall, Inc., 1998.
Introduction to a work included in a published edition	Washington, Margaret. Introduction to *Narrative of Sojourner Truth,* by Sojourner Truth. New York: Vintage Books, 1993. [According to CMS style, you should avoid this type of entry unless the introduction is of special importance to the work.]
Signed article in a weekly magazine	Wallace, Charles. "A Vodacious Deal." *Time,* 14 February 2000, 63.
Signed article in a monthly magazine	Gustaitis, Joseph. "The Sticky History of Chewing Gum." *American History,* October 1998, 30–38.
Unsigned editorial or story	*Wall Street Journal,* 11 February 2000. [CMS states that items from newspapers are seldom listed in a bibliography. Instead, the name of the paper and the relevant dates are listed.]
Signed pamphlet	[No style is offered under this heading.]
Pamphlet with no author, publisher, or date	[No style is offered under this heading.]
Filmstrips, slide programs, and videotape	Stevens, George. (director). *The Diary of Anne Frank.* 170 min. Beverly Hills, California: Twentieth Century Fox, 1994.
Radio or television program transcript	[No style is offered under this heading.]
Internet	[No style is offered under this heading.]
Newspaper	*Wall Street Journal,* 11 February 2000. [CMS states that items from newspapers are seldom listed in a bibliography. Instead, the name of the paper and the relevant dates are listed.]
Personal interview	[CMS states that, since personal conversations are not available to the public, there is no reason to place them in the bibliography. However, the following format should be followed if they are listed.] Jane Smith. Conversation with author. Wooster, Ohio, 10 February 2000.
CD (with multiple publishers)	Shakespeare, William. *Romeo and Juliet.* Oxford: Attica Cybernetics Ltd.; London: BBC Education; London: HarperCollins Publishers, 1995. CD-ROM.
Article from an encyclopedia	[According to CMS style, encyclopedias are not listed in bibliographies.]

Sample Works-Cited List (MLA)

Carwardine, Mark, Erich Hoyt, R. Ewan Fordyce, and
  Peter Gill. *The Nature Company Guides: Whales,
  Dolphins, and Porpoises.* New York: Time-Life
  Books, 1998.

Ellis, Richard. *Men and Whales.* New York: Knopf,
  1991.

Whales in Danger. "Discovering Whales." 18 Oct. 1999.
  <http://whales.magna.com.au/DISCOVER>

Sample Internal Citations (MLA)

It makes sense that baleen whales such as the
blue whale, the fin whale, the bowhead whale, the
humpback whale, and the sei whale (to name just
a few) grow to immense sizes (Carwardine 19–21).
The blue whale has grooves running from under its
chin to partway along the length of its underbelly.
As in some other whales, these grooves expand
and allow even more food and water to be taken in
(Ellis 18–21).

Author's
last name

page numbers
where
information
can be found

Internet Research Handbook

Introduction to the Internet

The Internet is a series of networks that are interconnected all over the world. The Internet allows users to have almost unlimited access to information stored on the networks. Dr. Berners-Lee, a physicist, created the Internet in the 1980's by writing a small computer program that allowed pages to be linked together using key words. The Internet was mostly text-based until 1992, when a computer program called the NCSA Mosaic (National Center for Supercomputing Applications at the University of Illinois) was created. This program was the first Web browser. The development of Web browsers greatly eased the ability of the user to navigate through all the pages stored on the Web. Very soon, the appearance of the Web was altered as well. More appealing visuals were added, and sound was also implemented. This change made the Web more user-friendly and more appealing to the general public.

Using the Internet for Research

Key Word Search

Before you begin a search, you should identify your specific topic. To make searching easier, narrow your subject to a key word or a group of key words. These are your search terms, and they should be as specific as possible. For example, if you are looking for the latest concert dates for your favorite musical group, you might use the band's name as a key word. However, if you were to enter the name of the group in the query box of the search engine, you might be presented with thousands of links to information about the group that is unrelated to your needs. You might locate such information as band member biographies, the group's history, fan reviews of concerts, and hundreds of sites with related names containing information that is irrelevant to your search. Because you used such a broad key word, you might need to navigate through all that information before you find a link or subheading for concert dates. In contrast, if you were to type in "Duplex Arena and [band name]" you would have a better chance of locating pages that contain this information.

How to Narrow Your Search

If you have a large group of key words and still don't know which ones to use, write out a list of all the words you are considering. Once you have completed the list, scrutinize it. Then, delete the words that are least important to your search, and highlight those that are most important.

These **key search connectors** can help you fine-tune your search:

AND: narrows a search by retrieving documents that include both terms. For example: *baseball AND playoffs*

OR: broadens a search by retrieving documents including any of the terms. For example: *playoffs OR championships*

NOT: narrows a search by excluding documents containing certain words. For example: *baseball NOT history of*

Tips for an Effective Search

1. Keep in mind that search engines can be case-sensitive. If your first attempt at searching fails, check your search terms for misspellings and try again.

2. If you are entering a group of key words, present them in order, from the most important to the least important key word.

3. Avoid opening the link to every single page in your results list. Search engines present pages in descending order of relevancy. The most useful pages will be located at the top of the list. However, read the description of each link before you open the page.

4. When you use some search engines, you can find helpful tips for specializing your search. Take the opportunity to learn more about effective searching.

Other Ways to Search

Using On-line Reference Sites

How you search should be tailored to *what* you are hoping to find. If you are looking for data and facts, use reference sites before you jump onto a simple search engine. For example, you can find reference sites to provide definitions of words, statistics about almost any subject, biographies, maps, and concise information on many topics. Some useful on-line reference sites:

On-line libraries
On-line periodicals
Almanacs
Encyclopedias

You can find these sources using subject searches.

Conducting Subject Searches

As you prepare to go on-line, consider your subject and the best way to find information to suit your needs. If you are looking for general information on a topic and you want your search results to be extensive, consider the subject search indexes on most search engines. These indexes, in the form of category and subject lists, often appear on the first page of a search engine. When you click on a specific highlighted word, you will be presented with a new screen containing subcategories of the topic you chose. In the screen shots below, the category *Sports & Recreation* provided a second index for users to focus a search even further.

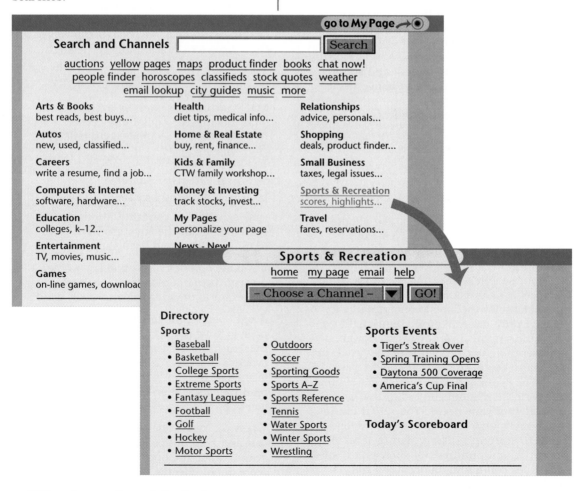

Evaluating the Reliability of Internet Resources

Just as you would evaluate the quality, bias, and validity of any other research material you locate, check the source of information you find on-line. Compare these two sites containing information on the poet and writer Langston Hughes:

Site A is a personal Web site constructed by a college student. It contains no bibliographic information or links to sites that he used. Included on the site are several poems by Langston Hughes and a student essay about the poet's use of symbolism. It has not been updated in more than six months.

Site B is a Web site constructed and maintained by the English Department of a major university. Information on Hughes is presented in a scholarly format, with a bibliography and credits for the writer. The site includes links to other sites and indicates new features that are added weekly.

For your own research, consider the information you find on Site B to be more reliable and accurate than that on Site A. Because it is maintained by experts in their field who are held accountable for their work, the university site will be a better research tool than the student-generated one.

Tips for Evaluating Internet Sources

1. Consider who constructed and who now maintains the Web page. Determine whether this author is a reputable source. Often, the URL endings indicate a source.

   - Sites ending in *.edu* are maintained by educational institutions.
   - Sites ending in *.gov* are maintained by government agencies (federal, state, or local).
   - Sites ending in *.org* are normally maintained by nonprofit organizations and agencies.
   - Sites with a *.com* ending are commercially or personally maintained.

2. Skim the official and trademarked Web pages first. It is safe to assume that the information you draw from Web pages of reputable institutions, on-line encyclopedias, on-line versions of major daily newspapers, or government-owned sites produce information as reliable as the material you would find in print. In contrast, unbranded sites or those generated by individuals tend to borrow information from other sources without providing documentation. As information travels from one source to another, the information has likely been muddled, misinterpreted, edited, or revised.

3. You can still find valuable information in the less "official" sites. Check for the writer's credentials and then consider these factors:

   - Don't let official-looking graphics or presentations fool you.
   - Make sure the information is updated enough to suit your needs. Many Web pages will indicate how recently they have been updated.
   - If the information is borrowed, see whether you can trace it back to its original source.

Respecting Copyrighted Material

Because the Internet is a relatively new and quickly growing medium, issues of copyright and ownership arise almost daily. As laws begin to govern the use and reuse of material posted on-line, they may change the way that people can access or reprint material.

Text, photographs, music, and fine art printed on-line may not be reproduced without acknowledged permission of the copyright owner.

Commonly Overused Words

When you write, use the most precise word for your meaning, not the word that comes to mind first. Consult this thesaurus to find alternatives for some commonly overused words. Consult a full-length thesaurus to find alternatives to words that do not appear here. Keep in mind that the choices offered in a thesaurus do not all mean exactly the same thing. Review all the options, and choose the one that best expresses your meaning.

about approximately, nearly, almost, approaching, close to

absolutely unconditionally, perfectly, completely, ideally, purely

activity action, movement, operation, labor, exertion, enterprise, project, pursuit, endeavor, job, assignment, pastime, scheme, task

add attach, affix, join, unite, append, increase, amplify

affect adjust, influence, transform, moderate, incline, motivate, prompt

amazing overwhelming, astonishing, startling, unexpected, stunning, dazzling, remarkable

awesome impressive, stupendous, fabulous, astonishing, outstanding

bad defective, inadequate, poor, unsatisfactory, disagreeable, offensive, repulsive, corrupt, wicked, naughty, harmful, injurious, unfavorable

basic essential, necessary, indispensable, vital, fundamental, elementary

beautiful attractive, appealing, alluring, exqui-site, gorgeous, handsome, stunning

begin commence, found, initiate, introduce, launch, originate

better preferable, superior, worthier

big enormous, extensive, huge, immense, massive

boring commonplace, monotonous, tedious, tiresome

bring accompany, cause, convey, create, conduct, deliver, produce

cause origin, stimulus, inspiration, motive

certain unquestionable, incontrovertible, unmistakable, indubitable, assured, confident

change alter, transform, vary, replace, diversify

choose select, elect, nominate, prefer, identify

decent respectable, adequate, fair, suitable

definitely unquestionably, clearly, precisely, positively, inescapably

easy effortless, natural, comfortable, undemanding, pleasant, relaxed

effective powerful, successful

emphasize underscore, feature, accentuate

end limit, boundary, finish, conclusion, finale, resolution

energy vitality, vigor, force, dynamism

enjoy savor, relish, revel, benefit

entire complete, inclusive, unbroken, integral

excellent superior, remarkable, splendid, unsurpassed, superb, magnificent

exciting thrilling, stirring, rousing, dramatic

far distant, remote

fast swift, quick, fleet, hasty, instant, accelerated

fill occupy, suffuse, pervade, saturate, inflate, stock

finish complete, conclude, cease, achieve, exhaust, deplete, consume

funny comical, ludicrous, amusing, droll, entertaining, bizarre, unusual, uncommon

get obtain, receive, acquire, procure, achieve

give bestow, donate, supply, deliver, distribute, impart

go proceed, progress, advance, move

good satisfactory, serviceable, functional, competent, virtuous, striking

great tremendous, superior, remarkable, eminent, proficient, expert

happy pleased, joyous, elated, jubilant, cheerful, delighted

hard arduous, formidable, complex, complicated, rigorous, harsh

help assist, aid, support, sustain, serve

hurt injure, harm, damage, wound, impair

important significant, substantial, weighty, meaningful, critical, vital, notable

interesting absorbing, appealing, entertaining, fascinating, thought-provoking

job task, work, business, undertaking, occupation, vocation, chore, duty, assignment

keep retain, control, possess

kind type, variety, sort, form

know comprehend, understand, realize, perceive, discern

like (adj) similar, equivalent, parallel

like (verb) enjoy, relish, appreciate

main primary, foremost, dominant

make build, construct, produce, assemble, fashion, manufacture

mean plan, intend, suggest, propose, indicate

more supplementary, additional, replenishment

new recent, modern, current, novel

next subsequently, thereafter, successively

nice pleasant, satisfying, gracious, charming

old aged, mature, experienced, used, worn, former, previous

open unobstructed, accessible

part section, portion, segment, detail, element, component

perfect flawless, faultless, ideal, consummate

plan scheme, design, system, plot

pleasant agreeable, gratifying, refreshing, welcome

prove demonstrate, confirm, validate, verify, corroborate

quick brisk, prompt, responsive, rapid, nimble, hasty

really truly, genuinely, extremely, undeniably

regular standard, routine, customary, habitual

see regard, behold, witness, gaze, realize, notice

small diminutive, miniature, minor, insignificant, slight, trivial

sometimes occasionally, intermittently, sporadically, periodically

take grasp, capture, choose, select, tolerate, endure

terrific extraordinary, magnificent, marvelous

think conceive, imagine, ponder, reflect, contemplate

try attempt, endeavor, venture, test

use employ, operate, utilize

very unusually, extremely, deeply, exceedingly, profoundly

want desire, crave, yearn, long

Commonly Misspelled Words

The list on these pages presents words that cause problems for many people. Some of these words are spelled according to set rules, but others follow no specific rules. As you review this list, check to see how many of the words give you trouble in your own writing. Then, read the instruction in the "Vocabulary and Spelling" chapter in the book for strategies and suggestions for improving your own spelling habits.

abbreviate	athletic	catastrophe	curious
absence	attendance	category	cylinder
absolutely	auxiliary	ceiling	deceive
abundance	awkward	cemetery	decision
accelerate	bandage	census	deductible
accidentally	banquet	certain	defendant
accumulate	bargain	changeable	deficient
accurate	barrel	characteristic	definitely
ache	battery	chauffeur	delinquent
achievement	beautiful	chief	dependent
acquaintance	beggar	clothes	descendant
adequate	beginning	coincidence	description
admittance	behavior	colonel	desert
advertisement	believe	column	desirable
aerial	benefit	commercial	dessert
affect	bicycle	commission	deteriorate
aggravate	biscuit	commitment	dining
aggressive	bookkeeper	committee	disappointed
agreeable	bought	competitor	disastrous
aisle	boulevard	concede	discipline
all right	brief	condemn	dissatisfied
allowance	brilliant	congratulate	distinguish
aluminum	bruise	connoisseur	effect
amateur	bulletin	conscience	eighth
analysis	buoyant	conscientious	eligible
analyze	bureau	conscious	embarrass
ancient	bury	contemporary	enthusiastic
anecdote	buses	continuous	entrepreneur
anniversary	business	controversy	envelope
anonymous	cafeteria	convenience	environment
answer	calendar	coolly	equipped
anticipate	campaign	cooperate	equivalent
anxiety	canceled	cordially	especially
apologize	candidate	correspondence	exaggerate
appall	capacity	counterfeit	exceed
appearance	capital	courageous	excellent
appreciate	capitol	courteous	exercise
appropriate	captain	courtesy	exhibition
architecture	career	criticism	existence
argument	carriage	criticize	experience
associate	cashier	curiosity	explanation

extension
extraordinary
familiar
fascinating
February
fiery
financial
fluorescent
foreign
forfeit
fourth
fragile
gauge
generally
genius
genuine
government
grammar
grievance
guarantee
guard
guidance
handkerchief
harass
height
humorous
hygiene
ignorant
illegible
immediately
immigrant
independence
independent
indispensable
individual
inflammable
intelligence
interfere
irrelevant
irritable
jewelry
judgment
knowledge
laboratory
lawyer
legible
legislature
leisure
liable

library
license
lieutenant
lightning
likable
liquefy
literature
loneliness
magnificent
maintenance
marriage
mathematics
maximum
meanness
mediocre
mileage
millionaire
minimum
minuscule
miscellaneous
mischievous
misspell
mortgage
naturally
necessary
negotiate
neighbor
neutral
nickel
niece
ninety
noticeable
nuclear
nuisance
obstacle
occasion
occasionally
occur
occurred
occurrence
omitted
opinion
opportunity
optimistic
outrageous
pamphlet
parallel
paralyze
parentheses

particularly
patience
permanent
permissible
perseverance
persistent
personally
perspiration
persuade
phenomenal
phenomenon
physician
pleasant
pneumonia
possess
possession
possibility
prairie
precede
preferable
prejudice
preparation
prerogative
previous
primitive
privilege
probably
procedure
proceed
prominent
pronunciation
psychology
publicly
pursue
questionnaire
realize
really
recede
receipt
receive
recognize
recommend
reference
referred
rehearse
relevant
reminiscence
renowned
repetition

restaurant
rhythm
ridiculous
sandwich
satellite
schedule
scissors
secretary
siege
solely
sponsor
subtle
subtlety
superintendent
supersede
surveillance
susceptible
tariff
temperamental
theater
threshold
truly
unmanageable
unwieldy
usage
usually
valuable
various
vegetable
voluntary
weight
weird
whale
wield
yield

Abbreviations Guide

Abbreviations, shortened versions of words or phrases, can be valuable tools in writing if you know when and how to use them. They can be very helpful in informal writing situations, such as taking notes or writing lists. However, only a few abbreviations can be used in formal writing. They are: *Mr., Mrs., Miss, Ms., Dr., A.M., P.M., A.D., B.C., M.A, B.A., Ph.D.,* and *M.D.*

The following pages provide the conventional abbreviations for a variety of words.

Abbreviations of Common Titles

Ambassador	Amb.	Lieutenant	Lt.
Attorney	Atty.	Major	Maj.
Brigadier-General	Brig. Gen.	President	Pres.
Brother	Br.	Professor	Prof.
Captain	Capt.	Representative	Rep.
Colonel	Col.	Reverend	Rev.
Commander	Cmdr.	Secretary	Sec.
Commissioner	Com.	Senator	Sen.
Corporal	Cpl.	Sergeant	Sgt.
Doctor	Dr.	Sister	Sr.
Father	Fr.	Superintendent	Supt.
Governor	Gov.	Treasurer	Treas.
Honorable	Hon.	Vice Admiral	Vice Adm.

Abbreviations of Academic Degrees

Bachelor of Arts	B.A. (or A.B.)	Esquire (lawyer)	Esq.
Bachelor of Science	B.S. (or S.B.)	Master of Arts	M.A. (or A.M.)
Doctor of Dental Surgery	D.D.S.	Master of Business	M.B.A.
Doctor of Divinity	D.D.	Administration	
Doctor of Education	Ed.D.	Master of Fine Arts	M.F.A.
Doctor of Laws	LL.D.	Master of Science	M.S. (or S.M.)
Doctor of Medicine	M.D.	Registered Nurse	R.N.
Doctor of Philosophy	Ph.D.		

Abbreviations of States

State	Traditional	Postal Service	State	Traditional	Postal Service
Alabama	Ala.	AL	Montana	Mont.	MT
Alaska	Alaska	AK	Nebraska	Nebr.	NE
Arizona	Ariz.	AZ	Nevada	Nev.	NV
Arkansas	Ark.	AR	New Hampshire	N.H.	NH
California	Calif.	CA	New Jersey	N.J.	NJ
Colorado	Colo.	CO	New Mexico	N.M.	NM
Connecticut	Conn.	CT	New York	N.Y.	NY
Delaware	Del.	DE	North Carolina	N.C.	NC
Florida	Fla.	FL	North Dakota	N.Dak.	ND
Georgia	Ga.	GA	Ohio	O.	OH
Hawaii	Hawaii	HI	Oklahoma	Okla.	OK
Idaho	Ida.	ID	Oregon	Ore.	OR
Illinois	Ill.	IL	Pennsylvania	Pa.	PA
Indiana	Ind.	IN	Rhode Island	R.I.	RI
Iowa	Iowa	IA	South Carolina	S.C.	SC
Kansas	Kans.	KS	South Dakota	S.Dak.	SD
Kentucky	Ky.	KY	Tennessee	Tenn.	TN
Louisiana	La.	LA	Texas	Tex.	TX
Maine	Me.	ME	Utah	Utah	UT
Maryland	Md.	MD	Vermont	Vt.	VT
Massachusetts	Mass.	MA	Virginia	Va.	VA
Michigan	Mich.	MI	Washington	Wash.	WA
Minnesota	Minn.	MN	West Virginia	W. Va	WV
Mississippi	Miss.	MS	Wisconsin	Wis.	WI
Missouri	Mo.	MO	Wyoming	Wyo.	WY

Common Geographical Abbreviations

Apartment	Apt.	National	Natl.
Avenue	Ave.	Park, Peak	Pk.
Block	Blk.	Peninsula	Pen.
Boulevard	Blvd.	Point	Pt.
Building	Bldg.	Province	Prov.
County	Co.	Road	Rd.
District	Dist.	Route	Rte.
Drive	Dr.	Square	Sq.
Fort	Ft.	Street	St.
Island	Is.	Territory	Terr.
Mountain	Mt.		

Abbreviations of Traditional Measurements

inch(es)	in.	ounce(s)	oz.
foot, feet	ft.	pound(s)	lb.
yard(s)	yd.	pint(s)	pt.
mile(s)	mi.	quart(s)	qt.
teaspoon(s)	tsp.	gallon(s)	gal.
tablespoon(s)	tbsp.	Fahrenheit	F.

Abbreviations of Metric Measurements

millimeter(s)	mm	liter(s)	L
centimeter(s)	cm	kiloliter(s)	kL
meter(s)	m	milligram(s)	mg
kilometer(s)	km	centigram(s)	cg
milliliter(s)	mL	gram(s)	g
centiliter(s)	cL	Celsius	C

Other Commonly Used Abbreviations

about (used with dates)	c., ca., circ.	manager	mgr.
and others	et al.	manufacturing	mfg.
anonymous	anon.	market	mkt.
approximately	approx.	measure	meas.
associate, association	assoc., assn.	merchandise	mdse.
auxiliary	aux., auxil.	miles per hour	mph
bibliography	bibliog.	miscellaneous	misc.
boxes	bx(s).	money order	M.O.
bucket	bkt.	note well; take notice	N.B.
bulletin	bull.	number	no.
bushel	bu.	package	pkg.
capital letter	cap.	page	p., pg.
cash on delivery	C.O.D.	pages	pp.
department	dept.	pair(s)	pr(s).
discount	disc.	parenthesis	paren.
dozen(s)	doz.	Patent Office	pat. off.
each	ea.	piece(s)	pc(s).
edition, editor	ed.	poetical, poetry	poet.
equivalent	equiv.	private	pvt.
established	est.	proprietor	prop.
fiction	fict.	pseudonym	pseud.
for example	e.g.	published, publisher	pub.
free of charge	grat., gratis	received	recd.
General Post Office	G.P.O.	reference, referee	ref.
government	gov., govt.	revolutions per minute	rpm
graduate, graduated	grad.	rhetorical, rhetoric	rhet.
Greek, Grecian	Gr.	right	R.
headquarters	hdqrs.	scene	sc.
height	ht.	special, specific	spec.
hospital	hosp.	spelling, species	sp.
illustrated	ill., illus.	that is	i.e.
including, inclusive	incl.	treasury, treasurer	treas.
introduction, introductory	intro.	volume	vol.
italics	ital.	weekly	wkly
karat, carat	k., kt.	weight	wt.
left	L.		

Proofreading Symbols Reference

Proofreading symbols make it easier to show where changes are needed in a paper. When proofreading your own or a classmate's work, use these standard proofreading symbols.

insert	I proofred. *a* ^
delete	Ip proofread.
close up space	I proof read.
delete and close up space	I proofreade.
begin new paragraph	¶ I proofread.
spell out	I proofread 10 papers. (sp)
lowercase	I Proofread. (lc)
capitalize	i proofread. (cap)
transpose letters	I proofraed. (tr)
transpose words	I only proofread her paper. (tr)
period	I will proofread⊙
comma	I will proofread and she will help.
colon	We will proofread for the following errors
semicolon	I will proofread she will help.
single quotation marks	She said, "I enjoyed the story The Invalid."
double quotation marks	She said, I enjoyed the story.
apostrophe	Did you borrow Sylvias book?
question mark	Did you borrow Sylvia's book ?/
exclamation point	You're kidding !/
hyphen	online /=/
parentheses	William Shakespeare 1564–1616

Student Publications

To share your writing with a wider audience, consider submitting it to a local, state, or national publication for student writing. Following are several magazines and Web sites that accept and publish student work.

Periodicals

Merlyn's Pen merlynspen.org

Skipping Stones P.O. Box 3939, Eugene, OR 97403
http://www.skippingstones.org

Teen Ink Box 30, Newton, MA 02461 teenink.com

On-line Publications

Kid Pub http://www.kidpub.org

MidLink Magazine http://www.ncsu.edu/midlink

Contests

Annual Poetry Contest National Federation of State Poetry Societies, Contest Chair, Kathleen Pederzani, 121 Grande Boulevard, Reading, PA 19608-9680

http://www.nfsps.com

Paul A. Witty Outstanding Literature Award International Reading Association, Special Interest Group for Reading for Gifted and Creative Students, c/o Texas Christian University, P.O. Box 297900, Fort Worth, TX 76129

Seventeen Magazine Fiction Contest *Seventeen* Magazine, 1440 Broadway 13th Floor, New York, NY 10018

The Young Playwrights Festival National Playwriting Competition Young Playwrights Inc., Dept WEB, 306 West 38th Street #300, New York, NY 10018

webmaster@youngplaywrights.org

Sentence Diagraming Workshop

Subjects, Verbs, and Modifiers

To diagram a sentence with just a subject and a verb, draw a horizontal line, place the subject on the left, the verb on the right, and then draw a vertical line to separate the subject from the verb.

EXAMPLE:
    S   V
Kathleen laughed.

Kathleen	laughed

When you diagram adjectives, place them on slanted lines directly below the nouns or pronouns they modify. Similarly, place adverbs on slanted lines directly below the verbs, adjectives, or other adverbs they modify.

EXAMPLE:
   ADV   ADJ   ADJ   ADV   ADV
Quite hesitant, my sister did not answer quickly.

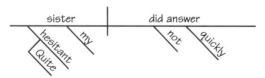

Orders and directions whose subjects are understood to be *you* are diagramed in the usual way, with parentheses around the understood subject. Inverted sentences also follow the usual subject-verb order in a diagram. The capital letter shows which word begins the sentence.

EXAMPLES:
     ORDER   QUESTION
     Stand up.   How are you?

Usually when *there* or *here* begins a sentence, it will function as an adverb modifying the verb. In this case, it should be diagramed on a slanted line below the verb.

Sometimes, however, *there* is used simply to get the sentence started. In this case, it is an expletive. Diagram an expletive by placing it on a short horizontal line above the subject. Diagram interjections and nouns of direct address in the same way.

EXAMPLES:

EXP
There was a storm.

INT   N of DA
Alas, my friend, you lost.

Exercise 1 Diagraming Subjects, Verbs, and Modifiers

Correctly diagram each sentence.
1. Mr. Ricardo, come here.
2. The ship wandered quite aimlessly.
3. Swallows soared overhead.
4. The beautiful white waterfall thunderously cascaded down.
5. There should be a parade today.

Adding Conjunctions

Conjunctions are diagramed on dotted lines drawn between the words they connect. In the example, coordinating conjunctions are used to join both adjectives and adverbs.

EXAMPLE:

CONJ   CONJ
The small but fierce dog barked loudly and steadily.

Conjunctions that connect compound subjects and compound verbs are also written on dotted lines drawn between the words they connect. Notice in the example on the next page how the horizontal line of the diagram is split so that each part of a compound subject or verb appears on a line of its own. Notice also the position of the correlative conjunctions *neither* and *nor*.

EXAMPLE:

CONJ   CONJ   CONJ
Neither Amanda nor Lisa wrote or called.

When a modifier modifies both parts of a compound subject or verb, however, it is placed under the main line of the diagram. In the example below, the adverb *confidently* modifies both parts of the compound verb, so it is placed under the main line.

EXAMPLE:

ADV   ADJ   ADJ
Confidently, the children and their parents

ADV   ADV
walked in and sat down.

▶ **Exercise 2** Diagraming Sentences With Conjunctions
Correctly diagram each sentence.
1. Wood can be painted or varnished.
2. Must pork and bacon be cooked thoroughly?
3. The unusual and colorful kite soared gracefully and slowly dipped.
4. Two obviously unhappy children and their desperately uncomfortable parents fidgeted anxiously and waited very impatiently.
5. The mechanical toy frog will not only croak but also jump far.

Complements

In a diagram, a direct object is positioned on the main horizontal line after the verb. A short vertical line is added to separate it from the verb. An indirect object is placed on a horizontal line extended from a slanted line directly below the verb.

EXAMPLES:

DO   IO   DO
Sue wore a gold chain.   I gave Ted advice.

Because an objective complement helps complete the meaning of a direct object, they are placed side by side. A short slanted line is added to separate the direct object from the objective complement.

EXAMPLE: The President named him Chief of Staff.

Both predicate nominatives and predicate adjectives are also placed on the main horizontal line after the verb. A short, slanted line is used to separate them from the verb.

EXAMPLES: My dog is a spaniel.   We felt grouchy.

As the following example shows, compound complements are diagramed by splitting the lines on which they appear. Conjunctions are placed on dotted lines drawn between the words they connect.

EXAMPLE: We showed Ellie and Tom the zoo and the museum.

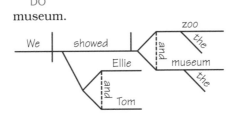

> **Exercise 3** Diagraming Complements Correctly diagram each sentence.
> 1. The irritable little boy pushed his food away.
> 2. This remarkable but true story taught Sally and me something.
> 3. His shy and cautious manner gave June and me courage.
> 4. The fresh, clean mountain air felt wonderful.
> 5. Her husband is a friend and a companion.

Prepositional Phrases

The diagram for a prepositional phrase has a slanted line for the preposition and a horizontal line for the object of the preposition. Modifiers are placed on slanted lines below the horizontal line. Adjective phrases are placed directly below the noun or pronoun they modify. Adverb phrases are placed directly below the verb, adjective, or adverb they modify.

PREP PHRASE   PREP PHRASE

EXAMPLE: The child *with the red ball* skipped *up the hill.*

An adjective phrase that modifies the object of the preposition of another prepositional phrase goes below the other phrase.

PREP PHRASE

EXAMPLE: I had salad *with pineapple in it.*

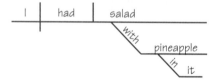

A prepositional phrase with a compound object is diagramed in the same way as the other compound parts of a sentence. The following example shows an adjective phrase that modifies a direct object.

PREP PHRASE

EXAMPLE: We need a house *with three bedrooms and a den.*

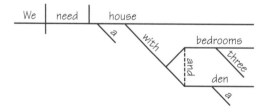

▶ **Exercise 4** Diagraming Prepositional Phrases Correctly diagram each sentence.
1. They flew in a private airplane across the Rockies.
2. Water trickled down Mark's neck.
3. Select a detergent for clothing with greasy stains and ground-in dirt.
4. Without much hope, Becky argued for more time.
5. Corina lives in an apartment with a balcony.

Appositives and Appositive Phrases

An appositive is placed in parentheses beside the noun or pronoun it identifies, renames, or explains. Any adjectives or adjective phrases included in an appositive phrase are placed directly beneath the appositive.

APPOSITIVE PHRASE

EXAMPLE: Harriet Danby, *her friend for many years,* is a lawyer.

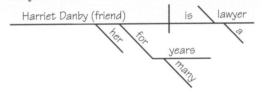

▶ **Exercise 5** Diagraming Appositives and Appositive Phrases Correctly diagram each sentence.
1. Gladys was a pianist, a very talented performer.
2. I know the author of that book, one of the top bestsellers.
3. The rat, a rodent, has one pair of upper incisors.
4. Mario prepared the meal, a lavish feast with six courses.
5. Their staircase, a spiral flight of steps, needs repair.

Participles and Participial Phrases

Because participles act as adjectives, they are placed directly beneath the noun or pronoun they modify. Unlike adjectives, however, participles are positioned partly on a horizontal line that extends from the slanted line. An adverb or adverb phrase that modifies a participle is placed below it. When a participle has a complement, the complement is also placed in its normal position, on the horizontal line with the participle, separated from the participle by a short vertical line. See the example on the next page.

EXAMPLE: *Carefully reviewing books for children,* Russell stays busy.

▶ **Exercise 6** Diagraming Participles and Participial Phrases

Correctly diagram each sentence.

1. He held a basket brimming with goodies.
2. Going without sleep, many volunteers worked into the night.
3. This deserted island offers peace and tranquillity.
4. From the beehive came a loud buzzing noise.
5. Stalling without warning, the car caused a traffic jam.

Gerunds and Gerund Phrases

   A gerund that acts as a subject, direct object, or predicate nominative is diagramed on a pedestal above the main horizontal line of the diagram. Modifiers and complements that are part of a gerund phrase are added to the diagram in the usual way. Notice the shape of the line on which the gerund rests.

GERUND PHRASE

EXAMPLE: The lease forbids *keeping any pets on the premises.*

   A gerund or gerund phrase that acts as an indirect object or an object of a preposition is placed on a line slanting down from the main horizontal line.

GERUND PHRASE

EXAMPLE: His lecture gave *traveling to South America* new dimensions.

A gerund or gerund phrase that acts as an appositive is placed on a pedestal, in parentheses, next to the noun or pronoun it accompanies. The example below shows a diagram containing an appositive modifying a direct object.

GERUND PHRASE

EXAMPLE: We mastered one sport, *playing tennis.*

> **Exercise 7** Diagraming Gerunds and Gerund Phrases
Correctly diagram each sentence.
1. His favorite activity was hiking through the woods.
2. Achieving the position of senator will be very difficult.
3. Their ability to harmonize made songwriting exciting.
4. Clark's fear, injuring his elbow, kept him on the bench.
5. All of Jill's friends like helping her with her projects.

Infinitives and Infinitive Phrases

Infinitives and infinitive phrases can act as nouns, adjectives, or adverbs. An infinitive acting as a noun is generally diagramed on a pedestal just as a gerund is, but the line on which the infinitive rests is simpler.

INFINITIVE PHRASE

EXAMPLE: She wanted *to show us her stamp collection.*

If an infinitive phrase has a subject, add it at the left.

INFINITIVE PHRASE

EXAMPLE: We asked her *to stay.*

An infinitive acting as an adjective or adverb is diagramed much as a prepositional phrase is.

INFINITIVE

EXAMPLE: Beth was proud *to try.*

When an infinitive in a sentence does not include the word *to,* add it to the sentence diagram in parentheses.

INFINITIVE PHRASE

EXAMPLE: Clancy helped me *climb the ladder to the attic.*

▶ **Exercise 8** Diagraming Infinitives and Infinitive Phrases
Correctly diagram each sentence.
1. Gordon's greatest accomplishment was to write a novel about etiquette during the sixteenth century.
2. Her mother let Susan go to the movies.
3. To focus on just one problem would be advisable.
4. Her inclination was to tell him the truth about his idea.
5. The person to see about tickets has left.

Compound Sentences

To diagram a compound sentence, just diagram each independent clause separately. Then, join them at the verbs with a dotted line on which the conjunction or semicolon is placed.

INDEPENDENT CLAUSE

EXAMPLE: *A gentle breeze blew across the lake,* and

INDEPENDENT CLAUSE
the raft floated inland.

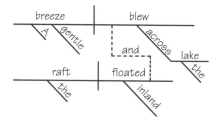

▶ **Exercise 9** **Compound Sentences** Diagram each sentence.

1. His temperature is high, but he remains alert.
2. Should I plant this cherry tree in that corner, or would you prefer it near the fence?
3. The steak was perfect, and the salad was excellent, but the dessert was too sweet.
4. Joan has little sense of her own worth; she never asserts herself.
5. Yesterday, we cleaned the attic and filled boxes with useless items; later, we went to the dump.

Complex Sentences

Complex sentences have an independent clause and one or more adjective, adverb, or noun clauses. Each clause is placed on a separate horizontal line.

Adjective Clauses To diagram a sentence with an adjective clause, first diagram the independent clause. Then, diagram the adjective clause beneath it. Connect the two clauses with a dotted line that extends from the modified noun or pronoun in the independent clause to the relative pronoun or relative adverb in the adjective clause. The position of the relative pronoun changes depending on its function in the adjective clause. In the following example, the relative pronoun is acting as the direct object of the adjective clause.

ADJECTIVE CLAUSE

EXAMPLE: My friend *whom you met yesterday* just called.

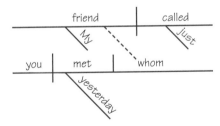

When a relative pronoun acts as an object of a preposition or as an adjective or when a clause is introduced by a relative adverb, the dotted line must be bent to connect the clauses.

ADJECTIVE CLAUSE

EXAMPLE: I need time *when I can study.*

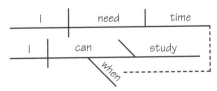

Adverb Clauses The main difference between a diagram for an adjective clause and one for an adverb clause is that the subordinating conjunction for an adverb clause is written on the dotted line. This line extends from the modified verb, adjective, adverb, or verbal in the main clause to the verb in the adverb clause.

ADVERB CLAUSE

EXAMPLE: To look *before you leap* is good advice.

Noun Clauses When diagraming a sentence with a noun clause, first diagram the independent clause. Then, place the entire noun clause on a pedestal extending upward from the position the noun clause fills in the sentence. Notice that the pedestal meets the noun clause at the verb.

NOUN CLAUSE

EXAMPLE: *Whatever you decide* is fine with me.

When an introductory word in a noun clause has no function in the clause, it is written alongside the pedestal.

NOUN CLAUSE

EXAMPLE: The question, *whether Jonas is truly sorry*, will be revealed in the next episode.

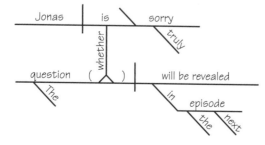

> **Exercise 10** Diagraming Complex Sentences Correctly diagram each sentence.
> 1. Barbara McClintock is a scientist whom I greatly admire.
> 2. He drives as if he were in a race.
> 3. They told us that they would be late.
> 4. We hope to complete this job while time remains.
> 5. The side lawn is the place where we always played croquet.

Compound-Complex Sentences

To diagram a compound-complex sentence, begin by diagraming and connecting each of the independent clauses just as you would if you were diagraming a compound sentence. Then, diagram and connect each subordinate clause.

ADVERB CLAUSE

EXAMPLE: *When we bought our microwave oven*, we considered that brand, but we decided *that it was too expensive.*

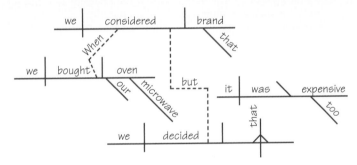

> **Exercise 11** Diagraming Compound-Complex Sentences Correctly diagram each sentence.
> 1. Because it rained, we missed the game that had been scheduled, but we still had a good time.
> 2. We waited until the plane landed, and then we rushed to the gate where the passengers would enter.

Index

Note: **Bold numbers** show pages on which basic definitions or rules appear.

A

a, an, 444
a while, awhile, **446**
Abbreviations
  capitalizing, **467**
  guide to, 686–689
  punctuating, **474**
-able, 586
Abstract Nouns, 216
Accent, 310
accept, except, **444**
Action, **54**, 603, 604
Action Verbs, **228**–229, 233
Active Voice, 57, **58**, **382**–385
ACT Test Preparation
  See SAT/ACT Test Preparation
adapt, adopt, **444**
Addresses, Punctuating, 487
Adjective Clauses, **323**–328
  combining sentences using, 20, 345–346
  essential and nonessential, 484
  introductory words for, 334
  relative adverbs with, 327
  relative pronouns with, 326
  semicolons with, 496
  See also Clauses
Adjective Phrases, **300**–301
  See also Prepositional Phrases
Adjectives, 240–251
  adjective phrases and, 300, 302
  capitalizing, **465**
  commas with, 74, **479**, **480**, 489
  compound, **246**
  coordinate, 74, **479**, 480
  cumulative, 479, 480
  defined, 242
  degrees of, **426**
  demonstrative, 247
  identifying, **255**–256
  indefinite, 248
  infinitives used as, 316
  interrogative, 247
  as modifiers, **242**–243
  noun clauses used as, 334
  nouns used as, **244**
  possessive, 247
  predicate, **296**
  pronouns used as, **247**–248, **326**
  proper, **245**, 465, 531
  verbs used as, **249**
  See also Modifiers; Using Modifiers
adopt, adapt, **444**
Adventure Stories, 49

Adverb Clauses, **328**–331
  combining sentences using, 20, 345–346
  elliptical, **330**–331
  introductory words for, 334
  subordinate, **328**–330
Adverb Phrases, **302**–303
  See also Prepositional Phrases
Adverbs, 240–241, 252–257
  adjective phrases and, 302
  conjunctive, 268–269, 482, **494**
  degrees of, 426
  identifying, **255**–256, 263, 267–268
  infinitives used as, 316
  as modifiers, **252**–253
  nouns used as, **253**–254
  opening sentences with, 352
  relative, 323, **327**
  See also Modifiers; Using Modifiers
Advertisements, 92–105
  defined, **93**
  drafting, 98
  editing and proofreading, 103
  model from literature, 94
  prewriting, 95–97
  publishing and presenting, 104
  revising, 99–102
  rubric for self-assessment, 104
  types of, 93
Advice Columns, 153
affect, effect, 444
after, 267
Agendas, Group Meeting, 631
Agreement, 168, **404**–423
  See also Pronoun-Antecedent Agreement; Subject-Verb Agreement
ain't, **444**
Aircraft, Names of, **464**, **515**
all-, **526**
all ready, already, **444**
all right, alright, **445**
all together, altogether, **445**
Allusion, 9
Almanacs, 620, 648
American Psychological Association (APA) Style, 170, 674, 676
among, between, 445
Amounts
  apostrophes with, 536
  subject-verb agreement for, 413
Analogies, **571**, 599, 626, 627
Analyses Papers, **195**
-ance, 90, 586
and, 265, **408**, **418**, 476, 493
and, but, 41

and, or, 276
Anecdotes, **33**
Animals, Proper Names of, **461**
ante-, anti-, 575
Antecedents, 417
  pronoun agreement with, 417–423
  of pronouns, 187, **220**, 225, 226
Anthologies, 61, 172, 621
Antonyms, **570**, 619
anxious, **445**
anywhere, **445**
APA Style. *See* American Psychological Association (APA) Style
Apostrophes, **534**–543
Appendices, in Textbooks, 589
Applications, Employment, **205**, 211
Appositive Phrases, **304**–306
Appositives, **303**–304
  essential, 304, 484
  nominative pronouns with, 390
  nonessential, 390, 484, **521**
  noun clauses as, **333**
  objective pronouns with, 393
  punctuation with, 496, 499–500, **521**
Appreciative Listening, 552
Arguments, Supporting, 84, 200, 549
  See also Evidence
Art, Fine, 559
  citing, 514
  See also Responding to Fine Art and Literature
Articles, Adjective, 243
as to, **445**
Asides, **523**
Assessment, 194–204
  defined, **195**
  types of, **195**
  See also Rubric for Self-Assessment; Writing for Assessment
at, **446**
Atlases, 554, 621
Audiences
  basing arguments on, 81
  choosing details for, 36, 66, 158, 180
  choosing language for, 142, 158, 180
  choosing tone for, 66
  creating profile for, 8
  evaluating topic for, 110
  impressing, in assessment, 197
  persuading, 96
  plan for identifying, 126

purpose planner and, 52
Audiotapes,
  practicing listening skills with, 551
  recording work on, 75, 549, 550
Authors' Strategies, 11, 33, 49, 63, 77, 93, 107, 123, 139, 155, 177, 195, 205
Autobiographical Writing, 32–47
  defined, **33**
  drafting, 38–39
  editing and proofreading, 46
  prewriting, 34–37
  publishing and presenting, 47
  revising, 40–45
  rubric for self-assessment, 47
  types of, 33
  See also Biographies
Awards, Names of, 464
awhile, a while, **446**

B

bad, badly, **429**, **446**
Balanced Comparisons, 433
Balances (transitions), for Paragraph Revision, 12
Bandwagon Appeals, **558**
Bar Graphs, 555
barely, 441
Basic Sentence Parts, 272–297
  direct objects, **287**–290
  indirect objects, **290**–291
  objective complements, **292**
  predicates, **274**–279
  subject complements, **294**–297
  subjects, 274–286
  test items for, 273
  See also Effective Sentences; Sentences
be, 231, 377, 541
because, **447**
because, since, 135
before, 267
"begging the question," 598
being as, being that, **447**
being, having, 307
beside, besides, **447**
between, among, **445**
Bias
  in media, 558
  in nonfiction, 596
  on Web sites, 622
Bibliographies, **674**
  sample entry for, 171
  textbook, 589
Biographies, **674**
  finding, in library, 614
  references for, 621

See also Autobiographical Writing
Blocks, Paragraph, 29
Blueprinting, 6, 34
Body, of Essays, 27
Books
  capitalizing titles of, **468**
  citing, **513**
  finding in library, 613–614
  punctuating titles of, 500
  See also Textbooks
"Borrowed" Words, 281, 310
Bracketing, 12
  See also Circling; Coding; Color-Coding; Highlighting; Underlining
bring, take, **447**
Brochures, **63**
Budgets, Developing, 637
Building Your Portfolio, **15**
  advertisements, 104
  anthologies, 61, 172
  assessment essays, 203
  audiotapes, 73
  book clubs, 190
  displays, 75
  e-mail, 136
  electronic essays, 120
  encouraging responses, 152
  guidance counselors, 203
  Internet publications, 172
  narratives, 47
  newspapers, 91, 190
  presentations, 120, 136
  problem-and-solution essays, 152
  storytelling, 47
  verbal sharing, 61
  Web sites, 104, 190
  See also Portfolios
Buildings, Names of, **462**
Bulletin Boards
  posting descriptions on, 75
Business Names
  apostrophes in, 536
  capitalizing, **463**
but, 265, 441, 476, 493
but, and, 41
by, buy, 103

C

Calendars, 636
Call Numbers, **613**, 614
Campaigns, 97
Capitalization, 456–470
  for first words, 458–460
  of parenthetical material, **524**
  of proper nouns, 218, **461**–464
  test items for, 457

in titles, 189, **466**–468
Captions, 590
Cases, 44, 388–395
  See also Nominative Case; Objective Case; Possessive Case
Catalogs
  electronic, 612
  library, **611**–612
  printed, 612
Cause-and-Effect Essays, 122–137
  defined, **123**
  drafting, 134–135
  editing and proofreading, 135
  prewriting, 124–127
  publishing and presenting, 136
  revising, 130–134
  rubric for self-assessment, 136
  types of, **123**
Cause-and-Effect Sequences, 599
CD-ROMs, 623
-cede, -ceed, -sede, 585
Chain of Events, 127
Chains, for Paragraph Revision, 12
Chapters, Punctuating Titles of, **516**
Characters
  developing, 52
  dialogue for, 55
  gathering details about, 53
  profiles for, 37
  sketches of, **63**
Charts, 561
Checklists, for Paragraph Revision, 185
Chicago Manual of Style, The (CMS), 170, 674, 677
Choosing a Form for Writing
  extensive, **4**
  focus on form, 10
  modes, **4**
  reflexive, **4**
Choosing Your Topic
  blueprinting, 6, 34, 64, 95
  bookshelves, browsing, 178
  calendars, browsing, 64
  celebrity lists, 156
  characters and settings, sketching, 50
  drawing and sketching, 64
  events, recalling, 34
  format for, 196
  freewriting, 50, 108
  geographical references, 156
  journal reviews, 178
  key words, 196
  listing, 108, 124, 178
  newspaper scans, 78, 124, 156
  peer discussions, 140, 178
  questions, skimming, 196

quicklists, 78
quotations, browsing, 50
scenes, sketching, 124
sentence starters, 78, 140
surveys, 95
See also Topic Bank Ideas
Chronological Order
  analyzing, 594
  for assessment, 198
  for cause-and-effect essays, 128
  creating coherence with, 26
  in descriptive writing, 69
  in research writing, 163
Circling
  important details, 99
  relationships, 130
  vague words, 72
  See also Bracketing; Coding;
    Color-Coding; Highlighting;
    Underlining
Circular Reasoning, 598
Citations
  in electronic indexes, 615
  elements for, 171
  guide for, 672–678
  internal, 678
  for literature, 183
  for quotations and figures, 113
  for speeches, 549
  See also Sources; Works-Cited
    Lists
Clarity
  commas for, **489**
  hyphens for, **528**
  prepositions for, 132
  revising for, 186
  semicolons for, 495
  transitions for, 132
  See also Coherence
Clauses, **298**–299, **322**–337
  adverb, **328**–331, 334
  combining sentences using,
    19–20, 345–346
  commas with, **478**
  defined, **298**
  elliptical, 330–331, **400**–401
  essential, 325
  introductory, **481**
  introductory words for, **333**–334
  negative words in, **441**
  nonessential, 325
  noun, **332**–335
  parallel, 86, **87**
  revising fragments of, **358**
  subject-verb agreement with,
    406
  See also Adjectives; Independent
    Clauses; Subordinate Clauses
Climaxes, **54**

Close Reading, 591
Closed Questions, **552**
Closings, Letter, **487**
Clubs, Names of, **463**
Cluster Diagrams, 594
  See also Topic Webs
CMS. *See Chicago Manual of Style*
  (CMS)
Coding, 100, 166
  See also Bracketing; Circling;
    Color-Coding; Highlighting;
    Underlining
Coherence
  in paragraphs, 25–26
  See also Clarity
Collections, Punctuating Titles of,
  517
Collective Nouns, 168, 216, **411**
Colons, **493**
  capitalization and, **458**
  expressions with, **505**
  parentheses and, 524
  quotation marks with, **508**
  rules for, **498**–501
Color-Coding
  elements, 186
  end marks, 100
  identifying support by, 85
  passive sentences, 57
  personal pronouns, 43
  related details, 131
  sentence types, 88
  structure, 114
  subject-verb patterns, 167
  subjects, 114, 186
  for unity, 69
  for variety, 42
  See also Bracketing; Circling;
    Coding; Highlighting;
    Underlining
Combining Sentences, 17–20,
  343–347
Commas, **476**
  vs. dashes, 521
  in dialogue, 60
  with expressions, **505, 506**
  parentheses and, 524
  quotation marks and, **508**
  rules for, 74, **476**–492
  run-ons and, 360
  semicolons and, 495, 496
Commercials, 557
Common Nouns, **218**
Communication, Verbal
  group, 547
  one-on-one, 629–630
  See also Listening Skills;
    Speaking Skills
Comparative Degree, 426

irregular forms of, **428**–431
regular forms of, **427**–428
rule for, **432**
Comparison-and-Contrast Essays,
  106–121
  assessment with, 195
  defined, **107**
  drafting, 112–113
  editing and proofreading, 119
  prewriting, 108–111
  publishing and presenting, 120
  revising, 114–118
  rubric for self-assessment, 120
  types of, **107**
Comparison-and-Contrast Order,
  26, 118, 198, 595
  See also Venn Diagrams
Comparison, Degrees of, **426**–437
complement, compliment, 292
Complements, **287**
  objective, **292**, 305
  subject, **294**
Complete Predicates, **274**
Complete Subjects, **274**
Complex Sentences, **42**
Compositions, **16**, 21–31
Compound Adjectives, **246**
Compound Direct Objects, **288**
Compound Nouns, **217, 536**, 538
Compound Objects, **343**
Compound Predicate Nominatives,
  390
Compound Prepositions, **260**
Compound Sentences, **42, 476,**
  344
  combining sentences into, 19,
    345
  creating, **344**
  objective pronouns in, 392
  punctuating, 119, **476**–477
  See also Sentences
Compound Subjects, 276–279
  combining sentences with, 18,
    343
  commas with, 476, **489**
  nominative pronouns in, 390
  verb agreement with, **408**–409
Compound Verbs, **277**–279
  combining sentences with, 18,
    343
  commas with, 476, 489
Compound Words, **527, 582**
Computers
  applying skills on, **639**
  creating visual aids on, 561, 562
  freewriting on, 36
  note-taking on, 610
  See also Word-Processing
    Programs

Conclusions
drawing, in reading fiction, 603
final paragraphs in essays, 27
matching introductions to,
184, 200
strengthening, 130
Concrete Nouns, **216**
Conflict, **54**
Conjugation, of Verbs, 376–379
Conjunctions, 19, 258–259,
265–271
connecting with, 116
coordinating, **117**, **265**, 360,
476
correlative, **117**, **265**
defined, **265**
identifying, 267–268
punctuating, 119
subordinating, **117**, **266**, 267,
328
types of, 117, 265–266
Conjunctive Adverbs, 19, **268**–269,
482, **494**
Connotation, **96**
in critical reading, 600
vs. denotation, **569**
Considering Your Audience and
Purpose. *See* Audiences;
Purpose for Writing
Contests, 659
Context
clues, **568**
historical, 604
Contractions
apostrophes with, 539, **541**–542
in dialogue, 56
possessive pronouns and, 394
Coordinate Adjectives, 74, **479**,
480
Coordinating Conjunctions, **117**
commas with, 476
list of, **265**
run-ons with, 360
Copyrights, 681
Correlative Conjunctions, 117,
265
Courses, Titles of, **468**
Creative Thinking, 634, 635
Credibility, Nonfiction, 596
Critical Listening, **551**–553
Critical Reading, 596–601
Critical Reviews, 177, 180
Critical Viewing Skills
analyze, 4, 32, 55, 68, 106, 128,
146, 150, 154, 161, 192, 194,
200, 204, 230, 237, 240, 243,
253, 256, 272, 282, 284, 291,
295, 296, 324, 386, 389, 392,
397, 433, 477, 489, 554, 591,
606, 608
apply, 73, 262, 369, 487, 507,
514, 525, 530, 539, 540,
543, 584
assess, 223
classify, 2
compare, 258, 329, 354, 359,
378, 434, 470, 612
compare and contrast, 31, 158,
197, 311, 340, 429, 435
connect, 16, 17, 76, 92, 217,
243, 249, 256, 267, 276, 362,
364, 366, 370, 383, 459, 466,
497, 505, 529, 579, 621, 628,
638
contrast, 338, 366, 383
deduce, 510, 548, 630
describe, 23, 29, 31, 228, 238,
261, 266, 309, 343, 345,
347, 360, 375, 391, 404,
410, 417, 421, 456, 460,
465, 482, 501, 523, 535
distinguish, 255, 438
draw conclusions, 399
evaluate, 317, 327
generalize, 188
identify, 214, 230, 244, 289,
424, 556
infer, 25, 221, 233, 303, 419,
546, 566, 570, 597
interpret, 62, 233, 449, 569,
577, 632
make a judgment, 137, 176,
357, 430
modify, 175
reflect, 89
relate, 84, 113, 122, 214, 306,
312, 334
respond, 217
speculate, 41, 48, 85, 138, 153,
173, 191, 218, 244, 315,
323, 408, 446, 464, 472,
495, 498, 517, 588, 601, 614
support, 221, 441, 581
Criticisms, Literary, 602
Cross-Curricular Connections
art, 432
fine art, 382
geography, 458
literature, 504
music, 350, 354, 426
physical education, 520
science, 242, 252, 294, 340,
396, 406, 472, 534
social studies, 216, 220, 228,
236, 260, 265, 274, 280,
287, 300, 322, 343, 368,
388, 417, 440, 444, 476,
493
Cubing, 67, 126
Cumulative Adjectives, **479**, 480

D

d', 542
Dangling Modifiers, 71
Dashes, **520**–522
Databases, Electronic, 623
Dates, Calendar
commas with, **486**
contractions in, 541
parentheses with, **523**
Days, Names of, **462**
Declarative Sentences, **101**, **340**
parentheses with, **524**
punctuating, **472**
Deductive Reasoning, 598
Degrees, Academic, 686
Degrees of Comparison, **426**–437
Deities, Capitalizing References
to, 463
Demonstrative Adjectives, **247**
Demonstrative Pronouns, **224**,
247
Denotation, **96**
vs. connotation, **569**
in critical reading, 600
Derived Words, Dictionary, 618
Description, 62–75
defined, **63**
drafting, 70–71
editing and proofreading, 74
prewriting, 64–67
publishing and presenting, 75
revising, 69–73
rubric for self-assessment, 75
telling through, 55
types of, **63**
Details
choosing, for audience, 66, 180
choosing, for purpose, 66, 180
circling important, 99
collecting, 143
color-coding related, 131
deleting unrelated, 40
historical, 84
order-of-importance for, 98
outlining, 69
underlining, 184
See also Gathering Details;
Providing Elaboration;
Supporting Details
Dewey Decimal System, **613**
Diagnostic Tests
for adjectives and adverbs, 241
for agreement, 405
for basic sentence parts, 273
for capitalization, 457
for effective sentences, 339

for modifiers, 425
for nouns, pronouns, and verbs, 215
for phrases and clauses, 299
for prepositions, conjunctions, and interjections, 259
for pronoun usage, 387
for punctuation, 471
for usage problems, 439
for verb usage, 367
Diagraming Sentences, 692–703
adjective clauses, 701
adverb clauses, 702
appositive phrases, 697
complements, 694–695
complex sentences, 701–703
compound sentences, 700–701
compound-complex sentences, 703
conjunctions, 693–694
gerunds and gerund phrases, 698–699
infinitives and infinitive phrases, 699–700
modifiers, 692–693
noun clauses, 702
participles and participial phrases, 697–698
prepositional phrases, 696–697
subjects and verbs, 692–693
Diagrams, 561
Dialects, 542
Dialogue
contractions in, 56, 542
developing plot with, 55
elaborating with, 39
formatting, 60
functional paragraphs with, 28
punctuating, 46, 60, 511–512
Diaries, 606
Diction, 30
Dictionaries, 572, **616–618**
different from, different than, **447**
Direct Address, Nouns of, 218
Direct Objects, **287–290**
adjective phrases and, 301
appositive phrases and, 305
compound, 288
gerunds used as, 312
indirect *vs.,* 291
infinitives used as, 316
noun clauses used as, **333**
pronouns used as, **392,** 393
relative pronouns used as, **326**
whom, whomever as, **398**
Direct Questions, 473
Direct Quotations
commas in, **488**
crediting sources of, 642

punctuating, **504**–512
Directions, Subjects in, **280**
Discussions, Group, 547, 567, **631**
Dividing Words, **530**–532
Documentaries, 137
described, 557
as reference tools, 623
Documentation, 171, 674–678
Documents
capitalizing names of, **462**
handwritten, 672
word-processed or typed, 673
doesn't, don't, **447**
done, **448**
Double Comparisons, 432
Double Negatives, **440,** 441, 442
Drafting, 5, **10**
from outlines, 145
thesis statements, 182
See also Providing Elaboration; Shaping Your Writing; Student Work in Progress, Drafting
Drama
interpretations, presenting, 565
reading, 604
See also Performances; Plays
due to, **448**

E

E-Mail,
sending essays via, 136
Editing and Proofreading, 5, **12–14**
for commonly confused words, 135
for *ie, ei* spelling errors, 202
in SAT/ACT, 670
mechanics for, 189
for punctuation errors, 46, 60, 74, 119
reference lists, 170–171
for spelling errors, 90, 586–587
test-taking and, **624**
that, which, 151
for *your, you're* usage, 103
Editorials, 77
effect, affect, **444**
Effective Sentences, 338–365
avoiding problems with, **354–365**
classifying functions of, **340–342**
combining for, **343**–349
creating variety for, 350–353
See also Basic Sentence Parts; Sentences
Effects, Organizing, 128
-efy, 586
ei, ie Words, 202, 585
Elaboration

in SEE technique, 10, 129
See also Providing Elaboration
-elect, **526**
Electronic Dictionaries, 616, 617
Electronic Indexes, 615
Electronic Maps, 621, 623
Elliptical Adverb Clauses, **330**–331
Elliptical Clauses, **330**–331, **400**–401
Elliptical Sentences, **488**
else, other, **434**–435
Empathic Listening, 552
"Empty" Words, 169, 201
-ence, 90, 586
Encyclopedias, 158, 620, 648
End Marks, **472**
color-coding, 100
correcting run-ons with, 360
parentheses with, 524
rules for, **472–475**
See also Exclamation Marks; Periods; Question Marks
Endnotes, 171
Entertaining Speeches, 548
-eous, 586
Episodes, Punctuating Titles of, **517**
-er, -est, **427,** 428, 432
-er, -or, 356
Essay Tests, **195,** 626
Essays
cause-and-effect, 122–137
comparison-and-contrast, 106–121
electronic, 120
personal, **195**
persuasive, 76–91
problem-and-solution, 138–153
punctuating titles of, **516**
sections in, 27
spelling in, 202
See also Exposition
Etymologies, **572,** 618
Euphemisms, 601
Evaluating Writing. *See* Peer Review; Reflecting on Your Writing; Rubric for Self-Assessment
Events
capitalizing names of, 462
gathering details about, 97
summarizing, in drama, 604
everywhere, **445**
Evidence
evaluating, in nonfiction, 596
methods for gathering, 82
types of, 84
See also Arguments
ex-, **526**

Exaggerations, 427
Examples
  citing, 143
  in dictionaries, 618
  elaborating with, 113, 199
  supporting, 23
except, accept, **444**
Exclamation Marks
  expressions with, **505, 506**
  quotation marks with, **508–509**
  rules for, **473**
Exclamatory Sentences, **101, 341**
  parentheses in, **524**
  punctuating, **473**
Exercises, in Textbooks, 590
Existence, Verbs Expressing, 231
Experiences, Personal
  connecting to literature, 9, 602, 603
Expert Testimony, 84
Explanations, Punctuating, 523
Expletives, 282
"Exploding the Moment," 39
Exposition, **123**
  in plots, **54**
  See also Cause-and-Effect Essays; Comparison-and-Contrast Essays; Essays; Problem-and-Solution Essays
Expressive Writing. *See* Description; Journals; Narration; Poems
Extemporaneous Speeches, **548**
Extension, in SEE Technique, 10, 129
Extensive Writing, **4**
Eyewitness Accounts, **33**

F

Fables, **49**
Fact Questions, **552**
Facts
  elaborating with, 113
  vs. opinions, 558, 597
  supporting, 23
Fading Technique, in videotaping, 564
Falling Action, **54**
Fantasies, **49**
farther, further, **448**
Fax (Facsimile) Cover Sheets, 210
Feminine Pronouns, 418
fewer, less, 448
Fiction
  analyzing and evaluating, 602
  finding, in library, **613**

strategies for reading, 603
Field Labels, in dictionaries, 618
Figurative Language
  recognizing and using, 94
  types of, **68**
Figures, Numerical, 113
Fill-in Questions, 625
Films
  citing, **514**
  evaluating historical information in, 603
Fine Art, 559
  See also Responding to Fine Art and Literature
First-Person Pronouns, 221, 222
Flashcards, 573
Flyers, 562
Footnotes, 171
for, 265, 476, 493
Foreign Words, 310, **515**
Form, in Writing Process, 10
Formal Language, 89
  in critical reviews, 180
  features of, 158
  vs. informal, 31, 188
  interjections in, 269
Formats
  computerized, 639
  for dialogue, 60
  for visual aids, 562
Forms, Business, **205, 210**–211
Fractions, Hyphenating, **526**
Fragments, **354**
  clause, **358**
  phrase, **356**–357
  recognizing, **354**–355
Freewriting, 36, 50
Functional Paragraphs, **28**, 41
further, farther, **448**
Future Perfect Tense, 149, 368, 369, 376
Future Tense, 149, 368, 369, 376

G

Gathering Details
  for advertisements, 97
  chain of events for, 127
  for characters, 37, 53
  citing examples for, 143
  cubing technique for, 67
  hexagonal writing for, 9, 181
  interviews for, 143
  note cards for, 127
  sensory word bins for, 9
  for settings, 37, 53
  sources for, 111
  surveys for, 143

using personal experiences for, 111
  See also Details; Providing Elaboration; Supporting Details
Gazetteers, 621
Gender, Agreement with, **417, 418**
General-to-Specific Organization, 69
Generalizations
  "glittering," **558**
  hasty, **598**
  in nonfiction, 596
Generating Topics. *See* Choosing Your Topic
Genre, reading in a wide variety of, 602–607
Geographical Terms, 475, **486**
  abbreviations for, 688
Gerund Phrases, **314**–315
Gerunds, **312**
  identifying, 313
  objects of, **392**
  possessive case with, **394**
  possessive pronouns and, 314
Glittering Generalities, **558**
Glossaries, 589
Goals
  personal, **633**
  professional, **633**
gone, went, **448**
good, well, 428
Government Bodies and Titles, 463
Grammar, Hands-on. *See* Hands-on Grammar
Grammar in Literature
  action verbs, **228**
  active and passive voice, 384
  adjectives, 245
  adverbs, 254
  apostrophes, 534
  commas, 479
  compound subjects, 277
  conjunctions, 267
  essential and nonessential phrases, 485
  modifiers, 430
  nominative and objective cases, 389
  noun clauses, 332
  nouns, 217
  past and present participles, 308
  personal pronouns, 223
  predicate nominatives, 295

prepositions, 261
punctuating dialogue, 512
semicolons, 497
sentence length, 351
subject-verb agreement, 407
subject-verb order, 283
use of *who*, 399
See also Hands-on Grammar
Grammar in SAT/ACT, 648–662
faulty parallelism, 654
faulty pronoun-antecedent
agreement, 652
faulty pronoun case, 650
faulty punctuation: comma use,
658
faulty punctuation: semicolon
use, 659
faulty subject-verb agreement,
648
faulty verb tense, 649
faulty word choice, 655
mixed constructions, 656
paragraph structure, 660
sentence fragments, 657
shifts in pronoun person, 653
transitions within a paragraph,
661
Grammar in Your Writing
active and passive voice, 58
agreement, 168
-ance, -ence words, 90
citing sources, 171
commas, 74
compound sentences, 119
conjunctions, 117
dangling and misplaced modifiers, 71
formatting and punctuating
dialogue, 60
homophones, 103
paragraphing dialogue, 46
parallel clauses, 87
pronoun cases, 44
pronouns and antecedents, 187
punctuating dialogue, 46
restrictive and nonrestrictive
clauses, 151
sentence functions, 101
styling titles, 189
transitional phrases, 133
use of *ie, ei*, 202
use of *since, because, then, than*,
135
verb tenses, 149
See also Hands-on Grammar
Graphic Organizers
creating, 560–562
charts, 561, 594

diagrams, 561
formatting, 562
graphs, 561
illustrations, 561
look at text structure to, 560
maps, 561
pictures, 561
set a purpose for, 560
tables, 561
Venn diagram, 595
See also Prewriting
interpreting
charts, 594
timeline, 594
Venn diagram, 595
Graphics
designing attractive, 98
effective use of, 560
in textbooks, 590
Graphs, 554–556, 561
Group Activities
discussions, 547, **567, 631**
reading aloud, 61, 152
Group Names, **463**
Guide Words, **616**

H

Hands-on Grammar
capitalization, 469
combining sentences with
phrases, 348
comparisons, 436
converting verbs to adjectives,
250
intransitive verbs, 234
inverted sentences, 285, 414
irregular verbs, 379
noun clauses, 335
prepositions and conjunctions,
271
pronoun usage, 402
semicolons, 502
usage problems, 454
See also Grammar in Literature;
Grammar in Your Writing
hardly, 441
Hasty Generalizations, **598**
having, being, 307
"He Said/She Said" Expressions,
505, 506
Headings, Textbook, 590
Helping Verbs
forming tenses with, 371–375
using negative, 440, 441
for verb phrases, **236**
here, there, 281–282
here's, there's, 410
Hexagonal Writing Technique,
9, 181

Highlighting
key words, 150
repeated words, 13
See also Bracketing; Circling;
Coding; Color-Coding;
Underlining
Historic Events and Periods,
Names of, **462**
Historical Articles, 123
Historical Details, 84
Holidays, Names of, **462**
Homophones, **570**
choosing correct, 103
spelling of, 202
Hyperbole, **68**
Hyphenated Words, **526**
Hyphens
function of, **520**
rules for, **526–532**

I

I, 459
-ible, 586
Ideas
adding dashes for dramatic,
520–522
connecting, 116, 146
extending, 101
in good writing, 3
incorporating, from research, 674
Idioms, 618
ie, ei, 202, 585
Illustrations, 23, 561
Images
envisioning, in poetry, 605
Imperative Sentences, **101, 341**
punctuating, **472, 473**
Importance, Order of, 26, 128,
163
Impressions, Writing, 52
in, into, **448**
Incidents, Autobiographical, **33**
Incomplete Questions
capitalizing, **458**
punctuating, **473**
Indefinite Adjectives, **248**
Indefinite Articles, 243
Indefinite Pronouns, 226
as adjectives, **248**
antecedent agreement with, **419**
possessive case with, **539**, 540
verb agreement with, **412**
Independent Clauses, **322–323**
colons with, **498**, 499–500
combining sentences with, 19,
344
punctuating, 476
semicolons with, **493–494**
See also Clauses

Indexes
  electronic, 615
  finding research clues in, 158
  literary, 621
  periodical, 615
  textbook, 589
  thumb, 616
Indirect Objects, **290**–**291**
  adjective phrases and, 301
  appositive phrases and, 305
  gerunds as, 312
  noun clauses as, **333**
  pronouns used as, **392**, 393
Indirect Questions, 472
Indirect Quotations
  punctuating, **504**
Inductive Reasoning, 598
Inferences
  drawing, in fiction, 603
  in nonfiction, 596
Infinitive Phrases, **133**, **319**
Infinitives, **316**–317, **318**
Inflated Language, 601
Inflected Forms, in dictionaries, 618
Informal Language, 89
  appropriate use of, 31
  example of, 158
  in journal entries, 180
  revising, 188
  in speeches, 548
Informal Tone, 150
Information
  gathering, from library, 159
  interpreting, oral, 551
Information Media, 557–558
  analyzing, 558
  and bias, 558
  commercial, 557
  documentary, 137, 557
  editorial, 77
  facts and opinions in, 558
  interview, 557
  loaded language and images, 558
  newscasts, 557
  nonprint materials as, 557
  purposes of, 557–558
  television news program, 557
Informative Speeches, **548**
-ing, **313**
Instances, Supporting, 23
Institutions, Names of, **463**
Intensive Pronouns, **222**
Interjections, **269**–**270**
  capitalizing, **458**
  punctuating, **473**
Internet
  art museums on, 559

catalogs on, 612
evaluating material on, 596
finding and evaluating information on, **622**–**623**
finding topics on, 9
learning to use, 639
narrowing a search, 679–681
printing information from, 127
researching on, 679–681
sharing research writing on, 172
See also Search Engines; Web Sites
Interpretations
  comparing and contrasting, 553
  preparing, 565
Interrogative Adjectives, **247**
Interrogative Pronouns, **225**
  as adjectives, **247**
Interrogative Sentences, **101**, **340**
  parentheses in, **524**
Interrupting Expressions, **506**
Interviews, 557
  conducting, 82
  gathering details through, 143
  in investigative research, 161
  keys to successful, **629**
Intransitive Verbs, **229**–230, 234
Introductions
  in essays, 27
  matching conclusions to, 184, 200
  strengthening, 130
  in textbooks, 589
Introductory Devices, 498–500
Introductory Words, **481**
  commas with, **481**
  for noun clauses, **333**–334
  punctuating, **505**
Inverted Sentences
  creating variety with, 167
  practice with, 414
  subject-verb agreement in, 168, **410**
  subject-verb order in, **280**–286
-ious, 586
Irony, 601
irregardless, 449
Irregular Verbs
  conjugating, 379
  principal parts of, **372**–375
Issues
  business, 139
  consumer, 139
  local, 139
  for problem-and-solution essays, 139
Italics
  rules for, **513**

in titles, 189
it's, its, 103, 202, 393, 539

J
Jargon, 601
Journals
  language and details in, 180
  reading, 606
  responding to literature in, 177
just, 449

K
Key Words
  finding topics with, 9
  highlighting, 150
  identifying, 197
  matching to thesis, 197
Key Words, Electronic
  finding information with, 373
  searching Internet with, 679
Keyboard Skills, 639
kind of, sort of, **449**
Know-Want-Learned (K-W-L) Charts, 159, 169

L
l', 542
Land Craft, Name of, **464**, **515**
Language(s)
  capitalizing names of, **463**
  choosing, for audience and purpose, 142, 158
  for effective speeches, 548
  evaluating, in nonfiction, 600–601
  formal *vs.* informal, 31, 89, 180, 188
  inflated, 601
  informal, 548
  rhetorical, 549
  standard and technical, 548
lay, lie, 450
Leads
  using enticing, 10
learn, teach, **450**
leave, let, **451**
Legibility
  cursive *vs.* print, 672
  manuscript preparation, 560
less, fewer, **448**
less, least, **427**
Letters
  business, **205**, **206**–**207**, 500
  to editors, 77
  reading, 606
Letters, of Alphabet
  citing, 515
  apostrophe and, **543**

Libraries
  on-line, 680
  planning research in, 159
  resources in, 611–614, 620–621
Library of Congress System, 614
like, **451**
Line Graphs, 555
Linking Verbs, **231**–233
  defined, **231**
  subject agreement with, **411**
Listening Skills
  asking questions, 547, 551
  critical listening, 551–553
  comparing personal interpreta-
    tions with those of others, 553
  distinguishing between fact and
    opinion, 558
  eliminating barriers to listening,
    551
  evaluating speeches, 550
  generating criteria for evalua-
    tions, 550
  identifying main idea and
    details, 551
  interaction, 629
  interviewing and, 629
  monitoring listening, 551
  nonverbal signals of speaker, 551
  preparing to listen, 551
  peer review and, 59, 73, 89,
    134, 150, 169, 188
  set a purpose for, 551, 552
  taking notes, summarizing and
    organizing, 551
  types of, 552
  vocabulary development
    through, 567
  See also Communication,
    Verbal; Speaking Skills
Listing, 200
Literary Analyses, 177
Literary Indexes, 621
Literary Writing, 602–605
Literature, Grammar in. *See*
  Grammar in Literature
Literature, Responding to. *See*
  Response to Literature
  See also Responding to Fine Art
    and Literature
Local Issues, 139
Logical Fallacies, 598
Logical Relationships, 118
Looping, 7, 80, 142
-ly, 254, 255, **527**

M

Magazines
  getting published in, 47
  punctuating titles of, 500

Web sites for, 615
Main Ideas
  developing single, 147
  locating and ranking, 200
  placement of, 99
  topic sentences and, 21–22
Main Points
  charting, 594
  color-coding support for, 11
  listing, 200
Maps, **554**, 561, 621, 623
Masculine Pronouns, 418
Math Skills, **638**
me, myself, I, 43
Measurements
  abbreviations for, 688
  subject-verb agreement for, 413
Mechanics
  in editing and proofreading, 189
  following conventions of, 14
Media, deconstructing informa-
    tion from, 558
Meeting Rooms, Names of, **462**
Meetings
  ground rules for, **631**
  minutes for, **205**, **208**–209
Memoirs, **33**
Memorials, Names of, **462**
Memory Aids, **580**
Messages
  responding to speakers', 551
Metaphors, **68**
Metric Measurement
    abbreviations, 688
Miscellaneous Problems in Usage,
    438–455
  list of common, 444–455
  negative sentences, 440–443
  test items for, 439
Misplaced Modifiers, **71**, 364–365
MLA Style. *See* Modern Language
    Association (MLA) Style
Models From Literature
  advertisements, 94
Modern Language Association
    (MLA) Style, 170, 674, 675,
    678
Modifiers, **71**
  adding to enhance description,
    70
  degrees of comparison for, 426
  hyphenating compound, **527**
  infinitives used as, 316
  irregular forms of, **428**–431

  misplaced, 361–364
  punctuating nonessential, **521**
  regular forms of, **427**–428
  See also Adjectives; Adverbs;

  Using Modifiers
Money Management, **637**
Months, Names of, **462**
Monuments, Names of, **462**
Mood
  creating, 68
more, most, **427**, 432
Movies. *See* Films
Multimedia
  working with, 563
Multimedia Presentations, 563
Multiple-Choice Questions, 625
Music
  citing titles of, **514**
  punctuating titles of, **517**

N

Names
  apostrophes with, 536
  capitalizing, 461–464
  citing, **515**
  contractions for, 542
  for family members, 218
  using commas with, **486**
Names, Organizational, 412
Narration, 49
  See also Autobiographical
    Writing; Short Stories
Narratives, Personal, **33**
Narrowing Your Response, 197
Narrowing Your Topic
  in advertisements, 96
  carbon paper for, 36
  cubing technique for, 126
  developing main character for,
    52
  looping for, 7, 80, 142
  research clues for, 158
  topic webs for, 68, 180
Nationalities, Names of, **463**
Negative Sentences, 440–443
News Media, Forms of, 557
News Programs, 623
Newspapers
  citing, **513**
  getting published in, 47
  reading, 606
  scanning for topics in, 124
  school and local, 91
  student, 190
  Web sites for, 615
Nominative Case
  for pronouns, **390**–391, 396–397
  usage of, 388–389
  use of, **44**
Nominatives, Predicate. *See*
    Predicate Nominatives
Nonfiction
  analyzing and evaluating, 596

applying modes of reasoning in, 598–599
distinguishing facts from opinions in, 597
finding, in library, **613**
identifying purpose and language in, 600–601
Nonrestrictive Appositives, 304
Nonrestrictive Clauses, **151**
Nonverbal Strategies, 549
nor, 265, 476, 493
not, 541
Notebooks, 609, 610
Notes
  elaborating on, 164
  marginal, 165
  methods for taking, **610**
  organizing details with, 127
  organizing findings with, 160
  preparing outline from, 162–163
  in research writing, 160
  taking, at meetings, 631
Noun Clauses, **332–335**
Nouns, 214–219
  as adjectives, 242, 244
  as adverbs, **253–254**
  capitalizing proper, **461–464**
  cases for, **388–389**
  categories of, **216**
  collective, 168, **216**, 411
  commas with, 489
  common and proper, **218**
  compound, **217**, **536**, 538
  concrete and abstract, **216**
  defined, **214**, **216**
  of direct address, 481, 482
  infinitives used as, 316
  opening sentences with, 352
  plural forms for, 581–582
  possessive case for, **394**, **535–538**
  proper, 245, 465, 531
  that look like plurals, 411
  See also Appositives; Gerunds
nowhere, **445**
Number
  concept of, 406
  pronoun-antecedent agreement with, **417–418**
Numbers
  apostrophes in, **543**
  citing, **515**
  colons with, 500
  hyphenating, **526**
  parentheses with, **523**
  using commas with, **488**

O

O, **459**

o', 542
Objective Case, **392**–393
  for pronouns, 396, 398
  usage of, **388**–389
  use of, **44**
Objective Complements, **292**
  appositive phrases and, 305
Objective Pronouns
  function of, 43
  usage of, **392**–393
  whom, whomever, 396, 398
Objective Tests, 624–626
Objects
  compound, 343
  descriptions of, **63**
  direct. *See* Direct Objects
  gathering details about, 97
  of gerunds, **392**
  indirect. *See* Indirect Objects
  of infinitives, **392**
  of participles, **392**
Objects of Prepositions
  appositive phrases and, 305
  direct objects *vs.*, 289
  gerunds as, 312
  indirect objects *vs.*, 291
  infinitives used as, 316
  noun clauses as, **333**
  in prepositional phrases, 262
  pronouns used as, **392**, 393
  relative pronouns as, **326**
  whom, whomever as, **398**
Observations, Personal, **63**, 199
of, **451**
Omissions, Commas for, **488**
only, **451**
Open-Book Essays, 202
Open-Ended Questions, 552
Openers, Sentence, 352
Opinions
  vs. facts, 558, 597
Optimistic Tone, 150
or, 265, 476, 493
or, and, 276
-or, -er, 356
or, nor, **408**–409, 417
Order
  for coherence, 26
  comparison-and-contrast, 26, 198, 595
  for details, 98
  of importance, 58, 128, 162
  part-to-whole, 162
  for research drafts, 163
  spatial, 26, 69
  subject-verb, **280**–286, 352
  See also Chronological Order; Organization
Orders, Verbal, 280

Organization
  in good writing, 3
  logical methods of, 128
  methods for, 198
  strategies for, 69, 162
  See also Shaping Your Writing; Order
Organizations, Names of
  apostrophes in, 536
  capitalizing, **463**
  subject-verb agreement and, 412
other, else, **434**–435
Outlines
  for details, 69
  drafting from, 145
  expanding on, 145
  modified, 610
  preparing, 162–163
  problem-solution, 144
  punctuation in, **474**
  for reading material, **593**
Overall Structure, Revising. *See* Revising Overall Structure, Strategies for
Overused Words, 134, 682–683
  list of, 682–683
  underlining and replacing, 134
Overviews, Textbook, 590
Ownership, Possessive Case for, **537**

P

Paintings
  capitalizing titles of, **468**
  citing titles of, **514**
Paragraphs, **16**
  in essays, 27–29
  focusing, 147
  functional, **28**, 41
  patterns for, 24
  quotation marks for, **511**
  strengthening unity among, 131
  structuring, with TRI/PS/QA, 83
  transitions, 661
  types of, 28–29
  writing effective, 21–26
  See also Revising Paragraphs, Strategies for
Parallel Structure
  creating, 86, 101
  creating, with adjectives, 478
Parallelisms
  faulty, 654
Paraphrases
  crediting sources of, 674
Parentheses
  function of, **520**
  rules for, **523–525**

Parenthetical Expressions
  commas with, **482**, 484
  dashes with, 521–**522**
Part-to-Whole Order, 162
Participation, Effective, **632**
Participial Phrases, **310**–311
  defined, **133**, **310**
  essential *vs.* nonessential, 484
  semicolons with, 496
Participles, **307**
  identifying, 309, 313
  opening sentences with, 352
  past and present forms of,
    307–308
Parts of Speech
  labels for, 618
  list of, 214
Passive Voice, 57, **58**, **382**–385
Past Participles, 307, 371–375
Past Perfect Tense
  basic and progressive forms for,
    149, 368
  conjugations for, 376
  expressing time through, 369
Past Tense
  basic and progressive forms for,
    149, 368
  conjugations for, 376
  expressing time through, 369
  verb forms for, 371–375
Patterns
  identifying subject-verb, 167
Peer Review
  asking questions for, 118, 150
  focusing for, 13
  K-W-L charts for, 169
  plus-and-minus charts for, 73
  point/counterpoint in, 89
  questioning, 102
  revising informal language for,
    188
  "say back" strategy for, 59, 134
  worksheets for, 45
Penmanship, 672
People
  capitalizing titles for, **466**–468
  descriptions of, **63**
  working with, 629–630
Performances, **550**, 565
  See also Drama; Plays
Periodicals
  capitalizing titles of, **468**
  citing, **513**
  finding and using, **615**
  on-line, 680
  punctuating titles of, 500
  student, 691
Periods
  with expressions, **506**

quotation marks with, **508**
  rules for, **472**, **474**
Person, Pronoun-Antecedent
    Agreement With, **417**, **418**
Personal Allusion, 9
Personal Essays, **195**
Personal Narratives, **33**
Personal Observations, **199**
Personal Pronouns, **221**, 223
  antecedent agreement with,
    417–418, 419, **420**–422
  conjugating tenses with,
    376–378
  evaluating, 63
  possessive case with, **539**, 540
Personification, **68**
Persuasion
  in advertising, 96
    See also Advertisements
  evaluating and critiquing, 558
  in nonfiction, 596
Persuasive Essays, 76–91
  defined, **77**
  drafting, 83–84
  editing and proofeading, 90
  planning, 664
  prewriting, 78–82
  publishing and presenting, 91
  revising, 85–89
  rubric for self-assessment, 91
  types of, **77**
Persuasive Speeches, **77**, **548**
Persuasive Techniques
  bandwagon appeal, **558**
  evaluating, 558
  in advertisements, 558
  glittering generalities, **558**
  symbols, 558
Phrases, **298**–321
  adjective, **300**–301
  adverb, **302**–303
  appositive, **304**–306
  combining sentences with, 17,
    347
  defined, **298**
  essential, 310
  gerund, **314**–315
  infinitive, 319
  introductory, **481**
  nonessential, 310
  parallel, 86
  parentheses with, **524**
  revising fragments of, 356–357
  subject-verb agreement with,
    406
  transitional, **133**
  verb, **236**–238
  verbal, **307**–321
  See also Participial Phrases;

Prepositional Phrases
Pictures, in textbooks, 590
Pie Graphs, **556**
Places, Names of
  capitalizing, **462**
  commas with, **486**
  descriptions of, 63
Plagiarism, **674**
Plays
  capitalizing titles of, **468**
  citing, **513**
  See also Performances; Drama
Plot Analyzers, 56
Plot
  diagrams, 38, 54
  elements of, **54**
  revealing through dialogue, 55
Plural Nouns
  possessive case for, **535**–536,
    538
  subject-verb agreement with,
    168
Plural Subjects, **406**–407
Plural Verbs, **406**–416
Plurals
  in dictionaries, 618
  spelling of, 581–582
Plus-and-Minus Charts, 73
Poems
  capitalizing titles of, **468**
  citing, **513**
  punctuating titles of, **516**
Poetry
  capitalizing words in, **459**
  reading, 605
Point-by-Point Organization, 112,
    198
Point/Counterpoint Peer Revision,
    89
Political Parties, Names of, **463**
Polls, Research, 161
Portfolios
  building and reviewing, 15
  See also Building Your Portfolio
Position Papers, **77**
Positive Degree, **426**
Possessive Adjectives, **247**
Possessive Case, **394**
  apostrophes with, **535**–540
  usage of, **388**–389
Possessive Pronouns
  as adjectives, **247**
  gerunds and, 314
  usage of, **394**
Predicate Adjectives, **296**
Predicate Nominatives, **294**–295,
    390
  adjective phrases and, 301
  appositive phrases and, 305

gerunds as, 312
infinitives used as, 316
noun clauses as, **333**
who, whoever as, **397**
Predicates, 274–279
complete, **274**
simple, **275–276**
Predictions, **123**
making, in reading, 603
Prefaces, 589
Prefixes
all-, **526**
ante-, anti-, 575
capitalizing, **465**, **467**
d', 542
dividing words with, **530**
ex-, **526**
hyphenating, **526**
l', 542
o', 542
rules for adding, **575–576**
self-, **526**
spelling words with, 583
Prepositional Phrases, 133, **262**
as adjectives, 300–301
as adverbs, 302–303
commas with, 476, **478**, 489
identifying, **318**
opening sentences with, 352
Prepositions, 258–264
compound, 260
defined, **260**
identifying, 263, 267–268
objects of. *See* Objects of
Prepositions
words used as, **260–261**
Present Participles, 307, 371–375
Present Perfect Tense
basic and progressive forms for,
149, 368
conjugations for, 376
expressing time through, 369
Present Tense
basic and progressive forms for,
149, 368
conjugations for, 376
expressing time through, 369
verb forms for, 371–375
Presentations
for cause-and-effect essay, 136
evaluating, 550
interpretive, 565
multimedia, 137, 563
performing and interpreting, 565
speech, 550
video, 564
See also Publishing and
Presenting
Prewriting, **5**, 6–9

See also Audiences; Choosing
Your Topic; Gathering Details;
Narrowing Your Topic; Purpose
for Writing; Student Work in
Progress, Prewriting
Primary Sources, 111
Print Media
getting published in, 47
Problem-and-Solution Essays,
138–153
defined, **139**
drafting, 144–145
editing and proofreading, 151
prewriting, 140–143
publishing and presenting, 152
revising, 146–150
rubric for self-assessment, 152
types of, **139**
Problem-and-Solution Paragraphs
examples of, 83, 115
outline for, 144
placing topic sentences with,
24
revising paragraphs with, 166
Problems
connecting solutions to, 146
steps in solving, **634**
Process Explanations, **123**
Profiles, Developing Audience, 8
Progressive Tenses
conjugations for, 377
examples of, 149, 368
Pronoun-Antecedent Agreement
indefinite pronouns, 419
personal pronouns, 417–418
reflexive pronouns, 420
special problems with, 420–422
Pronoun Usage, 386–403
cases, **398**–395
special problems in, 396–401
test items for, 387
Pronouns, 214–215, **220–227**
as adjectives, **247–248**
antecedents for, 187, 220, 225,
226
apostrophes with, **539–540**
cases for, 44, **388**–389
demonstrative, 224, 247
faulty antecedent agreement,
652
faulty case, 650
feminine/masculine, 418
intensive, 222
interrogative, 225, 247
nominative case for, **390–391**,
396–397
objective case for, **392–393**,
396, 398
possessive case for, 247, 314, 394

reflexive, 222, 420
relative, 224, 323, 326
shifts in person, 653
special problems with, 396–401
See also Appositives; Indefinite
Pronouns; Personal Pronouns
Pronunciation Keys, 617
Proofreading
key areas in, 14
in five minutes, 670
in research writing, 170
standard symbols for, **690**
See also Editing and
Proofreading
Proper Adjectives, **245**
capitalizing, **465**
dividing, **531**
Proper Nouns, **218**
capitalizing, **461–464**
dividing, **531**
as proper adjectives, 245
used as adjectives, 465
Providing Elaboration
adding dialogue for, 39
building with evidence for, 84
citing passages for, 183
citing quotations and figures
for, 113
creating figurative language, 68
elaborating on notes, 164
expanding outlines for, 145
"exploding the moment" for, 39
giving details for, 199
giving examples for, 113
including testimonials, statistics,
and graphics for, 98
providing facts for, 113
using dialogue for, 55
using SEE technique for, 10, 129
See also Details; Gathering
Details; Supporting Details
Public-Service Announcements,
93
Public Speaking, **548–550**
Publications
citing, **513**
Internet, 172
on-line, 691
student, 691
Publishing
in printed media, 47
Publishing and Presenting, **5**, **15**
strategies for, 15
*See also specific forms of writing,
e.g.,* Persuasive Essays
Punctuation, 470–543
in adjective clauses, 324–325
apostrophes, 534–543
colons, **498–501**

commas, **476**–492
for compound sentences, 119
for conjunctions, 119
dashes, 520–522
in dialogue, 46, 60, **511**–512
end marks, **472**–475
faulty comma use, 658
faulty semicolon use, 659
hyphens, 526–532
parentheses, **523**–525
of parenthetical material, **524**
quotation marks, **504**–513,
    516–518
reading according to, 605
semicolons, **493**–497
test items for, 471
underlining as, **513**–516
See also specific types
Purpose for Writing
in assessment situations, 197
choosing details and tone for,
    66
choosing language and details
    for, 158, 180
creating a planner for, 52
entertaining and informing, 36
evaluating a topic for, 110
identifying, 8
language types for, 142
in nonfiction, 596, 600
persuading and selling, 96
plan for identifying, 126
planner for, 81
Purpose Planners, 52, 81, 126

Q

QARs. *See* Question-Answer
    Relationships
Question and Answer Paragraphs
examples of, 83, 115
revising paragraphs with, 166
Question-Answer Relationships
    (QARs), 591
Question Marks, 472, **473**
with expressions, **505**, **506**
quotation marks with, **508**–
    509
Questions
capitalizing, **458**
direct, 473
direct objects in, 288
in group discussions, 547
incomplete, 473
indirect, **472**
parallel, 86
in peer revision, 118, 150
punctuating, **472**–474
in SQ4R method, **592**
subjects in, **280**

in textbooks, 590
types of, 552
types of tests, **625**–627
Quotation Marks
in dialogue, 46, **60**, **511**–512
rules for, **504**–512
with titles, 189, **516**–517
titles without, **518**
Quotations
books of, 621
capitalizing, **458**–459
citing for elaboration, 113
colons with, **498**–499
direct, 488, 674
indirect, **504**
proofreading, 165, 170
punctuating direct, **504**–512
punctuating quotations within,
    511

R

Radio
advertising on, 93
citing series on, **514**
Ratiocination, **11**
Reading
critical, for nonfiction, 596–601
developing vocabulary through,
    567
from literary writing, 602–605
outlines for, **593**
and replacing, 188
sources for, 606–607
in SQ4R method, **592**
strategies for, **591**–592
from textbooks, 589–590
Reading Aloud
checking grammar and style by,
    351
checking transitions while, 118
finding errors while, 151
sharing short stories by, 61
Reading Comprehension in
    SAT/ACT, 641–647
long passage, 642
paired reading passages, 644
short passage, 646
Reading Skills, 588–607
in literary writing, 602–605
methods and tools for, 589–595
in nonfiction, 596–601
question-answer relationships,
    591
sources for, 606–607
SQ4R method (survey, question,
    read, recite, record, review),
    592
Reasoning, applying modes of,
    598–599

Reciting, in SQ4R Method, **592**
Recording, in SQ4R method, **592**
Reference Skills
CD-ROM references, 623
dictionaries, **572**, 620–622
electronic catalogs, 612
electronic databases, 623
Internet and media
    resources, 622–623
library resources, 611–623
note-taking, 610
periodicals and periodical
    indexes, 615
thesaurus, **572**, 619
References
colons in, **500**
creating and checking lists of,
    170–171
in libraries, 614
on-line, 680
parenthetical, 171
types of, **620**–621
Reflecting on Your Reading, 607
Reflecting on Your Speaking,
    Listening, Viewing, and
    Representing, 565
Reflecting on Your Study,
    Reference, and Test-Taking
    Skills, 627
Reflecting on Your Vocabulary,
    Spelling, and Proofreading
    Skills, 587
Reflecting on Your Workplace
    Skills and Competencies, 639
Reflecting on Your Writing, **15**
for advertisements, 104
for assessments, 203
for autobiographical writing,
    47
for cause-and-effect essays, 136
for comparison-and-contrast
    essays, 120
for description, 75
for persuasive essays, 91
for problem-and-solution essays,
    152
for research writing, 172
for response to literature, 190
for short stories, 61
Reflective Listening, 552
Reflexive Pronouns
antecedent agreement with, 420
defined, **222**
Reflexive Writing, **4**
Regular Verbs, **371**–372
Relationships
adding transitions for, 118
circling to identify, 130
clarifying with transitions, 132

common analogy, 626
prepositions clarifying, 261
question-answer, 591
Relative Adverbs
adjective clauses with, **323**–324
within clauses, 327
Relative Pronouns
adjective clauses with, **323**–324
clauses with, **326**
defined, **224**
Reliability
evaluating, in nonfiction, 597
of Internet resources, 681
Religions, Capitalizing References
to, **463**
Representing Skills, 560–565
Research
finding unbiased, 82
incorporating ideas from, 674
information sources for, 620
investigative, 161
for speeches, 549
using Internet for, 158, 172,
679–681
See also Reference Skills;
Research Writing
Research Writing, 154–175
accessing prior knowledge for,
156–161
defined, **155**
drafting, 162–164
editing and proofreading, 170
generating research questions,
156–161
prewriting, 156–161
publishing and presenting, 172
revising, 165–169
rubric for self-assessment, 172
types of, **155**
Resolution, **54**
Responding to Fine Art and
Literature
for advertisements, 95
for autobiographical writing,
35
for cause-and-effect essays, 125
for comparison-and-contrast
essays, 109
defined, **177**
for description, 65
for persuasive essays, 79
for problem-and-solution
essays, 141
for research writing, 157
for response to literature, 179
for short stories, 51
types of, **177**
Response to Literature, 176–193
defined, **177**

drafting, 182–183
editing and proofreading, 189
prewriting, 178–181
publishing and presenting, 190
revising, 184–188
rubric for self-assessment, 190
types of, **177**
Restrictive Appositives, 304
Restrictive Clauses, 151
Résumés, 629
Reviewing, in SQ4R method, **592**
Reviewing Work. *See* Peer Review;
Reflecting on Your Writing;
Revising
Revising, **5, 11–13**
dialogue, 56
informal language, 89
systematic approach to, 11
See also Peer Review; Revising
Overall Structure, Strategies for;
Revising Paragraphs, Strategies
for; Revising Sentences,
Strategies for; Revising Word
Choice, Strategies for; Student
Work in Progress, Revising
Revising Overall Structure,
Strategies for
circling relationships, 130
color-coding by subject, 114
color-coding support for main
points, 11
color-coding supporting details,
85
connecting ideas, 146
deleting unrelated details, 40
listing main points, 200
marginal notes, 165
outlining details, 69
placement of main ideas, 99
underlining details, 184
using plot analyzers, 56
Revising Paragraphs, Strategies for
checklists, 185
circling important details, 99
coding to identify structure, 166
color-coding for unity, 69
color-coding related details, 131
creating parallelism, 86
forming functional, 41
locating and ranking main ideas,
200
questioning choices in, 147
using contractions, 56
using steps, stacks, chains, and
balances, 12
using TRI/PS/QA, 115
Revising Sentences, Strategies for
adding modifiers, 70
bracketing sentence openers, 12

checking beginnings, 201
clarifying relationships, 132
color-coding clues, 88
color-coding elements, 186
color-coding end marks, 100
color-coding for variety, 42
color-coding passive sentences,
57
color-coding subject-verb patterns, 167
combining, 17–20, 343–347
extending ideas, 101
naming verb tenses, 148
using conjunctions, 116
Revising Word Choice, Strategies
for
adding transitions, 118
color-coding personal pronouns, 43
deleting "empty and hedging
words," 201
deleting empty words, 169
evaluating tag words, 59
highlighting repeated words, 13
highlighting to change tone, 150
reading aloud, 118
reading and replacing, 188
replacing dull words, 102
replacing vague words, 72
revising informal language, 89
underlining repeated words,
134
Rhetorical Strategies, 549
Rising Action, **54**
Roots, Word, **574**–577
Rubric for Self-Assessment, 15
for advertisements, 104
for assessments, 203
for autobiographical writing, 47
for cause-and-effect essays, 136
for comparison-and-contrast
essays, 120
for description, 75
for persuasive essays, 91
for problem-and-solution essays,
152
for research writing, 172
for response to literature, 190
for short stories, 61
Run-on Sentences, **359**
correcting, 360–361
types of, 359

S

Salutations
colons in, 500
using commas with, **487**
SAT/ACT Test Preparation, 640–671
grammar, 648–662

reading comprehension,
641–647
writing, 662–671
"Say Back" Strategy, 59, 134
scarcely, 441
Schedule, Study, 609
Schools, Names of, 462
Science-Fiction Stories, **49**
Scriptures, Capitalizing References
to, **463**
Sculpture Titles, **514**
Sea Craft, Names of, **464**, **515**
Search Engines
tips for using, 679–680
Seasons, Names of, **462**
Second-Person Pronouns, 221,
222
Secondary Sources, 111
-sede, 585
SEE Technique. *See* Statement,
Extension, Elaboration (SEE)
Technique
seen, **451**
self-, **526**
-self, -selves, 222, **420**
Semicolons, **493**
connecting clauses with, 502
correcting run-ons with,
360–361
parentheses and, 524
quotation marks with, **508**
rules for, **493**–497
Sensory Word Bins, 9
Sentence Combining, 17–20,
343–347
Sentence Fluency, 3
Sentence Starters, to Choose
Topic, 78
Sentences, **274**
adding clauses to, 326
bracketing openers for, 12
capitalizing, **458**
coding to identify, 100
colons in, **499**
combining, **343**–349
combining, with appositive
phrases, 305
combining, with participial
phrases, 311
complex, **42**
correcting run-on, **359**–361
creating variety in, 30, 42, 88,
100, 201
declarative, 340, 472, 524
elliptical, 488
exclamatory, **101**, 341, 473, 524
fragments of, **354**–358, 657
functions of, **101**, **340**–342
imperative, **341**, 472, 473

interrogative, 340, 524
inverted, 167, **168**, **280**–286,
410
misplaced modifiers in, 361–364
negatives in, 440–443
parentheses in, **524**
topic, 21–24
varying length of, 350–351
varying openers and structures
in, 352
writing supporting, 23
See also Basic Sentence Parts;
Compound Sentences; Effective
Sentences; Revising Sentences,
Strategies for; Topic Sentences
Sentence Diagraming, 692–703
adjective clauses, 701
adverb clauses, 702
appositive phrases, 697
complements, 694–695
complex sentences, 701–703
compound sentences, 700–701
compound-complex sentences,
703
conjunctions, 693–694
gerunds and gerund phrases,
698–699
infinitives and infinitive phrases,
699–700
modifiers, 692–693
noun clauses, 702
participles and participial
phrases, 697–698
prepositional phrases, 696–697
subjects and verbs, 692–693
Sequences, Cause-and-Effect, **599**
Serial Commas, **74**
Series
colons with, **498**
commas with, **478**, **479**, 480
parentheses with, **523**
semicolons in, **496**, **497**
set, sit, **452**
Settings
envisioning, 603
gathering details for, 37, 53
Shaping Your Writing
arranging research findings for,
162
choosing form for, 10
choosing logical organization
for, 128
choosing organizational strategy
for, 163
creating mood for, 68
creating plots for, 38
enticing leads for, 10
ordering details for, 98
organizational methods for, 198

outlines for, 162–163
plot diagrams for, 54
point-by-point organization for,
112
problem-solution outline for, 144
subject-by-subject organization
for, 112
thesis statements for, 182
TRI/PS/QA for, 83
Short-Answer Tests, **195**, 626
Short Stories, 48–61
capitalizing titles of, **468**
defined, **49**
drafting, 54–55
editing and proofreading, 60
prewriting, 50–53
publishing and presenting, 61
revising 56–59
rubric for self-assessment, 61
types of, **49**
Similes, **68**
Simple Predicates, **275**–276
Simple Sentences, **42**
Simple Subjects, **275**–276
since, 267
since, because, 135
Singular Nouns, Possessive Case
for, **535**, 538
Singular Subjects, **406**–407
Singular Verbs, 406–416
sit, set, **452**
Skimming, 591
so, 265, **452**, 476, 493
Solutions
connecting problems to, 146
outlining, 144
somewhere, **445**
Songs
capitalizing titles of, **468**
punctuating titles of, **517**
sort of, kind of, **449**
Sources
cards for, 160
evaluating Internet, 681
primary and secondary, 111
for reading materials, 606–607
for speeches, 549
See also Citations; Works-Cited
Lists
Spacecraft, **464**, **515**
Spatial Order, 26, 69
Spatial Relationships, 118
Speakers
identifying, in poetry, 605
indicating quotations of, 506
punctuating change in, **511**–512
Speaking Skills, 546–550
class participation and, 547
evaluating, 550

interviews, 629
nonverbal strategies, 549
peer review and, 59, 73, 89, 134, 150, 169, 188
planning a speech, 549
preparation for, 549
preparing note cards for, 549
rhetorical strategies, 549
taking part in class discussions, 547
types of speeches, 548
verbal strategies, 549
and vocabulary development, 567
in the workplace, 629–632
See also Communication, Verbal; Listening Skills
Speeches
audience and, 548
delivering a speech, 549
evaluating speeches, 550
giving and getting feedback, 549–550
nonverbal language, 549
planning a speech, 549
preparing note cards for, 549
preparing outlines for, 549
providing main idea and details, 549
researching, 549
rhetorical strategies, 549
types, 548
volume, pitch, and tone, 549
Spell-Checking, Electronic, 14, 393, 445, 639
Spelling
of adjective forms of nouns, 242
of adverbs, 254
for *-ance, -ence* words, 356
applying rules for, 581–587
for *-ball* words, 527
of "borrowed" words, 281
for *complement, compliment*, 292
electronic checkers for, 14, 393, 445, 639
for *-er, -or* words, 356
of foreign words, 310
ie, ei rules for, **202**
improving, 578–587
of modifiers, 428
of negative verb forms, 440
notebooks for, **578**–579
of proper nouns, 218, 531
of suffixes, 356
of troublesome words, 684–685
SQ4R Method, **592**
Stacks (transitions), for Paragraph Revision, 12

Standard Language, 548
Statement, Extension, Elaboration (SEE) Technique, **10**, 129
States, Abbreviations for, 687
Statistics
analyzing, 638
building argument with, 84
including in ads, 98
supporting, 23
Steps (transitions), for Paragraph Revision, 12
Stories. *See* Short Stories
Structure
identifying, 165, 166
varying, in sentences, 352
Structure, Revising Overall. *See* Revising Overall Structure, Strategies for
Student Work in Progress, Drafting
citing literature passages for, 183
elaborating on notes, 164
elaborating with supporting details, 199
expanding outlines, 145
"exploding" the moment, 39
preparing outlines, 163
using point-by-point organization, 112
using SEE technique to elaborate, 129
Student Work in Progress, Final Drafts of
for advertisements, 105
Student Work in Progress, Prewriting
collecting details, 143
cubing to gather details, 67
doing newspaper scans, 124
freewriting to discover topic, 50
gathering details for events, 97
gathering evidence with T-charts, 82
gathering setting details, 53
hexagonal writing technique for, 181
K-W-L charts, 159
looping, 80
showing causes and effects, 127
taking notes, 160
using blueprints, 34
using sentence starters, 78
See also Choosing Your Topic
Student Work in Progress, Revising
adding conjunctions, 116
adding modifiers, 70
circling important details, 99
clarifying relationships, 132
color-coding characters, 186
color-coding passive voice, 57

color-coding personal pronouns, 43
color-coding related details, 131
color-coding sentence types, 88
color-coding structure, 114
color-coding subject-verb patterns, 167
color-coding supporting details, 85
creating parallelism, 86
deleting empty and hedging words, 201
deleting unrelated details, 40
fixing verb tenses, 148
focusing paragraphs, 147
identifying sentence types, 100
replacing vague words, 72
underlining details, 184
Study Plans, 609
Study, Reference, and Test-Taking Skills. *See* Reference Skills; Study Skills; Test-Taking Skills
Study Skills
developing plans for, 609
note-taking methods for, 610
Style in Reading
varying, 591
Style in Writing. *See* Audiences; Voice; Word Choice
Subheadings, Textbook, 590
Subject-by-Subject Organization, 112, 198
Subject Complements, **294**
Subject Pronouns, 43
Subject-Verb Agreement
collective nouns and, 168
compound subjects, 408–409
faulty, 648
singular and plural subjects, **406**–407
special problems with, 410–413
Subject-Verb Order, **280**–286, 352
Subjects, **274**–286
adjective phrases and, **300**–301
appositive phrases and, 305
color-coding, 114
color-coding for clarity, 186
complete, **274**
confusing, 410–413
gerunds as, 312
hard-to-find, 280–286
infinitives used as, 316
in inverted sentences, **280**–286
noun clauses as, **333**
on-line searches for, 648
in orders and directions, **280**
plural, 406–407
in questions, **280**–281
relative pronouns as, **326**

simple, **275**–276
singular, 406–407
who, whoever as, **397**
See also Compound Subjects
Subordinate Clauses, **322**–323
   adverb, **328**–331
   combining sentences with, **20**,
    345–346
   commas with, 476, 489
   noun, **332**–336
   revising fragments of, **358**
   See also Clauses
Subordinating Conjunctions, **117**
  in adverb clauses, 20, **328**
  identifying, 267
  list of, **266**
Subtopics, 594
Suffixes
  -able, 586
  adding to nouns, 242
  -ance, 90, 586
  -ball, 527
  capitalizing, **467**
  -cede, -ceed, -sede, 585
  dividing words with, **530**
  -efy, 586
  -elect, **526**
  -ence, 90, 586
  -eous, 586
  -er, -est, **427**, 428, 432
  -er, -or, 356
  hyphenating, **526**
  -ible, 586
  -ing, **313**
  -ious, 586
  -ly, **527**
  -or, -er, 356
  rules for adding, **576**–577
  -self, -selves, 222, **420**
  spelling words with, 356,
   583–587
  -sy, 586
  -uous, 586
Summaries, 610, **577**
  crediting sources of, 674
  note-taking and, 614
Summary Statements, Dashes in,
  520
Superlative Degree **426**–432
Supporting Details
  elaborating with, 199
  identifying, 85
  for topic sentences, 23
  See also Details; Gathering
   Details; Providing Elaboration
Supporting Sentences, 23
Surveys
  gathering details through, 143
  in investigative research, 161

in SQ4R method, 592
-sy, 586
Syllabification, 617
Symbols
  apostrophes in, 543
  citing, **515**
  in media, 558
Synonyms, **570**
  in thesaurus, 619

T

Tables, 561
Tables of Contents, 158, 589
Tag Words, 59
take, bring, **447**
Tape Recorders, 573
T-Charts, Gathering Evidence
  With, 82
teach, learn, **450**
Teamwork, 631
Technical Language, 548
Television
  citing series on, **514**
  information media on, 557
Tenses. *See* Verb Tenses
Test Preparation. *See*
  Writing for Assessment
Test-Taking Skills, 624–627
  See also Diagnostic Tests
Testimonials
  including in ads, 98
Testimony, Expert, 84
Tests
  timed, **195**, 202
  types of, **195**, 624–626
  See also Diagnostic Tests
Text-Organizers, Using to Locate
  Information
  glossary, 589
  graphic features, 590
  headings, 590
  tables of contents, 589
  textbook features, 590
  textbook sections, 589
Textbooks
  appendix, 589
  chapter introduction and
   summary, 590
  glossary, 589
  index, 589
  pictures and captions, 590
  questions and exercises, 590
  tables of contents, 589
  titles, headings, and subheadings, 590
Texts, Electronic, 607
Textual Evidence, 84
than, then, 135, **434**, 452
that, which, who, **452**

that, which, 151
Theater. *See* Drama; Performances;
  Plays
their, there, they're, **452**
them, **453**
there, here, **281**–282
there, they're, their, 202
there's, here's, 410
Thesaurus, 89, 572
Thesis, **619**, 639
  developing, 200
  matching key words to, 197
  for speeches, **549**
Thesis Statements
  drafting, 182
  examples of, 27
Third-Person Pronouns, 221, 222
Thumb Indexes, 616
till, 267
Time, Expressions of
  capitalizing, **462**
  punctuating, 500, 536
  verb tenses for, 369
Time Management
  software for, 609
  tools for, **636**
Timed Tests, **195**
  checking spelling on, 202
Timed Writing Prompts
  autobiographical essay about a
   humorous event, 35
  cause-and-effect essay about a
   historical event, 125
  comparison-and-contrast essay
   about middle school vs. high
   school, 109
  descriptive letter about a
   favorite class in school, 95
  descriptive writing about a
   favorite place, 65
  persuasive essay about the minimum legal driving age, 79
  persuasive letter about building
   a new facility at school, 141
  research report, 157
  response to literature, 179
  short story about your
   hometown, 51
  See also Topic Bank Ideas
Timelines, 594
Titles
  abbreviations for, 564
  apostrophes with, 536
  capitalizing, **466**–468
  citing, **513**–514
  colons in, 500
  quotation marks with, **516**–518
  styling, 189
  subject-verb agreement and, 412

textbook, 590
underlining, **518**
using commas with, **486**
to, 318
to, as, **445**
To-do Lists, 636
to, too, two, 103, 202, **453**
Tone
  choosing, to fit audience and
    purpose, 66
  creating and changing, 150
  writing style and, 30
Topic Bank Ideas
  anecdotes, 35
  autobiographical writing about
    a humorous event, 35
  blues music, 125
  business letters, 207
  cause-and-effect essay about a
    historical event, 125
  comparing and contrasting
    middle school and high
    school, 109
  comparing and contrasting
    poems, 179
  competing products, 109
  critical reviews, 179
  describing democracy, 65
  describing a favorite class, 95
  describing a favorite place, 65
  editorial on local issue, 141
  essay-test questions, 196
  historical personalities, 157
  historical *vs.* current events, 109
  math problems, 141
  meeting minutes, 209
  memoirs, 35
  nature stories, 51
  personal narratives, 35
  persuasive essay about the mini-
    mum driving age, 79
  persuasive letter about building
    a new school facility, 141
  persuasive speeches and essays,
    79
  rain forest changes, 125
  recalling challenge, 65
  research report, 157
  response to literature, 179
  school function ad, 95
  scientific phenomena, 157
  short story about your
    hometown, 51
  stories with themes, 51
  See also Choosing Your Topic;
    Narrowing Your Topic;
    Responding to Fine Art and
    Literature
Topic, Restatement, Illustration (TRI)

examples of, 83, 115
  placing topic sentences with, 24
  revising paragraphs with, 166
Topic Sentences
  main ideas and, 21–22
  paragraph blocks and, 29
  placing, 24
  supporting sentences for, 23
  tips for writing, 22
  See also Sentences
Topic Webs
  for narrowing topic, 66, 180
  See also Cluster Diagrams
Topical Paragraphs, **28**
Topics
  choosing. *See* Choosing Your
    Topic
  developing single, 147
  evaluating for audience and
    purpose, 110
  narrowing. *See* Narrowing Your
    Topic
  researching, for speeches, **549**
Transitional Phrases, **133**, **494**
Transitions
  clarifying relationships with, 132
  conjunctive adverbs as, 268
  connecting details with, 26
  expressing relationships with,
    118
  in functional paragraphs, 28
Transitive Verbs, **229–230**
TRI. *See* Topic, Restatement,
  Illustration
True-or-False Questions, 625

U
Underlining
  details, 184
  repeated words, 134
  rules for, **513–516**
  for titles, 189
  titles without, **518**
  See also Bracketing; Circling;
    Coding; Color-Coding;
    Highlighting
Understatement, 601
Understood Subjects, **280**
Understood Words, 326, 330, 334
Uniform Resource Locators
  (URLs), Electronic, 559
Unity
  among paragraphs, 131
  color-coding to check, 69
  creating, 40
  creating, in overall structure, 165
  maintaining paragraph, 25
until, 267
-uous, 586

URLs. *See* Uniform Resource
  Locators
Usage
  dictionary labels for, 618
  following conventions of, 14
  See also Miscellaneous Problems
    in Usage; Pronoun Usage;
    Verb Usage
Using Modifiers, 424–427
  degrees of comparison for,
    426–431
  making clear and logical com-
    parisons for, **432–437**
  See also Adjectives; Adverbs;
    Modifiers

V
Vague Words, 72
Variety, Sentence, 100
  adding, 88
  color-coding for, 42
  creating, 201
  inverting for, 167
  writing style and, 30
Venn Diagrams, 110, 595
  See also Comparison-and-
    Contrast Order
Verb Phrases, **236–239**
Verb Tenses, **368–381**
  basic and progressive forms for,
    149, **368**
  components of, **371–375**
  conjugating, **376–379**
  faulty, 649
  fixing shifts in, 148
Verb Usage, 366–385
  active and passive voice,
    382–385
  tenses, **368–381**
  test items for, 367
Verbal Phrases
  gerund, **314–315**
  infinitive, **319**
  participial, **310–311**
Verbals, **307**
  gerunds, **312–313**
  infinitives as, **316–317**
  participles, **307–309**
Verbs, 214–215, **228–239**
  action, **228–229**, 233
  active and passive voice for,
    58
  adverb phrases and, 302
  as adjectives, 249
  compound, **277–278**, 343, 476,
    489
  contractions with, **541**, 542
  helping, 236, 371–375, 440,
    441

identifying, 309, 313
intransitive, **229**–230, 234
in inverted questions, **280**
irregular, **372**–375, 379
linking, **231**–233, 411
plural, 406–407
principal parts of, **371**–375
regular, **371**–372
singular, 406–407
subject agreement with,
   406–416
transitive, **229**–230
vivid, 102
Videotapes
   producing, 564
   performances on, 550
   recording speeches on, 549
   as reference tools, 623
   viewing performances on, 604
Viewing Skills
   evaluating persuasive
      techniques, 558
   graphs, 555
      bar, 555
      line, 555
      pie, 556
   information media, 557–558
   maps, 554
   See also Critical Viewing Skills;
      Information Media;
      Responding to Fine Art and
      Literature
Visual Aids, **560**–561, 562
Vocabulary, 566–577
   development of, 567–571
   improving spelling of, 578–587
   notebooks for, 573
   systematic study for, 572–573
   word parts and origins in,
      574–577
Voice
   active *vs.* passive, 57, **58**,
      382–385
   in good writing, 3
   See also Audiences

W

Web Sites
   advertising on, 92
   art museums on, 559
   finding and evaluating,
      679–681
   finding information at, 373
   finding new words at, 576
   government, 400
   locating and evaluating, 622
   for periodicals, 615
   student, 190
   using company, 111

See also Internet; Search Engines
well, good, 428
went, gone, **448**
when, 266, 453
where, 266, 453
which, **452**
which, that, 151
who, **452**
who, whoever, **396**–397
who, whom, 396–399
whom, whomever, **396**, **398**
who's, whose, 103, 225, 396, **539**
will, 541
Word Choice, 3
   faulty, 655
   See also Revising Word Choice,
      Strategies for
Word Division, **530**–532
Word-Processing Programs
   Find feature in, 119
   finding words with, 134, 135
   formatting with, 562
   organizing writing with, 38
   spell-checking with, 14, 393,
      445, 639
   thesaurus in, 619
   using Find feature of, 60
   See also Computers
Wordiness, 169
Words
   in analogies, 571
   commonly confused, 135
   commonly misspelled, 684–685
   hearing and using new, 567
   origins of, 574–577
   problem, 579
   recognizing related, 570
   systematic study of, 572–573
   within words, 580
Workplace Skills and
      Competencies, 628–639
   applying computer skills, 639
   applying math skills, 638
   managing money, 637
   managing time, 636
   moving toward goals, 633
   solving problems, 634
   teamwork, 631–632
   thinking creatively, 635
   working with people, 629–630
Workplace Writing, 204–211
   business letters in, 206–207
   defined, **205**
   forms and applications in,
      210–211
   meeting minutes in, 208–209
   types of, **205**
Works-Cited Lists, **674**
   creating and checking, 170–171

examples of, 175
sample of, 646
See also Citations; Sources
Worksheets, Peer Review, 45
would, 541
Writers. *See* Authors
Writing
   types of, **4**
   using writing technologies, 639
   See also Autobiographical
      Writing; Cause-and Effect
      Essays; Comparison-and-
      Contrast Essays; Narration;
      Persuasive Essays; Problem-
      and-Solution Essays; Research
      Writing; Response to
      Literature; Short Stories;
      Writing for Assessment
Writing Activities, Ideas for
   See Cooperative Writing
      Timed Writing Prompts; Topic
      Bank Ideas
Writing for Assessment
   drafting, 198–199
   editing and proofreading, 202
   prewriting, 196–197
   publishing and presenting, 203
   revising, 200–201
   rubric for self-assessment, 203
   types of, **195**
Writing Process, **4**–15
   stages in, **5**
   types and modes in, **4**
Writing in SAT/ACT, 662–671
   the ACT writing test, 666
   introduction to the new SAT
      and ACT writing tests, 663
   the new SAT essay, 668
   planning the persuasive essay,
      664
   proofreading in five minutes,
      670
   reflecting on test preparation,
      671
   supporting an argument with
      examples, 665

Y

yet, 265, 476, 493
you, **280**, **421**
your, you're, 103

Z

Zooming Technique, 564

Acknowledgments

Staff Credits

The people who made up the *Prentice Hall Writing and Grammar: Communication in Action* team—representing design services, editorial, editorial services, electronic publishing technology, manufacturing and inventory planning, marketing, marketing services, market research, online services and multimedia development, product planning, production services, project office, and publishing processes—are listed below. Bold type denotes the core team members.

Betsy Bostwick, Evonne Burgess, **Louise B. Capuano, Sarah Carroll, Megan Chill,** Katherine Clarke, Rhett Conklin, Martha Conway, Harold Crudup, **Harold Delmonte,** Libby Forsyth, Maggie Fritz, Ellen Goldblatt, Elaine Goldman, Jonathan Goldson, **Rebecca Graziano, Diana Hahn,** Rick Hickox, Kristan Hoskins, Carol Lavis, **George Lychock, Gregory Lynch,** William McAllister, Loretta Moser, Margaret Plotkin, Maureen Raymond, Gerry Schrenk, **Melissa Shustyk,** Annette Simmons, Robin Sullivan, Julie Tomasella, **Elizabeth Torjussen, Doug Utigard.**

Additional Credits

Ernie Albanese, Diane Alimena, Susan Andariese, Michele Angelucci, Penny Baker, John Carle, Jaime Cohen, Angelo Focaccia, Kathy Gavilanes, Beth Geschwind, Jennifer Harper, Evan Holstrom, Raegan Keida, Leanne Korszoloski, Sue Langan, Rebecca Lauth, Dave Liston, Maria Keogh, Vicki Menanteaux, Gail Meyer, Artur Mkrtchyan, LaShonda Morris, Karyl Murray, Omni-Photo Communications, Kim Ortell, Carolyn Sapontzis, Mildred Schulte, Slip Jig Image Research Services, Sunnyside, NY, Debi Taffet

Grateful acknowledgment is made to the following for copyrighted material:

Susan Bergholz Literary Services

From "In Commemoration: One Million Volumes" Copyright © 1995 by Rudolfo A. Anaya. First published in *A Mill Stars*; Millionth Acquisition for U. of NM General Library, U. of NM Press, 1982. "Tepeyac" by Sandra Cisneros from *Vintage Cisneros.* Copyright © 2004 by Sandra Cisneros. All rights reserved.

Chana Bloch

From "Pride" from *The Window* by Dahlia Ravikovitch. Translated by Chana Bloch. Copyright © 1989. Reprinted by permission of Chana Bloch.

Brooks Permissions

"The Bean Eaters" by Gwendolyn Brooks from *Blacks.* Copyright © 1991 by Gwendolyn Brooks, published by Third World Press, Chicago. Reprinted by consent of Brooks Permissions.

Crown Publishers

"Damon and Pythias," from *Classic Myths to Read Aloud* by William F. Russell, copyright © 1989 by William F. Russell. Published by Crown Publishers. All rights reserved.

Harcourt, Inc.

"The Antigone of Sophocles" an English version by Dudley Fitts and Robert Fitzgerald. Copyright © 1939 by Harcourt, Inc. and renewed 1967 by Dudley Fitts.

The Barbara Hogenson Agency, Inc.

"The Dog That Bit People" from *My Life and Hard Times.* Copyright © 1933, 1961 by James Thurber.

Alfred A. Knopf, Inc.

From *Swimming to Antarctica: Tales of a Long-Distance Swimmer* by Lynne Cox. Copyright © 2004 by Lynne Cox. All rights reserved.

Oxford University Press, UK

"How Much Land Does a Man Need?" from *The Raid and Other Stories* (1999) by Leo Tolstoy edited by Louise & Aylmer Maude. Copyright © 1935 Oxford University Press.

G.P. Putnam's Sons

"Arthur Becomes King" Part I, Chapter XXII from *The Once and Future King* by T.H. White. Copyright © 1938, 1939, 1940, © 1958 by T. H. White renewed.

Jeremy P. Tarcher/Putnam

"Asorbic Acid" from *Napoleon's Buttons: How 17 Molecules Changed History* by Penny Le Couteur and Jay Burreson, copyright © 2003 by Micron Geological Ltd. All rights reserved.

Random House, Inc.

From "A Raisin in the Sun, Act I, Scene II" by Lorraine Hansberry from *A Raisin In The Sun.* Copyright © 1984 by Robert Nemiroff, as an unpublished work. Copyright © 1959, 1966, 1984 by Robert Nemiroff. All rights reserved.

Rogers, Coleridge and White, Ltd.

"Games at Twilight" from *Games at Twilight and Other Stories* by Anita Desai. Copyright © 1978 by Anita Desai. All rights reserved.

Heyden White Rostow

From "The American Idea" by Theodore H. White from *The New York Times Magazine, July 6, 1986.* Copyright © 1986 by Theodore H. White. All rights reserved.

David Unger

"The Censors," from *Open Doors: Stories* by Luisa Valenzuela. Copyright © translation by David Unger. All rights reserved.

Viking Penguin, Inc.

From *What Makes a Degas a Degas?* by Richard Muhlberger, published by The Metropolitan Museum of Art, New York, and Viking, a Division of Penguin Putnam Books for Young Readers, copyright © 1993 by The Metropolitan Museum of Art. All rights reserved.

Note: Every effort has been made to locate the copyright owner of material reproduced on this component. Omissions brought to our attention will be corrected in subsequent editions.

Photo Credits

Cover: Pearson Prentice Hall; **vi:** (top) LEA/ Omni-Photo Communications, Inc.; (bottom) Corel Professional Photos CD-ROM™; **vii:** (top & middle) Corel Professional Photos CD-ROM™; (bottom) David Young-Wolff/PhotoEdit; **ix:** Tony Stone Images; **x:** ©1997, G. & M. Kohler/FPG International Corp.; **xii:** image © Copyright 1998 PhotoDisc, Inc.; **xii:** Will Hart/ PhotoEdit; **xiii:** image © Copyright 1998 PhotoDisc, Inc.; **xiv:** image © Copyright 1998 PhotoDisc, Inc.; **xv:** F. Hoffmann/ The Image Works; **xvi:** © 1996, Walter Bibikow/FPG International Corp.; **xvii:** *Federal Brigade Commanded by General Winfield Scott,* Julian Scott, Smithsonian Institution; **xviii:** Kunsthistorisches Museum, Antikensammlung, Vienna, Austria, © Photograph by Erich Lessing/Art Resource, NY; **xix:** *Ballet Class,* Edgar Degas, Corel Professional Photos CD-ROM™; **xx:** (top) David Young-Wolff/PhotoEdit; (bottom) Bruce Ayres/Tony Stone Images; **xxi:** Corel Professional Photos CD-ROM™; **xxii:** (top) Corel Professional Photos CD-ROM™; (bottom) Courtesy of the Italian Government Tourist Board; **xxiii:** (top) Corel Professional Photos CD-ROM™; (bottom) Courtesy of the Library of Congress; **xxiv:** Corel Professional Photos CD-ROM™; **xxv:** Corel Professional Photos CD-ROM™; **xxvi:** (top & middle) Corel Professional Photos CD-ROM™; **xxvii:** (top) The Stock Market/Tom Stewart; (bottom) © The Stock Market/Jose L. Pelaez; **1:** *Femme Cousant,* Henri Lebasque, Christie's Images/ SuperStock, © 2001 Artists Rights Society (ARS), New York, ADAGP, Paris **2:** © Sven Martson/ The Image Works; **4:** Bob Daemmrich/Stock, Boston Inc./ PictureQuest; **16:** Tony Page/Tony Stone Images; **17:** Kindra Clineff/ Index Stock Photography, Inc.; **23:** Don Spiro/ Medichrome/The Stock Shop; **25:** AP/Wide World Photos; **29:** Corel Professional Photos CD-ROM™; **31:** © StockFood America/EISING; **32:** North Carolina Museum of Art/ CORBIS; **35:** *Backgammon,* 1976, Jane Freilicher, oil on canvas, 38 x 44 in., From the permanent collection of the Utah Museum of Fine Arts, Acc. 1979.008; **41:** LEA/ Omni-Photo Communications, Inc.; **48:** Richard Hutchings/PhotoEdit; **51:** *Students of Modeling and Painting,* Anonymous; Private Collection/ Bridgeman Art Library, NYC; **55:** Tony Freeman/ PhotoEdit; **62:** Gottlieb/ Monkmeyer; **65:** *Studio Interior,* 1982, Jane Freilicher, Tibor De Nagy; **68:** Kevin R. Morris/CORBIS; **73:** Michelle Bridwell/PhotoEdit; **76:** AP Photo/Jan Bauer; **79:** *Arrivals and Departures,* 1999, Chester Arnold, The Seven Bridges Foundation, Greenwich, CT. Photo courtesy of George Adams Gallery, New York; **84:** Bill Bachman/The Image Works; **85:** Tom Stack/Tom Stack &

Associates; **89:** Will Hart/PhotoEdit; **92:** image©Copyright 1998 PhotoDisc, Inc.; **94:** Costa Rica Tourist Board; **102:** Amy Etra/ PhotoEdit; **106:** Tony Arruza/COR-BIS; **109:** *Minor League,* Clyde Singer, Butler Institute of American Art; **113:** image©Copyright 1998 PhotoDisc, Inc.; **121:** Ken Karp/PH photo; **122:** *The Landing of Columbus at San Salvador (Guanahani) in Bahamas,* 12 October 1492, The Granger Collection, New York; **125:** *Rolling Power,* 1939, Charles Sheeler, Smith College Museum of Art, Northampton, Massachusetts. Purchased, Drayton Hillyer Fund, 1940; **128:** Ralph White/CORBIS; **137:** David Young-Wolff/PhotoEdit; **142:** Mary Kate Denny/PhotoEdit; **142:** David A. Northcott/CORBIS; **145:** *Unloading the Cargo,* 1942, Ralston Crawford; **150:** Corel Professional Photos CD-ROM™; **154:** The Kobal Collection; **154:** Corel Professional Photos CD-ROM™; **157:** *Federal Brigade Commanded by General Winfield Scott,* Julian Scott, Smithsonian Institution; **158:** Scribner's Publishing; **161:** PhotoEdit; **173:** Magnum Photos, Inc. © 1944 Robert Capa; **175:** Courtesy National Archives; **176:** © The Stock Market/Tom Stewart; **179:** *Children Dancing,* Robert Gwathmey, Butler Institute of American Art; **188:** Will Faller; **191:** *Penelope at the loom and Telemachus,* Museo Nazionale, Chiusi, Italy, © Photograph by Erich Lessing/Art Resource, NY; **192:** Kunsthistorisches Museum, Antikensammlung, Vienna, Austria, © Photograph by Erich Lessing/Art Resource, NY; **196:** © The Stock Market/Charles Gupton; **199:** (top & bottom) The Granger Collection, New York; **202:** Tony Stone Images; **204:** Bruce Ayers/Tony Stone Images; **212:** *Delta,* 1990, 40 x 40 inches, acrylic on canvas by Paul Giovanopoulos, Photograph Courtesy Louis K. Meisel Gallery, New York; **216:** Courtesy of the Library of Congress; **219:** Corel Professional Photos CD-ROM™; **220:** Courtesy National Archives; **223:** Corel Professional Photos CD-ROM™; **225:** Greater Houston Convention and Visitors Bureau; **230:** NASA; **232–263:** Corel Professional Photos CD-ROM™; **268:** Silver Burdett Ginn; **269:** Modern Curriculum Press; **272–309:** Corel Professional Photos CD-ROM™; **311:** Courtesy of the Library of Congress; **312–329** Corel Professional Photos CD-ROM™; **334:** Courtesy of the Italian Government Tourist Board; **338:** Silver Burdett Ginn; **340:** Pearson Education/Prentice Hall School; **343–351:** Corel Professional Photos CD-ROM™; **354:** Pearson Education/PH College; **357:** Silver Burdett Ginn; **359–362:** Corel Professional Photos CD-ROM™; **364:** Silver Burdett Ginn; **366–369:** Corel Professional Photos CD-ROM™; **370:** Courtesy, Museum of Fine Arts, Boston; **375:** Corel Professional

Photos CD-ROM™; **378:** © Archivo Iconografico, S.A./CORBIS; **383:** Corel Professional Photos CD-ROM™; **388:** Courtesy of the Library of Congress; **391:** Corel Professional Photos CD-ROM™; **393–394:** Courtesy of the Library of Congress; **399 & 401:** NASA; **404:** Corel Professional Photos CD-ROM™; **408:** NOAA; **410–435:** Corel Professional Photos CD-ROM™; **440 & 443:** Courtesy of the Library of Congress; **448–467:** Corel Professional Photos CD-ROM™; **468:** EMG—Education Management Group; **470:** Pearson Education/ Prentice Hall College; **472:** NASA; **477:** Pearson Education/Prentice Hall School; **482:** Corel Professional Photos CD-ROM™; **487:** Pearson Education/Prentice Hall College; **489:** Silver Burdett Ginn; **495:** *Snap the Whip,* Winslow Homer, Corel Professional Photos CD-ROM™; **497–498:** Corel Professional Photos CD-ROM™; **501:** New York Convention & Visitors Bureau; **505–508:** Corel Professional Photos CD-ROM™; **510:** Pearson Education/Prentice Hall College; **514:** Courtesy of the Library of Congress; **517:** Corel Professional Photos CD-ROM™; **523:** Pearson Education/Prentice Hall College; **525 & 529:** Corel Professional Photos CD-ROM™; **530:** image© Copyright 1998 PhotoDisc, Inc.; **535–543:** Corel Professional Photos CD-ROM™; **544:** *The Library,* 1960, Jacob Lawrence, National Museum of American Art, Washington, D.C. /Art Resource, NY; **546:** Paul Conklin/PhotoEdit; **548:** Morry Gash/AP/Wide World Photos; **559:** *Dancers in Pink and Green,* Edgar Degas, oil on canvas, H. 32-3/8 in. W. 29-3/4 in. (82.2 x 75.6 cm) Signed (lower right): Degas. The Metropolitan Musem of Art, Bequest of Mrs. H. O. Havemeyer, 1929. The H.O. Havemeyer Collection. (29.100.42). Photograph Copyright © 1980 By The Metropolitan Museum of Art; **566:** Dennis MacDonald/PhotoEdit; **569:** Corel Professional Photos CD-ROM™; **570:** David Young-Wolff/PhotoEdit; **577–579:** Corel Professional Photos CD-ROM™; **581:** © The Stock Market/Jose L. Pelaez; **584:** Corel Professional Photos CD-ROM™; **588:** Myrleen Ferguson/PhotoEdit; **591:** © The Stock Market/Gabe Palmer/Mug Shots; **597:** Tony Stone Images; **601:** Duomo/COR-BIS; **606:** The Granger Collection, New York; **608:** David Young-Wolff/PhotoEdit; **612:** Tony Freeman/ PhotoEdit; **614:** Michelle Bridwell/ PhotoEdit; **616:** CORBIS; **621:** Corel Professional Photos CD-ROM™; **628:** © The Stock Market/Tom Stewart; **630:** Ken Karp/PH Photo; **632:** Michael Newman/PhotoEdit; **638:** Kindra Clineff/Index Stock Photography, Inc.